Computer Vision

Edited by
Xiong Zhihui

Computer Vision

Edited by Xiong Zhihui

Republished by InTech

Janeza Trdine 9, 51000 Rijeka, Croatia

Additional hard copies can be obtained from orders@intechopen.com

Computer Vision, Edited by Xiong Zhihui
p. cm.
ISBN 978-953-7619-21-3

For EU product safety concerns:
IN TECH d.o.o., Prolaz Marije Krucifikse Kozulić 3, 51000 Rijeka, Croatia,
info@intechopen.com or visit our website at intechopen.com.

Preface

Computer vision uses digital computer techniques to extract, characterize, and interpret information in visual images of a three-dimensional world. The goal of computer vision is primarily to enable engineering systems to model and manipulate the environment by using visual sensing.

The field of computer vision can be characterized as immature and diverse. Even though earlier work exists, it was not until the late 1970s that a more focused study of the field started when computers could manage the processing of large data sets such as images.

There are numerous applications of computer vision, including robotic systems that sense their environment, people detection in surveillance systems, object inspection on an assembly line, image database organization and medical scans.

Application of computer vision on robotics attempt to identify objects represented in digitized images provided by video cameras, thus enabling robots to "see". Much work has been done on stereo vision as an aid to object identification and location within a three-dimensional field of view. Recognition of objects in real time, as would be needed for active robots in complex environments, usually requires computing power beyond the capabilities of present-day technology.

This book presents some research trends on computer vision, especially on application of robotics, and on advanced approachs for computer vision (such as omnidirectional vision). Among them, research on RFID technology integrating stereo vision to localize an indoor mobile robot is included in this book. Besides, this book includes many research on omnidirectional vision, and the combination of omnidirectional vision with robotics.

This book features representative work on the computer vision, and it puts more focus on robotics vision and omnidirectioal vision. The intended audience is anyone who wishes to become familiar with the latest research work on computer vision, especially its applications on robots. The contents of this book allow the reader to know more technical aspects and applications of computer vision. Researchers and instructors will benefit from this book.

Editor

Xiong Zhihui
College of Information System and Management,
National University of Defense Technology,
P.R. China

Contents

1

Behavior Fusion for Visually-Guided Service Robots

Mohamed Abdellatif
Ain Shams University, Faculty of Engineering
Egypt

1. Introduction

Mobile service robots are the class of robots that have tools to understand the environments at home and office. The development of mobile robots is increasing world-wide due to the availability of moderate price sensing and computing devices. Moreover, there is a strong belief that the market for service robots is just about to undergo a radical increase in the next few years.

Despite the huge literature of the mobile robot navigation, the development of intelligent robots able to navigate in unknown and dynamic environment is still a challenging task (Walther et al., 2003). Therefore, developing techniques for robust navigation of mobile robots is both important and needed.

The classical approach for mobile robot control used the "Model, Sense, Plan, Act", MSPA serial strategy, which proved to be inherently slow and totally fails if one module is out of order. We may call this approach as a planner-based control approach. The appearance of behavior-based navigation approach (Arkin, 1998; Brooks, 1986) was a remarkable evolution, in which the reactive behaviors were designed to run simultaneously in parallel giving tight interaction between sensors and actuators. The reactive behaviors allow for incremental improvements and addition of more application-specific behaviors. Building several behaviors, each concerned with a sole objective, will produce different decisions for the robot control parameters, and they have to be combined in some way to reach the final motion decision.

The fusion of independent behaviors is not an easy task and several approaches were proposed in the literature to solve this problem (Arkin, 1998; Borenstein & Koren, 1991; Carreras et al., 2001; Saffiotti, 1997). Coordination of behaviors can be classified into two further approaches, a competitive, as was originally proposed by (Brooks, 1986), and cooperative strategies (Carreras et al., 2001).

Depending on the environment, the competitive approach may fail and become unstable in critical situations demanding higher switching frequencies between behaviors. In the subsumption architecture (Brooks, 1986) behaviors are activated once at a time but this may be inadequate for a variety of situations requiring several behaviors to be active at the same time.

In the cooperative approach, all behaviors contribute to the output, rather than a single behavior dominates after passing an objective criterion. An example of the cooperative approach is proposed by (Khatib, 1985) using artificial potential fields to fuse control decisions from several behaviors. The potential field method suffers from being amenable to local minima which causes the control system to get stuck and become indecisive. Hybrid techniques from competitive and cooperative approaches were proposed in (Carreras et al., 2001). However, they used learning to build up the rule set which consumes a lot of time and effort.

The use of fuzzy logic for behavior fusion had been reported in (Saffiotti, 1997) where a hierarchy of behaviors was used for mobile robot guidance. Fuzzy logic approach, since its inception (Zadeh, 1965), have long been applied to robotics with many successful applications,(Luo et al., 2001; Saffiotti, 1997 ; Zimmermann, 1996) and regarded as an intelligent computational technique that enables the proper handling of sensor uncertainties. Fuzzy rules can be used to design the individual behaviors as well as the way they are integrated to reach a final decision (Arkin, 1998; Luo et al., 2001).

In this work, we propose a new method to integrate the behavior decisions by using potential field theory (Khatib, 1985) with fuzzy logic variables. The potential field theory proved to be very efficient especially for fast robots (Borenstein & Koren, 1991). The theory relies on the physical concept of force vector summation. Forces are virtual and describe the attractions and disattraction in the robot field. The potential field theory had been criticized for being susceptible to local minima and consequently unstable motion. We show that when the vector field is applied to the output from a single behavior, which is smooth due to the use of fuzzy logic, it can significantly enhance the performance of the robot navigation system. The control system is implemented and used to navigate a small indoor service robot so that it can track and follow an object target in an indoor flat terrain.

The chapter is arranged as follows, the next section presents the model of imaging and measurements of target location from the color image. In Section 3, we describe the design of fuzzy logic controller responsible for target tracking behavior, obstacle avoidance behavior and combining both behaviors. The results of robot control experiments for the behaviors are presented in Section 4. Conclusions are finally given in Section 5.

2. Measurement model

The RGB color space is the most popular color system since it is directly related to the acquisition hardware, but the RGB space is not perceptually uniform. The Hue, Saturation and Intensity, HSI color space is preferred when humans are involved, since it is perceptually uniform. The cylindrical representation of the HSI system is shown in Fig.1.

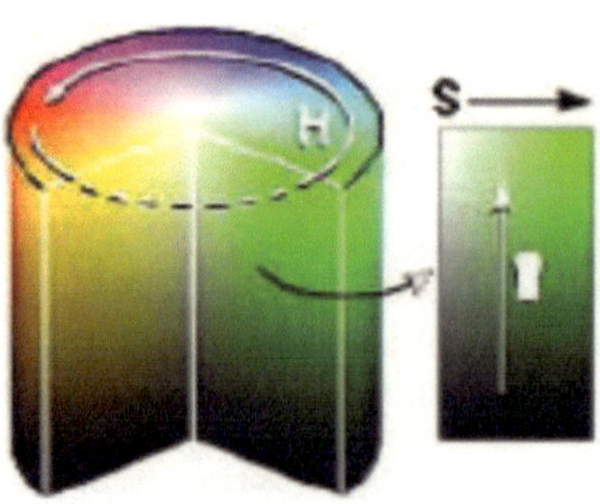

Fig. 1. The Hue-Saturation-Intensity (HSI) color space by cylindrical representation.

Perceptually Uniform, PU, color spaces are more suitable for color recognition than the RGB space, since the quality of recognition will always be judged by a human observer (Cheng & Sun, 2000 ; Kim & Park, 1996 ; Littmann & Ritter, 1997; Tseng & Chang, 1992).
The PU color space of HSI has the advantage that the object color is encoded mainly in the angle of the hue. This angle representation of color is easier in target color definition and less sensitive to changes of illumination intensity, but certainly changes when the illumination color is changed.
Therefore, we can compute the Hue, H and Saturation, S using the following formulae (Kim & Park, 1996) :

$$H = \arctan\left(\frac{\sqrt{3}(G-B)}{(2R-G-B)}\right) \tag{1}$$

$$I = (R+G+B)/3 \tag{2}$$

$$S = 1-\left(\frac{\min(R,G,B)}{I}\right) \tag{3}$$

The target object color is defined in terms of limiting hue angles and limiting saturation values describing the boundaries of a color zone in the H-S diagram that can be described by the following constraints:

$$H_{min} < H < H_{max}, \text{ and } S_{min} < S < S_{max} \tag{4}$$

Where subscript *min* refers to the minimum limit, and *max* refers to the maximum limit. The target is detected in the image by this selection criterion based on whether the pixel color lies within the boundaries of the H-S zone, known *apriori* for the target.
The segmented image is written into a monochromatic image, in which the target area color is written as white pixels and the background is written as dark pixels. The resulting binary image is then used to compute the area in pixels of the target area by counting the white pixels. This inherently uses the assumption that pixels are clustered in one group and that scattered pixels are a small portion in the image. The average horizontal coordinate of the target region is also computed and forwarded as input to the controller, as shown schematically in Fig. 2.

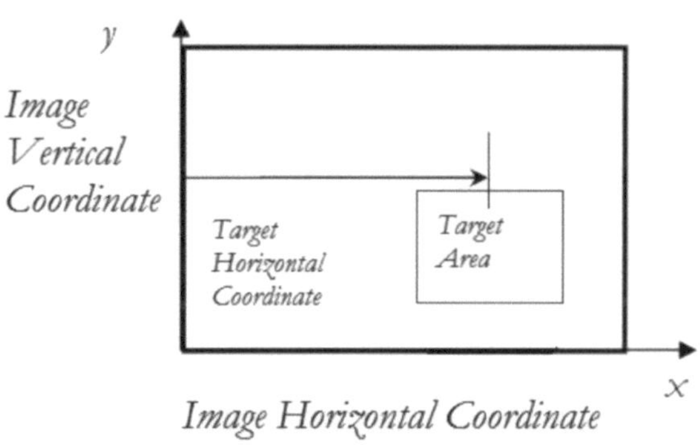

Fig. 2. Schematic representation of target measurement in the gray image showing extracted target region.

3. Design of controller

The goal of the controller is to enable the mobile robot to satisfy two objectives namely: target following and obstacle avoidance simultaneously. The objectives are implemented in separate behaviors which run independently in parallel and their output should be combined into a single command as shown in Fig.3. In this section, we describe the design of each behavior and then show how to combine their decisions.

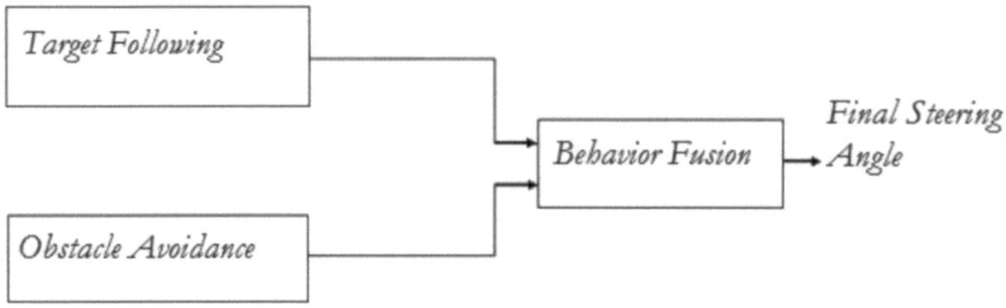

Fig. 3. Schematic of Robot Behaviors.

3.1 Design of target following behavior

The output of this behavior will decide the steering angle of the robot needed to make the target image appears continually in the middle of the image.

The sensory information available for the steering command is the average horizontal target position in the image, shown in Fig.2. The horizontal component of motion is only selected since the robot and target are both assumed to move on an indoor flat terrain and the camera orientation relative to the floor is fixed. The steering changes the target image position and hence, the motion attributes chosen as the input fuzzy linguistic inference layers for the FLC are selected to be:

1. Target image horizontal displacement
2. Target image horizontal velocity.

The membership functions for these two layers are shown in Fig.4. The fuzzy logic controller used to control the mobile robot employs triangular membership functions to fuzzify the data measured by the vision system. The input fuzzy variables are divided into three overlapping fuzzy set functions. In our implementation, the linguistic descriptors for the image horizontal displacement are defined as : 1) Left (L) , 2) Middle (M), and 3) Right (R), as shown in Fig.4. a.

The target image horizontal velocity is described by three fuzzy variables defined as : 1) Getting Left (GL), 2) Getting Middle (GM), and 3) Getting Right (GR), as shown in Fig.4.b. The shape and relative overlap of the fuzzy variables (that is tuning), are determined based on the experience gained from experiments with the robot. The shape of the membership function had been decided after studying the sensitivity of the mean of each membership function on the robot performance. The mean was changed across 10 % of its shown value and had been found to be stable over this range. The two fuzzy variables are then used to derive the output steering state. Three output states are used for steering namely, 1) Steer Right, SR, 2) go STRaight, STR and 3) Steer Left, SL, as shown in Fig.4.c. For each fuzzy linguistic interference process we define 3*3 fuzzy rule matrix as shown in Table 1.

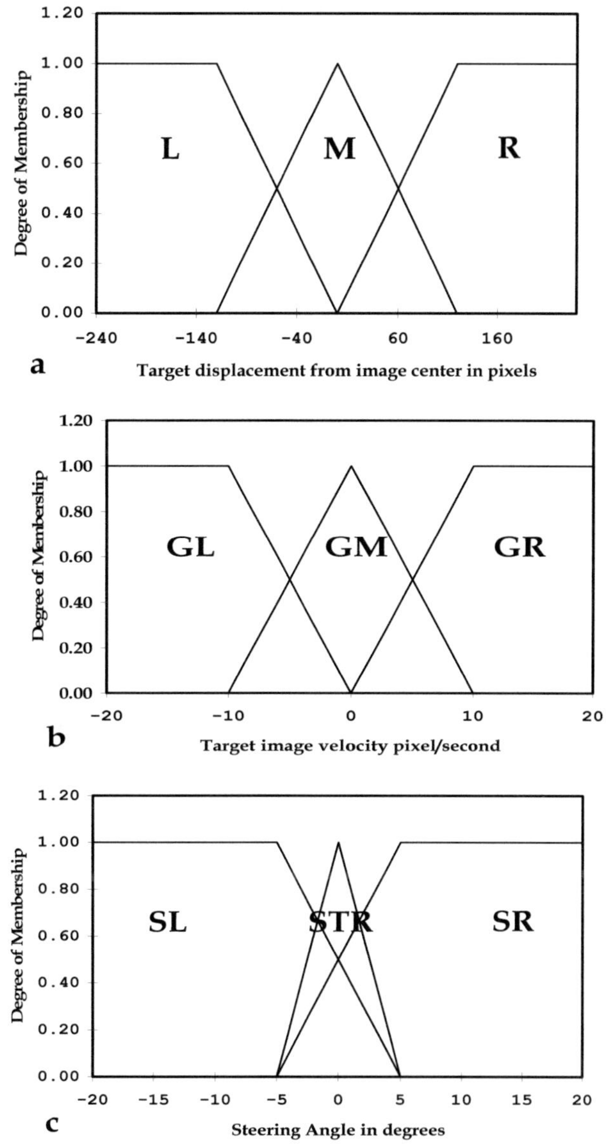

Fig. 4. Membership functions for the input variables of the steering FLC.

	GL	GM	GR
L	SL_1	SL_2	STR_1
M	SL_3	STR_2	SR_1
R	STR_3	SR_2	SR_3

Table 1. The Fuzzy Rule Matrix for the Target following FLC. (The columns show states for the target horizontal velocity, while the rows show states of target horizontal displacement).

The motion decision for the tracking behavior is calculated through the fusion of the image displacement and image velocity in the fuzzy logic inference matrix.
The values of matrix entry is calculated by finding the minimum of the two input variables. The three output variables are then computed using the root of sum squared of contributing variables. Finally, the normalized control command are defuzzified according to the center of gravity method.

3.2 Design of obstacle avoidance behavior

In the obstacle avoidance behavior, the reading of two ultrasonic range sensors are used as input variables for the FLC, while the output variable is the steering angle.
The flow chart of obstacle avoidance algorithm is shown in Fig.5, where the sensor reading are first read. Notations S1 and S2 denote signal of obstacle distance measured by left sensor and right sensor respectively. The sensor readings are then fuzzified (transformed into fuzzy linguistic variables) into three variables, namely, Near, N , Medium, M and Far, F.
The steering angle has three membership functions, Steer Left, SL, Steer Right, SR and STRaight, STR. Table 2, shows a list of the possible sensor states and the corresponding motion decision for avoiding the obstacle.

S1/S2	N	M	F
N	*Stop*	*SR*	*SR*
M	*SL*	*STR*	*SR*
F	*SL*	*SL*	*STR*

Table 2. The Fuzzy Rule Matrix for the Obstacle Avoidance FLC. (The columns show states for the right sensor, while the rows show states for the left sensor)

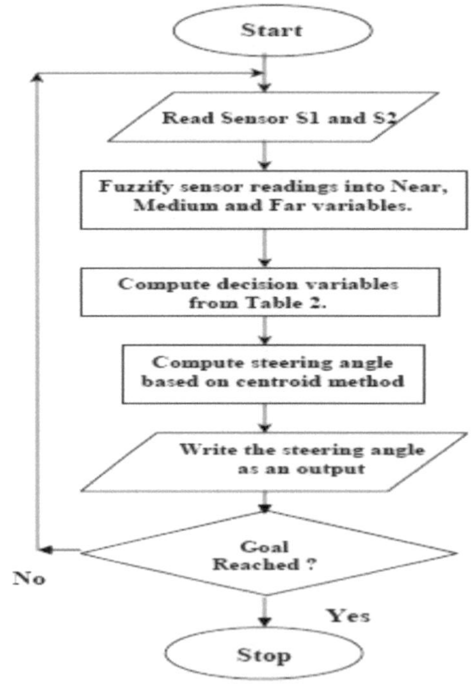

Fig. 5. Flow Chart of the Obstacle Avoidance Behavior.

It should be noted that based on the limit of the obstacle distance corresponding to the "N" linguistic variable, the robot may escape the obstacle by steering or may have to stop, in case the distance is very small to enable maneuvering without crash. The minimum distance in our case is 40 cm, and the robot speed is moderate, therefore we rarely get in the situation that the robot should stop unless it is besieged completely.
Then using the center of gravity methods, the steering angle is computed based on the decisions computed from Table 2 and made as a stand alone output signal that will be handled by the fusion algorithm.

3.3 Fusion of behaviors

We have two decisions for the steering angle computed from the two behavior implementations as shown before in Fig. 3. The decision is fused through using the potential field method by vector summation of the two vectors resulting from each behavior. The velocity vector from goal seeking behavior has a velocity amplitude maximum when steering is straight and decreases according to a linear model when the steering is off-axis. Then, using vector mechanics, the combined Euclidean magnitude and direction are computed and used to steer the vehicle. This method differs from the main potential field theory in the way the input vectors are generated, in our case it is generated through the fuzzy logic in each separate behavior in contrary to the direct construction of such vector in the main theory by linear scaling functions (Khatib, 1985; Saffiotti, 1997).

4. Experiments

4.1 System configuration

The robot had been constructed to have four wheels to move easily on flat terrain as shown in Fig.6. The two side wheels are driven by two independent servo motors, while the front and rear wheels are castor wheels and provided only to improve the mechanical stability of the robot. The robot consists of three layers of strong acrylic sheets supported by four long pillars. The lower level contains microcontroller circuit for controlling low level motor motion and reading of ultrasonic sensors and encoder readings. The second level carries the foursight vision processor and screen for displaying camera image, while the third carries the two cameras and the main microprocessor.
The robot is equipped with 16-ultrasonic sensors to enable perception of its environment. The resolution of the sensor measurement is around 1 cm. The robot has two color video cameras installed onboard. The cameras provide the image that is used by the target following behavior.
The main microprocessor receives data from the motion control system and the vision module. Inputs from both the cameras are fed into the Matrox Foursight module to process the image as a dedicated vision processor. The images received from the cameras are digitized via a Meteor II frame grabber and stored in the memory of the Foursight computer for online processing by specially designed software. We implemented algorithms that grab, calibrate the color image to eliminate the camera offset. The target color is identified to the system through measurement of it Hue-Saturation zone. The color attributes of the target are stored in the program for later comparison. Then the motion attributes of the target extracted area are computed and passed to main microprocessor where the data is needed for the FLC module. The movement of the vehicle is determined by the main microprocessor

with inputs from different components. All programs are implemented in C++ code and several video and data processing libraries are used, including Matrox Imaging Library, MIL and OpenCV.

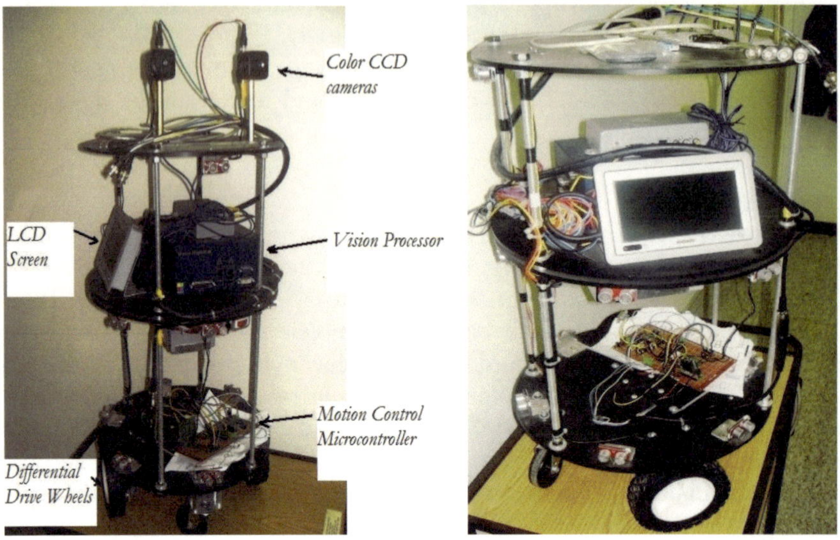

Fig. 6. Photograph of the mobile service robot.

The robot sensors and actuators communicate with the host computer via wired connections. The DC motor is controlled through a motor interface card utilizing the popular H-Bridge circuit with a high torque DC motor, of 8 kg.cm nominal torque at rated voltage of 12 Volts. Test programs were devised to ensure the right operation of the measurement and control system and to identify the resolution of measurements and control signal.
The robot main specifications are summarized in Table 3.

Item	Description
Size	40 cm diameter and 90 cm height.
Weight	20 kg
Power	12 V battery.
No. of Wheels	4
Steer and drive mode	Differential Drive
Camera type	Two Color CCD camera
Frame rate	30 frames per second
Image standard	NTSC
Image size	640×480 pixel × pixel
robot speed	Maximum 50 cm/s

Table 3. Specification of the mobile robot.

4.2 Results

An experimental program was conducted to explore the effectiveness of the control system in guiding the robot through the indoor environment according to desired behaviors.

Experiments were done for separate behaviors and then for the combined behavior. A sample result showing the extraction of target area is shown in Fig. 7. The left image shows original captured image and the extracted target area is shown in the right image.

Fig. 7. The segmented image showing the detected target area.

A computer program was devised to construct the Hue-Saturation, H-S histogram shown in Fig 8. The advantage of this representation is that it enables better extraction of the target when it had been well identified apriori. We show the histogram for a sample target, which is a red object in this particular case. The hue range is from 0 to 360 degrees and the saturation ranges from 0 to 255. It is worth noting that the hue angle is repeated and hence 0 degree vertical line coincides with the 360 degree vertical line, therefore the region shown can be described in limited bounds. The dark regions in the graph corresponds to a high number of pixels in the target area having the same H-S point. This defines the color zone mentioned earlier in this paper and the bounds are extracted from this figure. It is worth noting that the input image contains the target in several views and distances so that it almost encapsulates all the possible color reflections of the object in all views. For the target following experiments, the robot is adjusted at first to view the target inside the color image.

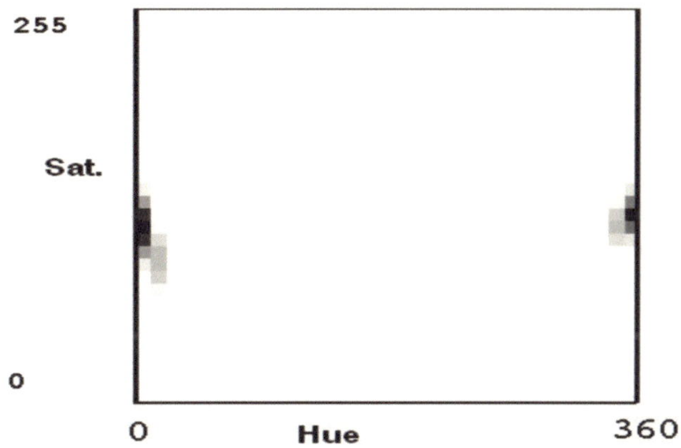

Fig. 8. The Hue-Saturation diagram showing regions of darker intensity as those corresponding to higher voting of the target object pixels.

The robot starts to move as shown in the robot track, Fig. 9 and keeps moving forward.

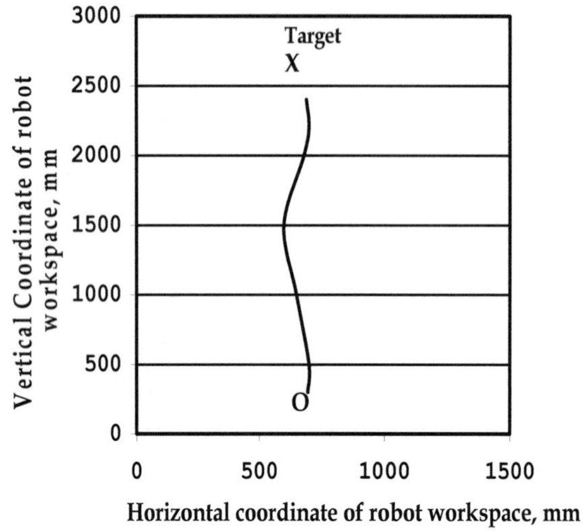

Fig. 9. The real track of the robot while following the colored target.

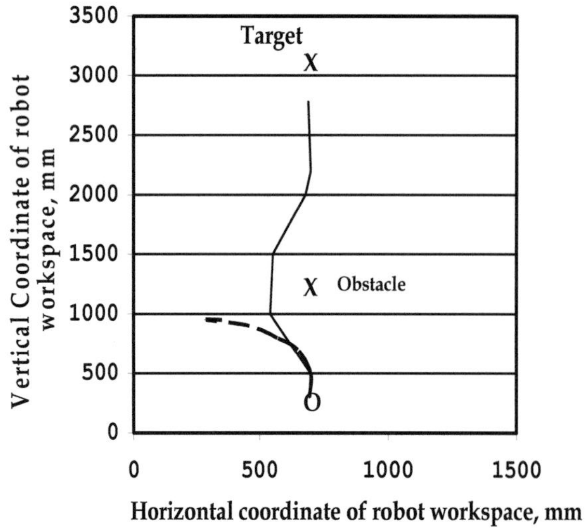

Fig. 10. The real track of the robot while following the colored target.

During the robot motion, the target continuously approach the image center and consequently the target area increases in the extracted target image. The robot followed the target even when it is moving in curved routes, as long as the target is visible in the robot camera and the target speed is comparable to robot speed.

An experiment for the obstacle avoidance behavior is shown in Fig 10. The dotted line shows the robot path when working with obstacle avoidance only. The robot evades the obstacles and move towards free areas based on the sequence of obstacles faced.

The robot stops when the target area in the image exceeds a certain empirical threshold so that the robot stops at about 25 cm in front of the target, or the sensors detect an obstacle less than 30 cm close to it.

The target following behavior is then integrated with the output from obstacle avoidance behavior using vector summation principle. The heading angle is then executed by the differential wheels.
An experiment showing the combined effect of both behaviors is shown also in Fig 10. The solid line shows the robot track when both behaviors are combined, the robot evades the right target but soon recovers and steer right toward the target.

5. Conclusion

We have implemented a control system that enables a mobile service robot to track and follow a moving target while avoiding obstacles. The system was experimentally validated using a real robot equipped with CCD cameras and ultrasonic range sensors. The algorithms for color image processing and extraction of the target image and measurement of target features had been developed. Fuzzy logic controllers had been designed to produce two concurrent behaviors of target following and obstacle avoidance and for combining the results of two behaviors into one set of commands for robot control. The control system succeeded in guiding the robot reliably in both tracking of the target and following it while keeping a reasonable distance between them that ensures the visibility of the target in the camera view. Fuzzy control provided smooth and reliable navigation that circumvents the inherent uncertainities and noise in the sensing process, as well as the smooth blending of behaviors.
Future directions of research include the use of more input information such as that from a human interface or an external planner. The goal is to create an autonomous service robot that will be able to navigate based on information from combined information from visual inputs, sonars and outdoor GPS data that will guide the vehicle in remote target points and have a user-friendly interface.

6. References

Arkin, R.C. (1998). *Behavior Based Robotics,* MIT Press, Cambridge Massachusetts.

Borenstein, J. & Koren, Y. (1991). The Vector Field Histogram A Fast Obstacle-Avoidance for Mobile Robots. *IEEE Journal of Robotics and Automation,* Vol. 7, No. 3., (1991), pp. 278-288.

Brooks, R.A. (1986). A Robust Layered Control System for a Mobile Robot. *IEEE Journal of Robotics and Automation,* Vol.2, No., (1986), pp 14-23.

Carreras, M.; Batlle, J. & Ridao, P. (2001). Hybrid Coordination of Reinforcement Learning-based Behaviors for AUV control, *Proceeding of IEEE/RSJIROS,* Vol.3, pp:1410-1415, Maui, HI, USA.

Cheng, H.D. & Sun, Y. (2000). A Hierarchical Approach to Color Image Segmentation Using Homogeneity. *In IEEE Transactions on Image Processing,* Vol. 9, No. 12, (2000), pp:2071-2082.

Khatib, O. (1985). Real-Time Obstacle Avoidance for Manipulators and Mobile Robots, *Proceeding of IEEE International Conference on Robotics and Automation,* pp. 500-505.

Kim,W. & Park, R. (1996). Color Image Palette Construction Based on the HSI Color System for minimizing the reconstruction error, *In Proceeding of IEEE International Conference on Image Processing,* pp: 1041-1044.

Littmann, E. & Ritter, H. (1997). Adaptive color segmentation—a comparison of neural and statistical methods. *IEEE Transactions on Neural Networks*, Vol. 8, No. 1, pp:175-185.

Luo, R.C. ; Chen, T.M. & Su, K.L. (2001). Target tracking using hierarchical grey fuzzy decision making method, *IEEE Transactions on Systems, Man and Cybernetics*, Part A Vol. 31 No.3, pp:179-186.

Saffiotti, A. (1997). The uses of fuzzy logic in autonomous robot navigation: a catalogue raisonne, Technical Report TR/IRIDIA/97-6, available from http://iridia.ulb.ac.be, Accessed: 2006-10-10.

Sei, I.; Tomokazu, S.; Koichiro Y. & Naokazu, Y. (2007). Construction of Feature Landmark Database Using Omnidirectional Videos and GPS Positions, *Proceeding of the Sixth International Conference on 3-D Digital Imaging and Modeling*, pp: 249–256.

Tseng, D.C. & Chang, C.H. (1992). Color Segmentation Using Perceptual Attributes, *In IEEE Int Conf. Image Processing*, pp: 228-231, Netherlands, The Hague.

Veera Ragavan, S. & Ganapathy V. (2007). A Unified Framework for a Robust Conflict-Free Robot Navigation, *International Journal of Intelligent Technology*, Vol.2, No.1, pp:88-94.

Walther, M.; Steinhaus, P. & Dillmann, R. (2003). A robot navigation approach based on 3D data fusion and real time path planning, *Proceeding IEEE International Conference on Multisensor Fusion and Integration for Intelligent Systems*, pp:45–50, Germany, July-2003, Karlsruhe.

Zadeh, L.A. (1965). Fuzzy sets Information and Control, 8, pp.338-353, 1965.

Zimmermann, H.J. (1996). Fuzzy set theory—and its applications (Third edition), Kluwer Academic Publishers, Norwell, MA, 1996.

2

Dynamic Omnidirectional Vision Localization Using a Beacon Tracker Based on Particle Filter

Zuoliang Cao, Xianqiu Meng and Shiyu Liu
Tianjin University of Technology
P.R. China

1. Introduction

Autonomous navigation is of primary importance in applications involving the usage of Autonomous Guided Vehicles (AGVs). Vision-based navigation systems provide an interesting option for both indoor and outdoor navigation as they can also be used in environments without an external supporting infrastructure for the navigation, which is unlike GPS, for example. However, the environment has to contain some natural or artificial features that can be observed with the vision system, and these features have to have some relationship to spatial locations in the navigation environment (Cao, 2001). The omni-directional camera system produces a spherical field of view of an environment. This is particularly useful in vision-based navigation systems as all the images, provided by the camera system, contain the same information, independent of the rotation of the robot in the direction of the optical axis of the camera. This makes the computed image features more suitable for localization and navigation purposes (Hrabar & Sukhatme, 2003; Hampton et al., 2004). The methods proposed have been developed for vision-based navigation of Autonomous Ground Vehicles which utilize an omni-directional camera system as the vision sensor. The complete vision-based navigation system has also been implemented, including the omni-directional color camera system, image processing algorithms, and the navigation algorithms. The actual navigation system, including the camera system and the algorithms, has been developed. The aim is to provide a robust platform that can be utilized both in indoor and outdoor AGV applications (Cauchois et al., 2005; Sun et al., 2004).
The fisheye lens is one of the most efficient ways to establish an omnidirectional vision system. The structure of the fisheye lens is relatively dense and well-knit unlike the structure of reflector lenses which consist of two parts and are fragile. (Li et al., 2006; Ying et al., 2006). Omnidirectional vision (omni-vision) holds promise of various applications. We use a fisheye lens upwards with the view angle of 185° to build the omni-directional vision system. Although fisheye lens takes the advantage of an extremely wide angle of view, there is an inherent distortion in the fisheye image which must be rectified to recover the original image. An approach for geometric restoration of omni-vision images has to be considered since an inherent distortion exists. The mapping between image coordinates and physical space parameters of the targets can be obtained by means of the imaging principle on the fisheye lens. Firstly a method for calibrating the omni-vision system is proposed. The method relies on the utilities of a cylinder on which inner wall including several straight

lines to calibrate the center, radius and gradient of a fisheye lens. Then we can make use of these calibration parameters for the correction of distortions. Several imaging rules are conceived for fisheye lenses. The regulations are discussed respectively and the distortion correction models are generated. An integral distortion correction approach based on these models is developed. A support vector machine (SVM) is introduced to regress the intersection points in order to get the mapping between the fisheye image coordinate and the real world coordinate. The advantage of using the SVM is that the projection model of fisheye lens which needs to be acquired from the manufacturer can be ignored.

Omni-directional vision navigation for autonomous guided vehicles (AGVs) appears definite significant since its advantage of panoramic sight with a single compact visual scene. This unique guidance technique involves target recognition, vision tracking, object positioning, path programming. An algorithm for omni-vision based global localization which utilizes two overhead features as beacon pattern is proposed. The localization of the robot can be achieved by geometric computation on real-time processing. Dynamic localization employs a beacon tracker to follow the landmarks in real time during the arbitrary movement of the vehicle. The coordinate transformation is devised for path programming based on time sequence images analysis. The beacon recognition and tracking are a key procedure for an omni-vision guided mobile unit. The conventional image processing such as shape decomposition, description, matching and other usually employed technique are not directly applicable in omni-vision. Vision tracking based on various advanced algorithms has been developed. Particle filter-based methods provide a promising approach to vision-based navigation as it is computationally efficient, and it can be used to combine information from various sensors and sensor features. A beacon tracking-based method for robot localization has already been investigated at the Tianjin University of Technology, China. The method utilizes the color histogram, provided by a standard color camera system, in finding the spatial location of a robot with highest probability (Musso & Oudjane, 2000; Menegatti et al., 2006).

Particle filter (PF) has been shown to be successful for several nonlinear estimation problems. A beacon tracker based on Particle Filter which offers a probabilistic framework for dynamic state estimation in visual tracking has been developed. We independently use two Particle Filters to track double landmarks but a composite algorithm on multiple objects tracking conducts for vehicle localization. To deal with the mass operations of vision tracking, a processor with the ability of effective computation and low energy cost is required. The Digital Signal Processor fits our demands, which is well known for powerful operation capability and parallel operation of instruction (Qi et al., 2005). It has been widely used in complicated algorithm calculation such as video/imaging processing, audio signal analysis and intelligent control. However, there are few cases that DSP is applied in image tracking as the central process unit. In our AGV platform, DSP has been implemented as a compatible on-board imaging tracker to execute the Particle Filter algorithm. An integrated autonomous vehicle navigator based on the configuration with Digital Signal Processor (DSP) and Filed-programmable Gate Array (FPGA) has been implemented. The tracking and localization functions have been demonstrated on experimental platform.

2. Calibration for fisheye lens camera

According to the fisheye imaging characteristics (Wang, 2006), the rectification of the fisheye image consists of two main phases. First the center of fisheye lens need to be calibrated.

Second, establish the mapping between the physical space coordinate and fisheye images coordinate.

The approach for geometric restoration of omni-vision images has been considered in some papers since the fisheye lens was used (Cao et al., 2007). Some parameters are primarily important in the geometric restoration, such as the center and focal length of the fisheye lens. The calibration by using distortion models has been discussed in recent papers (Wang et al., 2006; Li et al., 2006; Brauer-Burchardt. & Voss., 2001). The calibration parameters can be retrieved by the method of least square and mathematic models. The previous approach utilizes grids, which are drawn on a plan surface. The grids will distort after grabbed by the fisheye lens camera (Hartley & Kang, 2007). Here, another method for calibrating the center of omni-vision images is proposed.

If a straight line in physical space is parallel to the optical axis direction of the fisheye lens, the line will not distort in the fisheye image. Therefore, a cylinder model is proposed in this article. To construct the cylinder model, straight lines are drawn on the inner side of the cylinder, whose axis is parallel to the optical axis of the fisheye camera. Then enclose the camera lens with this cylinder. The image captured with fisheye camera using cylinder model is shown in Fig. 1. The intersection of all the lines is the fisheye lens center.

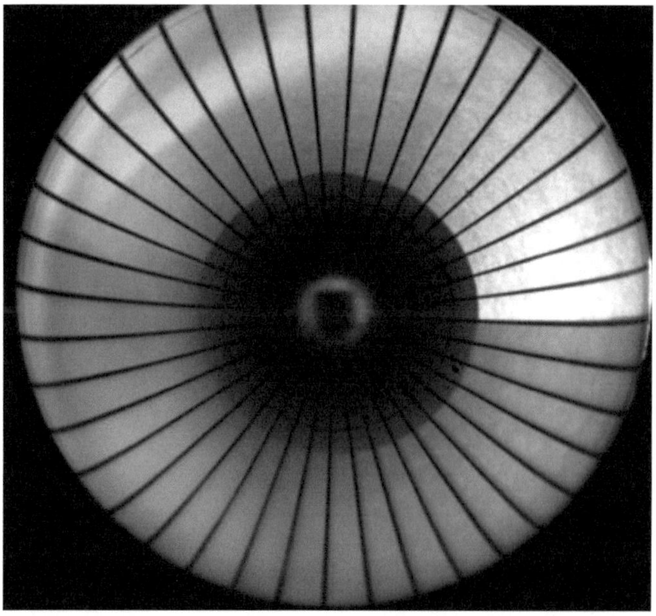

Fig. 1. Radial straight lines in fisheye lens image under cylinder model

To get the conversion relationship between the physical space coordinate and fisheye images coordinate, the following method is utilized. The lower vertex of the vertical strip which lies in the middle of the image is on the center of the fisheye optical projection that is the origin of the fisheye coordinate system as shown in Fig. 2. The horizontal strips have the same intervals and the intersection points of the vertical and horizontal strips have the equal radial distance between them in physical space. As a result of fisheye distortion, the distance between two consecutive intersection points are not equal in the image. But the corresponding coordinates of intersection points in the fisheye image is achieved.

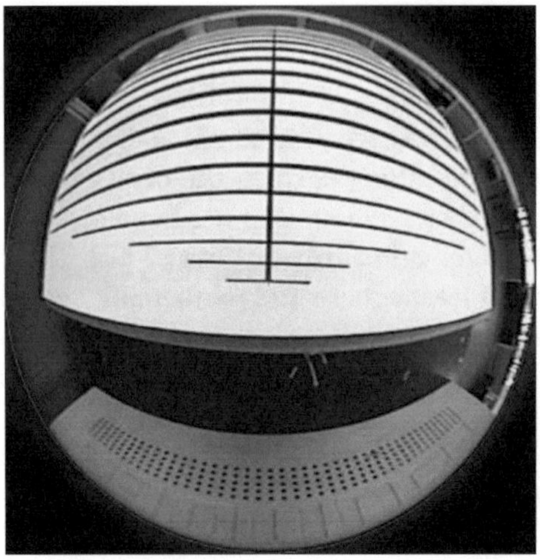

Fig. 2. Calibration for omnidirectional vision system

Then we use a support vector machine (SVM) to regress the intersection points in order to get the mapping between the fisheye image coordinate and the undistorted image coordinate. The advantage of using the SVM is that the projection model of fisheye lens which needs to be acquired from the manufacturer can be ignored.

3. Rectification for fisheye lens distortion

3.1 Fisheye Lens Rectification principle

The imaging principle of fisheye lens is different from that of a conventional camera. The inherent distortion of the fisheye lens is induced when a 2π steradian hemisphere is projected onto a plane circle. Lens distortion can be expressed as (Wang et al., 2006):

$$\begin{cases} u_d = u + \delta_u(u,v) \\ v_d = v + \delta_v(u,v) \end{cases} \tag{1}$$

Where u and v refer to the unobservable distortion-free image coordinates; u_d and v_d are the corresponding image with distortion; $\delta_u(u,v)$ and $\delta_v(u,v)$ are distortion in u and v direction.

Fisheye lens distortion can be classified into three types: radial distortion, decentering distortion and thin prism distortion. The first just arise the radial deviation. The other two produce not only the radial deviation but decentering deviation.

Generally, radial distortion is considered to be predominant, which is mainly caused by the nonlinear change in radial curvature. As a pixel of the image move along projection, the further it gets from the center of the lens, the larger the deformation is.

Owing to the different structure of lens, there are two types of deformation; one is that the proportion becomes greater while the range between the points and the center of radial distortion becomes bigger. The other is contrary. The mathematical model is as follow (Wang et al., 2006):

$$\begin{cases} \delta_{ur}(u,v) = u\left(k_1 r^2 + k_2 r^4 + k_3 r^6 + \cdots\right) \\ \delta_{vr}(u,v) = v\left(k_1 r^2 + k_2 r^4 + k_3 r^6 + \cdots\right) \end{cases} \tag{2}$$

Where k_1, k_2, k_3 are radial distortion coefficients; r is the distance from point (u, v) to the center of radial distortion.

The first term is predominant, and the second and third terms are usually negligible, so the radial distortion formula can usually be reduced as (Wang et al., 2006):

$$\begin{cases} \delta_{ur}(u,v) = k_1 u r^2 \\ \delta_{vr}(u,v) = k_1 v r^2 \end{cases} \tag{3}$$

Here, we just consider radial distortion, others are neglected. Let (u,v) be the measurable coordinates of the distorted image points, *(x,y)* be the coordinates of the undistorted image points, and the function f be the conversion relationship, which can be expressed as:

$$\begin{cases} x = f(u,v) \\ y = f(u,v) \end{cases} \tag{4}$$

Thus, the relationship between the fisheye image coordinate and physical world image coordinate is obtained.

3.2 Fisheye lens image rectification algorithm

In the conventional method, the approach to get parameters of distortion is complicated and the calculation is too intensive. Support Vector Machines (SVM) is statistical machine learning methods which perform well at density estimation, regression and classification (Zhang et al., 2005). It suits for small size example set. It finds a global minimum of the actual risk upper bound using structural risk minimization and avoids complex calculation in high dimension space by kernel function. SVM map the input data into a high-dimensional feature space and finds an optimal separating hyper plane to maximize the margin between two classes in this high-dimensional space. Maximizing the margin is a quadratic programming problem and can be solved by using some optimization algorithms (Wang et al., 2005). The goal of SVM is to produce model predicts the relationship between data in the testing set.

To reduce the computation complexity, we employ SVM to train a mapping from fisheye image coordinate to the undistorted image coordinate. SVM trains an optimal mapping between input date and output data, based on which the fisheye lens image can be accurately corrected.

In order to rectify fisheye image we have to get radial distortion on all of distorted image points. Based on the conversion model and the great ability of regression of SVM, we select a larger number of distorted image points (u,v) and input them to SVM. SVM can calculate the radial distortion distance and regress (u,v) to (x,y) (the undistorted image point); so that the mapping between the distortional images point and the undistorted image point can be obtained. The whole process of fisheye image restoration is shown in Fig. 3.

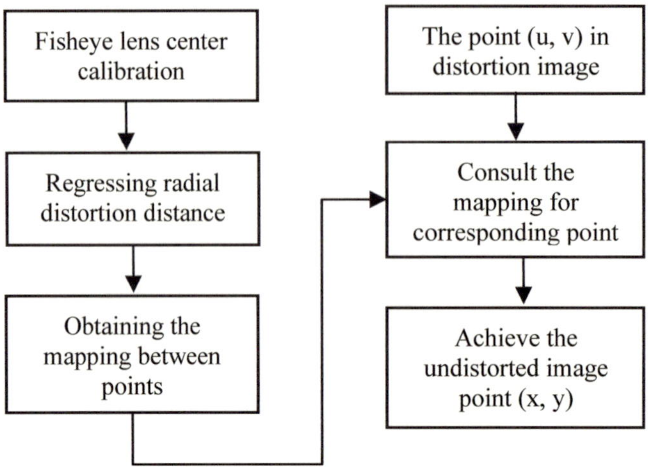

Fig. 3. Flow chart of fisheye image restoration algorithm

A number of experiments for fisheye lens image rectification have been implemented. By comparison, the results verify the feasibility and validity of the algorithm. The results are shown in Fig. 4.

Fig. 4. A fisheye image (above) and the corrected result of a fisheye image (below)

4. Omni-vision tracking and localization based on particle filter

4.1 Beacon recognition

Selecting landmark is vital to the mobile robot localization and the navigation. However, the natural sign is usually not stable and subject to many external influences, we intend to use indoor sign as the landmark. According to the localization algorithm, at least two color landmarks are requested which are projected on the edge of the AGV moving area. We can easily change the size, color and the position of the landmarks. The height of two landmarks and the distance between them are measured as the known parameters. At the beginning of tracking, the tracker has to determine the landmark at first. In our experiment, we use Hough algorithm to recognize the landmark at the first frame as the prior probability value. The Hough transform has been widely used to detect patterns, especially those well parameterized patterns such as lines, circles, and ellipses (Guo et al., 2006). Here we utilize DSP processor which has high speed than PC to perform the Circular Hough Transform. The pattern recognition by using CHT (Circular Hough Transform) is shown in Fig. 5.

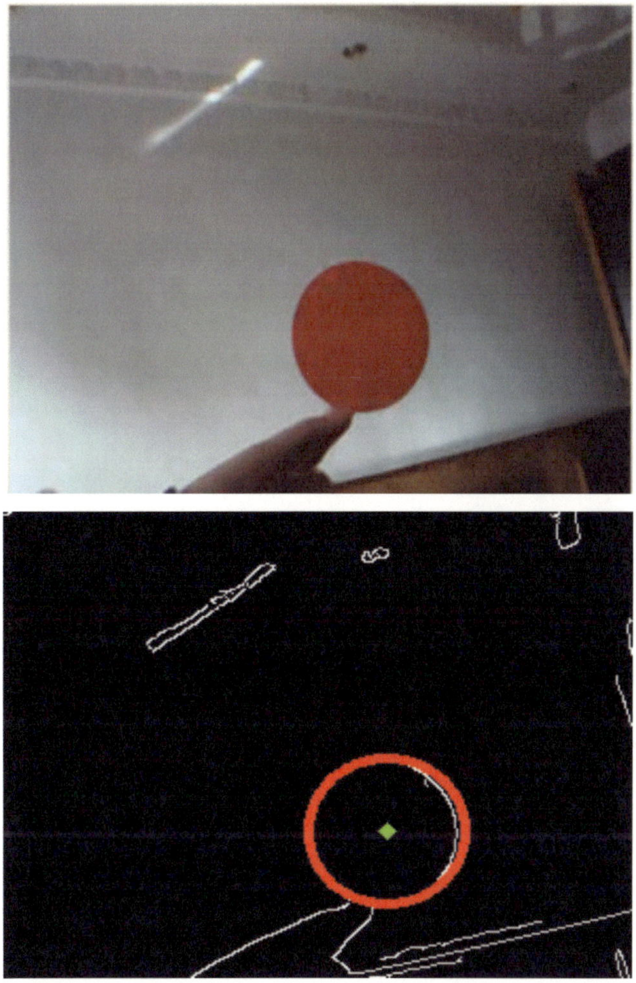

Fig. 5. A circle object (above) and the result of Circular Hough Transform (below)

4.2 Tracking based on particle filter

After obtain the initialization value, the two particle filters will track the landmark continuously. Particle filtering is a Monte Carlo sampling approach to Bayesian filtering. The main idea of the particle filter is that the posterior density is approximated by a set of discrete samples with associated weights. These discrete samples are called particles which describe possible instantiations of the state of the system. As a consequence, the distribution over the location of the tracking object is represented by the multiple discrete particles (Cho et al., 2006).

In the Bayes filtering, the posterior distribution is iteratively updated over the current state X_t, given all observations $Z_t = \{Z_1,...,Z_t\}$ up to time t, as follows:

$$p(X_t \mid Z_t) = p(Z_t \mid X_t) \cdot \int_{x_{t-1}} p(X_t \mid X_{1t-1}) \cdot p(X_{t-1} \mid Z_{t-1}) dx_{t-1} \quad (5)$$

Where $p(Z_t \mid X_t)$ expresses the observation model which specifies the likelihood of an object being in a specific state and $p(X_t \mid X_{t-1})$ is the transition model which specifies how objects move between frames. In a particle filter, prior distribution $p(X_{t-1} \mid Z_{t-1})$ is approximated recursively as a set of N-weighted samples, which is the weight of a particle. Based on the Monte Carlo approximation of the integral, we can get:

$$p(X_t \mid Z_t) \approx kp(Z_t \mid X_t) \sum_{i=1}^{N} w_{t-1}^{(i)} p(X_t \mid X_{t-1}^{(i)}) \quad (6)$$

The principal steps in the particle filter algorithm include:

STEP 1 Initialization

Generate particle set from the initial distribution $p(X_0)$ to obtain $\{X_0^{(i)}, w_0^{(i)}\}_{i=1}^{N}$, and set $k = 1$.

STEP 2 Propagation

For $i = 1,...,N$, Sample $X_k^{(i)}$ according to the transition model $p(X_k^{(i)} \mid X_{k-1}^{(i)})$.

STEP 3 Weighting

Evaluate the importance likelihood

$$w_k^{(i)} = \frac{w_k^{(i)}}{\sum_{j=1}^{N} w_k^{(j)}} \qquad i = 1,...,N \quad (7)$$

STEP 4 Normalize the weights

$$w_k^{(i)} = p(Z_k \mid X_k^{(i)}) \qquad i = 1,...,N \quad (8)$$

Output a set of particles $\{X_k^{(i)}, w_k^{(i)}\}_{i=1}^{N}$ that can be used to approximate the posterior distribution as

$$p(X_k \mid Z_k) = \sum_{i=1}^{N} w_k^{(i)} \delta(X_k - X_k^{(i)}) \quad (9)$$

Where $\delta(g)$ is the Dirac delta function.

STEP 5 Resample particles $X_k^{(i)}$ with probability $w_t^{(i)}$ to obtain N independent and identically distributed random particles $X_k^{(j)}$ approximately distributed according to $p(X_k \mid Z_k)$.

STEP 6 Set $k = k + 1$, and return to STEP 2.

4.3 Omni-vision based AGV localization

In this section, we will discuss how to localize the AGV utilizing the space and image information of landmarks. As it is shown in Fig. 6, two color beacons which are fixed on the edge of the AGV moving area as landmarks facilitate navigation. The AGV can localize itself employing the fisheye lens camera on top of it.

The height of two landmarks and the distance between them are measured as the known parameters. When the AGV is being navigated two landmarks are tracked by two particle filters to get the landmarks positions in the image.

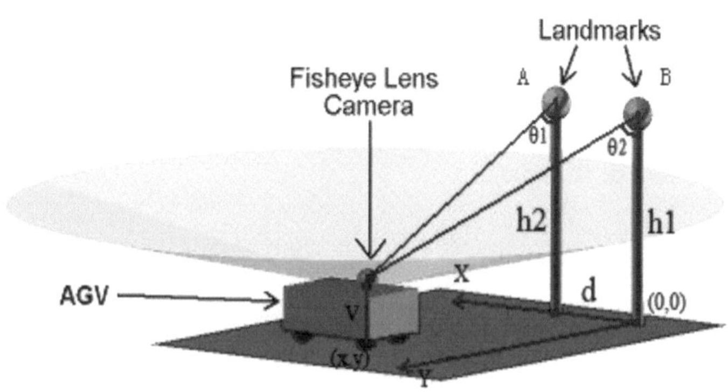

Fig. 6. Physical space coordinates system for landmarks localization

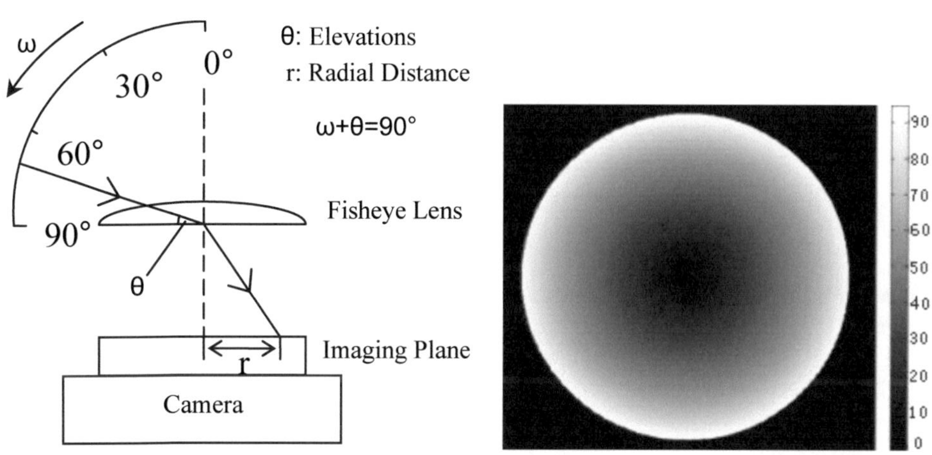

Fig. 7. Left figure shows that the relationship between incident angles and radial distances of fisheye lens. Right figure illustrates the values of corresponding incident angles with different grey levels in the whole area of fisheye sphere image

According to the Equal Distance Projection Regulation, the angle of view ω corresponds with the radial distance r between projection point and projection center. As shown in Fig. 7, the mapping between ω and r can be established. Based on this mapping, the image coordinate and space angle of the landmark are connected.
Utilizing the depressions obtained from images and demarcated parameters of landmarks, the physical space position of the AGV is confirmed. We tag the landmarks as A and B. In order to set up the physical coordinate system, A is chosen as the origin. AB is set as axis X and the direction from A to B is the positive orientation of axis X. Axis Y is vertical to Axis X. According to the space geometry relations, we can get:

$$\begin{aligned} x &= \frac{[\cot\theta_1(h_1 - v)]^2 - [\cot\theta_2(h_2 - v)^2] + d^2}{2d} \\ y &= \sqrt{[\cot\theta_1(h_1 - v)^2 - x^2]} \end{aligned} \tag{10}$$

where (x, y) is the physical space coordinate of lens, " h_1 " and " h_2 " are the height of two landmarks, " d " is the horizontal distance between two landmarks, " v " is the height from ground to lens, " θ_1 " and " θ_2 " are the depression angles from landmark A and B to lens. Here, y is nonnegative. Thus the moving path of AGV should keep on one side of the landmarks, which is half of the space.

5. Navigation system

5.1 Algorithm architecture of navigator

A dynamic omni-vision navigation technique for mobile robots is being developed. Navigation functions involve positional estimation and surrounding perception. Landmark guidance is a general method for vision navigation in structural environments. An improved beacon tracking and positioning approach based on a Particle Filter algorithm has been utilized. Some typical navigation algorithms have been already implemented such as the classic PID compensator, neural-fuzzy algorithm and so on. The multi-sensory information fusion technique has been integrated into the program. The hybrid software and hardware platform has been developed.
The algorithm architecture of the on-board navigator, as shown in Fig. 8, consists of the following phases: image collection, image pre-processing, landmark recognition, beacon tracking, vehicle localization and path guidance. The image distortion correction and recovery for omni-vision is a critical module in the procedures, which provides coordinate mapping for position and orientation.

5.2 Hardware configuration of navigator

The design of the navigator for mobile robots depends on considering the integration of the algorithm and hardware. Real-time performance is directly influenced by the results of localization and navigation. Most image processing platforms use a PC and x86 CPUs. This presents some limitations for an on-board navigator for vehicles because of redundancy resources, energy consuming and room utility.
This article presents a compatible embedded real-time image processor for AGVs by utilizing a Digital Signal Processor (DSP) and Field-Programmable Gate Array (FPGA) for the image processing component. The hardware configuration of the navigator is shown in Fig. 9.

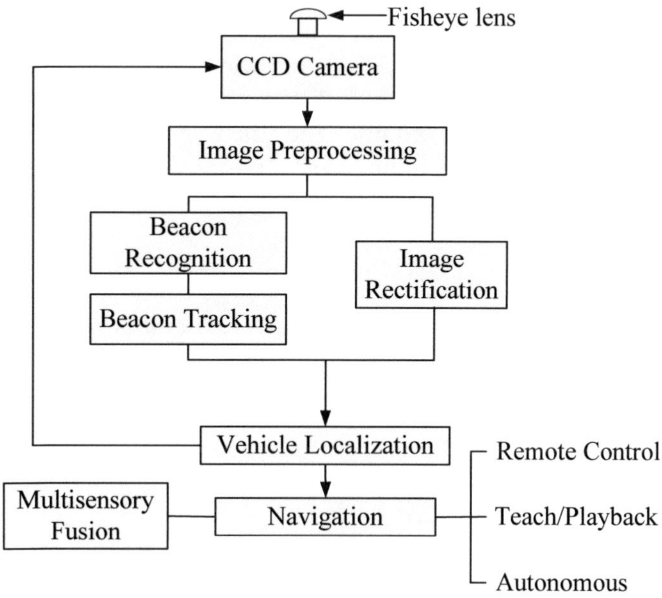

Fig. 8. The algorithm architecture of the navigator

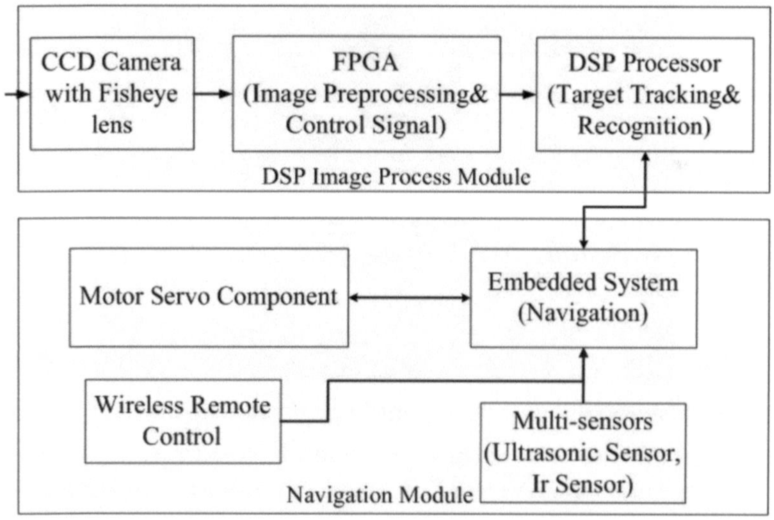

Fig. 9. Hardware configuration of the unique navigator

The DSP facilitates Enhanced DMA (EDMA) to transfer data between the DSP and external Navigation Module efficiently. Pipeline and code optimization are also required to move to sharply increase the speed. An efficient FPGA preprocessing uses binarized images with a given threshold before starting processing and also provides some necessary trigger signal functions. With this coprocessor, it is possible to accelerate all navigator processes. The DSP and FPGA can cooperate with each other to solve the real-time performance problems; the flexible frame is reasonable and practical.

The navigation module consists of an embedded platform, multi-sensors and an internet port. The embedded system is employed for a navigation platform, which consists of the following functions: vehicle localization, line following path error correction, obstacle avoidance through multi-sensory capability. There are three operation modes: remote control, Teach/Playback and autonomous. The internet port provides the wireless communication and human-computer interaction. The motor servo system is utilized for motion control. With the prototype we have obtained some satisfying experimental results.

6. Experimental result

The final system has been implemented by utilizing a real omni-directional vision AGV in an indoor environment which has been verified in terms of both the practicability and the feasibility of the design. The prototype experimental platform is shown in Fig. 10.

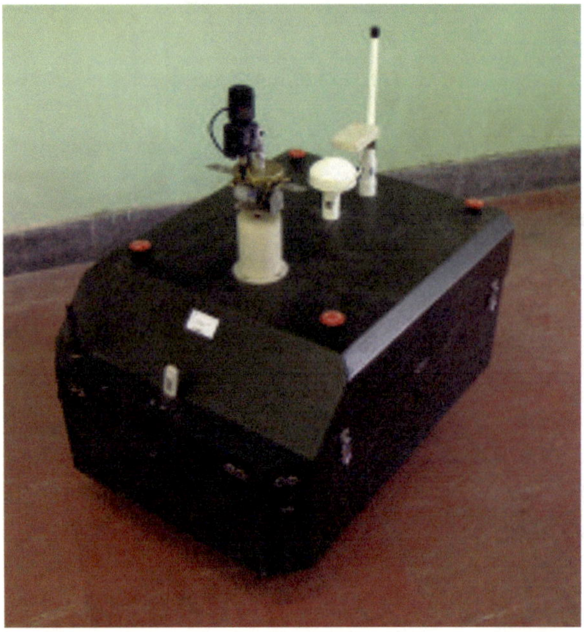

Fig. 10. Experimental autonomous guided vehicle platform

We perform the experiments twice to show the result. Two beacons with different colors are placed on the roof as landmarks. A color histogram was uses as the feature vector in particle filters. The experimental area we choose is about 30 square meters. The height of Landmarks A and B are 2.43m and 2.46m, respectively. The distance between them is 1.67m. The height of lens is 0.88m. At the initialization, the original positions of landmarks in the image are set for the tracker. The AGV guided by double color landmarks shown in Fig. 11. Driving path and orientation shown in Fig. 12. We can see the localization results are dispersed on the both sides of the moving path. The Fig. 12 demonstrates the results of AGV orientation corresponding to the positions in left figures from each localization cycle. The totally 16 fisheye images that were picked up are shown in Fig. 13 and Fig. 14. The numerical localization results are listed in the Table 1 and Table 2.

Fig. 11. Localization of the experimental AGV platform

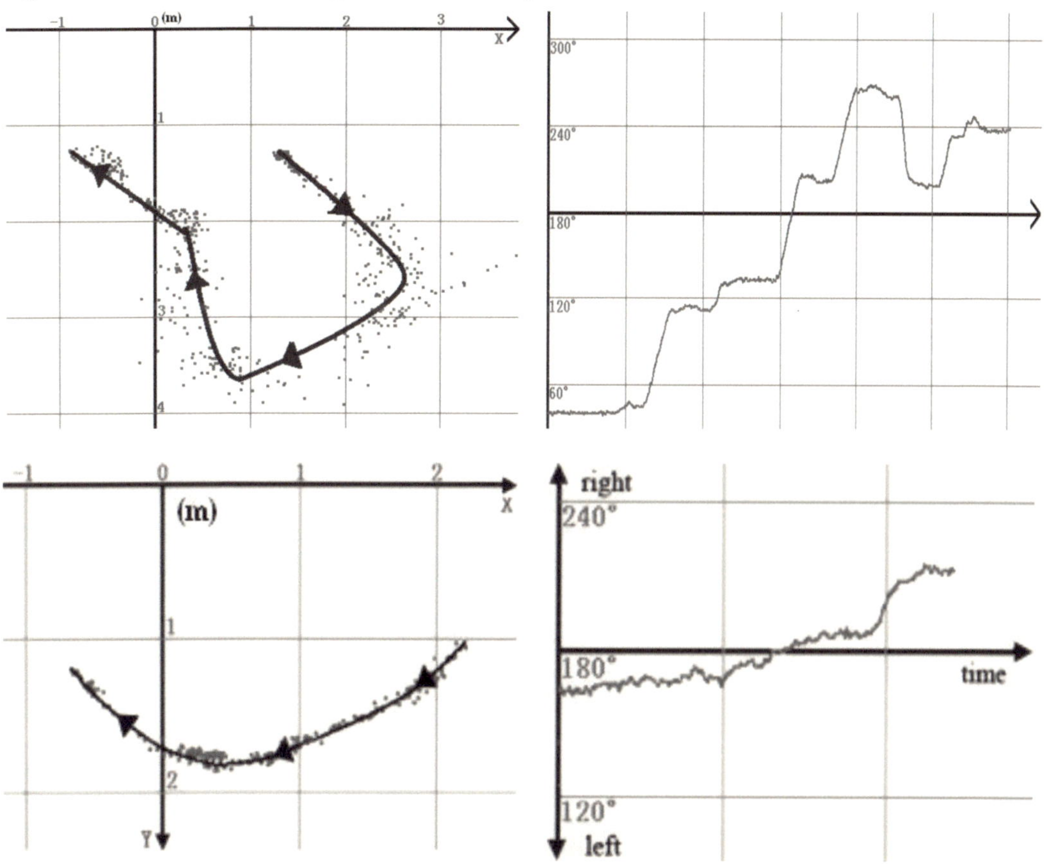

Fig. 12. Localization and orientation of autonomous vehicle in experiment 1 (above) and 2 (below) (the units are meter and degree (angle))

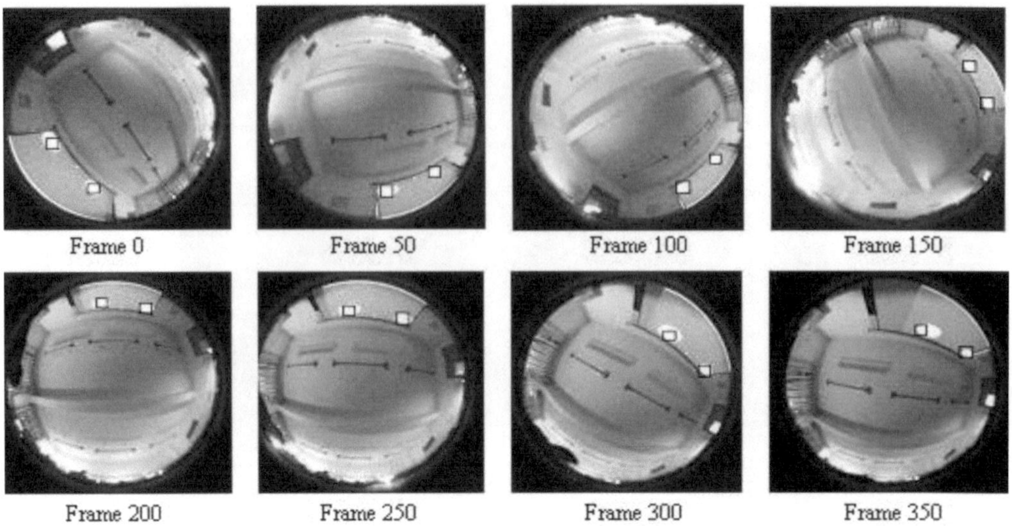

Fig. 13. Results of dynamic beacon tracking based on particle filters in experiment 1

(x, y, ϕ)	1	2	3	4
Actual Coordinates	(1.31, 1.35, 45°)	(2.00, 1.88, 68°)	(2.46, 2.67, 74°)	(2.34, 2.93, 144°)
Localization Coordinates	(1.47, 1.33, 43°)	(2.32, 1.93, 66°)	(2.33, 2.69, 79°)	(2.38, 2.96, 148°)
(x, y, ϕ)	5	6	7	8
Actual Coordinates	(1.35, 3.45, 162°)	(0.66, 3.00, 271°)	(0.00,1.94, 135°)	(-0.92, 1.33, 137°)
Localization Coordinates	(1.38, 3.47, 160°)	(0.68, 3.06, 276°)	(-0.18, 2.00, 132°)	(-0.88, 1.29, 135°)

Table 1. Localization results of experiment 1(units are meter and degree (angle))

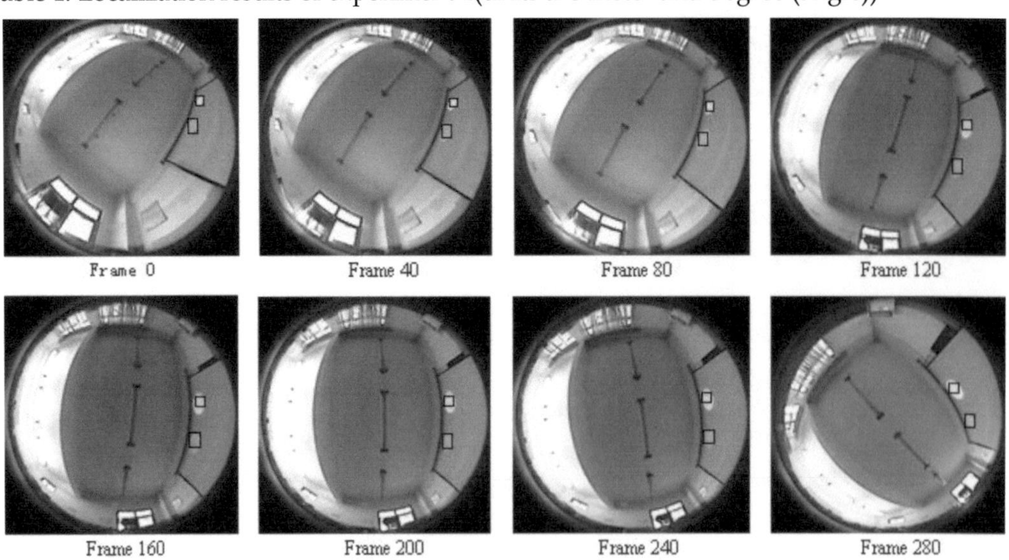

Fig. 14. Results of dynamic beacon tracking based on particle filters in experiment 2

(x, y, ϕ)	1	2	3	4
Actual Coordinates	(2.12, 1.06, 166°)	(2.05, 1.21,168°)	(1.53, 1.58,173°)	(1.07, 1.75, 176°)
Localization Coordinates	(2.23, 1.07, 165°)	(2.00, 1.18, 168°)	(1.55, 1.52,171°)	(1.00, 1.78 178°)
(x, y, ϕ)	5	6	7	8
Actual Coordinates	(0.52,1.93,179°)	(0.06,1.73,188°)	(-0.32,0.51,211°)	(-0.78,1.22,218°)
Localization Coordinates	(0.50,1.90,180°)	(0.00,1.70,191°)	(-0.35,0.50,210°)	(-0.75,1.20,220°)

Table 2. Localization results of experiment 2(units are meter and degree (angle))

7. Conclusion

We establish omni-directional vision system with fisheye lens and solve the problem of fisheye image distortion. A method for calibrating the omni-vision system is proposed to generate the center of a fisheye lens image. A novel fisheye image rectification algorithm based on SVM, which is different from the conventional method is introduced. Beacon recognition and tracking are key procedures for an omni-vision guided mobile unit. A Particle Filter (PF) has been shown to be successful for several nonlinear estimation problems. A beacon tracker based on a Particle Filter which offers a probabilistic framework for dynamic state estimation in visual tracking has been developed. Dynamic localization employs a beacon tracker to follow landmarks in real time during the arbitrary movement of the vehicle. The coordinate transformation is devised for path programming based on time sequence images analysis. Conventional image processing such as shape decomposition, description, matching, and other usually employed techniques are not directly applicable in omni-vision. We have implemented the tracking and localization system and demonstrated the relevance of the algorithm. The significance of the proposed research is the evaluation of a new calibration method, global navigation device and a dynamic omni-directional vision navigation control module using a beacon tracker which is based on a particle filter through a probabilistic algorithm on statistical robotics. An on-board omni-vision navigator based on a compatible DSP configuration is powerful for autonomous vehicle guidance applications.

8. Acknowledgments

This article contains the results of research of the international science and technology collaboration project (2006DFA12410) (2007AA04Z229) supported by the Ministry of Science and Technology of the People's Republic of China.

9. References

Brauer-Burchardt, C. & Voss, K. (2001). A new Algorithm to correct fisheye and strong wide angle lens distortion from single images, *Proceedings of 2001 International Conference on Image processing*, pp. 225-228, ISBN: 0-7803-6725-1, Thessaloniki Greece, October 2001

Cao, Z. L. (2001). Omni-vision based Autonomous Mobile Robotic Platform, *Proceedings of SPIE Intelligent Robots and Computer Vision XX: Algorithms, Techniques, and Active Vision*, Vol.4572, (2001), pp. 51-60, Newton USA

Cao, Z. L.; Liu, S. Y. & Röning, J. (2007). Omni-directional Vision Localization Based on Particle Filter, *Image and Graphics 2007, Fourth International Conference* , pp. 478-483, Chengdu China, August 2007

Cauchois, C.; Chaumont, F.; Marhic, B.; Delahoche, L. & Delafosse, M. (2005). Robotic Assistance: an Automatic Wheelchair Tracking and Following Functionality by Omnidirectional Vision, *Proceedings of the 2005 IEEE International Conference on Intelligent Robots and Systems*, pp. 2560-2565, ISBN: 0-7803-8912-3, Las Vegas USA

Cho, J. U.; Jin, S. H.; Pham, X. D.; Jeon, J. W.; Byun, J. E. & Kang, H. (2006). A Real-Time Object Tracking System Using a Particle Filter, Proceedings of the 2006 IEEE/RSJ International Conference on Intelligent Robots and Systems, pp. 2822-2827, ISBN: 1-4244-0259-X , Beijing China, October 2006

Guo, S. Y.; Zhang, X. F. & Zhang, F. (2006). Adaptive Randomized Hough Transform for Circle Detection using Moving Window, *Proceedings of 2006 International Conference on Machine Learning and Cybernetics*, pp. 3880-3885, ISBN: 1-4244-0061-9, Dalian

Hampton, R. D.; Nash, D.; Barlow, D.; Powell, R.; Albert, B. & Young, S. (2004). An Autonomous Tracked Vehicle with Omnidirectional Sensing. *Journal of Robotic Systems*, Vol. 21, No. 8, (August 2004) (429-437), ISSN: 0741-2223

Hartley, R. & Kang, S. B. (2007). Parameter-Free Radial Distortion Correction with Center of Distortion Estimation, *IEEE Transactions on Pattern Analysis and Machine Intelligence*, Vol. 29, No. 8, (August 2007) (1309-1321), ISSN: 0162-8828

Hrabar, S. & Sukhatme, G. S. (2003). Omnidirectional Vision for an Autonomous Helicopter, *Proceedings of the 2003 IEEE International Conference: Robotics and Automation*, Vol.1, pp. 558-563, Los Angeles USA, September 2003

Ishii, C.; Sudo, Y. & Hashimoto, H. (2003). An image conversion algorithm from fish eye image to perspective image for human eyes, *Proceedings of the 2003 IEEE/ASME International Conference on Advanced Intelligent Mechatronics*, pp. 1009-1014, ISBN: 0-7803-7759-1, Tokyo Japan

Li, S. G. (2006). Full-View Spherical Image Camera, *Pattern Recognition, 2006, ICPR 2006, 18th International Conference on Pattern Recognition*, pp. 386-390

Menegatti, E.; Pretto, A. & Pagello, E. (2006). Omnidirectional Vision Scan Matching for Robot Localization in Dynamic Environments, *Robotics and Automation IEEE Transactions*, Vol.22, No. 3, (June 2006) (523 - 535)

Musso, C. & Oudjane, N. (2000). Recent Particle Filter Applied to Terrain Navigation, *Proceedings of the Third International Conference on Information Fusion*, Vol. 2, pp. 26-33, ISBN: 2-7257-0000-0, Paris France

Qi, C; Sun, F. X. & Huang, T. S. (2005). The real-time image processing based on DSP, *Cellular Neural Networks and Their Applications*, 2005 9th International Workshop, pp. 40–43, ISBN: 0-7803-9185-3

Sun, Y. J.; Cao, Q. X. & Chen, W. D. (2004). An Object Tracking and Global Localization Method Using Omnidirectional Vision System, *Intelligent Control and Automation on 2004 Fifth Word Congress*, Vol. 6, pp. 4730-4735, ISBN: 0-7803-8273-0, Harbin China

Wang, L. P.; Liu, B. & Wan, C. R. (2005). Classification Using Support Vector Machines with Graded Resolution, *Proceedings of 2005 IEEE International Conference on Granular Computing*, Vol. 2, pp. 666 – 670, ISBN: 0-7803-9017-2, July 2005

Wang, J. H.; Shi, H. F.; Zhang, J. & Liu, Y. C. (2006). A New Calibration Model and Method of Camera Lens Distortion, *Proceedings of the 2006IEEE/RSJ national Conference on Intelligent Robots and Systems*, pp. 5317-5718, ISBN: 1-4244-0259-X, Beijing China, October , 2006

Wang, Y. Z. (2006). In: Fisheye Lens Optics, China Science Press, 26-61, ISBN: 7-03-017143-8, Beijing China

Ying, X. H. & Zha, H. B. (2006). Using Sphere Images for Calibrating Fisheye Cameras under the Unified Imaging Model of the Central Catadioptric and Fisheye Cameras, *ICPR 2006. 18th International Conference on Pattern Recognition*, Vol.1, pp. 539–542, Hong Kong

Zhang, J. P.; Li, Z. W. & Yang, J. (2005). A Parallel SVM Training Algorithm on Large-scale Classification Problems, *Proceedings of the Fourth International Conference on Machine Learning and Cybernetics*, Vol.3, pp. 1637–1641, Guangzhou China, August 2005

3

Paracatadioptric Geometry using Conformal Geometric Algebra

Carlos López-Franco
Computer Science Department, University of Guadalajara, Mexico

1. Introduction

Computer vision provides non-contact measurements of the world, extending the robot ability to operate in circumstances and environments which can not be accurately controlled. The use of visual observations to control the motions of robots has been extensively studied, this approach is referred in literature as visual servoing.

Conventional cameras suffer from a limited field of view. One effective way to increase the field of view is to use mirrors in combination with conventional cameras. The approach of combining mirrors with conventional cameras to enhance sensor field of view is referred as catadioptric image formation.

In order to be able to model the catadioptric sensor geometrically, it must satisfy the restriction that all the measurements of light intensity pass through only one point in the space (effective viewpoint). The complete class of mirrors that satisfy such restriction where analyzed by Baker and Nayar [1]. In [2] the authors deal with the epipolar geometry of two catadioptric sensors. Later, in [3] a general model for central catadioptric image formation was given. Also, a representation of this general model using the conformal geometric algebra was showed in [4].

Visual servoing applications can be benefit from sensors providing large fields of view. This work will show how a paracatadioptric sensor (parabolic mirror and a camera) can be used in a visual servoing task for driving a nonholonomic mobile robot.

The work is mainly concerned with the use of projected lines extracted from central catadioptric images as input of a visual servoing control loop. The paracatadioptric image of a line is in general a circle but sometimes it could be a line. This is something that should be taken into account to avoid a singularity in the visual servoing task.

In this work we will give a framework for the representation of image features in parabolic catadioptric images and their transformations. In particular line images in parabolic catadioptric images are circles. While of course conics and therefore circles can be represented in the projective plane we will provide a much more natural representation utilizing the conformal geometric algebra (CGA).

In CGA the conformal transformations are linearized using the fact that the conformal group on R^n is isomorphic to the Lorentz group on R^{n+1}. Hence nonlinear conformal transformations on R^n can be linearized by representing them as Lorentz transformations and thereby further simplified as versor representation. These versors can be applied not only to points but also to all the CGA entities (spheres, planes, circles, lines and point-pairs). In this model a b c represents the circle thought the three points. If one of these points is a null vector e_∞ representing the point at infinity, then $a \wedge b \wedge e_\infty$ represents the straight line trough a and b as a circle through infinity. This representation could not be available without the concept of null vector.

In contrast with other catadioptric sensors the paracatadioptric sensors have certain properties that make them very interesting. One important property is that paracatadioptric projection is conformal, this motivate us to use the conformal geometric algebra to represent it. Thus the paracatadioptric projection can be expressed linearly using versors of CGA. The advantage of our framework is that the projection can be applied to circles and lines in the same way as it does for points. That advantage has a tremendous consequence since the nonlinearity of the paracatadioptric image has been removed. As a result the input features for the visual servoing control loop can be handled effectively in order to design an efficient vision-based control scheme.

The rest of this paper is organized as follows: The next section will give a brief introduction to the conformal geometric algebra. In section 3 we show the equivalence between inversions on the sphere and the parabolic projections. Then, in section 4 we show the paracatadioptric image formation using the proposed framework. Later, in section 5 an application of a paracatadioptric stereo sensor is given. Finally, the conclusions are in section 6.

2. Conformal geometric algebra

In general, a geometric algebra [5] $\mathcal{G}^n$ is a n-dimensional vector space $\mathcal{V}^n$ over the reals $\mathcal{R}$. The geometric algebra is generated defining the *geometric product* as an associative and multilinear product satisfying the contraction rule

$$e_i^2 = \epsilon |e_i|^2, \ for \ e_i \ \in (V)^n \ , \tag{1}$$

where ϵ is −1, 0 or 1 and is called the signature of e_i. When $e_i \neq 0$ but its magnitude $|e_i|$ is equal to zero, e_i is called null vector.

The geometric product of a geometric algebra $\mathcal{G}_{p,q,r}$ for two basis e_i and e_j is defined as

$$e_i e_j = \begin{cases} 1 & \textbf{for } i = j \in \{1, 2, \ldots, p\} \\ -1 & \textbf{for } i = j \in \{p+1, \ldots, p+q\} \\ 0 & \textbf{for } i = j \in \{p+q+1, \ldots, n\} \\ e_{ij} = e_i \wedge e_j = -e_j \wedge e_i & \textbf{for } i \neq j \end{cases} \tag{2}$$

Thus, given a n-dimensional vector space V^n with an orthonormal basis $\{e_1, e_2, \ldots e_n\}$ its corresponding geometric algebra is generated using the geometric product. We can see that for a n-dimensional vector space, there are 2^n ways to combine its basis using the geometric product. Each of this product is called a basis blade. Together they span all the space of the geometric algebra $\mathcal{G}_n$.

We also denote with $\mathcal{G}_{p,q}$ a geometric algebra over $\mathcal{V}^{p,q}$ where p and q denote the signature of the algebra. If $p \neq 0$ and $q = 0$ the metric is euclidean $\mathcal{G}_n$, if non of them are zero the metric is pseudoeuclidean. A generic element in $\mathcal{G}_{p,q}$ is called a *multivector*. Every multivector M can be written in the expanded form

$$M = \sum_{i=0}^{n} \langle M \rangle_i \ , \tag{3}$$

where $\langle M \rangle_i$ represents the blade of grade i. The geometric product (denoted juxtaposition) of vectors is defined with a scalar part called the inner product and an outer product, which is a non scalar quantity, for example the outer product of **a** and **b** is

$$\mathbf{ab} = \mathbf{a} \cdot \mathbf{b} + \mathbf{a} \wedge \mathbf{b} \ , \tag{4}$$

The conformal geometric algebra [5] is the geometric algebra over an homogeneous conformal space. This framework extends the functionality of projective geometry to include circles and spheres. Furthermore, the dilations, inversions, rotations and translations in 3D becomes rotations in the 5D conformal geometric algebra. These transformations can not only be applied to points or lines, but to all the conformal entities (points, lines, planes, point pairs, circles and spheres).

In the conformal geometric algebra (CGA) we firstly add two extra vector basis e_+ and e_- to our $\mathcal{R}^3$ Euclidean space $\{e_1, e_2, e_3, e_-, e_+\}$, where $e_+^2 = 1$ and $e_-^2 = -1$. We denote this algebra with $G_{4,1}$ to show that four basis vectors square to +1 and one basis vector square to −1. In addition we define

$$e_0 = \frac{e_- - e_+}{2} \quad and \quad e_\infty = e_- + e_+ \ , \tag{5}$$

we note that they are null vectors since $e_0^2 = e_\infty^2 = 0$.. The vector e_0 can be interpreted as the origin of the coordinate system, and the vector e_∞ as the point at infinity. A few useful properties (easily proved) about this basis are

$e_+^2 = 1$	$e_-^2 = -1$	$e_\infty^2 = 0$	$e_0^2 = 0$
$e_\infty \wedge e_0 = E$	$e_0 \wedge e_\infty = -E$	$e_+ \wedge e_- = E$	$e_\infty \wedge e_- = E$
$e_+e_- = E$	$e_-e_+ = -E$	$ee_0 = -1 + E$	$e_0e = -1 - E$
$e_0 \cdot e_\infty = -1$	$e_\infty \cdot e_0 = -1$	$e_\infty \cdot E = e$	$E \cdot e_\infty = -e_\infty$
$E \cdot e_0 = e_0$	$e_0 \cdot E = -e_0$	$E^2 = 1$	$e_+ \cdot e_- = 0$
$Ee = -e$	$eE = e$	$Ee_0 = e_0$	$e_0E = -e_0$

(6)

Where $E = e_+ \wedge e_-$ is called the Minkowski plane.

To specify a 3-dimensional Euclidean point in an unique form in this 5-dimensional space, we require the definition of two constraints. The first constraint is that the representation must be homogeneous, that is αX and X represent the same point in the Euclidean space. The second constraint requires that the vector X be a null vector ($X^2 = 0$). The equation that satisfies these constraints is

$$X = \mathbf{x} + \frac{1}{2}\mathbf{x}^2 e_\infty + e_0 \tag{7}$$

where $\mathbf{x} \in \mathcal{R}^n$ and $X \in \mathcal{N}^{n+1}$. Note that this is a bijective mapping. From now and in the rest of the paper the points X are named conformal points and the points $\mathbf{x}$ are named Euclidean points. A conformal point (7) lies on the intersection of the null cone $\mathcal{N}^{n+1}$ and the hyperplane $\mathcal{P}^{n+1}(e_\infty, e_0)$, that is

$$\mathcal{N}^{n+1} \cap \mathcal{P}^{n+1}(e_\infty, e_0) = \{x \in \mathcal{R}^{n+1,1} | x^2 = 0, xe_\infty = -1\} . \tag{8}$$

A sphere on the *CGA* can be defined as

$$S = \mathbf{c} + \frac{1}{2}(\mathbf{c}^2 - r^2)e_\infty + e_0 . \tag{9}$$

To test for incidence of a point X with an entity S expressed in the *inner product null space* (IPNS) we use

$$X \cdot S = 0. \tag{10}$$

A point in the CGA is represented using (9), but setting the radius $r = 0$ we get (7). Also note that if $\mathbf{x} = 0$ in (7) we get the point e_0 of (5) corresponding to the origin of $\mathcal{R}^n$. One interesting thing about the conformal points is that their inner product

$$\begin{aligned} X_1 \cdot X_2 &= \left(\mathbf{x}_1 + \frac{1}{2}\mathbf{x}_1^2 e_\infty + e_0\right) \cdot \left(\mathbf{x}_2 + \frac{1}{2}\mathbf{x}_2^2 e_\infty + e_0\right) \\ &= \mathbf{x}_1 \cdot \mathbf{x}_2 - \frac{1}{2}\mathbf{x}_1^2 - \frac{1}{2}\mathbf{x}_2^2 = -\frac{1}{2}(\mathbf{x}_1 - \mathbf{x}_2)^2 \\ &= -\frac{1}{2}\|\mathbf{x}_1 - \mathbf{x}_2\|^2 \end{aligned} \tag{11}$$

is a directly representation of the Euclidean distance between the two points. Thus, the inner product has now a geometric meaning due to the concept of null vectors. Therefore, the square of a conformal point $X^2 = XX = X \cdot X + X \wedge X = X \cdot X = 0$ represents the Euclidean distance with itself.

In the CGA two multivectors represent the same object if they differ by just a non zero scalar factor, that is

$$M \approx \lambda \wedge M_2 \approx M_2 \wedge \lambda \approx \lambda M_2 \;\; \text{for } \lambda \in \mathcal{R} \text{ and } M \in \mathcal{G}_{4,1} \tag{12}$$

Thus, multiplying (9) with a scalar λ we get

$$\lambda S = \lambda \mathbf{c} + \frac{1}{2}\lambda(\mathbf{c}^2 - r^2)e_\infty + \lambda e_0 , \tag{13}$$

if we calculate the inner product of the above equation with respect to the point at infinity e_∞

$$\lambda S \cdot e_\infty = \lambda \mathbf{c} \cdot e_\infty + \frac{1}{2}\lambda(\mathbf{c}^2 - r^2)e_\infty \cdot e_\infty + \lambda e_0 \cdot e_\infty = 0 + 0 + \lambda e_0 \cdot e_\infty = -\lambda , \tag{14}$$

we have recover the scalar factor λ. Therefore, if we want to normalize a sphere S (i.e. $\lambda = 1$) we apply

$$S' = -\frac{S}{S \cdot e}\,, \tag{15}$$

The same equation can be applied to points, remember that they are nothing but spheres of zero radius. For other objects the common normalization is by its magnitude that is

$$M' = \frac{M}{|M|}, \quad |M| = \sqrt{\sum_{i=0}^{n} |\langle M\rangle_i \cdot \langle M\rangle_i|^2}\,, \tag{16}$$

where $\langle M\rangle_i$ represents the i-vector part of the multivector M.
An important operation that is used in the geometric algebra is called reversion, denoted by "~" and defined by

$$\left\langle \widetilde{M}\right\rangle_i = (-1)^{\frac{i(i-1)}{2}} \left\langle \widetilde{M_i}\right\rangle, \text{ for } M \in \mathcal{G}_n,\ 0 \le i \le n. \tag{17}$$

2.1 Geometric objects representation

The geometric objects can also be defined with the outer product of points that lie on the object. For example, with four points we define the sphere

$$S^* = A \wedge B \wedge C \wedge E\,. \tag{18}$$

The incidence of a point X with the sphere S^* expressed in the *outer product null space* (OPNS) is

$$X \wedge S^* = X \wedge (A \wedge B \wedge C \wedge D) = 0. \tag{19}$$

Both representation of the sphere (S and S^*) are dual to each other, i.e. orthogonal to each other in the representative conformal space. Therefore, the representations are equivalent if we multiply them by the pseudoscalar $I_c = e_1 \wedge e_2 \wedge e_3 \wedge e_+ \wedge e_-$, thus

$$M = M^* I_c^{-1} \quad \text{and} \quad M I_c^{-1} = M^* \text{ for } M \in G_{4,1} \tag{20}$$

If one of the points of the sphere (18) is the point at infinity, then the sphere becomes a plane (a flat sphere with infinite radius)

$$\Pi^* = A \wedge B \wedge C \wedge e_\infty\,. \tag{21}$$

Similarly, the outer product of three points defines a circle $C^* = A \wedge B \wedge C$, and if one of the points of the circle is at infinity ($C^* = A \wedge B \wedge e_\infty$) then the circle becomes a line (a flat circle with infinite radius), see (Table 1). The line can also be defined as the outer product of two spheres

$$L^* = S_1 \wedge S_2 \wedge e_\infty\,, \tag{22}$$

which is the line passing through the centers of the spheres S_1 and S_2. If instead of two spheres we take one sphere and a point

$$L^* = S \wedge X \wedge e_\infty \ , \tag{23}$$

then the line passes through the center of the sphere S and point X.
A complete list of the entities and their representations are given in (Table 1). The table shows a geometric object called *point-pair*, which can be seen as the outer product of two points

$$Q^* = X_1 \wedge X_2 \ . \tag{24}$$

The *point-pair* represents a 1-dimensional sphere, and it can be the result of the intersection between: a line and a sphere, two circles or three spheres. In addition, if one of the points is the point at infinity

$$Q^* = X_1 \wedge e_\infty \ . \tag{25}$$

then we get a special point-pair which is called *flat-point*. If the intersection between two lines exists, then they intersect in one point X and also at the point at infinity. It also can be the result of the intersection between a line and a plane.

Entity	IPNS Representation	OPNS Representation
Sphere	$S = \mathbf{c} + \frac{1}{2}(\mathbf{c}^2 - r^2)e_\infty + e_0$	$S^* = A \wedge B \wedge C \wedge D$
Point	$X = \mathbf{x} + \frac{1}{2}\mathbf{x}^2 e_\infty + e_0$	$X^* = S_1 \wedge S_2 \wedge S_3 \wedge S_4$
Plane	$\Pi = \mathbf{n} + \delta e_\infty$	$\Pi^* = A \wedge B \wedge C \wedge e_\infty$
Line	$L = (\mathbf{a} - \mathbf{b})I_E - e_\infty(\mathbf{a} \wedge \mathbf{b})I_E$	$L^* = A \wedge B \wedge e_\infty$
Circle	$Z = S_1 \wedge S_2$	$Z^* = A \wedge B \wedge C$
Point Pair	$Q = S_1 \wedge S_2 \wedge S_3$	$Q^* = A \wedge B$ $Q^* = A \wedge e_\infty$

Table 1. Entities in conformal geometric algebra

2.2 Conformal transformations

A transformation of geometric objects is said to be conformal if it preserves angles. Liouville was the first that proved that any conformal transformation on $\mathcal{R}^n$ can be expressed as a composite of *inversions* and *reflections* in hyperplanes. The *CGA* $\mathcal{G}_{4,1}$ allows the computation of inversions and reflections with the geometric product and a special group of multivectors called *versors*.

2.3 Objects rigid motion

In conformal geometric algebra we can perform rotations by means of an entity called rotor which is defined by

$$R = exp\left(\frac{\theta}{2}l\right) \ , \tag{26}$$

where **l** is the bivector representing the dual of the rotation axis. To rotate an entity, we simply multiply it by the rotor R from the left and the reverse of the rotor $\tilde{R}$ from the right, $X' = RX\tilde{R}$.
If we want to translate an entity we use a translator which is defined as

$$T = \left(1 + \frac{et}{2}\right) = exp\left(\frac{\mathbf{et}}{2}\right) . \tag{27}$$

With this representation the translator can be applied multiplicatively to an entity similarly to the rotor, by multiplying the entity from the left by the translator and from the right with the reverse of the translator: $X' = TX\tilde{T}$.
Finally, the rigid motion can be expressed using a *motor* which is the combination of a rotor and a translator: M= TR, the rigid body motion of an entity is described with $X' = MX\tilde{M}$.
For more details on the geometric algebra and CGA, the interested reader is referred to view [5–9].

3. Paracatadioptric projection and inversion

In this section we will see the equivalence between the paracatadioptric projection and the inversion. The objective of using the inversion is that it can be linearized and represented by a versor in the conformal geometric algebra. This versor can be applied not only to points but also to point-pairs, lines, circles, spheres and planes.
The next subsection shows the equivalence between the paracatadioptric projection and the inversion, later the computation of the inversion using will be shown.

3.1 Paracatadioptric projection

The parabolic projection of a point $\mathbf{x} = xe_1 + ye_2 + ze_3 \in \mathcal{G}_3$ is defined as the intersection of the line **xf** (where **f** is the parabola's focus) and the parabolic mirror, followed by an orthographic projection. The orthographic projection is to a plane perpendicular to the axis of the mirror.
The equation of a parabola with focal length *p*, whose focus is at the origin is

$$\frac{x^2 + y^2}{4p} - p = z. \tag{28}$$

The projection of the point **x** to the mirror is

$$\mathbf{x}_p = \lambda \mathbf{x} \tag{29}$$

where λ is defined as

$$\lambda = \frac{2p}{\|\mathbf{x}\| - z}. \tag{30}$$

Finally, the point $\mathbf{x}_p$ is projected onto a plane perpendicular to the axis of the parabola. The reason for this is that any ray incident with the focus is reflected such that it is perpendicular to the image plane.

3.2 Relationship between inversion and parabolic projection

The inversion of a point $\mathbf{x} \in \mathcal{G}_3$ with respect to sphere centered at the origin, and radius r, is a point $\mathbf{x}' \in \mathcal{G}_3$ lying on the line defined by the point $\mathbf{x}$ and the origin, if $\mathbf{x}'$ is the inverse of the point $\mathbf{x}$ then

$$\mathbf{x}\mathbf{x}' = r^2 \; . \tag{31}$$

When the sphere is centered at the point $\mathbf{c} \in \mathcal{G}_3$, the inverse of the point $\mathbf{x}$ is defined as

$$\mathbf{x}' = r^2 \frac{1}{\mathbf{x} - \mathbf{c}} + \mathbf{c} \tag{32}$$

As we already mention, the parabolic projection of a point $\mathbf{x}$ can be found with (30). Now, given a sphere centered at the origin with radius p, see Fig. 1. The projection of the point $\mathbf{x}$ on the sphere is simply

$$\mathbf{x}_s = p^2 \frac{\mathbf{x}}{||\mathbf{x}||} \tag{33}$$

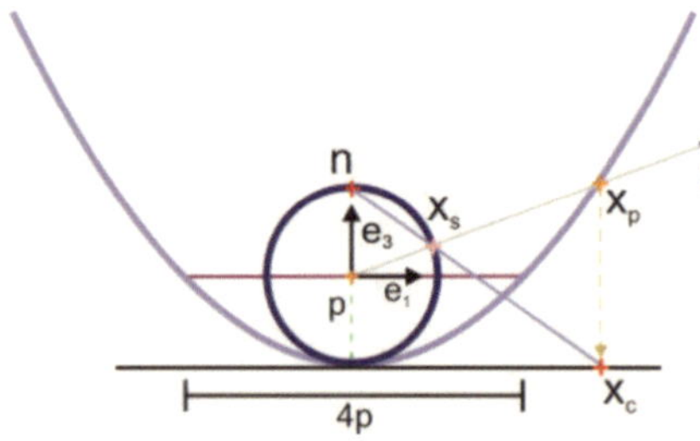

Fig. 1. Parabolic projection.

Note that there are three similar triangles in Fig. 1, which can be seen clearly in Fig. 2. The three triangles are : *NSQ*, *NPS* and *SPQ*. Therefore $\overline{NP} : \overline{NS} = \overline{NS} : \overline{NQ}$. Thus $\overline{NP} \cdot \overline{NQ} = \overline{NS}^2$, which is the exactly the *inversion* of a point with respect to a circle centered at N and radius $\overline{NS}$. Thus we have that

$$\sqrt{(\mathbf{x}_s - \mathbf{n})^2}\sqrt{(\mathbf{x}_c - \mathbf{n})^2} = (2r)^2 \; . \tag{34}$$

Thus, the parabolic projection of a point $\mathbf{x}$ is equivalent to the inversion of a point x_s, where the point lies on a sphere s centered at the focus of the parabola and radius p, with respect to a sphere s_0, centered at $\mathbf{n}$ and radius $2p$, see Fig. 3. To prove this equivalence we can use the definitions of the parabolic projection and inversion. With the definition of inversion (31) we have the following equation

$$\alpha ||\mathbf{x}_s - \mathbf{n}||^2 = (2p)^2 \tag{35}$$

where $\mathbf{n} = pe_3 \in \mathcal{G}_3$.

$$\alpha = \frac{(2p)^2}{||\mathbf{x}_s - \mathbf{n}||^2} = \frac{(2p)^2}{\frac{p^2(\mathbf{x} - ||\mathbf{x}||e_3)^2}{||\mathbf{x}||^2}} = \frac{4||\mathbf{x}||^2}{(\mathbf{x} - ||\mathbf{x}||e_3)^2} \tag{36}$$

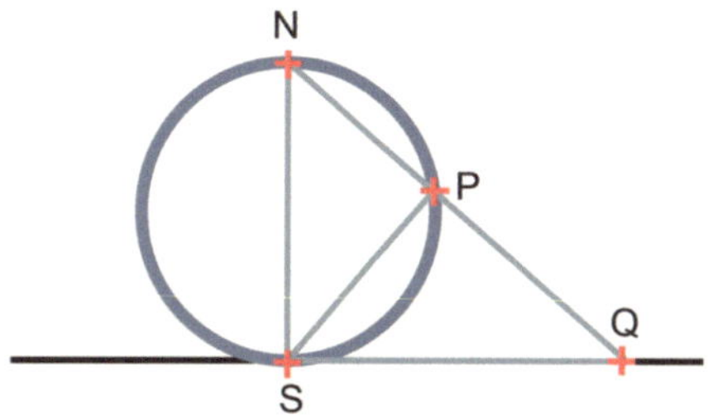

Fig. 2. The three similar triangles of the stereographic projection

thus, the projected point is

$$\mathbf{x}_c = \alpha \mathbf{x}_s = \alpha \frac{p}{\|x\|} \mathbf{x} \,. \tag{37}$$

The constant $\alpha \frac{p}{\|x\|}$ is equal to

$$\alpha \frac{p}{\|x\|} = \frac{4p\|\mathbf{x}\|^2}{2\|\mathbf{x}\|^2 - 2\|\mathbf{x}\|x \cdot e_3)^2} = \frac{2p}{\|\mathbf{x}\| - \mathbf{x} \cdot e3} = \frac{2p}{\|\mathbf{x}\| - z} \tag{38}$$

which is exactly the same value of the scalar λ from the parabolic projection (30). Therefore, we can conclude that the parabolic projection (29) and the inversion (37) of the point **x** are equivalent.

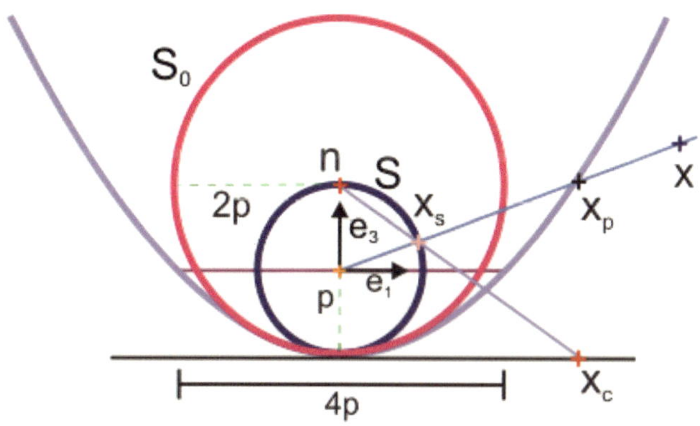

Fig. 3. Equivalence between parabolic projection and inversion

3.3 Inversion and the conformal geometric algebra

In the conformal geometric algebra, the conformal transformations are represented as versors [7]. In particular, the versor of the inversion is a sphere, and it is applied in the same way as the rotor, or the translator. Given a sphere of radius r centered at c represented by the vector

$$S = \mathbf{c} + \frac{1}{2}(\mathbf{c}^2 - r^2)e_\infty + e_0 \tag{39}$$

the inversion of a point X with respect to S is

$$X' = SX\tilde{S} \tag{40}$$

To clarify the above equation, let us analyze the special case when S is a unit sphere, centered at origin. Then S reduces to

$$S = -\frac{1}{2}e_\infty + e_0 = -\frac{1}{2}(e_- + e_+) + \frac{1}{2}(e_- - e_+) = -e_+ \tag{41}$$

thus (40) becomes

$$\begin{aligned} X' = SX\tilde{S} &= (-e_+)X(-e_+) = (-e_+)(\mathbf{x} + \frac{1}{2}\mathbf{x}^2 e_\infty + e_0)(-e_+) \\ &= e_+\mathbf{x}e_+ + \frac{1}{2}\mathbf{x}^2 e_+e_\infty e_+ + e_+e_0e_+ \ . \end{aligned} \tag{42}$$

The first term $e_+\mathbf{x}e_+$ is equal to

$$e_+\mathbf{x}e_+ = xe_+e_1e_+ + ye_+e_2e_+ + ze_+e_3e_+ = -xe_1 - ye_2 - ze_3 = -\mathbf{x} \ . \tag{43}$$

The term $e_+e_\infty e_+$ is equivalent to

$$e_+e_\infty e_+ = e_+(e_- + e_+)e_+ = (e_+e_- + 1)e_+ = -e_- + e_+ = -2e_0 \ . \tag{44}$$

Finally, the last term is

$$e_+e_0e_+ = e_+\frac{1}{2}(e_- - e_+)e_+ = \frac{1}{2}(e_+e_- - 1)e_+ = \frac{1}{2}(-e_- - e_+) = -\frac{1}{2}e_\infty \tag{45}$$

Rewriting (42) we have

$$X' = -\mathbf{x} - \frac{1}{2}e_\infty - \mathbf{x}^2 e_0 = \frac{1}{\mathbf{x}} + \frac{1}{2}\left(\frac{1}{\mathbf{x}}\right)^2 e_\infty + e_0 \ . \tag{46}$$

From the above equation we recognize the Euclidean point

$$\frac{1}{\mathbf{x}} = \frac{\mathbf{x}}{\mathbf{x}^2} = \frac{\mathbf{x}}{||\mathbf{x}||^2} \tag{47}$$

which represents the inversion of the point $\mathbf{x}$. The case of the inversion with respect to an arbitrary sphere is

$$\sigma X' = SX\tilde{S} = \left(\frac{\mathbf{x} - \mathbf{c}}{r}\right)^2 \left(f(\mathbf{x}) + \frac{1}{2}f(\mathbf{x})^2 e_\infty + e_0\right) \tag{48}$$

where $f(\mathbf{x})$ is equal to (37), the inversion in R^n. The value σ represents the scalar factor of the homogeneuos point.

The interesting thing about the inversion in the conformal geometric algebra is that it can be applied not only to points but also to any other entity of the *CGA*. In the following section we will see how the paracatadioptric image formation can be described in terms of the *CGA*.

4. Paracatadioptric image formation and conformal geometric algebra

In the previous section we saw the equivalence between the parabolic projection and the inversion. We also saw how to compute the inversion in the CGA using a versor, in this case the versor is simply the sphere where the inversion will be carried out. In this section we will define the paracatadioptric image formation using the CGA.
Given a parabolic mirror with a focal length p, the projection of a point in the space through the mirror followed by an orthographic projection can be handled by two spheres. Where the first sphere is centered at the focus of the mirror, and its radius is p. This sphere can be defined as

$$S = c + \frac{1}{2}c^2 e_\infty + e_0 \, . \tag{49}$$

The second sphere S_0 can be defined in several ways, but we prefer to define it with respect to a point N on the sphere S (i.e. $N \cdot S = 0$). If we compare the point equation (7) with the sphere equation (9), we can observe that the sphere has an extra term $-\frac{1}{2}r^2 e_\infty$, thus if we extract it to the point N we get a sphere centered at N and with radius r. The sphere S_0 is defined as

$$S_0 = N - \frac{1}{2}(2p)^2 e_\infty = n + \frac{1}{2}(n^2 - 4p^2)e_\infty + e_0 \, , \tag{50}$$

where $2p$ is the radius of the sphere. With these two spheres the image formation of points, circles and lines will be showed in the next subsections.

4.1 Point Images

Let X be a point on the space, its projection to the sphere can be found by finding the line passing through it and the sphere center, that is

$$L^* = S \wedge X \wedge e_\infty \, , \tag{51}$$

then, this line is intersected with the sphere S

$$Z_s^* = S \cdot L_1^* \, . \tag{52}$$

Where Z_s is a point-pair $(Z_s^* = X_s \wedge X_s')$, the paracatadioptric projection of this point can be found with

$$Z_c = S_0 Z_s \widetilde{S_0} \, . \tag{53}$$

which is also a point pair $(Z_c^* = X_c \wedge X_c')$. The paracatadioptric projection of the point closest to X, can be found with

$$X_s = \frac{Z_s^* - |Z_s^*|}{Z_s^* \cdot e} \, . \tag{54}$$

and then with

$$X_c = S_0 X_s \widetilde{S_0} \ . \tag{55}$$

The point X_c is the projection of the point X onto the catadioptric image plane, which is exactly the same point obtained through a parabolic and orthographic projections (Fig. 4).

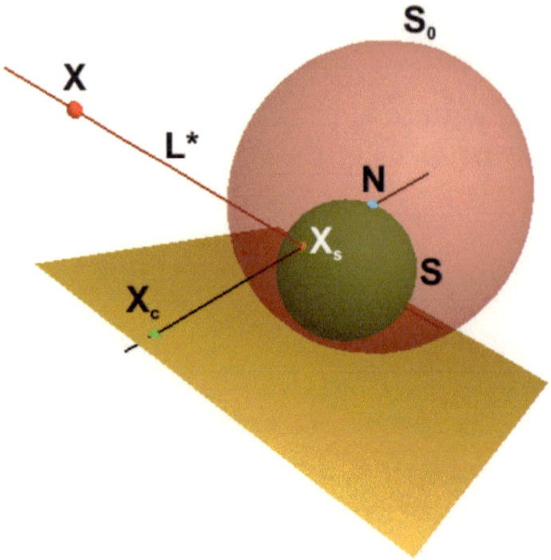

Fig. 4. Point projection onto the catadioptric image plane

4.2 Back projection of point images

Given a point X_c on the catadioptric image (Fig. 4), its projection to the sphere is simply

$$X_s = S_0 X_c \widetilde{S_0} \ . \tag{56}$$

Since the point X_s and the sphere center lie on the line L_1^*, it can be calculated as

$$L^* = P_1 \wedge S \wedge e_\infty \ . \tag{57}$$

The original point X lies also on this line, but since we have a single image the depth can not be determined and thus the point X can no be calculated.

4.3 Circle images

The circle images can be found in the same way as for points images. To see that, let X_1, X_2, X_3 be three points on the sphere S, the circle defined by them is

$$C^* = X_1 \wedge X_2 \wedge X_3 \ , \tag{58}$$

which can be a great or a small circle. The projection of the circle onto the catadioptric image is carried out as in (55)

$$C_2^* = S_0 C^* \widetilde{S_0} \ . \tag{59}$$

Where C_2^* could be a line, but there is no problem since it is represented as a circle with one point at infinity.
The back projection of a circle (or line) C_2^* that lie on the catadioptric image plane, can be found easily with

$$C^* = S_0 C_2^* \widetilde{S_0} \ . \tag{60}$$

In Fig. 5 the projection of circles on the sphere to the catadioptric image plane is shown.

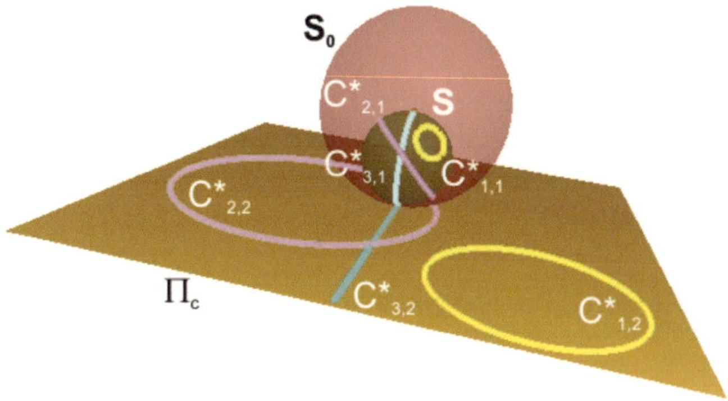

Fig. 5. Projection of circles on the sphere.

4.4 Line images

To find the paracatadioptric projection of a line L^* in the 3D space (Fig. 59), we first project the line to the sphere S. The plane defined by the line L^* and the sphere S is

$$\Pi^* = L^* \wedge S \ . \tag{61}$$

then the projection of the line L^* onto the sphere is

$$C_s^* = S \cdot \Pi^* \tag{62}$$

where C_s is a great circle. Finally the paracatadioptric projection of L^* can be found with the inversion of the circle C_s, that is

$$C_c^* = S_0 C_s^* \widetilde{S_0} \ . \tag{63}$$

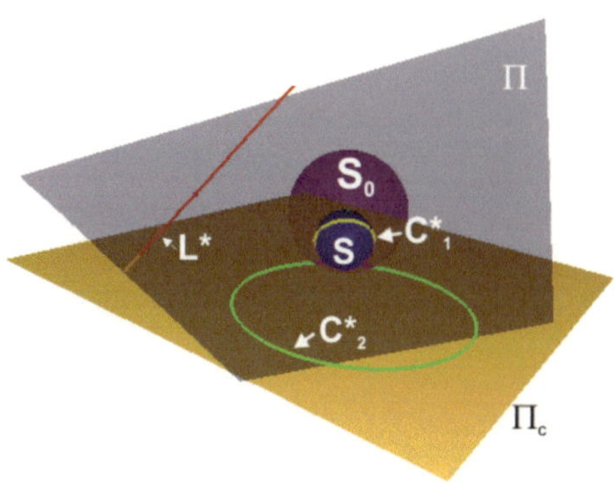

Fig. 6. Projection of a line in the space

5. Robot control using paracatadioptric lines

The problem to be solved is the line following with a mobile robot. The mobile robot is a nonholonomic system with a paracatadioptric system. We assume that the camera optical

axis is superposed with the rotation axis of the mobile robot. Thus, the kinematic screw is only composed with a linear velocity v along the e_1 axis and an angular velocity ω.
The problem will be solved using paracatadioptric image of lines. One of those lines is the paracatadioptric image of the desired line C_d and the other one is the current paracatadioptric image of the tracked line C. These lines will be projected to the sphere and then to a perspective plane Π_p, in this planes the image projection are straight lines. Finally, with the lines on the perspective plane we will compute the angular and lateral deviations.
Consider the paracatadioptric image C_d of the desired 3D line L_d^*, the inverse paracatadioptric projection of C_d can be found with

$$C_s^* = S_0 C_d^* \widetilde{S_0} \ . \tag{64}$$

Then the plane where the circle lies is defined as

$$\Pi_d^* = C_s^* \wedge e_\infty \ . \tag{65}$$

Finally, the intersection of the plane Π_d^* with the perspective plane Π_p^* is

$$L_{pd}^* = \Pi_d^* \cdot \Pi_v^* \ , \tag{66}$$

this line is the projection of the paracatadioptric image line C_d^* into the perspective plane Π_p^*. The perspective plane can be defined as

$$\Pi = \hat{\mathbf{n}} + \delta e_\infty \tag{67}$$

where $\hat{\mathbf{n}} = \mathbf{n}/|\mathbf{n}|$ and

$$\mathbf{n} = (S \wedge S_\wedge e_\infty) \cdot -E \ . \tag{68}$$

The expression $S \wedge S \wedge e_\infty$ represents the line passing through the centers of both spheres (S and S_0). The value of the scalar δ can be defined arbitrarily.
The current paracatadioptric line C can be projected into the line L in the perspective plane in similar way using the above equations, see Fig. 7.

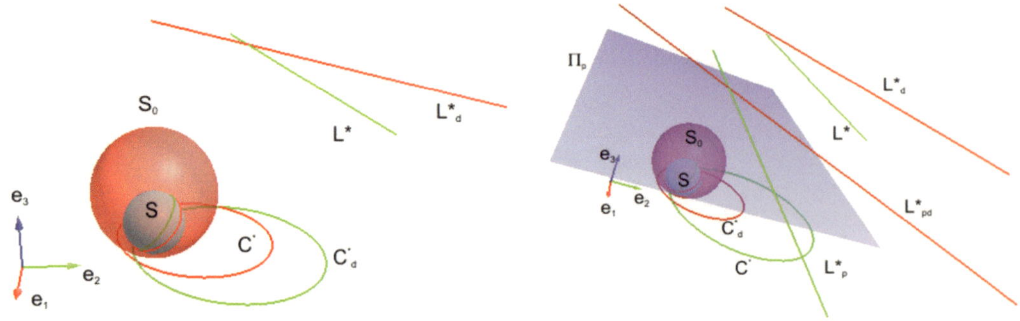

Fig. 7. a) Paracatadioptric projection of the desired and current line. b) Projection of the paracatadioptric lines into the perspective plane.

The lines L_p^* and L_{pd}^*, on the perspective plane, define a rotor which can be computed with

$$R = 1 + L_p^* L_{pd}^* \tag{69}$$

where $L_p^* L_{pd}^*$ represents the geometric product of the two lines. The angle between the lines is then

$$\theta = (R \cdot e_{12}) \langle R \rangle_0 \ . \tag{70}$$

which represents the angular deviation. The lateral deviation can be found with the signed distance between the lines, the signed distance between the lines is

$$d = (L^* \cdot e_{12} e_0) - (L_d^* \cdot e_{12} e_0) \ . \tag{71}$$

The angular and lateral deviations are used in a dynamic controller ,proposed in [10], to generate the robot's angular velocity. The dynamic controller is

$$\omega = -k_2 v d \frac{\sin\theta}{theta} - k_3 |v| \theta, \tag{72}$$

where the control gains are defined as

$$k_2 = \alpha^2 \tag{73}$$

$$k_3 = 2\xi\alpha^2 \ . \tag{74}$$

The value of α is left free to specify faster or slower systems, and where ξ is usually set to $1/\sqrt{2}$. The trajectories of the paracatadioptric images and the current paracatadioptric line are show in Fig. 8. These trajectories confirm that task is correctly realized. In Fig. 9 the angular an lateral deviations of the current paracatadioptric image with respect to the desired image are shown. These figures show that both deviations are well regulated to zero.

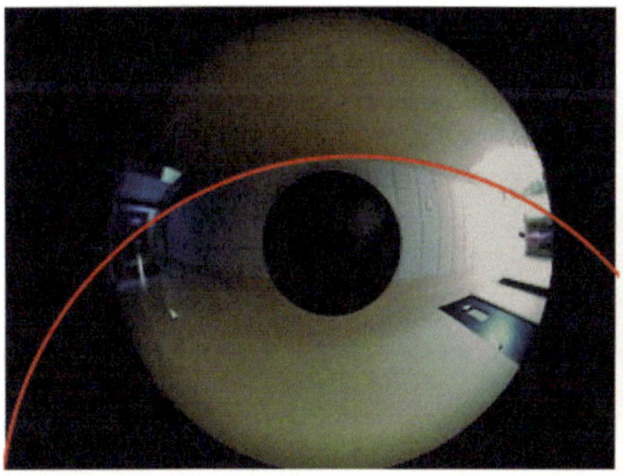

a)

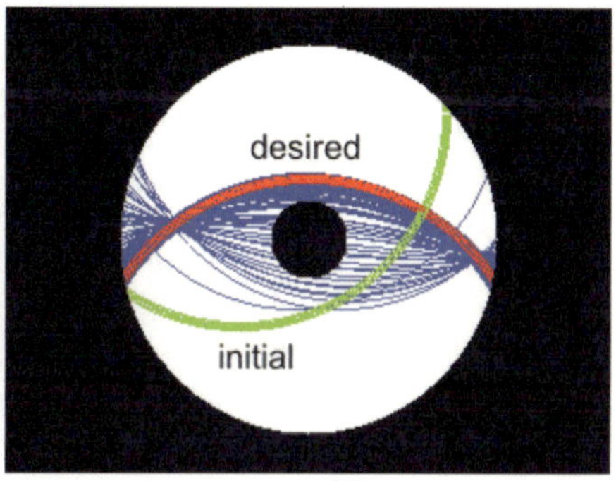

b)

Fig. 8. a) Tracked line in the paracatadioptric image. b) Trajectory of the projected lines in the paracatadioptric image.

6. Conclusions

In this work a comprehensive geometric model for paracatadioptric sensors has been presented. The model is based on the equivalence between paracatadioptric projection and the inversion. The main reason for using the inversion is that it can be represented by a versor (i.e. a special group of multivectors) in the CGA. The advantage of this representation is that it can be applied not only to points but also to point-pairs, lines, circles, spheres and planes.

The paracatadioptric projection and back-projection of points, *point-pairs*, circles, and lines is simplified using the proposed framework. This will allow an easier implementation of paracatadioptric sensors in more complex applications.

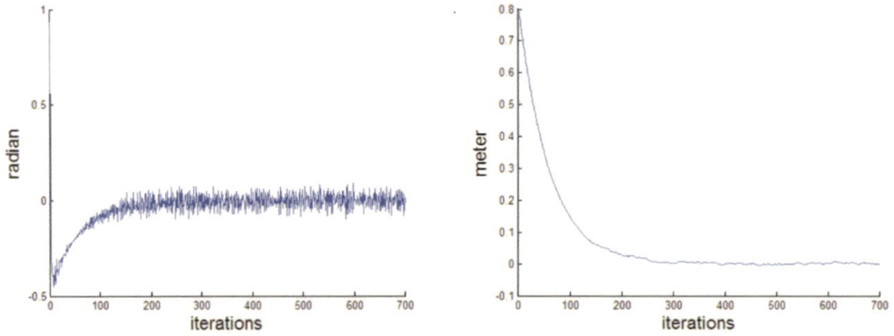

Fig. 9. a) Angular deviation. b) Lateral Deviation.

The proposed framework has been used to control a nonholonomic robot, with a paracatadioptric sensor. The input to the control scheme are the paracatadioptric images of the desired and current lines. With help of the proposed model the paracatadioptric images are back projected to sphere, and then projected to a perspective plane. Then, the lines on the perspective plane are used to compute the angular and lateral deviations. Finally, with these values the angular velocity of the robot can be computed using a dynamic controller. The application showed that is not necessary to have 3D measurements of the scene to solve the task, indeed it is possible to solve it from image data only.

7. References

Baker, S., Nayar, S.: A theory of catadioptric image formation. In Proc. Int. Conf. on Computer Vision (1998) 35–42

Svoboda, T., P.T., Hlavac, V.: Epipolar geometry for panoramic cameras. In Proc. 5th European Conference on Computer Vision (1998) 218–231

Geyer, C., Daniilidis, K.: A unifying theory for central panoramic systems and practical implications. Proc. Eur. Conf. on Computer Vision (2000) 445–461

Bayro-Corrochano, E., L´opez-Franco, C.: Omnidirectional vision: Unified model using conformal geometry. Proc. Eur. Conf. on Computer Vision (2004) 318–343

Hestenes, D., Li, H., Rockwood, A.: New algebraic tools for classical geometry. In Sommer, G., ed.: Geometric Computing with Clifford Algebra. Volume 24., Berlin Heidelberg, Springer-Verlag (2001) 3–26

Bayro-Corrochano, E., ed.: Robot perception and action using conformal geometric algebra. Springer- Verlag, Heidelberg (2005)

Li, H., Hestenes, D.: Generalized homogeneous coordinates for computational geometry. In Sommer, G., ed.: Geometric Computing with Clifford Algebra. Volume 24., Berlin Heidelberg, Springer-Verlag (2001) 27–60

Rosenhahn, B., Gerald, S.: Pose estimation in conformal geometric algebra. Technical Report Number 0206 (2002)

Perwass, C., Hildenbrand, D.: Aspects of geometric algebra in euclidean, projective and conformal space. Technical Report Number 0310 (2003)

Canudas de Wit, E., S.B., Bastian, G., eds.: Theory of Robot Control. Springer-Verlag (1997)

Geyer, C., Daniilidis, K.: Paracatadioptric camera calibration. IEEE Transactions on Pattern Analysis and Machine Intelligence 24 (2002) 687–695

4

Treating Image Loss by using the Vision/Motion Link: A Generic Framework

David Folio and Viviane Cadenat
CNRS; LAAS; 7, avenue du Colonel Roche, F-31077 Toulouse, and Université de Toulouse; UPS: Toulouse. France

1. Introduction

Visual servoing techniques aim at controlling the robot motion using vision data provided by a camera to reach a desired goal defined in the image (Chaumette & Hutchinson, 2006). Therefore, if the considered features are lost because of an occlusion or any other unexpected event, the desired task cannot be realized anymore. The literature provides many works dealing with this problem. A first common solution is to use methods allowing to preserve the visual features visibility during the whole mission. Most of them are dedicated to manipulator arms, and propose to treat this kind of problem by using redundancy (Marchand & Hager, 1998; Mansard & Chaumette, 2005), path-planning (Mezouar & Chaumette, 2002), specific degrees of freedom (DOF) (Corke & Hutchinson, 2001; Kyrki et al., 2004), zoom (Benhimane & Malis, 2003) or even by making a tradeoff with the nominal vision-based task (Remazeilles et al., 2006). In a mobile robotics context, the realization of a vision-based navigation task in a given environment requires to preserve not only the image data visibility, but also the robot safety. In that case, techniques allowing to avoid simultaneously collisions and visual data losses such as (Folio & Cadenat, 2005a; Folio & Cadenat, 2005b) appear to be limited, because they are restricted to missions where an avoidance motion exists without leading to local minima (Folio, 2007). As many robotic tasks cannot be performed if the visual data loss is not tolerated, a true extension of these works would be to provide methods that accept that occlusions may effectively occur without leading to a task failure. A first step towards this objective is to let some of the features appear and disappear temporarily from the image as done in (Garcia-Aracil et al., 2005). However, this approach is limited to partial losses and does not entirely solve the problem. Therefore, in this work, our main goal is to propose a generic framework allowing to reconstruct the visual data when they suddenly become unavailable during the task execution (camera or image processing failure, landmark loss, and so on). Thus, this work relies on the following central assumption: *the whole image is considered temporarily entirely unavailable*. This problem can be addressed using different methods such as tracking or signal processing techniques. However, we have chosen here to develop another approach for several reasons, which will be detailed in the chapter.
The proposed technique allows to reconstruct the visual features using the history of the camera motion and the last available features. It relies on the vision-motion link that is on the relation between the camera motion and the visual data evolution in the image.

The chapter is organized as follows. We first state the problem and introduce a new general framework allowing to reconstruct the visual features when they become unavailable. Then, we apply it to design a controller able to perform a vision-based navigation task despite the temporary total loss of the landmark during the mission. Finally, we present simulation and experimental results validating the developed approach. We end the chapter by providing a comparative analysis of the different proposed methods.

2. Visual data estimation

In this section, we address the problem of estimating (all or some) visual data s whenever they become unavailable during a vision-based task. Thus, the key-assumption, which underlies our works, is that the whole image is considered to be temporarily completely unavailable. Hence, methods which only allow to treat partial losses of the visual features such as (Garcia-Aracil et al., 2005; Comport et al., 2004) are not suitable here. Following this reasoning, we have focused on techniques dedicated to image data reconstruction. Different approaches, such as signal processing techniques or tracking methods (Favaro & Soatto, 2003; Lepetit & Fua, 2006) may be used to deal with this kind of problem. Here, we have chosen to use a simpler approach for several reasons. First, most of the above techniques rely on measures from the image which are considered to be totally unavailable in our case. Second, we suppose that we have few errors on the model and on the measures[1]. Third, as it is intended to be used in a visual servoing context, the estimated features must be provided sufficiently rapidly wrt. the control law sampling period *Ts*. Another idea is to use a 3D model of the object together with projective geometry in order to deduce the lacking data. However, this choice would lead to depend on the considered landmark type and would require to localize the robot. This was unsuitable for us, as we want to make a minimum assumption on the landmark model. Thus, we have finally chosen to design a new approach to reconstruct the image data when they are entirely lost. It relies on the vision/motion link that relates the variation of the visual features in the image to the camera motion. In the sequel, we define more precisely this notion and then present our estimation method.

2.1 The vision/motion link

In this part, we focus on the vision/motion link. We consider a camera mounted on a given robot so that its motion is holonomic (see remark 1). The camera motion can then be characterized by its kinematic screw $\mathbf{v}_c$ as follows:

$$\mathbf{v}_c = \begin{bmatrix} V_{C/F_c}^{F_c} \\ \Omega_{F_c/F_0} \end{bmatrix} = \mathbf{J}\dot{\mathbf{q}} \tag{1}$$

where $V_{C/F_c}^{F_c} = \left(V_{\vec{\mathbf{x}}_c}, V_{\vec{\mathbf{y}}_c}, V_{\vec{\mathbf{z}}_c}\right)$ and $\Omega_{F_c/F_0}^{F_c} = \left(\Omega_{\vec{\mathbf{x}}_c}, \Omega_{\vec{\mathbf{y}}_c}, \Omega_{\vec{\mathbf{z}}_c}\right)$ represent the translational and rotational velocity of the camera frame wrt. the world frame expressed in *Fc* (see figure 1). $\mathbf{J}$ represents the robot jacobian, which relates $\mathbf{v}_c$ to the control input $\dot{\mathbf{q}}$.

---

[1] In case where this assumption is not fulfilled, different techniques such as Kalman filtering based methods for instance may be used to take into account explicitly the system noises.

Remark 1: We do not make any hypothesis about the robot on which is embedded the camera. Two cases may occur: either the robot is holonomic and so is the camera motion; or the robot is not, and we suppose that the camera is able to move independently from it (Pissard-Gibollet & Rives, 1995).

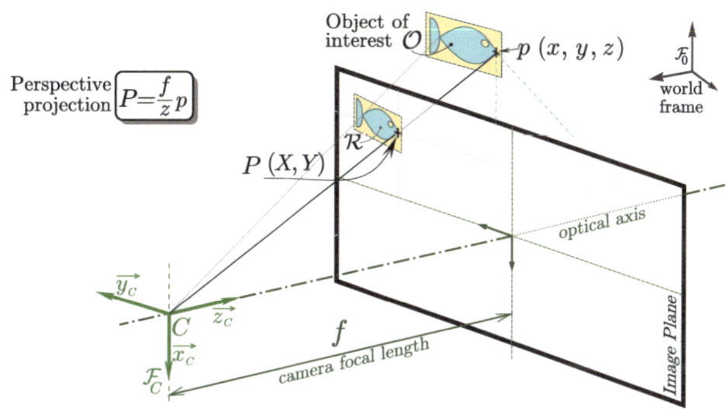

Fig. 1. The pinhole camera model.

Now, let us define the vision/motion link. In this work, we only consider fixed landmarks. We suppose that it can be characterized by a set of visual data s provided by the camera. We denote by **z** a vector describing its depth. As previously mentioned, the vision/motion link relates the variation of the visual signals $\dot{\mathbf{s}}$ to the camera motion. For a fixed landmark, we get the following general definition (Espiau et al., 1992):

$$\dot{\mathbf{s}} = \mathbf{L}_{(\mathbf{s},\mathbf{z})}\mathbf{v}_c = \mathbf{L}_{(\mathbf{s},\mathbf{z})}\mathbf{J}\dot{\mathbf{q}} \tag{2}$$

where $\mathbf{L}_{(\mathbf{s},\mathbf{z})}$ represents the interaction matrix. This matrix depends mainly on the type of considered visual data **s** and on the depth **z** representation. We suppose in the sequel that we will only use image features for which $L_{(s,z)}$ can be determined analytically. Such expressions are available for different kinds of features such as points, straight lines, circles in (Espiau et al., 1992), and for image moments in (Chaumette, 2004).

Our idea is to use the vision/motion link together with a history of the previous measures of image features and of the camera kinematic screw to reconstruct the visual data s. We have then to solve the differential system given by equation (2). However, this system depends not only on the visual features s but also on their depth **z**. Therefore, relation (2) cannot be directly solved and must be rewritten to take into account additional information about **z**. This information can be introduced in different ways, depending on the considered visual primitives. Therefore, in the sequel, we will first state the problem for different kinds of image data before presenting a generic formulation. We will then successively consider the case of points, of other common visual features and of image moments.

2.1.1 The most simple case: the point

The point is a very simple primitive, which can be easily extracted from the image. It is then commonly used in the visual servoing area. This is the reason why we first address this case. Therefore, we consider in this paragraph a visual landmark made of n interest points. Let us recall that, using the pinhole camera model, a 3D point p_i of coordinates (x_i, y_i, z_i) in F_c is projected into a point P_i (X_i, Y_i) in the image plane (see figure 1). We can then define the visual signals vector by a $2n$-dimensional vector $\mathbf{s} = [X_1, Y_1, \cdots, X_n, Y_n]^T$, where ($X_i$, Y_i) are the coordinates of each projected point. In this case, the interaction matrix $\mathbf{L}_{(\mathbf{s},\mathbf{z})} = [\mathbf{L}_{(P_1,z_1)}, \cdots, \mathbf{L}_{(P_n,z_n)}]^T$ is directly deduced from the optic flow equations. $\mathbf{L}_{(P_i,z_i)}$ is given by (Espiau et al., 1992):

$$\mathbf{L}_{(P_i,z_i)} = \begin{bmatrix} \mathbf{L}_{(X_i,z_i)} \\ \mathbf{L}_{(Y_i,z_i)} \end{bmatrix} = \begin{bmatrix} -\frac{f}{z_i} & 0 & \frac{X_i}{z_i} & \frac{X_i Y_i}{f} & \left(f + \frac{X_i}{f}\right) & Y_i \\ 0 & -\frac{f}{z_i} & \frac{Y_i}{z_i} & \left(f + \frac{Y_i}{f}\right) & -\frac{X_i Y_i}{f} & -X_i \end{bmatrix} \tag{3}$$

where f is the camera focal length. As one can see, $\mathbf{L}_{(P,z)}$ *explicitly* requires a model or an estimation of the depth z_i of each considered point P_i. Several approaches may be used to determine it. The most obvious solution is to measure it using dedicated sensors such as telemeters or stereoscopic systems. However, if the robotic platform is not equipped with such sensors, other approaches must be considered. For instance, it is possible to use structure from motion (SFM) techniques (Jerian & Jain, 1991; Chaumette et al., 1996; Soatto & Perona, 1998; Oliensis, 2002), signal processing methods (Matthies et al., 1989), or even pose relative estimation (Thrun et al., 2001). Unfortunately, these approaches require to use measures from the image, and they cannot be applied anymore when it becomes completely unavailable. This is the reason why we propose another solution consisting in estimating depth $\mathbf{z}$ together with the visual data $\mathbf{s}$ (see remark 3). To this aim, we need to express the analytical relation between the variation of the depth and the camera motion. It can be easily shown that, for one 3D point p_i of coordinates (x_i, y_i, z_i) projected into a point P_i (X_i, Y_i) in the image plane as shown in figure 1, the depth variation $\dot{z}_i$ is related to the camera motion according to: $\dot{z}_i = \mathbf{L}_{(z_i)} \mathbf{v}_c$, with $\mathbf{L}_{(z_i)} = [0,\ 0,\ -1,\ {}^{z_i Y_i}/_{f},\ {}^{z_i X_i}/_{f}, 0]$. Finally, the dynamic system to be solved for one point can be expressed as follows:

$$\begin{bmatrix} \dot{X}_i \\ \dot{Y}_i \\ \dot{z}_i \end{bmatrix} = \begin{bmatrix} \mathbf{L}_{(X_i,z_i)} \\ \mathbf{L}_{(Y_i,z_i)} \\ \mathbf{L}_{(z_i)} \end{bmatrix} \mathbf{v}_c \tag{4}$$

In the case of a landmark made of n points, introducing $\psi = (X_1, Y_1, z_1, \ldots, X_n, Y_n, z_n)^T$, we easily deduce that it suffices to integrate the above system for each considered point.

2.1.2 A more generic case: common geometric visual features

Now, we consider the case of other geometric visual primitives such as lines, ellipses, spheres, and so on. As previously, our goal is to determine the common dynamic system to be solved to compute these primitives when they cannot be provided anymore by the camera. Thus, let O be the observed fixed landmark. We denote by R the projected region of O in the image plane, as described in figure 1. Assuming that R has a continuous surface and closed contour, it can be shown that the depth z_i of each point p_i of O can be related to the coordinates (X_i, Y_i) of each point P_i belonging to R by the following relation (Chaumette, 2004):

$$\frac{1}{z_i} = \sum_{p\geq 0, q\geq 0} A_{pq} X_i^p Y_i^q \qquad (5)$$

$$\forall (X_i, Y_i) \in \mathrm{R}$$

where parameters A_{pq} depend on the nature of object O. For instance, if we consider a planar object and exclude the degenerate case where the camera optical center belongs to it, the previous equation can be rewritten as follows:

$$\frac{1}{z_i} = AX_i + BY_i + C \qquad (6)$$

$$\forall (X_i, Y_i) \in \mathrm{R}$$

where $A = A_{10}$, $B = A_{01}$ and $C = A_{00}$ in this particular case.
Now, let us suppose that it is possible to associate to O a set of n visual primitives leading to $\mathbf{s} = [\pi_1, \cdots, \pi_n]^T$, and that the depth $\mathbf{z}$ can be expressed using equation (5). In such a case, relation (2) can be rewritten as follows:

$$\dot{\mathbf{s}} = \begin{bmatrix} \dot{\pi}_1 \\ \vdots \\ \dot{\pi}_n \end{bmatrix} = \begin{bmatrix} \mathbf{L}_{(\pi_1, A_{pq})} \\ \vdots \\ \mathbf{L}_{(\pi_n, A_{pq})} \end{bmatrix} \mathbf{v}_c = \mathbf{L}_{(\pi_1, \cdots, \pi_n, A_{pq})} \mathbf{v}_c = \mathbf{L}_{(\pi, A_{pq})} \mathbf{v}_c \qquad (7)$$

where $\mathbf{L}_{(\pi, A_{pq})}$ is the interaction matrix related to the visual primitives π of $\mathbf{s}$ (see remark 2). The interested reader will find in (Espiau et al., 1992) different expressions of the interaction matrix for numerous kinds of common visual features (lines, cylinders, spheres, etc.). It is important to note that, here, $\mathbf{L}_{(\pi, A_{pq})}$ depends *implicitly* on the object depth through the A_{pq} 3D parameters. In this case, the estimation of the visual features by integrating differential system (7) will require to determine A_{pq}. Different methods may be used. A first natural idea is to use the 3D model of the object if it is known. If not, another nice solution is provided by dynamic vision that allows to recover the 3D structure, as in (Chaumette et al. 1996). Unfortunately, this approach requires to define a particular motion to the camera, which is not suitable in a visual servoing context. Another solution would be to use a similar approach to the case of points. The idea is then to first relate $\dot{A}_{pq}$ to the camera kinematic screw $\mathbf{v}_c$, and then to estimate A_{pq} together with $\mathbf{s}$. However, as $\dot{A}_{pq}$ depends on the considered visual features, it would be difficult to design a comprehensive formulation of the estimation problem. Therefore, to provide a generic framework, we propose to use (5) to identify A_{pq}. To this aim, we consider a set of l points P_i (X_i, Y_i) belonging to the region R (see remark 2). The A_{pq} 3D parameters can then be determined on the base of the coordinates (X_i, Y_i) using any identification method such as least-squares techniques. Finally, the geometric visual features will be computed using the four-step algorithm 1.

Algorithm 1: Computation of geometric visual features

1. Considering a set of l points belonging to R, define vector $\psi = (X_1, Y_1, z_1, \ldots, X_l, Y_l, z_l)^T$ as in the previous paragraph 2.1.1.
2. Solve system (4) to compute an estimation $\tilde{\psi}$ of ψ, that is an estimation of each triple (Xi, Yi, zi)
3. Use $\tilde{\psi}$ to identify the coefficients A_{pq} of the surface which fits the best way the l chosen points using a least-square method for instance.
4. Knowing parameters A_{pq}, integrate dynamic system (7) and deduce an estimation of vector $\mathbf{s} = [\pi_1, \cdots, \pi_n]^T$

Remark 2: In some cases, several objects O could be used to design the set of visual primitives involved in (7). In such a case, a solution is to associate a set of l points to each observed object and to follow algorithm 1 for each of these sets.

2.1.3 The most difficult case: image moments

Although image moments have been widely used in computer vision, they have been considered only recently in visual servoing (Chaumette, 2004; Tahri & Chaumette 2005). Indeed, they offer several interesting properties. First, they provide a generic representation of any simple or complicated object. Moreover, in the specific context of visual servoing, it can be shown that designing control laws with such features significantly improves the decoupling between translation and rotation in the camera motion (Tahri & Chaumette 2005). Therefore, we have also treated this specific case.

In this section, we first briefly recall some definitions before proposing a method allowing to determine these primitives when they cannot be extracted from the image. As previously, we will consider a fixed object O and will denote by R the projected region of O in the image plane. We will also assume that R has a continuous surface and a closed contour. However, as the proposed reasoning can be easily extended to non-planar landmarks, we will consider here only planar objects for the sake of simplicity. Further details about more complex shapes and different image moments are available in (Chaumette, 2004; Tahri & Chaumette 2005).

The $(i+j)^{th}$ order image moment m_{ij} of R in the image is classically defined by:

$$m_{ij} = \iint_{R} X^i Y^j dxdy \tag{8}$$

It can be shown that $\dot{m}_{ij}$ can be related to the camera kinematic screw by:

$$\dot{m}_{ij} = \mathbf{L}_{(m_{ij},A,B,C)} \mathrm{v}_c \tag{9}$$

where $\mathbf{L}_{(m_{ij},A,B,C)}$ is the corresponding interaction matrix. The 3D parameters A, B, C allow to define the depth in the case of a planar object as described by equation (6). The analytical expression of $\mathbf{L}_{(m_{ij},A,B,C)}$ expresses as follows (Chaumette, 2004):

$$\mathbf{L}_{(m_{ij},A,B,C)} = \begin{cases} m_{V\vec{x}_c} &= -i\left(Am_{ij} + Bm_{i-1,j+1} + Cm_{i-1,j}\right) - Am_{ij} \\ m_{V\vec{y}_c} &= -j\left(Am_{i+1,j-1} + Bm_{i,j} + Cm_{i,j-1}\right) - Bm_{ij} \\ m_{V\vec{z}_c} &= (i+j+3)\left(Am_{i+1,j} + Bm_{i,j+1} + Cm_{i,j}\right) - Cm_{ij} \\ m_{\Omega\vec{x}_c} &= (i+j+3)m_{i,j+1} + jm_{i,j-1} \\ m_{\Omega\vec{y}_c} &= (i+j+3)m_{i+1,j} - im_{i-1,j} \\ m_{\Omega\vec{z}_c} &= im_{i-1,j+1} - jm_{i+1,j-1} \end{cases} \tag{10}$$

As one can see, the time variation of a $(i+j)^{th}$ order moment depends on moments of higher orders (up to $i+j+1$) and on A, B and C. Therefore, as previously, the interaction matrix $\mathbf{L}_{(m_{ij},A,B,C)}$ depends implicitly on the object depth through the A, B and C parameters. Note that the same results hold for centered and discrete moments (Chaumette, 2004; Folio, 2007). Now, it remains to express the differential system to be solved to determine the desired primitives. Defining the visual features vector by a set of image moments, that is: $\mathbf{s} = [m_1, \cdots, m_n]^T$,and using equation (9) leads to:

$$\dot{\mathbf{s}} = \begin{bmatrix} \dot{m}_1 \\ \vdots \\ \dot{m}_n \end{bmatrix} = \begin{bmatrix} \mathbf{L}_{(m_1,A,B,C)} \\ \vdots \\ \mathbf{L}_{(m_n,A,B,C)} \end{bmatrix} \mathbf{v}_c = \mathbf{L}_{(m_1,\cdots,m_n,A,B,C)} \mathbf{v}_c \tag{11}$$

However, as mentioned above, the time derivative $\dot{m}_{ij}$ of a $(i+j)^{th}$ order moment depends on the moments of higher orders. Therefore, it is impossible to reconstruct the image moments m_{ij} using the dynamic system (11). To avoid this problem, we propose to estimate a set of visual primitives from which it is possible to deduce the m_{ij} image moments in a second step. Here, following a similar approach to the previous case, we propose to use l points belonging to the contour of R to approximate the image moments. We present below the final chosen algorithm 2:

Algorithm 2: Computation of image moments

1. Considering a set of l points belonging to the contour of R, define vector $\psi = (X_1, Y_1, z_1, \ldots, X_l, Y_l, z_l)^T$ as mentioned above.
2. Solve system (4) to compute an estimation $\tilde{\psi}$ of ψ, that is an estimation of each triple (Xi, Yi, zi)
3. Use $\tilde{\psi}$ to compute the different necessary moments m_{ij} and deduce an estimation of vector: $\mathbf{s} = (m_1, \cdots, m_n)^T$

Notice that the l points of the contour of R must be carefully chosen. In the particular case of polygonal shapes, these points may be defined by the vertices of the considered polygon, and the corresponding image moments can then be determined using the methods described in (Singer, 1993) or in (Steger, 1996). For more complex shapes, it is usually possible to approximate the contour by a polygon and obtain an estimate of the image moments by the same process. Finally, the image moments can be always analytically determined for simple geometric primitives, such as circles, ellipses and so on.

2.2 Generic problem statement

In the previous subsections, we have addressed the problem of reconstructing image data from the vision/motion link. Our goal is now to propose a generic formulation of this problem. Three cases have been highlighted[2] :

a. The interaction matrix $\mathbf{L}_{(\mathbf{s},\mathbf{z})}$ requires *explicitly* the depth and we suppose that $\dot{\mathbf{z}}$ can be directly related to the camera kinematic screw $\mathbf{v}_c$. In that case, we are brought back to the case of the point and we only have to solve a system similar to the one given by (4).

b. The interaction matrix $\mathbf{L}_{(\mathbf{s},\mathbf{z})}$ depends *implicitly* on a model of the depth through the A_{pq} coefficients for instance. In such a case, to provide a generic framework, we propose to apply the results obtained for the points to compute the needed parameters. It is then possible to determine the desired visual features by solving (7).

c. It is difficult or impossible to characterize some (or all) the elements of the differential system. In this last case, the estimation problem may be solved by estimating other more suitable visual features from which we can deduce the desired image data. We then retrieve the first two cases.

Hence, in order to reconstruct the visual data **s**, we propose to solve the following generic dynamic system:

$$\begin{cases} \dot{\psi} = \mathbf{L}_{(\psi)}\mathbf{v}_c = \varphi(\psi, t) \\ \psi(t_0) = \psi_0 \end{cases} \tag{12}$$

where ψ is the vector to be estimated and ψ_0 its initial value. Its expression depends on the previously mentioned cases:

in case (a), where the depth is explicitely required (e.g. points features): $\psi = (\mathbf{s}^T, \mathbf{z}^T)^T$. In the simple case of points, ψ is naturally given by $\psi = [P_1, \ldots, P_n, z_1, \ldots, z_n]^T$.

in case (b), where the depth is implicitely known, a two steps estimation process is performed: first, we set $\psi = [P_1, \ldots, P_l, z_1, \ldots, z_l]^T$ to reconstruct the l feature points P_i coordinates which allow to identify the $\tilde{A}_{pq}$ parameters; then we fix $\psi = [\pi_1, \ldots, \pi_l, \tilde{A}_{pq}]^T$ to estimate the desired set of visual primitives π (see algorithm 1).

in case (c), the expression of ψ is deduced either from case (a) or from case (b), depending in the primitives chosen to reconstruct the desired image features.

The previous analysis has then shown that the estimation of visual data can be seen as the resolution of the dynamic system given by expression (12). Recalling that ψ_0 is the initial value of ψ, it is important to note that it can be considered as known. Indeed, as the visual data is considered to be available at least at the beginning of the robotic task: $\mathbf{s}_0$ is directly given by the feature extraction processing, while the initial depth $\mathbf{z}_0$ can be characterized off-line (see remark 3).

Remark 3: While the image remains available (at least once at the begin), **s** is directly obtained from the image features extraction processing. In the case of points, their initial depth $\mathbf{z}_0$ can be computed using one of the previously mentioned methods (SFM methods, signal processing techniques, pose relative estimation approaches, etc). It follows that, for

---

[2] Note that the proposed approach can only be applied if an analytical expression of $\mathbf{L}_{(\mathbf{s},\mathbf{z})}$ is available.

other primitives, we can assume, without loss of generality, that parameters A_{pq} are known. Note also that ψ_0 being known, it is possible to determine ψ by iteratively applying our estimator from the task beginning. Finally, let us remark that, when the image is lost, ψ is provided by our estimator.

Now, let us address the resolution problem. A first idea is to integrate the above system (12) for any $t \in [t_0; t_f]$ where t_0 and t_f are respectively the initial and final instants of the task. However, in this case, the computation is then quite difficult to carry out. Therefore, we propose to discretize the problem and to solve system (12) during the time control interval $[t_k; t_{k+1}]$.

2.3 Resolution

2.3.1 Case of points: Towards an analytical solution

We focus here on specific features: the points. As previously shown, the differential system to be solved is given by equation (4). We will consider two approaches: in the first one, the obtained solution is independent from the robot structure on which is embedded the camera, while in the second one, it is closely related to it.

An analytical solution independent from the mechanical structure of the robot: In this part, our objective is to propose an analytical solution independent from the mechanical structure of the robot. It only depends on the type of the considered visual features, here points. A first idea is to consider that the camera kinematic screw $\mathbf{v}_c$ is constant during the control interval $[t_k; t_{k+1}]$. However, it is obvious that this property is not really fulfilled. This is the reason why we propose to sample this interval into $N \in \mathbb{N}_\Gamma$ sub-intervals and to consider that $\mathbf{v}_c$ is constant during $[t_n; t_{n+1}]$ where $t_n = t_k+(n-k)T_N$, $T_N = \frac{T_s}{N}$ and T_s is the control law sampling period. In this way, we take into account (at least a bit!) the variation of $\mathbf{v}_c$ during T_s.

First of all, let us analytically solve system (4) on the sub-interval $[t_n; t_{n+1}]$. Considering that $v_c(t_n)$ is constant during $[t_n; t_{n+1}]$ yields to:

$$\begin{cases} \dot{X} = -\frac{f}{z(t)} V_{\vec{x}_c}(t_n) + \frac{X(t)}{z(t)} V_{\vec{z}_c}(t_n) + \frac{X(t)Y(t)}{z(t)} \Omega_{\vec{x}_c}(t_n) + (f + \frac{X(t)^2}{f}) \Omega_{\vec{y}_c}(t_n) + Y(t)\Omega_{\vec{z}_c}(t_n) \\ Y = -\frac{f}{z(t)} V_{\vec{y}_c}(t_n) + \frac{Y(t)}{z(t)} V_{\vec{z}_c}(t_n) + (f + \frac{Y(t)^2}{f}) \Omega_{\vec{x}_c}(t_n) - \frac{X(t)Y(t)}{z(t)} \Omega_{\vec{y}_c}(t_n) - X(t)\Omega_{\vec{z}_c}(t_n) \\ \dot{z} = -V_{\vec{z}_c}(t_n) - \frac{z(t)Y(t)}{f} \Omega_{\vec{x}_c}(t_n) + \frac{z(t)X(t)}{f} \Omega_{\vec{y}_c}(t_n) \end{cases} \quad (13)$$

We set in the sequel $V_{\vec{x}_c} = V_{\vec{x}_c}(t_n)$, $V_{\vec{y}_c} = V_{\vec{y}_c}(t_n)$, $V_{\vec{z}_c} = V_{\vec{z}_c}(t_n)$, $\Omega_{\vec{x}_c} = \Omega_{\vec{x}_c}(t_n)$, $\Omega_{\vec{y}_c} = \Omega_{\vec{y}_c}(t_n)$ and $\Omega_{\vec{z}_c} = \Omega_{\vec{z}_c}(t_n)$ for the sake of simplicity. We also introduce the initial condition $X_n=X(t_n)$, $Y_n=Y(t_n)$ and $z_n=z(t_n)$, $\dot{z}_n=\dot{z}(t_n)$, and $\ddot{z}_n=\ddot{z}(t_n)$. It can be shown that (Folio, 2007)[3]:

1. If $\Omega_{\vec{x}_c} \neq 0$, $\Omega_{\vec{y}_c} \neq 0$, $\Omega_{\vec{z}_c} \neq 0$, hence $A_1 \neq 0$, $A_2 \neq 0$ and $A_3 \neq 0$, then:

---

[3] The interested reader will find in (Folio, 2007) a detailed proof of the proposed results.

$$X(t) = \frac{f\Omega_{\vec{x}_c} A_4 + \Omega_{\vec{y}_c} A_5}{\Omega_{\vec{z}_c} A_3 z(t)}, \; Y(t) = \frac{f\Omega_{\vec{x}_c} A_4 - \Omega_{\vec{y}_c} A_5}{\Omega_{\vec{z}_c} A_3 z(t)} \text{ and}$$

$$z(t) = -\tfrac{c_1}{A_1}\cos(A_1(t-t_n)) + \tfrac{c_2}{A_1}\sin(A_1(t-t_n)) + \tfrac{A_2}{A_1}(t-t_n) + \tfrac{c_1}{A_1} + z_n,$$

with $A_4 = \ddot{z}_n - \Omega_{\vec{x}_c} V_{\vec{y}_c} + z(t) A_3$ and $A_5 = f\Omega_{\vec{z}_c}(\dot{z}_n + V_{\vec{z}_c})$.

2. If $\Omega_{\vec{x}_c}=0$, $\Omega_{\vec{y}_c}=0$, $\Omega_{\vec{z}_c}=0$, hence $A_1=0$, $A_2=0$ and $A_3=0$, then:

$$X(t) = \frac{X_n z_n - fV_{\vec{x}_c}(t-t_n)}{z(t)}, \; Y(t) = \frac{Y_n z_n - fV_{\vec{y}_c}(t-t_n)}{z(t)} \text{ and } z(t) = z_n - V_{\vec{z}_c}(t-t_n)$$

5. If $\Omega_{\vec{x}_c} \neq 0$, $\Omega_{\vec{y}_c} \neq 0$, $\Omega_{\vec{z}_c}=0$, hence $A_1=\sqrt{\Omega_{\vec{x}_c}^2 + \Omega_{\vec{y}_c}^2}$, $A_2=0$ and $A_3=0$, then:

$$X(t) = \frac{X_n z_n - fV_{\vec{x}_c}(t-t_n) - f\Omega_{\vec{y}_c} A_6}{z(t)}, \; Y(t) = \frac{Y_n z_n - fV_{\vec{y}_c}(t-t_n) - f\Omega_{\vec{x}_c} A_6}{z(t)}$$

with $A_6 = -\frac{c_1}{A_1^2}\sin(A_1(t-t_n)) - \frac{c_2}{A_1^2}\cos(A_1(t-t_n)) + (\frac{c_1}{A_1} + z_n)(t-t_n) + \frac{c_2}{A_1^2}$.

6. If $\Omega_{\vec{x}_c}=0$, $\Omega_{\vec{y}_c}=0$, $\Omega_{\vec{z}_c} \neq 0$, then:

$$X(t) = \frac{c_3\Omega_{\vec{z}_c}\cos(\Omega_{\vec{z}_c}(t-t_n)) + c_4\Omega_{\vec{z}_c}\sin(\Omega_{\vec{z}_c}(t-t_n)) - fV_{\vec{y}_c}}{\Omega_{\vec{z}_c} z(t)},$$

$$Y(t) = \frac{-c_3\Omega_{\vec{z}_c}\sin(\Omega_{\vec{z}_c}(t-t_n)) + c_4\Omega_{\vec{z}_c}\cos(\Omega_{\vec{z}_c}(t-t_n)) + fV_{\vec{x}_c}}{\Omega_{\vec{z}_c} z(t)}$$

where $A_1=\sqrt{\Omega_{\vec{x}_c}^2 + \Omega_{\vec{y}_c}^2 + \Omega_{\vec{z}_c}^2}$, $A_2=-\Omega_{\vec{z}_c}(V_{\vec{x}_c}\Omega_{\vec{x}_c} + V_{\vec{y}_c}\Omega_{\vec{y}_c} + V_{\vec{z}_c}\Omega_{\vec{z}_c})$, $A_3=(\Omega_{\vec{x}_c}^2 + \Omega_{\vec{y}_c}^2)$, $c_1 = \ddot{z}$, $c_2 = \dot{z} - \frac{A_2}{A_1^2}$, $c_3 = -X_n z_n - f\frac{V_{\vec{y}c}}{\Omega_{\vec{z}c}}$ and $c_4 = Y_n z_n - f\frac{V_{\vec{x}c}}{\Omega_{\vec{z}c}}$.

The above expressions of ($X(t)$, $Y(t)$, $z(t)$) depend on the values of the camera kinematic screw at each instant t_n. These values must then be computed. To this aim, as $\mathbf{v}_c = \mathbf{J}(\mathbf{q})\dot{\mathbf{q}}$ (see equation (1)), it is necessary to evaluate the control input $\dot{\mathbf{q}}$ and $\mathbf{J}(\mathbf{q})$at t_n. Now, recalling that $\dot{\mathbf{q}}$ is hold during the time control interval, that is $\dot{\mathbf{q}}(t) = \dot{\mathbf{q}}(t_k)$, $\forall t \in [t_k; t_{k+1}]$, it is straightforward to show that $\dot{\mathbf{q}}(t_n) = \dot{\mathbf{q}}(t_k)$, $\forall t_n \in [t_k; t_{k+1}]$. It remains to compute $\mathbf{J}(\mathbf{q})$ and therefore the configuration $\mathbf{q}$ at instant t_n. To this aim, we propose to simply integrate the equation $\dot{\mathbf{q}}(t) = \dot{\mathbf{q}}(t_k)$ between t and t_k. It yields to:

$$\mathbf{q}(t) = (t - t_k)\dot{\mathbf{q}} + \mathbf{q}(t_k), \; \forall t \in [t_k; t_k+1] \tag{14}$$

where $\mathbf{q}(t_k)$ represents the robot configuration at instant t_k. The corresponding values can be measured using the embedded proprioceptive sensors. Then, on the base of $\mathbf{q}(t)$, it is possible to deduce the jacobian $\mathbf{J}(\mathbf{q}(t))$and therefore the camera kinematic screw on the sub-interval $[t_n; t_{n+1}]$. The latter being constant on this interval, the analytical expressions detailed above can be used to compute $\psi(t)=(X(t), Y(t), z(t))$ at t_{n+1}. The same computations must be performed at each instant t_n to obtain the value of ψ at t_{k+1}, which leads to algorithm 3.

Algorithm 3: Estimation of the points when vc is constant during $[t_n; t_{n+1}] \subset [t_k; t_{k+1}]$

```
Initialization: Determine ψ(t0) and set tk = t0 , ψ(tk ) = ψ(t0 )
For each control interval [tk; tk+1] do
        Set tn = tk , ψ(tn) = ψ(tk)
        For each integration interval [tn; tn+1] do
                Compute q(tn) thanks to relation (14)
                Deduce J(q(tn)) and vc(tn) = J(q(tn)) q̇ (tn)
                Evaluate ψ(tn+1)
        End for
End for
```

The proposed approach can be seen as a first step towards the introduction of the camera kinematic screw evolution into the reconstruction procedure. Its main advantage is that its realization is very simple and that it allows to remain independent from the robot mechanical structure. Naturally, the value of N must be carefully chosen: a large value reduces the estimation accuracy, especially if the control law sampling period Ts is large; a small value increases the computation time, but improves the precision, as it is getting closer to the true variable kinematic screw case.

Remark 4: Another equivalent idea to reconstruct the visual features in case of points would be to consider the exponential map approach and the direct measure of the camera velocity. This approach allows to determine the 3D coordinates of the point p_i (x_i, y_i, z_i) using the following relation (Soatto & Perona, 1998):

$$\dot{p}_i = -V_{C/F_c}^{F_c} - \Omega_{F_c/F_0}^{F_c} \wedge p_i(t) \leftrightarrow p_i(t_{k+1}) = \mathbf{R}(t_k)\, p_i(t_k) + \mathbf{t}(t_k)$$

where $\mathbf{R} \in SO_{(3)}$[4] and $\mathbf{t} \in R^3$ define respectively the rotation and translation of the moving camera. Indeed, $\mathbf{R}$ and $\mathbf{t}$ are related to the camera rotation $\Omega_{F_c/F_0}^{F_c}$ and translation $V_{C/F_c}^{F_c}$ motion thanks to an exponential map (Murray et al., 1994), that is:

$$\begin{pmatrix} \mathbf{R} & \mathbf{t} \\ 0 & 1 \end{pmatrix} = \exp\begin{pmatrix} [\Omega]_\times & V_{C/F_0} \\ 0 & 0 \end{pmatrix}$$

where $[\Omega]_\times$ belongs to the set of 3×3 skew-matrices and is commonly used to describe the cross product of $\Omega_{F_c/F_0}^{F_c}$ with a vector in R^3. However, this approach can be used only if the camera kinematic screw $\mathbf{v}_c$ can be assumed constant during the sampling period Ts, which is not usually the case. We are then brought back to a similar approach to the one presented above.

An analytical solution integrating the mechanical structure of the robot: As previously mentioned, the above analytical solution is restricted to the case where the camera kinematic screw remains constant during $[t_n; t_{n+1}] \subset [t_k; t_{k+1}]$. However, although it offers a general result independent from the robot mechanical structure, this assumption is rarely completely fulfilled in a real context. Indeed, only the control input $\dot{\mathbf{q}}$ can be considered to be really hold between t_k and t_{k+1}, whereas the camera motion $\mathbf{v}_c$ evolves during the same

[4] $SO_{(3)}$: special orthogonal group of Transformations of R^3.

period. This is the reason why our objective in this part is to relax the assumption about **v**c. To this aim, it is necessary to consider a particular robotic system in order to express the corresponding jacobian **J**. We have chosen here the robot Super-Scout II on which we have always realized our experimental tests up to now. This is a nonholonomic cart-like vehicle equipped with a camera mounted on a pan-platform (see figure 2). Its mechanical structure is then simple and the expression of its jacobian is given by (23). In this case, the control input is defined by $\dot{\mathbf{q}} = (v, \omega, \varpi)^T$, where v and ω are the cart linear and angular velocities, while ϖ is the pan-platform angular velocity. Our robot will be more precisely described in the next section dedicated to the application context.

As previously shown, our goal is now to analytically solve the dynamic system given by (4). Considering the particular mechanical structure of our robot, it is impossible to Transactionlate the camera along $\vec{x}_c$ and rotate it around axes $\vec{y}_c$ and $\vec{z}_c$, which leads to $V_{\vec{x}_c} = \Omega_{\vec{y}_c} = \Omega_{\vec{z}_c} = 0$. Taking into account this result into equation (4), the dynamic system to be solved for one point $P(X, Y)$ expresses as follows:

$$\begin{cases} \dot{X} = \frac{X(t)}{z(t)} V_{\vec{z}_c}(t) + \frac{X(t)Y(t)}{f} \Omega_{\vec{x}_c}(t) \\ \dot{Y} = -\frac{f}{z(t)} V_{\vec{y}_c}(t) + \frac{Y(t)}{z(t)} V_{\vec{z}_c}(t) + (f + \frac{Y(t)^2}{f}) \Omega_{\vec{x}_c}(t) \\ \dot{z} = -V_{\vec{z}_c}(t) - \frac{z(t)Y(t)}{f} \Omega_{\vec{x}_c}(t) \end{cases} \tag{15}$$

where $V_{\vec{y}_c}(t)$, $V_{\vec{z}_c}(t)$ and $\Omega_{\vec{x}_c}(t)$ are given by relation (23).

Now, let us determine the analytical solution of the differential (15). We denote by v_k, ω_k and ϖ_k the values of the velocities applied to the robot at instant t_k. For the sake of simplicity, we also introduce the following notations: $X_k = X(t_k)$, $Y_k = Y(t_k)$, $z_k = z(t_k)$ and finally $\vartheta_k = \vartheta(t_k)$ where ϑ represents the pan-platform orientation with respect to the mobile base. After some computations (a detailed proof is available in (Folio, 2007)), we get the following results for $z(t)$ depending on the control inputs ω_k and ϖ_k:

1. If $\omega_k \neq -\varpi_k$ and $\omega_k \neq 0$, then:
   $z(t) = c_1 \sin(A_1(t-t_k)) + c_2 \cos(A_1(t-t_k)) - D_x \cos(\vartheta(t)) + \frac{v_k}{\omega_k} \sin(\vartheta(t)) - C_x$
2. If $\omega_k = -\varpi_k \neq 0$, then:
   $z(t) = \frac{\omega_k}{\varpi_k} D_x (\cos(\vartheta(t)) - \cos(\vartheta_k)) - \frac{v_k}{\varpi_k} (\sin(\vartheta(t)) - \sin(\vartheta_k)) + z_k$
3. If $\omega_k = 0$, then:
   $z(t) = c_3 \sin(\varpi_k(t-t_k)) + c_4 \cos(\varpi_k(t-t_k)) - v_k(t-t_k)\cos(\vartheta(t)) + \frac{v_k}{2\varpi_k} \sin(\vartheta(t)) - C_x$
4. If $\omega_k = \varpi_k = 0$, then:
   $z(t) = z_k - v_k(t-t_k)\cos(\vartheta_k)$

(16)

with[5] $c_1 = \frac{v_k}{\omega_k}\cos(\vartheta_k) + D_x \sin(\vartheta_k) - \frac{Y_k z_k}{f} - C_y$, $c_2 = -\frac{v_k}{\omega_k}\sin(\vartheta_k) + D_x\cos(\vartheta_k) + z_k + C_x$, $c_3 = -\frac{v_k}{2\varpi_k}\cos(\vartheta_k) + \frac{Y_k z_k}{f} - C_y$, $c_4 = -\frac{v_k}{2\varpi_k}\sin(\vartheta_k) + z_k + C_x$ and $A_1 = (\omega_k + \varpi_k)$.

[5] (C_x, C_y) and D_x are geometric parameters of the robot and of the camera (see figure 2).

Now, we consider the determination of $X(t)$. From (15) we can write: $\frac{\dot{X}}{X(t)} = -\frac{\dot{z}}{z(t)}$. $X(t)$ can then be computed by integrating this last relation for $\forall t \in [t_k; t_k+1]$, and we get:

$$X(t) = \frac{z_k X_k}{z(t)} \quad (17)$$

Finally, $Y(t)$ is easily deduced from (15) as follows: $Y(t) = -f\frac{\dot{z}+V_{\dot{z}c}(t)}{z(t)\Omega_{\dot{x}c}(t)}$. Using the solution $z(t)$ given by (16), $Y(t)$ expresses as:

$$\begin{aligned}
&1.\ \text{If } \omega_k \neq -\varpi_k \text{ and } \omega_k \neq 0, \text{ then} \\
&\quad Y(t) = -\tfrac{f}{z(t)}\left(c_1 \cos(A_1(t-t_k)) - c_2 \sin(A_1(t-t_k)) - D_x \omega \sin(\vartheta(t)) - C_y(\omega+\varpi)\right) \\
&2.\ \text{If } \omega_k = -\varpi_k \neq 0, \text{ then} \\
&\quad Y(t) = \tfrac{f}{z(t)\varpi_k}\left(v\cos(\vartheta(t)) - \cos(\vartheta_k) + \varpi_k z_k Y_k\right) \\
&3.\ \text{If } \omega_k = 0, \text{ then} \\
&\quad Y(t) = -\tfrac{f}{z(t)}\left(c_1 \cos(A_1(t-t_k)) - c_2 \sin(A_1(t-t_k)) + v(t-t_k)\sin(\vartheta(t)) - \tfrac{v}{2\varpi}\cos(\vartheta(t)) + C_y\right) \\
&4.\ \text{If } \omega_k = \varpi_k = 0, \text{ then} \\
&\quad Y(t) = -\tfrac{f}{z(t)}\left(v_k(t-t_k)\sin(\vartheta_k) + z_k Y_k\right)
\end{aligned} \quad (18)$$

As one can see, the above solution requires the determination of $\vartheta(t)$. This angle can simply be computed by integrating $\dot{\vartheta}=\varpi$ between t_k and t. Some straightforward calculus leads to $\vartheta(t)=\varpi_k(t-t_k)+\vartheta_k$, where ϑ_k is the pan-platform angular value at t_k, which is usually provided by the embedded encoder.

The proposed approach takes fully into account the evolution of the camera kinematic screw in the reconstruction process of the triple $(X(t), Y(t), z(t))$ for all $t \in [t_k; t_{k+1}]$. Although the proposed approach is restricted to the considered robotic system and to points, its main advantage lies in its accuracy. As shown in the next section devoted to applications, the obtained results are significantly better with this method.

2.3.2 Numerical resolution: a generic framework

As previously mentioned, the analytical solutions are restricted to the case of points and, for one of them, to the robotic system. The question is now: "What to do if other kinds of image features are used"? In this part, we address this problem and we aim at designing a generic framework allowing to solve the dynamic system (12) in a general context. In such case, it appears to be difficult to keep on proposing an analytical solution to the considered system. This is the reason why we propose to use numerical methods to solve (12). In order to increase the accuracy of the different considered schemes, we propose to divide the $[t_k; t_{k+1}]$ control law interval into $N \in N^*$ sub-intervals $[t_n; t_{n+1}] \subset [t_k; t_{k+1}]$. In this way, it is possible to define the integration step $T_N = \frac{T_s}{N} = t_{n+1} - t_n$.

Using numerical techniques to solve (12) requires to characterize ψ and the different related interaction matrix (see paragraph 2.2.). We suppose in the sequel that such a characterization is possible. Moreover, the numerical algorithms will not be used in the same way depending on the camera kinematic screw is considered to be constant or not on the interval $[t_k; t_{k+1}]$. We can then distinguish the two following cases:

1. The camera motion **vc** can be considered as constant during the control law sampling period T_s. In this case, only one evaluation of **vc**(t_k) at time t_k is needed to compute $\varphi(\psi, t)$, $\forall t \in [t_k; t_{k+1}]$.
2. The camera motion **vc** varies with time in $[t_k; t_{k+1}]$. It is then necessary to calculate it at each instant t_n. Therefore, the computation of $\varphi(\psi, t)$ require an evaluation of **vc**(t_n) for each time t_n. Recalling that only $\dot{\mathbf{q}}$ is hold during T_s, and thanks to (14) we can then compute **vc**(t_n) = $\mathbf{J}(\mathbf{q}(t_n))\ \dot{\mathbf{q}}_k$ (or even using $\dot{\mathbf{q}}_n$ if available).

The literature provides many methods allowing to numerically solve differential equations. A large overview of such methods is proposed for example in (Butcher, 2008). In this work, we have compared several common numerical schemes to select the most efficient technique. Here, we consider the Euler, Runge-Kutta (RK), Adams-Bashforth-Moulton (ABM) and Backward Differentiation Formulas (BDF) numerical techniques. Hence, we first recall briefly the description of these schemes.

Euler Scheme: It is the simplest numerical integration method, but usually the less accurate. As a consequence, it requires a small integration step. The Euler integration method is classically given by:

$$\tilde{\psi}_{k+1} = \psi_k + T_n \varphi(\psi_k, t_k) \tag{19}$$

Runge–Kutta Schemes: The Runge–Kutta methods are an important family of iterative algorithms dedicated to the approximation of solutions of differential equations. The most commonly used scheme is the fourth order one, which is often referred as RK4. It expresses as follows:

$$\tilde{\psi}_{k+1} = \psi_k + \tfrac{1}{6}\left(K_1 + 2K_2 + 2K_3 + K_4\right), \quad \text{with}: \begin{cases} K_1 = T_n(\psi_k, t_k) \\ K_2 = T_n(\psi_k + \tfrac{1}{2}K_1, t_k + \tfrac{1}{2}T_n) \\ K_3 = T_n(\psi_k + \tfrac{1}{2}K_2, t_k + \tfrac{1}{2}T_n) \\ K_4 = T_n(\psi_k + K_3, t_k + T_n) \end{cases} \tag{20}$$

The methods presented above are known as one-step schemes because they are based only on one previous value to estimate $\tilde{\psi}_{k+1}$. Contrary to this case, techniques using more than one of the previous values (ie. ψ_k, ψ_{k-1}, ...ψ_{k-N}) are referred as multi-steps approaches. Two of them are described below.

Adams Schemes: The Adams based techniques are multistep methods which approximate the solution of a given differential equations by a polynomial. It usually works as a predictor/corrector pair called the Adams–Bashforth–Moulton (ABM) schemes. The method consists in a two-step approach: the value $\hat{\psi}_{k+1}$ is first predicted with an Adams–Bashforth scheme, and then corrected thanks to an Adams–Moulton algorithm to obtain the estimation $\tilde{\psi}_{k+1}$. For instance the fourth order Adams–Bashforth–Moulton (ABM4) is given by:

$$\begin{aligned} \hat{\psi}_{k+1} &= \psi_k + \tfrac{T_n}{24}\left(55\varphi_k - 59\varphi_{k-1} + 37\varphi_{k-2} - 9\varphi_{k-3}\right) && \text{Adams–Bashforth predictor} \\ \tilde{\psi}_{k+1} &= \psi_k + \tfrac{T_n}{24}\left(9\varphi(\hat{\psi}_{k+1}, t_{k+1}) + 19\psi_k - 5\psi_{k-1} + \psi_{k-2}\right) && \text{Adams–Moulton corrector} \end{aligned} \tag{21}$$

Gear's Methods: The Gear's methods, also known as Backward Differentiation Formulas (BDF), consist in using a polynomial which interpolates the N previous values ψ_k, ψ_{k-1},...,

ψ_{k-N} to estimate $\widetilde{\psi}_{k+1}$. They are mainly dedicated to stiff differential equations (see remark 5). We recall below the fourth order BDF4 scheme which have been used hereafter:

$$\widetilde{\psi}_{k+1} = \tfrac{48}{25}\psi_k - \tfrac{36}{25}\psi_{k-1} + \tfrac{16}{26}\psi_{k-2} - \tfrac{3}{25}\psi_{k-3} + \tfrac{12}{25}T_n\varphi(\hat{\psi}_{k+1}, t_{k+1}) \quad (22)$$

Remark 5: A problem is stiff if the numerical solution step size is more severely limited by the stability of the numerical technique than by its accuracy. Frequently, these problems occur in systems of differential equations involving several components which are varying at widely different rates. The interested reader will find more details in the survey by (Shampine & Gear 1979).

Therefore, these numerical methods provide an estimated value $\widetilde{\psi}_{k+1}$ after N integration steps over one control law sampling period T_s. The algorithm 4 given below details the different steps of calculus.

Algorithm 4: Estimation of the visual features using numerical schemes.

```
Initialization: Determine ψ(t0) and set tk = t0 , ψ(tk ) = ψ(t0 )
For each control interval [tk; tk+1] do
        If multiple step scheme and initialization not over then
                Initialization of the necessary previous values of ψ.
        End if
        If vc is considered to be constant during [tk; tk+1] then
                Evaluate vc only at instant tk .
        End if
        Set tn = tk , ψ(tn) = ψ(tk)
        For each integration interval [tn; tn+1] do
                If vc varies during [tk; tk+1] then
                        Evaluate vc at instant tn .
                End if
                Evaluate φ(ψ(tn), tn)
                Choose a numerical scheme and compute the corresponding value of
ψ(tn+1)
        End for
End for
```

Finally, numerical schemes can be used since an expression of $\varphi(\psi, t)$ and a history of successive values of ψ is available. In this way, dynamic system (12) can be solved in a general context, that is for any kind of image features and any robot mechanical structures.

2.4 Conclusion

In this section, we have proposed a set of methods allowing to reconstruct the visual features when they cannot be provided anymore by the camera. Most of the works which address this problem classically rely on information based on the image dynamics. In this work, we have deliberately chosen to consider the case where the image becomes totally unavailable. We have then used the vision/motion to link to estimate the lacking data. Our first contribution lies in the modelling step. Indeed, we have stated the estimation problem for different kinds of visual features: points, common geometric primitives and image moments. On the base of this analysis, we have shown that the considered problem can be expressed as a dynamic system to be solved. Our second contribution consists in the development of different techniques allowing to compute analytical and numerical solutions. The different proposed methods can be easily implemented on a real robot. Note that a careful choice of the different involved sampling periods is mandatory. Finally, these methods also require to have the necessary information for the algorithm initialization. This is particularly true for multi-step numerical methods which need a history of the values of ψ. Now, our goal is to validate and compare the different proposed approaches.

3. Applications

The proposed estimation methods can be used in many applications. For example, it has been recently successfully used to perform vision-based navigation tasks in cluttered environments. Indeed, in such a case, the visual features loss is mainly due to occlusions which occur when the obstacles enter the camera field of view. Integrating our reconstruction techniques in the control law allows to treat efficiently this problem and to realize the task despite the occlusion (Folio & Cadenat, 2007; Folio & Cadenat, 2008). Another interesting application area is to use the estimated visual features provided by our algorithms to refresh more frequently the control law. Indeed, as T_s is often smaller than the vision sensor sampling period T_c[6], the control law is computed with the same visual measures during several steps, which decreases its efficiency. Our work has then be successfully used to predict the visual features between two image acquisitions so as to improve the closed loop performances (Folio, 2007). Finally, it is also possible to apply our results to other related fields such as active vision, 3D reconstruction methods or even fault diagnosis for instance.
In this part, we still consider a visual servoing application but focus on a particular problem which may occur during the mission execution: the camera or the image processing failure. Our idea is here to use our estimation technique to recover from this problem so as the task can still be executed despite it. We first present the robotic system on which we have implemented our works. Then, we detail the mission to be realized and show how to introduce our estimation techniques in the classical visual servoing controller. Finally, we describe both simulation and experimental results which demonstrate the validity and the efficiency of our approach when a camera failure occurs.

3.1 Robotic system description and modelling

We consider the mobile robot Super-Scout II [7] equipped with a camera mounted on a pan-platform (see figure 2.a). It is a small cylindric cart-like vehicle, dedicated to indoor navigation. A DFW-VL500 Sony color digital IEEE1394 camera captures pictures in yuv 4:2:2 format with 640×480 resolution. An image processing module allows to extract the necessary visual features from the image. The robot is controlled by an on-board laptop running under Linux on which is installed a specific control architecture called GenoM (Generator of Module) (Fleury and Herrb, 2001).
Now, let us model our system to express the camera kinematic screw. To this aim, considering figure 2.b, we define the successive frames: $F_M(M,\vec{x}_M,\vec{y}_M,\vec{z}_M)$ linked to the robot, $F_P(P,\vec{x}_P,\vec{y}_P,\vec{z}_P)$ attached to the pan-platform, and $F_C(C,\vec{x}_c,\vec{y}_c,\vec{z}_c)$ linked to the

[6] On our experimental platform, T_s=50ms while T_c is between 100 and 150 ms.
[7] The mobile robot Super-Scout II is provided by the AIP-PRIMECA of Toulouse.

camera. Let ϑ be the direction of the pan-platform wrt. $\vec{x}_M$, P the pan-platform center of rotation and D_x the distance between the robot reference point M and P. The control input is defined by: $\dot{\mathbf{q}} = (v, \omega, \varpi)^T$, where v and ω are the cart linear and angular velocities, and ϖ is the pan-platform angular velocity wrt. F_M. For this specific mechanical system, the kinematic screw $\mathbf{v}_c$ is related to the control input by the robot jacobian $\mathbf{J}$: $\mathbf{v_c} = \mathbf{J}\dot{\mathbf{q}}$. As the camera is constrained to move horizontally, it is sufficient to consider a reduced kinematic screw: $\mathbf{v_c^r} = \left(V_{\vec{y}_c}, V_{\vec{z}_c}, \Omega_{\vec{x}_c}\right)^T$ involving only the controllable DOF. The corresponding reduced jacobian matrix $\mathbf{J_c^r}$ expresses as follows:

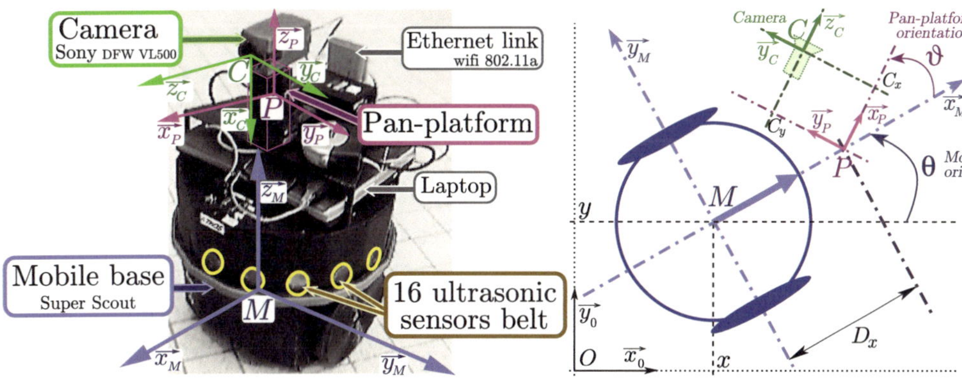

2.a - Nomadic Super-Scout II.

2.b - Cart-like robot with a camera mounted on a pan-platform.

Fig. 2. The robotic system.

$$\mathbf{v_c^r} = \begin{pmatrix} V_{\vec{y}_c}(t) \\ V_{\vec{z}_c}(t) \\ \Omega_{\vec{x}_c}(t) \end{pmatrix} = \begin{pmatrix} -\sin(\vartheta(t)) & D_x\cos(\vartheta(t)) + C_x & C_x \\ \cos(\vartheta(t)) & D_x\sin(\vartheta(t)) - C_y & -C_y \\ 0 & -1 & -1 \end{pmatrix} \begin{pmatrix} v \\ \omega \\ \varpi \end{pmatrix} = \mathbf{J_c^r}\dot{\mathbf{q}} \tag{23}$$

where C_x and C_y are the coordinates of C along axes $\vec{x}_P$ and $\vec{y}_P$ (see figure 2.b). Notice that $\mathbf{J_c^r}$ is a regular matrix as $\det(\mathbf{J_c^r}) = D_x \neq 0$.

3.2 Execution of a vision-based task despite camera failure

Our objective is to perform a vision-based task despite camera failure. We first describe the considered mission and state the estimation problem for this particular task before presenting the obtained results.

3.2.1 Vision-based task

Our goal is to position the embedded camera with respect to a visual landmark. To this aim, we have applied the visual servoing technique given in (Espiau et al., 1992) to mobile robots as in (Pissard-Gibollet & Rives, 1995). The proposed approach relies on the task function formalism (Samson et al., 1991) and consists in expressing the visual servoing task by the following task function to be regulated to zero:

$$e_{vs} = \mathbf{C}(\mathbf{s} - \mathbf{s}^*)$$

where **s*** represents the desired value of the visual signal, while **C** is a full-rank combination matrix allowing to take into account more visual features than available DOFs (Espiau et al., 1992). A classical controller $\dot{\mathbf{q}}_{(s)}$ making e_{vs} vanish can be designed by imposing an exponential decrease, that is: $\dot{e}_{vs} = -\lambda e_{vs} = \mathbf{CL}_{(s,z)}\mathbf{J}_c^r\dot{\mathbf{q}}_{(s)}$, where λ_{vs} is a positive scalar or a positive definite matrix. Fixing **C**= $\mathbf{L}_{(s^*,z^*)}$ as in (Espiau et al., 1992), the visual servoing controller $\dot{\mathbf{q}}_{(s)}$ can be written as follows:

$$\dot{\mathbf{q}}_{(s)} = \left(\mathbf{CL}_{(s,z)}\mathbf{J}_c^r\right)^{-1}(-\lambda)\mathbf{L}_{(s^*,z^*)}{}^{+}(\mathbf{s}-\mathbf{s}^*) \quad (24)$$

3.2.2 Control strategy

As previously mentioned, the goal is to perform a positioning vision-based task with respect to a landmark, despite visual data loss due to a camera failure. The robot will be controlled in different ways, depending on the visual data availability. Two cases may occur: either the camera is able to provide the visual data or not. In the first case, controller (24) can be directly applied to the robot and the task is executed as usually done. In the second case, we use our estimation technique to compute an estimation of the visual data vector $\tilde{\mathbf{s}}$. It is then possible to evaluate controller (24). Hence, during a camera failure, the vehicle is driven by a new controller: $\dot{\mathbf{q}}_{(\tilde{s})} = \left(\mathbf{CL}_{(\tilde{s},z)}\mathbf{J}_c^r\right)^{-1}(-\lambda)\mathbf{L}_{(s^*,z^*)}{}^{+}(\tilde{\mathbf{s}}-\mathbf{s}^*)$. Therefore, we propose to use the following global visual servoing controller:

$$\dot{\mathbf{q}}_{vs} = (1-\sigma)\dot{\mathbf{q}}_{(s)} + \sigma\dot{\mathbf{q}}_{(\tilde{s})} \quad (25)$$

where $\sigma \in [0; 1]$ is set to 1 when the image is unavailable. This reasoning leads to the control architecture shown in figure 3. Note that, generally, there is no need to smooth controller (25) when the image features are lost and recovered (if the camera failure is temporary). Indeed, when the failure occurs, as the last provided information are used to feed our reconstruction algorithm, the values of **s** and $\tilde{\mathbf{s}}$ are close and so are $\dot{\mathbf{q}}_{(s)}$ and $\dot{\mathbf{q}}_{(\tilde{s})}$. Usually, the same reasoning holds when the visual features are available anew. However, some smoothing may be useful if the camera motion has been unexpectedly perturbed during the estimation phase or if the algorithm has been given too inaccurate initial conditions. In such a case, it will be necessary to smooth the controller by defining σ as a continuous function of time *t* for instance.

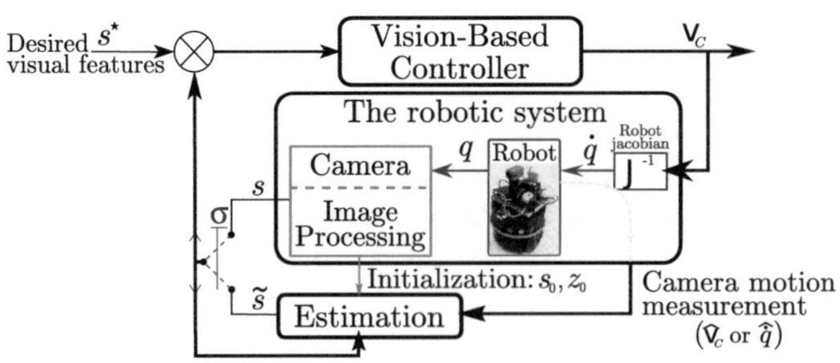

Fig. 3. The chosen control architecture.

3.3 Results

Our goal is then to position the embedded camera with respect to a given landmark despite camera failure. We will use controller (25). We propose hereafter some simulation results together with experimental tests to show the interest and the efficiency of the different proposed estimation techniques. We first present the obtained results in the two following subsections. Precise comments together with a detailed comparative analysis are provided in next part.

3.3.1 Simulation results

To validate our work, we have first realized numerous simulations using Matlab software. We have considered different kinds of visual features: points, ellipses and image moments. For each case, we have performed the same robotic task, starting from the same initial configuration to reach the same goal **s*** (see Figure 4). In a similar way, the camera failure occurs after 50 steps and lasts until the end of the mission. In this way, we guarantee that the multi-step numerical schemes can be correctly initialized6. The control law sampling period has been chosen equal to T_s = 50ms, which is close to its value on the robotic platform. The control interval has been divided in N=10 integration step, that is T_n=5ms.

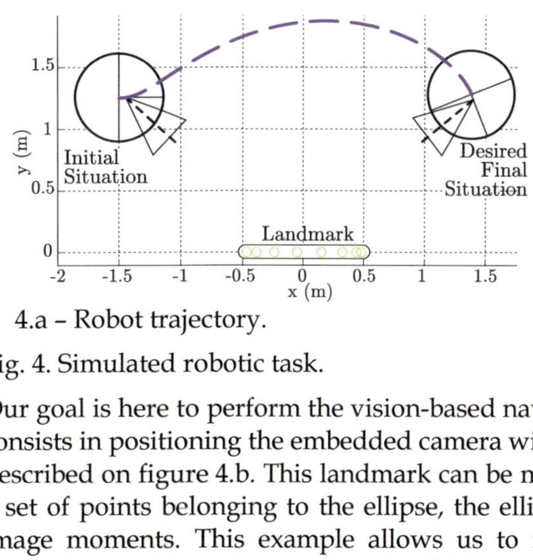

4.a - Robot trajectory.

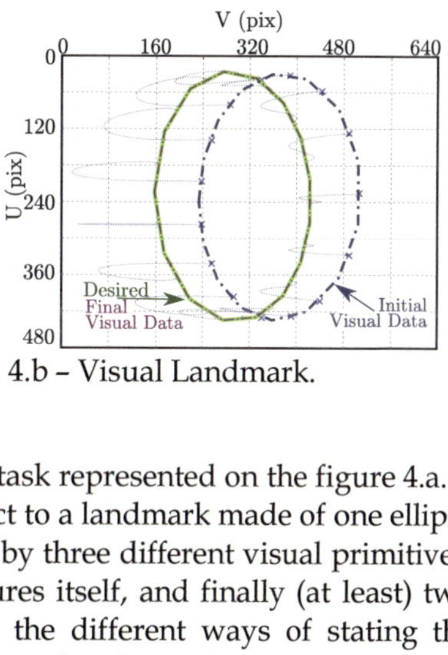

4.b - Visual Landmark.

Fig. 4. Simulated robotic task.

Our goal is here to perform the vision-based navigation task represented on the figure 4.a. It consists in positioning the embedded camera with respect to a landmark made of one ellipse described on figure 4.b. This landmark can be modelled by three different visual primitives: a set of points belonging to the ellipse, the ellipse features itself, and finally (at least) two image moments. This example allows us to illustrate the different ways of stating the estimation problem shown in section 2. We present below the obtained results for each of these primitives.

Case of points: In this case, we consider 10 points belonging to the ellipse. Thus, the image features vector is defined by: $\mathbf{s} = [X_1, Y_1, \cdots, X_{10}, Y_{10}]^T$, where ($X_i$, Y_i) are the coordinates of each projected point P_i. Let us recall that the dynamic system to be solved is given by (4).

The table 1 synthesis the simulation results obtained using the proposed numerical and analytical methods for points. More precisely, it shows the maximal and the standard deviation (std) error of the euclidean norm of the set of points (i.e. $\|\mathbf{s}-\tilde{\mathbf{s}}\|$) and of their depth (i.e. $\|\mathbf{z}-\tilde{\mathbf{z}}\|$).

	Euler error		RK4 error		ABM4 error	
	std	max	std	max	std	max
$\lvert \mathbf{s} \rvert$	$0.947 .10^{-3}$	$2.450 . 10^{-3}$	$0.299 . 10^{-3}$	$1.133 . 10^{-3}$	$0.136 . 10^{-3}$	$0.556 . 10^{-3}$
$\lvert \mathbf{z} \rvert$	$1.935 . 10^{-3}$	$8.949 . 10^{-3}$	$1.829 . 10^{-3}$	$7.624 . 10^{-3}$	$0.379 . 10^{-3}$	$1.906 . 10^{-3}$
	BDF4 error		Analytic error ($\mathbf{v}_c$ constant)		Analytic error ($\mathbf{v}_c$ variable)	
	std	max	std	max	std	max
$\lvert \mathbf{s} \rvert$	$0.311 .10^{-3}$	$2.109 . 10^{-3}$	$0.199 . 10^{-3}$	$0.863 . 10^{-3}$	$1.779 . 10^{-12}$	$31.724 . 10^{-12}$
$\lvert \mathbf{z} \rvert$	$0.892 . 10^{-3}$	$7.784 . 10^{-3}$	$0.968 . 10^{-3}$	$6.456 . 10^{-3}$	$8.795 . 10^{-12}$	$96.367 . 10^{-12}$

Table 1. Point simulation results ($\lvert \mathbf{s} \rvert$ in pixel, and $\lvert \mathbf{z} \rvert$ in mm).

Case of ellipse: We consider now the ellipse itself described on figure 4.b. Hence, we first recall that an ellipse can be defined by the following quadric equation:

$$X_i^2 + E_1 Y_i^2 + E_2 X_i Y_i + E_3 X_i + 2E_4 Y_i + E_5 = 0 \tag{26}$$

The visual features vector can expresses as: $\mathbf{s} = [E_1, E_2, E_3, E_4, E_5, X_1, Y_1, \cdots, X_{25}, Y_{25}]^T$, where (X_i, Y_i) are the coordinates of the points belonging to the ellipse. This set of l=25 points allows to identify the ellipse A_{pq} 3D parameters (see algorithm 2). The differential system to be solved can then be expressed as follows:

$$\dot{\mathbf{s}} = \begin{bmatrix} \mathbf{L}_{(E_1, A_{pq})} \\ \\ \mathbf{L}_{(E_5, A_{pq})} \\ \mathbf{L}_{(P_1, z_1)} \\ \\ \mathbf{L}_{(P_{25}, z_{25})} \end{bmatrix} \mathbf{v}_c = \mathbf{L}_{(E_1, E_2, E_3, E_4, E_5, A_{pq}, X_1, Y_1, \cdots, X_{25}, Y_{25})} \mathbf{v}_c \tag{27}$$

where $\mathbf{L}_{(P_i, z_i)}$ is the interaction matrix related to the point P_i given by (3) , and $\mathbf{L}_{(E_i, A_{pq})}$ is the interaction matrix related to the E_i ellipse quadric parameters. The $\mathbf{L}_{(E_i, A_{pq})}$ expressions are available in (Espiau et al., 1992). As the points were presented in the previous paragraph, we focus here on the ellipse. Thus, we focus on the ellipse quadric parameters E_i estimation results, for which only numerical techniques can be applied. Moreover, each estimated point P_i belonging to the ellipse has to fit the relation (26). Therefore, in this case, the estimator efficiency can be evaluated according to the following relation:

$$\varepsilon_{El} = \max_i \left(X_i^2 + E_1 Y_i^2 + E_2 X_i Y_i + E_3 X_i + 2E_4 Y_i + E_5 \right) \tag{28}$$

Hence, the table 2 summarizes the estimation error of E_i parameters and the ε_{El} error for each considered numerical scheme.

Case of moments: The landmark shown on figure 4.b has been characterized by points and ellipses. It is also possible to use the two following image moments: the area (i.e. m_{00}), and the gravity center, and the gravity center ($X_g = \frac{m_{10}}{m_{00}}, Y_g = \frac{m_{01}}{m_{00}}$) of the ellipse. In this case, the visual features vector is set to: $\mathbf{s} = [m_{00}, X_g, Y_g, X_1, Y_1, \cdots, X_{15}, Y_{15}]^T$. As previously mentioned the set of l=15 points allows to approximate the image moments features. The table 3 describes the image moments estimation error.

	Euler error		RK4 error		ABM4 error		BDF4 error	
	std	max	std	max	std	max	std	max
E_1	$6.194 . 10^{-4}$	$6.353 . 10^{-3}$	$2.181. 10^{-4}$	$5.469 . 10^{-3}$	$1.821 . 10^{-4}$	$3.846 . 10^{-3}$	$1.825 . 10^{-4}$	$3.477 . 10^{-3}$
E_2	$4.741 . 10^{-5}$	$2.315 . 10^{-4}$	$3.517. 10^{-5}$	$1.233 . 10^{-4}$	$2.878 . 10^{-5}$	$1.032 . 10^{-4}$	$3.092 . 10^{-5}$	$1.011 . 10^{-4}$
E_3	$4.967 . 10^{-5}$	$2.199 . 10^{-4}$	$3.995 . 10^{-5}$	$1.891 . 10^{-4}$	$3.179 . 10^{-5}$	$1.299 . 10^{-4}$	$3.101 . 10^{-5}$	$1.184 . 10^{-4}$
E_4	$4.569 . 10^{-4}$	$2.181 . 10^{-3}$	$3.157 . 10^{-4}$	$1.177 . 10^{-3}$	$2.357 . 10^{-4}$	$1.067 . 10^{-3}$	$2.109 . 10^{-4}$	$1.019 . 10^{-3}$
E_5	$2.328 . 10^{-4}$	$6.741 . 10^{-4}$	$1.314 . 10^{-4}$	$5.762 . 10^{-4}$	$1.087 . 10^{-4}$	$5.096 . 10^{-4}$	$1.006 . 10^{-4}$	$4.934 . 10^{-4}$
ε_{EI}	0.2027	0.8398	0.1512	0.7616	0.1284	0.5756	0.1071	0.6056

Table 2. Ellipse features simulation results.

	Euler error		RK4 error		ABM4 error		BDF4 error	
	std	max	std	max	std	max	std	max
m_{00}	6.1044	19.983	5.8346	18.1033	4.194	16.769	2.4298	10.3209
X_g	$1.768 .10^{-3}$	$4.253 .10^{-3}$	$1.278 .10^{-3}$	$3.526 .10^{-3}$	$0.805 .10^{-3}$	$2.404 .10^{-3}$	$0.449 .10^{-3}$	$1.923 .10^{-3}$
Y_g	$4.337 .10^{-3}$	$13.243 .10^{-3}$	$2.371 .10^{-3}$	$12.304 .10^{-3}$	$1.503 .10^{-3}$	$10.115 .10^{-3}$	$1.345 .10^{-3}$	$6.834 .10^{-3}$

Table 3. Image moments features simulation results (area m_{00} in pixel[2], and (X_g, Y_g) in pixel)

3.3.2 Experimental results

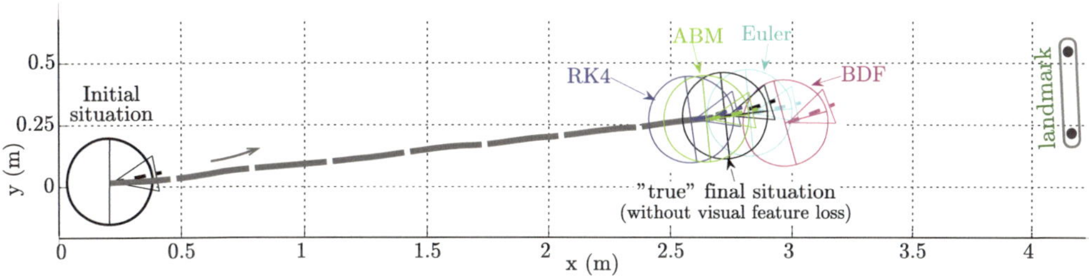

Fig. 5. Robot trajectory, using numerical schemes.

We have also experimented our approaches on our Super-Scout II. We have considered once again a vision-based navigation task which consists in positioning the embedded camera in front of a given landmark made of n=4 points. First of all, we address the validation of the proposed numerical schemes. For each of them, we have performed the same navigation task: start from the same configuration using the same **s*** (see figure 5). At the beginning of the mission, the robot is driven using the visual features available from the camera and starts converging towards the target. At the same time, the numerical algorithms are initialized and launched. After 10 steps, the landmark is artificially occluded to simulate a camera failure and, if nothing is done, it is impossible to perform the task. The controller is then evaluated using the computed values provided by our proposed method.

In a second step, we have validated the analytical method which take into account the vc time variation on our robotic platform (see figure 6). We have followed the same experimental procedure as for numerical schemes. Indeed, as previously, the visual data are available at the beginning of the task and the robot is controlled using (24). After a few steps, the landmark is manually occluded. At this time, the visual signals are computed by our estimation procedure and the robot is driven using controller. It is then possible to keep on executing a task which would have aborted otherwise.

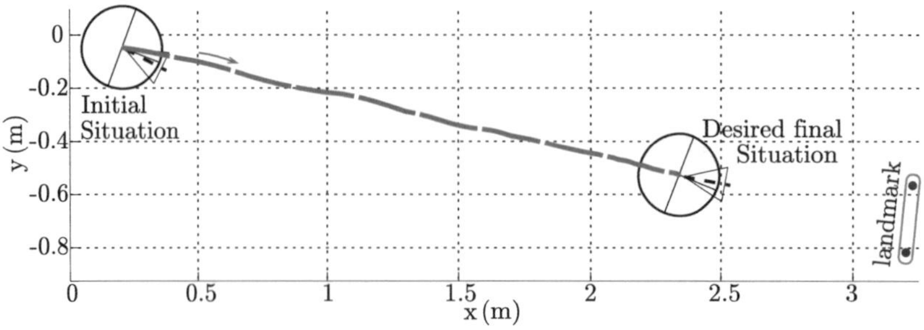

Fig. 6. Robot trajectory, using analytical method ($\mathbf{v}_c$ variable during $[t_k; t_{k+1}]$)

	Euler error		RK4 error		ABM4 error		BDF4 error		Analytic error ($\mathbf{v}_c$ variable)	
	std	max	std	max	std	max	std	max	std	max
$\|\mathbf{s}\|$	1.0021	9.6842	0.9092	7.0202	0.9003	5.9256	1.1172	7.6969	0.1275	0.7657
$\|\mathbf{z}\|$	0.0883	0.7233	0.0721	0.6385	0.0572	0.5064	0.1016	0.5989	0.0143	0.0637

Table 4. Experimental results ($|\mathbf{s}|$ in pixel, and $|\mathbf{z}|$ in m).

The table 4 summarizes the whole results obtained in the case of points. These errors remain small, which means that there are few perturbations on the system and, thanks to our estimation method, it is possible to reach a neighborhood of the desired goal despite the camera failure. Once again the analytical method gives the best estimation results. Moreover, for the proposed task, the ABM4 scheme is the most efficient numerical method, as it leads to the least standard deviation error (std) and to the smallest maximal error. The RK4 algorithm gives also correct performances, while Euler method remains the less accurate scheme as expected. As T_s is rather small, the BDF4 technique provides correct results but has been proven to be much more efficient when there are sudden variations in the kinematic screw (stiff context).

3.4 Comparative analysis and additional comments

The previous part has been devoted to the validation of the different reconstruction algorithms in the visual servoing context proposed in section 2. To this aim, we have focused on a specific problem which may occur during a vision-based task: the loss of the visual features due to a camera or an image processing failure. The presented simulation and experimental results have demonstrated the efficiency and the interest of our approach. Now, on the base of these results, our objective is to compare the different approaches and to exhibit their advantages and drawbacks. We also aim at giving some elements allowing to select the most suitable method depending on the context (considered visual features, task to be realized, and so on). All the tests have shown that the analytical solution integrating the true variation of the camera kinematic screw is the most accurate approach. This result is quite consistent because this solution explicitely takes into account the robot mechanical structure and appears to be the closest to the real system. Thus, the estimation errors appear to be negligible. In a similar way, the other analytical solution also leads to nice results (equivalent to the ones obtained with numerical approaches), but is less precise than the previous one. However, these two approaches are restricted to the case where the considered image features are points and cannot be used for other kinds of visual primitives. Moreover, as previously mentioned, one of them depends strongly on the mechanical structure of the robot on which is embedded the camera. To relax these restrictions, it is necessary to treat the problem using numerical schemes. Among them, the Gear's method (BDF4) and the Adams–Bashforth–Moulton scheme (ABM4) are the most accurate. It can be shown that the first one is particularly efficient when the dynamics of the system to be solved varies rapidly, that is when the problem becomes stiff. For example, this phenomenon has been observed when the robot has to avoid obstacles to safely perform the desired vision-based navigation task (Folio & Cadenat, 2007). In other cases (few variations on the camera kinematic screw), ABM4 scheme appears to provide better results, although it is sometimes limited by cumulative errors which occur when the visual primitives are reconstructed following several steps as in algorithms 1 and 2. Finally, the Runge–Kutta fourth order (RK4) algorithm and Euler schemes are the less accurate because they do not consider any history of the image features to be estimated. The above table 5 summarizes this comparative analysis.

Methods	Advantages	Drawbacks	Interest
Analytical solution $\mathbf{v}_c$ variable during $[t_k; t_{k+1}]$	High accuracy	Solution specific to a Super-Scout II-like robotic system and to points	+++
Analytical solution $\mathbf{v}_c$ constant during $[t_k; t_{k+1}]$	• Allows to consider different robotic systems • Good accuracy	Solution specific to points	+
Euler Scheme	Easy to implement	• The least accurate • Require small sampling period	--
RK4 Scheme	More accurate than Euler scheme		-
ABM4 Scheme	• Reconstruction based on a predictor/corrector pair. • The local truncation can be estimated.	• The scheme initialization requires a history of values of ψ obtained at previous instants. • Less accurate when successive approximations are performed.	+
BDF4 Scheme	The most efficient approach when $\mathbf{v}_c$ significantly varies	The scheme initialization requires a history of values of ψ obtained at previous instants.	++

Table 5. Comparative table

Only 4th order numerical schemes have been considered in this work. It is important to note that using greater orders does not necessarily lead to better results. Usually, a more suitable strategy is to reduce the integration step T_n. However, it must be noticed that in such a case the approximations are more and more cumulated and that the estimation error does not decrease anymore with T_n as one could have expected. Therefore, the most efficient way allowing to improve the quality of our algorithms is to reduce the control law sampling period.

Furthermore, as one could have expected, simulation provides better results than experimentation. In particular, when testing our algorithm, we have to deal with several constraints related to our robotic platform. First, the implementation of our algorithms requires to have the necessary data for initialization and to know precisely the values of T_s and T_n. These conditions are not necessarily fulfilled on experimental platforms, as it mainly depends on the operating system running on them. For instance, on the Super-Scout II, T_s cannot be precisely obtained. Moreover, our modelling does not take into account the noises which appear on the image features extraction processing and on the measurement of the robot velocities $\dot{\mathbf{q}}$.

Finally, let us recall that our main goal was to provide a generic framework to reconstruct the visual features whenever they become unavailable. In particular, we have shown that common visual primitives cannot be computed if the A_{pq} 3D parameters are not previously estimated. We have then proposed a solution consisting in using points to identify them. However, our validation work has demonstrated that this solution does not provide a totally efficient estimation because of the successive approximations induced by the procedure. Thus, the estimation algorithm could be improved by computing A_{pq} together with s as done for points. However, in such a case, the result would be restricted to the considered visual primitives, whereas the proposed solution based on points presents the advantage of the genericity.

In conclusion, the proposed reconstruction algorithms have been successfully validated in the vision-based navigation task. The obtained results have demonstrated the efficience and the relevancy of our approach to treat the specific problem of image features loss during a visual servoing task. Thanks to our method, as soon as an analytical expression of $\mathbf{L}_{(\mathbf{s},\mathbf{z})}$ is available, it is possible to reconstruct the visual data when needed and to keep on performing a task which should have been aborted otherwise.

4. Conclusion

In this chapter, we addressed the problem of computing the image features when they become unavailable during a vision-based task. To this aim, in a first step, we have elaborated different algorithms able to reconstruct the visual signals when they are lost. The proposed techniques rely on the camera kinematic screw and on the last measured perceptual cues. We have then shown that the problem can be expressed as the resolution of a dynamic system and we have developed different techniques allowing to solve it. We have proposed both analytical and numerical solutions. The first ones are very accurate, but appear to be limited to specific image features and dedicated to a particular robot mechanical structure. The second ones are less precise but present the advantage of genericity, as they can be applied in a general context (any kind of visual data and of robotic systems). It is then possible to obtain an estimation of any kind of image features independently from the robot on which is embedded the camera. In a second step, we have demonstrated the validity of our algorithm in the visual servoing context, considering the case of a positioning task during which a camera failure occurs. The obtained simulation and experimentation results have demonstrated the relevancy of our techniques to keep on performing the mission despite such a problem. Finally, we have ended our study by proposing a comparative analysis of the different elaborated algorithms.

These works have opened several interesting issues. First, the designed analytical solutions are restricted to the case of points and, for one of them, to the considered robotic system.

Although it is a priori difficult to develop such a solution for the general case, a natural extension would then to solve this problem for other kinds of robots and of visual primitives. Moreover, as the analytical solution directly provides an expression of the depth, it would be interesting to use it together with approaches such as tracking algorithms or camera pose reconstruction techniques. Finally, our results could also be successfully applied in other related fields than visual servoing. For example, it would be interesting to use them in a fault tolerance context to detect and correct errors in image processing algorithms.

5. References

Benhimane, S. & Malis, E. (2003). Vision-based control with respect to planar and non-planar objects using a zooming camera. *Proceedings of International Conference on Advanced Robotics*,Vol. 2, pp. 991–996, Coimbra, Portugal.

Butcher, J. C. (2008). *Numerical Methods for Ordinary Differential Equations* (2nd ed.). Wiley, ISBN:9780470723357.

Chaumette, F. (2004). Image moments: a general and useful set of features for visual servoing. *IEEE Transaction on Robotics*, Vol. 20, No. 4, pp. 713–723.

Chaumette, F.; Boukir, S.; Bouthemy, P. & Juvin, D. (1996, May). Structure from controlled motion. *IEEE Transaction Pattern Anal. Machine Intell.*, Vol. 18, No. 5, pp. 492–504.

Chaumette, F. & Hutchinson, S. (2006). Visual servo control, part I: Basic approaches. *IEEE Robotics and Automation Magazine*, Vol. 13, No. 4, pp. 82–90.

Comport, A. I.; Marchand, E. & Chaumette, F. (2004). Robust model-based tracking for robot vision. *Proceedings of IEEE/RSJ International Conference on Intelligent Robots and Systems*, Vol. 1, pp. 692–697, Sendai, Japan.

Corke, P. & Hutchinson, S. (2001). A new partitioned approach to image-based visual servo control. *IEEE Transaction Robotics and Automation*, Vol. 17, pp. 507–515.

Espiau, B., Chaumette, F.;, & Rives, P. (1992, June). A new approach to visual servoing in robotics. *IEEE Transaction Robotics and Automation*, Vol. 8, pp. 313–326.

Favaro, P. & Soatto, S. (2003). Seeing beyond occlusions (and other marvels of a finite lens aperture). *Proceedings of IEEE Computer Society Conference on Computer Vision and Pattern Recognition*, Vol. 2, pp. II-579–II-586, Saint -Louis, USA.

Fleury, S. & Herrb, M. (2001). GenoM: User Manual. LAAS-CNRS.

Folio, D. (2007). Stratégies de commande référencées multi-capteurs et gestion de la perte du signal visuel pour la navigation d'un robot mobile. PhD thesis, University of Toulouse, France.

Folio, D. & Cadenat, V. (2005a). A controller to avoid both occlusions and obstacles during a vision-based navigation task in a cluttered environment. *Proceedings of European Control Conference*, pp. 3898–3903, Seville, Spain.

Folio, D. & Cadenat, V. (2005b). Using redundancy to avoid simultaneously occlusions and collisions while performing a vision-based task amidst obstacles. *Proceedings of European Conference on Mobile Robots*, pp. 92–97, Ancona, Italy.

Folio, D. & Cadenat, V. (2007). A new controller to perform safe vision-based navigation tasks amidst possibly occluding obstacles. *Proceedings of European Control Conference*, pp. 1448–1454, Kos, Greece.

Folio, D. & Cadenat, V. (2008). A sensor-based controller able to treat total image loss and to guarantee non-collision during a vision-based navigation tasks. *Proceedings of IEEE/RSJ International Conference on Intelligent Robots and Systems*, Nice, France.

Garcia-Aracil, N.; Malis, E.; Aracil-Santonja, R. & Perez-Vidal, C. (2005). Continuous visual servoing despite the changes of visibility in image features. *IEEE Transaction Robotics and Automation*, Vol. 21, pp. 1214–1220.

Jerian, C. & Jain, R. (1991). Structure from motion: A critical analysis of methods. *IEEE Transaction on Systems, Man and Cybernetics*, Vol. 21, No. 3, pp. 572–588.

Kyrki, V., Kragic, D. & Christensen, H. (2004, October). New shortest-path approaches to visual servoing. *Proceedings of IEEE/RSJ International Conference on Intelligent Robots and Systems, pp. 349–355.*

Lepetit, V. & Fua, P. (2006). Monocular model-based 3d tracking of rigid objects. *Foundations and Trends in Computer Graphics and Vision*, Vol. 1, No. 1, pp. 1–89.

Mansard, N. & Chaumette, F. (2005). A new redundancy formalism for avoidance in visual servoing. *Proceedings of IEEE/RSJ International Conference on Intelligent Robots and Systems*, Vol. 2, pp. 1694–1700, Edmonton, Canada.

Marchand, E. & Hager, G. (1998). Dynamic sensor planning in visual servoing. *Proceedings of IEEE International Conference on Robotics and Automat.*, Vol. 3, pp. 1988–1993, Leuven, Belgium.

Matthies, L.; Kanade, T. & Szeliski, R. (1989). Kalman filter-based algorithms for estimating depth in image sequences. *International Journal of Computer Vision*, Vol. 3, No. 3, pp. 209–238.

Mezouar, Y. & Chaumette, F. (2002). Avoiding self-occlusions and preserving visibility by path planning in the image. *Robotics and Autonomous Systems*, Vol. 41, No. 2, pp. 77–87.

Murray, R.; Li, Z. & Sastry, S. (1994). *A mathematical introduction to robotic manipulation* (1st ed.). CRC Press, ISBN:0849379814, Boca Raton, FL, USA.

Oliensis, J. (2002, December). Exact two-image structure from controlled motion. *IEEE Transaction Pattern Anal. Machine Intell.*, Vol. 24, No. 12, pp. 1618–1633.

Pissard-Gibollet, R. & Rives, P. (1995). Applying visual servoing techniques to control a mobile hand-eye system. *Proceedings of IEEE International Conference on Robotics and Automation*, Vol. 1, pp. 166–171, Nagoya, Japan.

Remazeilles, A.; Mansard, N. & Chaumette, F. (2006). Qualitative visual servoing:application to the visibility constraInternational *Proceedings of IEEE/RSJ International Conference on Intelligent Robots and Systems*, pp. 4297–4303, Beijing, China.

Samson, C.; Borgne, M. L.; & Espiau, B. (1991). *Robot Control : The task function approach.* Oxford University Press, ISBN:0198538057, Oxford.

Shampine, L. F. & Gear, C. W. (1979). A user's view of solving stiff ordinary differential equations. *Society for Industrial and Applied Mathematics Review*, Vol. 21, No. 1, pp. 1–17.

Singer, M. (1993). Reducing structure from motion: A general framework for dynamic vision part 2: Implementation and experimental assessment. *Pattern Recognition*, Vol. 26, No. 7, pp. 1019–1028.

Soatto, S. & Perona, P. (1998). Reducing structure from motion: A general framework for dynamic vision part 2: Implementation and experimental assessment. *IEEE Transaction Pattern Analysis and Machine Intelligence*, Vol. 20, No. 9, pp. 943–960.

Steger, C. (1996). On the calculation of arbitrary moments of polygons. FGBV-96-05, Technische Universität München.

Tahri, O. & Chaumette, F. (2005). Point-based and region-based image moments for visual servoing of planar objects. *IEEE Transaction on Robotics*, Vol. 21, No. 6, pp. 1116–1127.

Thrun, S.; Fox, D.; Burgard, W.; & Dallaert, F. (2001). Robust mote-carlo localization for mobile robots. *Artifial Intelligence*, Vol. 128, No. 1-2, pp. 99–141.

5

Nonlinear Stable Formation Control using Omnidirectional Images

Christiano Couto Gava[1], Raquel Frizera Vassallo[1],
Flavio Roberti[2] and Ricardo Carelli[2]
[1]*Universidade Federal do Espítiro Santo*
[2]*Universidad Nacional de San Juan*
[1]*Brasil*
[2]*Argentina*

1. Introduction

There are a lot of applications that are better performed by a multi-robot team than a single agent. Multi-robot systems may execute tasks in a faster and more efficient way and may also be more robust to failure than a single robot. There are even some applications that can not be achieved by only one robot and just by a group of them (Parker, 2003; Cao et al., 1997). Another known advantage of multi-robot systems is that instead of using one expensive robot with high processing capacity and many sensors, sometimes one can use a team of simpler and inexpensive robots to solve the same task.

Some examples of tasks that are well performed by cooperative robots are search and rescue missions, load pushing, perimeter surveillance or cleaning, surrounding tasks, mapping and exploring. In these cases, robots may share information in order to complement their data, preventing double searching at an already visited area or alerting the others to concentrate their efforts in a specific place. Also the group may get into a desired position or arrangement to perform the task or join their forces to pull or push loads.

Although multi-robot systems provide additional facilities and functionalities, such systems bring new challenges. One of these challenges is formation control. Many times, to successfully perform a task, it is necessary to make robots get to specific positions and orientations. Within the field of robot formation control, control is typically done either in a centralized or decentralized way.

In a centralized approach a leader, which can be a robot or an external computer, monitores and controls the other robots, usually called followers. It coordinates tasks, poses and actions of the teammates. Most of the time, the leader concentrates all relevant information and decides for the whole group. The centralized approach represents a good strategy for small teams of robots, specially when the team is implemented with simple robots, only one computer and few sensors to control the entire group. In (Carelli et al., 2003) a centralized control is applied to coordinate the movement of a number of non-holonomic mobile robots to make them reach a pre-established desired formation that can be fixed or dynamic. There are also the so called leader-follower formation control as (Oliver & Labrosse, 2007; Consolini et al., 2007), in which the followers must track and follow the leader robot. The approach in (Oliver & Labrosse, 2007) is based on visual information and uses a set of images of the back of the leader robot that will be tracked by the follower robot. In (Consolini et al., 2007), a leader-follower formation control is introduced in which follower's position is not rigidly fixed but varies in suitable cones centered in the leader reference frame.

On the other hand, when considering a team with a large number of robots under a centralized control, the complexity significantly rises, demanding a greater computational capacity besides a larger communication system. In this case, a decentralized approach would be preferred. Usually in a decentralized control there is no supervisor and each robot makes its decisions based on its own duties and its relative position to the neighbouring teammates. Some researchers propose decentralized techniques for controlling robots' formation (Desai et al., 2001; Do, 2007) or cooperation on tasks such as exploration and mapping (Franchi et al., 2007; Correl & Martinoli, 2007; Rekleitis et al., 2005). There are also scalable approaches to control a large robotic group maintaining stability of the whole team control law (Feddema et al., 2002). Moreover some models are based on biologically-inspired cooperation and behaviour-based schemes using subsumption approach (Kube & Zhang, 1993; Balch & Arkin, 1998; Fierro et al., 2005). In these behaviour-based cases stability is often attained because they rely on stable controls at the lower level while coordination is done at a higher level.

The work presented in this chapter addresses the issue of multi-robot formation control using a centralized approach. Specifically, the principal concern is how to achieve and maintain a desired formation of a simple and inexpensive mobile robot team based only on visual information. There is a leader robot responsible for formation control, equipped with the necessary computational power and suitable sensor, while the other teammates have very limited processing capacity with a simple microcontroller and modest sensors such as wheel encoders for velocity feedback. Therefore, the team is composed of one leader and some simple, inexpensive followers. This hierarchy naturally requires a centralized control architecture. The leader runs a nonlinear formation controller designed and proved to be stable through Lyapunov theory. A nonlinear instead of linear controller was chosen because it provides a way of dealing with intrinsic nonlinearities of the physical system besides handling all configurations of the teammates, thus resulting in a more reliable option. It joins a pose controller with a compensation controller to achieve team formation and take the leader motion into account, respectively.

To control team formation it is necessary to estimate the poses of the robots that form the group. Computer vision has been used in many cooperative tasks because it allows localizing teammates, detecting obstacles as well as getting rich information from the environment. Besides that, vision systems with wide field of view also become very attractive for robot cooperation. One way of increasing the field of view is using omnidirectional images (360° horizontal view) (Nayar, 1997) obtained with catadioptric systems, which are formed by coupling a convex mirror (parabolic, hyperbolic or elliptic) and lenses (cameras) (Baker & Nayar, 1999). Such systems can really improve the perception of the environment, of other agents and objects, making task execution and cooperation easier.

Interesting works on cooperative robotics using omnidirectional images can be found in (Das et al., 2002; Vidal et al., 2004) and (Zhu et al., 2000). In (Das et al., 2002), all the robots have their own catadioptric system, allowing a decentralized strategy and eliminating the need for communication between the robots. The authors propose a framework in which a robot can switch between controllers to follow one or two leaders, depending on the environment. However, all the processing is done on an external computer and the use of many omnidirectional systems (one for each robot) makes the team expensive. In (Vidal et al., 2004), a scenario is developed in which each follower uses optical flow for estimating the leaders relative positions, allowing the group to visually mantain a desired formation. The computational cost for optical flow calculations is high and results are shown only through simulations. The work in (Zhu et al., 2000) proposes a cooperative sensing strategy through distributed panoramic sensors on teammate robots to synthesize virtual stereo sensors for human detection and tracking. The main focus is the stereo composing and it does not address team formation.

Now, in this work, we propose a formation controller based on omnidirectional vision and nonlinear techniques that runs onboard the leader robot. To drive all followers to a specific formation, the controller considers the desired formation parameters, the leader's linear and angular velocities and current followers' poses. The desired parameters and leader velocities are assumed to be known from a higher level controller that drives the leader robot to an appropriate trajectory. The followers' poses are estimated to feedback the controller using an omnidirectional vision system, formed by a hyperbolic mirror combined with a color camera and mounted on the leader, which allows it to see all followers by acquiring just one image. It is worth mentioning that although omnidirectional vision was used to estimate followers' positions and orientations, the proposed controller is independent of which sensor is used to implement the feedback.

Followers are identified by rectangles of different colors placed on the top of their platforms. Through a set of image processing techniques such as motion segmentation and color tracking, followed by Kalman filtering combined with Least Squares and RANSAC algorithm for optimization, followers' poses are reliably estimated. These poses are then used by the nonlinear controller to define followers' linear and angular velocities to achieve and maintain the desired formation. Notice that we focus on team formation during robot motion, while obstacle avoidance and task coordination are not addressed at this stage. Simulations and real experiments were carried out with different team formations. Current results show that the system performs well even with noisy and low resolution images.

The main contribution of this work is that stable formation control is achieved based solely on visual information totally processed onboard the leader. Also, there is no need for an absolute reference frame or a limited working area, since the vision system is carried by the leader and measurements are taken relative to it. Related works usually have an expensive robot team, use a fixed camera to observe the environment or even make all computations using an external computer.

This chapter is organized as follows. Section 2 describes the formation controller. Section 3 presents a method for estimating followers' poses based on omnidirectional images. One of the simulations carried out is presented in Section 4. In Section 5, some experiments with real robots are shown and the results are discussed. Finally, Section 6 concludes this chapter and outlines the next steps.

2. The controller

To make a mobile robot team (formed by one leader and n followers) navigate in an environment keeping a specific formation, a controller to command the follower robots was designed. The leader robot coordinates group navigation using an omnidirectional system, localizing each one of the followers on its own reference frame.

2.1 Definition

A nonlinear instead of linear controller was chosen because it provides a way of dealing with intrinsic nonlinearities of the physical system besides handling all configurations of the teammates, thus resulting in a more reliable option. This controller must provide the desired values for the follower velocities based on their coordinate and orientation errors. It integrates the functions of a pose controller, that brings the team to a desired formation, and a second controller, that compensates leader's linear and angular velocities. The generated velocities are considered as reference velocities for the followers and may be sent to the robots through different means of communication. Controller stability is proved using the Lyapunov method.

This controller is similar to that found in (Roberti et al.,2007), but differs in the saturation functions for the errors, which were adapted to fit our specific problem.

2.2 The pose controller

According to Figure 1, a vector containing the followers' coordinates can be defined as Equation 1.

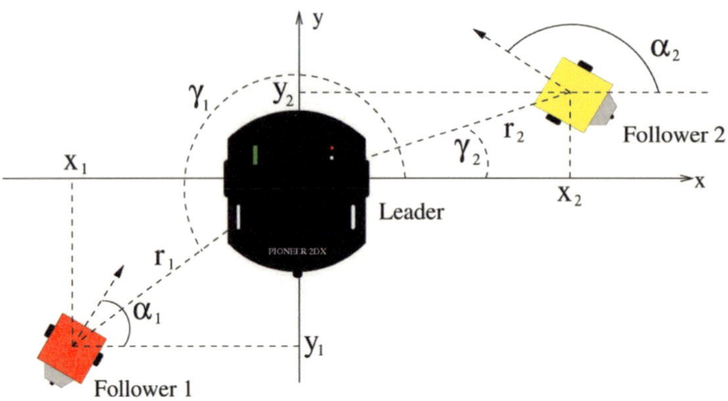

Fig. 1. Followers' pose representation on leader's reference frame.

$$\xi = \left(\xi_1 \;\; \xi_2 \;\; \cdots \;\; \xi_n\right)^T \quad \text{where} \quad \xi_i = \begin{pmatrix} x_i \\ y_i \end{pmatrix} = \begin{pmatrix} r_i \cos(\gamma_i) \\ r_i \sin(\gamma_i) \end{pmatrix} \tag{1}$$

where $\xi_i = (x_i \;\; y_i)^T$ stands for the real world coordinates of the i-th follower. To find a generic solution, the coordinate vector ξ can be considered as $\rho(\xi)$. This approach is interesting for the cases in which it is necessary to apply some coordinate transformation such as for vision systems (e.g. image coordinates) or define parameters associated to the formation (e.g. geometric parameters, baricenters, etc.). However, it is important to note that in our case $\rho(\xi) = \xi$, i. e., $\rho(\xi)$ is simply a vector containing the real world positions of the followers. We decided to keep the ρ notation for generality. By differentiating $\rho(\xi)$ with respect to time, we obtain Equation 2.

$$\dot{\rho} = J(\xi)\dot{\xi} \tag{2}$$

where $J(\xi)$ is the Jacobian of ξ.

From Equation 2, it is possible to define a formation control law given by Equation 3. The vector $\dot{\xi}_{fr}$ represents the desired formation velocities, i. e., the velocities, given at the leader reference frame, that the follower robots must have for achieving formation.

$$\dot{\xi}_{fr} = J^{-1}(\xi)\left(\dot{\rho}_d + f_{\tilde{\rho}}(\tilde{\rho})\right) \quad \text{with} \quad \tilde{\rho} = \rho_d - \rho \tag{3}$$

where $\tilde{\rho}$ is the vector of formation errors for the followers (Kelly et al., 2004) , ρ_d is the vector of desired formation parameters and ρ is the vector of the current formation parameters. Function $f_{\tilde{\rho}}(\tilde{\rho})$ is a saturation function for the error and defined as Equation 4.

$$f_{\tilde{\rho}}(\tilde{\rho}) = \mathrm{diag}\left[\frac{k_f(\tilde{\rho}_j)}{a + |\tilde{\rho}_j|}\right]\tilde{\rho} \qquad \text{with} \qquad k_f(\tilde{\rho}_j) = k_{f1} + k_{f2}\tanh\left(|\tilde{\rho}_j|\right) \tag{4}$$

where $k_{f1} + k_{f2}$ represents the saturation value and the gain for small errors is given by k_{f1}/a. This saturation function avoids applying velocities that might saturate the robots' motors.
In Equation 3, $J^{-1}(\xi)$ is the inverse Jacobian of ξ. Computation of inverse matrices is unattractive from the point of view of efficiency. Here it becomes clear why $\rho(\xi)$ was chosen to be equal to ξ: the Jacobian of ξ is simply an identity matrix and so is the inverse Jacobian. Then $\dot{\xi}_{fr}$ is obtained through the direct sum of vectors $\dot{\rho}_d$ and $f_{\tilde{\rho}}(\tilde{\rho})$, reducing the associated computational cost.
The action of the Pose Controller is illustrated in Figure 2, where it can be seen that $\dot{\xi}_{fr}$ does not have the orientation it would if the function $f_{\tilde{\rho}}(\tilde{\rho})$ were not used. It is due to the saturation of the formation error imposed by $f_{\tilde{\rho}}(\tilde{\rho})$ which makes the sum $\dot{\rho}_d + \tilde{\rho}$, represented in Figure 2 by $\dot{\xi}'_{fr}$, different from $\dot{\rho}_d + f_{\tilde{\rho}}(\tilde{\rho}) = \dot{\xi}_{fr}$ in both norm and orientation. However, this deviation does not affect this controller's stability because as the follower approximates a desired pose, $\|\tilde{\rho}\| \to 0$ and, therefore, $\dot{\xi}_{fr} \to \dot{\rho}_d$.

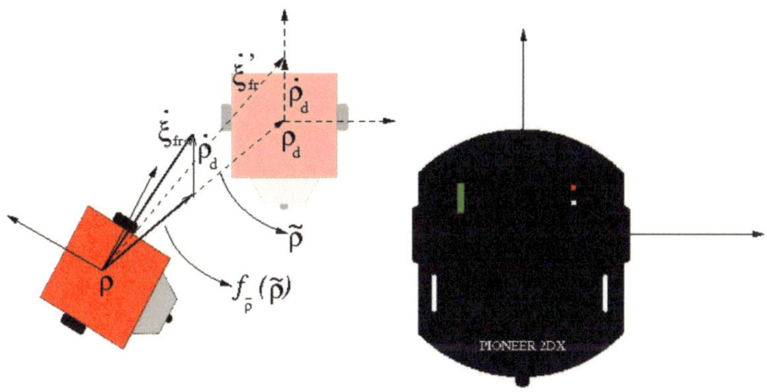

Fig. 2. Resulting $\dot{\xi}_{fr}$ after applying the Formation Controller.

Hence, the main idea for the Pose Controller is to generate velocity signals for all followers in order to bring them into formation, but taking the leader coordinate frame as reference,

which means it does not consider the leader motion. This is done by the Compensation Controller, which works in parallel with the Pose Controller.
It is known that the leader has its own linear and angular velocities, defined according to an absolute reference frame. These velocities must be considered when computing the follower velocities. In Equation 5, $\dot{\xi}_{fr}$ is added to $\dot{\xi}_{comp}$, a vector containing the compensations for the leader velocities. The resulting vector $\dot{\xi}_r$ provides the follower velocities needed to achieve at the same time the desired formation and compensate for the leader's motion.

$$\dot{\xi}_r = \dot{\xi}_{fr} + \dot{\xi}_{comp} \tag{5}$$

2.3 The compensation controller

The values of the elements of $\dot{\xi}_{comp}$ are computed to eliminate/overcome the effects caused by the leader's linear and angular velocities. Figure 3 shows an example in which the leader moves with linear (v_l) and angular (ω_l) velocities and the i-th follower is considered to be already at the desired position $(x_i \;\; y_i)^T$.
Once v_l and ω_l are known, r and r_i, the circles radii described by the leader and the follower, are given by Equation 6.

$$r = \frac{v_l}{\omega_l} \text{ and } r_i = \sqrt{(r + x_i)^2 + (y_i)^2} \tag{6}$$

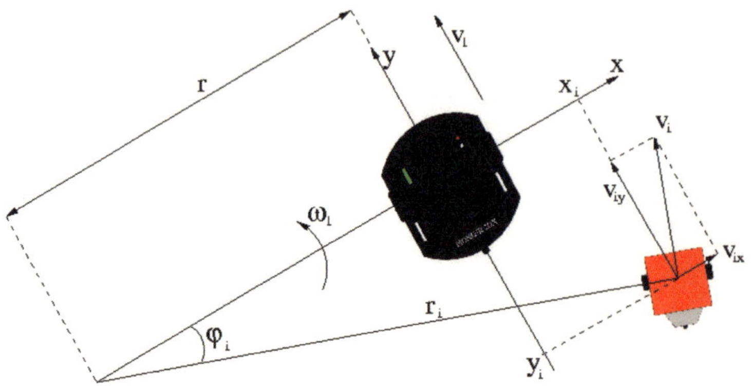

Fig. 3. Leader's velocities compensation.

Equations 7 - 9 describe the way compensation velocity is calculated for the i-th follower.

$$\varphi_i = \arctan\left(\frac{y_i}{r + x_i}\right) \text{ and } v_i = \omega_l r_i \tag{7}$$

$$v_{ix} = v_i \cos\left(\varphi_i + \frac{\pi}{2}\right) \tag{8}$$

$$v_{iy} = v_i \sin\left(\varphi_i + \frac{\pi}{2}\right) \tag{9}$$

where v_{ix} and v_{iy} are the follower compensation velocity components $\dot{\xi}_{comp}(v_{ix}, v_{iy})$ in the leader reference frame. It is also important to mention that when the leader robot has no angular velocity ($\omega_l = 0$), $\dot{\xi}_{comp}$ equals the leader linear velocity with $v_{ix} = 0$ and $v_{iy} = v_l$.

2.4 Generating commands

After obtaining $\dot{\xi}_r$, the linear and angular velocities to be sent to the i-th robot are defined by Equations 10 and 11.

$$v_{ci} = \left\|\dot{\xi}_{ri}\right\| \cos(\tilde{\alpha}_i) \quad (10)$$

$$\omega_{ci} = \dot{\alpha}_{ri} + f_{\tilde{\alpha}}(\tilde{\alpha}_i) + \omega_l \quad (11)$$

where $\left\|\dot{\xi}_{ri}\right\|$ is the desired velocity norm for the i-th follower and $\dot{\alpha}_{ri}$ is the change in its orientation during time. The term $\tilde{\alpha}_i$, defined as $\tilde{\alpha}_i = \alpha_{ri} - \alpha_i$, is the angular error, with α_{ri} and α_i representing the reference angle and the robot current orientation, all represented in the leader frame, as shown in Figure 4. Notice that, for simplifying Figure 4 in order to help understanding, we considered the leader angular velocity (ω_l) equal to zero.
The function $f_{\tilde{\alpha}}(\tilde{\alpha}_i)$, as before, is a saturation function for the error given by Equation 12.

$$f_{\tilde{\alpha}}(\tilde{\alpha}_i) = k_{\omega 1} \tanh^3(k_{\omega 2}\, \tilde{\alpha}_i) \quad (12)$$

where $k_{\omega 1}$ represents the saturation value of the orientation error and $k_{\omega 2}$ controls how fast this function reaches its saturation value. $f_{\tilde{\alpha}}(\tilde{\alpha}_i)$ has an interesting characteristic: its derivative tends to zero as the orientation error approaches zero, which means that transitions between positive and negative values are smooth, as can be seen in Figure 5. In practice, it avoids oscilations in the followers' trajectories.

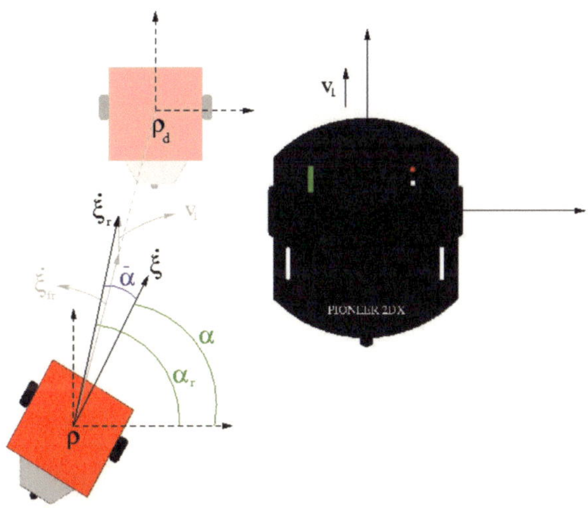

Fig. 4. Angles related to the linear and angular velocities sent to the followers.

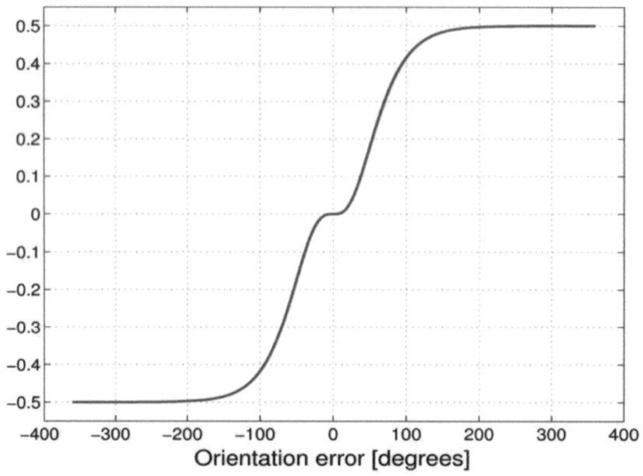

Fig. 5. Shape of $f_{\tilde{\alpha}}(\tilde{\alpha}_i)$ for $k_{\omega 1} = 0.5$ and $k_{\omega 2} = 1$.

The objective of $f_{\tilde{\alpha}}(\tilde{\alpha}_i)$ is to prevent initial orientation errors causing high angular velocity commands which would compromise control stability and submit robot motors to abrupt voltage variations.

2.5 Proof of stability

2.5.1 Proof for the pose controller

Due to their dynamics, the followers are not able to immediately achieve the desired formation velocities. However, these velocities are asymptotically achieved, represented by Equation 13, as it will be proved in Section 2.5.2.

$$\dot{\xi} \to \dot{\xi}_{fr} \tag{13}$$

where $\dot{\xi}$ is the vector of current velocities and $\dot{\xi}_{fr}$ is the vector containing the reference velocities for attaining formation. Equation 13 can also be written as Equation 14.

$$\dot{\xi}_{fr} = \dot{\xi} + \eta \quad \text{with} \quad \|\eta\| \to 0 \tag{14}$$

where η is the difference between the desired and current velocities. The control law for the Pose Controller is given by Equation 15, repeated here for convenience.

$$\dot{\xi}_{fr} = J^{-1}(\xi)\left(\dot{\rho}_d + f_{\tilde{\rho}}(\tilde{\rho})\right) \tag{15}$$

Equation 16 is obtained by the substitution of 14 in 15.

$$\dot{\xi} + \eta = J^{-1}(\xi)\left(\dot{\rho}_d + f_{\tilde{\rho}}(\tilde{\rho})\right) \tag{16}$$

Multiplying Equation 16 by $J(\xi)$ results in Equation 17.

$$J(\xi)\dot{\xi} + \eta_1 = \dot{\rho}_d + f_{\tilde{\rho}}(\tilde{\rho}) \text{ where } \eta_1 = J(\xi)\eta \tag{17}$$

As known from Equation 2, $\dot{\rho} = J(\xi)\dot{\xi}$, which leads to Equation 18.

$$\dot{\rho} + \eta_1 = \dot{\rho}_d + f_{\tilde{\rho}}(\tilde{\rho}) \tag{18}$$

The temporal derivative of $\tilde{\rho}$ produces Equation 19.

$$\dot{\tilde{\rho}} = \dot{\rho}_d - \dot{\rho} \quad \Rightarrow \quad \dot{\rho}_d = \dot{\tilde{\rho}} + \dot{\rho} \tag{19}$$

The substitution of 19 in 18 gives Equation 20.

$$\dot{\tilde{\rho}} = \eta_1 - f_{\tilde{\rho}}(\tilde{\rho}) \tag{20}$$

Then the following Lyapunov candidate function is proposed:

$$V = \frac{1}{2}\tilde{\rho}^T \tilde{\rho} \tag{21}$$

whose temporal derivative is

$$\dot{V} = \tilde{\rho}^T \dot{\tilde{\rho}} = \tilde{\rho}^T \eta_1 - \tilde{\rho}^T f_{\tilde{\rho}}(\tilde{\rho}) \tag{22}$$

For $\dot{V}$ to be definite negative it is necessary that:

$$\frac{\|k_f(\tilde{\rho})\|}{a + \|\tilde{\rho}\|}\|\tilde{\rho}\|^2 > \|\eta_1\|\|\tilde{\rho}\| \tag{23}$$

where $\|k_f(\tilde{\rho})\|$ is simply

$$\|k_f(\tilde{\rho})\| = k_f(\tilde{\rho}) = k_{f1} + k_{f2}\tanh(\|\tilde{\rho}\|) \tag{24}$$

Hence, the following condition must be satisfied:

$$\|\tilde{\rho}\| > \frac{a\|\eta_1\|}{k_{f1} + k_{f2}\tanh(\|\tilde{\rho}\|) - \|\eta_1\|} \tag{25}$$

As the followers achieve the desired velocities, $\|\eta\| \to 0$; and so $\|\eta_1\| \to 0$. Then the condition of Equation 25 will be satisfied for some finite time, which means that $\|\tilde{\rho}(t)\| \to 0$ with $t \to \infty$.

2.5.2 Proof for the generated commands

The temporal variation of the followers' orientations is expressed by

$$\dot{\alpha} = \omega_c - \omega_l \tag{26}$$

where the generated angular velocity ω_c, is given by

$$\omega_c = \dot{\alpha}_r + f_{\tilde{\alpha}}(\tilde{\alpha}) + \omega_l \tag{27}$$

Putting 27 into 26 results in Equation 28.

$$\dot{\alpha} = \dot{\alpha}_r + f_{\tilde{\alpha}}(\tilde{\alpha}) \tag{28}$$

Deriving $\tilde{\alpha}$ respect to the time gives

$$\dot{\tilde{\alpha}} = \dot{\alpha}_r - \dot{\alpha} \Rightarrow \dot{\alpha}_r = \dot{\tilde{\alpha}} + \dot{\alpha} \tag{29}$$

Then Equation 28 can be rewritten as

$$\dot{\tilde{\alpha}} + f_{\tilde{\alpha}}(\tilde{\alpha}) = 0 \tag{30}$$

Thus, the following Lyapunov candidate function is proposed

$$V = \frac{1}{2}\tilde{\alpha}^T \tilde{\alpha} \tag{31}$$

whose temporal derivative is

$$\dot{V} = \tilde{\alpha}^T \dot{\tilde{\alpha}} = -\tilde{\alpha}^T f_{\tilde{\alpha}}(\tilde{\alpha}) \tag{32}$$

As $f_{\tilde{\alpha}}(\tilde{\alpha})$ is an odd function, $\tilde{\alpha}^T f_{\tilde{\alpha}}(\tilde{\alpha}) > 0$ for $\tilde{\alpha} \neq 0$, which means that $\dot{V}$ is definite negative ($\dot{V} < 0$). Hence $\|\tilde{\alpha}(t)\| \to 0$ for $t \to \infty$. Finally, since $\cos(\tilde{\alpha}_i) \to 1$, we have $v_{ci} \to \|\dot{\xi}_{ri}\|$, concluding this proof.

3. Image processing and pose estimation

As said before, the leader robot is equipped with an omnidirectional vision system. Although omnidirectional images suffer from typical problems like loss of resolution and distortion, their wide field of view allows the leader to visualize all the region around itself, which facilitates localizing the teammates, avoiding obstacles and mapping the environment.

Each follower robot is identified by a colored rectangle placed on its platform. Their poses are estimated through color segmentation and Kalman filtering. Usually two colors are used on the top of the robots, so the orientation can be easily calculated (Santos-Victor et al., 2002). Because of the distortion of omnidirectional images, we decided to use just one color per robot. If two colors were used, each colored area would be reduced to half of the area seen on the image. Also image distortion increases as the robot moves away from the leader and could compromise robot localization if just a small part or none of the color of interest is seen on the image.

As discussed in the previous section, the leader must know the pose of each cellular robot belonging to the team in order for the team to navigate in formation. However, at the beginning, the leader does not know the follower's initial poses and colors. So it then needs to detect the initial position, color and orientation of each cellular robot. Once that is done the leader can start moving.

The image processing can then be divided into three main steps:

- Initial position detection;
- Tracking for initial orientation detection;
- Tracking for formation control.

In order to make the controller independent of image measurements (pixels), robot positions were converted to meters. One way of doing this and also eliminating image distortion is to

remap those images to *bird's eye view* (Vassallo et al., 2004; Pereira et al., 2005). Unfortunately this remapping depends on system calibration and requires more steps on image processing.
Instead a transform Γ, composed of a set of polynomial functions, was defined to recover robot world positions from image coordinates. The process of determining Γ is simple: first the region around the leader is divided into n sectors, each one defining a matching table relating distances on the image plane (pixels) and the real world (meters). Then each table is used to interpolate a polynomial function that estimates the follower positions.
Although the number of functions composing Γ can be high, it was decided to use just four, as illustrated in Figure 6, since they are enough for this application. It is important to note that this approach is much faster than using bird's eye view remapping.

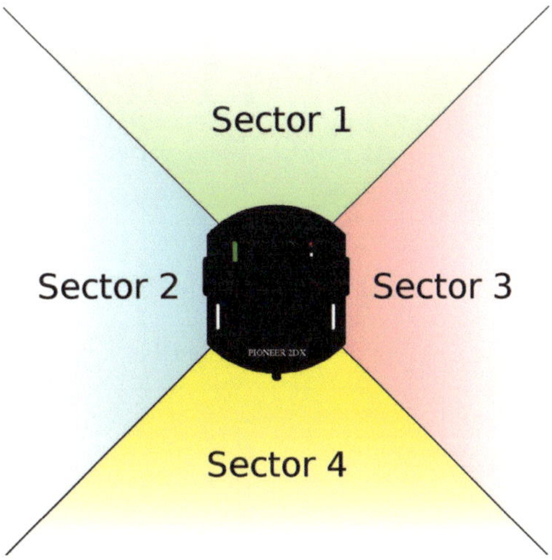

Fig. 6. Sectors used to define the Γ transform.

The polynomial functions obtained are plotted in Figure 7.

3.1 Detecting initial positions

Before starting to detect the followers' initial positions, the leader robot must focus its attention on a working area, the region around it in which all followers should be to be seen by the leader. That is because the distortion caused by omnidirectional images, which makes object detection impractical at some distance from the visual system. This region is defined by the mask exhibited in Figure 8-(a), which is applied to the omnidirectional image providing the result shown on Figure 8-(b), where a cellular robot is seen close to the leader.
This first step is accomplished by means of movement detection. Then it is not necessary to use color images, but only their grayscale version. In this work, movement detection is done based on a robust version of the background subtraction technique: instead of simply comparing a captured image with a previously constructed background, the leader compares two backgrounds. This procedure is necessary because of noise and the low resolution of omnidirectional images.
The leader starts by constructing the first background, called the *base* background -- Figure 9 -(a), while all robots are standing by. When that is finished, Follower 1 executes a short forward displacement and as soon as it stops another background is constructed, the

discriminant background -- Figure 9-(b). Then the leader compares both backgrounds and the result is thresholded, producing a blob as shown in Figure 9-(c), which represents the follower displacement and is used for estimating its initial position and color. After that the rectangle encompassing the blob -- Figure 9-(d) -- must be found because it will be used in the following steps by a tracking algorithm to estimate robot positions.

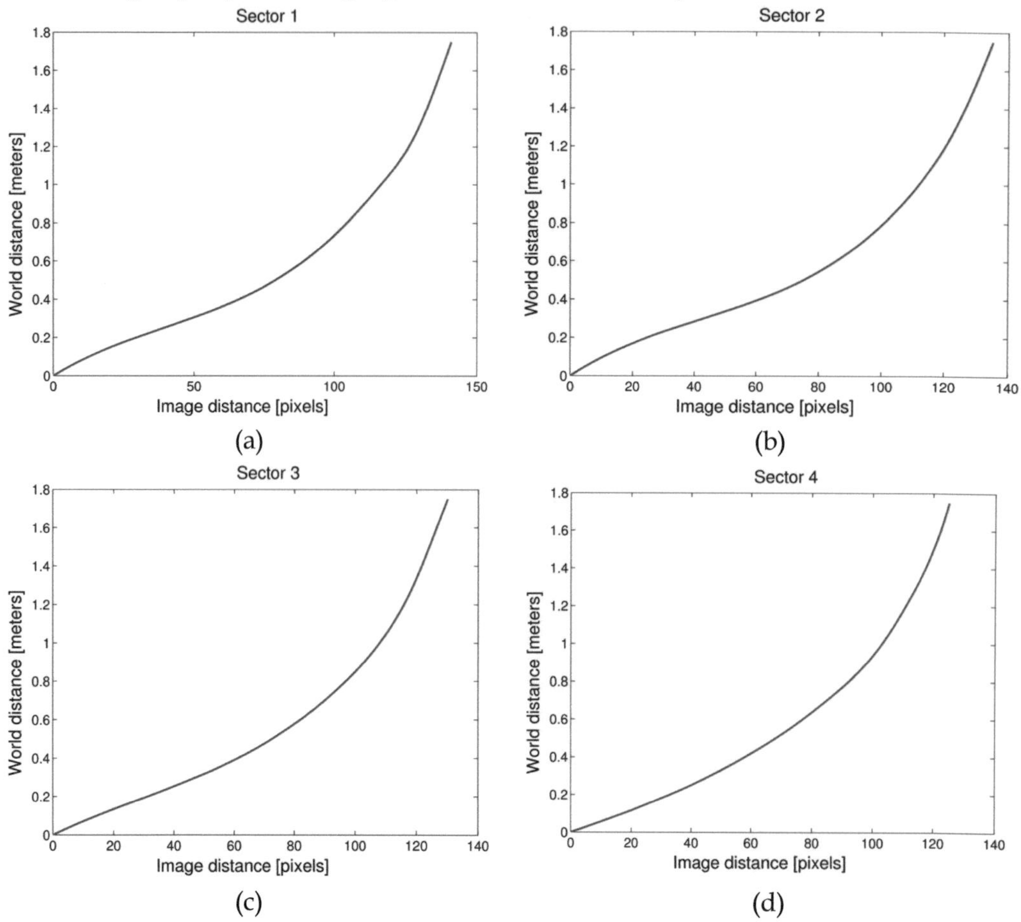

Fig. 7. Shape of each function composing the Γ transform.

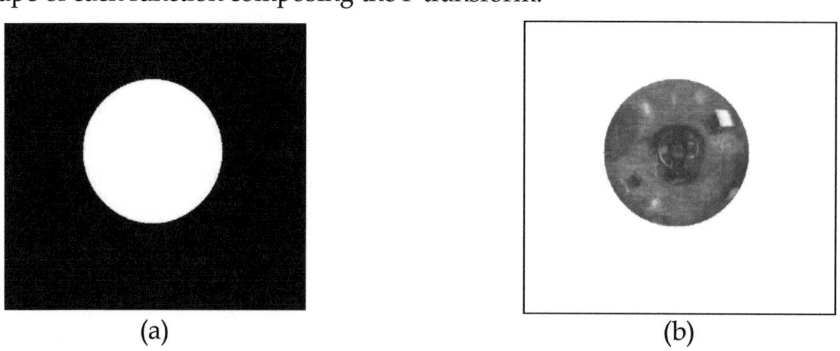

(a) (b)

Fig. 8. (a) Binary mask applied to omnidirectional image (b) Resulting working area.

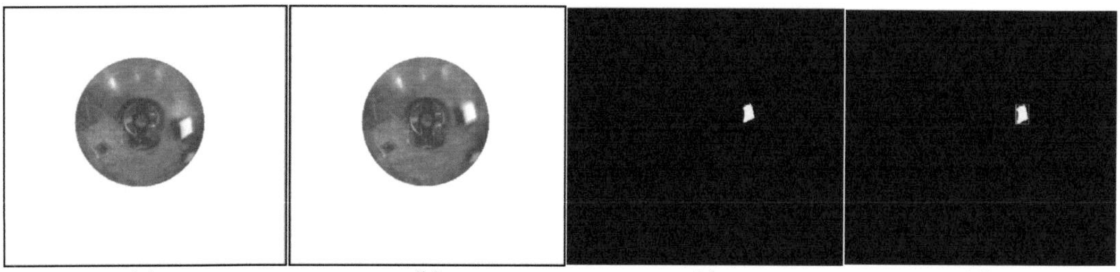

(a) (b) (c) (d)

Fig. 9. (a) Base background (b) Discriminant background (c) Blob obtained after thresholding the difference between the constructed backgrounds (d) Resulting encompassing rectangle.

Often, after executing its displacement, a cellular robot generates more than one blob, as shown by Figure 10-(a). So a filter algorithm had to be developed: it checks each blob's color; if it is the same and they are sufficiently close to each other, the encompassing rectangles are combined into a single encompassing rectangle; if not, only the larger one is retained - Figure 10-(b).

(a) (b)

Fig. 10. (a) Image with more than one blob (b) Filtered image.

The above procedure is executed to detect the initial position of just one follower. However, it is not necessary to construct two new backgrounds for the next follower to be detected, since the discriminant background related to the previous robot can be used as the base background for the next one. Then, for n followers $n+1$ backgrounds are constructed, instead of $2n$.

3.2 Detecting initial orientations

Once the color and the initial position of each follower is known, a tracking algorithm can be used for further estimate of robot positions. The CAMSHIFT (Continuously Adaptive Mean-SHIFT) algorithm, from OpenCV library, is attractive for this kind of application. Given a color histogram and an initial search window (both determined in the previous image processing step) it returns a new search window for the next image based on color segmentation. Such window is found using the dimensions of the segmented area and its centroid. This provides a fast and robust online performance for the tracking algorithm.

CAMSHIFT and Γ transform taken together allow the leader to estimate with adequate precision all follower positions. Then the procedure for finding the initial orientations is as follows: at the same time, all cellular robots execute again a forward displacement. While they are moving, the leader saves the trajectory described by each follower, as illustrated by Figure 11. Then the leader has, for each follower, a sequence of points describing a straight line, with its angular parameter corresponding to the relative orientation α_0. However, due to measurement noises, it is necessary to apply an algorithm like RANSAC (Fischler & Bolles, 1981) to eliminate outliers. After that, a Least Squares algorithm is used to find each follower orientation thus completing the initial pose estimation.

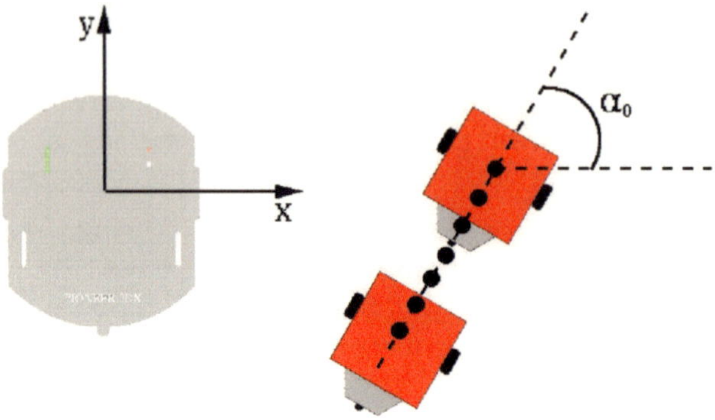

Fig. 11. Capturing a follower trajectory in order to determine its initial orientation α_0.

3.3 Tracking for formation control

Once the leader knows all followers' initial poses the logical next step would be to start moving and drive the team to the desired formation. However, there is a question that must be answered first: given a desired position, which follower should be driven to there? When a desired pose is achieved, because of the non-holonomic restriction, the respective follower must be aligned to the leader, i. e., its relative orientation must be 90°. This means that all final orientations are already known, but the final position that each follower should have is not known yet.

To solve this problem, a cost matrix C was defined - Equation 33 - where n is the number of cellular robots, c_{ij} represents the cost for the i-th follower to reach the j-th position. In other words, the i-th row of C is a vector containing the costs of the i-th follower relative to all desired positions.

$$C = \begin{bmatrix} c_{11} & c_{12} & \cdots & c_{1n} \\ c_{21} & c_{22} & \cdots & c_{2n} \\ \vdots & \vdots & \ddots & \vdots \\ c_{n1} & c_{n2} & \cdots & c_{nn} \end{bmatrix} \tag{33}$$

There are many ways of defining how to calculate the costs c_{ij}. In this work, it was decided to use the square of the euclidian distance between current and desired positions. Each possible followers-desired positions configuration can be viewed as a combination of n costs, taking each one from a different row and column of C. The associated cost is simply the sum of the n costs that compose such configuration. An advantage of this approach is that it permits an analogy with the energy spent by each follower to reach some desired position. Then, it is easy to see that the ideal configuration is that having the least associated cost.

After defining the ideal configuration, the leader starts to move. To drive the cellular robots into formation it is necessary to estimate their poses, which is based on the CAMSHIFT algorithm: robot positions are estimated using the centroids of the detected colored areas and passed to the Formation Controller. However, due to measurement noises, it is very difficult to have reliable orientation values if they are estimated on every acquired image. One way of doing that using just one color per robot is shown in (De La Cruz et al., 2006). Instead, it was decided to define a simpler method, based on the geometry of the robot trajectories, as shown in Figure 12. Each follower orientation is calculated after the robot has moved at least a minimum displacement Δs_{min}, defined in Equation 34 (these values were chosen empirically), whose objective is to reduce noise influence caused by image low resolution, mirror distortion and illumination changes.

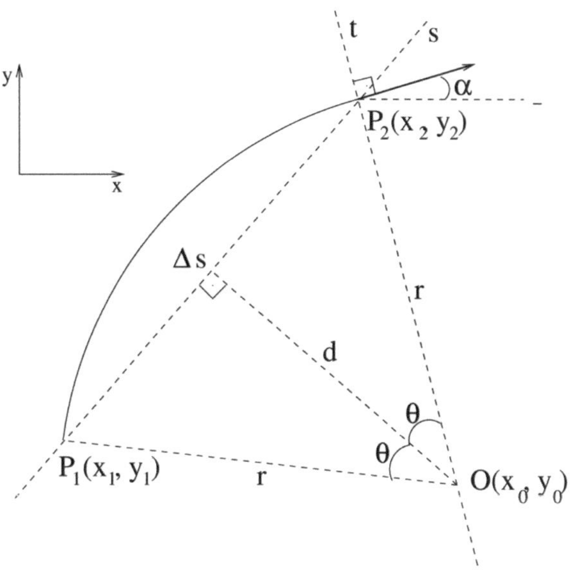

Fig. 12. Follower trajectory while its pose and velocities are not updated.

$$\Delta s_{min} = 0.02 + 0.03\tanh\left(2\|\tilde{\rho}\|\right) \tag{34}$$

The orientation α is estimated considering that, between two control signal updates, the robot maintains the previous linear and angular velocities and performs a curve trajectory. From Figure 12, the straight line s can be defined by Equation 35.

$$y = m_s x + l_s \quad \text{with} \quad m_s = \frac{y_2 - y_1}{x_2 - x_1} \quad \text{and} \quad l_s = y_2 - m_s x_2 \tag{35}$$

The distance d is obtained from the displacement Δs and the angle θ, using the follower's angular velocity ω and the time interval Δt spent to move from $P_1(x_1, y_1)$ to $P_2(x_2, y_2)$.

$$d = \frac{\Delta s}{2\tan(\theta)} \quad \text{where} \quad \theta = \frac{\omega \Delta t}{2} \tag{36}$$

Then d, the line s and the circle equation are used to find $O(x_O, y_O)$, which is used to calculate the angle α.

$$\alpha = \arctan\left(\frac{-1}{m_t}\right) \quad \text{where} \quad m_t = \frac{y_2 - y_O}{x_2 - x_O} \tag{37}$$

A special case is considered when $x_2 = x_1$: if $y_1 > y_2$, $\alpha = -\pi/2$, if not, $\alpha = \pi/2$. Then a Kalman Filter was applied to α, resulting in more stable estimates and reducing the errors for the next loop control. Kalman filtering was chosen because of its performance and low computational cost.
Figure 13 shows follower motion detection for the first pose estimation and the further tracking software running. White outlines involve the colorful rectangles segmented from an omnidirectional image.

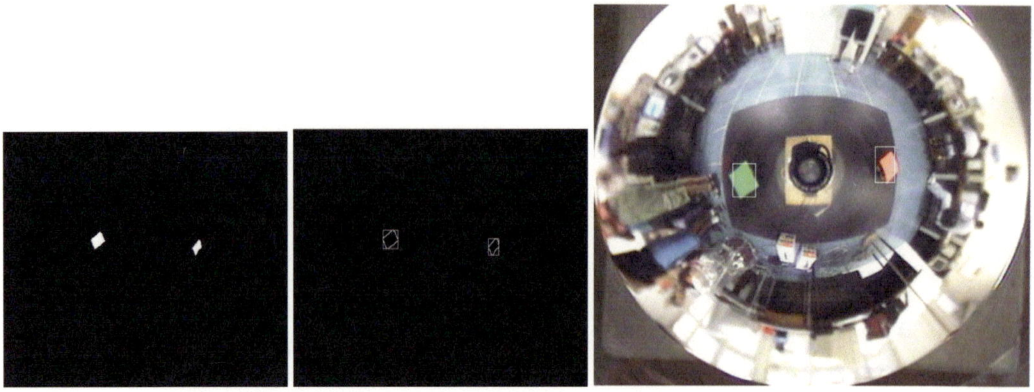

Fig. 13. Robots detection and the tracking software.

From the above equations it is clear that Δs must be known in order to determine robot orientations. It is computed while the team is moving and this is done based on a 2D geometric transformation, which is defined by composing a translation and a rotation, since the leader has, in general, both linear and angular velocities. The idea is to define two reference frames: the first corresponds to where the previous image was captured - S_0 - and the second to where the current image has been captured - S_1 - according to Figure 14, with dx and dy standing for x and y leader displacements and γ its rotation.
Then, knowing x_0, y_0, dx, dy and γ, Equation 38 shows how to obtain x_1 and y_1. It is important to note that $(x_1 \;\; y_1)^T$ do not mean the current follower position, but the previous position represented in the most recent frame S_1. Δs can now be calculated through the euclidian distance between the current position and $(x_1 \;\; y_1)^T$.

$$\begin{bmatrix} x_1 \\ y_1 \\ 1 \end{bmatrix} = \begin{bmatrix} \cos\gamma & -\sin\gamma & 0 \\ \sin\gamma & \cos\gamma & 0 \\ 0 & 0 & 1 \end{bmatrix} \begin{bmatrix} 1 & 0 & -dx \\ 0 & 1 & -dy \\ 0 & 0 & 1 \end{bmatrix} \begin{bmatrix} x_0 \\ y_0 \\ 1 \end{bmatrix} \tag{38}$$

Due to the projection geometry of omnidirectional visual systems, robot orientations are not affected by the translation of the coordinate system, only by its rotation. Figure 15 shows this effect, where α_0 and α_1 stand for a robot orientation on previous and current reference frame, respectively. Hence, it is easy to see that $\alpha_1 = \alpha_0 - \gamma$. Every time a follower presents a Δs greater than Δs_{min} its pose should be updated and passed to the controller in order to generate new control signals.

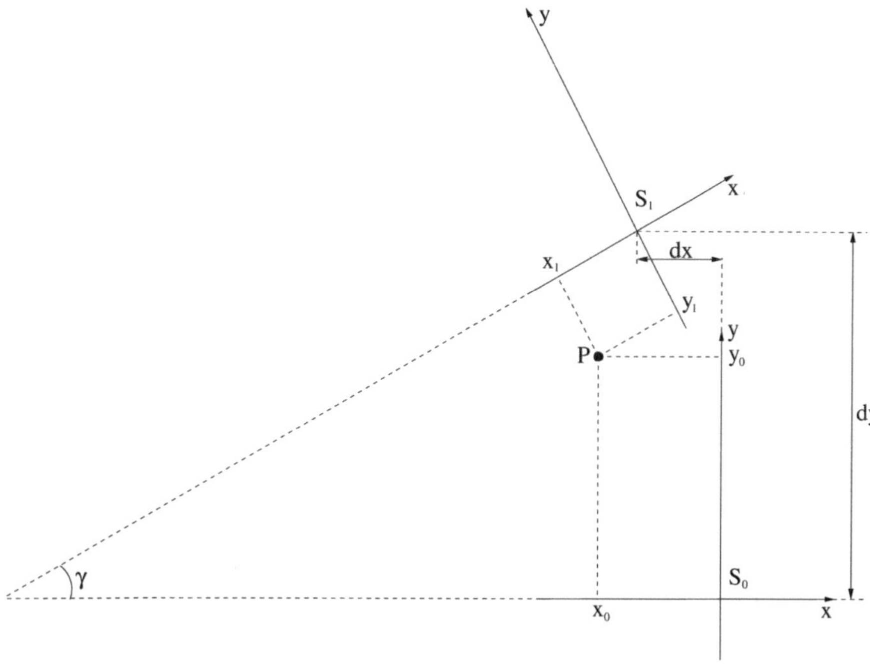

Fig. 14. Effects of leader's frame translation and rotation on a follower position representation.

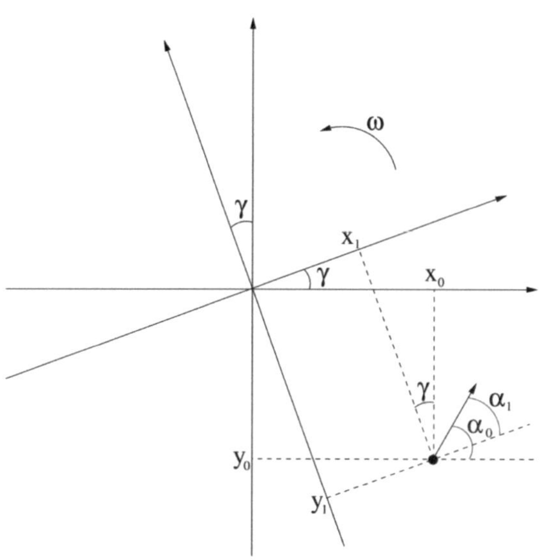

Fig. 15. Effect of leader's frame rotation over a follower orientation.

4. Simulation

Before testing on real robots, some simulations were carried out to evaluate the behavior of the proposed controller while varying some parameters, although not considering the team dynamics. Without loss of generality, the initial position of the leader is chosen to be coincident with the world frame origin. Several simulations were carried out with the same controller parameters used in the experiments.
The idea of the presented simulation is to reproduce an obstacle avoidance maneuver while maintaining formation, a common situation in navigation tasks. Figure 16 shows the trajectories described by the team during this simulation. The leader had a linear velocity of 60 mm/s and an angular velocity according to the function in Equation 39, which is the same function used in the last experiment shown in this chapter.

$$f_{\omega l}(t) = \begin{cases} k_1 \tanh(k_2(t_1 - t)) & \text{for} \quad 10 \le t \le 100\text{s} \\ 0 & \text{otherwise} \end{cases} \tag{39}$$

where k_1, k_2 and t_1 are auxiliary parameters used to control the desired shape of the leader's trajectory. For this simulation $k_1 = 1.5°/s$, $k_2 = 0.2$ and $t_1 = 55$ s, which means that for $10 < t < 100$ s the leader's angular velocity varied from -1.5°/s to 1.5°/s, reaching zero at $t = t_1 = 55$ s. The middle blue line indicates the leader's trajectory. The dashed outer lines represent the desired trajectories for the followers, that must stay on positions $\rho_{d1} = (-0.50 \quad -0.30)^T$ and $\rho_{d2} = (0.50 \quad -0.30)^T$ relative to the leader. The solid lines indicate the followers' trajectories that started from initial positions $\rho_{01} = (-0.70 \quad -0.80)^T$ and $\rho_{02} = (0.30 \quad -0.90)^T$. The red triangles indicate how the team gets into formation. Followers' initial orientations were 135° and 120°, respectively. The followers achieve their desired positions and successfully maintain the formation, describing the proposed trajectory.

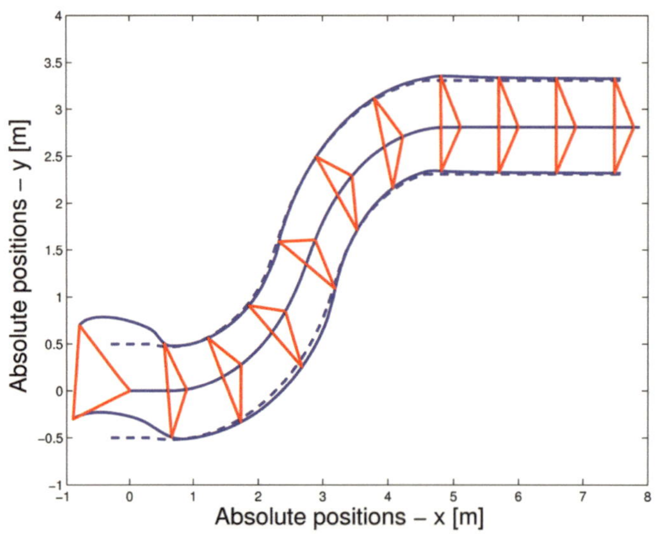

Fig. 16. Trajectory described by the team during this simulation.

Figure 17 exhibits the effect of the leader's angular velocity variation on followers' poses, in which (a) and (b) indicate followers' position errors while (c) shows their orientations. It is possible to see that abrupt variations or sign changes of the leader's angular velocity disturb the system, thus causing perturbations on followers' poses just after they happen. Since such perturbations are common during robot navigation, the controller must drive all followers to the desired poses regardless of that, which is shown by Figures 16 and 17.

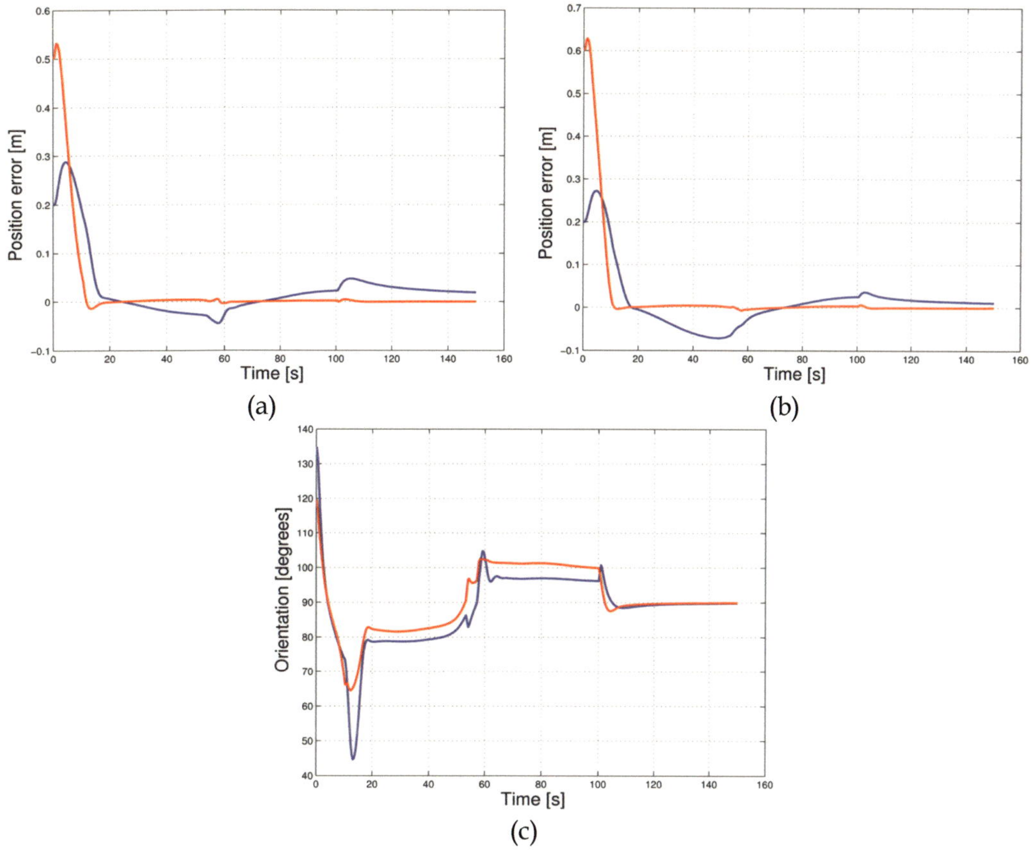

Fig. 17. Simulation results: position errors for (a) Follower 1 (b) Follower 2. (c) Followers orientations.

5. Experiments and results

The experiments presented here were performed with a robot team composed of a Pioneer 2DX (Pentium II, 266 MHz, 128 MB RAM) as leader and two cellular robots as followers. They are shown in Figure 18.

The leader has an omnidirectional system with a perspective color camera and a hyperbolic mirror. The two cellular robots were assembled in our lab and have about the size of 15 x 25 cm and 10 cm height. They are differential robots equipped with the MSP430F149 microcontroller and H-bridges TPIC0108B from *Texas Instruments* to drive the motors. Initially communication between leader and followers was accomplished by cables for serial communication, substituted later by a radio link.

Several experiments were also carried out. We decided to present three of them because they show the key features of the proposed controller.

Fig. 18. Robots used for the experiments.

5.1 Experiment 1

In this first experiment, the idea was to execute a simple translation in order to show the controller behaviour in a free corridor, for example. Then the leader has developed a straight line with 60 mm/s of velocity. Followers' initial positions were estimated at $\rho_{01} = (-0.50 \quad -0.40)^T$, $\rho_{02} = (0.35 \quad -0.50)^T$, while the desired positions were $\rho_{d1} = (-0.60 \quad 0.30)^T$, $\rho_{d2} = (0.60 \quad 0.30)^T$, that is, an isoceles triangle with followers in front of the leader. Initial orientations were approximately 135° and 60°, respectively.

Figure 19 shows the position errors for both followers, while Figure 20 gives the behaviour of their orientations. The error related to the x-coordinate is plotted in blue, while the red line indicates the error for the y-coordinate. In Figure 20, the calculated values for orientation are indicated in blue and the resultant values after Kalman Filtering are in red.

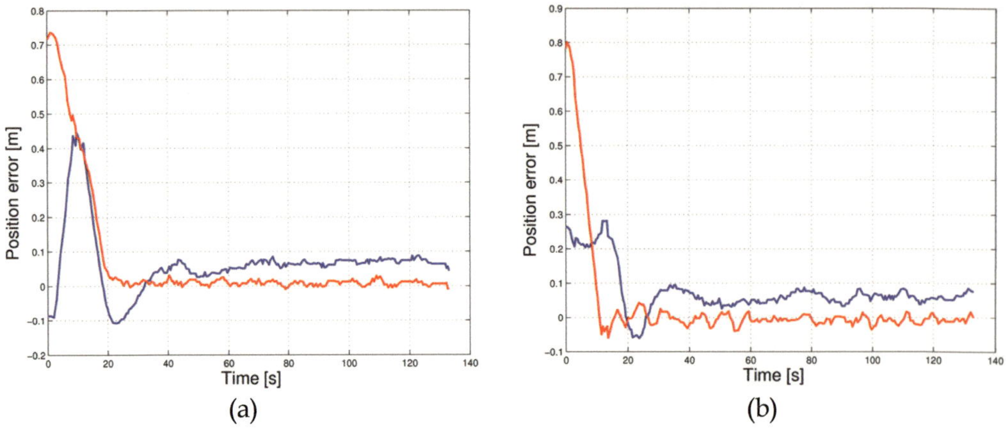

Fig. 19. Experiment 1: position errors (blue) x and (red) y for (a) Follower 1 (b) Follower 2.

From Figure 20 it is possible to see that after the transient stage, both orientations stay close to 90°. This result, together with the position errors shown in Figure 19, means that both followers achieve the desired poses and keep them until the end of the experiment.

The trajectory described by the group is illustrated in Figure 21, in which it is clear that it is not actually straight. The reason is a disalignment on the leader's left wheel, which affects encoder readings. As a result, the robot is unable to perform exactly the required linear and angular velocities. This effect is present in all experiments shown, but becomes more visible when the trajectory should be a straight line.

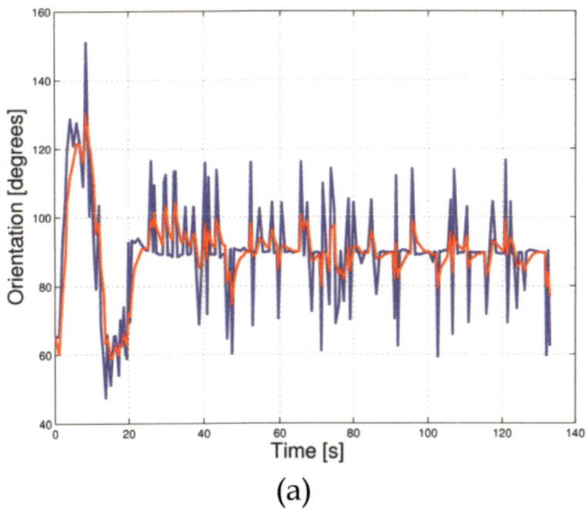

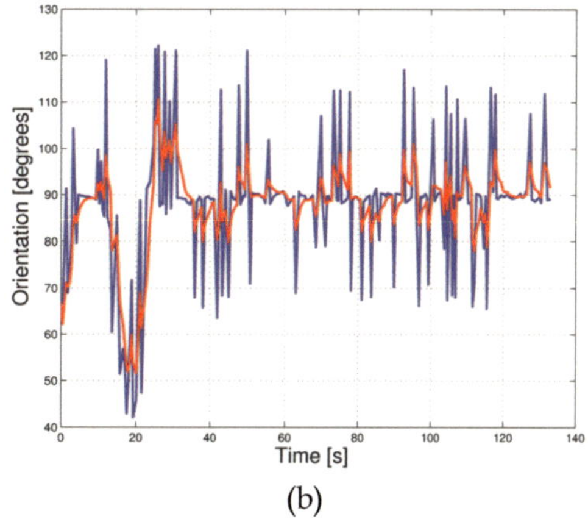

Fig. 20. Experiment 1: orientation behaviour (blue) before and (red) after filtering of (a) Follower 1 (b) Follower 2.

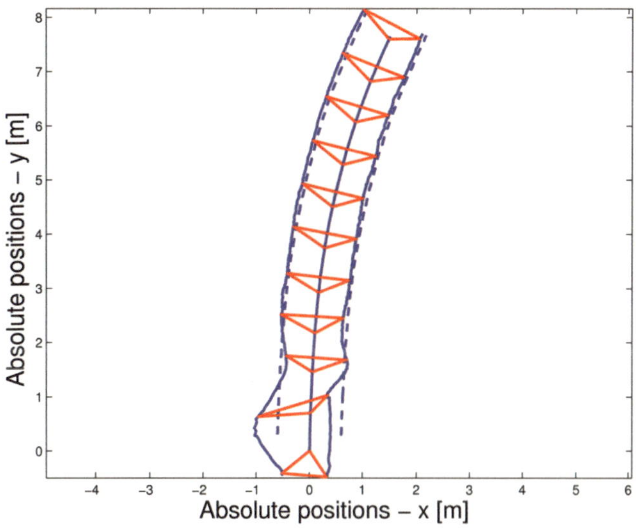

Fig. 21. Experiment 1: trajectory performed by the group.

5.2 Experiment 2

As has been shown in the first experiment, the leader navigated with fixed orientation. Now, the idea is to evaluate the controller behaviour when the reference frame is always changing its orientation. This second experiment was run with this purpose. Once again, leader's linear velocity was 60 mm/s, but its angular velocity was constant and equal to 1,5 °/s.

The followers were detected at positions given by $\rho_{01} = (-0.70 \quad 0.0)^T$, $\rho_{02} = (0.0 \quad -0.90)^T$ and their desired positions were $\rho_{d1} = (0.0 \quad 0.70)^T$, $\rho_{d2} = (0.0 \quad -0.70)^T$, which means that one follower should stay in front of the leader and the other behind it, as shown by Figure 22. Initial orientations were both estimated as being 85°.

Figure 22 serves also to see that the radii described by the followers are greater then that described by the leader and they are related by $r_i = \sqrt{r^2 + y_i^2}$, with i = 1, 2. The position errors obtained are depicted in Figure 23 and Figure 24 shows the evolution of both followers' orientations.

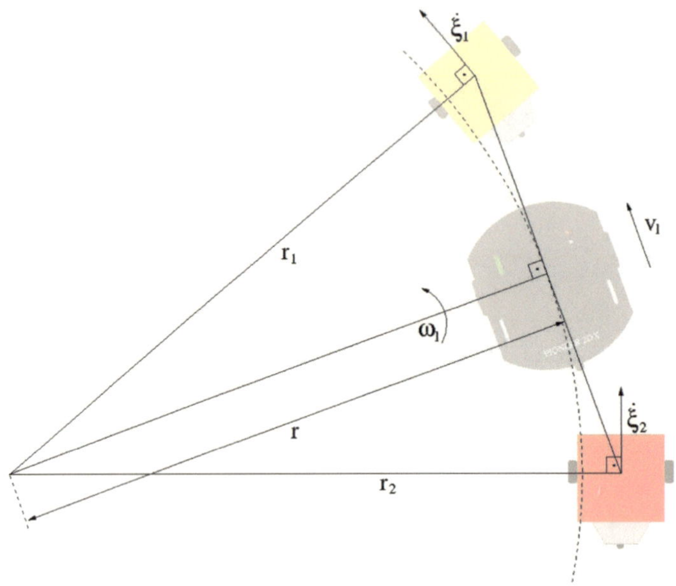

Fig. 22. Expected geometry formation for the second experiment.

Here it is worth mentioning the reason for the negative peak relative to the second follower's x-error (Figure 23-(b)) after about 60 seconds of experiment: this robot got stuck for a moment and could not follow the leader. But as soon as it could move again, the controller brought it back to the desired pose. We decided to present this particular experiment also because it shows the robustness of the controller on dealing with disturbances.

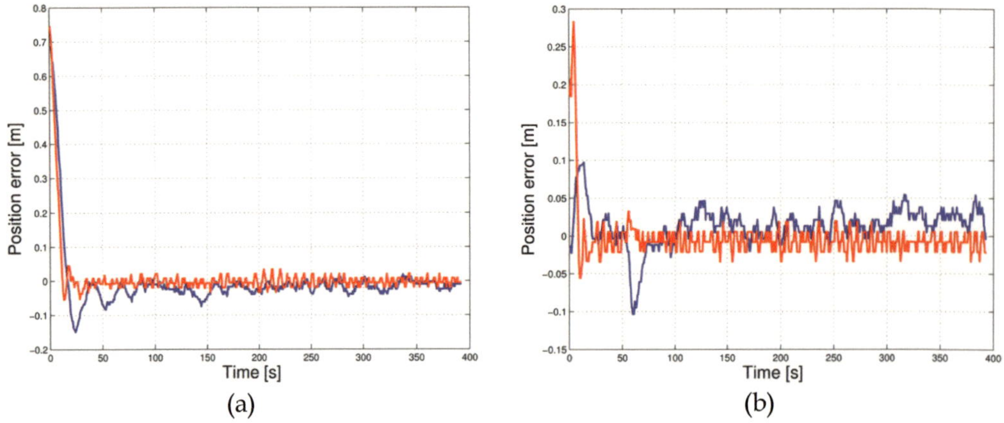

Fig. 23. Experiment 2: position errors (blue) x and (red) y for (a) Follower 1 (b) Follower 2.

Another important observation can be done with respect to the orientations presented by the cellular robots. According to Figure 24 the followers' orientations did not achieve the steady state around 90°, but close to 100° and 80°, respectively. This fact was already expected and can be easily explained by Figure 22, where it can be seen that for a counterclockwise rotation the robot that is going in front of the leader must have an angle greater than 90° relative to the leader frame, while the other robot must present an orientation less than 90°. As might be expected, the relation between these angles is inverted for a clockwise rotation.

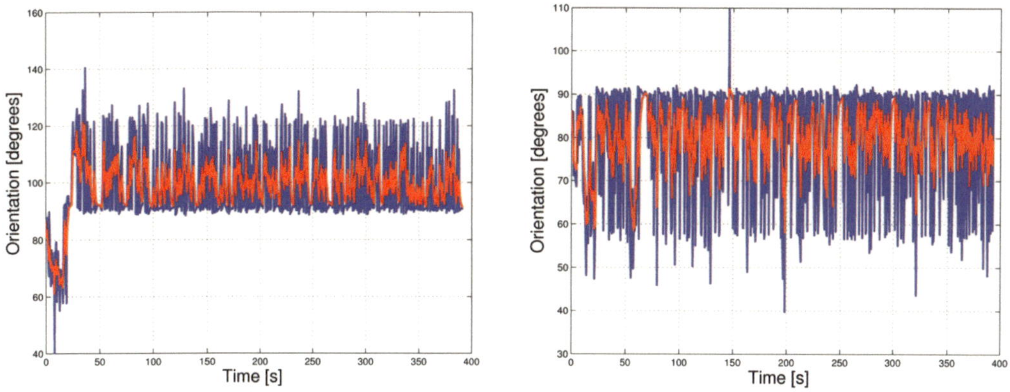

(a) (b)

Fig. 24. Experiment 2: orientation behaviour before (blue) and after filtering (red) of (a) Follower 1 (b) Follower 2.

The resulting trajectory is illustrated in Figure 25 in which the team was moving counterclockwise, since leader's angular velocity was positive. It should be noted that the robots rapidly achieved the desired formation and maintained it until closing the circle, as shown by the triangle representing team formation, almost becoming a straight line.

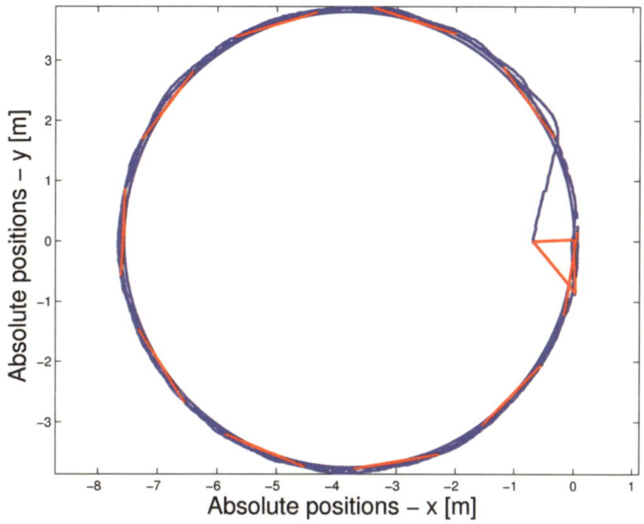

Fig. 25. Experiment 2: trajectory performed by the group.

5.3 Experiment 3

The simulation presented above, although not considering robots' dynamics, illustrates the controller behaviour in a common situation in which the team needs to get into formation and avoid an obstacle at the same time. The objective of this last experiment was to evaluate the controller in the same situation, but using real robots.

Hence, in this experiment the leader navigated with the same velocities it had in the simulation and followers' initial positions were approximately $\rho_{01} = (-0.40 \quad -0.80)^T$ and $\rho_{02} = (0.25 \quad -0.85)^T$, while their desired positions were $\rho_{d1} = (-0.50 \quad -0.30)^T$ and $\rho_{d2} = (0.50 \quad -0.30)^T$. Initial orientations were estimated as being 105° and 80°, respectively. Figure 26 gives the position errors and Figure 27 shows the followers' orientations obtained with this experiment.

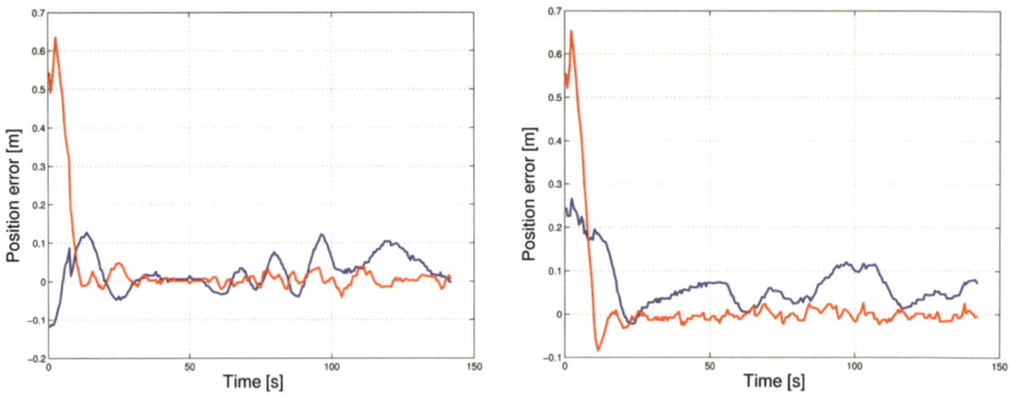

(a) (b)

Fig. 26. Experiment 3: position errors (blue) x and (red) y for (a) Follower 1 (b) Follower 2.

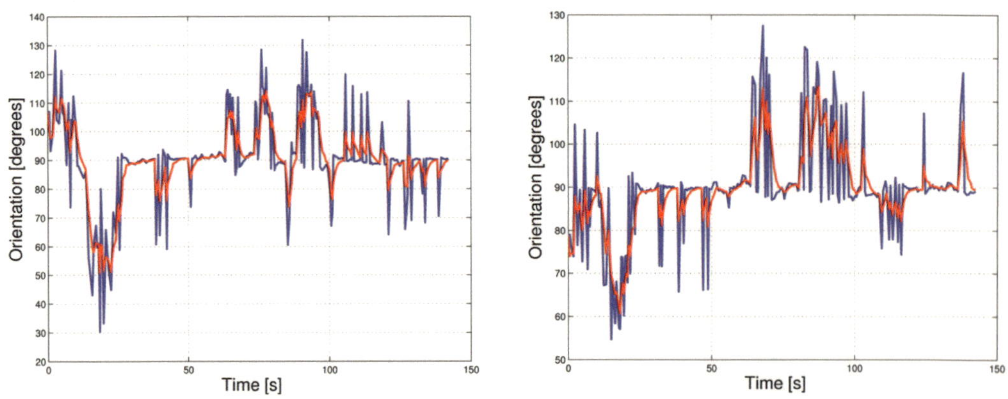

(a) (b)

Fig. 27. Experiment 3: orientation behaviour before (blue) and after filtering (red) of (a) Follower 1 (b) Follower 2.

As in the simulation, followers' poses suffered from leader's angular velocity variations, but the controller successfully drove the robots to the desired formation. Figure 28 shows the performed trajectory, which is not exactly the same of that obtained in the simulation because of the disalignment on the leader's left wheel.

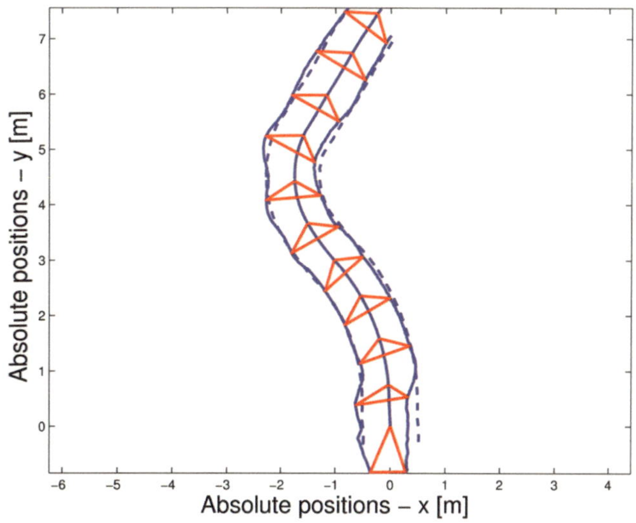

Fig. 28. Experiment 3: trajectory performed by the group.

5.4 Remarks

The experiments shown demonstrate that the robot team has achieved the desired formation and maintained it until the end of the respective experiment, even suffering the influence of image noise, low resolution of the camera and reduced useful image area. Position errors were limited to 10 cm in most experiments.

The use of Kalman Filter provided more reasonable orientation values, thus significantly improving the controller performance through better robot's pose estimation. As a result, the generated commands are smoother than those obtained without filtering.

6. Conclusion and future work

This chapter has presented a multirobot formation control strategy based on nonlinear theory and omnidirectional vision. The objective is to drive a team of simple and inexpensive mobile robots to a desired formation using only visual information. Because of the limitations of the celular robots they must be led by a leader robot having the necessary processing capacity and equipped with an adequate sensor. Thus, the formation control is done using a centralized approach.

Group formation is accomplished by a stable nonlinear controller designed to drive the followers into formation during navigation regardless of which sensor is used to implement the feedback. In this work, feedback was implemented using a single omnidirectional vision system because it allows the leader to localize all followers by acquiring just one image.

An important advantage of our approach is that the working area is not limited since the vision system is attached to the leader and so is the reference frame, which means all measurements are taken relative to the leader. Besides that, all computations are carried out onboard the leader, discarding the use of an external computer.

Through a set of image processing techniques followers' poses are reliably estimated. That includes motion segmentation, morphological filtering and color tracking, complemented by

Kalman filtering combined with Least Squares and RANSAC algorithm for optimization. Followers' positions and orientations are then used by the controller to define desired velocities for the robots to attain formation.
Simulations and experiments were carried out to evaluate the controller performance and current results show that the system performs well even with noisy and low resolution images. As future work, the controller shall be improved and obstacle avoidance will be included. Optical flow on omnidirectional images might play an important role on obstacle avoidance, and time to collision can be used to provide a safe team navigation.
Finally, this work may represent a good step towards applications that require using a large number of robots while keeping costs within reason. Combining centralized and decentralized strategies could be used to make a large robot group divide itself into smaller teams each having one leader. Leaders would negociate navigation and task execution among themselves while controlling the follower teammates. This approach would provide stable formation control and robustness against the failure of a leader. In this case, other leaders could adopt the "orphan" followers and the task in charge would be handled with reduced impact.

7. Acknowledgment

The authors would like to thank FAPES, through the projects FUNCITEC 30897360/2005 and FUNCITEC 38425025/2007, CAPES (Brazil) and SPU (Argentina), through the binational program CAPG-BA, for their financial support. A partnership between UFES, Brazil, and INAUT-UNSJ, Argentina, allowed Christiano Couto Gava to stay three months in San Juan, and Flavio Roberti to stay three months in Vitória, where part of this work was developed. It is also important to thank Fabricio Bortolini de Sá and Marino Frank Cypriano (undergraduate students) for their commitment on assembling the follower robots and Celso De La Cruz Casaño for his assistence.

8. References

Parker, L. E. (2003). Current Research in Multirobot Systems. Artificial Life Robotics, Vol. 7, No. 1-2 (March 2003) pp. 1-5, ISSN 1433-5298.

Cao, Y. U.; Fukunaga, A. S.; Kahng, A. B. (1997). Cooperative Mobile Robotics: Antecedents and Directions. Autonomous Robots, Vol. 4, No. 1 (March 1997), pp. 7-27, ISSN 0929-5593.

Carelli, R.; De La Cruz, C.; Roberti, F.(2006). Centralized formation control of non-holonomic mobile robots. Latin American Applied Research, Vol.36, No.2 (2006), pp.63-69.

Oliver, J.; Labrosse, F. (2007). Towards an appearance-based approach to the leader-follower formation problem, Proceedings of Taros 2007 - Towards Autonomous Robotic Systems, pp. 137-144, United Kingdom, September, 2007.

Consolini, L.; Morbidi, F.; Prattichizzo, D.; Tosques, M. (2007). A Geometric Characterization of Leader-Follower Formation Control, Proceedings of ICRA 2007 - IEEE International Conference on Robotics and Automation, pp. 2397-2402, ISBN 1-4244-0601-3, Roma, Italy, April 2007.

Desai, J. P.; Ostrowski, J. P.; Kumar, V. (2001). Modeling and Control of Formations of Nonholonomic Mobile Robots, IEEE Transactions on Robotics and Automation, Vol. 17, No. 6 (December 2001), pp. 905-908, ISSN 1042-296X.

Do, K. D. (2007). Bounded Controllers for Decentralized Formation Control of Mobile Robots with Limited Sensing, International Journal of Computers, Communications & Control, Vol. 2, No. 4 (2007), pp 340-354.

Franchi, A.; Freda, L.; Oriolo, G.; Venditteli, M. (2007). A Randomized Strategy for Cooperative Robot Exploration, Proceedings of ICRA 2007 - IEEE International Conference on Robotics and Automation, pp. 768-774, ISBN 1-4244-0601-3, Roma, Italy, April 2007.

Correl, N.; Martinoli, A. (2007) Robust Distributed Coverage using a Swarm of Miniature Robots, Proceedings of ICRA 2007 - IEEE International Conference on Robotics and Automation, pp. 379-384, ISBN 1-4244-0601-3, Roma, Italy, April 2007.

Rekleitis, I.; Peng New, A.; Choset, H. (2005) Distributed Coverage of Unknown/Unstructured Environments by Mobile Sensor Networks, In: Multi-Robot Systems. From Swarms to Intelligent Automata. Volume III, Editors Parker, L.; Schneider, F. E.; Schultz, A. C., pp. 145-155, Springer, ISBN 978-1-4020-1185-6.

Feddema, J. T.; Lewis, C.; Schoenwald, D. A. (2002). Decentralized Control of Cooperative Robotic Vehicles: Theory and Application, IEEE Transactions on Robotics and Automation, Vol. 18, No. 5 (October 2002), pp. 852-864, ISSN 1042-296X.

Kube,R. C.; Zhang, H. (1993). Collective robotics: From social insects to robots, Adaptive Behavior, Vol. 2, No. 2 (1993), pp. 189-218, ISSN1059-7123.

Balch, T.; Arkin, R. C. (1998). Behavior-based formation control for multi-robot teams, IEEE Transactions on Robotics and Automation, Vol. 14, No. 6 (December 1998), pp. 926-939, ISSN: 1042-296X.

Fierro, R.; Clark, J.; Hougen, D.; Commuri, S. (2005). A Multi-Robot Testbed for Biologically-Inspired Cooperative Control, In: Multi-Robot Systems. From Swarms to Intelligent Automata. Volume III, Editors Parker, L.; Schneider, F. E.; Schultz, A. C., pp. 171-182, Springer, ISBN 978-1-4020-1185-6.

Nayar, S. K. (1997). Omnidirectional Vision, Proceedings of the 8th International Symposium on Robotics Research, Hayama, Japan, October 1997.

Baker, S.; Nayar, S. K. (1999). A Theory of Single-Viewpoint Catadioptric Image Formation, International Journal of Computer Vision, Vol. 35, No. 2 (November 1999), pp. 175-196, ISSN 0920-5691.

Das, A. K.; Fierro, R.; Kumar, V.; Ostrowski, J. P., Spletzer, J.; Taylor, C. J. (2002). A Vision-Based Formation Control Framework, IEEE Transactions on Robotics and Automation, Vol. 18, No. 5 (October 2002), pp. 813-825, ISSN: 1042-296X.

Vidal, R.; Shakernia, O.; Sastry, S. (2004). Following the Flock, IEEE Robotics & Automation Magazine, Vol. 11, No.4 (December 2004), pp. 14-20, ISSN 1070-9932.

Zhu, Z.; D. Rajasekar, K.; Riseman, E. M.; Hanson, A. R. (2000). Panoramic Virtual Stereo Vision of Cooperative Mobile Robots for Localizing 3D Moving Objects, Proceedings of IEEE Workshop on Omnidirectional Vision - OMNIVIS'00, pp. 29-36, ISBN 0-7695-0704-2, Hyatt Regency, USA, June 2000.

Roberti, F.; Toibero, J. M.; Carelli, R.; Vassallo, R. F. (2007). Stable formation control for a team of wheeled mobile robots, Proceedings of XII Reunión de Trabajo en Procesamiento de la Información y Control, 6 p., Rio Gallegos, Argentina, 2007.

Kelly, R.; Carelli, R.; Zannatha, J. M. I.; Monroy, C. (2004). Control de una Pandilla de Robots Móviles para el Seguimiento de una Constelación de Puntos Objetivo, Proceedings of VI Congreso Mexicano de Robótica, pp. 83-89, COMRob, Torreón, Coahuila, México, 2004.

Santos-Victor, J. A.; Carelli, R.; Van Zwaan, S. (2002). Nonlinear Visual Control of Remote Cellular Robots, Proceedings of the10th Mediterranean Conference on Control and Automation, Lisbon, Portugal, July 2002.

Vassallo, R. F.; Encarnação, L. F.; Santos-Victor, J. A.; Schneebeli, H. J. A. (2004). Bird's Eye View Remapping and Path Following Based on Omnidirectional Vision, Proceedings of XV CBA - Congresso Brasileiro de Automática, Gramado, Brasil, September 2004.

Pereira, F. G.; Gava, C. C.; Vassallo, R. F.; Sarcinelli-Filho, M. (2005). Calibração de Sistemas Catadióptricos e Detecção da Pose de Robôs Móveis por Segmentação de Imagens Omnidirecionais, Proceedings of VII SBAI - Simpósio Brasileiro de Automação Inteligente, 8p., São Luís, Brasil, September 2005.

Fischler, M. A.; Bolles, R. C. (1981). Random Sample Consensus: A Paradigm for Model Fitting with Applications to Image Analysis and Automated Cartography, Communications of the ACM, Vol. 24, No.6 (June 1981), pp. 381-395.

De La Cruz, C.; Carelli, R.; Gava, C. C. (2006). Control Centralizado de Formación Usando Una Cámara Omnidireccional, Proceedings of IV Jornadas Argentinas de Robótica, 6p., Córdoba, Argentina, November 2006.

6

Dealing with Data Association in Visual SLAM

Arturo Gil, Óscar Reinoso, Mónica Ballesta and David Úbeda
Miguel Hernández University
Systems Engineering Department
Elche (Alicante), Spain

1. Introduction

This chapter presents a stereo vision application to Mobile Robotics. In particular we deal with the problem of simultaneous localization and mapping (SLAM) (Dissanayake et al., 2001; Montemerlo et al., 2002) and propose a stereo vision-based technique to solve it (Gil et al., 2006). The problem of SLAM is of paramount importance in the mobile robotics community, since it copes with the problem of incrementally building a map of the environment while simultaneously localizing the robot within this map. Building a map of the environment is a fundamental task for autonomous mobile robots, since the maps are required for different higher level tasks, such as path planning or exploration. It is certainly an ability necessary to achieve a true autonomous operation of the robot. In consequence, this problem has received significant attention in the past two decades.

The SLAM problem is inherently a hard problem, because noise in the estimate of the robot pose leads to noise in the estimate of the map and viceversa. The approach presented here is feature based, since it concentrates on a number of points extracted from images in the environment which are used as visual landmarks. The map is formed by the 3D position of these landmarks, referred to a common reference frame. The visual landmarks are extracted by means of the Scale Invariant Feature Transform (SIFT) (Lowe, 2004). A rejection technique is applied in order to concentrate on a reduced set of highly distinguishable, stable features. The SIFT transform detects distinctive points in images by means of a difference of gaussian function (DoG) applied in scale space. Next, a descriptor is computed for each detected point, based on local image information at the characteristic scale (Lowe, 2004). We track detected SIFT features along consecutive frames obtained by a stereo camera and select only those features that appear to be stable from different views. Whenever a feature is selected, we compute a more representative feature model given the previous observations. This model allows to improve the Data Association within the landmarks in the map and, in addition, permits to reduce the number of landmarks that need to be maintained in the map. The visual SLAM approach is applied within a Rao-Blackwellized particle filter (Montemerlo et al., 2002; Grisetti et al., 2005).

In this chapter we propose two relevant contributions to the visual SLAM solution. First, we present a new mechanism to deal with the data association problem for the case of visual landmarks. Second, our approach actively tracks landmarks prior to its integration in the map. As a result, we concentrate on a small set of stable landmarks and incorporate them in the map. With this approach, our map typically consists of a reduced number of landmarks compared to those of (Little et al., 2002) and (Sim et al., 2006), for comparable map sizes. In addition, we have applied effective resampling techniques, as exposed in (Stachniss et al., 2004). This fact reduces the number of particles needed to construct the map, thus reducing computational burden.

Our system has been implemented and tested on data gathered with a mobile robot in a typical office environment. Experiments presented in this chapter demonstrate that our method improves the data association and in this way leads to more accurate maps.

The remainder of the chapter is structured as follows. Section 2 introduces related work in the context of visual SLAM. Next, Section 3 defines the concept of visual landmark and their utility in SLAM. Section 4 explains the basics of the Rao-Blackwellized particle filter employed in the solution. Next, Section 5 presents our solution to the data association problem in the context of visual landmarks. In Section 6 we present our experimental results. Finally, Section 7 sums up the most important conclusions and proposes future extensions.

2. Related work

Most work on SLAM so far has focussed on building 2D maps of environments using range sensors such as SONAR or laser (Wijk and Christensen, 2000; Thrun, 2001). Recently, Rao-Blackwellized particle filters have been used as an effective means to solve the SLAM problem using occupancy grid maps (Stachniss et al., 2004) or landmark-based maps (Montemerlo et al., 2002). Fig. 1 shows an example of both kind of maps. Recently, some authors have been concentrating on building three dimensional maps using visual information extracted from cameras. Typically, in this scenario, the map is represented by a set of three dimensional landmarks related to a global reference frame. The reasons that motivate the use of vision systems in the SLAM problem are: cameras are typically less expensive than laser sensors, have a lower power consumption and are able to provide 3D information from the scene.

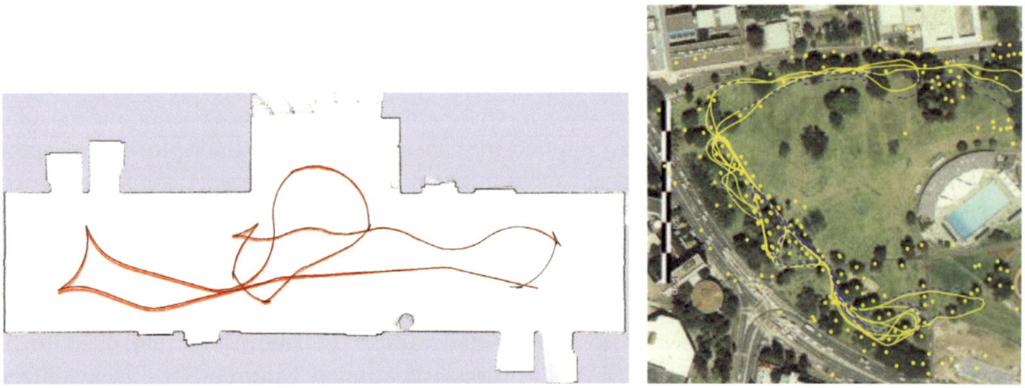

a) b)

Fig. 1. Two typical maps. Fig. 1(a) occupancy-grid map. Fig. 1(b) landmark-based map: landmarks are indicated with (grey/yellow dots).

In (Little et al., 2001) and (Little et al., 2002) stereo vision is used to track 3D visual landmarks extracted from the environment. In this work, SIFT features are used as visual landmarks. During exploration, the robot extracts SIFT features from stereo images and

computes relative measurements to them. Landmarks are then integrated in the map with an Extended Kalman Filter associated to it. However, this approach does not manage correctly the uncertainty associated with robot motion, and only one hypothesis over the pose of the robot is maintained. Consequently it may fail in the presence of large odometric errors (e.g. while closing a loop). In (Miró et al., 2005) a Kalman filter is used to estimate an augmented state constituted by the robot pose and N landmark positions (Dissanayake et al., 2001). SIFT features are used too to manage the data association among visual landmarks. However, since only one hypothesis is maintained over the robot pose, the method may fail in the presence of incorrect data associations. In addition, in the presence of a significant number of landmarks the method would be computationally expensive.
The work presented in (Sim et al., 2006) uses SIFT features as significant points in space and tracks them over time. It uses a Rao-Blackwellized particle filter to estimate both the map and the path of the robot.

3. Visual landmarks

In our work, we use visual landmarks as features to build the map. Two main processes can be distinguished when observing a visual landmark:

- The detection phase: This involves extracting a point in the space by means of images captured from the environment. The detection algorithm should be stable to scale and viewpoint changes, i.e. should be able to extract the same points in space when the robot observes them from different angles and distances.
- The description phase: Which aims at describing the appearance of the point based on local image information. The visual descriptor computed in this phase should also be invariant to scale and viewpoint changes. Thus, this process enables the same points in the space to be recognized from different viewpoints, which may occur while the robot moves around its workplace, thus providing information for the localization process. The descriptor is employed in the data association problem, described in Section 5.

Nowadays, a great variety of detection and description methods have been proposed in the context of visual SLAM. In particular, in the work presented here we use SIFT features (Scale Invariant Feature Transform) which were developed for image feature generation, and used initially in object recognition applications (Lowe, 2004; Lowe, 1999). The Scale-Invariant Feature Transform (SIFT) is an algorithm that detects distinctive keypoints from images and computes a descriptor for them. The interest points extracted are said to be invariant to image scale, rotation, and partially invariant to changes in viewpoint and illumination. SIFT features are located at maxima and minima of a difference of Gaussians (DoG) function applied in scale space. They can be computed by building an image pyramid with resampling between each level. Next, the descriptors are computed based on orientation histograms at a 4x4 subregion around the interest point, resulting in a 128 dimensional vector. The features are said to be invariant to image translation, scaling, rotation, and partially invariant to illumination changes and affine or 3D projection. SIFT features have been used in robotic applications, showing its suitability for localization and SLAM tasks (Little et al., 2001; Little et al., 2002; Sim et al., 2006).
Recently, a method called Speeded Up Robust Features (SURF) was presented (Bay et al., 2006). The detection process is based on the Hessian matrix. SURF descriptors are based on sums of 2D Haar wavelet responses, calculated in a 4x4 subregion around each interest point. For example, in (Murillo et al., 2007) a localization method based on SURF features is presented.

Finally, in (Davison & Murray, 2002) monocular SLAM is implemented using the Harris corner detector and the landmarks are described by means of a gray patch centered at the points.
To sum up, different detectors and descriptors have been used in visual SLAM approaches. In our opinion, there exists no consensus on this matter and this means that the question of which interest point detector and descriptor is more suitable for visual SLAM is still open. However, the evaluation presented by (Mikolajczyk & Schmid, 2005) proved the great invariability and discriminant power of the SIFT descriptors. On the other hand, the study presented in (Ballesta et al.,2007), demonstrated that the points obtained with the DoG detector where highly unstable. As a consequence, in the work presented here, a tracking of the points is performed in order to reject unstable points.

4. Rao-Blackwellized SLAM

We estimate the map and the path of the robot using a Rao-Blackwellized particle filter. Using the most usual nomenclature, we denote as s_t the robot pose at time t. On the other hand, the robot path until time t will be denoted $s_t = \{s_1, s_2, \cdots, s_t\}$. We assume that at time t the robot obtains an observation z_t from a landmark. The set of observations made by the robot until time t will be denoted $z^t = \{z_1, z_2, \cdots, z_t\}$ and the set of actions $u^t = \{u_1, u_2, \cdots, u_t\}$. The map is composed by a set of different landmarks $L = \{l_1, l_2, \cdots, l_N\}$. Therefore, the SLAM problem can be formulated as that of determining the location of all landmarks in the map L and robot poses s_t from a set of measurements z^t and robot actions u^t. Thus, the SLAM problem can be posed as the estimation of the probability:

$$p(L \mid s_t, z_t, u_t, c_t) \tag{1}$$

While exploring the environment, the robot has to determine whether a particular observation z_t corresponds to a previously seen landmark or to a new one. This problem is known as the Data Association problem and will be further explained in Section 5. Provided that, at a time t the map consists of N landmarks, the correspondence is represented by c_t, where c_t 2 $[1 \ldots N]$. In consequence, at a time t the observation z_t corresponds to the landmark c_t in the map. When no correspondence is found we denote it as $c_t = N+1$, indicating that a new landmark should be initialized. The conditional independence property of the SLAM problem implies that the posterior (1) can be factored as (Montemerlo et al., 2002):

$$p\left(s^t, L \mid z^t, u^t, c^{t\}}\right) = p\left(s^t \mid z^t, u^t, c^t\right) \prod_{k=1}^{N} p\left(l_k \mid s^t, z^t, u^t, c^t\right) \tag{2}$$

This equation states that the full SLAM posterior is decomposed into two parts: one estimator over robot paths, and N independent estimators over landmark positions, each conditioned on the path estimate. This factorization was first presented by Murphy (Murphy, 1999). We approximate $p(s_t \mid z_t, u_t, c_t)$ using a set of M particles, each particle having N independent landmark estimators (implemented as EKFs), one for each landmark in the map. Each particle is thus defined as:

$$S_t^{[m]} = \left\{s^{t,[m]}, \mu_{1,t}^{[m]}, \Sigma_{1,t}^{[m]}, \mu_{2,t}^{[m]}, \Sigma_{2,t}^{[m]}, \cdots, \mu_{N,t}^{[m]}, \Sigma_{N,t}^{[m]}\right\} \tag{3}$$

where $\mu_{k,t}^{[m]}$ is the best estimation at time t for the position of landmark based on the path of the particle m and $\Sigma_{k,t}^{[m]}$ its associated covariance matrix. Each landmark is thus described as: $l_k=\{\mu_k, \Sigma_k, d_k\}$, where d_k is the associated SIFT descriptor. The SIFT descriptor allows to differentiate between landmarks, based on their visual appearance. The set of M particles, each one with its associated map will be denoted $S_t=\{S_t^1, S_t^2, \cdots, S_t^M\}$. The particle set S_t is calculated incrementally from the set S_{t-1}, computed at time t-1 and the robot control u_t. Thus, each particle is sampled from a proposal distribution $p(s_t \mid s_{t-1}, u_t)$, which defines the movement model of the robot. Particles generated by the movement model are distributed following the probability distribution $p(s^t \mid z^{t-1}, u^t, c^{t-1})$, since the last observation of the robot z_t has not been considered. On the contrary, we would like to estimate the posterior: $p(s^t \mid z^t, u^t, c^t)$, in which all the information from the odometry u^t and observations z^t is included. This difference is corrected by means of a process denoted sample importance resampling (SIR). Essentially, a weigth is assigned to each particle in the set according to the quality by which the pose and map of the particle match the current observation z_t. Following the approach of (Montemerlo et al., 2002) we compute the weight assigned to each particle as:

$$\omega_t^{[m]} = \frac{1}{\sqrt{\left|2\pi Z_{c_t,t}\right|}} \exp\left\{-\frac{1}{2}\left(z_t - \hat{z}_{c_t,t}\right)^T \left[Z_{c_t,t}\right]^{-1} \left(z_t - \hat{z}_{c_t,t}\right)\right\} \tag{4}$$

Where z_t is the current measurement and $\hat{z}_t$ is the predicted measurement for the landmark c_t based on the pose $s_t^{[i]}$. The matrix $Z_{c_t,t}$ is the covariance matrix associated with the innovation $v = (z_t - \hat{z}_t)$. Note that we implicitly assume that each measurement z_t has been associated to the landmark c_t of the map. This problem is, in general, hard to solve, since similar-looking landmarks may exist. In Section 5 we describe our approach to this problem. In the case that B observations $z_t=\{z_{t,1}, z_{t,2}, \cdots, z_{t,B}\}$ from different landmarks exist at a time t, we compute a weight for each observation $\omega_{t,1}^{[m]}, \omega_{t,2}^{[m]}, \cdots, \omega_{t,B}^{[m]}$ following Equation (4), next the total weight assigned to the particle as:

$$\omega_t^{[m]} = \prod_{i=1}^{B} \omega_{t,i}^{[m]} \tag{5}$$

The weights are normalized so that $\sum_{i=1}^{M} \omega_t^{[i]} = 1$, so that they ressemble a probability function. In order to assess for the difference between the proposal and the target distribution, each particle is drawn with replacement with probability proportional to this importance weight. During resampling, particles with a low weight are normally replaced by others with a higher weight. It is a well known problem that the resampling step may delete good particles from the set and cause particle depletion. In order to avoid this problem we follow an approach similar to (Stachniss et al., 2004). Thus we calculate the number of efficient particles N_{eff} as:

$$N_{eff} = \frac{1}{\sum_{i=1}^{M} \left(\omega_t^{[i]}\right)^2} \tag{6}$$

We resample each time N_{eff} drops below a pre-defined threshold (set to M/2 in our application). By using this approach we have verified that the number of particles needed to achieve good results is reduced.

5. Data association

While the robot explores the environment it must decide whether the observation z_t corresponds to a previously mapped landmark or to a different one. The observation z_t is a relative three-dimensional relative measurement obtained with a stereo camera. Associated to the observation is a visual SIFT descriptor d_t. To find the data association we find a set of landmark candidates using the current measurement z_t and the following Mahalanobis distance function:

$$d = \left(z_t - \hat{z}_{c_t,t}\right)^T \left[Z_{c_t,t}\right]^{-1} \left(z_t - \hat{z}_{c_t,t}\right) \tag{7}$$

The landmarks with d below a pre-defined threshold d_0 are considered as candidates. Next, we use the associated SIFT descriptor d_t to find the correct data association among the candidates. Each SIFT descriptor is a 128-long vector computed from the image gradient at a local neighbourhood of the interest point. Experimental results in object recognition applications have showed that this description is robust against changes in scale, viewpoint and illumination (Lowe, 2004). In the approaches of (Little et al., 2001), (Little et al., 2002) and (Sim et al., 2006), data association is based on the squared Euclidean distance between descriptors. In consequence, given a current SIFT descriptor, associated to the observation z_t and the SIFT descriptor d_i, associated to the i landmark in the map, the following distance function is computed:

$$E = (d_t - d_i)(d_t - d_i) \tag{8}$$

Then, the landmark i of the map that minimizes the distance E is chosen. Whenever the distance E is below a certain threshold, the observation and the landmark are associated. On the other hand, a new landmark is created whenever the distance E exceeds a pre-defined threshold. When the same point is viewed from slightly different viewpoints and distances, the values of its SIFT descriptor remain almost unchanged. However, when the same point is viewed from significantly different viewpoints (e.g. 30 degrees apart) the difference in the descriptor is remarkable. In the presence of similar looking landmarks, this approach produces a remarkable number of incorrect data associations, normally causing an inconsistent map.

We propose a different method to deal with the data association in the context of visual SLAM. We address the problem from a pattern classification point of view. We consider the problem of assigning a pattern d_t to a class C_i. Each class C_i models a landmark. We consider different views of the same visual landmark as different patterns belonging to the same class C_i. Whenever a landmark is found in an image, it is tracked along p frames and its descriptors $\{d_1, d_2, \ldots, d_p\}$ are stored. Then, for each landmark C_i we compute a mean value d_i and estimate a covariance matrix S_i, assuming the elements in the SIFT descriptor independent. Based on this data we compute the Mahalanobis distance:

$$D = (d_t - d_i)S_i^{-1}(d_t - d_i) \tag{9}$$

We compute the distance D for all the landmarks in the map of each particle and assign the correspondence to the landmark that minimizes D. If none of the values exceeds a predefined threshold then we consider it a new landmark. In order to test this distance function we have recorded a set of images with little variations of viewpoint and distance (see Figure 2). SIFT landmarks are easily tracked across consecutive frames, since the variance in the descriptor is low. In addition, we visually judged the correspondence across images. Based on these data we compute the matrix S_i for each SIFT point tracked for more than 5 frames. Following, we compute the distance to the same class using Equation (8) and (9). For each observation, we select the class that minimises its distance function and as we already know the correspondences, we can compute the number of incorrect and correct matches. Table 1 shows the results based on our experiments. A total of 3000 examples where used. As can be clearly seen, a raw comparison of two SIFT descriptors using the Euclidean distance does not provide total separation between landmarks, since the descriptor can vary significantly from different viewpoints. As can be seen, the number of false correspondences is reduced by using the Mahalanobis distance. By viewing different examples of the same landmark we are able to build a more complete model of it and this permits us to better separate each landmark from others. We consider that this approach reduces the number of false correspondences and, consequently produces better results in the estimation of the map and the path of the robot, as will be shown in Section 6.

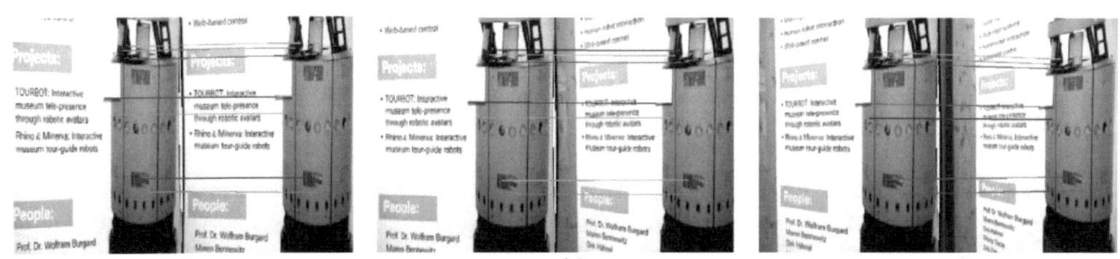

a) b) c)

Fig. 2. Tracking of points viewed from different angles and distances.

6. Experimental results

During the experiments we used a B21r robot equipped with a stereo head and a LMS laser range finder. We manually steered the robot and moved it through the rooms of the building 79 of the University of Freiburg. A total of 507 stereo images at a resolution of 320x240 were collected. The total traversed distance of the robot is approximately 80m. For each pair of stereo images a number of correspondences were established and observations $z_t = \{z_{t,1}, z_{t,2}, \cdots, z_{t,B}\}$ were obtained, each observation accompanied by a SIFT descriptor $\{d_{t,1}, d_{t,2}, \cdots, d_{t,B}\}$. After stereo correspondence, each point is tracked for a number of frames. By this procedure we can assure that the SIFT point is stable and can be viewed from a significant number of robot poses. In a practical way, when a landmark has been tracked for more than p=5 frames it is considered a new observation and is integrated in the filter. After the tracking, a mean value d_i is computed using the SIFT descriptors in the p views and a diagonal covariance matrix is also computed. In consequence, as mentioned in Section 5, each landmark is now represented by (d_i, S_i). Along with the images, we captured laser data using the SICK laser range finder. These data allowed us to estimate the path followed by the robot using the approach of (Stachniss, 2004). This path has shown to be very precise and is used as ground truth.

	Correct matches	Incorrect matches
Euclidean distance	83.85	16.15
Mahalanobis distance	94.04	5.96

Table 1. Comparison of correct and incorrect matches using the Euclidean distance and the Mahalanobis distance in the data association.

Figure 3 shows the map constructed with 1, 10, and 100 particles. A total number of 1500 landmarks were estimated. With only 1 particle the method fails to compute a coherent map, since only one hypothesis is maintained over the robot path. It can be seen that, with only 10 particles, the map is topologically correct. Using only 100 particles the map is very precise. On every figure we show the path followed by the robot (blue continuous line), the odometry of the robot (magenta dotted line) and the path estimated using the visual SLAM approach presented here (red dashed line). As can be seen in the figures, some areas of the map do not possess any landmark. This is due to the existence of featureless areas in the environment (i.e. texture-less walls), where no SIFT features can be found.

Figure 4 shows the error in localization for each movement of the robot during exploration using 200 particles. Again, we compare the estimated position of the robot using our approach to the estimation using laser data. In addition, we have compared both approaches to data association as described in Section 5. To do this, we have made a number of simulations varying the number of particles used in each simulation. The process was repeated using both data association methods. As can be seen in Figure 5 for the same number of particles, better localization results are obtained when the Mahalanobis distance is used (red continuous line), compared to the results obtained using the Euclidean distance (blue dashed line). Better results in the path estimation imply an in the quality of the estimated map.

Compared to preceeding approaches our method uses less particles to achieve good results. For example, in (Sim et al., 2006), a total of 400 particles are needed to compute a topologically correct map, while correct maps have been built using 50 particles with our method. In addition, our maps typically consists of about 1500 landmarks, a much more compact representation than the presented in (Sim et al., 2006), where the map contains typically around 100.000 landmarks.

7. Conclusion

In this Chapter a solution to SLAM based on a Rao-Blackwellized particle filter has been presented. This filter uses visual information extracted from cameras. We have used natural landmarks as features for the construction of the map. The method is able to build 3D maps of a particular environment using relative measurements extracted from a stereo pair of cameras. We have also proposed an alternative method to deal with the data association problem in the context of visual landmarks, addressing the problem from a pattern classification point of view. When different examples of a particular SIFT descriptor exist (belonging to the same landmark) we obtain a probabilistic model for it. Also we have compared the results obtained using the Mahalanobis distance and the Euclidean distance. By using a Mahalanobis distance the data association is improved, and, consequently better results are obtained since most of the false correspondences are avoided. Opposite to maps created by means of occupancy or certainty grids, the visual map generated by the approach presented in this paper does not represent directly the occupied or free areas of the environment. In consequence, some areas totally lack of landmarks, but are not necessary free areas where the robot may navigate through. For example, featureless areas such as blank walls provide no information to the robot. In consequence, the map may be used to effectively localize the robot, but cannot be directly used for navigation. We believe, that this fact is originated from the nature of the sensors and it is not a failure of the proposed approach. Other low-cost sensors such as SONAR would definitely help the robot in its navigation tasks.

As a future work we think that it is of particular interest to further research in exploration techniques when this representation of the world is used. We would also like to extend the method to the case where several robots explore an unmodified environment and construct a visual map of it.

8. Acknowledgment

The work has been supported by the Spanish government under the project: SISTEMAS DE PERCEPCION VISUAL MOVIL Y COOPERATIVO COMO SOPORTE PARA LA REALIZACIÓN DE TAREAS CON REDES DE ROBOTS. Ref. DPI2007-61197, (Ministerio de Educación y Ciencia).

9. References

Ballesta, M.; Martínez-Mozos, O.; Gil. A. & Reinoso, O. (2007). A Comparison of Local Descriptors for Visual SLAM. In Proceedings of the Workshop on Robotics and Mathematics (RoboMat 2007). Coimbra, Portugal.

Bay, H.; Tuytelaars, T. & Van Gool, L. (2006). Object recognition from local scale-invariant features. In: *European Conference on Computer Vision.*

Davison, A.J. & Murray, D.W. (2002). Simultaneous localisation and map-building using active vision. *IEEE Transactions on Pattern Analysis and Machine Intelligence.*

Dissanayake, G.; Newman, P.; Clark, S.; Durrant-Whyte, H. & Csorba, M. (2001). A solution to the simultaneous localization and map building (SLAM) problem, *IEEE Trans. on Robotics and Automation,* 17:229–241.

Gil, A.; Reinoso, O.; Burgard, W.; Stachniss, C. & Martínez Mozos, O. (2006). Improving data association in rao-blackwellized visual SLAM. *In: IEEE/RSJ Int. Conf. on Intelligent Robots & Systems.* Beijing, China.

Grisetti, G.; Stachniss, C. & Burgard, W. (2007). Improved techniques for grid mapping with Rao-blackwellized particle filters. *IEEE Transactions on Robotics* 23(1).

Little, J.; Se, S. & Lowe, D. (2002). Global localization using distinctive visual features. *In: IEEE/RSJ Int. Conf. on Intelligent Robots & Systems (ICRA).*

Little, J.; Se, S. & Lowe, D. (2001). Vision-based mobile robot localization and mapping using scale-invariant features. *In: IEEE Int. Conf. on Robotics & Automation.*

Lowe, D. (2004). Distinctive image features from scale-invariant keypoints. *Int. Journal of computer Vision,* 2(60).

Lowe, D. (1999). Object recognition from local scale invariant features. In *International Conference on Computer Vision,* pages 1150–1157.

Mikolajczyk, K. & Schmid, C. (2005). A performance evaluation of local descriptors. *IEEE Transactions on Pattern Analysis and Machine Intelligence* 27(10).

Miró, J. V.; Dissanayake, G. & Zhou, W. (2005). Vision-based SLAM using natural features in indoor environments. *In Proceedings of the 2005 IEEE International Conference on Intelligent Networks, Sensor Networks and Information Processing*, pages 151–156.

Montemerlo, M.;Thrun, S.; Koller, D. & Wegbreit, B. (2002). Fastslam: A factored solution to the simultaneous localization and mapping problem. *In Proc.~of the National Conference on Artificial Intelligence* (AAAI). Edmonton, Canada.

Murillo, A. C.; Guerrero, J.J. & Sagüés, C. (2007). SURF features for efficient robot localization with omnidirectional images. In: *IEEE Int. Conf. on Robotics & Automation.*

Murphy, K. (1999). Bayesian map learning in dynamic environments. *In Neural Information Processing Systems (NIPS).*

Sim, R.; & Little, J. J. (2006). Autonomous vision-based exploration and mapping using hybrid maps and Rao-Blackwellised particle filters. *In: IEEE/RSJ Int. Conf. on Intelligent Robots & Systems*. Beijing, China.

Stachniss, C.; Hähnel, D. & Burgard, W. (2004). Exploration with active loop-closing for FastSLAM. In *IEEE/RSJ Int. Conference on Intelligent Robots and Systems.*

Stachniss, C.; Hähnel, D. & Burgard, W. (2005). Improving grid-based slam with rao-blackwellized particle filters by adaptive proposals and selective resampling. *In IEEE Int. Conference on Robotics and Automation (ICRA).*

Thrun, S. (2001). A probabilistic online mapping algorithm for teams of mobile robots. *International Journal of Robotics Research*, 20(5):335–363.

Wijk, O. & Christensen, H. I. (2000). Localization and navigation of a mobile robot using natural point landmarks extracted from sonar data. *Robotics and Autonomous Systems*, 1(31):31–42.

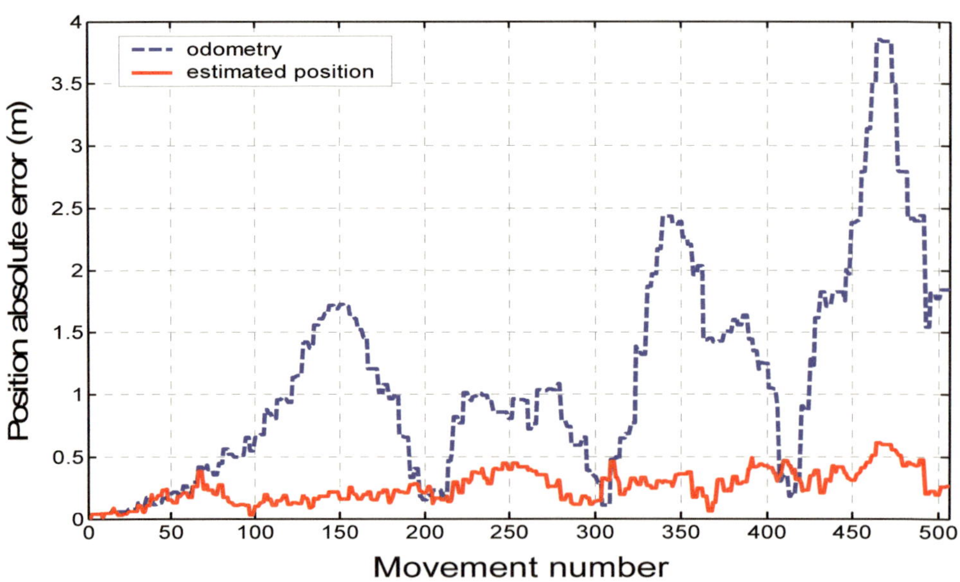

Fig. 4. Absolute position error in odometry and visual estimation.

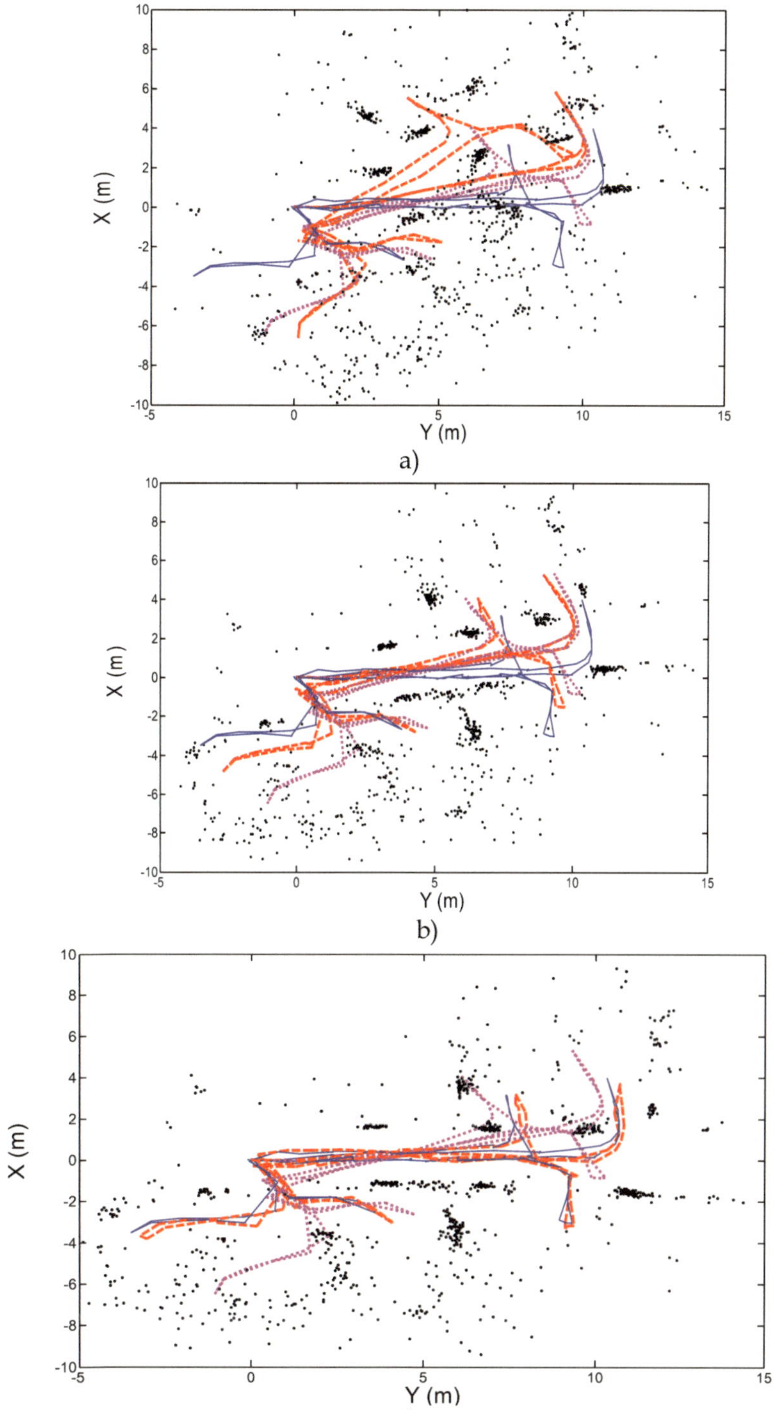

Fig. 3. Maps built using 1, 10 and 100 particles. A 2d view is showed where landmarks are indicated with black dots.

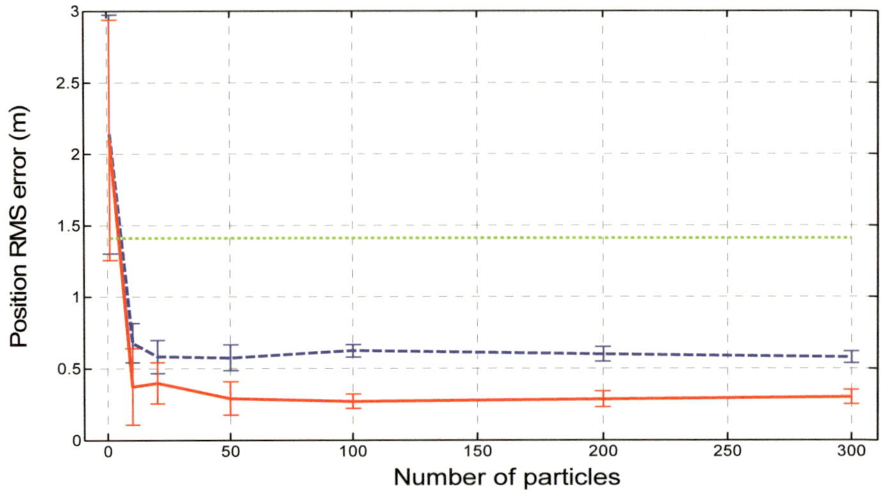

Fig. 5. RMS error in position for different number of particles.

7

Precise and Robust Large-Shape Formation using Uncalibrated Vision for a Virtual Mold

Biao Zhang[a], Emilio J. Gonzalez-Galvan[b], Jesse Batsche[a], Steven B. Skaar[a], Luis A. Raygoza[b] and Ambrocio Loredo[b]

[a] *Aerospace and Mechanical Engineering Department. University of Notre Dame. Notre Dame, IN 46556*

[b] *Centro de Investigación y Estudios de Posgrado. Facultad de Ingeniería. Universidad Autónoma de San Luis Potosí. San Luis Potosí, S.L.P. 78290, México*

1. Introduction

Consider four flat-surface regions each of which has been placed, with varying positions and orientations, within the workspace of a robot, as suggested in Figure 1. Assume that the robot is kinematically able to reach each surface in the sense of delivering a cutting and an abrading tool to the poses needed in order to remove material from a blank to the point of recovering each of these surfaces.

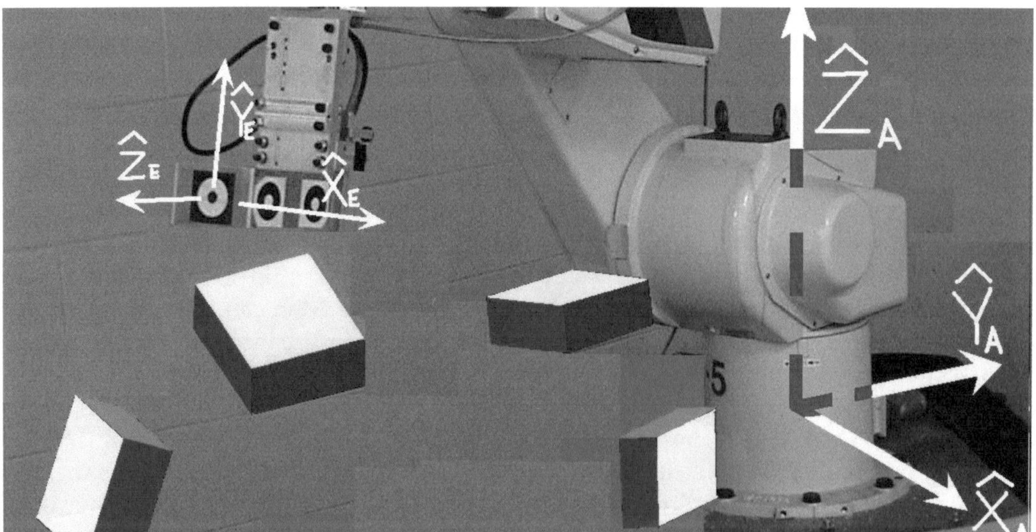

Fig. 1. The four flat surfaces which are to be duplicated via robot machining and abrasive action - precisely in their respective locations.

We pose the task as one of recovering to within a maximum error of 0.1mm, each of the four surfaces of Fig. 1 using the robot with end-of-arm machining and abrading equipment.

Rather than using internal-angle-dependent, calibrated, kinematical relationships of Figure 1's E frame relative to the A frame, as might be used with a CNC machine as the basis for this recovery of geometry, we instead apply uncalibrated, stationary cameras, in numbers and locations such that each of the four target surfaces of Fig. 1 is clearly viewed by at least two cameras. Laser spots are cast onto the four original surfaces, as indicated in Fig. 2, and, through image differencing, registered and located in the uncalibrated cameras' image planes or "camera spaces". Similar laser spots are cast onto the various intermediate forms of the fashioned blank as it approaches the prototype geometry of Figure 1.

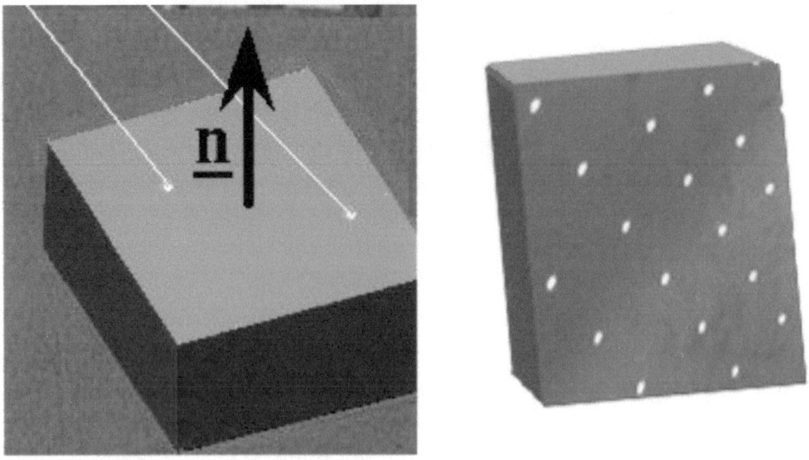

Fig. 2. Hundreds of laser-spot centers may be "collected" in each participant camera space by way of image differencing. Individual spots (left) and multiple spots (right) may be cast. These lead to the unit normal **n** in a special reference frame: the frame with respect to which the nominal kinematics model of the robot is locally virtually perfect.

The robot's degrees of freedom are guided using camera-space manipulation [1]. As such, there is no need to calibrate the robot kinematics just as there is no need to calibrate the cameras. The forward kinematics model in terms (say) of Denavit-Hartenberg parameters, is considered known but not especially accurate globally, as is typical for such industrial robots. Importantly, knowledge of the location of the base of the robot is not used; the base may be introduced into the scene in any way that is convenient for the operation at hand.

The proposition of the paper is, first, that extremely high precision can be achieved in this surface-recovery process provided the cameras remain stationary throughout. The second point is that more arbitrarily curved surfaces - surfaces that would be of interest in countless kinds of real-world applications - can also be recovered using variations on the same strategy. Thus, a new possibility for replacing CNC machining is introduced - a possibility not predicated on a data base but rather a large number of laser spots incident upon the prototype surface and registered in the uncalibrated cameras, followed by robot-based, camera-guided machining and abrading using one or, equally feasible, several conveniently, arbitrarily positioned robots. Presuming the prototype piece is shaped as desired (it need not of course be of the same material as the duplicate), the accuracy of the final form of one end-juncture of the duplicate with respect to an opposite end juncture will be completely independent of the extent of those two points' separation, or the number of base positions of robots engaged to achieve the shape recovery. Put another way, the absolute accuracy of the surfaces' final contour will be the same whether it is a small object fashioned by a single machine or a huge one (imagine for example the Statue of Liberty) fashioned using many portable dexterous machines, or a single robot repositioned arbitrarily throughout the shape-recovery process. Alternative means such as contact probes for monitoring accuracy are unnecessary. The one requirement is that cameras not shift from initial spot detection as those spots are reflected off the prototype piece through to formation of the replica.

2. Laser-assisted robot operation using camera-space manipulation

The high precision of replicating the four surfaces is achieved in a three-stage process. The first stage entails identification of the surfaces by the process of "spot matching" among those cameras that have a clear view of any one of the four original surfaces. Matched spots, then, are used to map a relationship between 2D camera-space junctures of the surface as they locate in one of the pertinent cameras and camera-space location in each of the other cameras with visual access to a given surface region.
As indicated in Figure 3, the grayscale differenced image that includes a single laser spot may be conditioned or smoothed using a mask applied to each differenced image.

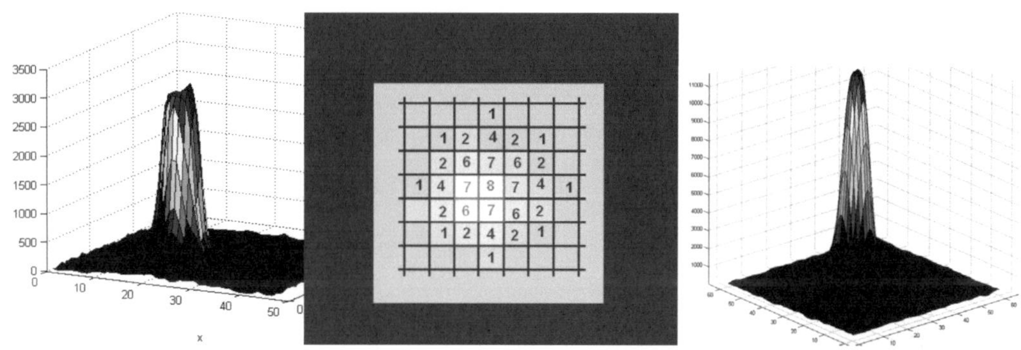

Fig. 3. Raw grayscale, differenced image of a laser spot (left) followed by application to each pixel of a smoothing mask (center) produces a smoothed differenced image with a clearer peak or center location in camera space (right).

Thousands of laser-spot centers may be "collected" in each participant camera space and mapped among the regionally pertinent cameras by way of image differencing of large numbers of images, each with the spots directed slightly differently onto any one prototype-surface plane. As indicated in Fig. 4, it is possible to difference two images with laser spots "on", provided the multiple-beam laser pointer is shifted between images. The identity of the spots with pan/tilt position in such an image is based upon the "up" or "down" orientation. These samples aggregate leading to the unit normal **n**, as depicted in Fig. 2, in a special 3D physical reference frame: the frame with respect to which the nominal kinematics model of the robot is locally virtually perfect. This does not imply "calibration" in the usual sense, as it is never known - from region to region of the robot's workspace within which operation occurs - exactly how this special reference frame is positioned and oriented. Rather, the philosophy of "camera-space manipulation" is used to identify the "camera-space kinematics" in each locally pertinent camera.

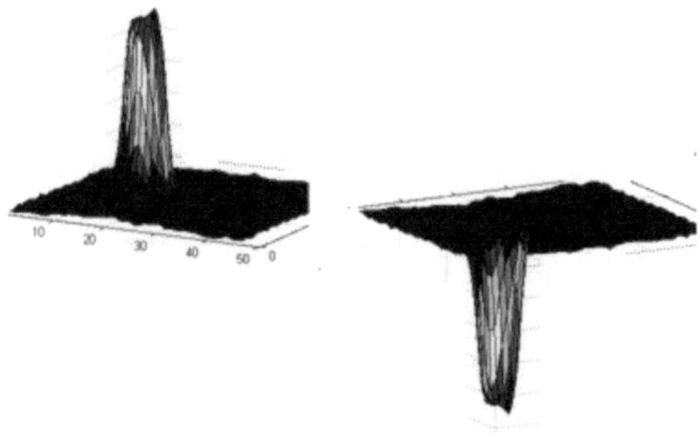

Fig. 4. By differencing two images with pan/tilt-shifted laser spots, it is possible to separate those peaks which pertain to the first image's blast from those of the second image's "blast" by noting the "up" or "down" orientation.

As discussed below, this approach allows for three-dimensional locating of each matched spot's center in a 3D reference frame that "drifts" as action is applied across the various regions of operation.

The identification of components of $\underline{\mathbf{n}}$ in the drifting3D frame in which the kinematics are locally virtually perfect, is achieved through judicious camera-space sampling of the circular cues of Figure 1 - together with corresponding robot internal joint rotations - as the end member approaches for subsequent machining, in accordance with camera-space manipulation [2]-[5]. Provided circular end-member cues are densely sampled in the very small robot-joint region where machining would occur, the benefit of having these relationships in hand is that local movement of the internal degrees of freedom can then be commanded in such a way as to recreate the surface whose unit normal is this same $\underline{\mathbf{n}}$.

The next step entails calculation, via nominal kinematics, of the 3D coordinates of each matched spot relative to the aforementioned 3D reference frame. From these many spots the best fit of $\underline{\mathbf{n}}$ and the location along $\underline{\mathbf{n}}$ of the plane are determined. The second stage of the process involves calculation from the nominal forward kinematics of the robot, and execution, of passes of the arm that will approach the final surface but not quite reach it, and that will have the same surface normal $\underline{\mathbf{n}}$ previously calculated. Intermediate sets of passes leading up to this near-terminal plane are based upon reflections of laser spots off of intermediate stages of the forming body and reflected into the controlling cameras. We have the ability to calculate these passes and execute them in such a way as to create with extreme precision a new surface that is parallel to and slightly extended beyond the prototype surface in physical space.

The third and final step in the process entails replacement of the cutting tool with an abrasion tool and sanding down to realize a polished final surface in the exact location as the original surface. This transition is indicated in the left image of Fig. 5. Part of the reason for the change in tool is that many real-world applications benefit from the last bit of material removal occurring in a polishing mode. The other part has to do with final-surface accuracy: The camera-space kinematics on the basis of which the surface calculation is made are as good as the apriori rigid-body specification of circular-cue and tip locations. While this relationship can be extremely good, tool wear is likely to make it somewhat imperfect. Fortunately, there is the prospect of a more-frequent application of the large number of laser spots in the final phases of material removal. Extreme sub-pixel, sub-millimeter precision is afforded by frequently alternating sanding passes with laser-spot application.

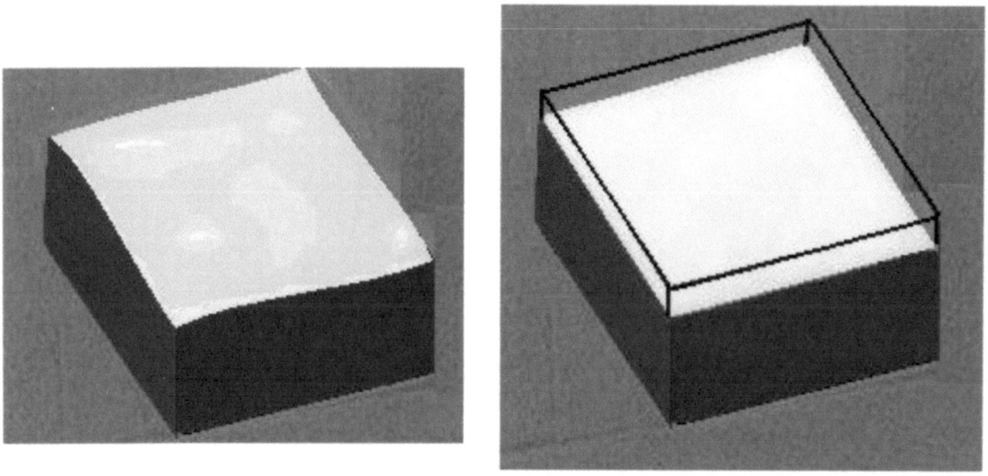

Fig. 5. The image on the left indicates the outline of the initially machined surface of orientation **n**, and the contained target surface with the same orientation. Vagaries of the sanding process used to recover the latter from the former can produce gradual, unwanted valleys and peaks in the intermediate surfaces as indicated on the right. New laser spots incident upon these intermediate surfaces can be used to adjust slightly the CSM-based sanding motion in order compensate or level the surface as movement proceeds.

Vagaries of the sanding process used to recover the final plane can produce gradual, unwanted valleys and peaks in the intermediate surfaces as indicated in Fig 5's right image. (Although experimental evidence indicates that even without measures explicitly taken to counter this variation, less than a tenth of a tenth of a mm of variation over a 20 mm^2 area attends a 1.5mm depth of material removal by sanding [3].) New laser spots incident upon these intermediate surfaces can be used to adjust slightly the CSM-based sanding motion in order to compensate or level the surface as movement proceeds. Several possible strategies may be combined to achieve such leveling, including a proportional increase over the course of the normal sanding passes of interference across those regions which are determined from intermediate-surface laser spots to be relative - if extremely gradual - peaks. "Interference" in this context is the extent of intrusion of the sanding surface beneath the current surface that would occur absent the current surface's actual, resisting, physical presence.

With this ability - using discrete, flat surfaces - the question remains: Can a similar procedure be made useful for more general surfaces which are not comprised of perfectly flat surface subdomains? We make a case below that it can.

The first part of the case returns to the argument for the four surfaces but looks at the reduction in replication accuracy as surface size diminishes. The second part considers ways in which such reduction in accuracy - both of **n** and location of the surface along **n** - will be mitigated with knowledge of adjacent-surface slope and position continuity. Finally, the argument moves to ways in which a CAD representation of the nominal shape of the body could be used to facilitate this process of exploiting continuity near the region of interest. Importantly, this is the only place in the process (apart from fabrication of the prototype piece itself, which could be achieved using a softer or otherwise more easy-to-form material) where use of any CAD data come into play; and the actual enforcement of final form is not directly based upon this information even if it is used, but rather on the laser-spot characterization of the prototype body in the images of the participant, uncalibrated cameras.

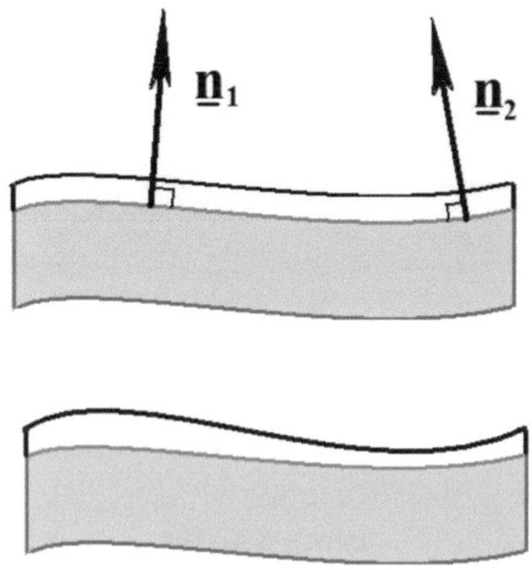

Fig. 6. Approximations $\underline{\mathbf{n}}_1$ and $\underline{\mathbf{n}}_2$ to closely spaced unit normals is established using laser spots reflected off the prototype surface. Using interpolation the outer surface is machined to approximate with upper line of the lower image the actual surface. Abrasion is finally used to remove material using relatively more interference across regions where the remaining layer is thicker.

As the sizes of the individual surfaces of Fig. 1 diminish, the separation of laser spots incident upon the prototype flats likewise diminish. This reduces the accuracy of $\underline{\mathbf{n}}$, and the points along $\underline{\mathbf{n}}$ where the surfaces are located (in the aforementioned "special" 3D coordinate system). Consideration of a continuously curving, but otherwise general, surface can be thought of as a limiting process of this flat-surface size reduction. Establishment of $\underline{\mathbf{n}}$, however, can be achieved across a larger finite region provided, at each point, the surface's third spatial derivatives are small compared to the second, i.e. locally the surface is symmetric. Surface location along $\underline{\mathbf{n}}$ will require the reduced number of more-local spots.
The initial step, indicated in Fig. 6, of approximating $\underline{\mathbf{n}}_1$ and $\underline{\mathbf{n}}_2$ can, due to local symmetry about any given surface point, be achieved using spots that fall upon the larger surface subdomain. The machining event can compensate for less accuracy of position of original-surface junctures by leaving a greater tolerance to be sanded as indicated in the lowermost of the images of Figure 6. Interpolation of approximations $\underline{\mathbf{n}}_1$ and $\underline{\mathbf{n}}_2$ to closely spaced unit normals is established using laser spots reflected off the prototype surface. Using interpolation among the closely spaced junctures would result in a variable, but similarly generous, margin across the outer surface. This is indicated with the upper line of the lower image of Fig. 6. Abrasion is finally used to remove material using relatively more interference across regions where the remaining layer is thicker.

The latter process would be limited in precision in accordance with the curvature of the prototype/replica surface at the points of interest were it not for the availability of the CAD data. To the extent that these data allow for identification of the prototype with the design information, a functional form for the region may be used to fit laser spot reflections of both original (prototype-surface) and evolving replica surfaces across a larger finite region, increasing the accuracy of the final product.

3. Experimental verification

As discussed above, laser-assisted characterization of the geometry of the object surface is based on 3D-coordinate data of the surface points. A fundamental experiment aimed at verifying shape formation would be the surface-reduction-gauging testing. In this experiment, laser-spot-assisted, 3D image analysis is applied to gauge thickness changes of a surface. The physical thickness change after removal of a flat, thin layer of material is measured by caliper and compared with the thickness change estimated using laser-spot measurement.

The robot-vision system that was set up for the surface-reduction-gauging experiment consists of a Kawasaki JS5 six DOF robot, a personal computer, three off-the-shelf CCD, monochrome, analog, industrial video cameras (JAI model CV-M50) and one single-dot laser pointer and one laser-grid pointer mounted on a pan/tilt unit. The cameras are connected to a frame grabber board (Data Translation model DT-3152), which is installed in the computer. The laser pointers cast laser spots onto the object surface. On/off of the laser pointers is controlled with a digital I/O board (CyberResearch model CYDIO-24) installed in the computer. The pan/tilt unit is a computer controlled 2-DOF mechanism. It carries the two laser pointers to illuminate the object surface and accumulates enough density of laser spots on the surface by shifting the projected laser grid.

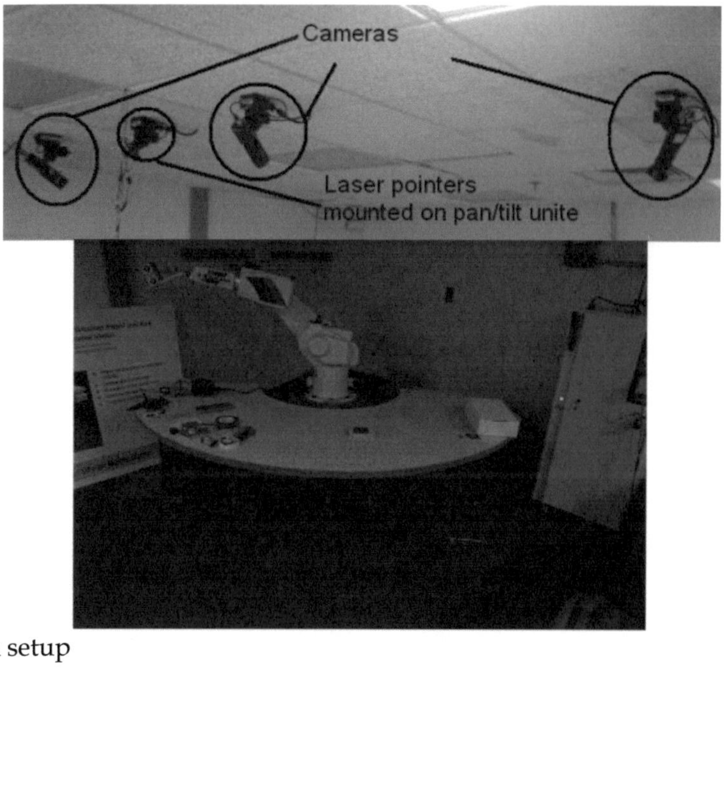

Fig. 7. System setup

The system configuration is shown in Fig. 7. Three static cameras are mounted on the ceiling, about 3 meters away from the work space. This is contained within a volume of a cube of approximately 1 m^3. The pixel resolution of the camera is 640 by 480 pixels. Each pixel represents about 2mm projected from physical space.

Two pieces of square aluminum plates were stacked on the top of each other and placed inside the workspace volume. The thickness of the top plate was measured both by calipers and laser spots. In order to test the precision of the laser-spot measurement, the variations that exist in the plate surfaces should be very small. Two 50 by 50 mm square pieces of aluminum were used in the experiment. The pieces were cut and then machined to have less than 0.01 mm surface variation. The thickness of the plate is 3.20 mm ±0.01mm.

The experiment procedure for assessing the accuracy of this approach for gauging surface reduction is briefly described here. As shown in Figure 8, the two flat plates of aluminum described above, are placed in the workspace.

Fig. 8. Metal plates

The procedure is as follows,

Step 1: Laser spots are cast down onto the top surface of the top plate. Using image differencing, detection and matching process described above, the 2D coordinates of the laser-spot centers on the top surface of the top plate are identified in three CSM cameras.

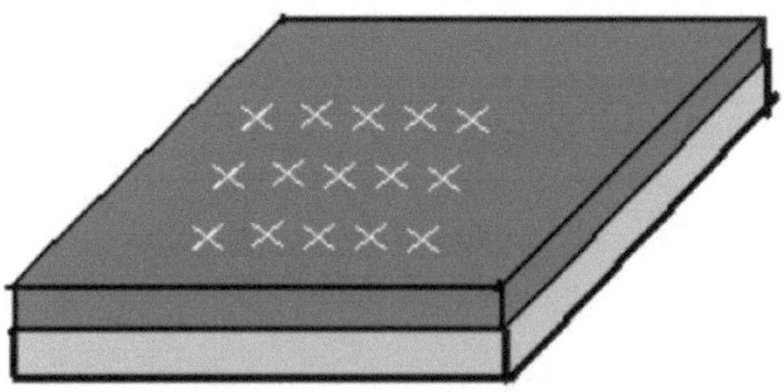

Fig. 9. Laser spots cast on the top surface of top plate

Step 2: The top plate is removed as illustrated in Fig. 10. Therefore, the thickness change of the surface is the thickness of the top plate. Laser spots are cast onto the top surface of the lower plate. The 2D coordinates of the laser-spot centers on the top surface of the lower plate are identified in the same three CSM cameras.

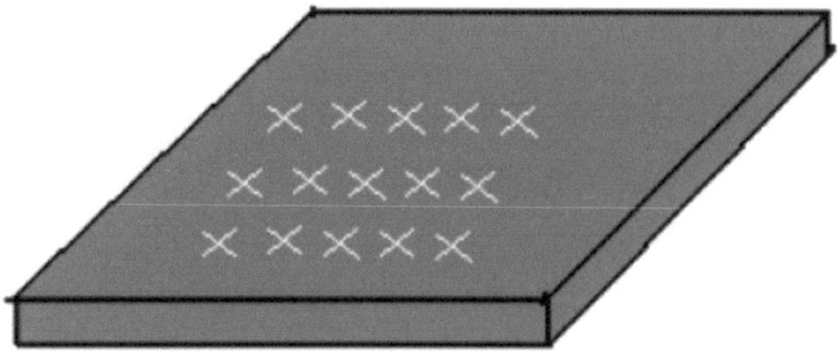

Fig. 10. Laser spots cast on the top surface of lower plate

Step 3: After the two sets of laser-spot 2D-coordinate data are stored in computer memory, cue-bearing plates mounted on the robot are introduced into the same physical region as the two stacked plates, as shown in Fig.11.

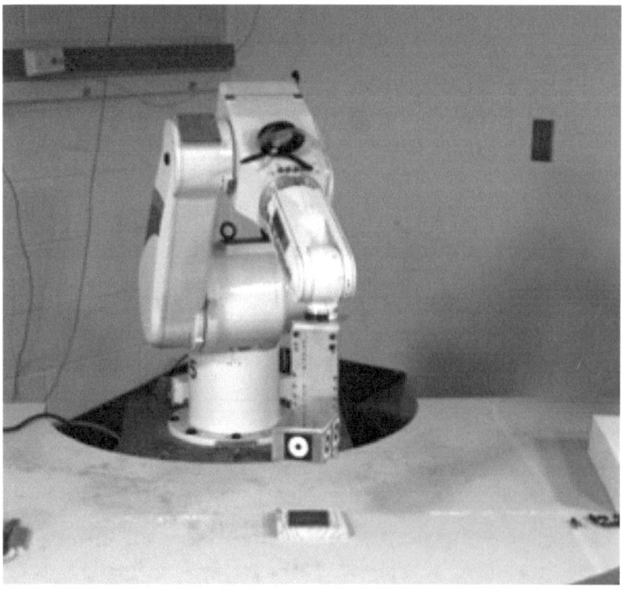

Fig. 11. Cue-bearing plates approach workpiece

Step 4: Newly sampled cues and the joint coordinates of the robot in corresponding poses were used to update, locally, the camera-space kinematics. Then, with the new local mapping model and the two sets of laser-spot 2D-coordinate data in each camera space, the 3D coordinates of surface spots were estimated relative to the nominal world frame.

Step 5: The surface points on the top plate are fit to a plane using least squares. The distance from the plane to the surface points on the lower plate are calculated. The average distance is the estimate of the thickness of the removed plate. In step 1 and step 2 the number of laser spots cast on the top surface is varied from 100 to 2000 in various tests. The laser-spot-array direction can be shifted slightly using the pan/tilt unit to cast down new surface spots, allowing for accumulation of a virtually unlimited density of points on the surface regions of interest. A different test consisted of placing multiple paper cues on the top surface of the lower plate, instead of the laser spots, as illustrated in Fig. 12.

Fig. 12. Multiple paper cues on surface

The paper cues placed on the surface are the same circular geometry as those borne on the plate mounted on the robot end effector. The 2D coordinates of the cues were identified in three CSM cameras and nominal 3D coordinates of the cues were estimated as the surface-point data, which was applied in same process as step 5, in order to calculate the thickness of the removed plate

4. Experiment result and discussion

The known thickness of the metal plate is 3.20 mm±0.01mm. The calculated average thickness using about 100 spots (accumulated from multiple images) for estimation is listed in Table 1.

Test Number	Thickness measured (mm) by 100 laser spots vs. 100 laser spots	Thickness measured (mm) by 100 laser spots vs. 100 cues
1	3.27	3.28
2	3.15	3.18
3	3.21	3.18
4	3.16	3.25
5	3.17	3.10

Table 1. Experiment result

The precision of thickness gauging is consistently within one tenth of a millimeter. It is one order of magnitude higher than image resolution. This sub-pixel level of accuracy was consistent throughout the robot's workspace, and for a range of plate orientations.
Why is the laser-spot-assisted, 3D image analysis able to estimate the CSM target shift with sub-pixel accuracy despite the large random error from the coarse pixel quantization of camera space together with error associated with the 3D-coordinate estimation of laser spots in CSM nominal world frame? An error consists of two parts, deterministic error and random error. The deterministic error was cancelled because the thickness assessment is from the difference of two sets of laser spots, which have the same deterministic offset due to the proximity in distance and continuous mapping of surfaces points in camera space to the same body's position and orientation. Therefore, only the random error was left in thickness gauging results and the each laser spot's position assessment is virtually zero-mean. With the advantage of the effect of averaging to filter out the image-discretization and other noise, a large number of laser spots could achieve high certainty and precision. The above experimental result is the proof. The histogram summary of 10 trials is shown in Fig. 13. The data clearly show that the error of thickness gauging is random with normal distribution.

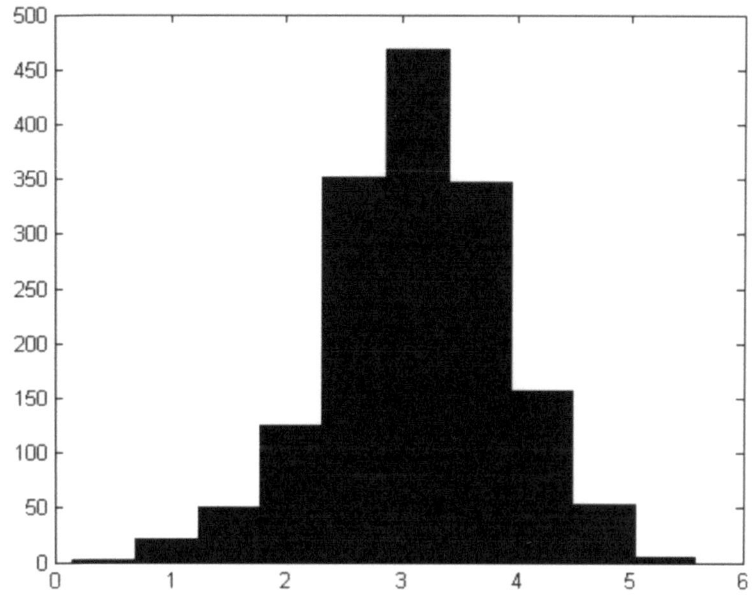

Fig. 13. Histogram of surface points vs. thickness

The normal distribution of the random error brings up the issue of level of certainty. The practical question pertaining to this certainty issue is what a sufficient number of laser spots cast on the surface of an object needs to be in order to guarantee each individual assessment is within a certain prescribed precision. In another words, what is a sufficient density of laser spots cast on the surface, in spots per unit area on a flat surface in order to characterize the geometry of the surface with designated accuracy? The variation of the error is measured by standard deviation (STD σ) in statistics. It allows one to deduce the relationship between the number of laser spots (samples) and the certainty of the individual assessment (mean μ) for answering the question. Table 2 shows STD σ of the individual assessments of plate thickness for the five tests.

Test Number	Mean (μ) of thickness (mm) with 100 samples	STD (σ) of individual assessment of thickness (mm) with 100 samples
1	3.27	0.772
2	3.11	0.7653
3	3.21	0.7383
4	3.12	0.7347
5	3.14	0.7732
STD of the mean of the 5 tests	0.068	

Table 2. Standard deviation of the individual assessments of plate thickness

As illustrated in Fig. 14, the individual thickness assessments have about a 68% probability of falling within the range between mean (μ)−STD (σ) and mean (μ)+STD(σ), as expected with a normal distribution.

As presented in [6], consider a random process with standard deviation σ_1. A second random process can derived from the first one by taking out m samples (m>1) from the first process and average their values to be a sample for the second process. The samples from the second random process have a standard deviation of σ_m. The relationship between the σ_m and σ_1 is:

$$\sigma_m^2 = \sigma_1^2/m$$

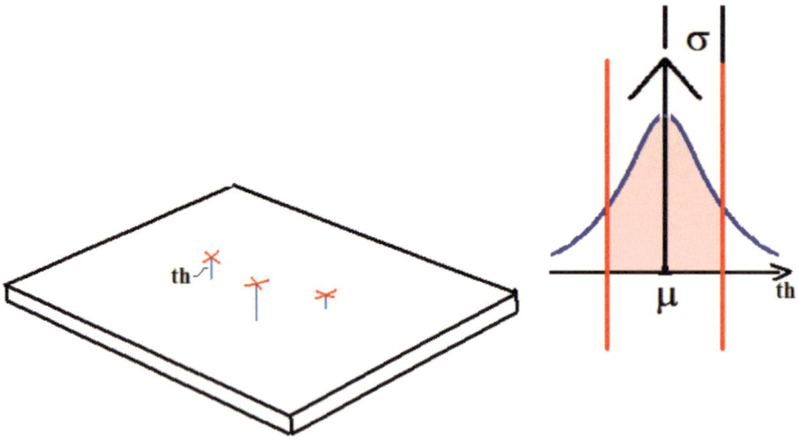

Fig. 14. Normal distribution of individual thickness assessment

In the present case, the predicted (σ_{100}), STD of 100 samples' mean in the thickness-gauging experiment result, is about 0.07 according to this statistical analysis. The actual STD of the mean of the 5 tests with 100 samples is 0.068, which agrees with the statistical analysis. This relationship was also proven using 2000 spots tests.

In the experiment results of Table 2, the third column shows that the same high precision of thickness gauging occurred in the test of placing multiple paper cues on the surface of the lower plate instead of casting laser spots after the top plate was removed. This result proves that there is no significant detection bias between the laser-spot detection and cue detection in camera space. In other words, there is no bias between 2D position of the detected center of cue and laser spot in camera space if they occupy same physical location. (The "physical location" of the laser-spot center is not, strictly speaking, actually defined. What the tests indicate is that, on average, the software places each camera's camera-space center of a given laser spot in such a way as to represent the same surface juncture in all three cameras.) This seems unsurprising, but thinking how different are the appearances of the cue and laser spot in physical space, there are enough reasons to doubt this no-bias result to warrant physical proof. Among the reasons for a possible bias is the fact that laser spots are incident on the surface from a particular angle, and this angle will vary with any shift in the workpiece or laser-pointer base.

The CSM targets established by laser-spot-assisted, 3D image analysis are ultimately for the robot to position the point of interest on a robot's end effector with high precision. CSM's high precision is fundamentally based on the premise that a point or juncture attached on the robot end effector collocates the target point in 3D physical space when these two junctures collocate in at least two cameras' camera spaces. So the non-bias detection of position between cue and laser spot is a critical premise to extend the CSM high-precision positioning where laser spots are used to establish camera-space targets.

In step 3 of the thickness-reduction experiment, cue-bearing plates mounted on the robot were introduced into the same physical region as the two stacked plates. The newly sampled cues and the joint coordinates of the robot in corresponding poses were applied to update local mapping between the camera space object is 2D coordinates and robot joint coordinates. Then, with the new local mapping and the two sets of laser-spot 2D camera-space coordinates stored in computer memory, the 3D coordinates of surface spots were estimated relative to nominal world frame. Though, in the thickness-gauging experiment, the robot doesn't need to position its end effector to the target with high precision, in real world applications the CSM targets established by laser-spot-assisted 3D image analysis are used for robot positioning. So the experimental studies of step 3 were performed in same situation as real applications.

5. Summary and conclusion

The surface-reduction-gauging experiment proves the ability of laser-spot assisted, 3D image analysis to characterize the geometry of the surface and provide the CSM target with high precision. It also discloses the extent of measurement precision of surface-reduction gauging and reveals the relationship between the density of laser spots cast on the surface, in spots per unit area, to the accuracy of the characterized geometry of surface.

The experimental results also prove the following three premises of the surface extent application of laser spots using CSM-based 3D nominal World-frame-coordinate estimation:

Though the nominal optical model and nominal robot kinematics model in the CSM system are globally imperfect, the premise is that as long as the laser spots are close enough to each other within the asymptotic-limit region or volume the relative error between them is close to zero-mean. Therefore, any error on the CSM side does not propagate into the measurement of surface reduction relative to an as-located original surface. The experiment repeatedly proves the premise for a range of surface positions and orientations.

Another premise is that error in thickness assessment with laser-spot data is unbiased and random. This means that, provided they are matched, a laser-spot center detected in each camera corresponds to one single physical juncture on the object's surface. In other words, only error in thickness assessment with laser-spot data can be averaged out by applying a large amount of laser-spot data on the surfaces. The results of the above experiment repeatedly verify this premise.

There is no bias between 2D position of the detected center of a circular cue and that of a laser spot in camera space if they occupy same physical location. (The "physical location" of the laser-spot center is not, strictly speaking, actually defined. What the tests indicate is that, on average, the software places each camera's camera-space center of a given laser spot in such a way as to represent the same surface juncture in all three cameras.)

High-precision surface-change gauging extends the vision-guided-robot system based on CSM into a more potent surface-operating system, one that in practice only can be done by humans, and this in an imprecise, non-uniform, and often ineffective way. A number of surface-finishing tasks entail application of force or pressure combined with in-plane motion in order to achieve a scrubbing, polishing or sanding effect. Such tasks often make use of human dexterity and effort, which can result in repetitive-motion injury and incomplete or uneven treatment of the surface. But with high-precision surface reduction gauging and

CSM, our vision-guided robot system can accomplish these tasks efficiently and uniformly. Material removal can be monitored and surface reduction gauged and controlled to within approximately one tenth of a millimeter.

6. References

Steven B. Skaar and Guillermo Del Castillo Revisualizing Robotics: New DNA for Surviving a World of Cheap Labor, 2006.

González-Galván E.J., Loredo-Flores A., Cervantes-Sanchez J.J., Aguilera-Cortes L.A., Skaar, S.B., "An Optimal Path-generation Algorithm for Surface Manufacturing of Arbitrarily Curved Surfaces using Uncalibrated Vision". Robotics and Computer-Integrated Manufacturing. Vol. 24, No. 1, pp. 77-91. 2008.

Zhang, Biao. Three-dimensional laser-assisted image analysis for robotic surface operation with camera-space manipulation. Ph.D. Dissertation. University of Notre Dame. 2007.

Gonzalez-Galvan E.J., Pazos-Flores F., Skaar S.B., Cardenas-Galindo A., "Camera Pan/Tilt to Eliminate the Workspace Size/Pixel-Resolution Tradeoff with Camera-Space Manipulation". Robotics and Computer-Integrated Manufacturing, 18(2), Elsevier Science Press, pp. 95-104. 2002.

Gonzalez-Galvan,E.J., Skaar,S.B., Korde,U.A., Chen,W.Z. "Application of a Precision Enhancing Measure in 3-D Rigid-Body Positioning Using Camera-Space Manipulation" The International Journal of Robotics Research ISSN 0278-3649. Vol. 16, No.2, pp.240-257. 1997.

Dietrich C., Uncertainty, Calibration and Probability: The Statistics of Scientific and Industrial Measurement, 2nd edition. Page 29, CRC Press, January, 1991.

8

Humanoid with Interaction Ability Using Vision and Speech Information

Junichi Ido*, Ryuichi Nisimura**, Yoshio Matsumoto*
and Tsukasa Ogasawara*
**Nara Institute of science and technology,*
***Wakayama university*
Japan

1. Introduction

Recently, there are many research on harmonized human robot interaction in the real environment (Honda; Suzuki et al., 2002). Speech recognition is useful for human-robot communication, and there are many robots that have such interface (Asoh et al., 2001) (Matsusaka et al., 2001). Some interface use non-verbal information such as facial expression and gaze, which are also seen as important for interaction. We have developed a reception guidance humanoid robot "ASKA", which can interact with humans using verbal and non-verbal information such as gaze direction, head pose and lip motion (Ido et al., 2003).

Fig. 1. Humanoid robot HRP-2 interacting with a user using vision and speech information

In this paper, we introduce a humanoid robot system for human-robot communication research. Fig.1 shows the overview of our humanoid robot HRP-2. This humanoid robot system with interaction ability was developed at NAIST (Nara Institute of Science and Technology) under the collaboration of Robotics and Speech Laboratories. It is used as a research platform to develop an intelligent real-world interface using various information technologies studied in our institute. The following functions are implemented for human-robot interaction:

1. Speech recognition
2. Voice synthesizing
3. Facial information measurement
4. Portrait drawing
5. Gesture recognition

The dialogue system which use a large vocabulary continuous speech recognition, and the eye contact system, which use a facial information measurement system, are the unique features of this robot. The rest of this paper is organized as follows: First, the design concepts are discussed in Section 2. The hardware and software system configuration are described separately in Section 3. In Section 4, the voice interface implemented in this system is explained. The interaction modules using visual information are explained in Section 5. In section 6, are explained the demonstration and the experiment in which a person interacts with the humanoid. Finally, we summarize our research and future works in Section 7.

2. Design concept

Our robot system has been designed based on two concepts: (1) as a research platform for various information technologies, and (2) as an achievement of human-robot interaction.

2.1 Research platform

The main objective in the early stage of its development was to build a research platform for various information technologies using a robot. The software architecture was designed based on this concept. Fig.4 shows a simple configuration in which each module communicates its own status and sensory information to the server. Each module runs independently and can start and stop at an arbitrary timing. This modularity enables rapid development and easy maintenance of the modules.

2.2 Human-robot interaction

The information utilized for face-to-face communication is classified in two major categories, "verbal" and "non-verbal" information. Although the primary information in communication is the former, the latter, such as facial direction, gaze and gesture, is recently emphasized as a mean of natural human-robot interaction. We focus on face direction and gesture information in this research and try to achieve more natural interaction by combining them with speech information. In the next section, we describe how the software and the hardware of our system are constructed. The typical scenario of the interaction is also described.

3. System configuration

3.1 Hardware configuration

The system is composed of a humanoid body, stereo cameras, hand-held microphones, a speaker and several PCs as shown in Fig.2. HRP-2 (KAWADA Industries, Inc.) is used as the humanoid body. A stereo camera system with four IEEE1394 cameras (Flea, Point Grey Research Inc.), eight tiny microphones and an 8ch A/D board (TD-BD-8CSUSB, Tokyo Electron Device Ltd.) are installed in the head of HPR-2. Eight built-in microphones attached to the head are connected to the on-board vision PC via A/D board, and 8ch speech signals can be captured simultaneously. Additionally, a hand-held microphone can be connected to an external PC for speech recognition. Switching between these two microphone systems is achieved by software. The use of the hand-held microphone enables the interaction in places where the background noise is large to such an extent that recognition using the built-in microphone fails. Two external PCs are used besides the PC built into the robot. One of them is used for the speech recognition and speech synthesis, and the other is used as the terminal PC of the robot.

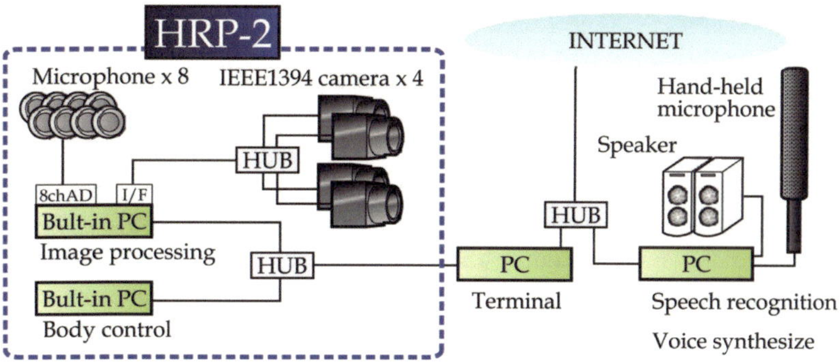

Fig. 2. Hardware configuration

A special chair, as shown in Fig. 3, was built in order for HRP-2 to sit down drawing the experiment. Regrettably, HRP-2 cannot seat itself because it has to be bolted to the chair for stability as shown Fig. 3.

Fig. 3. HRP-2 fixed on a chair

3.2 Software configuration

The basic software of this system consists of six modules:

- Speech Recognition Module
- Speech Synthesizing Module

- Face Tracking Module
- Gesture Recognition Module
- Portrait Drawing Module
- Body Gesture Controller Module

In our system, the Face Tracking Module, the Gesture Recognition Module and the Portrait Drawing Module are all used as Visual Measurement Modules, and they are connected to the vision subserver. The speech recognition module has an independent interface called "adintool" to record, split, send and receive speech data. These interfaces enable to select the speech input with no influence on the other modules.

These modules run on the distributed PCs and communicate with a server program by socket communication over TCP/IP protocols as shown in Fig. 4. This is a simple implementation of the blackboard system (Nii, 1986). The server collects all the information (sensory information and status of execution) from all the client modules. Each client module can access the server to obtain any information in order to decide what actions to take. Each module runs independently and can start and stop at an arbitrary timing. This modularity enables the rapid development and easy maintenance of the modules.

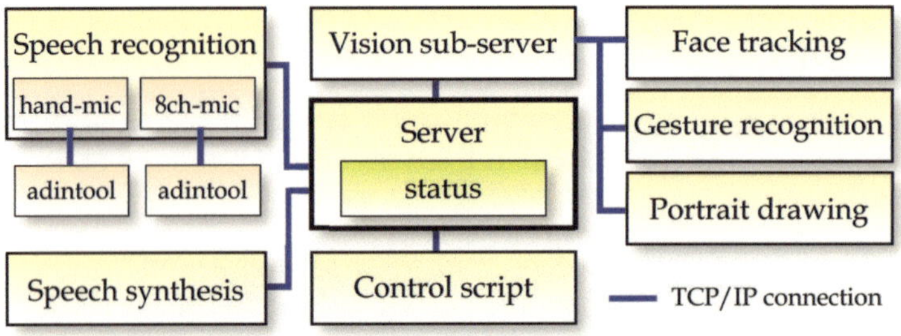

Fig. 4. Software configuration

3.3 Interaction scenario

HRP-2 sitting opposite to a user across a table can detect face and gaze directions of the user and recognize the question asked by the user. The typical scenario of the interaction between a user and the humanoid is as follows:

1. The humanoid detects the direction of the user's face.
2. When the face direction of the user is detected to be facing the humanoid, the user is regarded as having an intention to talk to the humanoid. The user can then talk with gestures to humanoid.
3. The humanoid recognizes the question and makes a response with voice and gesture or carries out an ordered task.

The speech dialogue system of the humanoid can answer the following questions:

- Office and laboratory locations
- Extension telephone numbers of staffs
- Locations of university facilities
- Today's weather report, news and current time
- Greetings

In addition to these questions, commands such as "pass the objects" or "draw a portrait" can be recognized and carried out. The training corpus used for speech recognition is described in the following section.

The motions comprising the gesture responses are defined beforehand using a dedicated software, "Motion Creator" (Nakaoka et al., 2004). These responses are linked to its corresponding sentences manually.

4. Voice interface using speech and noise recognition

The voice interface of our system was developed to contain two parallel sound recognition methods to be able to have flexible interactions with users. We implemented a spoken dialogue routine based on a continuous speech recognition technology with a large vocabulary dictionary for accepting users' various utterances. We also introduced a nonstationarynoise recognition program based on likelihood measurements using Gaussian Mixture Models (GMMs). It realizes not only rejection mechanisms of environmental noises, but also novel human-robot interaction schemes by discerning unintended user's voices such as laughter, coughing, and so on. This section explains about the speech recognition and the noise recognition.

4.1 Speech recognition

The continuous speech recognition has accomplished remarkable performance. However, sufficient accuracy when recognizing natural spontaneous utterances has not been attained yet. To obtain higher accuracy, we needed to organize task-suitable statistical models beforehand.

Our speech recognition engine, "Julius" (Lee et al., 2001) requires a language model and an acoustic model as statistical knowledge.

For an acoustic model, we use the speaker-independent PTM (Lee et al., 2000) triphone HMM (Hidden Markov Model). The model can deal with an appearance probability of phonemes with considering context dependent co-articulations consisting of the current phoneme and its left and right phonemes.

An acoustic model for the HRP-2 was trained from the following data using HTK (Hidden Markov Model Toolkit) (Young et al., 2002):

- **Dialog** Natural users' utterances in using actual dialogue system (24,809 utterances).
- **JNAS** Reading style speech by speakers, extracted from the JNAS (Japanese Newspaper Article Sentences) (Itou et al., 1999) database (40,086 utterances).

Dialog data are actual human-machine dialogue data extracted from utterance logs collected by a long-term field test of our spoken dialogue system "Takemaru-kun System" (Nisimura et al., 2005), which has been deployed in a public city office since November 2002 and operated every business day. We have obtained over 300,000 recorded inputs as of February 2005. The accuracy improvement of natural utterance recognition can be obtained efficiently by using these actual conversation data. We can also say that the built model can obtain better performance for recognition of child voices because the **Dialog** data contains many voices uttered by children. See (Nisimura et al., 2004) for details.

The training data of the acoustic model included the **JNAS** data due to the necessities of holding a large amount of speech data in building the model.

We adopted a word trigram model as the language model, which is one of the major statistical methods in modeling appearance probabilities of a sequence of words (Jelinek, 1990). There are two well-known task description approaches in continuous speech recognition: (1) finite state network grammar, and (2) word trigram language model. Finite state network grammar is usually adopted for small restricted tasks. By using a statistical method instead of a network grammar, some utterances even in out-of-domain task are correctly recognized. Utterances including various expression styles can also be recognized more flexibly than with the network grammar based recognition. In order to train the model, a training corpus consisting of the following texts was prepared:

- **Dialog** Transcribed utterances collected by the field testing Takemaru-kun system (15,433 sentences).
- **Web** Texts extracted from web pages (826,278 sentences).
- **Chat** Texts extracted from Internet Relay Chat (IRC) logs (2,720,134 sentences).
- **TV** Texts of request utterances in operating a television through a spoken dialogue interface (4,256 sentences).

We produced a vocabulary dictionary which includes 41,443 words, each appearing 20 or more times in the corpus. Then, language model tools provided from IPA Japanese free dictation program project (Itou et al., 2000) was used to build a baseline model. Finally, a task-dependent network grammar was adapted to the model. We wrote a finite state network grammar for the HRP-2 task, which included 350 words. Adaptation was performed by strengthening the trigram probabilities in the baseline model on the basis of word-pair constraints in the written grammar. This method enables more accurate recognition of in-task utterances while keeping the acceptability of statistical model against unexpected utterances.

Class	# of training data
Adult voice	7,497
Child voice	7,503
Laughter	849
Coughing	321
Beating by hand	101
Beating by soft hammer	104
Background noise	5,000
Other noise	6,380

Sampling rate/bit	16 kHz, 16 bit
Window width/shift	25/19 msec
Parameter	MFCC (12 dim.), ΔMFCC, ΔPower
Mixtures of Gaussian	64

Table 1. Training Conditions of GMMs

4.2 Noise recognition

We introduced noise recognition programs to the HRP-2 to realize a novel human-robot interaction that mediates unintended sound inputs, such as coughing, laughing, and other impulsive noises. Although noises have been deleted as needless inputs in a general dialogue system (Lee et al., 2004), the proposed system can continue to dialogue with humans while recognizing a noise category.

We investigated sound verification to determine whether the inputted voice was intended by comparison of acoustic likelihood given by GMMs. GMMs have proven to be powerful for text-independent speech verification technique. Although conventional speech verification studies have only focused on environmental noises, our previous studies found that GMMs can also discriminate more utterance-like inputs.

Table 1 shows the training conditions of GMMs, where training data were recorded through a microphone used when performing a spoken dialogue for the HRP-2. When laughter or coughing is recognized, the response corresponding to the recognition result is returned to the user. To realize the identification of the voice and non-voice, adult and child's voices were included in the training data. If the input is identified as voice, the system executes a normal spoken dialogue routine. "Beating by hand" and "Beating by soft hammer" indicate impulsive noises when a user beats the head of HRP-2 by hand or by a soft hammer. The system will use the identification result of beatings for dealing with mischief from users when the robot is installed in a house.

8-class GMMs with 64 Gaussian mixtures were made from each class training data. As for an acoustic parameter, we adopted the mel frequency cepstral coefficients (MFCC), which is a major parameter when analyzing human voices for speech recognitions. The class of GMM that has the highest acoustic likelihood against parameters of input sound is chosen as an output.

4.3 Dialogue strategy

The spoken dialogue strategy of our system was designed based on a simple principle. Candidate responses to a user's question are prepared beforehand. Selection of a suitable response among the candidates is performed by keyword or key-phrase matching mechanism. We defined keywords for each candidate. After recording the user's voice, the number of keywords matched with recognized text is totaled for all prepared candidates. The system will choose the most matched candidate as a response. In this procedure, the N-best output is used as the speech recognition result that complements recognition errors.

5. Interaction system using visual information

Our system obtains gray-scale images from the stereo camera system installed in the head, and the following three vision based functions were implemented; facial information measurement, pointing gesture recognition and portrait drawing. These functions are described in the following sections.

5.1 Facial information measurement

The face and gaze information provides important information showing intentions and interests of a human. In a previous study, it is shown that humans tend to be conscious of an object at the time of utterance (Kendon, 1967). Facial module is based on a facial measurement system (Matsumoto et al., 2000) and sends measured parameters such as the pose and the position of the head and the gaze direction to the server via network. This module tracks the face using a 3D facial model of the user, and measures various facial information such as head position and orientation, gaze direction, blinks and lip motions. **Fig. 5** illustrates the 3D facial model, which consists of template images of facial features and their 3D coordinates. The position and orientation of the head is calculated by fitting the 3D facial model to the set of 3D measurements of the facial features based on the following equation:

$$E = \sum_{i=0}^{N-1} w_i (Rx_i + t - y_i)^T (Rx_i + t - y_i)$$

where E is the fitting error, N is the number of facial features, x_i is the position vector of each feature in the 3D facial model, y_i is the measured 3D position of the corresponding feature obtained from the current image, and w_i is the reliability of the measurements. T and R are the translation vector and the rotation matrix to be estimated. The problem of achieving the best fitting boils down to finding a set of T and R which minimizes the fitting error E, and can be solved by Steepest Descent Method.

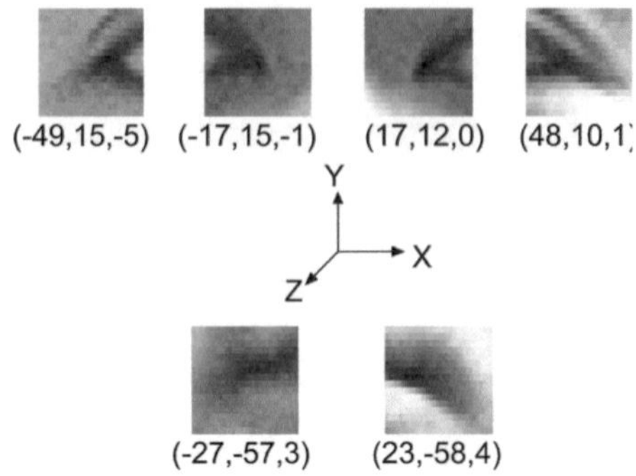

Fig. 5. 3D facial model

How to estimate the gaze direction is illustrated in Fig. 6. As the position and orientation of the head is estimated, the position and the size of the eyeball in the image can be estimated assuming that it is located at a fixed position inside the head. If the position of the iris (or the pupil) can be detected in the image, the relative (vertical and horizontal) position of the iris and the center of the eyeball in the image produces the 3D direction of the gaze. Fig. 7 shows how the facial information is measured. In this figure, rectangles indicate feature areas in a face utilized for tracking, and the two lines indicate gaze direction. The main purpose of this measurement is to detect valid speech period. The speech input is recognized only after the user turns his face to HRP-2. Therefore, the robot does not recognize utterances directed to other people. We regard this function as a simple implementation of "eye contact."

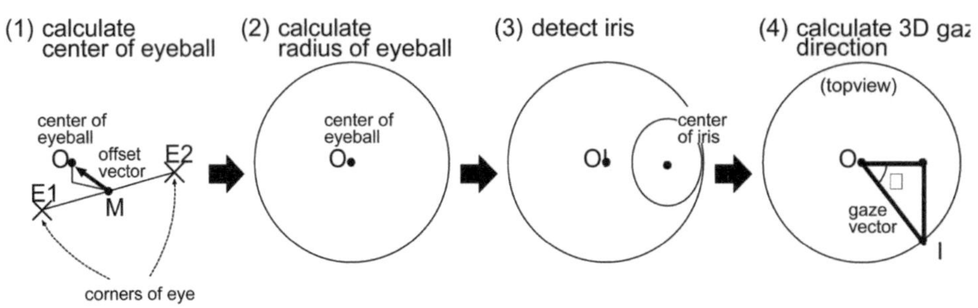

Fig. 6. Modeling of gaze

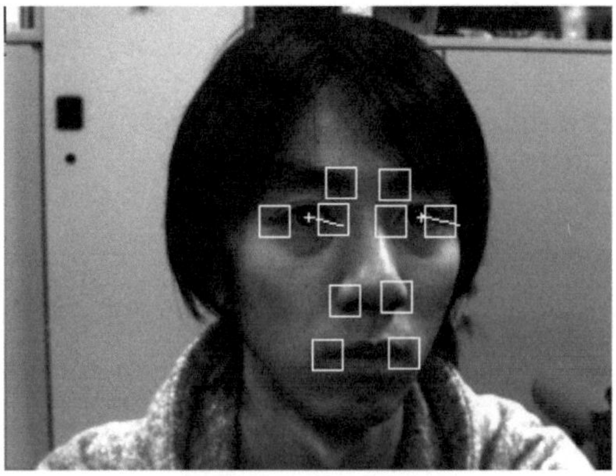

Fig. 7. Facial information measurement

5.2 Point gesture recognition

The gesture recognition module which recognizes simple pointing gesture is described. Gestures such as motion of the head help attain clearer communication. Furthermore, gestures which points to directions are important when considering guiding tasks. If the robot can recognize only speech it is difficult to make natural communication because demonstrative pronouns are often used in such a situation. Pointing gesture recognition module used depth information generated by correlation based on SAD (Sum of Absolute Difference). Fig. 8 is an example of the disparity map. The process of recognizing the pointing gesture is as follows:

1. The disparity map is generated after correcting for lens distortion.
2. The pointing direction is detected on the supposition that the closest part of the user to the robot in the disparity map is the user's hand.

The recognition of the pointing gesture enables HRP-2 to respond, even if a user gives questions with demonstrative pronoun. For example, HRP-2 can choose and pass a proper newspaper to the user when it is asked "Pass me that newspaper" with a pointing gesture.

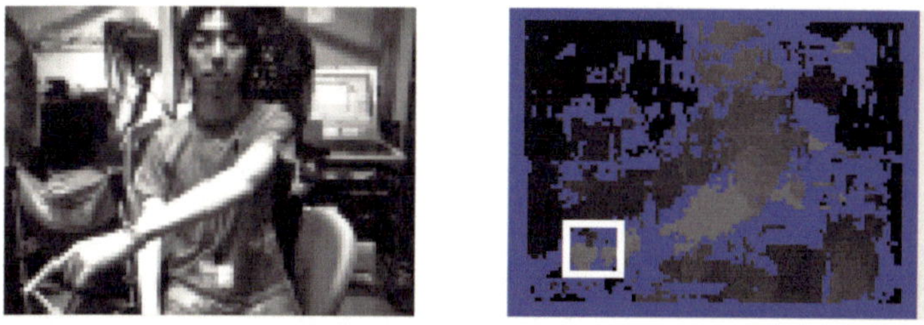

Fig. 8. Pointing gesture recognition based on depth image

5.3 Portrait drawing

The third module using vision information, the portrait drawing module, is described here. This module literally provides the functionality of drawing a portrait as shown in Fig. 9. This function was implemented to show that HRP-2 can perform skillful tasks with its motion in addition to communicating with a user in the demonstration. From a technical viewpoint, portrait drawing requires the segmentation of the face region from the background. The procedures to draw the portrait of a user are as follows:

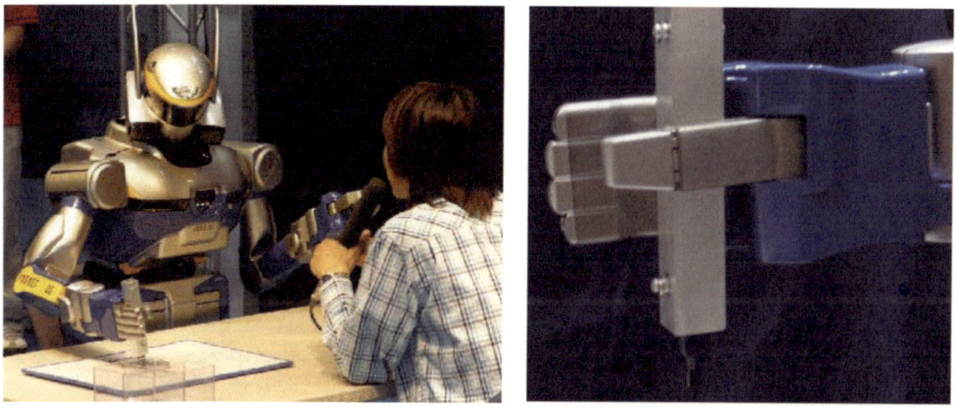

(a) HRP-2 while drawing portrait (b) Pen holder

Fig. 9. HRP-2 drawing portrait of a user

1. When the module detects using the foregoing facial information that the user has turned his face to HRP-2, a still image of the user is captured.
2. A canny edge image, a depth mask image and an ellipsoid mask image are generated.
3. The face region is extracted from the edge image using the mask data.
4. The face image is converted to a sequence of points by chain method.
5. The sequence of points are sorted and thinned.
6. HRP-2 draws a portrait using the generated data.

When the user requests a portrait to be drawn by HRP-2, it asks the user to pass the pen and to turn the user's face toward the robot. Then it captures an image as shown in Fig.10 (A). An edge image using Canny's algorithm (Fig. 10 (B)) is generated by the appropriate face image. A depth mask image (Fig. 10 (C)), and an ellipsoid mask image (Fig. 10 (D)) are generated by two kinds of data, the stereo image pair and the measurement value of face position. Fig. 10 (E) shows the facial part extracted from the whole edge image using the masks. The portrait is drawn on an actual white-board by HRP-2 using the sequence data generated. Inverse kinematics for eight degrees of freedom is solved under the condition that the pose of the pen is kept vertical. After the sequence of hand positions is determined, the hand moves interpolating these points. Fig. 10 (F) shows the resulting image drawn on the whiteboard. When HRP-2 actually draws a portrait, it uses a felt-tip pen with a holder that was designed to help it grasp and absorb the position errors of the hand by a built-in spring (Fig. 9 (b)).

6. Experiment

6.1 Facial information while talking with the robot

We implemented the dialog system using simple "eye contact." However, it is not clea whether a user looks at the robot's face when talking with the humanoid robot. Therefore we conducted an interaction experiment in a public exhibition to answer this question. To investigate the facial information of users while talking with the humanoid robot, images from the camera attached to its head were stored for subsequent analysis. Some examples of these images are shown in Fig.11. Subjects were fifteen visitors who consist of five men, five women and five children. After we gave a simplified explanation about the robot, users talked with the robot freely. In this experiment, the robot sitting opposite to a user across a table always respond to the user's utterances without face and gaze information. Users spoke to the robot for about 14 seconds on average, which included about 10 sentences. Users sometimes spoke to other people such as staffs or their accompanying persons. The total time for talking to others beside the robot averages about 4 seconds per person.

We analyzed how often users turned their face and gaze to the robot's face when speaking to the robot. As a result, users gazed at the robot at a rate of 69% and turn their face to it at the rate of 95% on average when speaking to the humanoid robot.

This result shows that people tend to look at the face when they talk to a humanoid robot. It also indicates that our dialog system using eye contact works well regardless of user's age or gender.

6.2 Interaction experiment with two users

In order to investigate accuracy of our dialogue system using "eye contact", we experimented on an interaction with two people. Two users sat opposite to the robot across a table. One of them talked to the other and to the robot based on the scenario given before. The built-in microphones were used for speech recognition. The number of subjects was 10 pairs. The scenario was composed of 7 "person-to-person" sentences, 4 "person-to-robot" sentences and 4 responses from the robot.

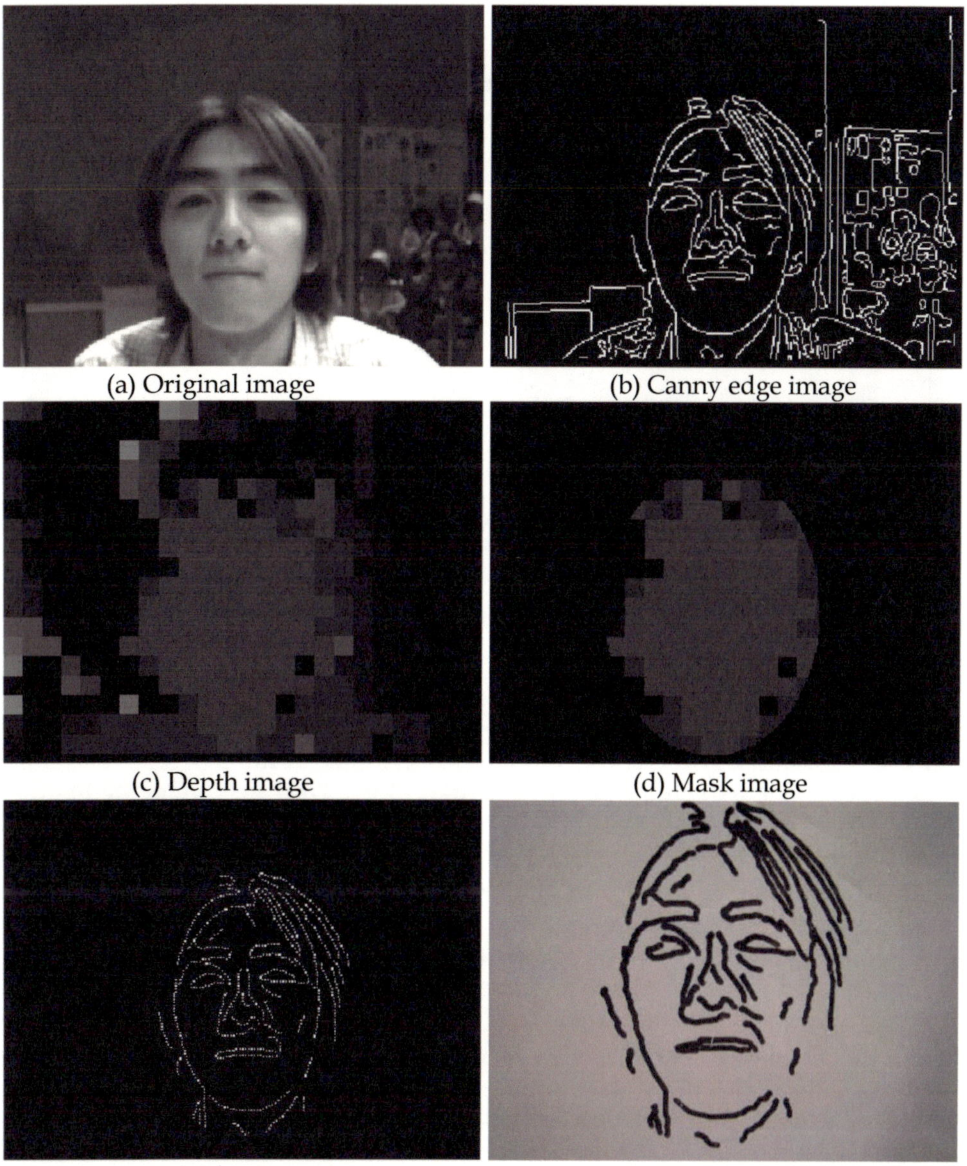

(a) Original image (b) Canny edge image

(c) Depth image (d) Mask image

(e) Line segment data (f) Resulting image

Fig. 10. Portrait drawing process

Fig. 11. Visitors talking to the humanoid robot

Fig.12 shows the ratio of false responses to the conversations between the users. Without using eye contact, this ratio was 75.7[%] on average, and it dropped down to 4.3 [%] when the robot utilized eye contact information effectively. This result shows that the utilization of eye contact information improved the accuracy of response.

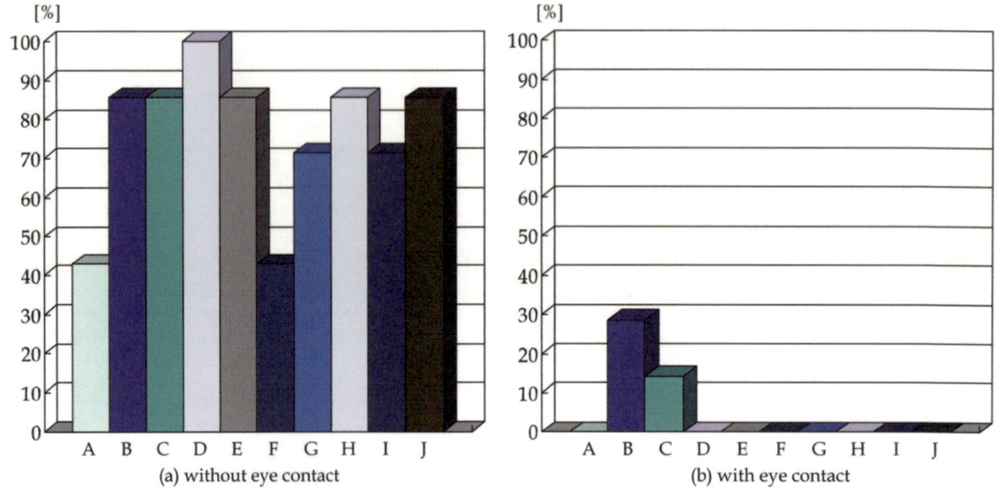

Fig. 12. Ratio of false response

6.3 Demonstration

We verified the usefulness of our system in a real environment through a demonstration in the Prototype Robot Exhibition at Aichi World EXPO 2005 as shown in Fig.13. The exhibition area was so noisy, full of audience and with simultaneously held demonstrations that hand-held microphone was utilized in the demonstration. The nonstationary noise recognition system was utilized for recognizing users' coughing to start talking about cold in the demo scenario. When connected to the Internet, HRP-2 can answer questions on weather information, news headlines and so on.

The uncontrollable lighting condition was also crucial for image processing. However, since our method does not relies on skin color detection which is known to be sensitive to lighting condition, the face measurement and gesture recognition was robust enough in such an environment. HRP-2 was also able to draw a portrait by extracting the face of the user from cluttered background. Our demonstration was successfully carried-out for two weeks without problems.

7. Conclusion

The HRP-2 is a speech-oriented humanoid robot system which realizes natural multi-modal interaction between human and robot. This system has a vision and a speech dialogue system to communicate with visitors. The voice interface that has two aspects was implemented on the HRP-2 to realize flexible interactions with users. One is the spoken dialogue routine based on a continuous speech recognition technology with a large vocabulary dictionary, and the other is a non-stationary noise recognition system. We also implemented the face measurement function in order for the humanoid to realize "eye contact" with the user. In addition, the pointing gesture recognition function was implemented based on depth-map generation. By integrating speech information and gesture information, HRP-2 can recognize questions that include a demonstrative pronoun. The feasibility of the system was demonstrated at EXPO 2005. Some issues and demands have been gradually clarified by the demonstration and the experiment.

Fig. 13. Demonstration in the Aichi EXPO 2005

The future work in vision and speech involve several aspects. Since the current system doesn't fully make use of the microphone array, there is a room for improvement in this regard. For example, the realization of Blind Source Separation (BSS) using multiple microphones will enable dialogue with multiple users simultaneously. The strengthening of noise robustness and improvements of the dialogue system will be also necessary. The improvement of the number of the recognizable gestures is also an important issue for a more natural interaction.

8. References

Asoh, H. Motomura, Y. Asano, F. Hara, I. Hayamizu, S. Itou, K. Kurita, T. Matsui, T. Vlassis, N. Bunschoten, R. Kroese, B. (2001). Jijo-2: An office robot that communicates and learns, *IEEE Intelligent Systems*, vol. 16, no. 5, pp. 46–55

Honda, Asimo robot, http://world.honda.com/ASIMO/

Ido, J. Myouga, Y. Matsumoto, Y. & Ogasawara, T. (2003). Interaction of receptionist ASKA using vision and speech information, in *IEEE Conference on Multisensor Fusion and Integration for Intelligent Systems*, pp. 335–340

Itou, K. Shikano, K. Kawahara, T. Takeda, K. Yamada, A. Itou, A. Utsuro, T. Kobayashi, T. Minematsu, N. Yamamoto, M. Sagayama, S. & Lee, A. (2000). Ipa Japanese dictation free software project, in *Proc. International Conference on Language Resources and Evaluation*, pp. 1343–1349

Itou, K. Yamamoto, M. Takeda, K. Takezawa, T. Matsuoka, T. Kobayashi, T. Shikano, K. & Itahashi, S. (1999). Jnas: Japanese speech corpus for large vocabulary continuous speech recognition research, *The Journal of the Acoustical Society of Japan (E)*, vol. 20, no. 3, pp. 199-206

Jelinek, F. (1990). Self-organized language modeling for speech recognition, *Language Processing for Speech Recognition*, pp. 450–506

Kendon, A. (1967). Some functions of gaze-direction in social interaction, *Acta Psychologica*, vol. 26, pp. 22–63

Lee, A. Kawahara, T. & Shikano, K. (2001). Julius–an open source real-time large vocabulary recognition engine, in *Proc. ISCAEUROSPEECH2001*, pp. 1691–1694

Lee, A. Kawahara, T. Takeda, K. & Shikano, K. (2000). A new phonetic tiedmixture model for efficient decoding, in *Proc. ICASSP2000*, pp. 1269–1272

Lee, A. Nakamura, K. Nisimura, R. Hiroshi, S. & Shikano, K. (2004). Noise robust real world spoken dialogue system using gmm based rejection of unintended inputs, *In Proc. INTERSPEECH2004*, vol. 1, pp. 173–176

Matsusaka, Y. Fujie, S. & Kobayashi, T. (2001). Modeling of conversational strategy for the robot participating in the group conversation, in *Proc. ISCA-EUROSPEECH2001*, pp. 2173–2176

Matsumoto Y. & Zelinsky, A. (2000). An algorithm for real-time stereo vision implementation of head pose and gaze direction measurement, *In Proc. of Fourth Int. Conf. on Automatic Face and Gesture Recognition*, pp. 499–505

Nakaoka, S. Nakazawa, A. & Ikeuchi, K. (2004). An efficient method for composing whole body motions of a humanoid robot, in *In Proc. of the Tenth International Conference on VIRTUAL SYSTEMS and MULTIMEDIA*, pp. 1142–1151

Nii, H. P. (1986). The blackboard model of problem solving and the evolution of blackboard architectures, *AI Magazine*, pp. 38–53

Nisimura, R. Lee, A. Saruwatari, H. & Shikano, K. (2004). Public speech-oriented guidance system with adult and child discrimination capability, in *Proc. ICASSP2004*, vol. 1, pp. 433–436

Nisimura, R. Lee, A. Yamada, M. & Shikano, K. (2005). Operating a public spoken guidance system in real environment, in *Proc. INTERSPEECH2005*

Suzuki, K. Hikiji R. & Hashimoto, S. (2002). Development of an autonomous humanoid robot, iSHA, for harmonized human-machine environment, *Journal of Robotics and Mechatronics*, vol. 14, no. 5, pp. 324–332

Young, S. Evermann, G. Hain, T. Kershaw, D. Moore, G. Odell, J. Ollason, D. Povey, D. Valtchev, V. & Woodland, P. (2002). The HTK book (for HTK version 3.2.1). http://htk.eng.cam.ac.uk/

9

Development of Localization Method of Mobile Robot with RFID Technology and Stereo Vision

Songmin Jia, Jinbuo Sheng and Kunikatsu Takase
University of Electro-Communications
1-5-1 Chofugaoka, Chofu-City, Tokyo 182-8585,
Japan

1. Introduction

Many service robotic systems have been developed in order to improve care costs and the quality of the elderly people in the aging population [L. Nagi et al., 2002; Vogl, M.et al., 2005]. Our Human- Assistance Robotic System Project (HARSP) project has been developing a network distributed Human-Assistance Robotic System since 2000 [S. Jia et al., 2002, 2004, 2005]. We developed a hardware base, key technologies and implemented several Common Object Request Broker Architecture (CORBA) application servers to provide some basic services to aid the aged or disabled. Localization and obstacle recognition in indoor environments for mobile robots are main topics in order to navigate a mobile robot to perform a service task at facilities or at home. Many efforts have been made to solve this problem using sensors such as cameras and laser ranger scanners [A. Davision, 2003; W. Shen et al., 2005; H. Surmann et al., 2003]. In our previously developed system, the indoor Global Positioning System (iGPS) has been developed to localize a mobile robot [Y. Hada et al., 2004]. Recently, some research has used radio frequency identification (RFID) technology for indoor mobile robot localization as the information written in ID tags can be easily read out by an RFID reader. Kulyukin et al. used RFID to localize a mobile robot within a coarse position and decided the next movement based on the information written in ID tags [V. Kulyukin et al., 2004]. Kim et al. developed an RFID system including three orthogonal antenna, which determines the direction and distance of a tag by comparing the signal strength in each direction [M. Kim et al., 2004; W. Lin et al., 2004]. In this paper, a novel method is proposed for indoor environmental obstacle recognition and localization of a mobile robot by using an RFID system with a stereo camera as it is inexpensive, flexible and easy to use in the practical environment. As the information (such as type, colour, shape or size of the obstacles) can be written in ID tags in advance, the proposed method enables easy and quick obstacle recognition. The proposed method is also helpful to improve dynamic obstacle recognition (such as a chair or person) and occlusion problems that are very difficult to solve. This is because the communication between the ID reader and ID tags uses RF, and the information written in ID tags can be simultaneously read by an RFID reader. RF is not so stable, so determining the accurate position of obstacle objects is difficult. In order to localize the ID tags accurately, the Bayes rule was introduced to calculate the probability where the ID tag exists after the tag reader detects a tag. Then the stereo camera starts to process the Region Of Interest (ROI) determined by the results of the Bayes rule. As the proposed method does not need to process all input images, and some information about environment was obtained from the ID tag, this decreases the image processing computation, and enables us to detect the obstacles easily and quickly. Research on RFID technology integrating stereo vision to localize an indoor mobile robot has also been performed. This paper introduces the architecture of the proposed method and gives some experimental results.

The rest of the paper consists of seven sections. Section 2 describes the structure of the hardware of the developed system. Section 3 presents the localization of ID tags using RFID system. Section 4 introduces the proposed method of obstacle localization and detection, Section 5 details obstacle avoidance with RFID technology and stereo vision. Section 6 explains the principle of the developed indoor mobile robot localization method. The experimental results are given in Section 7. Section 8 concludes the paper.

2. System description

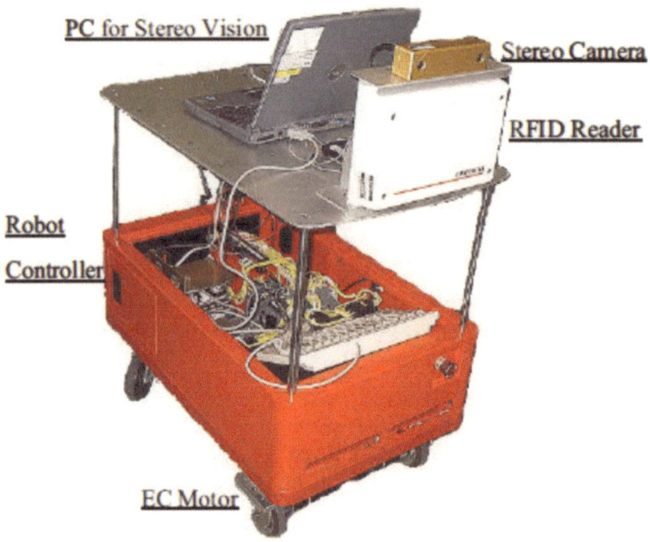

Fig. 1. The structure of developed mobile robot platform.

In the previously developed system, an omnidirectional mobile robot was used to perform service tasks. Owing to the specific structure of its wheel arrangement, it is difficult for a mobile robot to pass over a bump or enter a room where there is a threshold. Another important point is to lower costs and decrease the number of motors so that the battery can supply enough electricity for a mobile robot to run for a longer time. Figure 1 illustrates the developed mobile robot platform. In our new system, we developed a non-holonomic mobile robot that was remodeled from a commercially available manual cart. The structure of the front wheels was changed with a lever balance structure to make the mobile robot move smoothly and the motors were fixed to the two front wheels. It has low cost and can easily pass over a bump or gap between the floor and rooms. We selected the Maxon EC motor and a digital server amplifier 4-Q-EC 50/5 which can be controlled via RS-232C. For the controller of the mobile robot, a PC104 CPU module (PCM-3350 Geode GX1-300 based) is used, on which RT-Linux is running. For communication between the mobile robot and the mobile robot control server running on the host computer, a wireless LAN (PCMCIA-WLI-L111) is used.

The Kenwood series was used in the developed system. The tag reader S1500/00 communicates with tags via 2.45-GHz radio waves. Figure 2 illustrates the specification of RFID system. Since there is a communication area between the ID tag and tag reader (the communication between the mobile robot controller and tag reader is via RS-232C), if the ID tag comes into the communication area while mobile robot moves to a close to the ID tag, the ID tag can be detected and the information written in it can simultaneously be read by the tag reader mounted on the mobile robot. When the working domain of the mobile robot is changed or extended, what needs to be done is just putting the new ID tags in a new environment and registering these ID tags to the database. It is also helpful to improve dynamic obstacle recognition (such as a chair or person).

Item	Specification
Frequency	2.45GHz
Card Memory size	72byte
The maximum communication distance	4m
Interface	RS-485,RS-232C
Power requirement	DC24(V) 1.0(A)
Weight (reader)	2kg
Dimension (reader)	263x176x53mm (WxLxH)

Fig. 2. The specifications of KENWOOD RFID system.

The Bumblebee (Point Grey Research) stereo camera and MDCS2 (Videre Design) camera are usually used in the robotics field. In our system, we selected the Bumblebee to integrate RFID technology to localize the service mobile robot. The Bumblebee two-camera stereo vision system provides a balance between three dimensional (3-D) data quality, processing speed, size and price. The camera is ideal for applications such as people tracking, mobile robotics and other computer vision applications. It has a resolution of 640 x 480 or 1024 x 768 (640 x 480 at 30 FPS or 1024 x 768 at 15 FPS). The size of the camera is approximately 160 x 40 x 50 mm and the weight is about 375 g. It has features such as: two 1/3-inch progressive scan CCDs to provide significantly better light collection and signal-to-noise ratio; high-speed IEEE-1394 digital communication allowing powering of the camera and camera control through a single cable; and accurate precalibration for lens distortions and camera misalignments and automatic intercamera synchronization, useful for acquiring 3-D data from multiple points of view. A notebook computer (Intel Pentium 3M 1.00 GHz, memory SDRAM 512, Windows XP Professional) was used to process images. Figure 3 illustrates the specifications of Bumblebee stereo camera, and Figure 4 shows the connection of developed robot system. Tag reader communicated with PC 104 robot controller via RS-232C, and Bumblebee stereo camera was connected with a note PC via IEEE1394 bus.

Item	Specification
Baseline	12 cm
Focal Lengths	6mm with 43°
Frame Rates	48 FPS(640x480)
Interfaces	6-pin IEEE-1394a
Power Consumption	2.5W at12V
Dimensions	157 x 36 x 47.4mm
Mass	342 grams
Signal To Noise	Ratio 60dB
Gain	Automatic/Manual

Fig. 3. The specification of Bumblebee stereo camera.

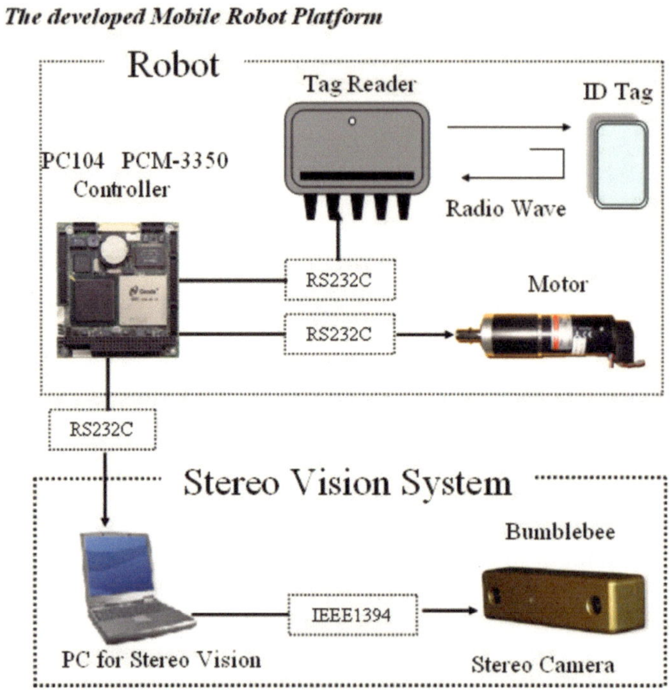

Fig. 4. Connection of the developed mobile robot system.

3. Localization of ID tag using RFID system

3.1 RFID probability model

Obstacle recognition; specially, dynamic obstacle recognition such as chair or human person is a difficult problem. For human being, it is easy to avoid the obstacles such as chairs, tables to perform a task, but for mobile robot, it is very difficult. We proposed the method of indoor environmental obstacle recognition for mobile robot using RFID. Because the information of obstacle such as size, color can be written in ID tags in advance, so the proposed method enables the obstacle recognition easily and quickly. By considering the probabilistic uncertainty of RFID, the proposed method introduces Bayes rule to calculate probability where the obstacle exists when the RFID reader detects a ID tag. In our research, for the obstacle objects like chairs and tables, we attached the ID tags on them, and the system can detect them when the mobile robot moves the place where ID tags enters the communication range of RFID reader. Simultaneously, the data written in the ID tags can also be read out. But localizing accurately the position of obstacle objects is difficult just using RFID because the antenna directivity of RFID system is not so good. We introduce Bayes rule to calculate probability where the ID tag exists after the tag reader detects a tag [E. Shang et al., 2005].

Bayes' theorem relates the conditional and marginal probabilities of two events E and O, where O has a non-vanishing probability.

$$P_t(E|O) \propto P(O|E)P_{t-1}(E)$$

In our method, O is phenomenon of the reception of the signal by the tag reader, E is phenomenon of the existence of the obstacle (ID tag), $P_t(E|O)$ is the conditional probability the tag exists after t times update, $P(O|E)$ is sensor probability model of RFID, and $P_{t-1}(E)$ is the prior or marginal probability after the tag exists t-1 times update. To determine the model for RFID antennas, we attached an RFID tag to a fixed position, and the mobile robot moves in different paths. We repeated this for different distances and counted for every point in a discrete gird the frequency of detections of ID tags. In order to overcome the multipath effect of electric wave, we set ID tags detection buffer for saving latest 10 times detecting results. "1" means the ID tag was detected, "0" means the ID tag was not detected. If the results of 9 times are "1", we think the ID tag can be detected with 0.9 probability. Additionally, we use the recursive Bayesian to calculate probability where the ID tag exists, which can improve multipath effect. According to the experimental results, we can get the data distribution shown in Figure 5. The points means the RFID tag can be detected (0.9 probability). According to this result, we can simplify the RFID sensor model shown in Figure 6. The likelihood of the major detection range for each antenna is 0.9 in this area. The likelihood for the other range is setup as 0.5.

When the user commands a mobile robot to perform a service task, the mobile robot starts to move in the office, or at home. In order to enable a mobile robot to finish a task autonomously, it is necessary for mobile robot to have perfomance to detect the obstacles in indoor environment and avoid them. Many researchers used many sensors to solve this problem. In our system, we proposed the method using RFID and stereo vision to recognize the obstacle. RFID reader system was mounted on the mobile robot platform. When the mobile robot starts to move for performing a task, RFID reader system was started simultaneously to detect the ID tags arround the mobile robot. There are communication area for different RFID system. The Kenwood series used in the developed system has communication range about 4x1.8m^2. When the mobile robot moves to place close to ID tags, the ID tag can be detected and the information written in ID tag can also be read out simultaneously. When RFID system detected a obstacle ID tag, a map 4×4m^2 (cell size 4×4cm^2, the public precision in the field of robot navigation) will generated. Figure 7 illustrates the initial probability map after the RFID reader detected a obstacle with ID tag. In order to know the obstacle is on the left or on the right of mobile robot, and narrow the area where the obsatcle with ID tag exists, the mobile robot moves along the detection

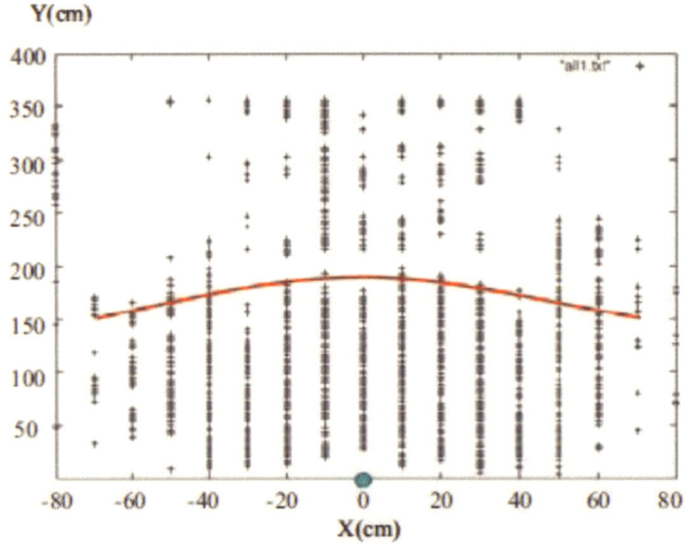

Fig. 5. The data distribution of the RFID.

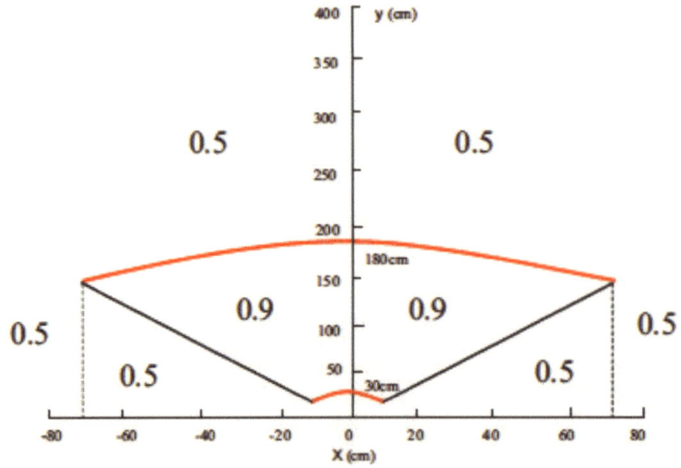

Fig. 6. Simplified sensor model for antenna.

trajectory. Because the relative offset between ID tag and antenna affects on the P(O|E), the posterior $P_t(E|O)$ is different when the robot changes its relative position. Whenever the reader mounted on the robot detects a ID tag after robot was changing its relative position, the posterior $P_t(E|O)$ of each cell of map is updated according to recursive Bayesian equation and using sensor model (Figure 6), and a new probability map was generated. The cell center position of the maximum probability in the latest map after mobile robot finishes its detection trajectory is considered as the position of obstacle with ID tags. Figure 8 illustrates the detection trajectory when the RFID detects a obstacle with ID tag. We have done some experimental results for different angle of curve of detection trajectory, and $\alpha = 30^{\circ}$ was best.

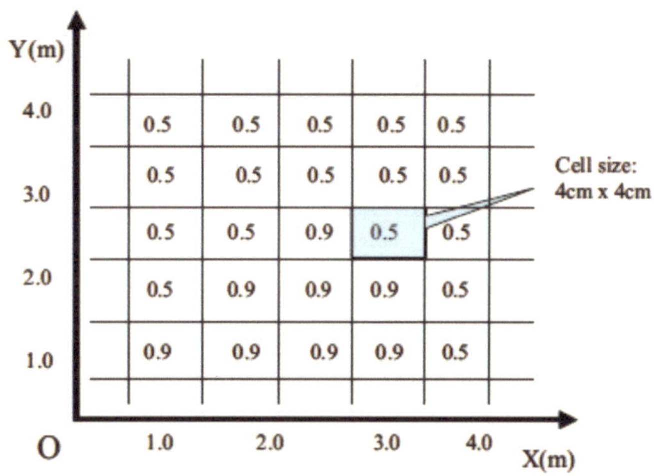

Fig. 7. Probability map of mobile robot.

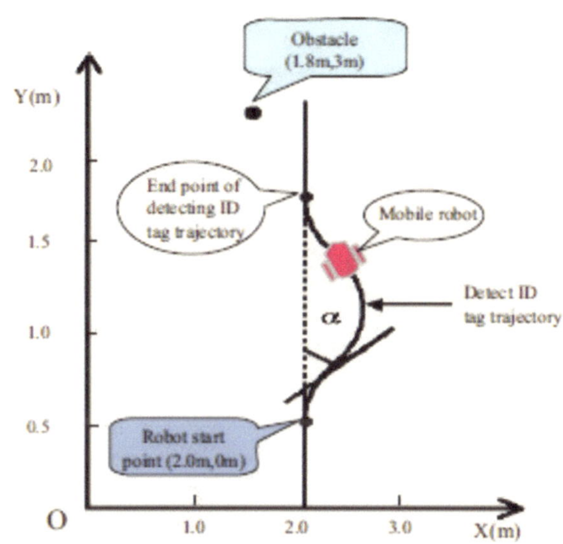

Fig. 8. Detection trajectory for localizing ID tag.

3.2 Simulation and experimental results of obstacle detection using RFID

When the ID tag reader detects a obstacle ID tag, system will generate a 4×4m² map, and do cell splitting. The cell size is 4×4cm², which is regarded as the accepted precision in navigation research fields. Mobile robot moves alone a trajectory and updates the probability of each cell at a constant time stamp, then we can calculate the cell which has maximum probability. Figure 9 shows some simulation results and Figure 10 shows some experimental results. According to the results shown in Figure 9 and Figure 10, we can localize the RFID tag within the area about 0.1m² for simulation results, for experimental results, it is about 0.26m². So, the error of experiment results of localization of mobile robot is bigger than the results of simulation. This is because that the communication between ID Reader and ID Tags uses Radio Frequency, Radio Frequency is not so stable, and the sensor model is not so accurate. In order to improve the accuracy of localization of obstacles just using RFID tag, we will use stereo camera to recognize the obstacle objects further according to the information of obstacle written in ID tags.

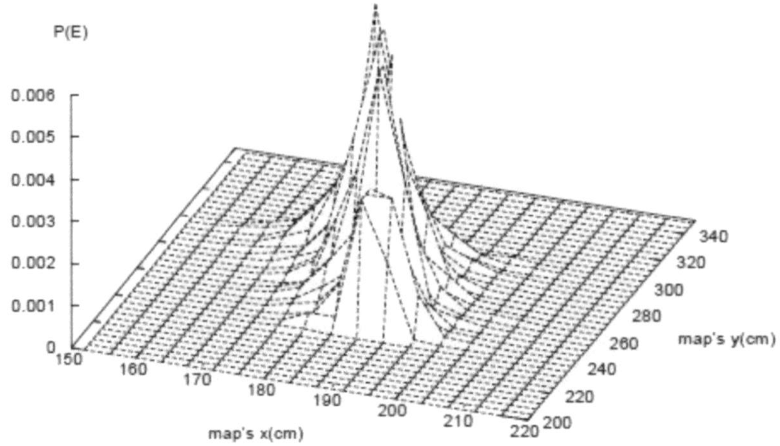

Fig. 9. Simulation results of localizing ID tag using Bayes rule.

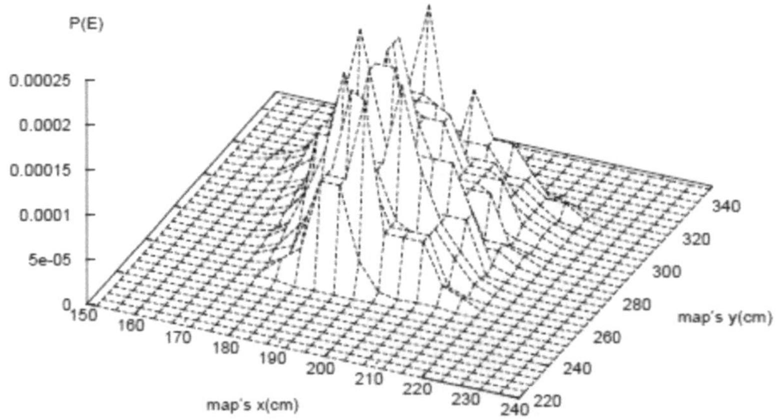

Fig. 10. Experimental results of localizing ID tag using Bayes rule.

4. Obstacle localization using RFID and stereo camera

Bayes rule was introduced to calculate the maximum probability where the obstacle exists, but the precision is not enough for navigating a mobile robot. Thus, we use the results of the Bayes rule to determine the ROI that stereo vision needs to process in order to get the posture of the obstacles much more precisely. For obstacles such as chairs, we developed the processing algorithm as follows:

- Open the stereo camera to grab images.
- Set up the configuration of the camera.
- Preprocess the images taken by the stereo camera.
- Do RGB–HSV conversion, morphologic operation and labeling processing according to the information about the obstacle written in the ID tag for the ROI of the input image obtained by the Bayes rule.
- Calculate the position (x, y) and orientation (θ) of the obstacle according to the results of the imaging process
- Get the depth of the obstacle by the information of the depth image obtained from stereo vision.

Human detection is indispensable when the mobile robot performs a service task in an indoor environment (office, facilities or at home). Detection of the human body is more complicated than for objects as the human body is highly articulated. Many methods for human detection have been developed. Papageorgiou and Poggio [C. Papageorgiou et al., 2000] use Haar-based representation combined with a polynomial support vector machine. The other leading method uses a parts-based approach [P. Felzenszwalb et al., 2005]. Our approach first uses the Bayes rule to calculate the probability where the human exists when the RFID reader detects a human with the ID tag, then the stereo camera starts to perform image processing for the ROI determined by Bayes rule results. The depth information of the ROI from the depth image can be obtained from stereo vision and the histogram of pixels taken for the same distance of the obstacles was built:

$$P_{\text{obstacle}}(m) = \sum_{i=0}^{w} \sum_{j=0}^{h} f_m[i, j]$$

Here, $P_{obstacle}$ is the number of pixels for the m obstacle having the same depth in the image. W is the width variable of object, h is the height variable of the object. For each $P_{obstacle}$, the values of pixel aspect ratio are calculated by image processing, and then the most fitting value to the human model was selected as candidate of human body. Because the human part from shoulder to face is easy to be recognized and is insensitive to the variations in environment or illumination, we make the second order model of human. We calculate the vertical direction projection histogram and horizontal direction projection histogram. The top point of vertical direction projection histogram can be thought the top of head. The maximum point in vertical axis around the top of head was thought as the width of head. According to the human body morphology, the 2.5 to 3 times height of the width of head can be thought the height of human from face to shoulder. Figure 11, 12, 13 shows one sample of second order model of human.

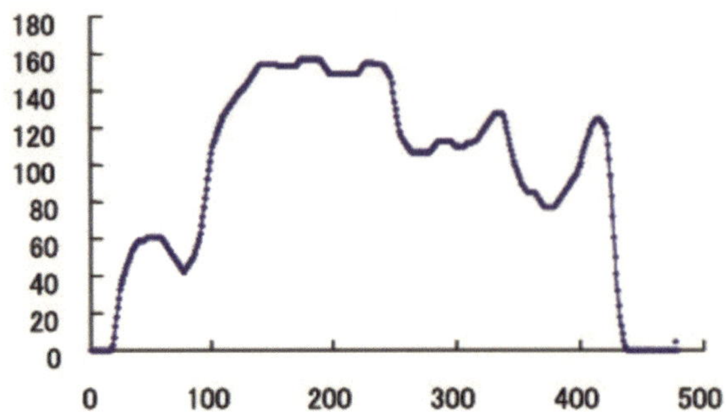

Fig. 11. Vertical direction projection histogram.

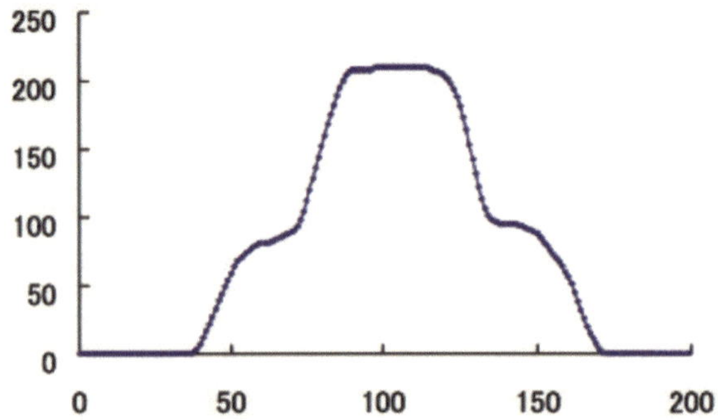

Fig. 12. Horizontal direction projection histogram.

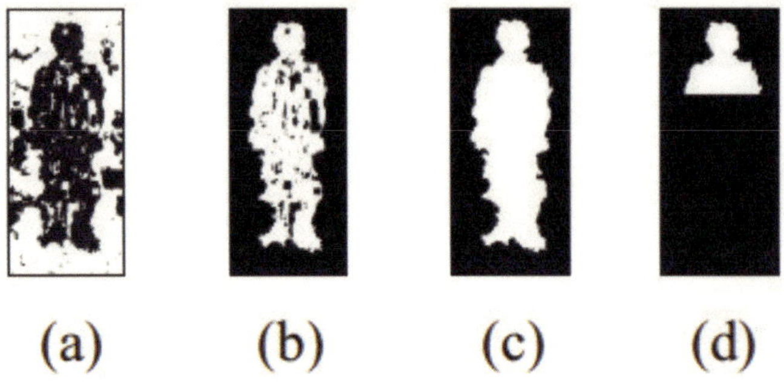

Fig. 13. The second order model of human.

For the obstacle having the same aspect ratio with human body, we introduce Hu moments invariants as feature parameters to recognize second order human body model further. Hu moment invariants are recognition method of visual patterns and characters independent of position, size and orientation. Hu moment defined the two-dimensional (p+q)th order moments in discrete can be defined as following equation.

$$m_{pq} = \sum_{i=0}^{N} \sum_{j=0}^{K} i^p j^q f(i,j)$$

Here, p, q=0, 1, 2....
The central moments $m\mu_{pq}$ are defined as

$$mu_{pq} = \sum_{i=0}^{N}\sum_{j=0}^{K}(i-\bar{x})^p(j-\bar{y})^q f(i,j)$$

Here, $\bar{x}$ =m_{10}/m_{00}, $\bar{y}$ =m_{01}/m_{00}.
It is well known that under the translation of coordinates, the central moments do not change. The (p+q)th order central moments for image f(i, j) can be express as:

$$\eta = \mu_{pq}/\mu_{00}^{r}$$

Here, r= (p+q+2)/2, p+q>2. For the second and third order moments, we can induce six absolute orthogonal invariants and one skew orthogonal invariant. Using these seven invariants moments can accomplish pattern identification not only independently of position, size and orientation but also independently parallel projection. Using this method first learned a number of patterns for human and chair, then calculated the seven invariants moments. According to the results, the seven invariants moments of human are almost the same in spite of the position of human in image changing, and the seven invariants moments of chair is different from that of human (Figure 14). The average value of seven invariants moments of a number of patterns for human was used as character parameters for human recognition. For the new input ROI image, first calculate the seven invariants moments of the obstacle, then get the Euclid distance by the equation

$$d_i = \sqrt{\sum_{i=0}^{6}(X_o{}^r - X_i^h)}$$

Here, X_i^h is the seven invariants moments of human calculated in advance, and X_o^i is the seven invariants moments of the obstacle. If $d_i < L_i$ is satisfied, the obstacle is recognized as human.

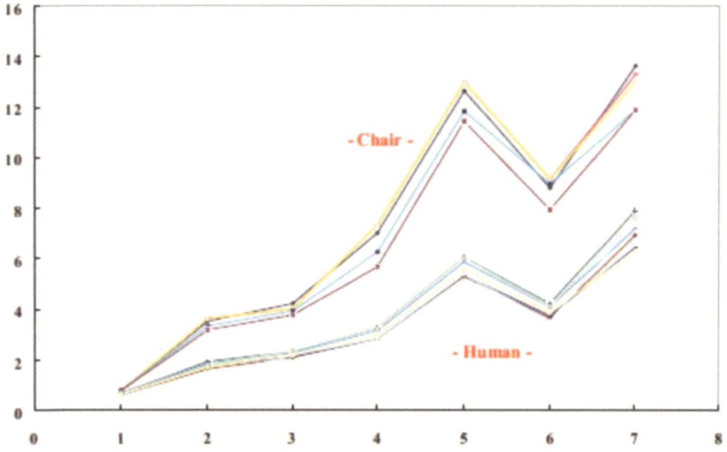

Fig. 14. Hu seven invariants moments of human.

5. Obstacle avoidance

The Obstacle Avoidance Module calculates the avoidance area and route for the mobile robot to avoid the obstacle after the obstacle has been detected. After the tag reader detects the ID tag and localizes the obstacle using the Bayes rule, the mobile robot will determine how to avoid this obstacle. Figure 15(a) shows the flowchart of obstacle avoidance algorithm. Figure 15(b) shows the real obstacle-avoiding route that was calculated. First, the mobile robot will determine the avoidance area (R) to judge if the mobile robot can directly pass obstacle. The avoidance route will be generated for the mobile robot by the Obstacle Avoidance Module if the mobile robot cannot pass directly:

$$R = r + r_{\mathrm{err}}$$

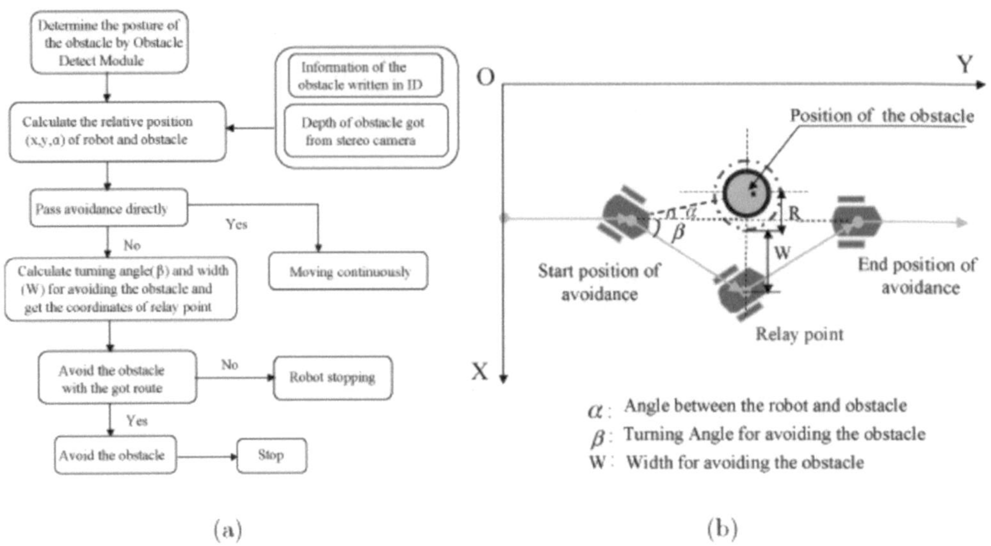

Fig. 15. Flowchart and route of obstacle avoidance.

where r is the radius of the circumscribed circle of the obstacle and r_{err} is the error of the position of the detected obstacle.

6. Robot localization using RFID and stereo camera

The Robot Localization Module localizes the mobile robot when the tag reader detects the ID tags of localization. We propose the localization method for an indoor mobile robot using RFID technology combining stereo vision. First, the RFID reader detects the ID tags and judges whether they are localization tags or not. If ID tags for localization are detected, then the system starts the stereo camera system to recognize the ID tags, and calculates the pose of the mobile robot according to the information written in the tags and the results of image processing. The Bumblebee camera was used and was connected with a notebook computer, and the image processing calculation was run on a notebook computer. The results of information about the position and orientation of the mobile robot were sent to the mobile robot controller and the mobile robot controller sends the commands to adjust the pose of the mobile robot to return its desired position to finish a task.

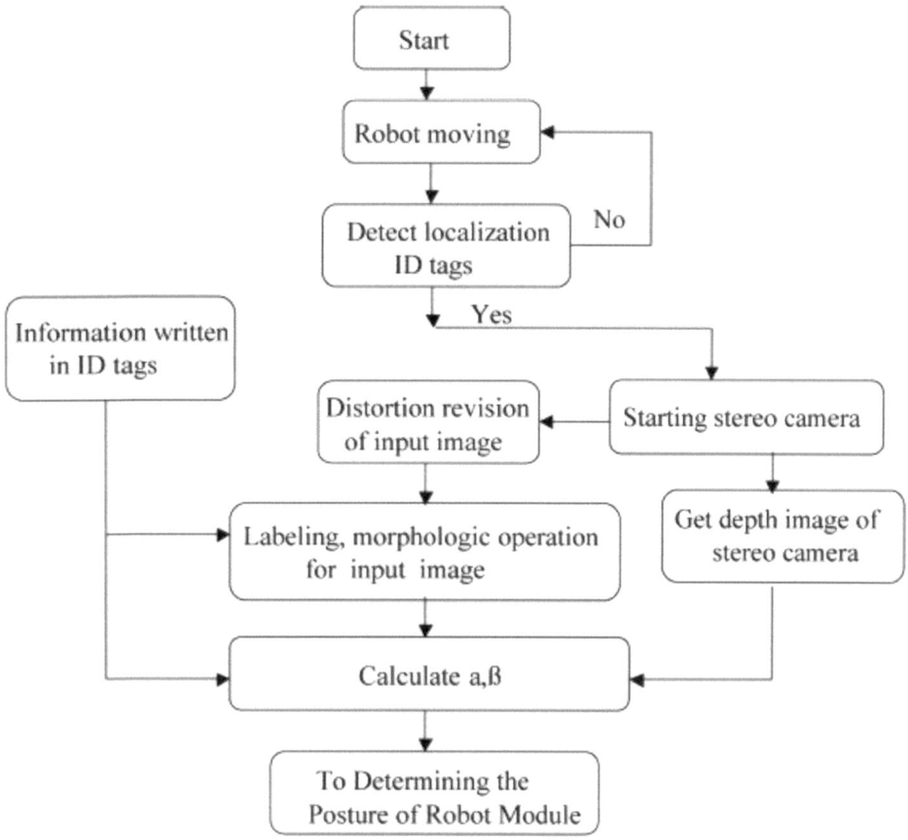

Fig. 16. Flowchart of localization of the mobile robot.

6.1 Landmark recognition

Landmark Recognition Module is used to take the images of the environment when the ID tags for localization are detected, perform image processing and localize the ID tags. Landmark recognition [K. E. Bekris., 2004] for localization of a mobile robot is a popular method. The image processing computation of the usual landmark recognition methods is enormous because the vision system needs to recognize all kinds of landmarks in real-time while the mobile robot moves. As the system can get tag information of the environment such as their world coordinates when the RFID detects a tag, the proposed method of the localization method of a mobile robot just does image processing after the RFID system detects ID tags for localization. It is helpful to decrease the image processing computation and to improve dynamic obstacle recognition (e.g., a person or chair). Figure 16 illustrates the flowchart of localization of the mobile robot. The image processing of recognizing the ID tags for localization includes:

- Open the stereo camera to grab images.
- Set up the configuration of the camera.

- Preprocess the images taken by the stereo camera.
- Perform RGB binary processing, exclude noise, perform template matching with threshold.
- Get the coordinates of the ID localization tags of the left and right images.
- Perform stereo processing to get the world coordinates of the ID tags.
- Calculate α and β (see Fig. 17) in order to determine the position and orientation of the mobile robot.

6.2 Determining the posture of the robot

Determining the Posture of the Robot Module is used to calculate the position and orientation of the mobile robot using the information of the Landmark Recognition Module and the information written in the ID tags. Figure 17 illustrates the principle of the proposed method of localization of the mobile robot. Four ID localization tags are used as one set and

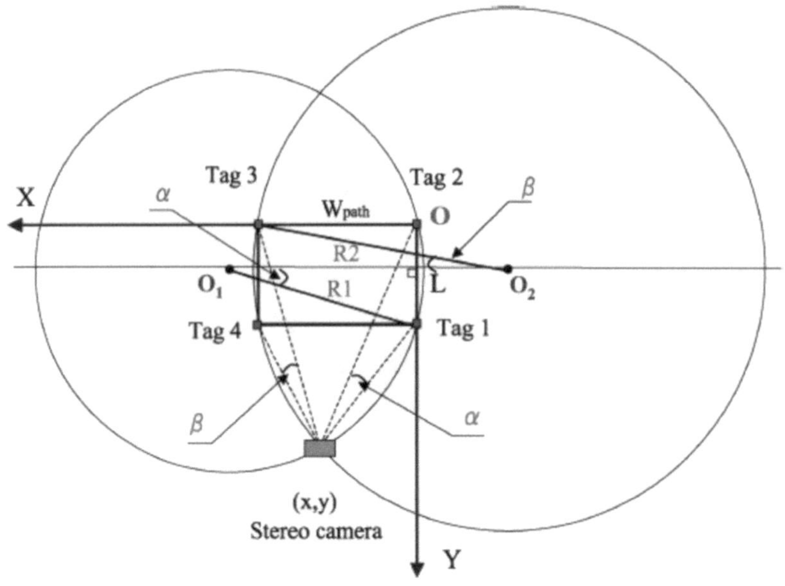

Fig. 17. Principle of localization of the mobile robot.

are affixed in the environment. Since the ID tag's absolute coordinates are written in them in advance, the RFID reader can read out their information simultaneously when it detects tags. α and β can be determined by the Landmarks Recognition Module, the position (x, y) and orientation (ε) of the mobile robot can be calculated by

$$x = \frac{(W_{\text{path}} - R_2 \cos\beta)^2 + R_1^2 \sin\alpha^2 - R_2^2}{2(W_{\text{path}} - R_2 \cos\beta - R_1 \cos\alpha)}$$

$$y = \frac{L}{2} + \sqrt{R_1^2 - (x - R_1 \cos\alpha)^2}$$

$$\epsilon = \arctan\frac{x}{(y - L)} - \delta,$$

where W_{path} is the width of the passage, L is the distance between tag 1 and tag 2 or tag 3 and tag 4, R_1 is the radius of circle 1 and R_2 is the radius of circle 2. α is the angle between the center of the camera to tag 1 and the center of the camera to tag 2. β is the angle between the center of the camera to tag 3 and the center of the camera to tag 4. δ is the angle between the orientation of the camera and the centerof the camera to tag 1.

6.3 Path planning

A Path Planning is necessary and improtant issue for calculating the optimal route for the mobile robot to move in order to perform a service task autonomously in indoor environment. Many reseachers give their effrot on path planning for mobile robot to finish a task costly and efficiently. In our research, we also proposed method of path planning for our mobile robot system. As we know, each ID localization tag has a unique ID, so each ID localization node (consisting of four ID localization tags; the center of the four ID localization tags is defined as the position of the ID localization node) can indicate an absolute position in the environment. All the nodes make up a topologic map of the indoor environment in which the mobile robot moves. For example, if the mobile robot moves from START point A to GOAL point F, the moving path can be described with the node tree shown in Fig. 18. The system searched the shortest path between the START and GOAL node (e.g., the shortest path between A and F is A→B→ C→D→F) by tracing the branches between them.

In order to navigate a mobile robot in an indoor environment, building a map is a big problem. Generally, there are two kinds of map, one is geometric approaches, and the second is topological map which can be thought of as robot-centric, or representations in sensor space. In our system, the topological map based on RFID and vision for the mobile robot was developed. For building a topological map, we use a 6-bit decimal numbe to represent the connectivity of ID localization nodes and the relative direction angles between every two adjacent ID nodes.

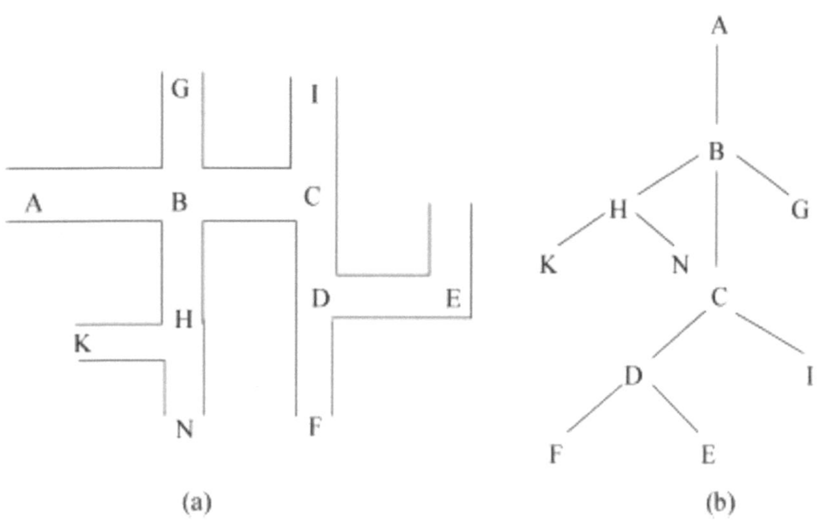

Fig. 18. Movement path and its description with nodes.

7. Experimental results

The experiment of obstacle detection was performed by the proposed method using RFID technology and stereo vision. ID tags were affixed to the obstacles of the environment. When the mobile robot mounted on the RFID reader moves close to the chair, the tag reader can detect the ID tags. When the mobile robot detected an obstacle using the RFID system, the area of the obstacle existing in high possibility was determined using Bayes rule together with the information about the obstacle written in the ID tag. Then the ROI value of the image to be processed can also be determined. Figure 19(a) shows one sample of the distortion revision of the input image from stereo camera. Figure 19(b) shows the depth image for the input image from the stereo camera. Figure 19 illustrates one sample of image processing for a ROI image to recognize the obstacle (chair). We have done some experiments for comparison of the processing image time using the proposed method. The experiments were done by image processing from taking raw images (640×480), doing HSV conversion, morphologic operation, and labelling processing. For the common method, the average processing image time was about 295ms, and that of the proposed method was about 125ms.

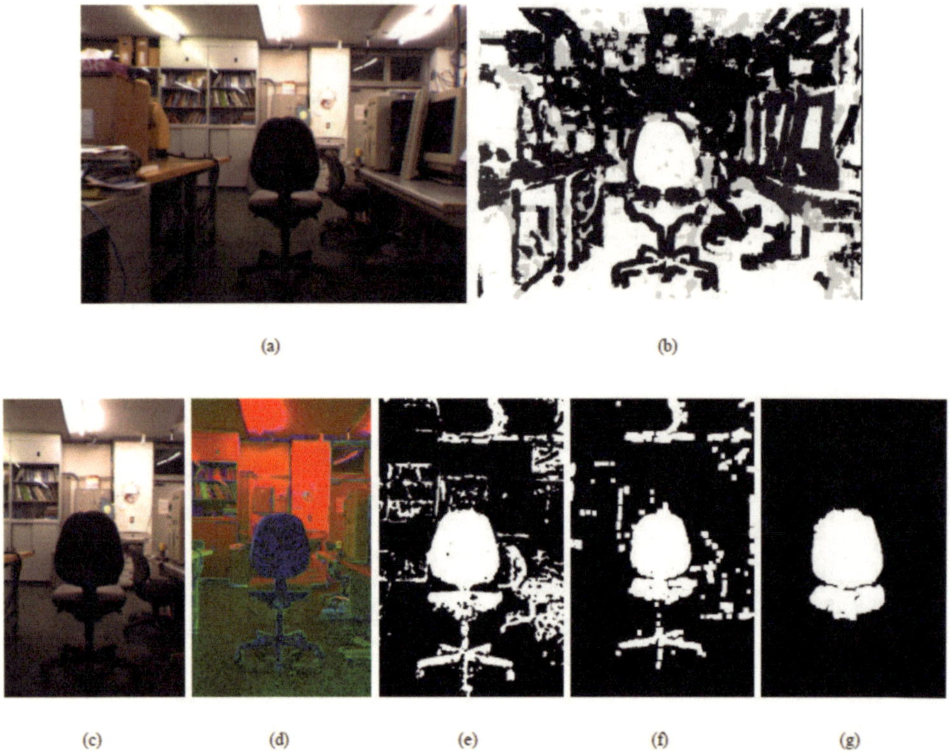

Fig. 19. Obstacle recognition experimental results using the proposed system.

Human detection experiments were also performed in our laboratory. Figure 20 illustrates the results of detecting a human body using the proposed algorithm. Figure 20(a) is the input image with distortion revision from the stereo camera and Figure 20(b) is the depth image. We used the Bayes rule to calculate the probability to narrow the human location and then determined the ROI value (Figure 20(c)). Figure 20(d) is the histogram built according to the depth image. Comparing the human pixel aspect ratio in the image, we can successfully detect the centre of gravity of the human as shown in Fig. 20(g).

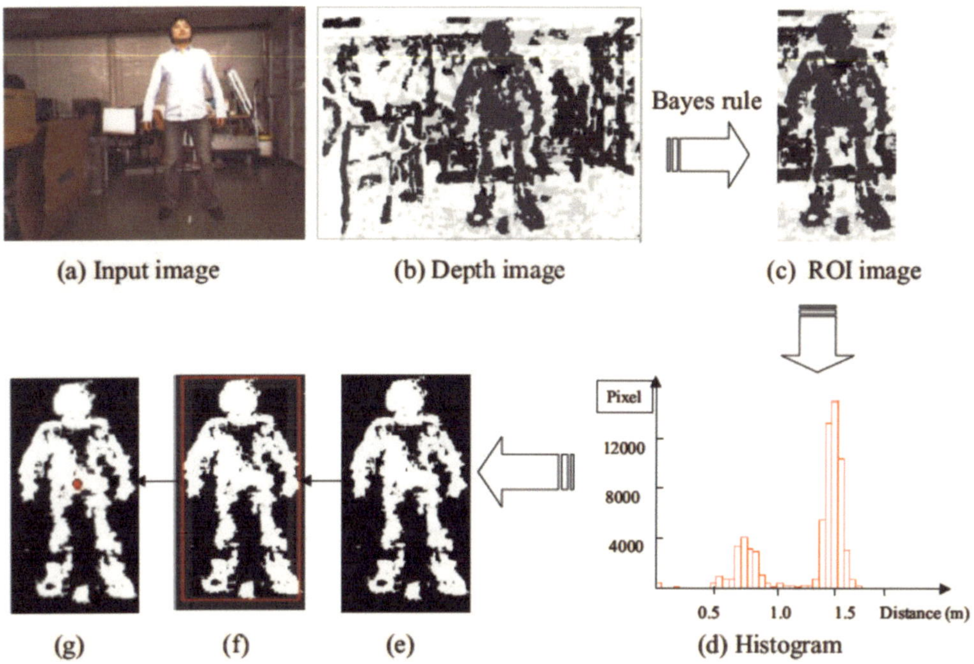

Fig. 20. Human detection experiment: (a) input image, (b) depth image, (c) ROI image after narrowing the human using Bayes rule, (d) histogram, (e) binary image, (f) image with human pixel aspect ratio detected and (g) resulting image with the centroid detected.

The obstacle avoidance experiments have been performed in an indoor environment. When the position of the obstacle was localized, the avoidance area and route were determined for the mobile robot to avoid it. Figure 21 shows the experimental results of the mobile robot avoiding the obstacle (chair) using the proposed method of integrating RFID and stereo vision. Figure 21(a–e) shows the obstacle on the right of the mobile robot and Figure 21(k–o) shows the obstacle on the left of the mobile robot. Figure 21(f–j) shows that the mobile robot was not disturbed by the obstacle and the mobile robot did not need to change its movement route. According to the experimental results of Figure 21, we know that the proposed method can detect an obstacle and enable an indoor mobile robot to avoid the obstacle (chair) successfully in different cases.

We proposed a localization method of an indoor mobile robot using RFID combining stereo vision to decrease the image processing computation and improve dynamic obstacle recognition (such as a person or chair). When the RFID system detects ID tags for localization of a mobile robot, the stereo camera will start to recognize the ID localization tags as landmarks. Then the position and orientation of the mobile robot can be calculated according to the information written in the ID tags. This experiment of localization of mobile robot was performed in a passage (width: 233 cm) in our corridor of our lab, and the tags were fixed on the wall at 117 cm intervals. The mobile robot moved from a random position and orientation and, after localization, it can move back to the centreline of the passage. The average error of localization of the mobile robot is about 8.5 cm. Figure 22 illustrates some experimental results of localization of an indoor mobile robot. According to the experimental results, we know the proposed method of localization for mobile robot using RFID and stereo vision was effective.

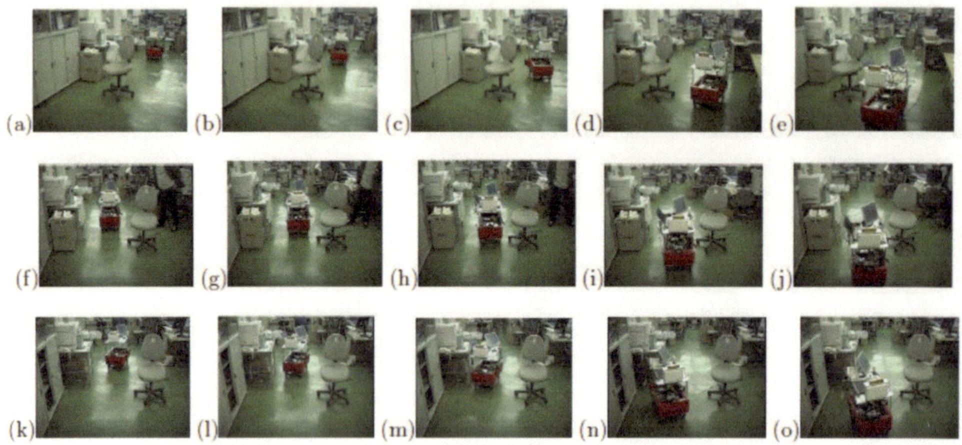

Fig. 21. Obstacle avoidance experimental results using the proposed system.

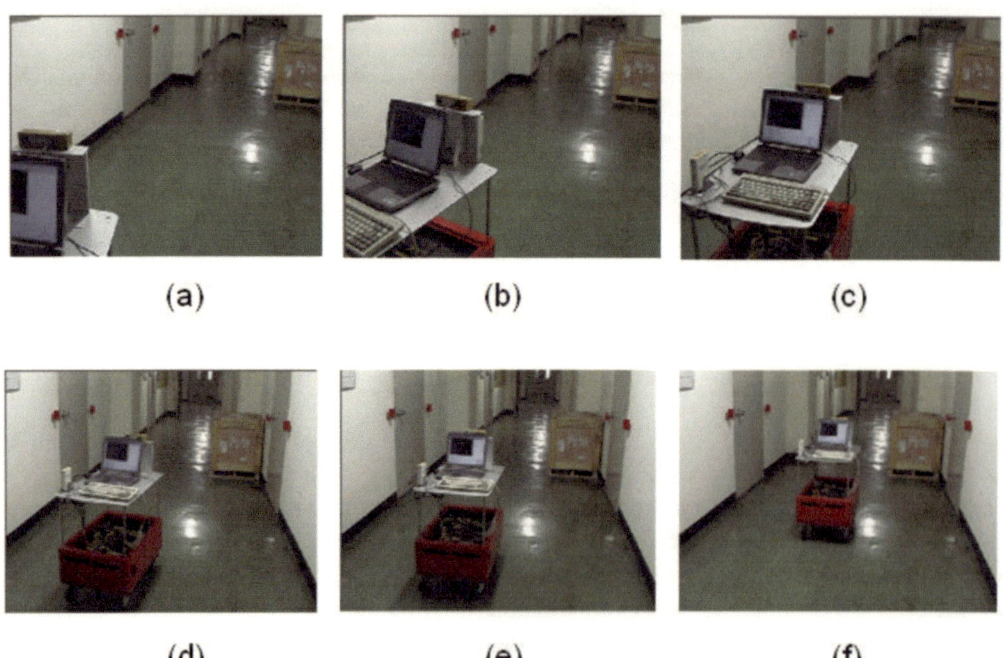

Fig. 22. Experiments of localization of a mobile robot.

8. Conclusion

This paper presents the proposed method of obstacle recognition and localization of a mobile robot with RFID technology and stereo vision. We developed hardware and software such as the Obstacle Detecting Module, Obstacle Avoidance Module, Robot Localization Module, Landmark Recognition Module, Determine the Posture of Robot Module, Path Planning Module and Communication Module. In order to improve the accuracy of localizing the ID tags, Bayes rule was introduced to calculate the probability where the ID tag exists after the tag reader detects a tag. Experiments with RFID technology integrating stereo vision for obstacle detection and localization of an indoor mobile robot have been performed. As the system can obtain tag information of the environment such as obstacle and the world coordinates when the RFID detects a tag, the proposed method is helpful to decrease the image processing computation, and improve dynamic obstacles recognition (such as a person or chair) and occlusion problem. The experimental results verified that the proposed method was effective. The main topic for future work will be performing home service tasks by using the proposed method to aid the aged or disabled.

9. Acknowledgements

The obstacle recognition and localization for mobile robot using RFID and stereo vision was developed with funding by the New Energy and Industrial Technology Development Organization (NEDO) of Japan.

10. References

Nagi, W. S. Newman and V. Liberatore, An experiment in Internet-based, human-assisted robotics, in: Proc. IEEE Int. Conf. on Robotics and Automation, Washington, DC, pp. 2190–2195 (2002).

R. Vogl, M. Vincze and G. Biegelbauer, Finding tables for home service tasks and safe mobile robot navigation, in: Proc. IEEE Int. Conf. on Robotics and Automation, New Orleans, LA, pp. 3046–3051 (2005).

S. Jia, Y. Hada, G. Ye and K. Takase, Distributed telecare robotic systems using CORBA as a communication architecture, in: Proc. IEEE Int. Conference on Robotics and Automation,Washington, DC, pp. 2002–2007 (2002).

S. Jia, Y. Hada and K. Takase, Distributed telerobotics system based on common object request broker architecture, Int. J. Intell. Robotic Syst. 39, 89–103 (2004).

S. Jia, Y. Hada, T. Ohnishi, H. Gakuhari, K. Takase and T. Abe, Development of intelligent service robotic system based on robot technology middleware, in: Proc. 3rd Int. Conf. on Computational Intlligence, Robotics and Autonomous System, Singapore (2005).

A. Davision, Real-time simultaneous localization and mapping with a single camera, in: Proc. Int. Conf. on Computer Vision, Nice, pp. 1403–1410 (2003).

W. Shen and J. Gu, Fuzzy approach for mobile robot positioning, in: Proc. IEEE/RSJ Int. Conf. on Intelligent Robots and Systems, Edmonton, Alberta, pp. 2906–2910 (2005).

H. Surmann, A. Nüchter and J. Hertzberg, An autonomous mobile robot with a 3D laser finder for 3D exploration and digitalization of indoor environments, Robotics Autonomous Syst. 45, 181–198 (2003).

Y. Hada, K. Takase, K. Ohagaki et al., Delivery service robot using distributed acquisition, actuators and intelligence, in: Proc IEEE/RSJ Int. Conf. on Intelligent Robots and Systems, Sendai, pp. 2997–3002 (2004). V. Kulyukin, C. Gharpure, J. Nicholosn and S. Pavithran, RFID in robot-assisted indoor navigation for the visually impaired, in: Proc IEEE/RSJ Int. Conf. on Intelligent Robots and Systems, Sendai, pp. 1979–1984 (2004).

M. Kim, T. Takeuchi and N. Y. Chong, A 3-axis orthogonal antenna for indoor localization, in: Proc. 1st Int. Workshop on Networked Sensing Systems, Tokyo, pp. 59–62 (2004).

W. Lin, S. Jia, F. Yang and K. Takase, Topological navigation of mobile robot using ID tag and web camera, in: Proc. Int. Conf. on Intelligent Mechatronics and Automation, Chengdu, pp. 644–649 (2004).

S. Ikeda and J. Miura, 3D indoor environment modeling by a mobile robot with omnidirectional stereo and laser range finder, in: Proc. IEEE/RSJ Int. Conf. on Intelligent Robots and Systems, Beijing, pp. 3435–3440 (2006).

H. Koyasu, J.Miura and Y. Shirai, Real-time Omnidirectional stereo obstacle detection in dynamic environment, in: Proc. IEEE/RSJ Int. Conf. on Intelligent Robots and Systems, Honolulu, HI, pp. 31–36 (2001).

D. Castro, U. Nunes and A. Ruano, Obstacle avoidance in local navigation, in: Proc. 10th Mediteranean Conf. on Control and Automation, Lisbon, pp. 9–12 (2002).

M.Watanabe, N. Takeda and K. Onoguchi,Moving obstacle recognition using optical flow pattern analysis for mobile robot, Advanced Robotics 12, 791–816 (1999).

E. Shang, S. Jia, T. Abe and K. Takase, Research on obstacle detection with RFID technology, in: Proc. 23st Annu. Conf. of the Robotic Society of Japan, Tokyo, p. 1B34 (2005).

C. Papageorgiou and T. Poggio, A trainable system for object detection, Int. J. Comp. Vis. 38, 15–33 (2000).

P. Felzenszwalb and D. Huttenlocher, Pictiorial structure for object recognition, Int. J. Comp. Vis. 61, 55–79 (2005).

K. E. Bekris, A. A. Argyros and L. E. Kavraki, Angle-based methods for mobile robot navigation: reaching the entire plane, in: Proc. IEEE Int. Conf. on Robotics and Automation, New Orleans, LA, pp. 2373–2378 (2004).

10

An Implementation of Humanoid Vision - Analysis of Eye Movement and Implementation to Robot

Kunihito Kato, Masayuki Shamoto and Kazuhiko Yamamoto
Gifu University
Japan

1. Introduction

Humanoid robots are becoming like human and imitating human behaviour (HONDA ASIMO)(NAGARA-3). They usually have cameras (Onishi et al., 2005), and then we consider that eyes for the humanoid robot have to be "Humanoid Vision" (Mitsugami et al., 2004).

Humanoid Vision is the vision system which is focused on human actions of the robot, and emulation of human beings. We considered that the human beings is optimized for human frameworks, thus the Humanoid Vision will be the best vision system for humanoid robots which has human like. We used a humanoid robot "YAMATO" which is installed two cameras on his eyes.

We analyzed the human action of tracking an object by the eyes and head. Then, based on this analysis, we made a model for the humanoid robot, and we implemented the obtained features which are tracking actions of the human.

From implementation results, the actions of the humanoid robot became natural motion such like the human beings, and we show the effectiveness of the Humanoid Vision.

2. Humanoid vision

2.1 Introduction of YAMATO

Humanoid robot "YAMATO" is shown in Fig.1 to implement the humanoid vision. Its height is 117cm, and it has 6 DOF on the arms, and 9 DOF on the head. Table 1 shows the detail of DOF on the arm and the head (Mitsugami et al., 2004). It can act various expressions with all 21 DOF.

The humanoid robot has twelve SH2 processors and one SH4 processor. Twelve SH2 processors control motors, and one SH4 processor is main control unit. We can control the robot by a PC through the RS-232C. Then we send the angle of each joint to make him posture or motion.

Magellan Pro is used in the lower body. It has sixteen sonar sensors, sixteen IR sensors and sixteen tactile sensors. Its size is 40.6 cm in diameter and 25.4 cm in height. Linux is installed on it. It can move forward and backward, and traverse.

Fig. 1. Humanoid robot "YAMATO"

Part		Degree of Freedom
Arm	Shoulder	3
	Elbow	2
	Hand	1
Head	Eye	3
	Neck	4
	Mouth	2

Table 1. Title of table, left justified

3. Analysis of eye and head movement

3.1 Camera setting

First, we analyzed how to move eyes and head to track an object. Fig. 2 shows overview of our camera system setting. In this, we used two screens. The moving marker was projected by a projector on a screen (screen1). Another screen (screen2) was used to observe the head movement.

Fig. 3 shows a camera which can take only eyes movement even if his/her face moves. We call this camera as "Eye coordinate camera". This camera system consists of a small camera and a laser pointer which are mounted on a helmet. A laser points on screen2 surface. We can observe the head coordinate by using this screen as shown in Fig. 4. Lines on this screen are written every 10 degrees from center of screen. We took the movement of laser by using another camera. We call this camera as "Head coordinate camera".

Fig. 5 shows the moving marker that is presented for subjects. This is projected on the screen1. To capture human movement, moving marker was moved left or right after stop for several seconds. Its movement speed was 20, 30 and 40deg/s, and its movement range was set from +60 degrees to –60 degrees.

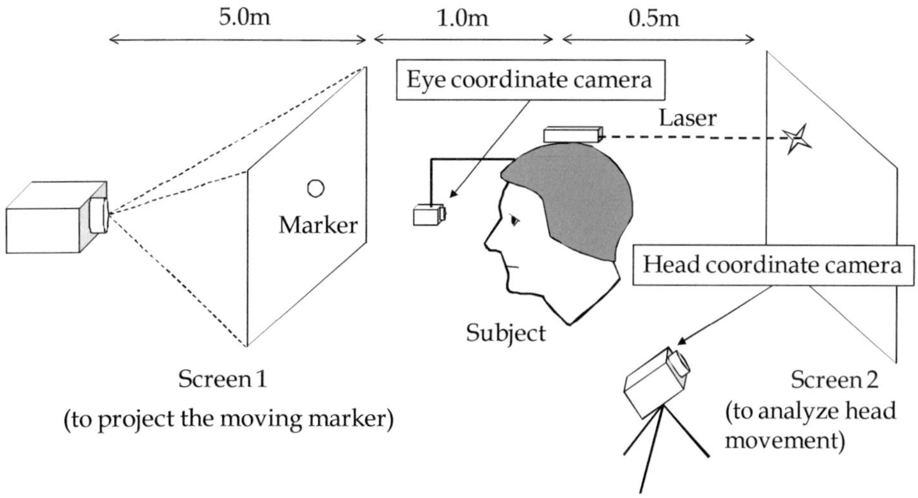

Fig. 2. Experimental setting

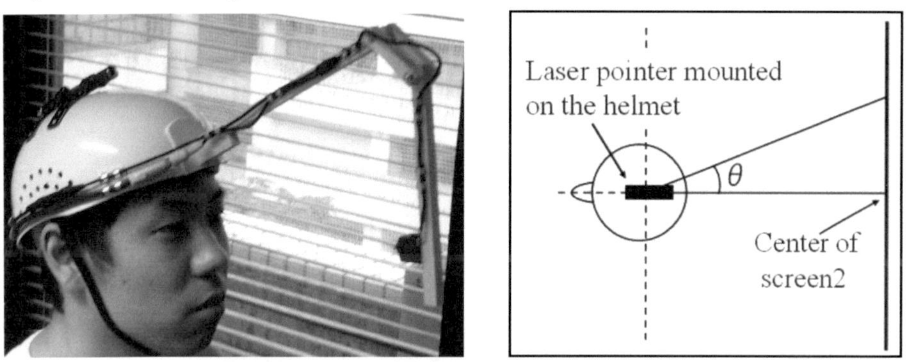

Fig. 3. Eye coordinate camera system (θrange is from +60 degrees to -60 degrees.)

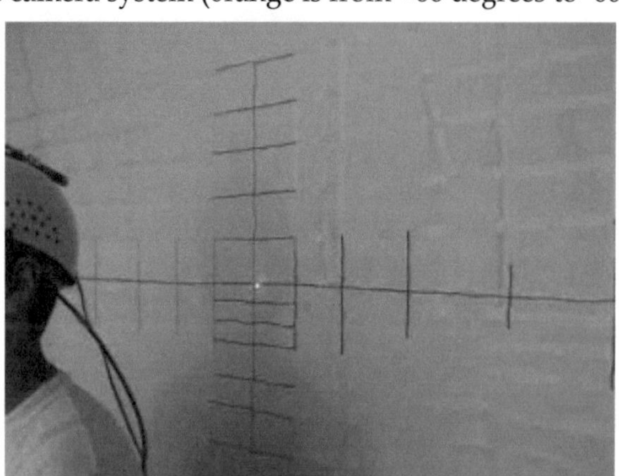

Fig. 4. Screen2 (to analyze head movement)

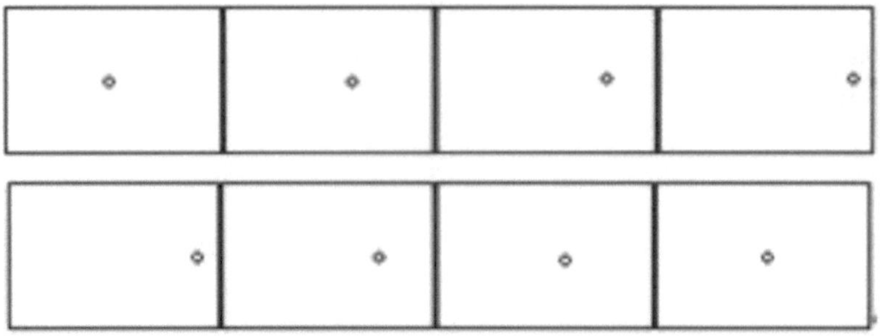

Fig. 5. Example of moving marker images

3.2 Analysis of eye and head movement

Fig. 6 shows images that were taken from the head coordinate camera. White point of images is a point which is illuminated by the laser. From these images, we can measure that the laser pointer is moved on the screen 2. Fig. 7 shows images that are taken from the eye coordinate camera as Fig. 3. The face doesn't move in these images, and these images obtain only changes of eyes and background. Each image as shown in Fig. 6 is corresponding to images as shown in Fig. 7.

We analyzed that how to track an object from these images. Facial movement was analyzed a position that the laser illuminates on the screen2. Eyes movement was analyzed center of the right iris. Eyes movement is assumed that both eyes are same movement. In this analysis, we extracted only x-coordinate of left and right movement. X-coordinate is head angle or eye angle.

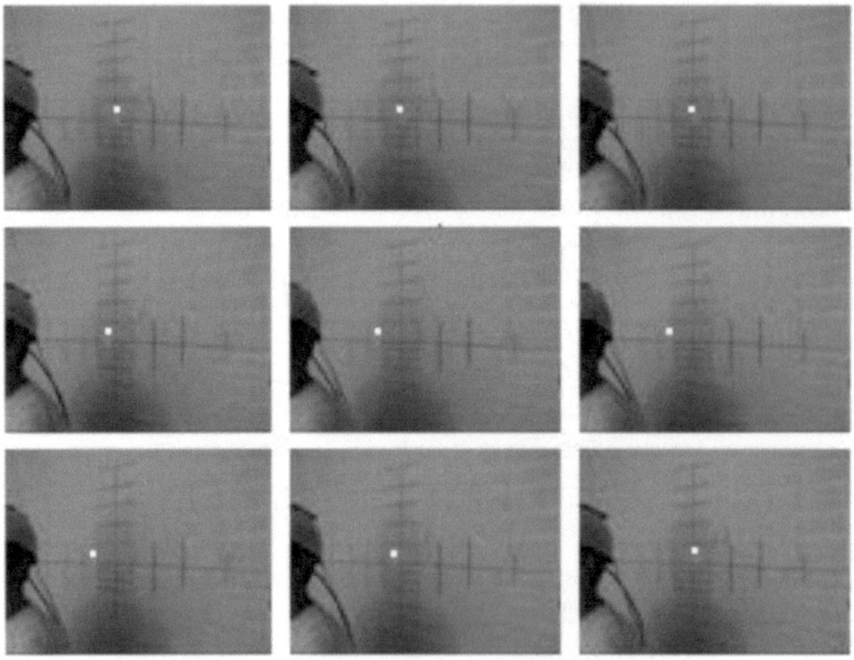

Fig. 6. Head coordinate images

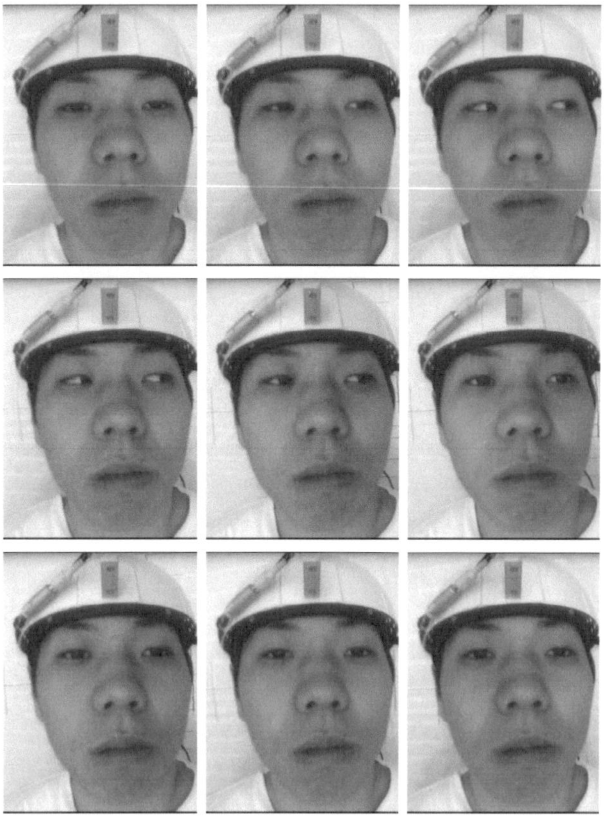

Fig. 7. Eye coordinate images

4. Consideration of eye and head movement

Fig. 8 shows a graph that is observed 20deg/s of moving marker speed. Horizontal axis shows number of frames, and vertical axis shows the head's and eye's x-coordinate in each frame. Each coordinate of frame 0 is defined as baseline. If values are smaller than the value of frame 0, it shows that the subject is moved his face to the right. If values are rather than 0, it shows that he moved his face to the left. In this graph, line of the head is changed after eye is moved. This shows that the moving marker is tracked by using only head after tracking by using only eyes. When the moving marker returned to center, it was tracked by using only eyes again. The moving marker was tracked by using head after eyes returned. From these results, as the moving marker speed was slow, we understood that eyes were used preferentially and tracked it. This velocity is understood that smooth pursuit eye movement is possible.

Fig. 9 shows a graph that is observed 30deg/s of moving marker speed. First, the eyes move to some extent, and next the head started to move. This movement shows that the moving marker was tracked by using the head. In this time, the eyes were holding on the left. When the moving marker returned to the center (after frame 50), eyes moved slightly faster than head. In the graph, eye is used preferentially to track. From these results, some features are given corresponding to the moving marker speed.

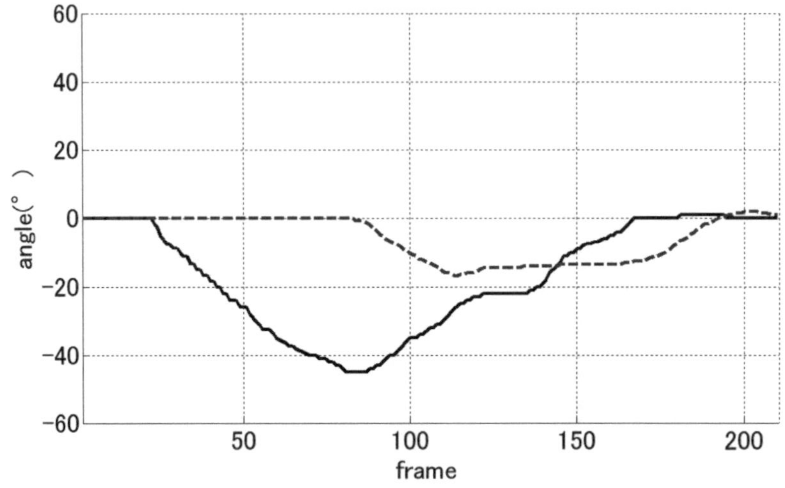

Fig. 8. Movement graph of experiment 20deg/s

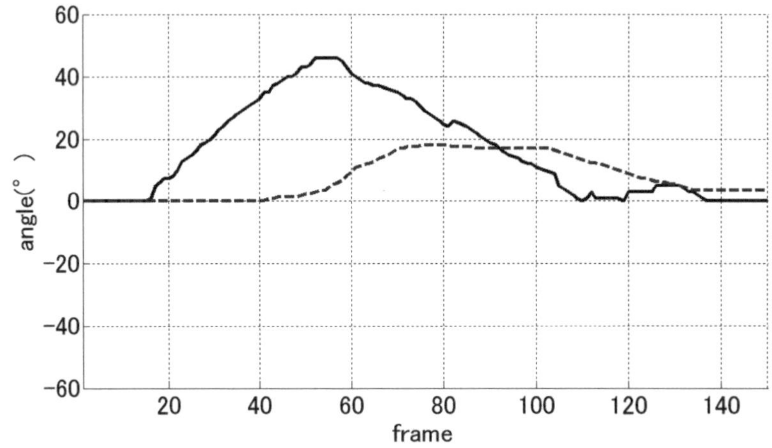

Fig. 9. Movement graph of experiment 30deg/s

Fig. 10 shows a graph that is observed 40deg/s of moving marker speed. In this graph, the eyes move to some extent, and after the head started to move. Between frame 0 and frame 35, change of graphs is similar to Fig. 8 and 9. This shows that the moving marker is tracked by using only head after tracking by using only eyes. But when the moving marker returned to center (after frame 35), head and eye values are changed at the same time. It shows the human uses both face and eyes to track an object (Nakano et al., 1999). Change of eye movement is smooth because of he used both face and eyes to track an object. From this result, smooth pursuit eye movement is possible at 40deg/s (Sera, & Sengoku, 2002) (Tabata et al., 2005).

As the above results, two kind of features of 20~30 deg/s and 30~40 deg/s were obtained.

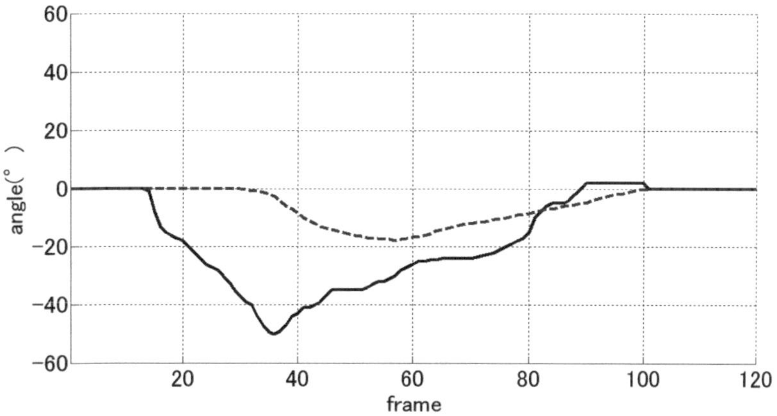

Fig. 10. Movement graph of experiment 40deg/s

5. Making of object tracking model

We made a model based on features obtained by analysis of eye and head movement. This model is shown in Fig. 11. We implemented the humanoid vision with this model to the humanoid robot YAMATO. In conditions, there is an object in the center of the image, and smooth pursuit eye movement is possible. YAMATO detects an object and determines its speed. In the feature of 20~30deg/s, eyes are used first to track an object, and head is used to do it. When an object is returned, eyes are used again. In the feature of 30~40deg/s, eyes are used first to track an object, and head is used to do it. When an object is returned, eyes and head are used to track it in the same time.

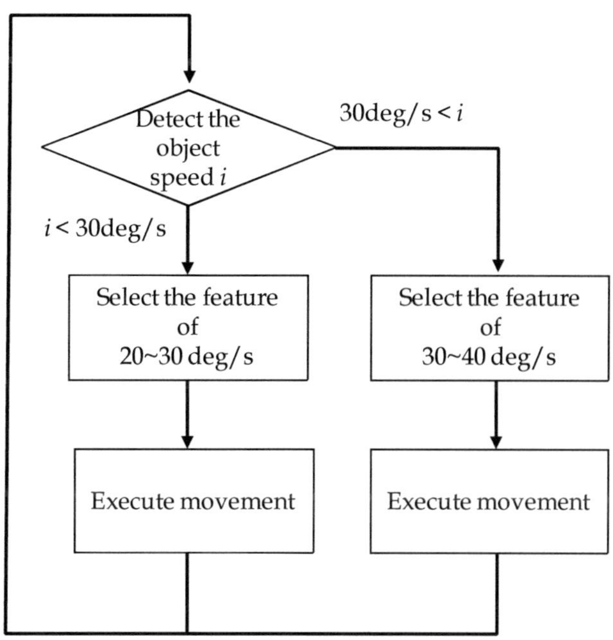

Fig. 11. Implementation model

6. Implementation to the robot

We implemented a model introducing at the previous section. We used a red ball as the target object. A ball was moved sideways, constant speed, and 60 degrees to the left. We repeated it. The distance from YAMATO to a ball was around 1m. Fig. 12 shows a scene of an experiment.

Fig. 13 shows images of movement that YAMATO expressed features of 20~30deg/s. In these images, YAMATO moved his eyes in the first. After he finishes moving his eyes, then head is moved. When a ball was returned to the front, the head and eyes were moved in the sideway.

Fig. 14 shows images of movement that YAMATO expressed features of 30~40deg/s. In these images, YAMATO moved eyes and head. These results show that YAMATO expresses the implementation model.

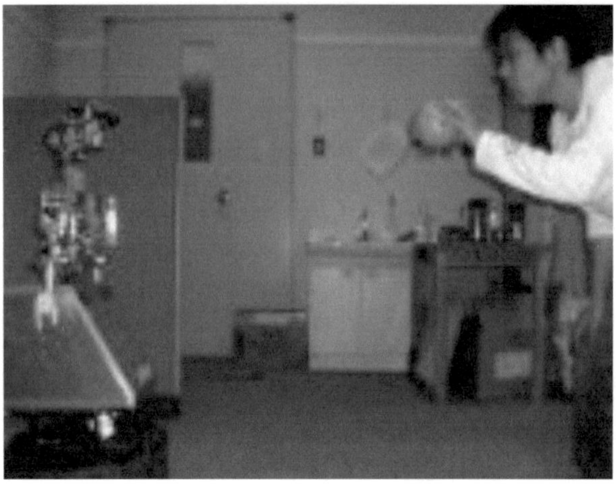

Fig. 12. A scene of an experiment

Fig. 13. Expression of 20~30deg/s

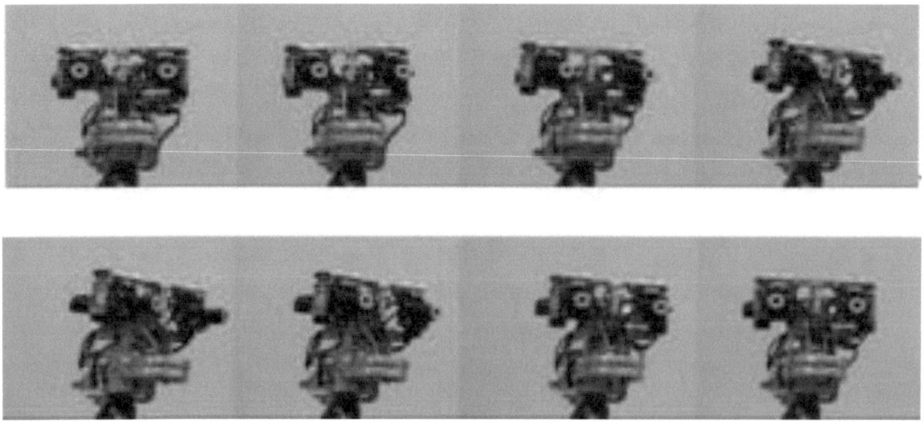

Fig. 14 Expression of 30~40deg/s

7. Conclusion

In this research, we considered that "the humanoid robot has to have humanoid functions", and eyes for humanoid robot have to be "Humanoid Vision". Therefore, we analyzed the human action of tracking an object by the eyes and implemented the obtained features to a humanoid robot "YAMATO". From implementation results, we showed the effectiveness of humanoid vision. Our future works are analysis of longitudinal movement and complicated movements to movement of a robot.

8. References

HONDA ASIMO, http://www.honda.co.jp/ASIMO/

NAGARA-3, http://www.ifujidesign.jp/work/nagara.html

M Onishi, T Odashima, & Z Luo, Cognitive Integrated Motion Generation for Environmental Adaptive Robots, IEEJ trans. EIS, Vol.125(6), pp.856-862, 2005. (in Japanese)

H. Mitsugami, K. Yamamoto, & K. Kato, Motion Emulation System with Humanoid Robot and Image Processing, Proc. of AISM2004, pp.716-721, 2004.

H. Mitsugami, K. Yamamoto, K. Kato, & Y. ogawa, Development of Motion Emulation System Using Humanoid Robot, Proc. of VSMM2004, pp.1136-1141, 2004.

E. Nakano, H. Imamizu, R. Osu, Y. Uno, H. Gomi, T. Yoshitaka, & M. Kawato, Quantitative Examinations of internal representations for arm trajectory planning: Minimum commanded torque change model , Journal of Neurophysiology 81., pp.2140-2155, 1999.

A. Sera, & Y. Sengoku, Saccade Mixture Rates in Smooth Pursuit Eye Movement and Visual Perception of Learning Disabled Children, JAOT trans., Vol21, p.307, 2002. (in Japanese)

H. Tabata, K. Miura, & K. Kawano, Preparation for Smooth Pursuit Eye Movements Based on the Expectation in Humans, IEICE Trans., Vol.J88-D-Ⅱ(12), pp.2350-2357, 2005.(in Japanese)

11

Methods for Postprocessing in Single-Step Diffuse Optical Tomography

Alexander B. Konovalov[1], Vitaly V. Vlasov[1], Dmitry V. Mogilenskikh[1], Olga V. Kravtsenyuk[2] and Vladimir V. Lyubimov[2]
[1]*Russian Federal Nuclear Center – Zababakhin Institute of Applied Physics, Snezhinsk*
[2]*Institute for Laser Physics of Vavilov State Optical Institute Corporation, St.Petersburg*
Russia

1. Introduction

The methods of computed tomography - X-ray computed tomography, magnetic resonance imaging, single-photon emission computed tomography, positron emission tomography, ultrasonic reflectivity tomography and others (Webb, 1998) are now widely used in the practice of medical imaging and their importance increasingly grows. These methods allow the real time reproduction and visual analysis of the inner spatial structure of tissue on the display, which on whole helps increase the quality of diagnostics. However, in the context of problems to be resolved in oncology, the efficiency of currently available commercial tomography methods remains relatively low. One of the reasons is the lack of methods that would allow reliable differentiation between malignant and benign tumors on reconstructed tomograms. The recent clinical studies (Boas et al., 2001; Gibson et al., 2005) show that rapidly developing diffuse optical tomography (DOT) is very likely to help out. DOT is unique in its ability to separately reconstruct the spatial distributions of optical parameters (absorption and scattering coefficients) which helps visualize the spatial pattern of blood volume and oxygen saturation. As a result, it becomes possible to differentiate and spatially localize such phenomena as cancerous tissue vascularisation and angiogenesis and hence detect cancer in the early stage of its development.

DOT implies that tissue is probed by near-infrared radiation from the so-called therapeutic window (700-900 nm) where absorption by tissue is minimal. Position dependent measurements are taken, i.e. near-infrared light from an array of sources is observed with an array of receivers. Then an inverse problem, i.e. the tomographic reconstruction problem is solved to infer the spatially localized optical properties of tissue. The main problem of DOT is the low spatial resolution because of the multiple scattering of photons that do not have regular trajectories and are distributed in the entire volume V being probed. As a result, each volume element significantly contributes to the detected signal. The basic equation of DOT is written as

$$g(\mathbf{r}_s,\mathbf{r}_d) = \int_V f(\mathbf{r}) W(\mathbf{r},\mathbf{r}_s,\mathbf{r}_d) d^3 r , \qquad (1)$$

where $g(\mathbf{r}_s, \mathbf{r}_d)$ is the optical projection measured for source position $\mathbf{r}_s$ and receiver position $\mathbf{r}_d$ (usually the relative signal disturbance due to optical inhomogeneities), $f(\mathbf{r})$ is the sought function of optical inhomogeneity distribution (later on the object function), and $W(\mathbf{r}, \mathbf{r}_s, \mathbf{r}_d)$ is a weight function which provides for the contribution of each volume element to the signal formed between the points $\mathbf{r}_s$ and $\mathbf{r}_d$. Equation (1) and hence the inverse problem of DOT are strongly nonlinear because of the nonlinear dependence of photon flux on optical parameters. The local linearization of the inverse problem is performed, as a rule, by using multistep reconstruction algorithms (Arridge, 1999; Yodh & Chance, 1995) based on the variational formulation of the equation that describes the radiation transport model. A classical example of these algorithms is the Newton-Raphson algorithm with the Levenberg-Marquardt iterative procedure (Arridge, 1999). The multistep algorithms allow gaining relatively high spatial resolution (0.3~0.5 cm) for diffusion tomograms, but they are not as fast as required for real time diagnostics. The reason is that the forward problem of DOT, i.e. the problem of radiation propagation through tissue is solved numerically many times and at each step of linearization it is necessary to adjust the matrix of the system of algebraic equations that describe the discrete reconstruction model.

As shown in our earlier papers (Kalintsev et al., 2005; Konovalov et al., 2003; 2006b; 2007a; 2007b; Lyubimov et al., 2002; 2003), there exists a unique opportunity to make the reconstruction procedure much faster by changing over in equation (1) from volume integration to integration along an effective trajectory from source to receiver. The photon average trajectory method (PAT method) we have developed finds such a trajectory using a probabilistic interpretation of light energy transfer by photons from source to receiver. The method introduces the density of the conditional probability $P[\mathbf{r}, \tau\ (\mathbf{r}_s, 0) \rightarrow (\mathbf{r}_d, t)]$ that a photon migrating from a space-time source point $(\mathbf{r}_s, 0)$ to a space-time receiver point $(\mathbf{r}_d, t)$ reaches a point $\mathbf{r} \in V$ at time τ $(0 \leq \tau \leq t)$. The effective trajectory is a photon average trajectory (PAT) described by the mass center of the spatial distribution P over a time t. If we deal with absorbing inhomogeneities, then in the approximation of perturbation theory by Born or Rytov, integral (1) can be written as the fundamental equation of the PAT method (Kravtsenyuk & Lyubimov, 2000; Lyubimov et al., 2002; 2003)

$$g(\mathbf{r}_s, \mathbf{r}_d, t) = \int_L v(l) \left\{ \int_V f(\mathbf{r}) P[\mathbf{r}, \tau | (\mathbf{r}_s, 0) \rightarrow (\mathbf{r}_d, t)] d^3 r \right\} dl, \tag{2}$$

where L is the PAT from the source point $\mathbf{r}_s$ to the receiver point $\mathbf{r}_d$, l is distance along the PAT, and $v(l)$ is a factor meaning the inverse relative velocity of the mass center of the distribution P along the PAT. The volume integral in the braces is the sought object function $f(\mathbf{r})$ averaged over the spatial distribution of the photons that contribute to the signal recorded at time t. If denote the averaging operator by $<\cdot>$, we can write (2) in a more compact form as

$$g = \int_L v(l) < f(\mathbf{r}) > dl\,. \tag{3}$$

Equation (3) is an analog of the Radon transform and can be inverted for the function $< f(\mathbf{r}) >$ with the fast algorithms of projection tomography.

It is well known (Kak & Slanay, 1988; Herman, 1980) that there are two different approaches to the solution of type (3) integral equations. The first is based on their analytical solution and the use of the resulted inversion formulas for finding the object function in discrete points of space. The second consists in the representation of the integral equation as a system of linear algebraic equations which is solved for the set of unknowns that define the discrete values of the object function. Replacing volume integral (1) by trajectory integral (3) in both the approaches makes it possible to change over from multistep to single-step reconstruction. For the first approach this means that the integral formulas for inverting equation (3) are linear and no linearization steps are needed. For the second approach the single-step reconstruction means that the system of algebraic equations describing the discrete model is only once inverted and the matrix needs no adjustment.

In our previous papers we provided some examples of 2D reconstruction from data simulated for the time-domain measurement technique to show that the PAT method can be implemented with integral algorithms (Konovalov et al., 2003; 2007b; Lyubimov et al., 2003) as well as with algebraic ones (Konovalov et al., 2006b; 2007a; Lyubimov et al., 2002). Compared with the multistep algorithms, the former give a terrific gain (a factor of about 100) in calculation time, but are too inaccurate in the reconstruction of optical inhomogeneities near the boundaries of the study object. This is since the implementation of the integral inversion formulas has to be done through a linear (or rough piecewise-linear) approximation of PATs that really bend near boundaries because of avalanche photon migration outside the object. The algebraic algorithms are not so fast, but successfully treat the bended trajectories partly compensating for this shortcoming. However on the whole one must admit that the integral and algebraic algorithms inverting equation (3) are severely behind the multistep algorithms in accuracy because they reproduce the function $< f(\mathbf{r}) >$, i.e., reconstruct the tomograms that are a priori blurred due to averaging. In fact the singlestep reconstruction helps localize an inhomogeneity, but it cannot say anything about its size and shape. In order to compensate for blurring and get useful information for the successful structure analysis and proper diagnosis in the end, the reconstructed tomograms must be subject to posprocessing.

This chapter describes two methods of postprocessing that are complementary and used successively one after another. The first implies iterative restoration with the use of the spatially variant blurring model by Nagy et al. (2004) which is described by a system of linear algebraic equations, whose matrix contains information on blurring in different regions of the image being restored. The system is inverted using iterative algorithms which solve systems with very sparse matrices. The method was developed for restoring aerospace photographs and we adapted it to diffuse optical images (Konovalov et al., 2007b) as well as to X-ray radiograms taken in X-pinch rays (Konovalov et al., 2006c). Section 2 of this chapter gives a detailed description of the method and gives examples on the restoration of model diffusion tomograms reconstructed with the PAT method. It is shown that space-varying restoration helps significantly clear the blurring and offset inhomogeneity shape distortions present on blurred tomograms. Unfortunately, the method is incapable of the accurate restoration of step functions and inhomogeneities defined by constant values of optical parameters are still reproduced with blurred boundaries. The second phase of postprocessing implies the use of nonlinear color interpretation methods (Mogilenskikh, 2000) developed at the Russian Federal Nuclear Center - Zababakhin Institute of Applied Physics for the purpose of getting more informative images of hydrodynamic plasma objects. The methods are based on the generation of nonlinear analytical and statistical functions of correspondence (hereafter correspondence function - CF) between image intensity and color space. They are described in Section 3 of this chapter. Nonlinear CFs are applied to restored tomograms to segment and identify inhomogeneity boundaries. It is shown that in case of simple model objects (absorbing macro-inhomogeneities in a homogeneous scattering medium) it is possible to find a combination of nonlinear CFs which allows the boundaries of inhomogeneities to be reconstructed completely. Section 4 formulates basic inferences and outlines further research to improve the methods of diffusion tomogram postprocessing.

2. Space-varying restoration of diffusion tomograms

2.1 Validation of linear spatially variant blurring model

In the theory of linear systems and transforms (Papoulis, 1968) the image blurring caused by systematic errors of a visualization system is described with a model of a linear filter. Such a model is successfully used in projection tomography for estimating the accuracy of the spatial structure reproduction (Konovalov et al., 2006a; Very & Bracewell, 1979). It introduces into consideration a point spread function (PSF) that is defined as the image of an infinitesimally small point object and specifies how points in the image are distorted. A diffuse optical tomograph in general is not a linear filter because of the absence of regular rectilinear trajectories of photons. However, the PAT method that we use for reconstruction possesses a number of features which in our opinion warrant the application of a model of a linear filter in the given particular case of DOT. These features are as follows:

a. Our concept proposes the conditional PATs to be used for reconstruction as regular trajectories.
b. The PATs are close to straight lines inside the object and bend only near its boundaries.
c. The algorithms where all operations and transformations are linear are used for reconstruction.

Therefore, the PSF at the first order approximation may be assumed for describing the blurring due to reconstruction.

Let us consider at once the variance of the PSF against spatial shift. The time integral of the function $P[\mathbf{r},\tau\,(\mathbf{r}_s\,,0) \rightarrow (\mathbf{r}_d\,,t)]$ for each τ describes instantaneous distribution of diffuse photon trajectories. At time moment $\tau = t$ this distribution forms a zone of the most probable trajectories of photons migrated from $(\mathbf{r}_s\,,0)$ to $(\mathbf{r}_d\,,t)$. This zone is shaped as a banana (Lyubimov et al., 2002; Volkonskii et al., 1999) with vertices at the points of source and receiver localizations on the boundary of the scattering object. The effective width of this zone estimates the theoretical spatial resolution and is described by the standard rootmean-square deviation of photon position from the PAT as follows

$$\Delta(\tau) = \left[\int_V |\mathbf{r} - \mathbf{R}(\tau)|^2 P[\mathbf{r},\tau \,|\, (\mathbf{r}_s,0) \rightarrow (\mathbf{r}_d,t)]\, d^3 r \right]^{1/2}, \tag{4}$$

where $\mathbf{R}(\tau)$ is a radius-vector describing the PAT. According to equation (4), as the object boundary is approached, the theoretical resolution tends to zero. In the center, the resolution is worst and depends on the object size. Thus, the resolution and, therefore, the PSF describing the PAT tomogram blurring are strongly variant against the spatial shift. It means that the spatially variant blurring model may exclusively be assumed for restoration of the PAT tomograms.

The generic spatially variant blurring would require a point source at every pixel location to fully describe the blurring operation. Since it is impossible to do this, even for small images, some approximations should be made. There are several approaches to the restoration of images degraded by the spatially variant blurring. One of them is based on a geometrical coordinate transformation (Sawchuk, 1974) and uses coordinate distortions or known symmetries to transform the spatially variant PSF into one that is spatially invariant. After applying a spatially invariant restoration method, the inverse coordinate distortion is used to obtain the result. This approach does not satisfy us because the coordinate transformation functions need to be known explicitly. Another approach considered, for example, in (Fish et al., 1996), is based on the assumption that the blurring is approximately spatially invariant in small regions of the image domain. Each region is restored using its own spatially invariant PSF, and the results are then sewn together to obtain the restored image. This approach is laborious and also gives the blocking artifacts at the region boundaries. To restore the PAT tomograms, we use the blurring model recently developed by Nagy et. al. (2004). According to it the blurred image is partitioned into many regions with the spatially invariant PSFs. However, rather than deblurring the individual regions locally and then sewing the individual results together, this method interpolates the individual PSFs, and restores the image globally. It is clear that the accuracy of such method depends on the number of regions into which the image domain is partitioned. The partitioning where the size of one region tends to a spatial resolution seems to be sufficient for obtaining a restoration result of good quality.

2.2 Description of blurring model

Let **f** be a vector representing the unknown true image of the object function $f(\mathbf{r})$ and let $<\mathbf{f}>$ be a vector representing the reconstructed image $<f(\mathbf{r})>$ blurred due to averaging. The spatially variant blurring model of Nagy et al. (2004) is described by a system of linear algebraic equations

$$<\mathbf{f}> = \mathbf{A}\cdot\mathbf{f}\,, \tag{5}$$

where **A** is a large ill-conditioned matrix that models the blurring operator (blurring matrix). If the image is partitioned into m regions, the matrix **A** has the following structure

$$\mathbf{A} = \sum_{j=1}^{m} \mathbf{D}_j \mathbf{A}_j\,, \tag{6}$$

where $\mathbf{A}_j$ is a matrix that contains information on the spatially invariant PSF assigned to the j-th region of the image and $\mathbf{D}_j$ is a diagonal matrix satisfying the condition

$$\sum_{j=1}^{m} \mathbf{D}_j = \mathbf{I}\,, \tag{7}$$

where **I** is the identity matrix. The piecewise constant interpolation implemented implies that the i-th diagonal entry of $\mathbf{D}_j$ is one if the i-th pixel is in the j-th region, and zero otherwise. The matrix $\mathbf{A}_j$ is uniquely determined by a single column $\mathbf{a}_j$ that contains all of the non-zero values in $\mathbf{A}_j$. This vector $\mathbf{a}_j$ is obtained from the invariant PSF $\mathbf{PSF}_j$ corresponding to the j-th region as follows

$$\mathbf{a}_j = vec(\mathbf{PSF}_j^{\,T})\,, \tag{8}$$

where the operator $vec(\cdot)$ transforms matrices into vectors by stacking the columns.

0	0	0
0	f	0
0	0	0

f	f	f
f	f	f
f	f	f

f_{rc}	f_r	f_{rc}
f_c	f	f_c
f_{rc}	f_r	f_{rc}

Fig. 1. Standard boundary conditions: (a) zero, (b) periodic, (c) reflexive (f_c is obtained by the transposition of columns f, f_r by the transposition of rows f, f_{rc} by the transposition of rows and columns)

The blurring matrix **A** accounts for a priori information on the extrapolation of the restored image beyond its boundaries, i.e. boundary conditions. This is necessary to compensate for near-boundary artifacts caused by Gibbs effect. The blurring model implements three type of "standard" boundary conditions: zero, periodic and reflexive. The zero boundary conditions correspond to image extension by zeros (Figure 1(a)). The periodic boundary conditions assume that the image is periodically repeated (extended) in all directions (Figure 1(b)). Finally, the reflexive boundary conditions mean that the image is specularly (i.e., normally) reflected at the boundary (Figure 1(c)). The matrix $\mathbf{A}_j$ is banded block Toeplitz matrix with banded Toeplitz blocks (Kamm & Nagy, 1998) if the zero boundary conditions are used, or the banded block circulant matrix with banded circulant blocks (Andrews & Hunt, 1977) for the periodic boundary conditions, or the sum of banded block Toeplitz matrix with banded Toeplitz blocks and the banded block Hankel matrix with banded Hankel blocks (Ng et al., 1999) for the reflexive boundary conditions. The "banding" of matrix $\mathbf{A}_j$ means that the matrix-vector multiplication product $\mathbf{D}_j\mathbf{A}_j\mathbf{z}$, where $\mathbf{z}$ is any vector defined into the image domain, depends on the values of $\mathbf{z}$ in the j -th region, as well as on values in other regions within the width of the borders of the j -th region. The matrix-vector multiplication procedure is implemented by means of the 2D discrete fast Fourier transform and is fully described in (Nagy & O'Leary, 1997). Note that the standard boundary conditions may give the bandpass artifacts, if the image contains complex structures adjoining to the boundary. In this case a special approach to image extrapolation is needed (Konovalov et al., 2006c).

To simulate the invariant PSF corresponding to an individual region, first of all we must choose a characteristic point and specify a point inhomogeneity in it. It is advisable to choose the center of the region for location of the point inhomogeneity. Then we must perform two steps as follows:

a. Simulate optical projections from the point inhomogeneity.
b. Reconstruct the tomogram with PSF by the PAT method.

The optical projections from the point inhomogeneity are simulated via the numerical solution of the time-dependent diffusion equation with the use of the finite element method (FEM). To guarantee against inaccuracy of calculations, we optimize the finite element mesh so that it is strongly compressed in the vicinity of the point inhomogeneity location. For FEM calculations the point inhomogeneity is assigned by three equal values into the nodes of the little triangle on the center of the compressed vicinity. The example of the mesh for the circular scattering object 6.8 cm in diameter is given in Figure 2.

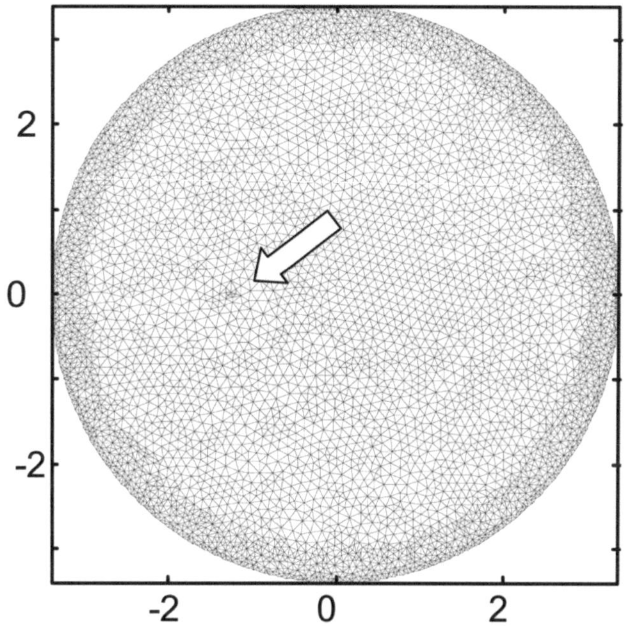

Fig. 2. High-resolution finite element mesh with the compressed vicinity

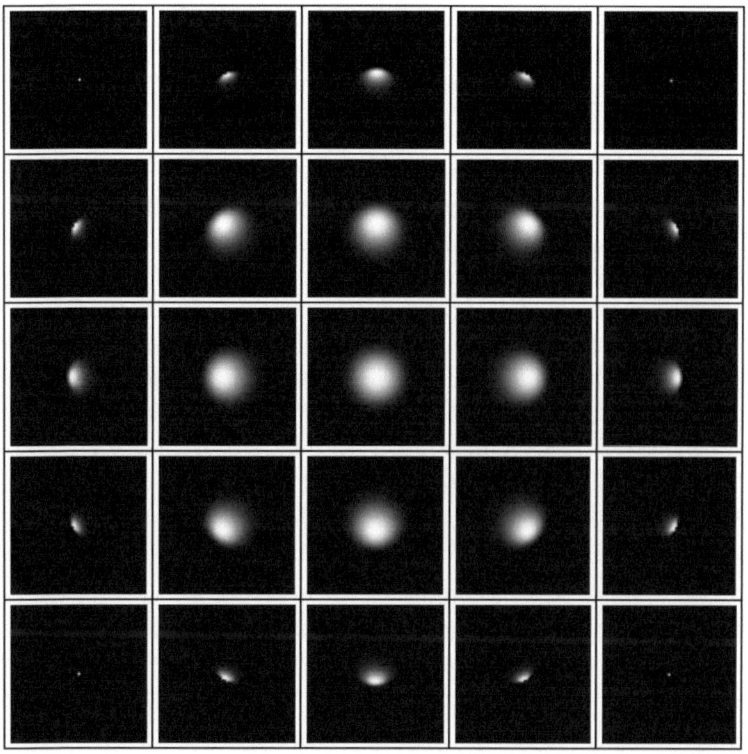

Fig. 3. The 5×5 array of the invariant PSFs corresponding to individual regions of the image domain

CGLS	MRNSD
$\mathbf{f} = <\mathbf{f}>$	$\mathbf{f} = <\mathbf{f}>$
$\mathbf{r} = <\mathbf{f}> - \mathbf{Af}$	$\mathbf{g} = \mathbf{A}^T(\mathbf{Af} - <\mathbf{f}>)$
$\mathbf{g} = \mathbf{A}^T\mathbf{r}$	$\mathbf{F} = diag(\mathbf{f})$
$\gamma = \\|\mathbf{g}\\|^2$	$\gamma = \mathbf{g}^T\mathbf{F}\mathbf{g}$
for $k = 1,2,\ldots$	for $k = 1,2,\ldots$
if $k == 1$, $\mathbf{s} = \mathbf{g}$	$\mathbf{s} = -\mathbf{F}\mathbf{g}$
otherwise $\mathbf{s} = \mathbf{g} + (\gamma / \gamma_{old})\mathbf{s}$	$\mathbf{u} = \mathbf{As}$
$\mathbf{u} = \mathbf{As}$	$\alpha = \min(\gamma / \mathbf{u}^T\mathbf{u}, \min_{s_i<0}(-f_i / s_i))$
$\alpha = \gamma / \\|\mathbf{u}\\|^2$	$\mathbf{f} = \mathbf{f} + \alpha\mathbf{s}$
$\mathbf{f} = \mathbf{f} + \alpha\mathbf{s}$	$\mathbf{F} = diag(\mathbf{f})$
$\mathbf{r} = \mathbf{r} - \alpha\mathbf{u}$	$\mathbf{z} = \mathbf{A}^T\mathbf{u}$
$\mathbf{g} = \mathbf{A}^T\mathbf{r}$	$\mathbf{g} = \mathbf{g} + \alpha\mathbf{z}$
$\gamma_{old} = \gamma$, $\gamma = \\|\mathbf{g}\\|^2$	$\gamma = \mathbf{g}^T\mathbf{F}\mathbf{g}$
end	end

Fig. 4. The step sequences describing the restoration algorithms

Figure 3 presents the array of the invariant PSFs calculated for the case of image partitioning into 5×5 regions.

2.3 Restoration algorithms

After constructing the blurring matrix $\mathbf{A}$, an acceptable algorithm should be chosen to solve system (5) for unknown vector **x**. Because of the large dimensions of the linear system, iterative algorithms are typically used to compute approximations of **f**. They include a variety of least-squares algorithms (Bjorck, 1996), the steepest descent algorithms (Kaufman, 1993), the expectation-maximization algorithms (Bertero & Boccacci, 1998), and many others. Since non of the iterative algorithm is optimal for all image restoration problems, the study of iterative algorithms is an important area of research. In present paper we consider the conjugate gradient algorithm CGLS (Bjorck, 1996) and the steepest descent algorithm MRNSD (Kaufman, 1993). These algorithms represent two different approaches: a Krylov subspace method applied to the normal equations and a simple descent scheme with enforcing a nonnegativity constraint on solution. The step sequences describing the algorithms are given in Figure 4. The operator $\|\cdot\|$ denotes a Euclidian norm, the function $diag(\cdot)$ produces the diagonal matrix containing the initial vector.

Both CGLS and MRNSD are easy to implement and converge faster than, for example, the expectation-maximization algorithms. Both the algorithms exhibit a semi-convergence behavior with respect to the relative error $\|\mathbf{f}_k - \mathbf{f}\| / \|\mathbf{f}\|$, where $\mathbf{f}_k$ is the approximation of **f** at the k -th iteration. It means that, as the iterative process goes on, the relative error begins to decrease and, after some optimal iteration, begins to rise. By stopping the iteration when the error is low, we obtain a good regularized approximation of the solution. Thus, the iteration number plays the role of the regularization parameter. This is very important for us, as the matrix **A** is severely ill-conditioned and regularization must be necessarily incorporated. To estimate the optimal iteration number, we use the following blurring residual that measures the image quality change after beginning the restoration process:

$$\beta_k = \|\mathbf{f}_k - \mathbf{f}\| / \| < \mathbf{f} > - \mathbf{f}\| \% . \tag{9}$$

Like the relative error, the blurring residual has a minimum that corresponds to the optimal iteration number. Note that we do not know the true image (vector **f**) in clinical applications of DOT. However, using criterion $\beta_k \to \min$, it is possible to calibrate the algorithms in relation to the optimal iteration number via experiments (including numerical experiments) with phantoms. In general many different practical cases of optical inhomogeneities can be considered for calibration. In clinical explorations, the particular case is chosen from a priori information, which the blurred tomograms contain after reconstruction. Further, regularization can be enforced in a variety of other ways, including Tikhonov (Groetsch, 1984), iteration truncation (Hanson & O'Leary, 1993), as well as mixed approaches. Preconditioned iterative regularization by truncating the iterations is an effective approach to accelerate the rate of convergence (Nagy et al., 2004). In general, preconditioning amounts to finding a nonsingular matrix $\mathbf{C}$, such that $\mathbf{C} \approx \mathbf{A}$ and such that **C** can be easily inverted. The iterative method is then applied to preconditioned system

$$\mathbf{C}^{-1} < \mathbf{f} > = \mathbf{C}^{-1}\mathbf{A} \cdot \mathbf{f} . \tag{10}$$

The appearance of matrix **C** is defined by the regularization parameter $\lambda < 1$ that characterizes a step size at each iteration. In this paper we consider two methods for calculating λ: generalized cross validation (GCV) method (Hanson & O'Leary, 1993) and method based on criterion of blurring residual minimum. In the first case we assume that a solution computed on a reduced set of data points should give a good estimate of missing points. The GCV method finds a function of λ that measures the errors in these estimates. The minimum of this GCV function corresponds to the optimal regularization parameter. In the second case we calculate blurring residual (9) for different numbers of iterations and different discrete values of λ, taken with the step $\Delta\lambda$. The minimum of blurring residual corresponds to optimal number of iterations and the optimal regularization parameter.

The main reason of choosing MRNSD for PAT tomogram restoration is that this algorithm enforces a nonnegativity constraint on the solution approximation at each iteration. Such enforcing produces much more accurate approximate solutions in many practical cases of nonnegative true image (Kaufman, 1993). In DOT (for example, optical mammotomography), when the tumor structure is detected, one can expect that the disturbances of optical parameters are not randomly inhomogeneous functions, but they are smooth or step nonnegative ones standing out against a close-to-zero background and forming the macroinhomogeneity images. Indeed, the typical values of the absorption coefficient are between 0.04 and 0.07 cm^{-1} for healthy breast tissue, and between 0.07 and 0.1 cm^{-1} for breast tumor (Yates et al., 2005). Thus, we have the nonnegative true image $f(\mathbf{r})$. This a priori information gives the right to apply constrained MRNSD and change negative values for zeros after applying unconstrained CGLS.

2.4 Restoration results

To demonstrate the effect of blurring reduction on PAT-reconstructed tomograms, a numerical experiment was conducted, wherein circular and rectangular scattering objects with absorbing inhomogeneities were reconstructed from model optical projections and then restored. In this chapter we present processing results for five objects whose description and parameters are given in Table 1. To simulate the optical projections, we solved the timedependent diffusion equation with the instantaneous point source for photon density by the FEM. The signals of the receivers were found as photon fluxes on the object boundary. Each optical projection was calculated as logarithm of the non-perturbed signal determined for the homogeneous medium to the signal perturbed due to inhomogeneities. For all objects from Table 1 we used the measurement ratio 32×32 (32 sources and 32 receivers). The circular objects were reconstructed by the backprojection algorithm with convolution filtering (Konovalov et al., 2003; 2007b; Lyubimov et al., 2003) and the rectangular ones with the modified multiplicative algebraic reconstruction technique (Konovalov et al., 2006b; 2007a). To restore the reconstructed tomograms, in all cases we partitioned the image domain into 5×5 regions and applied the reflexive boundary conditions.

Description	Visual model	Sizes, cm	Optical parameters			
			f^{obj} cm^{-1}	f^{inh} cm^{-1}	D cm	n
Circular object with 1 cm-in-diam inhomogeneity		Ø6.8	0.05	0.075	0.066	1.4
Circular object with two 1 cm-in-diam inhomogeneities						
Circular object with two 1.4 cm-in-diam inhomogeneities	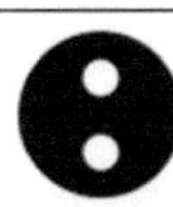					
Rectangular object with two 1 cm-in-diam inhomogeneities		11×8			0.034	
Rectangular object with two 1 cm-in-diam inhomogeneities and RIC	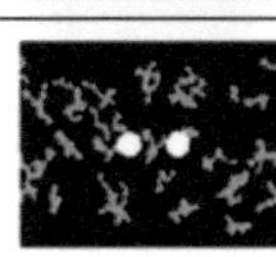			0.075 (inhom) 0.06 (RIC)		

Table 1. Description and parameters of the model scattering objects: f^{obj}, absorption coefficient of the object; f^{inh}, absorption coefficient of the inhomogeneities; D, diffusion coefficient; n, refraction index; RIC, randomly inhomogeneous component

Figure 5 shows results of restoration for the circular object with the inhomogeneity 1 cm inndiameter in comparison with its blurred tomogram. The results are presented as gray level images. The axes are graduated in centimeters and the palette scale is in inverse centimeters. The points on the images present the positions of the sources on the boundary of the object. The circle on the left image shows the true boundary of the inhomogeneity. It is seen that restoration allows getting closer to its actual size.

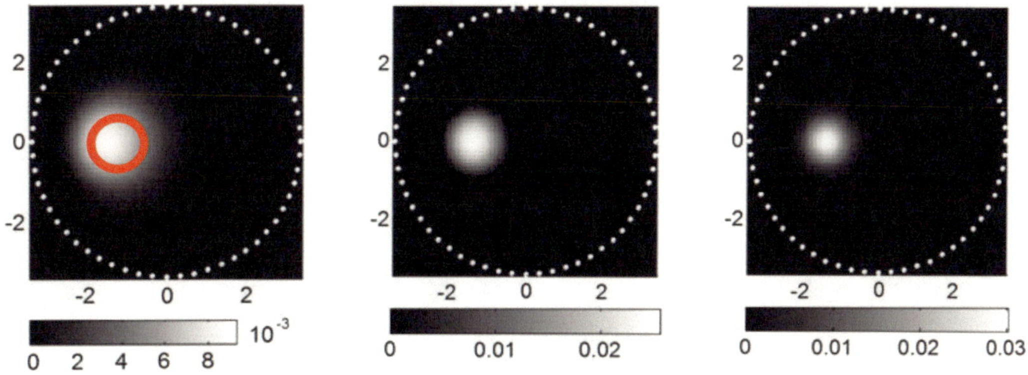

Fig. 5. Reconstruction and restoration results for the circular object with the inhomogeneity 1 cm in diameter: blurred tomogram (left) and results of its restoration by CGLS and MRNSD (center and right)

Figure 6 shows pseudo-3D plots representing the same results for the circular object with two inhomogeneities that form a periodic structure. Digits on the plots show the values of the modulation transfer coefficient estimated as the relative depth of the dish between two peaks. This figure demonstrates that restoration helps significantly increase the modulation transfer coefficient and hence the spatial resolution of tomograms. For all restorations presented in Figures 5 and 6 we used the unpreconditioned algorithms (CGLS and MRNSD). The optimal iteration number obtained by the criterion of blurring residual minimum is equal to 15 in the case of CGLS and to 9 in the case of MRNSD, respectively.

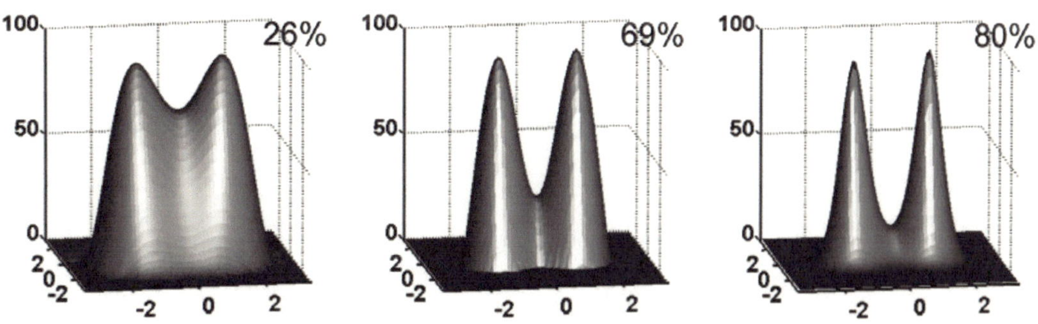

Fig. 6. Reconstruction and restoration results for the circular object with two inhomogeneities 1 cm in diameter: blurred tomogram (left) and results of its restoration by CGLS and MRNSD (center and right)

Figure 7 presents the restoration results obtained with the use of preconditioned MRNSD. The left image corresponds to the regularization parameter calculated by the GCV method ($\lambda = 0.003$). To obtain the central restoration, we used preconditioner with $\lambda = 0.1$. This value of the regularization parameter was found by the criterion of blurring residual minimum. The right image in Figure 7 shows the result of restoration by unpreconditioned MRNSD for comparison. The optimal iteration number in the cases of preconditioned algorithm was equal to 3. Thus, preconditioners allow the restoration procedure to be accelerated. But, as it follows from Figure 7, preconditioned algorithms distort the form of inhomogeneities being restored. We can conjecture that the image partitioning into 5×5 regions is not enough to obtain good quality of restoration by preconditioned algorithms. As we save computational time, in future the image partitioning number may be increased.

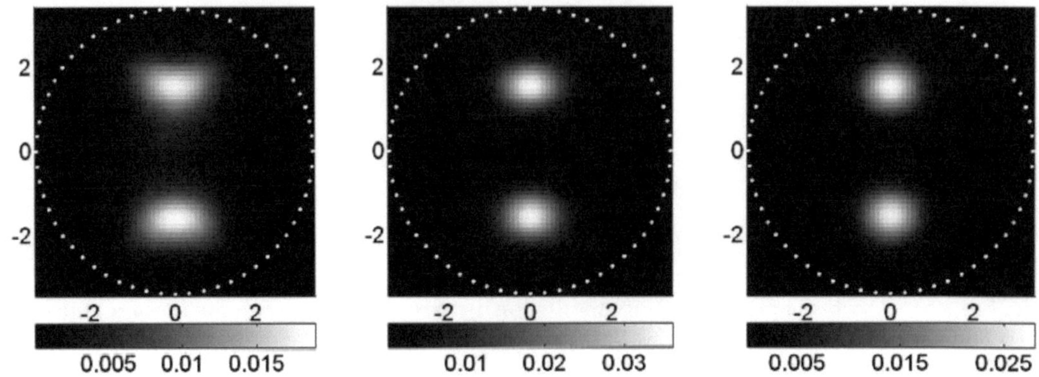

Fig. 7. Comparison of the restoration results obtained with the use of preconditioned MRNSD (left and center) and unpreconditioned one (right) for the circular object with two inhomogeneities 1.4 cm in diameter

Figure 8 demonstrates results obtained in the testing of unpreconditioned MRNSD for noise immunity. The left image shows the 20%-noised sinogram that is a gray level map of optical projection distributions over the index ranges of the source and the receiver. The sinogram abscissa is the receiver index and the sinogram ordinate is the source index. The palette scale is graduated in relative units. Despite the fact that the reconstructed tomogram (center) is strongly blurred, the restored image (right) has only low distortion in the shape of inhomogeneities. Thus, the restoration algorithm demonstrates good immunity to measurement noise.

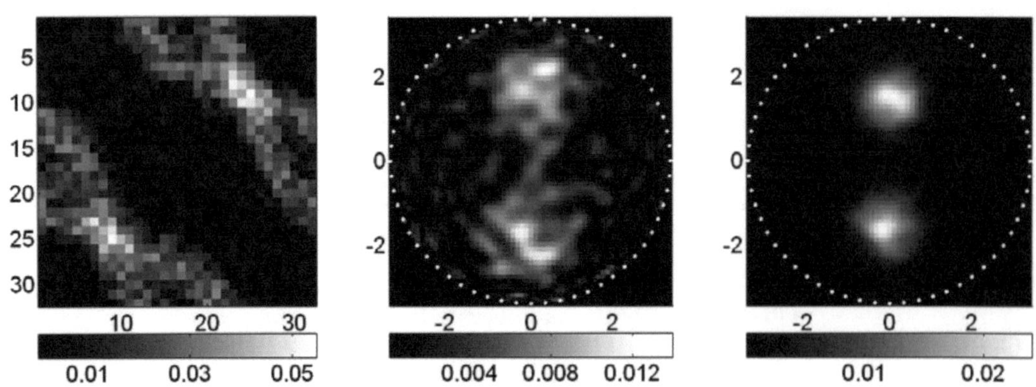

Fig. 8. 20%-noised sinogram (left), blurred tomogram (center) and restoration with unpreconditioned MRNSD (right) for the circular object with two inhomogeneities 1.4 cm in diameter

Figure 9 compares the spatially variant model by Nagy and a spatially invariant model that is described by one PSF defined in the center of the tomogram domain. In the latter case the centers of inhomogeneities are seen to be abnormally shifted from their true positions marked with crosses.

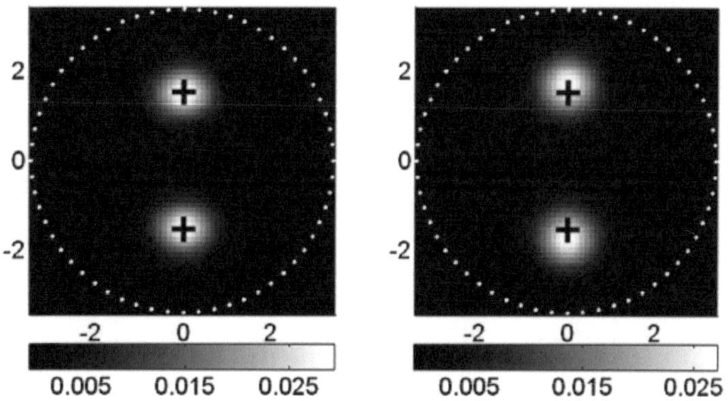

Fig. 9. Restoration results for the circular object with two inhomogeneities 1.4 cm in diameter, obtained with spatially variant (left) and spatially invariant (right) blurring models

Finally Figure 10 presents reconstruction and restoration results for the rectangular object with two inhomogeneities 1 cm in diameter (and without RIC). Here unpreconditioned MRNSD was applied.

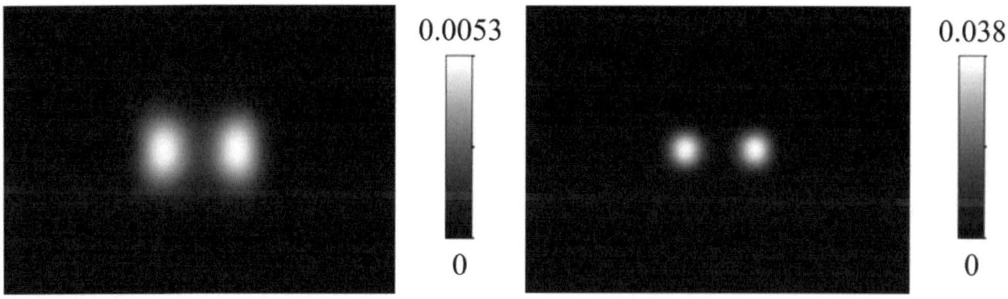

Fig. 10. Reconstruction and restoration results for the rectangular object with two inhomogeneities 1 cm in diameter: blurred tomogram (left) and the result of its MRNSD restoration (right)

The results presented thus confirm that blurring of PAT tomograms can be reduced through iterative restoration. The spatially variant model helps adequately estimate the actual size of inhomogeneities, but as follows, for instance, from Figure 6, further processing is needed to reconstruct inhomogeneity boundaries and get reliable information on its shape because even after restoration inhomogeneity profiles have a "gaussian" form, being far from the ideal steps typical of true images.

3. Segmentation with nonlinear CFs

3.1 CF generation algorithms

To segment restored diffusion tomograms, i.e. to reconstruct the boundary and shape of optical inhomogeneities, we use nonlinear color interpretation methods (Konovalov et al., 2007; Mogilenskikh, 2000) based on the generation of nonlinear analytical and statistical

functions of correspondence between image intensities (values of the restored object function) and palette colors. A palette is an ordered set of colors from color space where each color is assigned a number. If the pallet is linear, then the set of its colors create a straight trajectory in color space. The curvilinear trajectory corresponds to the nonlinear palette.
The analytical CFs imply the use of nonlinear color coordinate scales for attaining correspondence between intensity and color in a cell. Elementary functions and their algebraic combinations are used for this purpose. What particular combination is taken depends on the operator and a priori information contained in restored tomograms.
The nonlinear statistical CFs are generated using statistical information on the distribution of colors of an initially chosen palette (as a rule, linear) over image cells. The algorithm we have implemented can be described in brief by the following steps.

a. A linear CF is generated, i.e. a color $G\ (f_{kl})$ from the linear palette chosen is assigned to image intensity f_{kl} in a cell with indexes k and l.
b. The number of cells $N_G^{cells}\ (f_{kl})$ of each color from the palette is calculated; then a weight vector, whose size is equal to the number of colors in the palette, is calculated as

$$W_G(f_{kl}) = N_{col}\,\mathrm{norm}\left[\frac{N_G^{cells}(f_{kl})+1}{N^{cells}}\right], \tag{11}$$

where N_{col} is the number of colors in the palette, N^{cells} is the total number of cells in the image and norm(·) is a normalization operator.
c. The statistical CF is calculated from the collected statistics as a spline. We use the following simple spline:

$$G^{stat}(f_{kl}) = \left[G(f_{kl}) - N_{col}\mathrm{norm}(f_{kl})\right]\cdot\left[W_G(f_{kl}) - W_{G+1}(f_{kl})\right] + W_G(f_{kl})\,. \tag{12}$$

d. The nonlinear CF is generated by summing the statistical CF (12) and the initial linear CF.

Our experience (Konovalov et al., 2007) suggests that combinations of nonlinear analytical and statistical CFs give best results in the context of the segmentation problem solution. Indeed, the use of the statistical CF is needed to ultimately get a step palette. And before that it is advisable to "focus" the boundary of the inhomogeneity, which is clearly "gaussian" after space-varying restoration, by applying a nonlinear smooth function. Also inhomogeneity images after restoration exhibit a large percentage of background (zero or almost zero) values and before applying the statistical CF it is advisable to somewhat "level" statistics with respect to background values and inhomogeneity intensities.
Note that such a segmentation method based on the generation of nonlinear CFs compares favorably with the standard threshold filtration where some part of the image is rejected and replaced by a background value of the object function which may result in the loss of important details in the reproduction of randomly inhomogeneous structures. Nonlinear CFs are applied to all pixels in the image and if their parameters are well chosen, we manage not to lose, but effectively segment the informative details of the image.

3.2 Examples of nonlinear CF application to restored tomograms

For the analytical CF we tried power and exponential functions and found the latter to be more effective. An exponential function written as $G(f) = \exp(B_1 f) + B_2$ was parametrized so that the coefficients B_1 and B_2 were determined from the equality of volumes of the figures bounded by the object function $f(x, y)$ before and after image transformation that consisted in the successive application of the analytical and statistical CFs. The statistical CF was automatically generated with the algorithms described in Section 3.1. For the purpose of parametrization we had to state and solve the problem of minimizing the difference between figure volumes. Since image transformation on the whole does not have the analytical representation, the optimal parameters were found with a simple direct search algorithm (Lagarias et al., 1998) that does not require the numerical or analytic calculation of gradients.

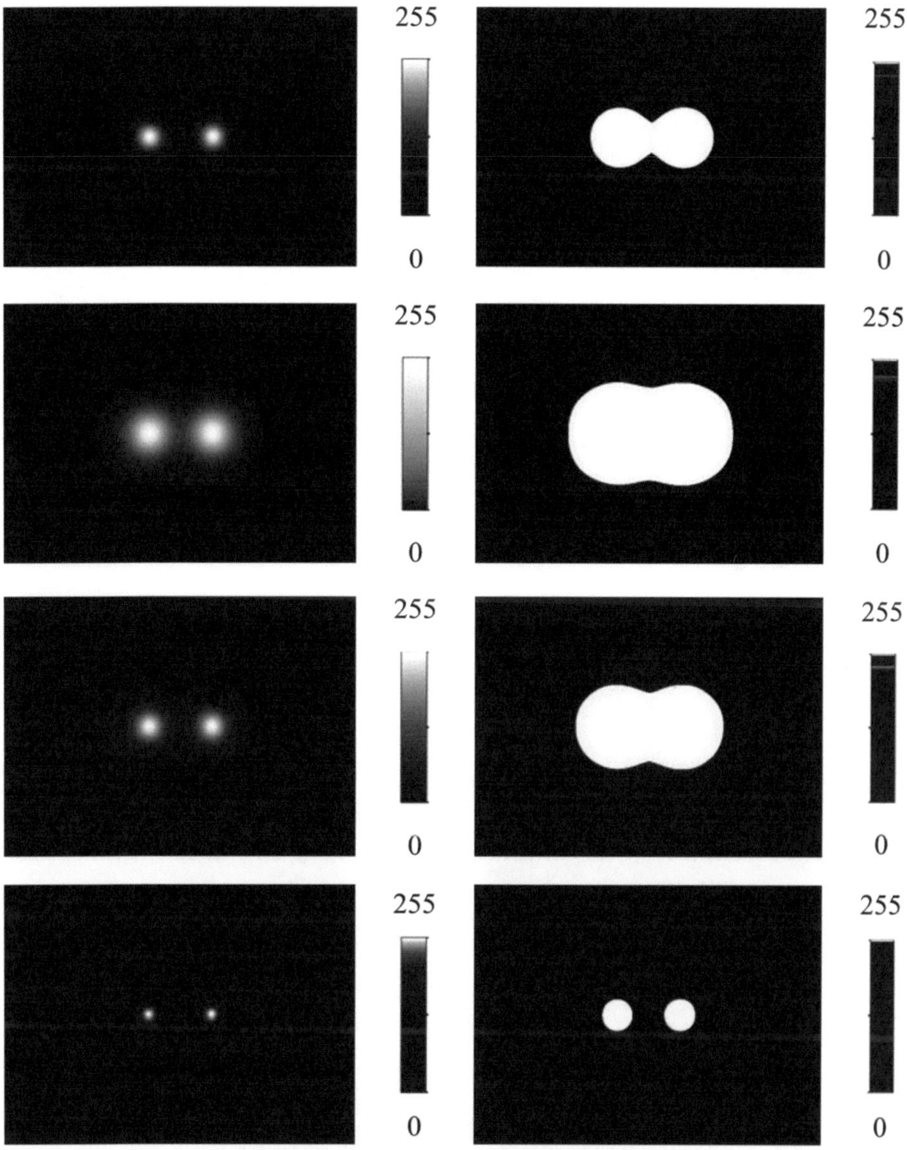

Fig. 11. Examples of nonlinear CF application to the restored tomogram of the rectangular object with two inhomogeneities 1.0 cm in diameter

Figure 11 illustrates examples of nonlinear CF application to the restored tomogram of the rectangular object with two inhomogeneities 1.0 cm in diameter (see the right image of Figure 10). The left column of images shows the effects of the analytical CFs (top down): the power function $G(f) = f^2$, the power function $G(f) = f$, the exponential function $G(f) = \exp(f)$ and the parametrized exponential function $G(f) = \exp(B_1 f) + B_2$. The right column demonstrates what was obtained after applying statistical CFs. Image intensities are normalized. It follows from Figure 11 that for "simple" models (absorbing macro-inhomogeneities in a homogeneous scattering medium), it is possible to obtain such a combination of nonlinear CFs that allows the true structure of inhomogeneities to be reconstructed almost completely. Indeed, if apply subtraction to the lowest right image of Figure 11 and the normalized true image of the inhomogeneities, we obtain the three-tone pattern shown in Figure 12 (coincidence is in grey and difference is in black and white).

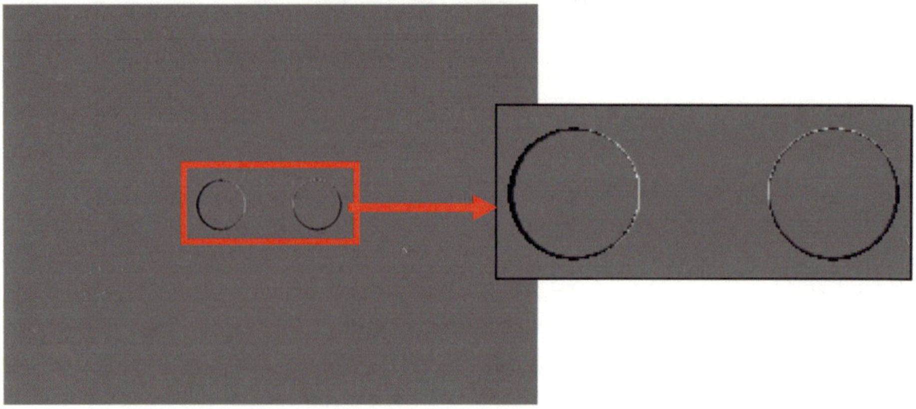

Fig. 12. The three-tone pattern characterizing how the result of postprocessing agrees with the true image

Figure 13 shows an object defined on a finite element mesh, which models a randomly inhomogeneous medium with macro-inhomogeneities and Figure 14 demonstrates results of its reconstruction (upper left), restoration (upper right) and nonlinear postprocessing (lower left and right).

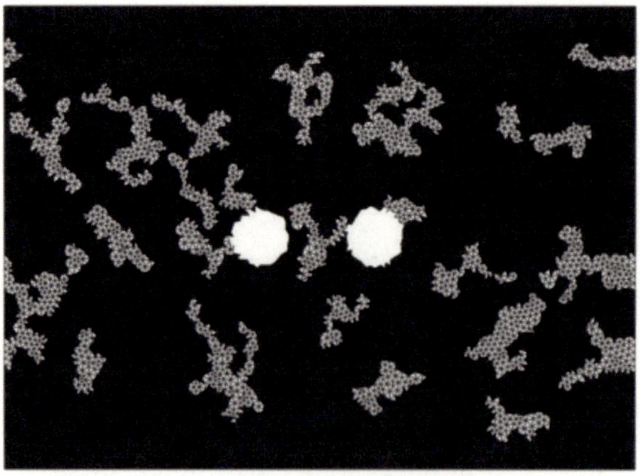

Fig. 13. The rectangular object with two inhomogeneities 1.0 cm in diameter and RIC

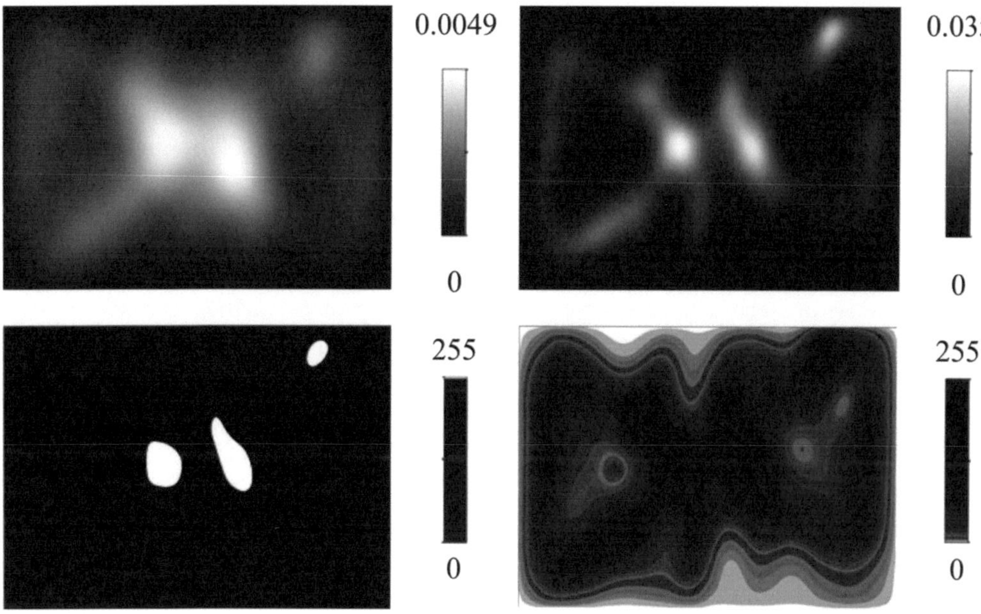

Fig. 14. Reconstruction and postprocessing results for the object of Figure 13

The lower left image resulted from the successive application of the parametrized exponential and statistical CFs to the restored tomogram and the lower right image was obtained after applying the statistical CF without preprocessing with analytical functions. It is seen that our segmentation method in the case of the complex model of Figure 13 give inhomogeneity shape distortions and artifacts (the upper structure on the lower left image) which may however be removed on the basis of a priori information contained in restored tomograms. The lower right image demonstrates an attempt to segment inhomogeneities with no use of analytical CFs. One must admit that the visual examination of reproduced results in this case is much more inconvenient.

In conclusion we should note that the two-step postprocessing of one image on Intel PC with the 1.7-GHz Pentium 4 processor and 256-MB RAM in MATLAB takes less than 30 seconds. The reconstruction of blurred tomograms takes to 5 seconds if integral algorithms are applied and to 30 seconds if iterative algebraic ones are used. The total time is thus below 1 minute. The comparative analysis of computational speed presented in (Lyubimov et al., 2002) suggests that the use of the well-known package TOAST (Temporal Optical Absorption and Scattering Tomography, Schweiger & Arridge, 2008) which implements the Newton-Raphson algorithm will make the time of restoration several times longer. It should also be noted that there are good prospects for making the postprocessing procedure yet faster by using not MATLAB, but a faster programming environment and optimizing the measurement ratio. Our investigation (Konovalov et al., 2007a) suggests that the number of sources can be reduced from 32 to 16 almost with no loss in reproduction quality.

4. Conclusion

In this chapter we have demonstrated the effective application of two-step postprocessing to the diffuse optical tomograms restored from model optical projections with the photon average trajectory method. The first step involves iterative restoration with the spatially variant blurring model and the second is segmentation with nonlinear palettes and nonlinear functions of correspondence between image intensities and palette colors. The first step helps reduce blurring due to averaging over the spatial distribution of diffuse photons and get information on the actual size of reproduced inhomogeneities. The boundary and shape of inhomogeneities are segmented at the second step. It is shown that the true image can almost completely be reconstructed for simple model objects (circular absorbing macro-inhomogeneities in a homogeneous scattering medium). For complex models of randomly inhomogeneous media, the proposed method of postprocessing may give distortions and artifacts. Therefore of certain interest is further investigation into methods that would help optimize the algorithms of correspondence function generation and obtain images without artifacts.

5. Acknowledgments

The authors would like to thank V. N. Ananijchuk, S. V. Kolchugin, V. M. Kryukov and G. N. Rykovanov for their considerable long-standing encouragement and support.

6. References

Andrews, H. & Hunt, B. (1977). *Digital Image Restoration*, Prentice-Hall, Englewood Cliffs, New York.

Arridge, S. R. (1999). Optical tomography in medical imaging. *Inverse Problems*, Vol. 15, No. 2, April 1999, pp. R41–R93.

Bertero, M. & Boccacci, P. (1998). *Introduction to Inverse Problem in Imaging*, IOP, London.

Bjorck, A. (1996). Numerical Methods for Least Square Problems, SIAM, Philadelphia.

Boas, D. A.; Brooks D. N.; Miller, E. L.; DiMarzio, C. A.; Kilmer, M.; Gaudette, R. J. & Zhang, Q. (2001). Imaging the body with diffuse optical tomography. *IEEE Signal Processing Magazine*, Vol. 18, No. 6, November 2001, pp. 57-75.

Fish, D. A.; Grochmalicki, J. E. & Pike, R. (1996). Scanning singular-value-decomposition method for restoration of images with space-variant blur. *Journal of the Optical Society of America A: Optics, Image Science & Vision*, Vol. 13, No. 3, March 1996, pp. 464-469.

Gibson, A. P.; Hebden, J. C. & Arridge, S. R. (2005). Recent advances in diffuse optical imaging. *Physics in Medicine & Biology*, Vol. 50, No. 4, February 2005, pp. R1–R43.

Groetsch, C. W. (1984). The Theory of Tikhonov Regularization for Fredholm Integral Equations of the First Kind, Pitman, Boston.

Hanson, P. C. & O'Leary, D. P. (1993). The use of the L-curve in the regularization of discrete ill-posed problems. *SIAM Journal on Scientific Computing*, Vol. 14, No. 6, November 1993, pp. 1487–1503.

Herman, G. T. (1980). Image Reconstruction from Projections: The Fundamentals of Computerized Tomography, Academic, New York.

Kak, A. C. & Slaney, M. (1988). *Principles of Computerized Tomographic Imaging*, IEEE Press, New York.

Kalintsev, A. G.; Kalintseva, N. A.; Kravtsenyuk, O. V. & Lyubimov, V. V. (2005). Superresolution in diffuse optical tomography. *Optics & Spectroscopy*, Vol. 99, No. 1, July 2005, pp. 152–157.

Kamm, J. & Nagy, J. G. (1998). Kronecker product and SVD approximation in image restoration. *Linear Algebra & Its Applications,* Vol. 284, No. 1-3, November 1998, pp. 177-192.

Kaufman, L. (1993). Maximum likelihood, least squares, and penalized least squares for PET. *IEEE Transactions on Medical Imaging,* Vol. 12, No. 2, February 1993, pp. 200–214.

Konovalov, A. B.; Kiselev, A. N. & Vlasov V. V. (2006a). Spatial resolution of few-view computed tomography using algebraic reconstruction techniques. *Pattern Recognition & Image Analysis,* Vol. 16, No. 2, April 2006, pp. 249-255.

Konovalov, A. B.; Lyubimov, V. V.; Kutuzov, I. I.; Kravtsenyuk, O. V.; Murzin, A. G.; Mordvinov, G. B.; Soms, L. N. & Yavorskaya, L. M. (2003). Application of the transform algorithms to high-resolution image reconstruction in optical diffusion tomography of strongly scattering media. *Journal of Electronic Imaging,* Vol. 12, No. 4, October 2003, pp. 602-612.

Konovalov, A. B.; Mogilenskikh, D. V.; Vlasov, V. V. & Kiselev, A. N. (2007a). Algebraic reconstruction and post-processing in incomplete data computed tomography: from X-rays to laser beams, In: *Vision Systems: Applications,* Obinata, G. & Dutta, A. (Eds.), Chapter 26, pp. 487-518, I-Tech Education and Publishing, Vienna.

Konovalov, A. B.; Vlasov, V. V.; Kalintsev, A. G.; Kravtsenyuk, O. V. & Lyubimov, V. V. (2006b). Time-domain diffuse optical tomography using analytic statistical characteristics of photon trajectories. *Quantum Electronics,* Vol. 36, No. 11, November 2006, pp. 1048-1055.

Konovalov, A. B.; Vlasov, V. V.; Kravtsenyuk, O. V. & Lyubimov, V. V. (2007b). Spacevarying iterative restoration of diffuse optical tomograms reconstructed by the photon average trajectories method. *EURASIP Journal on Advances in Signal Processing,* Vol. 2007, No. 3, March 2007, ID 34747.

Konovalov, A. B.; Vlasov, V. V.; Uglov, A. S.; Shelkovenko, T. A. & Pikuz, S. A. (2006c). Iterative restoration of X-ray images taken in X-pinch rays. *Proceedings of the 2nd International Symposium on Communications, Control and Signal Processing (ISCCSP'2006),* on CD-ROM, Marrakech, March 2006, Suvisoft Oy Ltd. publisher, Tampere.

Kravtsenyuk, O. V. & Lyubimov, V. V. (2000). Application of the method of smooth perturbations to the solution of problems of optical tomography of strongly scattering objects containing absorbing macroinhomogeneities. *Optics & Spectroscopy,* Vol. 89, No. 1, July 2000, pp. 107–112.

Lagarias, J. C.; Reeds, J. A.; Wright, M. H. & Wright, P. E. (1998). Convergence properties of the Nelder-Mead simplex method in low dimensions. *SIAM Journal on Optimization,* Vol. 9, No. 1, January 1998 pp. 112-147, 1998.

Lyubimov, V. V.; Kalintsev, A. G.; Konovalov, A. B.; Lyamtsev, O. V.; Kravtsenyuk, O. V.; Murzin, A. G.; Golubkina, O. V.; Mordvinov, G. B.; Soms L. N. & Yavorskaya L. M. (2002). Application of photon average trajectories method to real-time reconstruction of tissue inhomogeneities in diffuse optical tomography of strongly scattering media. *Physics in Medicine & Biology,* Vol. 47, No. 12, June 2002, pp. 2109-2128.

Lyubimov, V. V.; Kravtsenyuk, O. V.; Kalintsev, A. G.; Murzin, A. G.; Soms, L. N.; Konovalov, A. B.; Kutuzov, I. I.; Golubkina O. V. & Yavorskaya, L. M. . (2003). The possibility of increasing the spatial resolution in diffusion optical tomography. *Journal of Optical Technology*, Vol. 70, No. 10, October 2003, pp. 715–720.

Mogilenskikh, D. V. (2000). Nonlinear color interpretation of physical processes, *Proceedings of the 10th International Conference on Computer Graphics and Vision (GRAPHICON'2000)*, pp. 201-211, Moscow, August-September 2000, Moscow State University publisher, Moscow.

Nagy, J. G. & O'Leary, D. P. (1997) Fast iterative image restoration with a spatiallyvarying PSF, In: *Advanced Signal Processing: Algorithms, Architectures, and Implementations VII*, Luk, F. T. (Ed.), *Proceedings of SPIE*, Vol. 3162, pp. 388-399, SPIE, Bellingham.

Nagy, J. G.; Palmer, K. & Perrone, L. (2004). Iterative methods for image deblurring: a Matlab object oriented approach. *Numerical Algorithms,* Vol. 36, No. 1, May 2004, pp. 73–93.

Ng, M. K.; Chan, R. H. & Tang, W.-C. (1999). A fast algorithm for deblurring models with Neumann boundary conditions. *SIAM Journal on Scientific Computing,* Vol. 21, No. 3, November-December 1999, pp. 851–866.

Papoulis, A. (1968). Systems and Transforms with Applications in Optics, McGraw-Hill, New York.

Sawchuk, A. A. (1974). Space-variant image restoration by coordinate transformations. *Journal of the Optical Society of America,* Vol. 64, No. 2, February 1974, pp. 138–144.

Schweiger, M. & Arridge, S. R. (2008). http://web4.cs.ucl.ac.uk/research/vis/toast.

Very, J. G. & Bracewell, R. N. (1979). Blurring in tomograms made with X-ray beams of finite width. *Journal of Computer Assisted Tomography,* Vol. 3, No. 5, May 1979, pp. 662–678.

Volkonskii, V. B.; Kravtsenyuk, O. V.; Lyubimov, V. V.; Mironov, E. P. & Murzin, A. G. (1999). The use of the statistical characteristics of the photons trajectories for the tomographic studies of the optical macroheterogeneities in strongly scattering objects. *Optics & Spectroscopy*, Vol. 86, No. 2, February 1999, pp. 253–260.

Webb, S. (1998). *The Physics of Medical Imaging*, Institute of Physics Publishing, Bristol.

Yates, T.; Hebden, J. C.; Gibson, A.; Everdell, N.; Arridge, S. R. & Douek, M. (2005). Optical tomography of the breast using a multi-channel time-resolved imager. *Physics in Medicine & Biology,* Vol. 50, No. 11, June 2005, pp. 2503-2517.

Yodh, A. & Chance, B. (1995). Spectroscopy and imaging with diffusing light. *Physics Today,* Vol. 48, No. 3, March 1995, pp. 34–40.

12

Towards High-Speed Vision for Attention and Navigation of Autonomous City Explorer (ACE)

Tingting Xu, Tianguang Zhang, Kolja Kühnlenz and Martin Buss
Institute of Automatic Control Engineering
Technische Universität München
80333, Munich,
Germany

1. Introduction

In the project Autonomous City Explorer (ACE) a mobile robot should autonomously, efficiently and safely navigate in unstructured urban environments. From the biological aspect, the robot should not only plan its visual attention to acquire essential information about the unknown real world but also estimate the ego motion for the navigation based on vision with definitely fulfilled real-time capability. To achieve this, a multi-camera system is developed, which contains a multi-focal multi-camera platform, the camera head, for attentional gaze control and two high-speed cameras mounted towards the grounds for accurate visual odometry in extreme terrain.

How to apply the human visual attention selection model on a mobile robot has become an intensively investigated research field. An active vision system should autonomously plan the robot's view direction not only based on a specific task but also for stimulus-based exploration of unknown real-world environment to collect more information. Moreover, psychological experiments also show that the familiarity of the current context also strongly influences the human attention selection behavior. To solve this context-based attention selection problem, we propose a view direction planning strategy based on the information theory. This strategy combines top-down attention selection in 3D space and bottom-up attention selection on the basis of a 2D saliency map. In both spaces the information content increases are defined. The optimal view direction is chosen which results in a maximum information gain after a camera view direction change. The main contribution is that a concerted information-based scalar is inserted to evaluate the information gains in the both sides. Moreover, the robot behavior, the choice of attention selection mechanism, can be adaptive to the current context.

In addition, we implemented the compute-intensive bottom-up attention on Graphics Processing Units (GPUs) using the Compute Unified Device Architecture (CUDA), which provides an excellent speed-up of the system, due to the highly parallelizable structure. Using 4 NVIDIA GeForce 8800 (GTX) graphics cards for the input images at a resolution of 640 x 480, the computational cost is only 3.1ms with a frame rate of 313 fps. The saliency map generation on GPUs is approximately 8.5 times faster than the standard CPU implementations.

Angle-encoders on the wheels of the platform are normally used for the odometry. But if ACE moves on the ground which is not flat or has sands, it will slide. The encoders can not provide accurate information any more. Using a high-speed camera with 200 Hz, an elaborated concept for visual odometry based on optical flow is implemented. Utilizing Kalman Filter for data fusion, a distinctly local, low-latency approach that facilitates closed-loop motion control and highly accurate dead reckoning is proposed. It helps ACE determine the relatively precise position and orientation. Image processing at high frequency can decrease the time delay of close-loop control and improve the system stability.
The various vision-based modules enable an autonomous view direction planning as well as visual odometry in real time. The performance is experimentally evaluated.

2. Overview of ACE and its high-speed vision system

The ACE project (Lidoris et al., 2007) (see Fig. 2.1 left) envisions to develop a robot that will autonomously navigate in an unstructured urban environment and find its way through interaction with humans. This project combines the research fields of robot localization, navigation, human-robot interaction etc..
Seen from the biological aspect, the visual information provided by the camera system on ACE is very essential for attention as well as navigation. Another prerequisite of the vision system is the image processing efficiency. The real-time requirement should be fulfilled during the robot locomotion.
The vision system of ACE consists of a multi-focal stereo camera platform (Fig. 2.2 middle) for the interaction and attention and a high-speed camera (Fig. 2.2 right) for visual odometry. The camera platform comprises several vision sensors with independent motion control which strongly differ in fields of view and measurement accuracy. High-speed gaze shift capabilities and novel intelligent multi-focal gaze coordination concepts provide fast and optimal situational attention changes of the individual sensors. Thereby, large and complex dynamically changing environments are perceived flexibly and efficiently. The detailed description of the camera platform is in (Kühnlenz, 2006a; Kühnlenz, 2006b). Currently in our application, only the wide-angle stereo-camera is used to demonstrate the attentional saccade caused by the saliency in the environment.

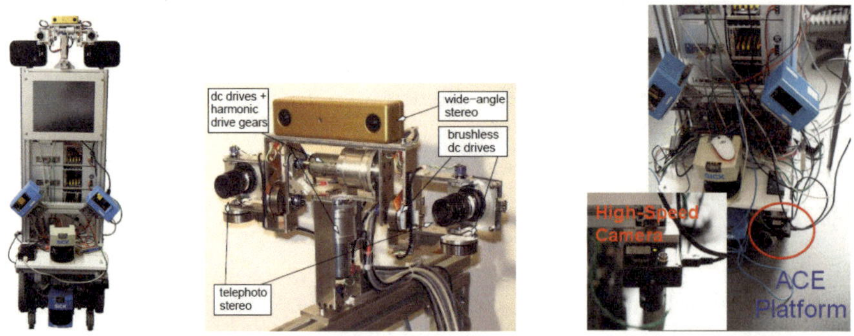

Fig. 2.1. Autonomous City Explorer (ACE) (left), the camera platform (middle) and the high-speed camera (right)

Moreover, a dragonfly® express camera (Point Grey Research Inc.), fitted with a normal wide-angle lens, is mounted on the mobile platform, facing the ground. This camera can work at 200 fps with the resolution of 640x480 pixels and be applied for visual odometry.

3. Information-based visual attention of mobile robots

3.1 Related work

In the robotics domain a variety of approaches to the view direction planning of active vision systems has been already proposed. The most concepts are based on the predefined robot tasks and in a top-down way. Above all, robot self-localization using active vision is well studied. In (Davison, 1998) visual information is used for simultaneous localization and map-building for a robot operating in an unknown environment. Point features are used as visual landmarks. The active cameras can re-detect the previously seen features and adjust their maps. In (Pellkofer & Dickmanns, 2000) an approach to an optimal gaze control system for autonomous vehicles is proposed in which the perceptive situation and subjective situation besides the physical situation are also predicted and the viewing behavior is planned and optimized in advance. For gaze control of humanoid robot the basic idea of (Seara & Schmidt, 2005) is based on maximization of the predicted visual information content of a view situation. A task decision strategy is applied to the view direction selection for individual tasks.

In the last few years, bottom-up saliency based attention selection models also become focus of robot view direction planning. A saliency map model was firstly proposed in (Itti et al., 1998). In the saliency map model the salient positions in a static image are selected by low-level features. The saliency map predicts the bottom-up based visual attention allocation. No high-level object recognition is required to drive a robot's attention, if bottom-up signals are also taken into account.

By now, the top-down and the bottom-up attention selections are only combined in the 2D image-space. In (Ouerhani et al., 2005) a visual attention-based approach is proposed for robot navigation. The trajectory lengths of the salient scene locations are regarded as a criterion for a good environment landmark. In (Frintrop, 2006) a biologically motivated computational attention system VOCUS is introduced, which has two operation modes: the exploration mode based on strong contrasts and uniqueness of a feature and the search mode using previously learned information of a target object to bias the saliency computations with respect to the target. However, the task accomplishment is evaluated in the image space which can only contain the information which is currently located in the field of view, although the performance evaluation in robotics domain is usually executed in the task-space.

Another key factor which has an influence on attention mechanism is the scene context. The context has already been used to facilitate object detection in the natural scenes by directing attention or eyes to diagnostic regions (Torralba & Sinha, 2001) and scene recognition (Im & Cho, 2006). In both cases the scene context is only statically observed. In (Remazeilles & Chaumette, 2006) vision-based navigation using environment representation is proposed. An image memory, a database of images acquired during a learning phase, is used to describe the path which the robot should follow. However, there is no dynamical context-based behavior adaptation considered.

3.2 Strategy overview

The objective is to plan the robot view direction with visual information from the input image, considering the competition of the task-based top-down attention and the stimulus-based bottom-up attention as well as behavior adaptation on the current context. Fig. 3.1 illustrates the view direction planning strategy architecture.

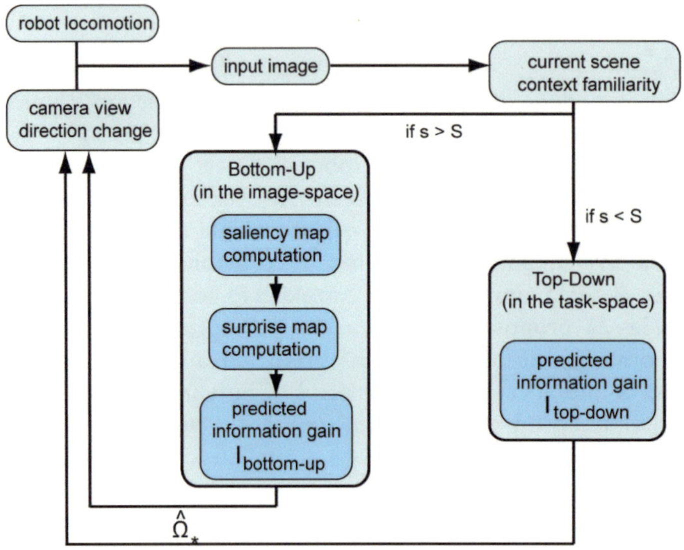

Fig. 3.1. View direction planning strategy architecture

We define the optimal view direction as the view direction with the estimated maximum information gain, calculated as the relative entropy/Kullback-Leibler (KL) divergence.

$$\hat{\Omega}_*^{k+1|k} = \arg\max_{\hat{\Omega}}(\nu(s) \cdot I_{top-down}(\hat{\Omega}) + (1-\nu(s)) \cdot I_{bottom-up}(\hat{\Omega})) \tag{1}$$

with

$$\nu(s) = \begin{cases} 1 \text{ if } s < S \\ 0 \text{ if } s > S \end{cases} \tag{2}$$

$I_{top-down}$ and $I_{bottom-up}$ indicate the relative entropies acquired from the top-down and bottom-up sides with $\nu(s)$ the context-based weighting factor for the top-down attention. The total visual attention is 100%. Therefore, the weight of the bottom-up attention is $1-\nu(s)$. The detailed definition of v(s) is described in Section 3.5. $\hat{\Omega}$ and $\hat{\Omega}_*$ stand for the possible view directions and the optimal view direction of the camera.

3.3 Information-based modeling of the top-down attention

For the top-down attention we model the system state $\underline{x}$ as 2D Gaussian distributions with the average value $\underline{\mu}$ and the covariance matrix $R_{\underline{x}}$ in the task-space. p and q are the prior and the predicted posterior probability density functions (pdf) with the continuous variable $\underline{x}$ for specific tasks

$$p(\underline{x}) = \frac{1}{(\sqrt{2\pi})^n \cdot \left|R_{\underline{x}}^k\right|} \cdot \exp(-\frac{1}{2}(\underline{x}^k - \underline{\mu}^k)^T \cdot R_{\underline{x}}^{k-1}(\underline{x}^k - \underline{\mu}^k)) \tag{3}$$

and

$$q(\underline{x},\hat{\Omega}) = \frac{1}{(2\pi)^{n} \cdot |R|} \cdot \exp(-\frac{1}{2}(\underline{x}^{k+1|k} - \underline{\mu}(\hat{\Omega})^{k+1|k})^{T} R^{-1} \cdot (\underline{x}^{k+1|k} - \underline{\mu}(\hat{\Omega})^{k+1|k})) \tag{4}$$

with the dimension n of the state variable $\underline{x}$ and with

$$R = R_{\underline{x}}(\hat{\Omega})^{k+1|k} . \tag{5}$$

The relative entropy is then computed as follows:

$$I_{top-down} = KL(p_{top-down} \,||\, q_{top-down}) = \iint_{D} p(\underline{x}) \cdot \log \frac{p(\underline{x})}{q(\underline{x},\hat{\Omega})} \text{ in [bit]} \tag{6}$$

3.4 Information-based modeling of the bottom-up attention

Besides the task accomplishment, the robot should also have the ability to explore the world, acquire more information, update the knowledge and also react to the unexpected events in the environment. In order to achieve this, a bottom-up attention selection is integrated. Here we consider the static outliers as well as the temporal novelty in the image-space.

For the static outliers we use the saliency map model proposed in (Itti et al., 1998). As known, human is much more attracted by salient objects than by their neighbourhood. The bottom-up saliency map is biology-inspired and can predict the position of the salient regions in a real-scene image.

In Fig. 3.2 the saliency map model is visualized. Firstly, an input image is sub-sampled into a dyadic Gaussian pyramid in three channels (intensity, orientation for 0°, 45°, 90°, 135°, opponent colour in red/green and blue/yellow). Then a centre-surround difference is calculated for the images in the Gaussian pyramid. In this phase feature maps are generated in which the salient pixels with respect to their neighbourhood are highlighted. Using across-scale combinations the feature maps are combined and normalized into a conspicuity map in each channel. The saliency map is the linear combination of the conspicuity maps. The bright pixels are the salient and interesting pixels predicted by the saliency map model.

For the temporal novelty we applied a similar Bayesian definition like (Itti &Baldi, 2005) for the information content of an image, but directly on the saliency map. The notion "surprise" is used here to indicate the unexpected events. Only the positions spatially salient and temporally surprising are taken to draw the robot's attention. Therefore, we build a surprise map on two consecutive saliency maps without camera movement to find the unexpected event.

Firstly, as an example, the saliency maps of images at the resolution of 640 x 480 are rescaled into 40 x 30 pixels. Thus, each pixel represents the local saliency value of a 16 x 16 region.

Secondly, we model the data D received from the saliency map as Poisson distribution $M(\lambda(x_i, y_i))$. $\lambda(x_i, y_i)$ stands for the saliency value with $x_i = 1, \cdots, 40$ and $y_i = 1, \cdots, 30$. Therefore, a prior probability distribution $p_i(x_i, y_i)$ can be defined as a Gamma probability density (Itti & Baldi, 2005) for the i-th pixel:

$$p_i(x_i, y_i) = \gamma(\lambda, \alpha, \beta) = \frac{\beta^{\alpha} \lambda^{\alpha-1} e^{-\beta\lambda}}{\Gamma(\alpha)} \tag{7}$$

with the shape $\alpha > 0$, the inverse scale $\beta > 0$, and $\Gamma(\cdot)$ the Euler Gamma function.

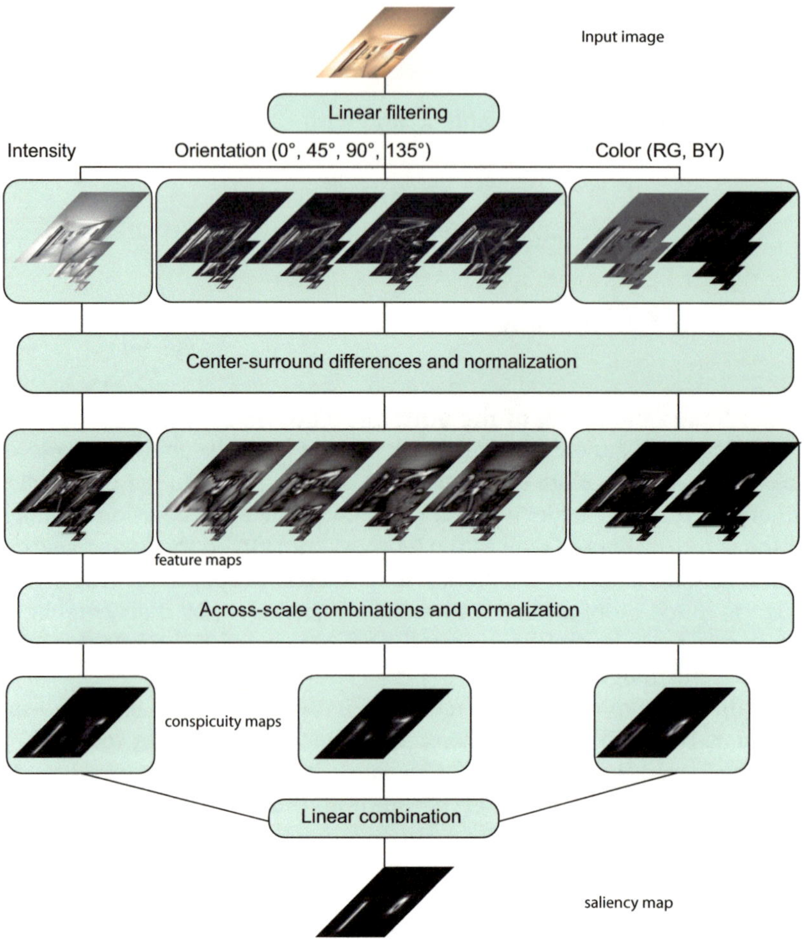

Fig. 3.2. The saliency map computation model

The posterior probability distribution $p((x_i, y_i) | D)$ is obtained from the 2. saliency map with the new saliency value $\lambda'(x_i, y_i)$. The parameters α and β are supposed to change into α' and β', while

$$\begin{aligned} \alpha' &= \xi\alpha + \lambda', \text{ and} \\ \beta' &= \xi\beta + 1 \end{aligned} \tag{8}$$

Then, the surprise map with surprise value τ is estimated as the KL-divergence as follows:

$$\tau(x_i, y_i) = KL(p_i(x_i, y_i), p_i(x_i, y_i | D)) \tag{9}$$

The predicted information gain is then quantified as the KL-divergence of the prior and the predicted estimated posterior probability distributions over all the interesting pixels in the surprise map.

P and Q are the normalized prior and the predicted posterior probability mass functions (pmf) with discrete variables: the pixel indexes x_i, y_i.

$$I_{bottom-up} = KL(P_{bottom-up} \,||\, Q_{bottom-up}) = \\ = \sum_{x_i=\chi_1} \sum_{y_i=\chi_2} P(x_i, y_i) \cdot \log \frac{P(x_i, y_i)}{Q((x_i, y_i), \hat{\Omega})} \text{ in [bit]} \tag{10}$$

where

$$P(x_i, y_i) = \frac{\tau^k(x_i, y_i)}{d^k(x_i, y_i)} \tag{11}$$

$$Q((x_i, y_i), \hat{\Omega}) = \frac{\tau^{k+1|k}(x_i, y_i)}{d^{k+1|k}((x_i, y_i), \hat{\Omega})} \tag{12}$$

with the surprise value τ of the pixel (x_i, y_i) and the weighting factor d indicating the distance between the pixel (x_i, y_i) and the image centre of the camera lens.

3.5 Context-based combination of top-down and bottom-up attention selections

There are two dominated arts of context recognition approach: the object-based context recognition and the gist-based context recognition. For the object-based context recognition the robot recognizes certain objects as the symbols of certain scenes and adapts its behaviour and tasks to this situation. On the other side, the gist-based context recognition provides the robot a rough idea about what kind of scene the robot is located. In the case that the robot has no previous knowledge about the situation, we consider here only the latter one and try to determine how familiar the current context is and how the robot should adapt its attention selection to this kind of context.

Firstly, we consider the static environment as familiar environment for the robot and the dynamic environment as less familiar environment because of the moving objects causing change and danger. Therefore, we define the context familiarity using motion map histograms computed by three successive input images.

Each normalized histogram of motion map can be regarded as a discrete distribution. Because the perception of human is expectation-based, we calculated the relative entropy s of the histograms of the two consecutive motion maps as the chaos degree of the context. A threshold S should be experimentally specified and applied to determine the weighting factor $\nu(s)$ (see Eq. 2).

3.6 Experiments and results

To evaluate the performance of our view direction planning strategy, the following experiments were conducted. Firstly, four different scenes are investigated to calculate the chaos degree threshold S. Then, experiments in a robot locomotion scenario are conducted, in an environment without surprising event as well as in an environment with a surprising event.

3.6.1 Experiment setup

The experiments are executed in a corridor using ACE (see Fig. 3.4). Four artificial landmarks are installed at the same height as the camera optical axis.

Fig. 3.4. Experiment scenario using ACE and four artificial landmarks

The mobile platform moved straight forward. About every 0.5m a view direction planning is executed and an optimal view direction will be applied for the next 0.5m. We define the view direction Ω as the angle between the locomotion direction and the camera optical axis in the horizontal plane. At the start point (0, 1.25)m the camera has an initial view direction 0° towards the locomotion direction.

3.6.2 Context investigation

Firstly, we specified the chaos degree threshold S. We gathered four different scenes, shown in Fig. 3.5, and calculated their chaos degrees s.

- scene 1: a floor with no moving objects present (Fig. 3.5, column 1)
- scene 2: a square with crowded people (Fig. 3.5, column 2)
- scene 3: a floor with people suddenly appearing (Fig. 3.5, column 3)
- scene 4: a street with a vehicle moving very fast (Fig. 3.5, column 4)

The rows show the consecutive time steps k-2, k-1 and k at a frame rate of 30pfs. It is obvious that the context almost does not change in the first scene. Therefore, the chaos degree is very small, namely 0.0526. In comparison to the first scene, in the scene 4 the environment changes very much because of the vehicle movement. Hence, the chaos degree in this context is very large, namely 1.1761. For the second scene we have obtained a small chaos degree, namely 0.0473, because the context change is relatively small although there is motion. This context can be regarded as a familiar context, since no surprise exists. In the third scene the chaos degree is large, because a person appeared suddenly in the second image and therefore, the context change is relatively large. For the further experiments we will set S equal 1.0.

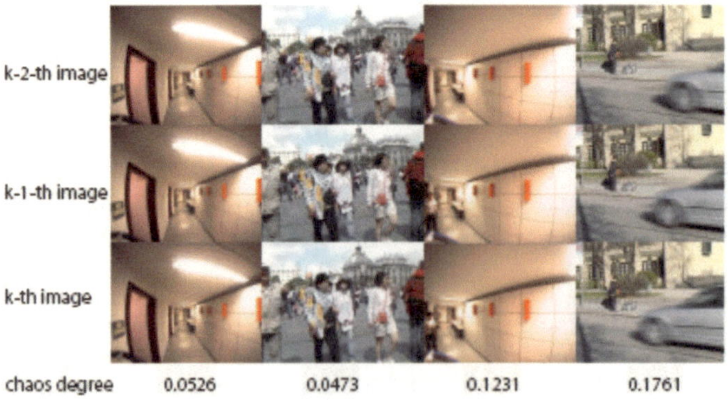

Fig. 3.5. The context chaos degrees in four various scenes

3.6.3 Robot locomotion with and without surprising events

Firstly, the robot moved in a static environment with a constantly low context chaos degree, accomplishing the self-localization task. The image sequence and the respective optimal view directions are shown in Fig. 3.6. If there is no surprising event in the environment, the camera directed its gaze direction to the task-relevant information -- the landmarks (row 1).

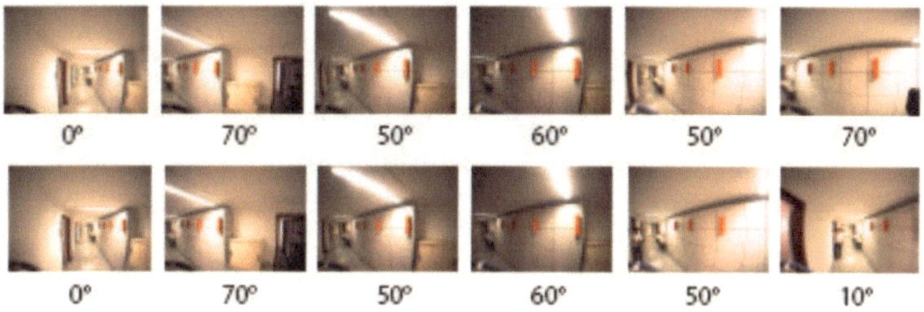

Fig. 3.6. The image sequence and the respective camera view directions in an environment without surprising event (row 1) and with surprising event (row 2)

Fig. 3.6 (row 2) also illustrates an image sequence with the optimal view directions during the locomotion in an environment with surprising event. Most of the time the environment was static with a low context chaos degree (see Fig. 3.5, column 1) and the robot planned its view direction based on the top-down model for the localization task. At the fifth step a person appeared suddenly. Because of the high context chaos degree caused by the surprising event at this moment (see Fig. 3.5, column 3) the camera planned its view direction based on bottom-up attention, tried to locate the surprising event in the environment and changed its view direction from 50° to 10°.

4. GPU aided implementation of bottom-up attention

4.1 Related work

Because of the essential real-time capability of the bottom-up attention, various implementations are proposed. A real-time implementation of the saliency-based model of visual attention on a low power, one board, and highly parallel Single Instruction Multiple Data (SIMD) architecture called Protoeye is proposed in (Ouerhani et al., 2002) in 2002. The implemented attention process runs at a frequency of 14 fps at a resolution of 64 x 64 pixels.
In 2005 another real-time implementation of a selective attention model is proposed (Won et al., 2005). In this model intensity features, edge features, red-green opponent features and blue-yellow opponent features are considered. Their model can perform within 280ms at Pentium-4 2.8GHz with 512MB RAM on an input image of 160 x 120 pixels.
In the same year a distributed visual attention on a humanoid robot is proposed in (Ude et al., 2005). In this system five different modalities including colour, intensity, edges, stereo and motion are used. The attention processing is distributed on a computer cluster which contains eight PCs. 4 run Windows 2000, 3 Windows XP and 1 Linux. Five of the PCs are equipped with 2x2.2 GHz Intel Xeon processors, two with 2x2.8 GHz Intel Xeon processors, and one with 2 Opteron 250 processors. A frequency of 30 fps with input images with 320 x 240 pixels is achieved.
In 2006 a GPU based saliency map for high-fidelity selective rendering is proposed (Longhurst et al., 2006). This implementation is also based on the saliency map model proposed in (Itti et al., 1998). In this implementation a motion map and a depth map as well

as habituation are also integrated. However, they use a Sobel filter instead of the complex Gabor filter to produce the orientation maps. No iterative normalization is computed. For an input image at a resolution of 512 x 512 the saliency map generation takes about 34ms using NVIDIA 6600GT graphics card. No CUDA technology is used.
The most comparable implementation to our implementation is proposed in (Peters & Itti, 2007), because both of them use the same parameter values as those set in (Itti et al., 1998; Walther & Koch, 2006). For a 640 x 480 colour input image, running in a single-threaded on a GNU/Linux system (Fedora Core 6) with a 2.8GHz Intel Xeon processor, the CPU time required to generate a saliency map is 51.34ms at a precision of floating-point arithmetic and 40.28ms at a precision of integer arithmetic. Computed on a cluster of 48 CPUs a 1.5-2 times better result is achieved. Currently, the fastest computation of saliency map is 37 fps using multi-threaded mode.

4.2 Graphics processing unit (GPU)

In the last few years, the programmable GPUs have become more and more popular. GPU is specialized for compute-intensive, highly parallel computation. Moreover, the CUDA, a new hardware and software architecture issued by NVIDIA in 2007, allows issuing and managing computations on the GPU as a data-parallel computing device without the need of mapping them in a graphics API (CUDA, 2007). It is the only C-language development environment for the GPU.
The saliency map computation consists of compute intensive filtering in different scales, which is nevertheless highly parallelizable. For real-time application we implemented the computation of saliency map on GeForce 8800 (GTX) graphics cards of NVIDIA, which support the CUDA technology. The GeForce 8800 (GTX) consists of 16 multiprocessors which consists of 8 processors each. All the processors in the same multi-processor always execute the same instruction, but with different data. This concept enables a high-gradely parallel computation of a large amount of similar data. The multi-GPU performance is strongly dependent on an efficient usage of the thread-block concept and the different memories.

A. Thread Batching

Programming with CUDA, the GPU is called *compute device*. It contains a large amount of threads which can execute an instruction set on the device with different data in parallel. A function which is compiled to those instruction set is called *kernel*. In comparison with GPU, the main CPU is called *host*. The goal is to execute the data-parallel and compute-intensive portions of applications on the GPU instead of on the CPU.
Fig. 4.1 shows the thread batching model of the GPU. For each *kernel* function the GPU is configured with a number of threads and blocks. The respective grid of a *kernel* consists of two dimensional blocks. Each block contains up to 512 threads. The input data are divided into the threads. All the threads in a grid execute the same kernel functions. With the thread index *threadIdx* and the block index *blockIdx* we know which data will be processed in which thread. With this structure an easy programming and a good scalability are realized.

B. Memory

The memory access is also a focus for an efficient programming on GPU. There are six different memories in GPU:

- read-write per-thread registers

- read-write per-thread local memory
- read-write per-block shared memory
- read-write per-grid global memory
- read-only per-grid constant memory
- read-only per-grid texture memory

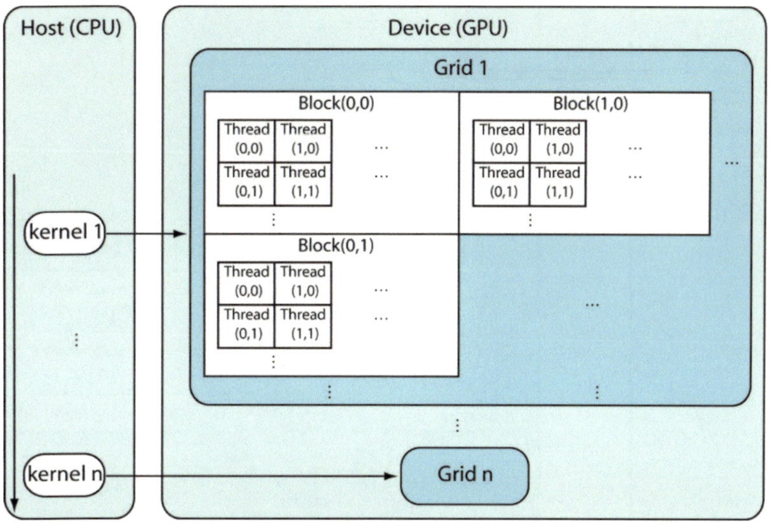

Fig. 4.1. The thread batching model of GPU

Above all, the shared memory and the texture memory are cached, while the read or write access in the not cached global memory always takes 400-600 clock cycles. Only the texture memory and the global memory can be used for a large amount of data. Moreover, the texture memory is optimized for 2D spatial locality and supports many operations such as interpolation, clamping, data type conversion etc.. However, the texture is read-only. The results must be saved in the global memory, which requires data copy between memories.

4.3 Multi-GPU implementation details

In Fig. 4.2 a data flow diagram of our GPU-implementation is illustrated. After an initialization, an input image is firstly converted into 32-Bit floating point such that a high accuracy and a high efficiency will be achieved in the following computation phases. The Gaussian dyadic pyramid is created in the shared memory together with the generation of intensity maps (I-maps), opponent red-green (RG-maps) and blue-yellow maps (BY-maps). We use the Gabor filter to calculate the Orientation-maps (O-maps). The Gabor filter kernel is firstly calculated in the CPU. To spare computational cost, the convolution of the subsampled images with Gabor filter in the space domain is displaced by the multiplication in the frequency domain using Fast Fourier Transform (FFT). Here we conducted a Cuda-image which contains all the images to be filtered by the in the initialization transformed Gabor filter such that only one FFT and eight IFFT are needed for the convolution. The images should be assembled before the transformation and disassembled after the transformation in the texture memory. After that, 9 I-maps, 18 C-maps and 36 O-maps are generated.

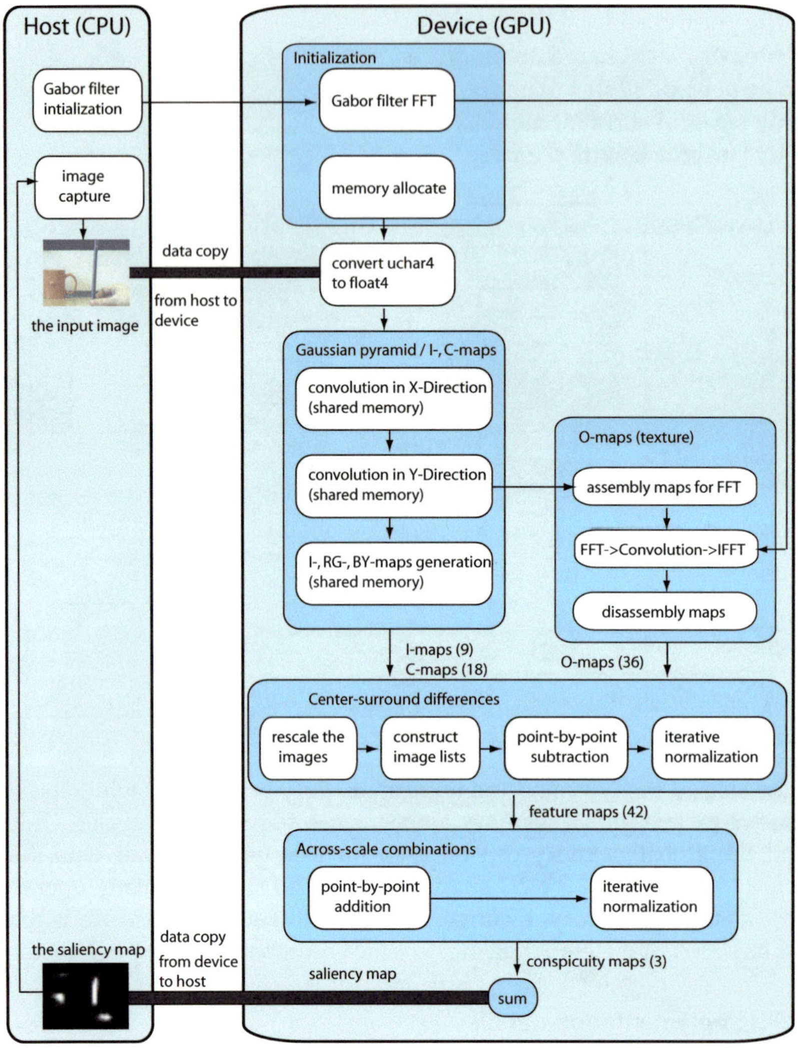

Fig. 4.2. Data flow diagram for GPU-implementation of the saliency map computation

Furthermore, to ease the center-surround differences and the cross-scale combinations, the available maps at different scales are rescaled into the same size. A point-to-point subtraction followed by an iterative normalization is calculated. On the resulting 42 feature maps a point-to-point addition and its following normalization are executed. One conspicuity map in each channel is obtained. At the end, a summation of the conspicuity maps into the saliency map is completed. The detailed description is as follows:

A. Initialization

Firstly, the GPU should be initialized. For the reason that the memory allocation in GPU takes very long, the memory is firstly allocated for different images such as the input images, the images in the Gaussian dyadic pyramids, the feature maps, the conspicuity maps, the rescaled feature and conspicuity maps at the same size as well as the final saliency map.

Since the filter kernel will not be changed during the saliency map computation, we also calculate the Gabor filter in the initialization phase in the CPU and then transform it into the frequency domain. The implementation of the Gabor filter and the FFT-transformation of the Gabor filter will be described in Section 4.3-E in detail.

B. Data type conversion

The input image has the resolution of 640 x 480 and three 8-bit channels, namely red, green and blue. The image data are copied from the CPU into the global memory of the GPU. Since the global memory is not cached, it is essential to follow the right access pattern to get maximum memory bandwidth. The data type must be such that *sizeof(type)* is equal to 4, 8, or 16 and the variables of type *type* must be aligned to *sizeof(type)* bytes (CUDA, 2007). If the alignment requirement is not fulfilled, the accesses to device memory are very costly. The image width fulfills the alignment requirement, while the data amount of each pixel is 3 x 8 = 24 Bytes which does not fulfill the alignment requirement. Therefore, we must extend the pixel width with *padding* and insert an extra 8-bit channel (see Fig. 4.3).

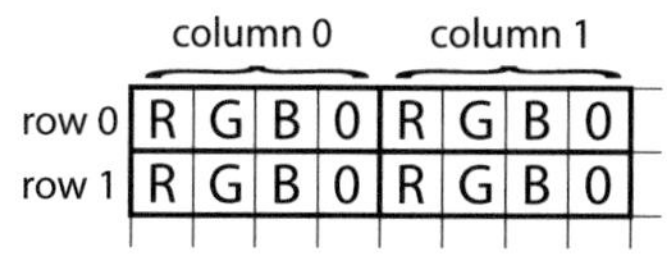

Fig. 4.3. Image data padding

After the *padding* we convert the image data type with *uchar4* into *float4* to achieve the high precision for the following computation using the implicit type conversion of the texture.

C. Gaussian dyadic pyramid computation

In (Walther & Koch, 2006) a 6 x 6 separable Gaussian kernel [1 5 10 10 5 1]/32 is used for the image size reduction. A two-dimensional convolution contains 6 x 6 = 36 multiplications for each output pixel, while a convolution with separable filters only requires 6 + 6 = 12 multiplications for each output pixel. Therefore, we separate the Gaussian dyadic pyramid computation into two convolutions: one convolution in the horizontal direction to reduce the horizontal dimension, and one convolution in the vertical direction, respectively.

Since each access in the uncached global memory takes 400-600 clock cycles, it is necessary to compute the convolutions in the faster texture memory or shared memory. Bounding the images to a texture requires the data copy between the global memory and the texture memory. Moreover, the data are only readable by kernels through texture fetching. It is more costly than loading the data into the shared memory and compute the convolution there. Therefore, the convolution is computed in the shared memory.

For the convolution in the horizontal direction, the thread and block number are so specified that a block consists of as many threads as the number of the output image columns and a grid has as many blocks as the number of the output image rows. For example, for the subsampling from an input image at 640 x 480 into an output image at 320 x 480, each block has 320 threads, while each grid has 480 blocks. Each thread computes only one pixel in the output image.

Attention must be paid to the threads synchronization, because the convolution in the thread n is dependent on the pixels loaded by thread n-1 and n+1.

To deal with the convolution on the image border, we use [10 10 5 1]/26 on the left border and [1 5 10 10]/26 on the right border.

After that, a following subsampling in the vertical direction can be similarly solved. The input image at 640 x 480 is subsampled into 8 other scales: 320 x 240 (scale $\sigma = 1$), 160 x 120 ($\sigma = 2$), ..., 2 x 1 ($\sigma = 8$).

D. C-maps and I-maps computation

In the saliency map computation the I-, RG- and BY-maps are required (Walther & Koch, 2006). To make the computation more efficient, we integrate the computation of the I-maps and the C-maps into the Gaussian filter convolution in the vertical direction, because the image data are already in the shared memory after the convolution. Thus, we can spare the time for loading the data from the global memory.

E. O-maps computation

1) Gabor filter: To compute the O-maps in different scales, the Gabor filter truncated to 19 x 19 pixels is used (Walther & Koch, 2006). The Gabor filter is formulated as follows:

$$G_\psi(x, y, \theta) = \exp(\frac{x'^2 + \gamma^2 y'^2}{2\delta^2}) \cdot \cos(2\pi \frac{x'}{\lambda} + \psi) \tag{13}$$

With

$$x' = x\cos(\theta) + y\sin(\theta), \quad y' = -x\sin(\theta) + y\cos(\theta) \tag{14}$$

(x, y) is the pixel coordinate in the Gabor filter. The parameter values of our implementation are according to (Walther & Koch, 2006). γ stands for the aspect ratio with the value 1, while λ is the wavelength and has the value of 7 pixels. The standard deviation δ is equal 7/3 pixels, and $\psi \in \{0, \frac{\pi}{2}\}$. θ stands for the orientation angles with $\theta \in \{0°, 45°, 90°, 135°\}$.

As defined in Eq. 14, a Gabor filter consists of a combination of a 2D Gaussian bell-shaped curve and a sine ($\psi = \pi/2$) and cosine function ($\psi = 0$). In each direction, the image should be filtered twice and summed as follows:

$$M_\theta(\sigma) = \|M_I(\sigma) * G_0(\theta)\| + \|M_I(\sigma) * G_{\pi/2}(\theta)\| \tag{15}$$

with $M_I(\sigma)$ the I-Maps at scale σ.

2) FFT and IFFT: Since a convolution with the 19 x 19 Gabor filter is too costly, we use FFT and IFFT to accelerate this process significantly. The Gabor filter and the to be convoluted images should be converted into the frequency domain using FFT at first, and multiplied with each other. Then, the result is converted from the frequency domain into the space domain using IFFT. In doing this, the complexity sinks from $O(n^4)$ (2D convolution) to $O(n^2 \log n)$ (2D FFT).

As mentioned in 4.3-A, the FFT of the Gabor filter should be computed in the initialization, because it will never be modified in the saliency map generation. Using CUFFT library (CUDA CUFFT, 2007) we compute from the original Gabor filter eight FFTs with four different orientations and two different forms (sine and cosine).

Due to the fact that the input image (640 x 480) and the subsampled image at scale 1 (320 x 240) are not used for the following saliency map computation, 7 x 4 x 2 = 56 convolutions for the O-maps are needed (7 scales, 4 orientations and 2 forms). We assembly the images in 7 scales together into an Cuda-image (see Fig. 4.5, left) such that just 1 FFT and 8 IFFTs instead of 7 FFT and 56 IFFTs are computed. For an input image with 640 x 480 pixels, an image with 256 x 256 is big enough to have all the images into itself.

Using the texture a modus named "clamp-to-border" is supported, which makes the image copy very simple. If a pixel outside the texture border is accessed, this pixel has the same color as the border. Therefore, instead of copying the pixel from (0, 0) to (n-1, n-1), we copy the pixel from (-9, -9) to (n+8, n+8) of an image with n x n pixels. In doing this we get the border extension for the convolutions.

Before we compute the FFT of the Gabor filter, we should resize the Gabor filter kernel (19 x 19) into the same size as the to be convoluted image (256 x 256), because the convolution using FFT only can be applied on the input data of the same size (Podlozhnyuk, 2007). The expansion of the Gabor filter kernel to the image size should be executed as shown in Fig. 4.5 right: cyclically shift the original filter kernel such that the kernel center is at (0, 0).

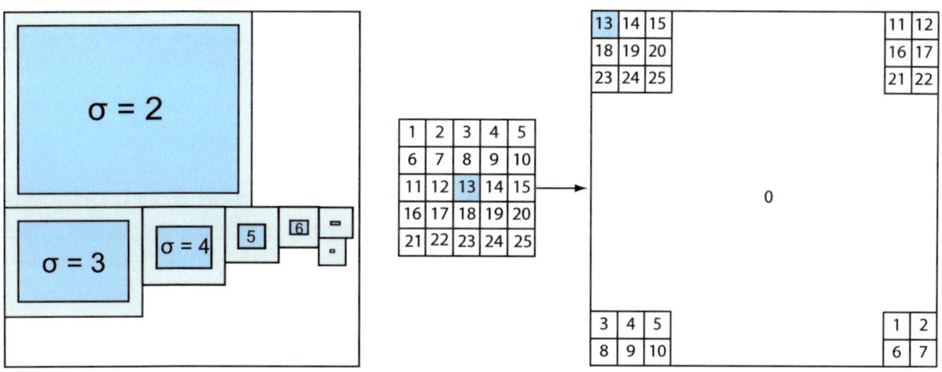

Fig. 4.5. The image (left) and the filter kernel (right) prepared for FFT

In the center-surround differences, 6 feature maps in the intensity channel, 12 feature maps in the color channel and 24 feature maps in the orientation channel are computed between the selected fine scale maps and the coarse maps. To execute this subtraction, the images should be enlarged or reduced into the same size and then a point-by-point subtraction is accomplished. We reduce the images at scale 2 and 3 into scale 4 and enlarge the images at scale 5, 6, 7, 8 also into scale 4. At the end all the images are at scale 4 and have 40 x 30 pixels. For those enlargements and reductions we use the texture concept again by bounding them to the textures.

	I-maps							O-maps					
list center	2	2	3	3	4	4	...	2	2	3	3	4	4
list surround	5	6	6	7	7	8	...	5	6	6	7	7	8
list difference	2-5	2-6	3-6	3-7	4-7	4-8	...	2-5	2-6	3-6	3-7	4-7	4-8

Fig. 4.6. The image lists configuration

Since the images are rescaled into 40 x 30 pixel at this step, we construct three lists to make the computation as parallelly as possible. Fig. 4.6 shows the configuration of the lists. Each list contains 6 x 7 = 42 images with different scale number (but in the same size 40 x 30) and channels. The threads and blocks are so parametrized that 42 blocks are configured. Each block is responsible for one image in the list. 42 images are processed in only one kernel function parallelly. This list-concept is also used for the iterative normalization and the cross-scale combinations.

G. Iterative normalization

The iterative normalization N(.) is an important component in the whole computation. It simulates local competition between neighboring salient locations (Itti et al., 1998). Each iteration contains self-excitation and neighboor-induced inhibition, which can be implemented using a difference of Gaussian filter (DoG) (Itti & Koch, 1999):

$$DoG(x,y) = \frac{c_{ex}^2}{2\pi\sigma_{ex}^2} e^{-\frac{x^2+y^2}{2\pi\sigma_{ex}^2}} - \frac{c_{inh}^2}{2\pi\sigma_{inh}^2} e^{-\frac{x^2+y^2}{2\pi\sigma_{inh}^2}} \tag{16}$$

with $\sigma_{ex} = 2\%$ and $\sigma_{inh} = 25\%$ of the input image width, $c_{ex} = 0.5$, $c_{in} = 1.5$ and the constant inhibitory term $C_{inh} = 0.02$. At each iteration the given image M is computed as follows (Itti & Koch, 1999):

$$M \leftarrow |M + M * DoG - C_{inh}|_{\geq 0} \tag{17}$$

The inseparable DoG filter is divided into two separable convolution filters, one Gaussian filter for excitation with 5 x 5 pixels and one Gaussian filter for inhibition with 29 x 29 pixels for an input image at 40 x 30. The larger the input image is, the bigger are the filter kernels. The kernel size can be computed as follows:

$$size_{(ex|inh)} = 2 \cdot floor(\sigma_{(ex|inh)} \cdot \sqrt{-2 \cdot \ln(1/100)}) + 1 \tag{18}$$

The 153 iterations on 51 images are very costly. Although the shared memory size is limited, the images at 40 x 30 and the respective filter kernels (4916 Byte) can fit into it. In doing this, a 10 times acceleration is obtained, whereas the lists mentioned in 4.3-F are also used.

H. Combination into the saliency map

In the following cross-scale combinations no image rescaling is needed. It is only a question of point-by-point integration of the feature maps into conspicuity maps $\overline{I}$, $\overline{C}$ and $\overline{O}$. The saliency map is a linear combination of the normalized conspicuity maps.

I. Multi-GPU utilization

A parallel utilization of multi-GPU enables a significant acceleration of the saliency map computation. To avoid the intricateness of a multi-process mode, a multi-threaded mode is used to manage the multi-GPU utilization. In a multi-threaded mode, in addition to a main thread several threads are utilized. Each thread is responsible for one GPU. Fig. 4.7 illustrates the multi-threaded mode in a petri-net. Two semaphores are used to ensure the synchronization of the threads. The semaphore 1 sends a signal to the main thread if one or more GPUs are idle and is initialized with the number of the applied GPUs. The semaphore 2 starts one of the GPU-threads. Interestingly, in the main thread, at $t_{0,4}$ a thread is started, while at $t_{0,5}$ a saliency map is ready to be taken. Using this multi-threaded mode the frame rate can be significantly increased.

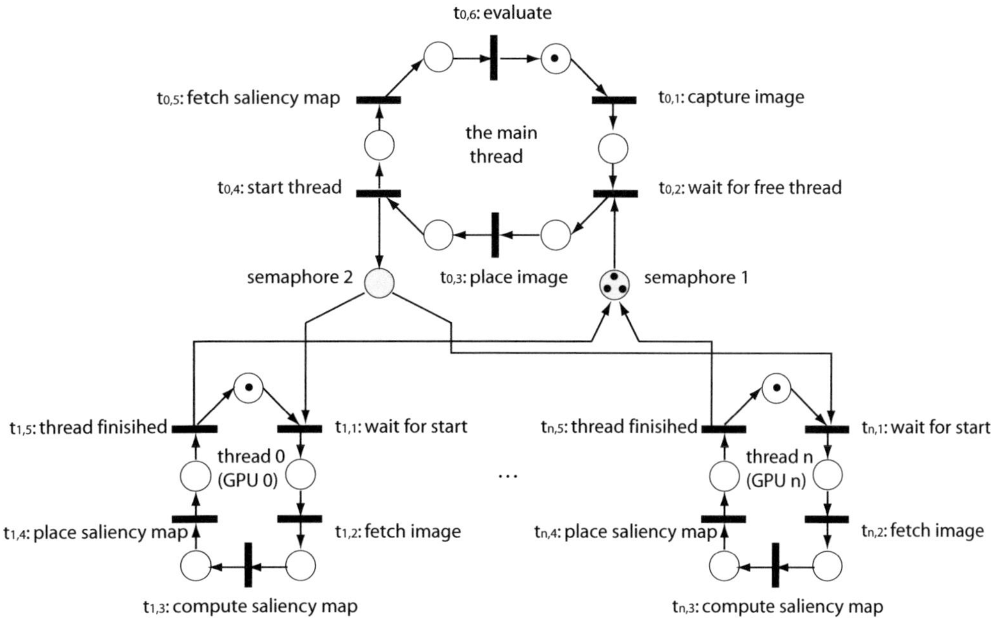

Fig. 4.7. The petri-net structure for multi-threaded mode

4.4 Results and discussion

We tested our multi-GPU implementation using 1 to 4 NIVDIA GeForce 8800 (GTX) graphics cards. The computers are equipped with different CPUs and 64-bit linux systems. The computational time is the average processing time of 1000 input images at a resolution of 640 x 480 pixels.

Tab. 4.1 shows the detailed processing time protocol. The most costly step is the initialization which has a computational time of 328ms. The memory allocation happens only once and needs almost 50MB RAM. The saliency map computation takes only about 10.6ms with a frame rate of 94.3 fps, respectively. In the GFLOPS performance estimation, only the floating-point operations are considered. The address-pointer-arithmetic, the starting of the CUDA functions and the memory copy accesses, which are very time-consuming and have, therefore, a strong influence on the computational time, are not considered.

Saliency map computation	**Time**	**FLOP**	**GFLOPS**
initialization	328ms		
Gaussian pyramid I-, C-maps	2,10ms	6.482.049	3,09
FFT, convolution, IFFT	2,39ms	27.867.923	11,66
image rescaling	0,89ms	294.000	0,33
center-surround differences	0,16ms	151.200	0,95
iterative normalization	4,74ms	34.876.690	7,36
Integration into saliency maps	0,33ms	62.390	0,19
total	10,61ms	69.734.252	6,57

Table 4.1. Computational time registration using 1 GPU

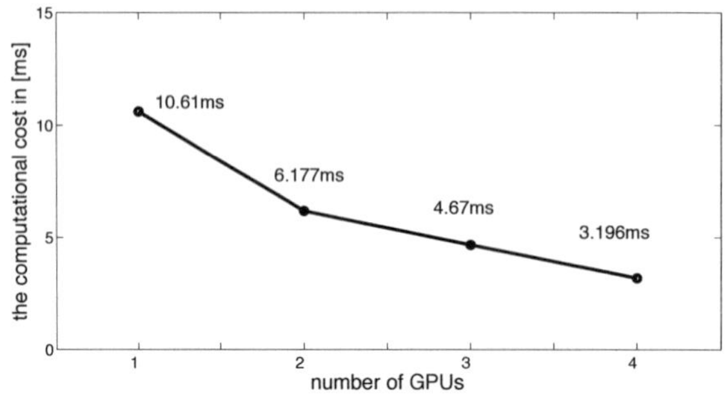

Fig. 4.8. Comparison of computational time using 1 to 4 GPUs

Fig. 4.8 illustrates the computational time using 1 to 4 GPUs, which shows a very good scalability of the multi-GPU implementation.

In Tab. 4.2 the performance of the iLab's implementation (Peters & Itti, 2007) and our implementation is compared. Working on the images with the same resolution and the same precision, iLab uses the 2.8GHz Intel Xeon processor and achieves a frequency of 19.48 Hz, while using our implementation a frequency of 313 Hz is obtained. Using multi-threaded mode, the maximum speed of iLab is 37 fps which is still about 8.5 times slower than our implementation.

	iLab´s implementation	**our implenentation**
resolution	640 x 480	640 x 480
hardware	2.8GHz Intel Xeon processor	4 NVIDIA GeForce 8800 (GTX)
precision	floating-point	floating-point
computational time	51.34ms	3.196ms
frequency	19.48 Hz	313 Hz

Table 4.2. Comparison between iLab's implementation and our implementation

5. Visual odometry for ACE

The goal of ACE is to navigate in an unpredictable and unstructured urban environment. For achieving the aim, accurate pose estimation is one of the preconditions. As humans, we use visual information to estimate the relative motion between ourselves and a reference object. If we close our eyes, we can still estimate the motion by feeling the foot step. Even if we move in a car and close our eyes, we can use inertial sensor in the body, such as inner ear, to tell how our motion is. By now, ACE only has the information from the angle-encoders on the wheels. If there are sands, cobblestone on the ground, the wheels will slip, which causes an inaccurate localization. Therefore, we want to use the visual information to support the localization. We mount a high-speed camera in the front of ACE. The camera looks straight towards the ground.

In this section a visual odometry system is presented to estimate the current position and orientation of ACE platform. The existing algorithms of optical flow computation are analyzed, compared and an improved sum-of-absolute difference (SAD) algorithm with high-speed performance is selected to estimate the camera ego-motion. The kinematics model describing the motion of ACE robot is set up and implemented. Finally the whole odometry system was evaluated within appropriate scenarios.

5.1 Background
How to locate the position and orientation of a moving object has long been a research focus of the computer vision community. The probably existing problems could be being robust against complicated environment, different ground situations and changing brightness. Most visual odometry methods include three phases: firstly, a suitable optical flow computation algorithm should be selected to determine the optical flows in a series of successive images. Then, the translation and rotation of the camera should be estimated according to these optical flows acquired in the first step. At last, a geometry model denoting the relation between camera and robot should be established so that the localization of the robot can be deduced from the position of the camera.

5.1.1 Optical flow techniques
The computation of optical flows has been a key problem discussed in the processing of image sequences for many years (Barron et al., 1994). Nowadays there are two most popular techniques: Matching-based method and differential method. Block-based matching is applied in many aspects of computer vision area. It's also one of the most important techniques for optical flow computation. Two simple algorithms, sum-of-absolute difference (SAD) and sum-of-squared difference (SSD), are usually used to find the best match. They are more efficient than the other techniques. Lucas & Kanade is a typical and classical differential technique, which is based on the gradient constraint. It has a comparative robustness and accuracy in the presence of noise and is feasible in reality.

5.1.2 Pose estimation using optical flow information
Pose estimation is the procedure to compute the position and orientation of a camera relative to the world coordinate. Using image Jacobian matrix, the relationship between object velocity in 3-D world and its image-plane velocity on the image sensor is described as follows:

$$\begin{bmatrix} \dot{u} \\ \dot{v} \end{bmatrix} = \begin{bmatrix} \frac{\lambda}{z} & 0 & -\frac{u}{z} & -\frac{uv}{\lambda} & \frac{\lambda^2+u^2}{\lambda} & -v \\ 0 & \frac{\lambda}{z} & -\frac{v}{z} & \frac{-\lambda^2-u^2}{\lambda} & \frac{uv}{\lambda} & u \end{bmatrix} \cdot \begin{bmatrix} T_x \\ T_y \\ T_z \\ \omega_x \\ \omega_y \\ \omega_z \end{bmatrix} \quad (19)$$

where T_x, T_y, T_z are translation velocities of the camera in world coordinate in three directions, ω_x, ω_y, ω_z angular velocities in three directions. $\dot{u}$ and $\dot{v}$ are the pixel velocity along x and y directions in image plane, while u and v are the corresponding pixel coordinates in image plane. Normally we have more than 3 feature points on the image plane, so the equation system is redundant.

5.1.3 Related work
Jason Campbell et al. (Campbell et al. 2005) designed a model using monocular camera mounted at the robot's front and viewing front and underside of the ground. The flow

vectors are divided into three parts: a dead zone near the horizon is defined and discarded in the computational processing; the vectors above the horizon are used to calculate the robot rotation while the vectors below the horizon are used to estimate the robot translation. Similar to the model established by Campbell, the monocular camera in Wang's model (Wang et al. 2005) focuses only on the locally planar ground, and calculates the translation and rotation together. Both of the models use Lucas & Kanade method to obtain the optical flow. Utilizing the Harris corners detection and normalized correlation, Nister presented a system (Nister et al. 2004) that provides an accurate estimation but works relative slowly. In Fernadez's work (Fernadez & Price 2004), utilizing the task-sharing abilities of the operating system, the problem of synchronization across multiple frame-grabbers can be solved. In order to have a better efficiency, the SAD algorithm is used here. In Dornhege's work (Dornhege & Kleiner, 2006) the salient features are tracked continuously over multiple images and then the differences between features that denotes the robot's motion are computed. An inertial measurement unit (IMU) is employed here to estimate the orientation.

5.2 Hardware and modeling

5.2.1 Hardware description

Fig. 5.1 illustrates the hardware configuration. A high-speed camera and a 1394b PCI-express adapter are used in our system to capture and transfer the images to the computational units. The dragonfly® express camera (Point Grey Research Inc.), fitted with a normal wide-angle lens, can work at 200 fps with the resolution of 640x480 pixels. Utilizing the IEEE-1394B (Firewire 800) interface, the camera is connected to our vision processing computer with an AMD Phenom 9500 @2.2GHz Quad-Core processor and 4 GB memory.

Fig. 5.1. Hardware configuration

5.2.2 Kinematics modeling

Because ACE will explore the outdoor urban environments, e.g. the city centre of Munich, and communicate frequently with the humans, so the camera for visual odometry may not gaze directly forward. For avoiding the disturbance of moving crowd, the camera is mounted in the front of ACE and the optical axis is perpendicular to the ground.

The camera is firmed on ACE such as represented in Fig. 5.2. The relative position between the camera and the robot does not change in the whole process. Any actuated motion of the robot will result in a movement of the camera relative to its original position. Because the displacement between camera and ground in z-direction is much smaller than the distance between camera and ground z, we can approximately assume that the ground is a flat plane and the ACE-platform displaces without any roll and pitch angle. Based on this assumption only 3 variables must be considered: the movements in x and y directions and the orientation around the z axis. We divide the movement of robot in two parts (see Fig. 5.3).

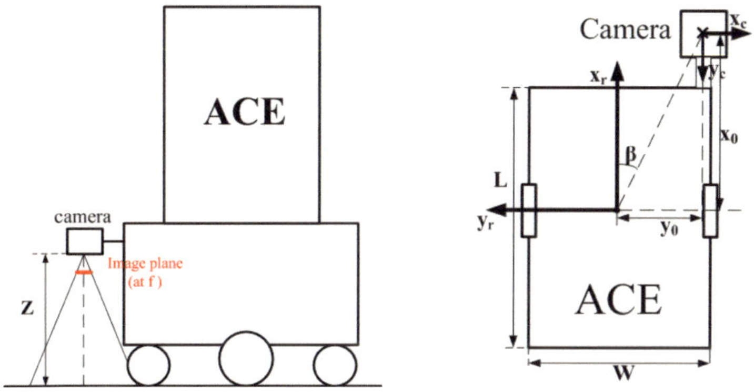

Fig. 5.2. Cutaway and planform of the visual odomery configuration

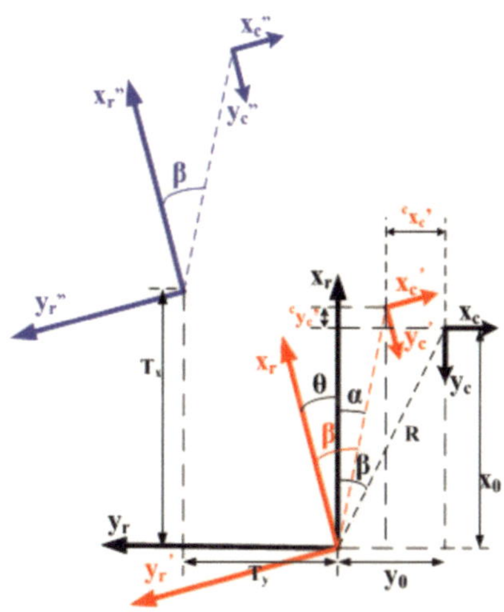

Fig. 5.3. Geometry relationship between robot and camera in motion with frames and variables definition

Firstly, it rotates with an angle of θ without any translation. Then, the robot has movement of (T_x, T_y). After that, the three variables of camera relative to its original position can be denoted as:

$$\begin{aligned} \theta_c &= \theta_r \\ X_c &= y_0 - R \cdot \sin(\beta + \theta_c) - T_y \\ Y_c &= x_0 - R \cdot \cos(\beta + \theta_c) - T_x \end{aligned} \qquad (20)$$

where $R = \sqrt{x_0^{\,2} + y_0^{\,2}}$ and $\beta = \arctan(\frac{y_0}{x_0})$.

5.3 Motion estimation

Our long-term objective is to fuse the visual information at 200 Hz and the information provided by the angle-encoders at 30 Hz to achieve a high accuracy visual odometry. Currently, we focus on the visual information. The vision processing is as follows: the input images will be undistorted at first. Then, using SAD the optical flow is computed. The relationship between optical flow and the camera ego-motion is indicated by image Jacobian. To reduce the noise and optimize the results of the redundant equations, a Kalman filter is applied.

5.3.1 Optical flow algorithm – elaborated SAD

Compared with other optical flow computation algorithms, SAD performs more efficiently and less system resources are required. The size of our images is 640x480 pixels and the central 400x400 pixels are chosen as interest area. A searching window of 20x20 is defined so there are totally 400 windows in this interest area. SAD algorithm is used in every window with a block size of 8x8 pixels. This block is regarded as original block in frame n-1 and compared with the corresponding neighbour blocks within the searching window in frame n. The block with the least SAD values in frame n will be taken as the matching block. The distance between the original block and the matching block is defined as optical flow value of this searching window. After SAD matching 400 sets of optical flow values have been acquired and a further elaboration is fulfilled as follows: The searching windows on the boundary of the interest area are abandoned and the remaining 18x18 windows can be separated into 36 groups. Each group consists of 3x3 windows as show in Fig. 5.4. In every group we set a limit to eliminate some windows whose optical flow values seem not to be ideal enough. The average optical flow values of remaining windows in every group should be determined and could be seen as a valid optical flow value of this group. Every group can be considered as a single point and we just calculate the optical flow values of 36 feature points with a better accuracy.

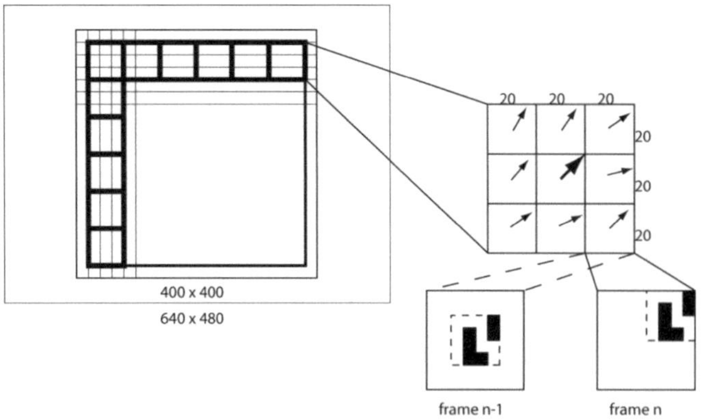

Fig. 5.4. Elaborated SAD algorithm

5.3.2 State estimation – Kalman filter

After calculating optical flow values with an elaborated SAD algorithm, we apply Kalman filter to determine the redundant equations based on image Jabobian matrix. The basic thought of Kalman filter is to predict the state vector x_k according to the measurement vector z_k. Based on the assumption we have made in kinematics model, only T_x, T_y and ω_z are required and therefore the state vector is composed of only three elements. The measurement vector z_k comprises the 36 sets of points velocities acquired from optical flow values of 36 feature points. The measurement matrix is a simplified image Jacobian matrix J, the redundant equations can be described as follows:

$$\begin{bmatrix} \dot{u}_1 \\ \dot{v}_1 \\ \vdots \\ \dot{u}_{36} \\ \dot{v}_{36} \end{bmatrix} = \begin{bmatrix} \frac{\lambda}{z} & 0 & -v_1 \\ 0 & \frac{\lambda}{z} & u_1 \\ \vdots & \vdots & \vdots \\ \frac{\lambda}{z} & 0 & -v_{36} \\ 0 & \frac{\lambda}{z} & u_{36} \end{bmatrix} \cdot \begin{bmatrix} T_x \\ T_y \\ \omega_z \end{bmatrix} \tag{21}$$

The basic process of Kalman filter in our experiment is as follows:

$$\begin{aligned} x_k &= x_{k-1} + w_k \\ z_k &= J \cdot x_{k-1} + v_k \end{aligned} \tag{22}$$

Random variables w_{k-1} and v_k represent the process noise and measurement noise respectively. The estimation process can be divided into two parts: predict part and correct part. At the beginning, the camera velocity vector, which is also the state vector in Kalman filter, is initialized with null vector, after the predict part, prior camera velocity estimation and prior error covariance estimation are transferred to the correct part. In correct part the posterior camera velocity estimation are computed by incorporating current point velocity vector, which is also the measurement vector. A posterior error covariance is also calculated in correct part and together with posterior camera velocity estimate transferred as initialization of the next step. In every step the posterior camera velocity estimation is the result of the redundant equations.

5.4 Experiments results

In the ACE platform there is an encoder which can estimate the current position of ACE. We read the data from the encoder at a frequency of 4-5Hz and consider them as ground truth. The camera mounted on ACE works at a frequency of 200Hz. Our experiment data is obtained when ACE is moving in the environment of stone sidewalk. The experiment is divided into two parts. In the first part, ACE ran about 6,7m in a straight line, which is taken as pure translation. The second part is pure rotation test. ACE only rotated at the starting point and passes about 460 grads. Two series of images are captured and saved, and then the experiment is carried out offline. The motion estimation computation works also at 200Hz.

Fig. 5.5 left shows the results of estimating the robot displacements in pure translation. The red curve indicates the displacement in x-direction measured by encoder, and the blue curve indicates the displacement in x-direction estimated by visual odometry.

The right part of Fig. 5.5 shows the angular result in pure rotation. The red curve indicates the ground truth from encoder, and the black curve indicates the estimation result from visual odometry.

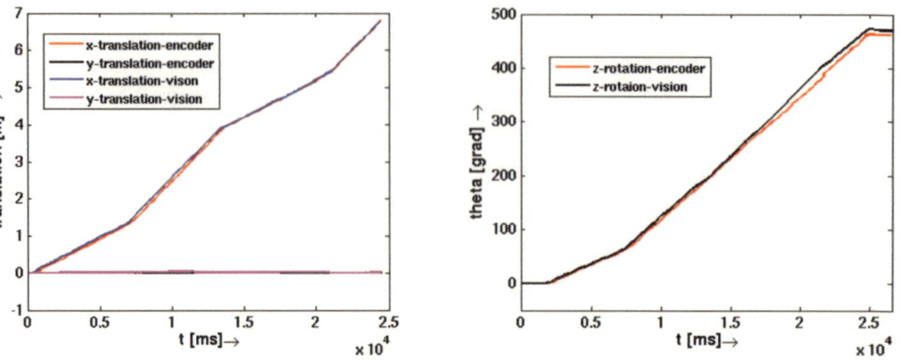

Fig. 5.5. Position estimation in pure translation (left) and in pure rotation (right)

The right part of Fig. 5.5 shows the angular result in pure rotation. The red curve indicates the ground truth from encoder, and the black curve indicates the estimation result from visual odometry.

6. Conclusions and future work

In this chapter, two high-speed vision systems are introduced, which can acquire and process visual information in real time and are used for the visual attention and navigation of the Autonomous City Explorer (ACE).

An information-based view direction planning is proposed to rapidly detect the surprising event in the environment during accomplishing predefined tasks. This high performance is facilitated and ensured by high-speed cameras and high-speed processors such as Graphics Processing Units (GPUs). A frequency of 313 fps on input images at 640 x 480 pixels is achieved for the bottom-up attention computation, which is about 8.5 times faster than the standard implementation on CPUs. For the high speed visual odometry, our algorithm performs well according to the experiments results. The time delay of close-loop control can be decreased and the system stability can be improved.

Further development based on these two high-performance vision systems is planned to improve the self-localization and navigation accuracy. Besides, a suitable data fusion algorithm should be selected to combine data from encoder and visual. The visual attention system should also be extended for the application of human-robot interaction.

7. Acknowledgment

This work is supported in part within the DFG excellence initiative research cluster *Cognition for Technical Systems* – **CoTeSys**, see also www.cotesys.org.

8. References

Barron, J.; Fleet, D. & Beauchemin, S. (1994). Performance of optical flow techniques, *International journal of computer vision*, Vol.12, No. 1, February 1994, pp. 43-77, ISSN: 0920-5691.

Campbell, J.; Sukthankar, R.; Nourbakhsh, I. & Pahwa, A. (2005). A robust visual odometry and precipice detection system using consumer-grade monocular version,

Proceedings of the 2005 IEEE International Conference on robotics and automation, pp.3421 - 3427, ISBN: 0-7803-8915-8 , Barcelona, April 2005
CUDA (2007). *Programming Guide Version 1.1.* NVIDIA
CUDA CUFFT Library (2007). NVIDIA
Davison, A.J. (1998). *Mobile Robot Navigation Using Active Vision.* PhD thesis. Robotics Research Group, Department of Engineering Science, University of Oxford
Dornhege, C. & Kleiner, A. (2006). Visual odometry for tracked vehicles, *Proceeding of the IEEE international workshop on safety, security and rescue robotics*, Gaithersburg, USA, 2006
Fernadez, D. & Price, A. (2004). Visual odomerty for an outdoor mobile robot, *Proceeding of the 2004 IEEE conference on robotics and mechatronics*, Singapore, December 2006
Frintrop, S. (2006). *VOCUS: A Visual Attention System for Object Detection and Goal-directed search.* PhD thesis
Im, S. & Cho, S. (2006). Context-Based Scene Recognition Using Bayersian Networks with Scale-Invariant Feature Transform, *ACIVS 2006*, LNCS 4179, pp. 1080-1087
Itti, L.; Koch, C & Niebur, E. (1998). A model of saliency-based visual attention for rapid scene analysis, *Pattern Analysis and Machine Intelligence*, vol. 20, pp. 1254-1259
Itti, L. & Koch, C. (1999). A comparison of feature combination strategies for saliency-based visual attention systems, *SPIE human vision and electronic imaging IV* (HVEI'99), San Jose, CA pp 473-482
Itti, L. & Baldi, P. (2005). A Principled Approach to Detecting Surprising Events in Video, *Proceedings of the IEEE International Conference on Computer Vision and Pattern Recognition (CVPR)*, June, 2005
Kühnlenz, K. (2006a). *Aspects of Multi-Focal Vision*, PhD thesis, Technische Universität München.
Kühnlenz, K., Bachmayer, M. and Buss, M. (2006b). A Multi-Focal High-Performance Vision System, *Proceedings of the International Conference of Robotics and Automation (ICRA)*, pp. 150-155, Orlando, USA, May 2006.
Lidoris, G., Klasing, K., Bauer, A., Xu, T., Kühnlenz, K., Wollherr, D. & Buss, M. (2007). The Autonomous City Explorer Project: Aims and System Overview, *Proceedings of the IEEE/RSJ International Conference on Intelligent Robots and Systems (IROS)*, 2007.
Longhust, P.; Debattista, K. & Chalmers, A. (2006). A GPU based Saliency Map for High-Fidelity Selective Rendering, *AFRIGRAPH 2006*, Cape Town, South Africa
Nister, D., Naroditsky, O., Bergen, J. (2004). Visual odometry, *Proceedings of the 2004 IEEE computer society conference on computer Vision and Pattern Recognition*, Vol.1, pp. 652-659, ISBN: 0-7695-2158-4, Washington DC, July 2004
Ouerhani, N.; Hügli, H.; Burgi, P.Y. & Ruedi, P.F. (2002). A Real Time Implementation of the Saliency-Based Model of Visual Attention on a SIMD Architecture, *DAGM 2003*, LNCS 2449, pp. 282-289
Ouerhani, N.; Hügli, H.; Gruener, G. & Codourey, A. (2005). A Visual Attention-Based Approach for Automatic Landmark Selection and Recognition, *WAPCV 2004*, LNCS 3368, pp. 183-195
Pellkofer, M. & Dickmanns, E.D. (2000). EMS-Vision: Gaze Control in Autonomous Vehicles, *Proceedings of the IEEE Intelligent Vehicles Symposium 2000*, Dearborn, USA

Peters, R.J. & Itti, L. (2007). Applying computational tools to predict gaze direction in interactive visual environments, *ACM Transactions on Applied Perception*, May 2007, Pages 1-21

Podlozhnyuk, V. (2007). *FFT-based 2D convolution*. NVIDIA

Remazeilles, A. & Chaumette, F. (2006). Image-based robot navigation from an image memory, *Robotics and Autonomous Systems*

Seara, J.F. & Schmidt, G. (2005). Gaze Control Strategy for Vision-Guided Humanoid Walking, *at-Automatisierungstechnik*, vol. 2, pp. 49-58

Torralba, A. & Sinha, P. (2001). Statistical Context Priming for Object Detection. Proceedings of the International Conference on Computer Vision (ICCV), pp. 763-770, Vancouver, Canada

Ude, A.; Wyart, V.; Lin, L.H. & Cheng, G. (2005). Distributed Visual Attention on a Humanoid Robot, *Proceedings of 2005 5-th IEEE-RAS International Conference on Humanoid Robots*

Walther, D. & Koch, C. (2006). Modeling attention to salient proto-objects, *Science Direct, Neural Networks*, vol. 19, pp. 1395-1407

Wang, H.; Yuan, K.; Zou, W. & Zhou, Q. (2005). Visual odometry based on locally planar ground assumption, *Proceeding of the 2005 IEEE international conference on information acquisition*, Hong Kong and Macau, China, June 2005

Won, W. J.; Ban, S. W. & Lee, M. (2005). Real Time Implementation of a Selective Attention Model for the Intelligent Robot with Autonomous Mental Development, *IEEE ISIE 2005*, June 20-23, Dubrovnik, Croatia

13

New Hierarchical Approaches in Real-Time Robust Image Feature Detection and Matching

M. Langer and K.-D. Kuhnert
University of Siegen
Germany

1. Introduction

The detection of robust image features of high distinctiveness forms a ubiquitous problem in digital image processing. Robust image features are the first step and the key to reliably detect patterns or objects in images, which subsequently leads to object classification and semantic interpretation of the objects in a given image.

The ideal situation for object recognition and classification is to find unambiguous traits of patterns or objects that are to be processed. For anyone delving into this matter, the subject presents itself as a challenging task. Besides the often not obvious object traits, there are a lot of other issues that have to be taken into account. For instance, lighting conditions can vary as well as the objects' scales and rotations; image noise or partial occlusion also is likely to occur. Unless one conducts experiments under laboratory conditions, where some of these problems might be ruled out, all these issues have to be addressed properly. So the challenging task is to find image features that are distinct and robust under the varying conditions just stated before.

An obvious method for detecting objects is to examine their shape and, as an abstraction of it, their *contours*. Contour matching usually works well, if the distinct object classes have strong variations in their shape (like the shape of any automobile is quite different compared to the shape of a human). The contour can be represented by a classic chain-code (or its many derivates). For the matching process both contour representations undergo a transformation to achieve scale and rotation invariance and are then compared to each other. The comparison can either be done directly on the transformed image coordinates or on measures deduced from the earlier representation (i.e. the moments, distances, polygonal, or Fourier descriptors yielded from the contour points).

Besides those methods, one popular approach is to detect certain local *interest points* at distinctive locations in the image, such as corners, blobs, or T-junctions. The interest point detector is supposed to be repeatable under varying viewing conditions (e.g. different lighting or different viewing angles). Having found distinctive interest points in an image, the interest points are examined more closely regarding their neighbourhood. Taking the neighboring pixels into account forms an *image feature* or *image descriptor*, which has to fulfill certain criteria regarding distinctiveness, robustness against noise, detection errors, and image deformations. These image features can then be matched to features computed from other images. Matching features indicate a high likeliness of correspondence between the two images. Hence patterns or objects in one image can be detected in other images employing this method. An advantage of this method is that detection of interest points takes place at one of the first stages of the image processing pipeline: in *scale-space*. All the interest point detectors and image descriptors discussed in section 3 will exploit the scale-space representation of an image. Hence a short review of scale-space computation is provided in the following section.

2. Structural information and scale-space representation of an image

In this section a short review about scale-space construction on digital images is given. One of the most thorough and comprehensive researches on the topic of scale-space representation was done in (Lindeberg, 1994). In his work, Lindeberg first states the principle problem about detecting the characteristic structure of objects in images regarding the scale level the image was taken. A good example is the structure of a tree that varies over different scaling levels. At a very coarse level, the observer may only recognize a green blob-like structure of the treetop, whereas at finer scales, branches and leaves may be noticeable. As the scale-space is a continuous and infinite space, this can go as far as the tree may degenerate to a single unnoticeable green spot or to a level where leaf-fibres can be examined. Which scale intervals are best suited totally depends on the image processing task at hand. A method for automatic scale selection for characteristic image features in this regard is presented in (Lindeberg, 1998).

Scale-space representations span a broad range of applications in image processing (i.e. feature detection, feature classification, shape computation, or even stereo matching). In this work, though, we are mainly interested in exploiting scale-space for object recognition. It will be shown that scale-space representations of images allow for effective extraction of distinctive image features, which can be matched with features from other images in the context of object recognition. To compute these distinctive features one has to transform the image into scale-space first, so that the interest point detectors and image descriptors introduced in section 3 can build upon this representation. The *multi-scale* representation of a digital image is well-known and widely used in image processing in forms of quad-trees, image pyramids, or (the relatively more recent) wavelets. The scale-space is just a special type of a multi-scale transformation.

2.1 Scale-space construction of continuous signals

The scale-space of a digital image is directly related to the scale-space in signal processing, whereas the scale-space representation of a one-dimensional signal is defined by *embedding* this signal into a one-parameter family of derived signals computed by convolution with a one-parameter *Gaussian kernel* with increasing width (Witkin, 1983). In (Lindeberg, 1994) a proof is provided that the Gaussian kernel is a *unique* choice for scale-space processing. The Gaussian kernel alone fulfills all necessary requirements for scale-space computation like basical linearity, spatial shift and scale invariance, and preserving the constraint that no new structures (maxima or minima in the image) will be created. It is also shown that the scale-space abides by the laws of a mathematical semi-group. The formal mathematical notion for constructing the scale space is as follows: Let $f : \mathbb{R} \to \mathbb{R}$ stand for the original signal. Then, the scale space representation $L : \mathbb{R}^N \times \mathbb{R}_+ \to \mathbb{R}$ is defined by $L(\cdot; 0) = f$ and

$$L(\cdot; t) = g(\cdot; t) * f \tag{1}$$

where $t \in \mathbb{R}_+$ is the scale parameter, and $g : \mathbb{R}^N \times \mathbb{R}_+ \backslash \{0\} \to \mathbb{R}$ is the Gaussian kernel. The kernel itself is defined by

$$g(x;t) = \frac{1}{(2\pi t)^{N/2}} e^{-x^T x(2t)} = \frac{1}{(2\pi t)^{N/2}} e^{-\sum_{i=1}^{N} x_i^2/(2t)} \qquad (x \in \mathbb{R}^N, x_i \in \mathbb{R}). \quad (2)$$

$\sigma = \sqrt{t}$ is the standard deviation of kernel g. It is a natural measure of spatial scale in the smoothed signal at scale t.
Another equivalent way to construct the scale-space L is by solving the differential heat diffusion equation

$$\partial_t L = \frac{1}{2}\nabla^2 L = \frac{1}{2}\sum_{i=1}^{N} \partial_{x_i^2} L \quad (3)$$

with initial condition $L(\cdot;0) = f$, which is the well-known physical formula describing how a heat distribution L evolves over time t in a homogeneous medium with uniform conductivity, given the initial heat distribution stated above. From Eq. (1)-(3) multi-scale spatial derivates can be defined by

$$L_{x^n}(\cdot;t) = \partial_{x^n} L(\cdot;t) = g_{x^n}(\cdot;t) * f, \quad (4)$$

where g_{x^n} denotes a derivative of some order n.
The main goal of the scale-space construction is that fine scale information (i.e. amplitude peaks or noise at high frequencies) shall vanish with increasing scale parameter t. Witkin (Witkin, 1983) noticed that new local extrema cannot be created, if the scale-space is contructed in the above described manner. Because differentiation and convolution are commutative,

$$\partial_{x^n} L(\cdot;t) = \partial_{x^n}(g(\cdot;t) * f) = g(\cdot;t) * \partial_{x^n} f, \quad (5)$$

this non-creation property holds for any nth degree spatial derivative. This feature enables detection of significant image structures over scales and is exploited by the algorithms described in section 3.
An important statement in (Koenderink, 1984) is that without a priori knowledge of specific image structures, the image has to be processed at *all* scales *simultaneously*. In this regard the images forming the scale-space are *strongly coupled* and not just a set of unrelated derived images.

2.2 Scale-space construction of discrete signals

Because digital image processing deals with discrete signals, the equations presented above need to be adapted. The interesting question here is how this adjustment needs to be performed so that the scale-space properties are preserved. It turns out that there is only one way to construct a scale-space for discrete signals. For an in-depth look into the derivation of the following formula see (Lindeberg, 1994). Given a signal $f : \mathbb{Z} \to \mathbb{R}$ the scale-space representation $L : \mathbb{Z} \times \mathbb{R}_+ \to \mathbb{R}$ is given by

$$L(x;t) = \sum_{n=-\infty}^{\infty} T(n;t) f(x-n) \quad (6)$$

where $T : \mathbb{Z} \times \mathbb{R}_+ \to \mathbb{R}$ is a kernel named the "discrete analogue of the Gaussian kernel", which is defined in terms of a modified Bessel function given by $T(n;t) = e^{-\alpha t} I_n(\alpha t)$.

It can be shown that the discrete scale-space family $L : \mathbb{Z}^N \times \mathbb{R}_+ \to \mathbb{R}$ of a discrete signal $f : \mathbb{Z}^N \to \mathbb{R}$ must satisfy

$$\partial_t L = \alpha_1 \nabla_3^2 L \tag{7}$$

$$\partial_t L = \alpha_1 \nabla_5^2 L + \alpha_2 \nabla_{\times^2}^2 L \tag{8}$$

in one and two dimensions for constants $\alpha_1 \geq 0$ and $\alpha_2 \geq 0$. ∇_5^2 and $\nabla_{\times^2}^2$ denote two discrete approximations of the Laplace operator. They are defined by

$$(\nabla_5^2 f)_{0,0} = f_{-1,0} + f_{+1,0} + f_{0,-1} + f_{0,+1} - 4f_{0,0}\,,$$

$$(\nabla_{\times^2}^2 f)_{0,0} = \frac{1}{2}\,(f_{-1,-1} + f_{-1,+1} + f_{+1,-1} + f_{+1,+1} - 4f_{0,0}).$$

The function subscripts are the indices at which position in the image an intensity value shall be taken. With $\alpha_2 = 0$, the two-dimensional scale-space representation of a digital image is given by convolution with a one-dimensional Gaussian kernel along each direction. What remains to say is that the spatial derivatives of the Gaussian kernel can be approximated by *differences of Gaussian* (DoG) kernels at different spatial locations.

2.3 Image features from scale-space representations

To exploit scale-space for image feature detection, one has to deal with differential geometry. Some methods are required for further processing the output of the Gaussian derivative operators to gain meaningful and distinct image features. It is mandatory to base the analysis on image descriptors that do not depend on the actual coordinate system of the spatial and intensity domain, because a single partial derivative contains no useful geometric information. So it is required that the scale-space representation shall be *invariant* with respect to *translation, rotation,* and *scale changes*. Unfortunately complete affine invariance (i.e. non-uniform rescaling) is harder to achieve. This issue is also addressed in (Lindeberg, 1998).

Scale-space representation of an image is especially well-suited to detect sub-pixel *edges, junctions* and *blob-like* structures. For this, it is helpful to define a local orthonormal coordinate system for any point of interest in the image. A useful definition would be that for any Point P_0, normal *(x,y)* image coordinates are translated into a *(u,v)* coordinates with the v-axis aligned along the gradient direction and the u-axis perpendicular to it (which also aligns with the tangent orientation). This leads to $e_u = (\sin\alpha, -\cos\alpha)^T$ and $e_v = (\cos\alpha, \sin\alpha)^T$ for example, where

$$e_v|_{P_0} = \begin{pmatrix} \cos\alpha \\ \sin\alpha \end{pmatrix} = \frac{1}{\sqrt{L_x^2 + L_y^2}} \begin{pmatrix} L_x \\ L_y \end{pmatrix}. \tag{9}$$

In terms of Cartesian coordinates, the local directional operators can be expressed by

$$\begin{pmatrix} \partial_u \\ \partial_v \end{pmatrix} = \begin{pmatrix} \sin\alpha & -\cos\alpha \\ \cos\alpha & \sin\alpha \end{pmatrix} \begin{pmatrix} \partial_x \\ \partial_y \end{pmatrix}. \tag{10}$$

Note that $L_u = 0$, because of e_u being parallel to the tangent at point P_0.

With these definitions *edge detection* in scale-space can be computed by a non maximum suppression in the gradient direction. The following conditions need to be fulfilled:

$$\begin{cases} L_{vv} = 0 \\ L_{vvv} < 0 \end{cases}. \tag{11}$$

With Eq.(9) and (10) it is possible to convert these statements back to Cartesian coordinates. *Junction detection* is expressed in terms of curvature of level curves in gray level images. In derivative terms the curvature can be expressed by

$$\kappa = \frac{L_{uu}}{L_v}. \tag{12}$$

The curvature is usually multiplied by the gradient magnitude L_v raised to some power *k*. This provides stronger responses at edges. In (Brunnström, 1992) *k=3* is chosen leading to

$$|\widetilde{\kappa}| = \left|L_v^2 L_{uu}\right| = \left|L_y^2 L_{xx} - 2L_x L_y L_{xy} + L_x^2 L_{yy}\right|. \tag{13}$$

A point P_0 has to fulfill the following conditions to be considered a junction-point:

$$\begin{cases} \partial_u(\widetilde{\kappa}) = 0, \\ \partial_v(\widetilde{\kappa}) = 0, \\ \mathcal{H}(\widetilde{\kappa}) = \widetilde{\kappa}_{\mathcal{H}} = \widetilde{\kappa}_{uu}\widetilde{\kappa}_{vv} - \widetilde{\kappa}_{uv}^2 > 0, \\ \operatorname{sign}(\widetilde{\kappa})\widetilde{\kappa}_{uu} < 0. \end{cases} \tag{14}$$

Blob detection can be performed by calculating the zero-crossings of the Laplacian, where

$$\nabla^2 L = L_{uu} + L_{vv} = L_{xx} + L_{yy} = 0. \tag{15}$$

All the introduced feature detectors in section 3 first do a scale-space transformation and then employ Eq. (11)-(15) to detect interest points. At these points the local image descriptors are then computed and used for the later matching process.

3. Technology review of interest point detectors and image descriptors

Usually the computation of distinctive image features is split into two phases. First, interest points are computed at locations that are considered to be promising for the later descriptor calculation. A reliable (and in this regard reproducible) interest point detector is crucial for the feature determination. Then, after the locations of the interest points have been determined, for each such point a local image descriptor is computed by processing the neighbouring intensity values of the current interest point's location. This yields a set of image features that are supposed to be distinctive to the objects in the image. These features can then be used in object recognition or object tracking by matching features yielded from one image to those from another.

3.1 Interest point detectors

Classic interest point detectors used simple attributes like edges or corners. Among these, the probably most widely used, is the Harris corner detector (Harris, 1988). It is based on eigenvalues of the second-moment (also called auto-correlation) matrix. Unfortunately, this detector lacks scale-invariance.

Lindeberg tried to extend the Harris corner detector experimenting with the determinant of the Hessian matrix as well as the Laplacian to detect blob-like shapes (Lindeberg, 1998). He also examined methods for automatic scale selection for image feature computation.

(Mikolajczyk & Schmid, 2004) refined this method exploiting a combination of the Harris detector to determine the location, and the Laplace matrix for scale selection of an image feature. It is basically a combination of the Harris corner detector with the automatic scale selection methods proposed by Lindeberg. This yields the desired scale-invariance. Their image descriptors proved to be highly distinctive, scale invariant, rotation invariant, and highly tolerant against illumination effects.

(Lowe, 2004) mainly focused on speeding up this computational costly processing by replacing the Laplacian of Gaussian (LoG) by a Difference of Gaussian filter (DoG). In 2004 he presented his method called SIFT (scale invariant feature transform) to the public. SIFT features embody the same tolerance to (uniform) changes in scale, rotation, and illumination effects. This also qualifies SIFT as an ideal candidate for pattern and object recognition.

The main difference between SIFT and the feature detector described in (Mikolajczyk & Schmid, 2004) is that the former interest point detector aims at blob-like structures and the latter at corners and highly textured points in images. Thus it can be concluded that the two interest point detectors generate complementary feature.

One basic problem with these sophisticated interest point detectors is that they are computationally complex and hence cannot match hard real-time constraints (i.e. analyzing a video stream of a constant 25fps online). This problem was addressed in (Bay *et al.*, 2006). The group showed that SIFT could be speeded up further almost without losing any of its matching quality. Their work is based on certain approximations (and simplifications) of Lowe's work and was coined "*speeded up robust features*" (SURF). For instance, the research group proved that the approximation of the LoG by a DoG filter can be pushed even further to a *difference of means* (DoM) filter. This filter can be implemented very efficiently exploiting integral images, thus achieving constant runtime behavior. Also the components of the resulting feature vector are cut in half, which provides faster matching speed between different feature vectors.

Usually some interpolation steps are applied over scale-space to accurately locate the interest points before the image descriptor is computed. In (Mikolajczyk & Schmid, 2004) an iterative approach is taken based on displacement calculations using Eq. (16) by starting at the initially detected point for affine normalized windows around this point. In (Lowe, 2004) a 3D quadratic function is fitted to local sample points to interpolate the location of the maximum. This is employed by using the Taylor expansion introduced in (Brown & Lowe, 2002).

A common drawback to all these interest point detectors is their strong responses at edges or contours. This can be mitigated to a certain degree by selecting the scale at which the trace *and* the determinant of the Hessian matrix assume a local extremum.

3.2 Image descriptors

Image descriptors are computed from the location around the previously detected interest points.

(Mikolajczyk & Schmid, 2004) use Gaussian derivates computed in the local neighborhood of each interest point. They convolve these derivatives on small image patches normalized with a matrix U of the form

$$U = \prod_{k} \left(\mu^{-\frac{1}{2}}\right)^{(k)} U^{(0)}. \tag{16}$$

with μ denoting the (scale-space adapted) second moment matrix of the Harris corner detector and k denoting the step width of this iterative algorithm. $U^{(0)}$ is the initial concatenation of square roots of the second moment matrices. To gain invariance to rotation, the derivatives are aligned at the direction of the gradient. The gradient orientation at each interest point is averaged with the gradient orientations in the neighborhood and goes into the descriptor.

Fig. 1. SIFT feature matches applied to a self recorded scene. The blue sugar box on the left side of the image was found in the right complex scene. The SIFT matching software yielded 16 matches (shown as white lines). Note that only 3 matches would have sufficed to correctly identify an object. Also note the partial occlusion and difficult lighting conditions under which the images were taken. The digital camera used to record both images was a Canon Powershot A75 with 3.2 megapixels. The camera was set to automatic mode. The images also underwent a lossy JPEG compression.

Lowe determined his descriptor components by computing the gradient magnitude and orientation for each sample point neighboring the interest point. These values are weighted by a Gaussian window. The samples are then accumulated into orientation histograms, which summarize the contents of 4x4 subregions around the interest point. Over each such subregion the 8 predominant gradient orientations are computed. These values make for the image descriptor. Hence the descriptor consists of 128 components. A visual example of the image feature matching with our own implementation of the SIFT operator is shown in Fig. 1.
The SURF descriptor is determined by the following steps. First, a square region is constructed around the interest point and aligned along the dominant orientation obtained by haar wavelet filter responses at the interest point. The side length of the wavelet is four times the scale level at which the point was detected. The dominant orientation is estimated

by calculating the sum of all responses within a sliding window covering an angle of $\frac{\pi}{3}$. Then, the horizontal and vertical responses over these windows are summed and contribute to the components of the vector of the estimated orientation. The size of this sliding window needs to be determined experimentally (see Bay *et al.*, 2006). The square region size around the interest point is of size 20s (s denoting the scale parameter). The region is split into 4x4 subregions like in (Lowe, 2004). For each such subregion a few simple features (again employing the directional Haar wavelet responses) at 5x5 regularly spaced sample points are computed. Finally, the responses are accumulated over the regions and provide a first set of entries to the image descriptor. Also the sum of the absolute response values is calculated. This yields a four-dimensional vector for each subregion of the form $\mathbf{v} = (\sum d_x, \sum d_y, \sum |d_x|, \sum |d_y|)$, with d_x denoting the Haar wavelet response in x-direction and d_y respectively. Such vectors form a single descriptor vector for all four subregions. Hence the resulting descriptor vector is of size 64 – half the size of a SIFT-descriptor.
There are yet some derivations the introduced image descriptors, i.e. (PCA-SIFT, U-SURF, GLOH etc.) that are not discussed here. These derivates mainly vary in the way how the final descriptor computation is done aiming at lesser component numbers than the original version to speed up object matching.

4. Performance evaluation of local image features

This section is contributed to a short overview of the performance of local image features regarding their *object recognition ratio* and their *computational speed* when implemented on modern computers. Also the issue of exploiting image features for *object classification* is addressed at the end of this section.
In (Leibe & Schiele, 2003) a systematic comparison between contour based, shape based, and appearance based approaches regarding their effectiveness for object recognition is performed. For their evaluation they constructed an own database of small objects, coined the *ETH-80* database. It consists of 80 objects from 8 self chosen categories (i.e. fruit and vegetables, animals, human-made small objects, and human-made big objects). For each category 10 objects are provided that span in-class variations while still clearly belonging to that category. The test mode is of the form leave-one-object-out-crossvalidation, which means that the object recognition system is trained with 79 objects (randomly taken out of the 8 categories) and tested against the one remaining object. The measurements were performed over object sets taken of each category and the results were averaged.
The algorithms used for testing were

- a simple *colour histogram* driven approach,
- *texture based* methods over scale-space (which directly corresponds to the image feature detectors from section 3.1-3.2); these are split into a *rotation variant* method (first order derivatives in *x* and *y* direction) and a *rotation invariant* method (gradient magnitude and Laplacian over 3 scales - also see (Love, 2004)),
- *global shape*: PCA-based methods either based on *one single global eigenspace* for all categories or *separate eigenspaces* for each category,
- and *local shape* using the contours of each object represented by a discrete set of sample points; these points are later matched with points from other images with a *dynamic programming* and a *one-to-one point matching* (using a greedy strategy) approach.

The results found in (Leibe & Schiele, 2003) show that contour-based (local shape) methods perform best, with an average object recognition ratio of 86.4%. Second place were global-shape based PCA variation with 83.4% and 82.9% respectively, but with the texture histograms only slightly behind with 82.2%. As expected, colour histograms performed worst with just 64.9%. Yet, nothing is stated about the different runtime behaviour of the different methods, because this paper deals with quantitative evaluation of the recognition ratio. It can reasonably be assumed that the global and local contour matching algorithms, besides showing the best recognition ratio are also the most costly ones to compute.
Leibe & Schiele also examined combinations for the above described methods. Cascading object recognition systems were constructed using different permutations of these algorithms. They showed that certain combinations could raise the overall object recognition ratio up to 93%. In section 5.1 we show our own approach for a cascading object recognition system aimed to fulfil certain real-time constraints, yet preserving high recognition ratios.
(Mikolajczyk *et al.*, 2005a) evaluated interest region descriptors among themselves and how they perform in different situations; they concentrated especially on all kinds of affine transformations, blurring, and JPEG compression artefacts. They concerned with all the image feature detectors described in section 3 and their common variations and also proposed their own extension to the SIFT operator. In their results section they conclude that the *gradient orientation and location histogram* (GLOH) - a variation of the original SIFT operator - performs best regarding object recognition ratio, closely followed by SIFT. We also employ SIFT features for our cascading object recognition system (see section 5.1).
Another highly noteworthy contribution is presented in (Mikolajczyk *et al.*, 2005b), where local image features are examined regarding their applicability on *object classification*. The interesting question here is, whether the image features, which perform well in scenarios like pattern matching and object recognition, contain useful information that can be applied as features for object classification. They pursue a cluster-driven approach of image features for classification. They computed the distribution of features in the cluster and defined a similarity measure between two clusters by

$$\frac{1}{NM}\sum_{m}^{M}\sum_{n}^{N}(f_{km}-f_{lm})^2=\sigma_k^2+\sigma_l^2+(\mu_k-\mu_l)^2\leq v \tag{17}$$

with N and M denoting the numbers of features in clusters k and l; μ_k and μ_l represent the cluster centres; σ_k^2 and σ_l^2 denote the variances, and v an experimentally determined threshold value.
Mikolajczyk *et al.*, evaluated image feature detectors employing Hessian-Laplace and Salient region, Harris-Laplace, SIFT, PCA-SIFT, and GLOH detectors. The challenging object classification task was to detect pedestrians crossing a street in an urban scenario. Again, the GLOH descriptors exploiting regions around interest points found by Hessian-Laplace obtained the best results; salient region detectors also performed well. Hence, it can be concluded that scale-space image feature detectors are also applicable to object classification beyond their originally intended domain (pattern and object matching).

5. Extending local image features for real-time object recognition

All the previously described image features from section 3 show excellent robustness on object recognition under real-world conditions. Regarding object recognition by matching features of different images, the image features prove to be

- scale-invariant,
- rotational invariant,
- *partially* affine invariant (non-uniform scale changes are problematic),
- highly tolerant against changes in illumination, and
- insensitive to noise (to a certain reasonable degree).

Yet, one important issue has not been fully addressed: the real-time processing of image features or feature matching respectively. In many scenarios, online computation of image features for real-time object matching is desirable. In this regard it is common to imply that a constant video stream needs to be analyzed in real-time, which in this case would mean that the image feature computation software had to cope with 25fps in camera-like image resolutions. The high robustness of the scale-invariant image features comes at the prize of high computation-time, which renders them applicable only partially to these scenarios.

Constructing the scale-space and finding reliable interest points is one of the bottlenecks in this case; another is the component size of the image descriptors, which have to be used for the later matching process. Many extensions to the image features have been applied to address this problem and especially the latest of these, the SURF operator, aims at better runtime speed. The idea in (Bay *et al.*, 2006) is to simplify the costly difference of Gaussian (DoG) filter, which is used during scale-space computation, to a *difference of means* (DoM) filter. The DoM is just a simple box filter. Bay *et al.* showed that this approximation of the DoG filter is permissible, because the DoG filters, which are supposed to be infinite, are actually cropped when they are applied to the image. Thus DoG filters are, when it comes to applying them in discrete digital image processing, an approximation of the theoretical DoG filters themselves. The DoM filter has the nice property that it can be computed very efficiently employing integral images. An integral image is defined by

$$I_{\Sigma}(x,y) = \sum_{i=0}^{i \le x} \sum_{j=0}^{j \le y} I(i,j). \tag{18}$$

After I_{Σ} is constructed, it takes just four additions to calculate the DoM filter of *any size* at any point. This is a major saving of computation time compared to the full application of a Gaussian filter at any point.

Bay *et al.* also reduce the length of the image descriptor to 64 components in contrast to the 128 components of the SIFT operator. This saves time when feature matching is applied, because during the matching process each image descriptor from one image has to be compared (usually by employing some common metric, i.e. the Euclidian distance) to each descriptor of the image that is to be matched.

These measures mitigate the problem of time consuming computations and in fact the SURF operator with all its optimizations only needs 33% the time of the SIFT operator to perform its tasks.

5.1 Cascading object recognition approach

Yet, we seek even better run-time performance than the optimized SURF operator. The SURF operator still cannot satisfy the hard real-time constraints stated in the last section. So we came up with a cascading approach for object recognition. The precondition to our approach is that *a priori knowledge* of the objects to be recognized can be assumed, which is the case in many classic object recognition and classification scenarios. In particular you need to know with which objects the system is supposed to deal with to construct sensible training data sets for an initial teaching of the system.

The main idea of our contribution is to employ a *two-stage cascading approach*: a fast decision-tree based pre-classifier, which sorts out the objects to recognize with a recognition ratio of 66%-75% accuracy, and a later performed image feature matching exploiting SIFT and SURF operators. The recognized objects from the first stage need not be processed by the costly operators anymore. The time savings go directly into equation

$$t_o = t_p + (1 - r)t_s + t_d \tag{19}$$

with t_0 denoting the overall system processing time, t_p the time for pre-computation (system initialization etc.), t_s the time for the SIFT/SURF matching process, and t_d the dead-time of the system (consumed e.g. by memory management and other administrative tasks). r is the ratio of correctly classified objects from the earlier pre-processing stage. Considering the fact that $t_p << t_s$, applying the pre-computation yields better overall timing.

We use the Coil-100 image database[1] as a testbed for our algorithms. This library consists of 100 different, small, everyday use objects, which have about the same size. Each object is rotated around the Y-axis 72 times at a 5° angle each step, thus covering the full 360 degree, which yields 7,200 object view images in total. Each image has a size of 128x128 pixels. The methods and results presented in the following sections all refer to this database.

5.2 Decision tree construction

Decision trees are a classic tool rooting in artificial intelligence and are mainly used for data mining purposes. Decision trees in our work are exploited to classify objects. For an in-depth look into the structure of general decision trees and methods to generate them the reader is referred to (Quinlan, 1983), who was the first to introduce decision trees in his work and (Russel, 2003), who provides a quick and practice oriented overview of decision trees.

We use a fast classification method in the first stage for our object recognition software exploiting *binary decision trees*. Decision trees, once trained, provide means to classify large amounts of objects (several thousands) in just a few milliseconds. The idea is to recursively divide the feature space into sets of similar sizes and feed these sets to nodes into the decision tree. To classify an object, the object features are matched with the class feature sets each node holds. Each node decides whether an object belongs to one (or none) of its two class-feature sets. The decision made by the node determines the next sub-tree, which has to deal with the classification. This process is repeated until a leaf-node is reached. The feature represented by this leaf node yields the class the object belongs to. Because the tree needs not necessarily be built up completely, whole class or feature sets can be represented by leaf nodes.

We pursue a simple colour cluster driven approach to train the decision tree based classificators. The training data sets are taken out of the Coil100 image database. Although

[1] http://www1.cs.columbia.edu/CAVE/software/softlib/coil-100.php

yielding high performance, the training of the decision trees proved to be difficult regarding classification quality, which is at 66% of correctly classified objects on average. This is mainly due to the simple colour based features we use. To gain the features, we apply Alg. 1.

Algorithm 1: Generating a decision tree

```
Data: training sets S of images
Result: generated decision tree d
begin
    C ← ∅
    forall I ∈ S (with I ⊂ S) do
        G ← ∅
        repeat
            A ← P ← ∅
            forall i ∈ I do
                P ∪ GaussPyr(i)
                avg_RGB ← P(i)|max. pyramid level
                A ∪ avg_RGB
            G ∪ CalcCOGs(A)
        until |S| = 2
        C ∪ G    (C holds all CoG subsets)
    d ← BuildDecisionTree(C)
    return d
end
```

Each node divides the center of gravity set (and so the associated class set) into half. This way we achieve a runtime complexity of $\mathcal{O}(M \log(N))$ with N denoting the number of classes and M the number of objects to classify.

The problem of low classification quality can be mitigated by moving to *decision forests* (see Zhao, 2005). Decision forests integrate more than one decision tree into their decision process. These trees are trained with varying datasets which may lead to different classification results. Among all the trees in the forest a quorum is made and the decision taken which should be correct most likely; usually this is done by proclaiming the largest subset of trees, which made the same decision, the winning subset using their decision as the classification result. Applying this method raises the correctly classified objects rate to 75%, but also increases the runtime complexity to $\mathcal{O}(kM \log(N))$ with k denoting the number of trees in the forest.

The rate of correctly classified objects in this stage may seem to be quite low compared to other more sophisticated classificators found in literature, but it is important to note that we employ the pre-stage system only to speed up the later main-stage object recognition process. Every correctly recognized object at the end of this phase means, that no costly image transformation, and no exhaustive search through an image feature database comparing all the descriptor vectors with each other needs to be performed. Hence a classification rate of 66% to 75% means an overall time reduction of the entire system at almost the same rate. As we will show next, this will get us closer to the desired real-time behavior of the object recognition system.

5.3 Performance evaluation

The two-stage image feature matching approach yields a very efficient object recognition method providing highly accurate results. The pre-processing of the algorithm drastically reduces the search-space at minimal computational costs of a few milliseconds.
A typical feature match of a Coil-DB image with the SIFT feature database performs at 75ms. Applying the pre-processing, which yields 75% of correctly classified objects, which is the average rate for well trained decision forests in our implementation, the processing time reduces to 21ms. This time reduction is correlated linearly to the rate of correctly classified objects of the pre-processing phase and follows Eq. (19).

feature distance	correct positive	false positive
40,000	49.30%	0.00%
60,000	65.38%	0.09%
80,000	85.66%	1.74%
100,000	95.10%	8.85%
120,000	97.55%	31.78%

Tab. 1. Results of the object recognition process employing SIFT image features.

Tab. 1 shows some results regarding the object recognition ratio applying SIFT. It clearly shows the high accuracy and reliability employing SIFT features. The matching parameter denotes the threshold that is taken for feature comparison. Features are compared to each other using the squared Euclidian distance over the 128 dimensional feature vectors. Only feature distances that are below this threshold are considered to be equal enough to yield a match. As it can be seen, at a certain value of the threshold (in this particular case 100,000) we yield a rate of correctly classified objects of 95%. Increasing the threshold value any further increases the false positive rate of the matched features drastically (from 9% to 32%) yet improving the correct positive rate at only 2%. We averaged our results over several objects that were taken out of the Coil-100 database randomly. The images we used were to be found in a subset of the database that consisted of all objects and object views from an angle of 60°. Angles between 60° and 90° cannot be reliably matched with the SIFT operator anymore. Values beyond 90° are impossible to use with SIFT, because the object views now show their backside of the object whereas the reference object view shows its front side. For SIFT this is equivalent to a total occlusion of the object. The optimal feature distance for a concrete image set is determined experimentally and changes according to different environments.
Exchanging the SIFT with the SURF operator the values from Tab. 1 stay almost the same (with only slight deviations), except for the even better run-time performance of the system. We could verify that the SURF operator is indeed almost 3 times faster than SIFT as stated in (Bay *et al.*, 2006). The overall computation time of 21ms reduces to 10ms, if SIFT is replaced by SURF in the main-processing stage.

We also took our own image sets with standard CMOS cameras at standard sizes of 320x240 pixels. The object recognition system is capable of processing at a rate of 11fps (SIFT) and 16fps (SURF). This gets us closer to the desired real-time behaviour of 25fps, yet exploiting all the benefits of the SIFT and SURF operators.

6. Conclusion and future work

In this chapter we gave an overview about current object recognition methods exploiting scale-space transformation and showed an extension to the very reliable and accurate methods SIFT and SURF. We focused on speeding up these two operators even further targeting at real-time behaviour (at least 25fps for 320x200 pixel sized images). We used a pre-processing step exploiting decision trees to sort out as much data as possible in an early stage, trying to employ the costly SIFT and SURF matching process only at falsely recognized objects. We showed that this method is capable of further reducing overall computation time by the formulas given in section 5.1.

We intend to use this hierarchical approach for use in an *analysis by synthesis* system (Todt, 2008). This system is supposed to reliable detect real-world objects from synthetic three dimensional scene models, which are generated by a photo-realistic 3D lumigraph renderer for the synthesis part. The generation of this renderer uses the recently appeared PMD cameras (see Stommel & Kuhnert, 2006; Kuhnert *et al.*, 2007). Because this is an iterative computational process approximating, the best synthesis parameters for a given real-world object, one faces hard real-time constraints. We are confident, that our approach presented in this paper embodies the potency to fulfil these constraints.

We also plan on implementing this object recognition system on our mobile outdoor robot AMOR (see Kuhnert & Seemann, 2007; Seemann & Kuhnert, 2007) for passive object tracking purposes. It is supposed to support the active laser scanner sensors in tracking a vehicle that drives in front of AMOR. This is done by analyzing a constant video stream taken from a camera on the front side of the robot. Hard real-time constraints apply here as well.

There are still many optimizations remaining, e.g. software parallelization exploiting modern multi-core processors has yet to be implemented. The filter operations in particular are excellent candidates for this approach, because there are no data dependencies. This also leads to purely GPU based image filter algorithms (see Staudt, 2008). Modern graphic cards have shown high potential in processing large streams of independent data. We hope in implementing these optimizations, the costs for image feature computation can be reduced even further and that we get closer to the above stated real-time behaviour.

7. References

Bay, H.; Tuytelaars, T. & Gool, L. V. (2006). Surf: Speeded up robust features. *9th European Conference on Computer Vision,* 2006

Brown, M. & Lowe, D. G. (2002). Invariant features from interest point groups. In *British Machine Vision Conference*, Cardiff, Wales, pp. 656-665, 2002

Brunnström, K.; Lindeberg, T. & Eklundh, J.-O. (1992). Active detection and classification of junctions by foveation with a head-eye system guided by the scale-space primal sketch. *In Proc. 2nd European Conf. on Computer Vision* (G. Sandini, ed.), vol. 588 of *Lecture Notes in Computer Science*, pp. 701-709, Springer-Verlag, 1992

Harris, C. & Stephens, M. (1988). A combined corner and edge detector. In *Proceedings of the Alvey Vision Conference*, pp. 147 - 151, 1988

Koenderink, J. J. (1984). The structure of images. In *Biological Cybernetics*, 50, pp. 363-370, 1984

K.-D. Kuhnert, M. Langer, M. Stommel, & A. Kolb. (2007). Dynamic 3D-Vision, In *volume 4 of Vision Systems, Applications*, chapter 18, pages 311–334. I-Tech Education and Publishing, Vienna, Austria, June 2007. ISBN 978-3-902613-01-1.

Kuhnert, K.-D. & Seemann, W. (2007). Planning of minimal-time trajectories for high speed autonomous vehicles. In *The 2007 IEEE Intelligent Vehicle Symposium* (IV'07), Istanbul, Turkey, June 13-15, 2007.

Lindeberg, T. (1994). Scale-space theory. A basic tool for analysing structures at different scales. *Journal of Applied Statistics*, 21(2), pp. 224-270, 1994

Lindeberg, T. (1998). Feature detection with automatic scale selection. *Int. Journal of Computer Vision*, 30, 2, pp. 79—116, 1998

Lowe, D. G. (2004). Distinctive image features from scale-invariant keypoints. *Int. Journal of Computer Vision*, 20, pp. 91–110, 2004

Mikolajczyk, K. & Schmid, C. (2001). Indexing based on scale invariant interest points. *ICCV*, 1, pp. 525–531, 2001

Mikolajczyk, K. & Schmid, C. (2004). Scale & affine invariant interest point detectors. In *Int. Journal of Computer Vision*, 60(1), pp. 63-86, Kluwer Academic Publishers, 2004

Mikolajczyk, K. & Schmid, C. (2005a). A performance evaluation of local descriptors. In *IEEE Transactions on Pattern Analysis and Machine Intelligence*, 27(10), October, 2005

Mikolajczyk, K.; Leibe, B. & Schiele B. (2005b). Local features for object classification. In *Tenth IEEE International Conference on Computer Vision (ICCV 2005)*, 2, pp. 1792-1799, 17-21 Oct, 2005

Quinlan, J. (1983). *Machine Learning: an artificial intelligence approach*, pages 463–482. Morgan Kaufmann, 1983

Russel, S. & Norwig, P. (2003). *Artificial Intelligence - A Modern Approach*, Prentice Hall, pp. 653—664, 2003

Seemann, W. & Kuhnert, K.-D. (2007). Design and realization of the highly modular and robust autonomous mobile outdoor robot amor. In *The 13th IASTED International Conference on Robotics and Applications*, Würzburg, Germany, August 29-31, 2007.

Staudt, A.; Langer M. & Kuhnert, K.-D. (2008). Comparison of two real-time image processing system approaches. *Proceedings of the 10th IASTED International Conference on Computer Graphics and Imaging*, 2008

M. Stommel & K.-D. Kuhnert. (2006). Fusion of stereo-camera and PMD-camera data for real-time suited precise 3D environment reconstruction. In *IEEE/RSJ International Conference on Intelligent Robots and Systems (IROS)*, pages 4780–4785, October 9-15, 2006. Also presented at the Robotic 3D Environment Cognition Workshop at the *Spatial Cognition*, Bremen, Germany, September 24-28, 2006.

Todt, S.; Langer, M.; Rezk-Salama, C.; Kolb, A. & Kuhnert, K.D. (2008). Spherical light-field rendering in application for analysis by synthesis. *IJISTA N3/4*, 5, 2008

Witkin, A. P. (1983). Scale-space filtering. In *Proc. 8th Int. Joint Conf. on Art. Intell.*, Karlsruhe, Germany, pp. 1019-1022, Aug. 1983

Zhao, H. & Sinha, A. (2005). An efficient algorithm for generating generalized decision forests. In *IEEE Transactions on Systems, Man and Cybernetics, Part A*, 35, pp. 754–762, 2005

14

Image Acquisition Rate Control Based on Object State Information in Physical and Image Coordinates

Feng-Li Lian and Shih-Yuan Peng
Department of Electrical Engineering, National Taiwan University
Taipei, Taiwan

1. Introduction

Recently, three-dimensional (3-D) vision applications play an important role in industry and entertainment. Among these applications, interactivity and scene reality are the two key features affecting the 3-D vision performance. Depending on the nature of the applications, the interactivity with the users (or the players) can be regarded as an important need, for example, in the applications of 3-D games and 3-D virtual reality. On the other hand, 3-D vision scenes can be generated based on physical or virtual models. In order to improve the scene reality, a new trend in 3-D vision system is to generate the scene based on some physical or real-world models.

For the 3-D reconstruction, research topics mainly focus on the static cases and/or the dynamic cases. For the static cases, the reconstructed scenes do not change with the observed scenes. For the dynamic cases, the reconstructed scenes change with the observed scenes. For both static and dynamic cases, the 3-D positioning of moving objects in the scene is the major component of obtaining the object states in the physical coordinate. A typical 3-D positioning system is shown in Figure 1. Cameras shown in Figure 1 are used to capture the images of moving objects in the physical coordinate. The image acquisition rate of Camera X is denoted as Rate X. After one camera captures the images using its designated acquisition rate, the captured images are stored and analyzed in the computer. After analyzing the images, the object states, e.g., position and velocity, in the physical coordinate can be estimated by any 3-D positioning method.

The 3-D positioning plays an important role of obtaining the object states in the physical coordinate. In general, cameras are designated as the input devices for capturing images. Fundamental components of 3-D positioning are shown in Figure 2. First of all, images are captured by the input devices such as cameras. Before the image acquisition, the camera calibration should be done. Based on the calibration result, the relationship between the physical coordinate and the image coordinate in the captured images can be obtained. Since the quality of the captured images may be influenced by noise, some image processes should be performed to eliminate the noise. After the image processing, the captured images can be analyzed to extract the object information for further 3-D positioning. Finally, any 3-D positioning method is used to find the object states such as the position and/or velocity in the physical coordinate.

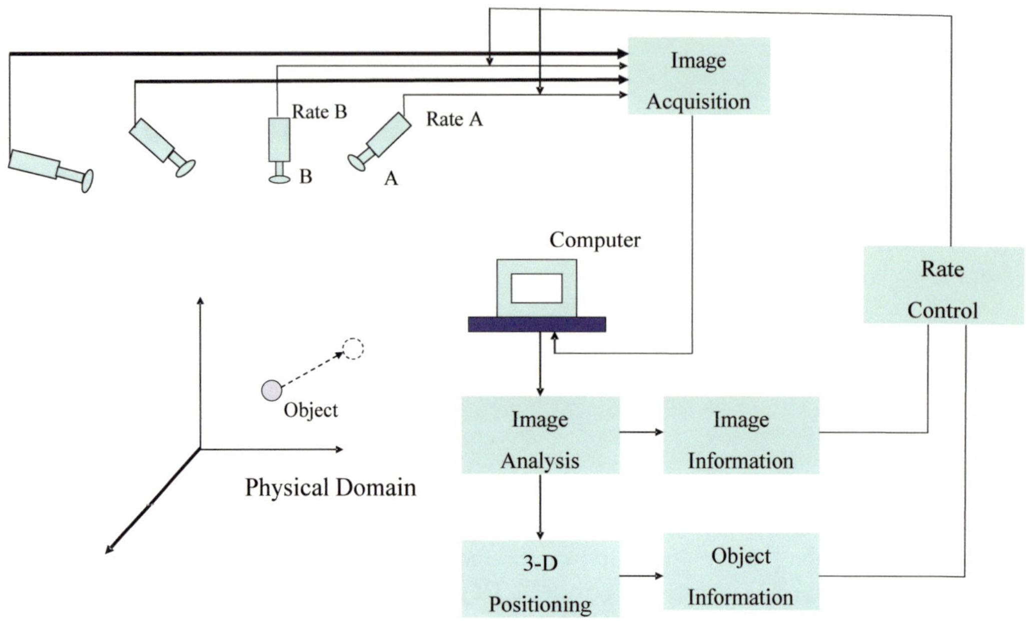

Fig. 1. A general 3-D positioning system

Due to the limitation on computational load, data storage, and communication bandwidth, the image acquisition rate may not be able to set at the highest rate for each camera. For example, the computation load of estimating the object trajectory in the physical coordinate may be too heavy and the data storage of all the captured images for future image analysis may be huge. Hence, a method of properly controlling the image acquisition rate is required for the purpose of saving the memory cost and/or reducing the computational load. For designing a proper method to adaptively control the image acquisition rate, the object states in the image coordinate (after proper image processing) and/or in the physical coordinate (after proper image/positioning processing) should be considered in the acquisition rate control. Therefore, a rate control method as shown in Figure 2 is used to adjust the image acquisition rate based on the result of image analysis and the estimation of the object states.

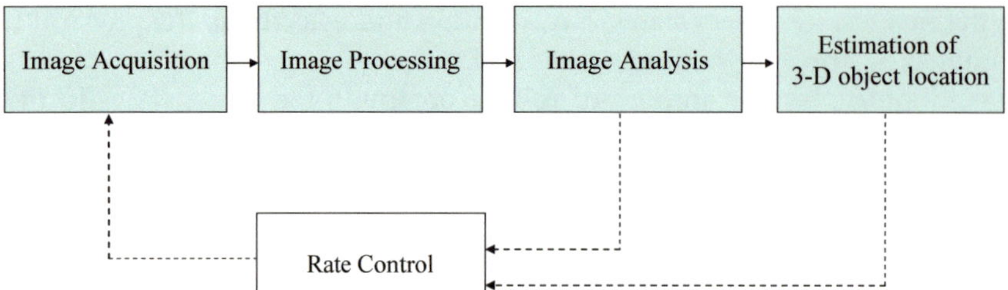

Fig. 2. Fundamental components of 3-D positioning

In this chapter, three methods of controlling the image acquisition rate are designed. With a suitable method for adjusting the acquisition rate, the ultimate goal is to reduce the computational load of the 3-D positioning, the memory cost, and the communication bandwidth for the captured images. The first method is to adjust the image acquisition rate by analyzing the object states in the physical coordinate. The second method considers the adjustment by analyzing the object states in the image coordinate. The third method deals with the issue of acquisition asynchronization among multiple cameras. The proposed methodologies have been experimentally tested using a two-camera setup within the MATLAB programming environment. Performance of using the proposed methods has been compared with that of using fixed-rate methods. Experimental results show that the proposed approaches achieve satisfactory performance and reduce computational load and data storage.

1.1 Outline

The rest of the chapter is organized as follows. Section 2 surveys related research work in camera control, 3-D positioning, object extraction, esimation of object position, database analysis, and visualization interface. Section 3 presents the three control methods of adjusting image acquistion rate based on image and physical coordinates. Section 4 illustrates experimental tests of the proposed image acqusition methods. Finally, Section 5 summarizes this chpater and discusses future tasks.

2. Related research work

In the literature, key 3-D vision applications for controlling the image acquisition rate is the 3-D positioning of moving balls. Similar methodology can be applied to other objects or scenarios. A general framework of the 3-D positioning system is shown in Figure 3. The performance of image acquisition mainly depends on camera control. Different camera control methods can decide the quantity and quality of the information contained from the captured images for further image analysis. After the image acquisition, the captured images can be analyzed by the 3-D positioning methods for extracting the object states contained in these images. Once the image analysis of the object states is obtained, the analyzed result is stored in the database and further visualization interface is used to generate a 3-D animation. Related research works on these issues are summarized in detail in the following.

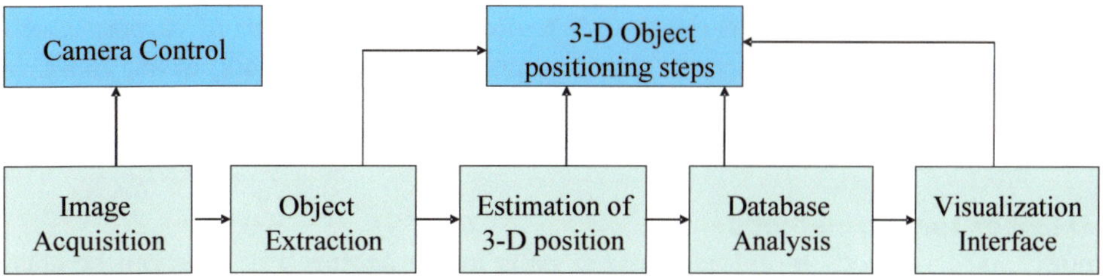

Fig. 3. General framework of 3-D image reconstruction system

2.1 Camera control

Images captured by cameras are used for further analysis in the 3-D reconstruction of scenes or the 3-D positioning of objects. Hence, the information obtained from the captured images is directly related to the issues on the location and the number to allocate these cameras. An example of the 3-D reconstruction from constrained views by using three cameras placed in the orthogonal directions is discussed in (Shin & Shin, 1998).

Generally speaking, the information in the captured images is influenced by the temporal and spatial factors. Hence, the information can be related to the image acquisition rate of cameras. If the image acquisition rate is high, more information can be obtained through the captured images. However, using a high acquisition rate takes much computational time for data processing and consumes a large amount of memory. Hence, properly controlling the image acquisition rate is a method that can reduce the computational load.

The amount of information in captured images is related to the image acquisition rate of the cameras. If the image acquisition rate is high, more information can be obtained through the captured images. However, a high acquisition rate might take more computation time for data processing and more storage memory. Therefore, the control method for adjusting image acquisition rate could help reduce the computational load as well as storage size. Since this kind of control methods adjust the sampling rate of input devices, they are classified as the handling of the temporal factors. In general, the inputs of the control methods for adjusting image acquisition rate are the current status of process system such as the computational load, or the states of interested object that are obtained by analyzing the captured images. The criterion for adjusting image acquisition rate might depend on the percentage of computational load and/or the guaranteed amount of information in the captured images. For example, in (Hong, 2002), the criterion of the controlling the acquisition rate is specified as the amount of computational load and defined by the number of data management operations per unit time.

For the zoom and focus control of cameras, the main goal is to maintain required information of the captured images in the spatial resolution. The input for the zoom and focus control method is often regarded as the percentage of the target shown in the image search region. For example, in (Shah & Morrell, 2004), the camera zoom is adjusted by the target position shown in the captured images. An adaptive zoom algorithm for tracking target is used to guarantee that a given percentage of particles can fall onto the camera image plane.

On the other hand, the pan-tilt motion controls of camera deal with the issue of guaranteeing enough spatial and temporal resolutions in the captured images. The camera is commanded to track the target and the target is required to be appeared in a specific region of the captured images. The inputs for the pan-tilt motion controls are often regarded as the percentage of target appeared in the search region and the velocity of camera motion to track the target in order to guarantee real-time performance. In (Wang et al., 2004), a real-time pan-tilt visual tracking system is designed to control the camera motion where the target is shown in the center area of the captured images.

2.2 3-D ball extraction methods

Commonly used methods to extract moving balls in the captured images can be classified based on the color information, geometric features of the balls, and the frame differencing technique. A comparison of related ball extraction methods is summarized in Table 1.

Ball Extraction Method	References
Color information	(Theobalt et al., 2004; Andrade et al., 2005; Ren et al., 2004)
Geometric features	(Yu et al., 2004; Yu et al., 2003b; D'Orazio et al., 2002)
Frame differencing	(Pingali et al., 2001)

Table 1. Methods of extracting ball movement from captured images

First of all, a ball detection method based on the color of balls is studied in (Theobalt et al., 2004). The motion for a variety of baseball pitches is captured in an experimental environment where the floor and walls are covered with black carpet and cloth. Foreground object segmentation is facilitated by assigning the background with the same color. In order to record the rotation and spin of the ball along its trajectory, the entire surface of the ball is assigned with different markers. Similar idea used to track a ball by its color is also shown in (Andrade et al., 2005) and (Ren et al., 2004).

Secondly, the ball extraction can also be achieved by related geometric features of the ball. In (Yu et al., 2004) and (Yu et al., 2003b), several trajectory-based algorithms for ball tracking are proposed. From recorded image sequences, the candidates of possible ball trajectory are extracted. These trajectory candidates are detected by matching all the ball features such as circularity, size, and isolation. In (D'Orazio et al., 2002), a ball detection algorithm based on the circle hough transform of the geometric circularity is used for soccer image sequences.

Another method proposed in (Pingali et al., 2001) is based on the frame differencing between current and previous images. Supposing that the balls move fast enough and the background does not change, the balls in the foreground can be extracted by comparing the image sequences.

2.3 Estimation of 3-D ball position

Based on the extraction results, the ball states such as position and velocity can be estimated. Typical 3-D ball positioning methods include triangulation, trajectory fitting by physical models, and the estimation of the ball position by the Kalman filter. Related methods for the ball positioning are summarized in Table 2.

Methods for Ball Positioning	References
Triangulation	(Ren et al., 2004)
Trajectory fitting to physical models	(Ohno et al., 2000)
Kalman filter	(Yu et al., 2003a)

Table 2. A comparison of different estimation methods for ball positioning

In (Ren et al., 2004), the 3-D positioning of a soccer is achieved by intersecting a set of two rays through two cameras and the observed ball projection on the ground in the images. Since these two rays usually have no intersection, a 3-D position of the object is employed as the point that has a minimum distance to both of these two rays.

In (Ohno et al., 2000), the ball position in a soccer game is estimated by fitting a mathematical ball model in the physical coordinate. The estimated position in each image frame depends on the initial position and the initial velocity of the ball in the physical coordinate. The overall trajectory of the soccer can then be determined by the equation specified by the gravity, air friction and timing parameters.

In (Yu et al., 2003a), the ball positions in the 3-D space are predicted by the Kalman filter which utilizes the information of past measured positions. By iteratively estimating the ball positions, the whole ball trajectory can be generated.

2.4 Database analysis

Database analysis focuses on calculating ball positions in all captured images or recorded video. Once all the ball positions are estimated, further analysis on the changes of ball trajectory can be obtained. For example, from the ball positions in the analyzed images or the ball trajectories in the physical coordinate, the speed and orientation can be calculated.

In (Shum & Komura, 2004), the speed and orientation of a baseball between two image frames are analyzed. The key events in a match can then be observed by reconstructing the baseball trajectory from the database. In (Yu et al., 2003b), the curves of soccer velocity in a match are generated for the analysis of special events. When a person touches the soccer, the trajectory of the soccer generates a local minimum point that changes with time. The local minimal velocity points in a velocity curve may also be caused by the ball bouncing that changes the soccer direction. The information of these events can help analyze the game strategy.

2.5 Visualization interface

The visualization interface is designed for users to watch the reconstructed animation such as the ball trajectory or the landing positions of a ball. In (Pingali et al., 2000), the authors show a virtual replay of a tennis game and the landing position. In (Pingali et al., 2001), a virtual replay environment which can let the users watch a replay at any speed and from any viewpoint is designed. Since the database stores all the ball information, the users can decide to visualize any interesting part of the game independently. If a visualization interface can also take into account of the practical situation in a match, the reality of the visualization can be improved. For example, an enrichment system of visualization interface is proposed in (Yan et al., 2004). This system can reconstruct a sport game in 3-D display and enrich the performance with related music and illustrations. Hence, the users can enjoy a comfortable viewing experience through a better visualization interface.

In this chapter, the methods for controlling image acquisition rate are designed. In order to test the control methods, several case studies of the 3-D object positioning are proposed. The ball extraction methods are based on the color information of the objects. Also, the triangulation method is used to estimate the position of balls in the physical coordinate. The visualization interface for the virtual replay of object positions is performed in the MATLAB programming environment.

3. Methods for controlling image acquisition rate

By selecting an appropriate image acquisition rate, the computational load of the 3-D positioning as well as the memory cost can be reduced. The proposed methods are based on the states of moving objects by analyzing the sequence of images obtained from the cameras. Two categories of information are used for designing the rate control methods. The first one is based on the object states in the physical coordinate and the second one is based on those directly in the image coordinate of captured images. Since multiple cameras are used and may have different acquisition rates, the captured images may not be synchronized. Hence, two types of reconstruction mechanisms are used for the information obtained in the image coordinate. Furthermore, a criterion is proposed to judge the performance of different image acquisition rates

3.1 Control method based on object states in the physical coordinate (case A)

After the 3-D positioning, the object states such as position and velocity in the physical coordinate can be computed. These object states can then be used as the key information for deciding the image acquisition rate. For example, when an object moves fast, the image acquisition rate should be set as high as possible to capture the object motion clearly. If an object moves slowly or is only in a stationary status, a high acquisition rate is not required. Using a high acquisition rate may waste the memory storage and the computational cost in image processing. On the other hand, using a low acquisition rate may lose the reality of the object motion. Hence, in order to balance the tradeoff between the computational cost and the accuracy of the 3-D positioning result, the control method for adjusting different image acquisition rates should be properly designed.

The proposed procedure is discussed in detail in the following. First of all, images are captured by multiple cameras. Since the quality of captured images may be influenced by noise, a spatial Gaussian filter is then used to smooth the captured images within the RGB color channels. Based on a set of predefined features of the objects in terms of the RGB color channels, the moving objects can be extracted from the images. After the objects are extracted, the region occupied by the objects in a captured image is stored in a new gray-scale image. These gray-scale images can be further transformed into binary images by a specific threshold value. Some lighting influences on the objects may change the result of color analysis on the object surfaces. The object surfaces in the binary image might not be necessarily shown in a regular shape. Hence, the image dilation method can be used to enlarge the analyzed image area, and to improve the object shapes in these binary images. Finally, by the triangulation approach on the images, a set of 3-D information about the objects in the physical coordinate can be computed. Also, since the time of captured images and the corresponding estimated object position are recorded, the object velocity in the physical domain can be estimated. By analyzing the position and velocity of the object, the image acquisition rate for the next frame can then be adjusted based on the computed information.

In this case (named as Case A), the key feature of controlling the image acquisition rate is to analyze the object states in the physical coordinate. Assume that there are N levels of image acquisition rates, and each level only represents a specific range of values for the object states. Hence, by analyzing these object states, a corresponding image acquisition rate can be determined. Figure 4 shows an example of the mapping between the ball velocity (i.e., the object state) and the set of image acquisition rates. V_0, V_1, V_2 ,..., V_N, are the values of ball velocity in the physical coordinate. Rate 1, Rate 2, ..., Rate N, are different levels of image acquisition rates arranged from the lowest value to the highest value. By analyzing the ball velocity, the corresponding image acquisition rate can be determined. That is, if the ball velocity is between V_{i-1} and V_i, the corresponding image acquisition rate is set as Rate i.

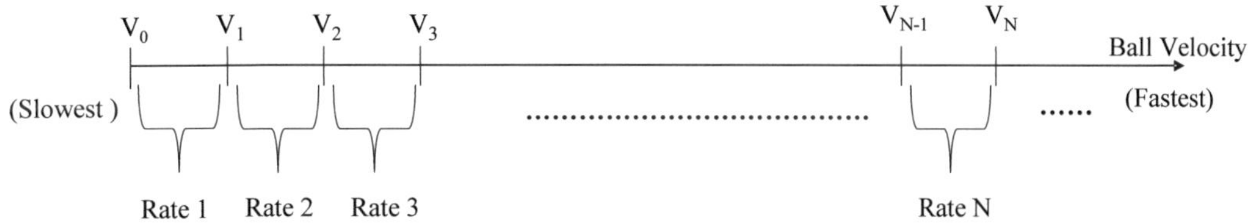

Fig. 4. An example of mapping different image acquisition rates by the ball velocity (object state)

The pseudo code of the control algorithm for an example of three levels of acquisition rates is shown in Figure 5, where related variables used are defined in Table 3. The cases with more levels of image acquisition rates can be easily extended. Also, all the cameras are designed to adjust their image acquisition rates at the same time. For generating a complete replay, the object positions in the physical coordinate that are not calculated in the 3-D positioning can be predicted by using methods such as interpolation, extrapolation, or data fitting.

Initialization
(All cameras are set to the high level of image acquisition rate at first.)
for each camera C_K $(K = 1 \sim n)$
$F_{C_K} \leftarrow F_H$
Adjusting of image acquisition rate
(All cameras adjust their image acquisition rate synchronously.)
for each incoming $V(T_i)$
if ($(V(T_i)! = empty)$ **and** ($V(T_{i-1})! = empty)$) **then**
Get $V(T_i)$ and $V(T_{i-1})$ from database as bases
Generate $V_P(T_i + T_L)$ and $V_P(T_i + T_N)$
end if
for each camera C_K $(K = 1 \sim n)$
if ($(V_S < V_P(T_i + T_L) < V_F)$ **and** $(V_S < V_P(T_i + T_N) < V_F)$) **then**
$F_{C_K} \leftarrow F_N$
else if ($(V_P(T_i + T_L) < V_S)$ **and** $(V_P(T_i + T_N) < V_S)$) **then**
$F_{C_K} \leftarrow F_L$
else
$F_{C_K} \leftarrow F_H$
end if

Fig. 5. Pseudo code of the algorithm in Case A

When the objects are far away from the cameras and move in a similar direction, the objects shown in the corresponding image coordinate are almost stationary. That is, the objects may move fast in the physical coordinate, but the information shown in the corresponding image coordinate does not reveal the fact. Therefore, the 3-D positioning result may not reveal correct object states in the physical coordinate. The type of failure is due to that little image information is used for the 3-D positioning. Hence, the control method should be modified to reflect the richness of image information from each individual camera. The amount of image information should be regarded as a decision factor for controlling the acquisition rate. The modified control methods are discussed in the following sections.

Symbol	Definition	Unit
C_K	index of camera $(K = 1 \sim n)$	none
F_{C_K}	the image acquisition rate for the specific index of camera	times/sec
$\max(F_{C_K})$	the maximum image acquisition rate of the all cameras C_K $(K = 1 \sim n)$	times/sec
F_L	the specific low level of image acquisition rate	times/sec
F_N	the specific normal level of image acquisition rate	times/sec
F_H	the specific high level of image acquisition rate	times/sec
T_i	the recorded time of the captured image which is index i	sec
T_L	the corresponding image acquisition time to the lower level of image acquisition rate $(T_L = 1/F_L)$	sec
T_N	the corresponding image acquisition time to the normal level of image acquisition rate $(T_N = 1/F_N)$	sec
$P(t)$	the object velocity in the pixel coordinate domain at time t	pixel/sec
$P_{P_{C_K}}(t)$	the predictive object velocity in the image domain at time t (the subscript C_K means the index of camera)	pixel/sec
P_S	the threshold value of slow object velocity in the image domain	pixel/sec
P_F	the threshold value of fast object velocity in the image domain	pixel/sec
$V(t)$	the object velocity in the physical coordinate at time t	mm/sec
$V_P(t)$	the predictive object velocity in the physical coordinate at time t	mm/sec
V_S	the threshold value of slow object velocity in the physical coordinate	mm/sec
V_F	the threshold value of fast object velocity in the physical coordinate	mm/sec

Table 3. The meanings of the symbols in the control algorithm

3.2 Control method based on object states in the image coordinate (case B and case C)

In Case A, the method for controlling the image acquisition rate is based on the object states in the physical coordinate. In this section, novel methods to control the image acquisition rate directly based on the object states in the image coordinate are proposed. The reason of using the object states in the image coordinate is that the acquisition rates can be effectively adjusted based on the actual available information instead of the projected information in the physical coordinate. Based on different synchronization scenarios among the cameras, two cases for adjusting the image acquisition rates are discussed. In the first case (named as Case B), each camera adjusts the image acquisition rate independently to other cameras, while in the second case (named as Case C) all the cameras adjust their image acquisition rates cooperatively.

3.2.1 Independently controlling image acquisition rate (case B)

In Case B, each camera is designed to control its image acquisition rate independently based on the information in the image coordinate. The object states are first analyzed independently in the image coordinate of each camera and then each camera adjusts the acquisition rate based on the significance of the analyzed image. The significance can be used as a function of the mobility or the geometric feature of the object. Since all the cameras do not capture image simultaneously, the numbers of captured images at each camera are neither the same nor synchronized. Hence, during the 3-D reconstruction, the images from some cameras may be missed. To overcome this drawback, an interpolation or extrapolation method should be applied for those missing images. The advantage of only capturing the most significant images is to reduce the computational load for reconstructing useless images in the physical coordinate, and/or the transmission bandwidth. The algorithm for the adjustment of three-level image acquisition rates is shown in Figure 6. The definition of the variables in the algorithm is also listed in Table 3. Cases with more levels of image acquisition rates can be easily extended.

Initialization

(All cameras are set to the high level of image acquisition rate at first.)

for each camera C_K $(K = 1 \sim n)$

$F_{C_K} \leftarrow F_H$

Adjusting of image acquisition rate

(Each camera adjusts the image acquisition rate by itself.)

for each camera C_K $(K = 1 \sim n)$

for each incoming $P_{C_K}(T_i)$

if $((P_{C_K}(T_i)! = empty)$ **and** $(P_{C_K}(T_{i-1})! = empty))$ **then**

Get $P_{C_K}(T_i)$ and $P_{C_K}(T_{i-1})$ from database as bases

Generate $P_{P_{C_K}}(T_i + T_L)$ and $P_{P_{C_K}}(T_i + T_N)$

end if

if $((P_S < P_{P_{C_K}}(T_i + T_L) < P_F)$ **and** $(P_S < P_{P_{C_K}}(T_i + T_N) < P_F))$

then $F_{C_K} \leftarrow F_N$

else if $((P_{P_{C_K}}(T_i + T_L) < P_S)$ **and** $(P_{P_{C_K}}(T_i + T_N) < P_S))$

then $F_{C_K} \leftarrow F_L$

else

$F_{C_K} \leftarrow F_H$

end if

Fig. 6. Pseudo code of the algorithm in Case B

In Case A, all the cameras adjust their image acquisition rates simultaneously, so that the captured images are always in pairs for further processing. Hence, the object states in the physical coordinate can be directly reconstructed. In Case B, since these cameras adjust their image acquisition rate independently, the acquisition efficiency of each camera could be improved, but the captured images may not be necessarily in pairs. The missing images can be recovered by an interpolation or extrapolation estimation based on the captured images. Therefore, the 3-D reconstruction of the objects in the physical coordinate can also be performed.

However, in some scenarios, if the reconstruction by interpolation or extrapolation generates unacceptable errors, it is advised to increase the acquisition rates of some cameras in a cooperative way. The cooperation increases the acquisition rates of some cameras and hence improves the reconstruction performance. However, the total number of captured images is still smaller than that in Case A. Therefore, the computational cost is still reduced. The cooperation mechanism is discussed in next section.

3.2.2 Cooperatively controlling image acquisition rates (case C)

In this case, the method for controlling image acquisition rate is also based on the information obtained in the image coordinate. In additions, all cameras try to adjust its image acquisition rate synchronously. In order to achieve the synchronization, these acquisition rates should first be compared. The comparison works as follows. Each camera first predicts an image acquisition rate for the next image frame. The control algorithm then compares the prediction of each camera and then a designated image acquisition rate is chosen as the highest of all the predicted image acquisition rates. Finally, all the cameras adjust to their acquisition rates synchronously. Therefore, the captured images from all the cameras can be used for the 3-D reconstructions simultaneously.

The algorithm for the case of three levels of image acquisition rates is shown in Figure 7. The definition of the variables in the algorithm is also listed in Table 3. Cases with more levels of image acquisition rates can be easily extended. Initially, all the cameras are set to the higher level of image acquisition rate and, hence, capture some images in the meantime. Therefore, the set of captured images are in pairs. After that, the image is further analyzed and, because the image information obtained is different among these cameras, each camera may adjust its acquisition rate independently. Next, at each camera, the image acquisition rate for the next image frame is analyzed and predicted based on the captured images. In order to capture the next image frame synchronously, all the cameras are adjusted to the highest level of all the predicted image acquisition rates and the image frames can be guaranteed to be captured at the same time.

By using this algorithm, the cameras can compare their predicted image acquisition rates and adopt the highest rate for the next image frame. Since the algorithm in Case C adjusts the image acquisition rate before analyzing the object information in the physical coordinate, this algorithm could performs more efficiently than that of Case A. A preliminary comparison of the three control algorithms is listed in Table 4.

In addition to the synchronization effect and reconstruction performance, other factors can also be considered when selecting a suitable algorithm for controlling the image acquisition rate. The most important concept is that the adjustment of the acquisition rate should depend on the image quality captured by each camera. In order to characterize the outcome of the proposed control methods, a performance criterion is proposed in the next section.

Initialization

(All cameras are set to the high level of image acquisition rate at first.)

for each camera C_K $(K = 1 \sim n)$

$F_{C_K} \leftarrow F_H$

Adjusting of image acquisition rate

(All cameras adjust their image acquisition rate synchronously.)

for each camera C_K $(K = 1 \sim n)$

if $((P_{C_K}(T_i)! = empty)$ **and** $(P_{C_K}(T_{i-1})! = empty))$ **then**

Get $P_{C_K}(T_i)$ and $P_{C_K}(T_{i-1})$ from database as bases

Generate $P_{P_{C_K}}(T_i + T_L)$ and $P_{P_{C_K}}(T_i + T_N)$

end if

for each incoming $P_{C_K}(T_i)$

if $((P_S < P_{P_{C_K}}(T_i + T_L) < P_F)$ **and** $(P_S < P_{P_{C_K}}(T_i + T_N) < P_F))$ **then**

$F_{C_K} \leftarrow F_N$

else if $((P_{P_{C_K}}(T_i + T_L) < P_S)$ **and** $(P_{P_{C_K}}(T_i + T_N) < P_S))$ **then**

$F_{C_K} \leftarrow F_L$

else $F_{C_K} \leftarrow F_H$

end if

Find $\max(F_{C_K})$

Set the image acquisition rate of all cameras as $\max(F_{C_K})$

Fig. 7. Pseudo code of the algorithm in Case C

	Case A	Case B	Case C
The time to carry out the algorithm	Long	Short	Normal
Are captured images always in pairs?	Yes	No	Yes

Table 4. The comparison of control algorithms designed in this study

3.3 Criterion for characterizing image acquisition

These methods proposed for controlling the image acquisition rate could reduce computational cost and memory space for the captured images. For the 3-D positioning, the object position, for example, in the physical coordinate can be estimated based on the information of analyzing the captured images. In order to compare the performance of different control methods, the following criterion is designed:

$$R = W_s \times s - W_d \times d \qquad (1)$$

where s denotes the saving percentage of image quantity, d denotes a reference value representing the percentage of image distortion, and W_s, W_d are two weighting factors. Specifically, s can be described as follows:

$$s = 1 - \frac{N_1}{N_2}, \tag{2}$$

where N_1 denotes the number of captured images when carrying out the control method and N_2 denotes the number of captured images when all the cameras are set at the highest acquisition rate. For example, if 240 images are captured using the highest acquisition rate, and only 200 images are recorded by performing one of control methods, then the percentage of image saving is estimated as follows:

$$s = 1 - \frac{200}{240} \cong 0.167 = 16.7\%.$$

Furthermore, W_s can be regarded as a function of memory saving. For example, the function can be defined as follows:

$$W_s = \alpha(\xi), \tag{3}$$

where $\xi = M_1 / M_2$ and M_1 denotes the quantity of memory used to record all the captured images by using the highest acquisition rate, and M_2 denotes the quantity of memory assigned by the computer in advance. For example, if it needs 100MB to record all the captured images and the memory size assigned by the computer is 80MB, ξ can be calculated as follows:

$$\xi = \frac{100}{80} = 1.25.$$

If $\xi > 1$, then saving the number of captured images can be considered an important goal. W_d can be regarded as a function of the object states and the image acquisition rate. For example, W_d is described as follows:

$$W_d = \beta(v, k), \tag{4}$$

where v characterizes the object states such as position or velocity, and k is the highest acquisition rate used in a practical application. If the object states have a large impact on the image processing (for example, the object speed is large), and the image acquisition rate is low, it is likely that the outcome of the image processing will be distorted and the value of W_d should be increased. In summary, $W_s \times s$ can be regarded as the advantage for carrying out the control method, while $W_d \times d$ can be regarded as the disadvantage for carrying out the control method.

When the value of R is equal to zero, the performance of the control method is just the same as that without any acquisition rate control because all the images are just captured by the highest image acquisition rate and occupy all the available memory. Hence, in order to guarantee the performance of the control method, the value of R should be a positive number. If several control methods are available for the users to choose, they can be compared based on the criterion.

4. Experimental results

In this section, the 3-D positioning of solid balls are experimentally tested for the three methods of controlling image acquisition rates. The test-bed is shown in Figure 8(a). The image coordinates of the two cameras is shown in Figure 8(b), where the camera centers are denoted as P_1 and P_2, respectively, and π_1 and π_2 are the image frames of the two camera, repsectively. Since three balls of different colors are used in these experiments, the foreground object segmentation can be easily performed. The background of the scene is only white broads. Also, two cameras are used to capture the images which are stored and analyzed at one single computer.

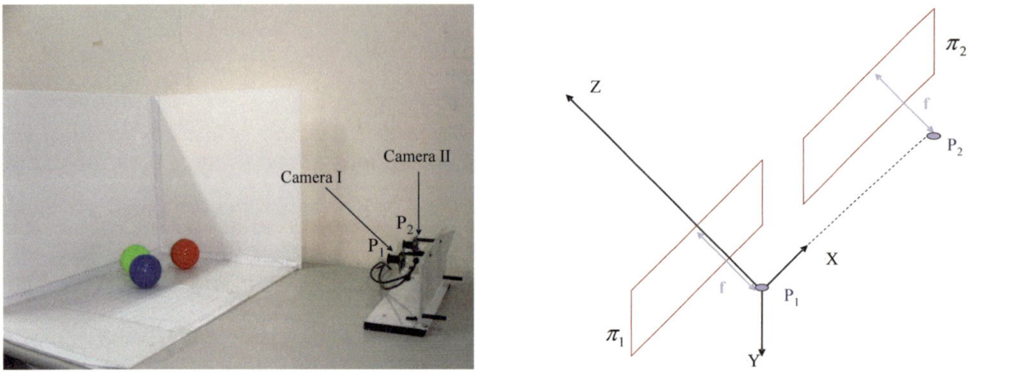

(a) (b)

Fig. 8. (a) A snapshot of experimental environment for 3-D positioning, (b) the image coordinates of the two cameras

In this study, assume that the radius of these balls is known in advance. Hence, the goal of the 3-D positioning is only to identify the center of these balls. In order to locate the ball centers in the physical coordinate, the ball center shown in each camera should be processed first by proper image processing operations. Once the position of the ball center in the image coordinate of each camera is found, the position of ball center in the physical coordinate can then be computed by the triangulation method used in the 3-D mapping.

4.1 Image processing results

The captured images are stored in the memory of the computer and processed by the image processing step. First of all, the original captured images loaded from the memory are full-color images, i.e., with red, green and blue color channels. The spatial Gaussian filter is then used to process these color channels, independently. In order to distinguish these three balls shown in the image, each ball is identified from the image by the color analysis. Supposing that a ball region is extracted after the color analysis, the region is stored and transformed into a gray-scale image. The gray-scale image can be further transformed into a binary image. Finally, the image dilation method is used to further characterize the shape of ball region shown in the binary image.

In the color analysis step, all pixels in a captured image are processed by a color analysis method. That is, a pixel shown in the captured images can be judged as either a part of color ball or a part of background. When a pixel does not belong to the region of the three balls, the pixel is regarded as a part of background. This color analysis method is designed to process all pixels in the captured image. Supposing that the balls are not blocked by others, this color analysis method can identify every ball region. An example of using the color analysis method to find a ball region is shown in Figure 9.

In Figure 9(a), an original captured image is shown. Next, the extraction result of the green ball is shown in Figure 9(b), where a binary image is obtained. It is clear that the ball shape is incorrect after the color analysis. Hence, the image dilation method is used to further improve the result of ball region extraction. The result after the image dilation is shown in Figure 9(c), where the ball shape is better than that shown in Figure 9(b).

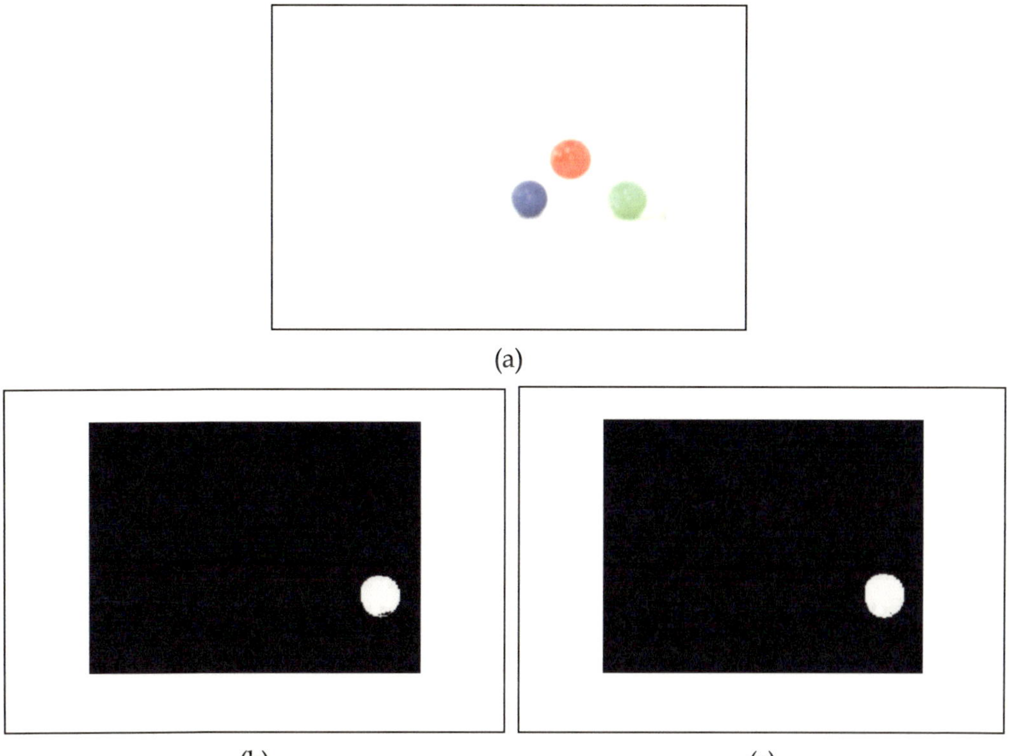

(a)

(b) (c)

Fig. 9. The results of ball extraction and image dilation in the captured image. (a) The original image. (b) After ball extraction. (c) After image dilation

4.2 3-D positioning results

In this study, the target for 3-D positioning are the centers of the balls. In order to find the positions of ball centers in the physical domain, the ball centroid shown in images are first calculated by the image processing step discussed in previous section. Once the positions of ball centroid shown in images are found, the position of ball center in the physical domain can be found by the triangulation method. Supposing that a ball center s is the target for 3-D positioning, an example of the corresponding points of s in the image planes of the two cameras used in this study is shown in Figure 10.

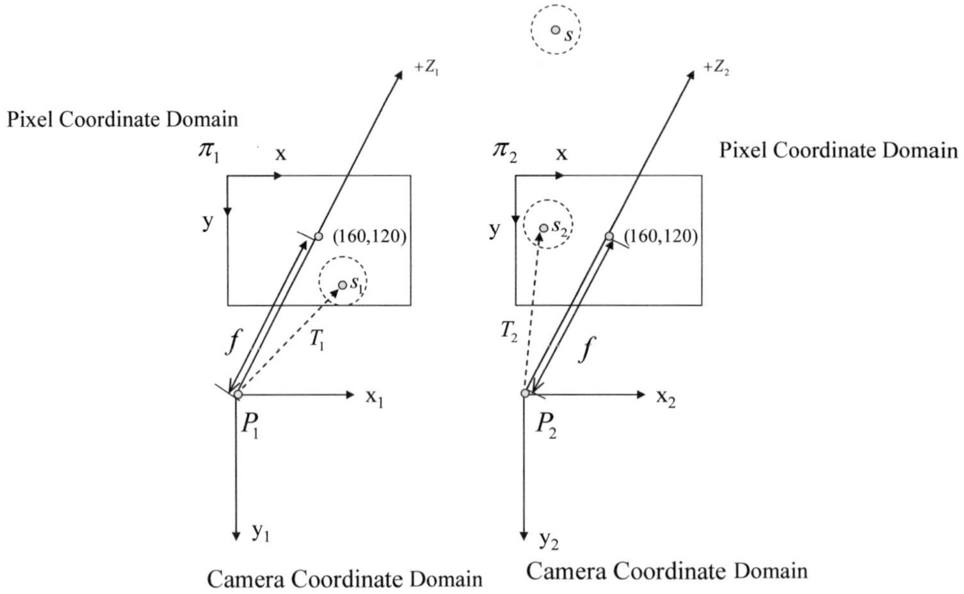

Fig. 10. An example for describing the corresponding points of a ball center in the image planes

The centers of the two camera coordinate domains are denoted by P_1 and P_2, respectively, and the image planes are denoted by π_1 and π_2, respectively. Assume that the range of the image plane is 320*240 in pixel and the center of the image coordinate is then denoted as (160, 120). The focal length is denoted by f. The ball center s is the target of the 3-D positioning, and the corresponding point of s shown in the two image coordinates are denated as s_1 and s_2, respectively. Hence, the coordinates of s_1 and s_2 in π_1 and π_2, respevtively, can be described as follows:

$$s_1 = (x_1, y_1) \tag{5}$$

$$s_2 = (x_2, y_2) \tag{6}$$

Supposing that the unit of the focal length f is in terms of pixel, the two 3-D vectors T_1 and T_2 can be described as follows

$$T_1 = (x_1 - 160, y_1 - 120, f) \tag{6}$$

$$T_2 = (x_2 - 160, y_2 - 120, f) \tag{7}$$

where T_1 denotes the 3-D vector from P_1 to s_1 and T_2 denotes the 3-D vector from P_2 to s_2. After finding the two vectors, the position of s can be calculated by the triangulation method as shown in Figure 11.

In Figure 11, the coordinate domain is in the physical domain. Line L_1 in the physical domain can be determined by the information of Point P_1 and Vector T_1. Line L_2 in the physical domain can be determined by the information of Point P_2 and Vector T_2. On Line L_1, s_1' is the point closest to Line L_2, and, on Line L_2, s_2' is the point closest to Line L_1. Point s is the target point for 3-D positioning and is calculated by finding the midpoint of s_1' and s_2'.

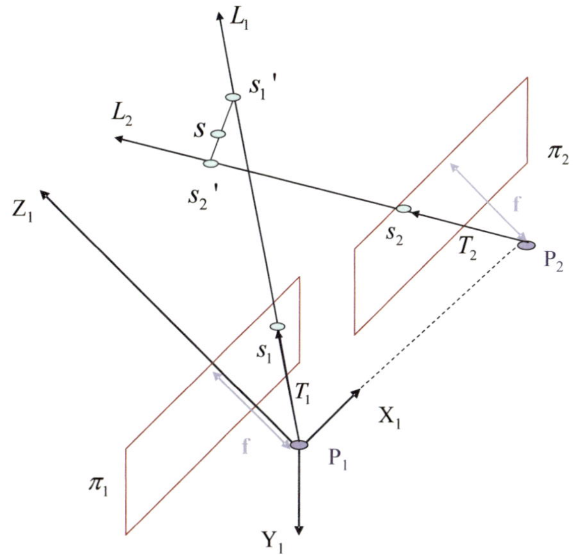

Fig. 11. An example of finding the position of ball center in the physical domain by the triangulation method

After all the captured images are processed by the 3-D positioning step, the trajectories of these balls can be reconstructed in a virtual environment, for example, in the 3-D plotting in MATLAB. In the virtual environment, these balls can be shown in different viewpoints. An example of the 3-D positioning for the three balls is shown in Figure 12. The original placement of the three balls is shown in Figure 12(a), and the 3-D positioning result in the virtual environment from three different viewpoints are shown in Figure 12(b), (c), and (d), respectively.

For testing the three cases of rate control, three levels of image acquisition rates are used. They are characterized as the higher level: 4 frames/sec, the normal level: 2 frames/sec, and the lower level: 1 frames/sec. In each case, twenty experiments are tested for 60 seconds. In each test, the ball velocity in the physical coordinate can be calculated based on the 3-D positioning of the ball center and the sampling time interval. Hence, two threshold values V_S and V_F used in Case A can then be determined based on the analyzed data. In the study, V_S and V_F are set as 32.47 and 48.46 mm/sec, respectively. Similarly, the threshold values P_S and P_F used in Case B and Case C are set as 9.80 and 17.05 pixel/sec, respectively.

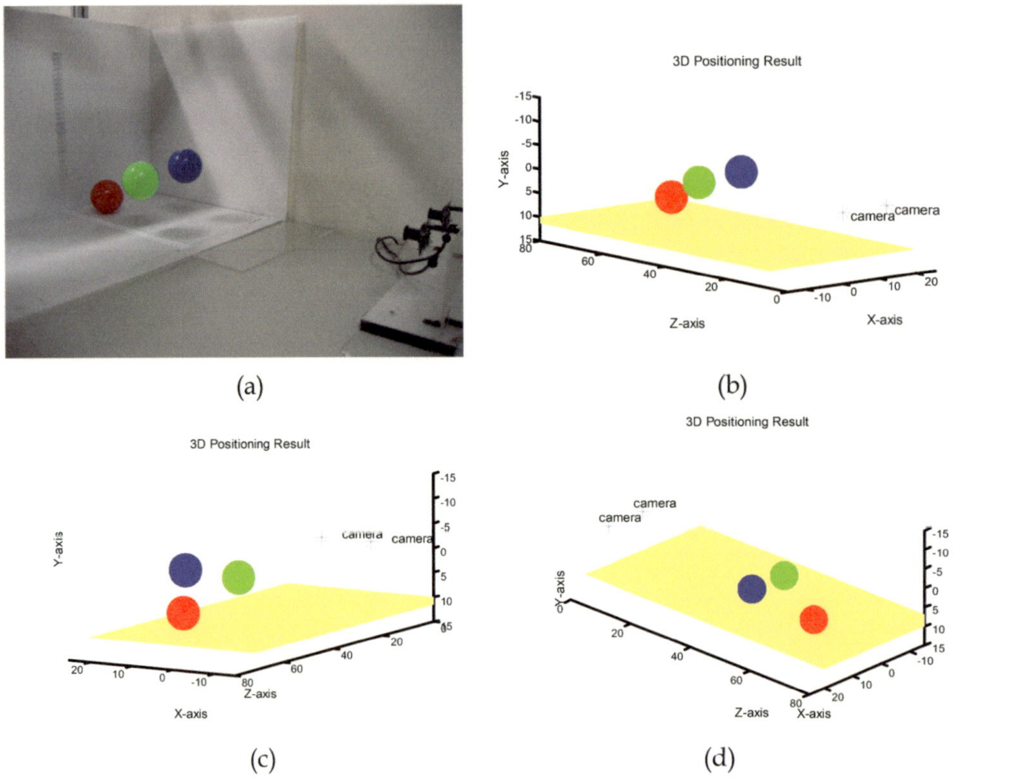

Fig. 12. An example of the 3-D positioning of the three balls. (a) A snapshot of the original placement. (b) The 3-D positioning reconstructed in the MATLAB environment. (c) and (d) The 3-D positioning results shown in the different viewpoints

Furthermore, for the evaluation of the control methods, the root-mean-square-error (RMSE) of the difference between the tests with and without rate control is calculated. The definition of RMSE is described as follows:

$$RMSE = \sqrt{\frac{1}{n}\sum_{i=1}^{n}(q_i - \hat{q}_i)^2} \tag{8}$$

where n is the number of predicted results, q denotes the original image quality, and $\hat{q}$ denotes the predicted image quality. When there are no corresponding images, the 3-D positioning results are estimated by the interpolation, extrapolation, or data fitting to a line by the least squares approximation.

In this study, the three control methods discussed in Section 3 are performed and compared by the average value of RMSE. In each case, five similar experiments are performed. The images in the five experiments are captured first by the higher level of image acquisition rate. Each experiment lasts for 60 seconds and 240 images are captured in each experiment. The result of the percentage of image saving is shown in Table 5. Since the original 3-D positioning results in the five experiments are calculated in advance, the values of RMSE for different control methods can be calculated. By using the interpolation method to predict unknown 3-D positions, the calculated results for RMSE is shown in Table 6. By using the extrapolation method to predict unknown 3-D positions, the calculated results for RMSE is shown in Table 7. Finllay, by using the method of least squares approximation to predict unknown 3-D positions, the calculated results for RMSE is shown in Table 8. Also, the timing data of the image acquisition by uisng the three control methods and the fixed rate cases are shown in Figure 13.

When all the images are captured by a fixed, normal image acquisition rate, the percentage of image saving is the smallest. In Case C, the image acquisition rate is adjusted before comparing the image processing result of the two cameras. Once one camera determines the time to capture next image, the other camera also capture the image no matter what its original decision is. Hence, the percentage of image saving for Case C is smaller than that of Case A and Case B.

For the prediction performance, since Case C acquires more images than Case A and Case B do, the RMSE for Case C are smaller than those for Case A and Case B. In Case B, the two cameras do not utilize identical image acquisition rate synchronously. Hence, the position of the ball in the image coordinate is then predicted. In Case A and Case B, the image acquisition rate for the two cameras is adjusted synchronously. Therefore, the RMSE in Case B is larger than those Case A and Case C.

	Percentage of image saving				
Index of experiments	Case A	Case B	Case C	Fixed rate (normal level)	Fixed rate (lower level)
1	71.67%	70.42%	52.08%	50%	75%
2	71.67%	70.21%	54.58%	50%	75%
3	72.50%	70.21%	56.67%	50%	75%
4	72.92%	70.63%	63.75%	50%	75%
5	72.92%	68.13%	52.08%	50%	75%
Average	72.34%	69.92%	55.83%	50%	75%

Table 5. The percentage of image saving in the experiments

	RMSE (by the interpolation method) (Unit: mm)				
Index of experiments	Case A	Case B	Case C	Fixed rate (normal level)	Fixed rate (lower level)
1	32.122	63.279	25.957	22.951	33.863
2	33.417	54.744	33.129	22.347	35.781
3	29.328	47.472	26.531	20.588	30.771
4	33.403	68.569	32.773	23.019	34.769
5	31.169	109.168	27.352	21.224	32.368
Average	31.888	68.646	29.142	22.026	33.510

Table 6. The RMSE of prediction performance when all unknown 3-D positioning results are predicted by the interpolation method

	RMSE (by the extrapolation method) (Unit: mm)				
Index of experiments	Case I	Case II	Case III	Fixed rate (normal level)	Fixed rate (lower level)
1	56.811	148.509	57.446	43.265	59.658
2	67.293	103.541	63.782	44.111	63.331
3	60.500	109.406	57.555	36.308	55.947
4	59.374	134.716	67.257	41.649	55.583
5	61.874	225.318	58.105	39.891	61.883
Average	61.170	144.298	60.229	41.045	59.280

Table 7. The RMSE of prediction performance when all unknown 3-D positioning results are predicted by the extrapolation method

	RMSE (by the method of data fitting to a line) (Unit: mm)				
Index of experiments	Case A	Case B	Case C	Fixed rate (normal level)	Fixed rate (lower level)
1	56.628	122.772	51.346	39.219	56.959
2	62.361	103.874	63.106	41.516	59.385
3	57.299	102.364	52.468	36.267	53.805
4	59.218	136.043	59.807	38.435	54.829
5	56.965	210.031	53.714	41.380	56.788
Average	58.494	135.017	56.088	39.363	56.353

Table 8. The RMSE of prediction performance when all unknown 3-D positioning results are predicted by the method of data fitting to a line

Finally, the performance criterion, defined in Section 3.3, of these three cases is summarized in Table 9. The performance criteria in Case A are larger than those in Case B and Case C. Hence, the performance of Case A is the best. Also, it is advised to use a control method with a positive R. Therefore, the performance of Case B is not good enough. Also, the statistic suggests that the performance of using interpolation to predict the missing data is better than that of using extrapolation and data fitting.

	R		
	Case A	Case B	Case C
Interpolation	0.2440	-0.1614	0.1139
Extrapolation	-0.1842	-1.0421	-0.3477
Data fitting	-0.1520	-0.9354	-0.2723

Table 9. The performance criterion R

In summary, Case A has a better result in the percentage of image saving and the performance criterion. For Case B, due to the asynchronization in image acquisition, the 3-D positioning results cannot be predicted properly and may generate bigger errors than that in Case A and Case C. Therefore, if the cameras can be placed in an appropriate position to avoid the problem of obtaining too little object information, Case A should be a better choice for practical application than Case C.

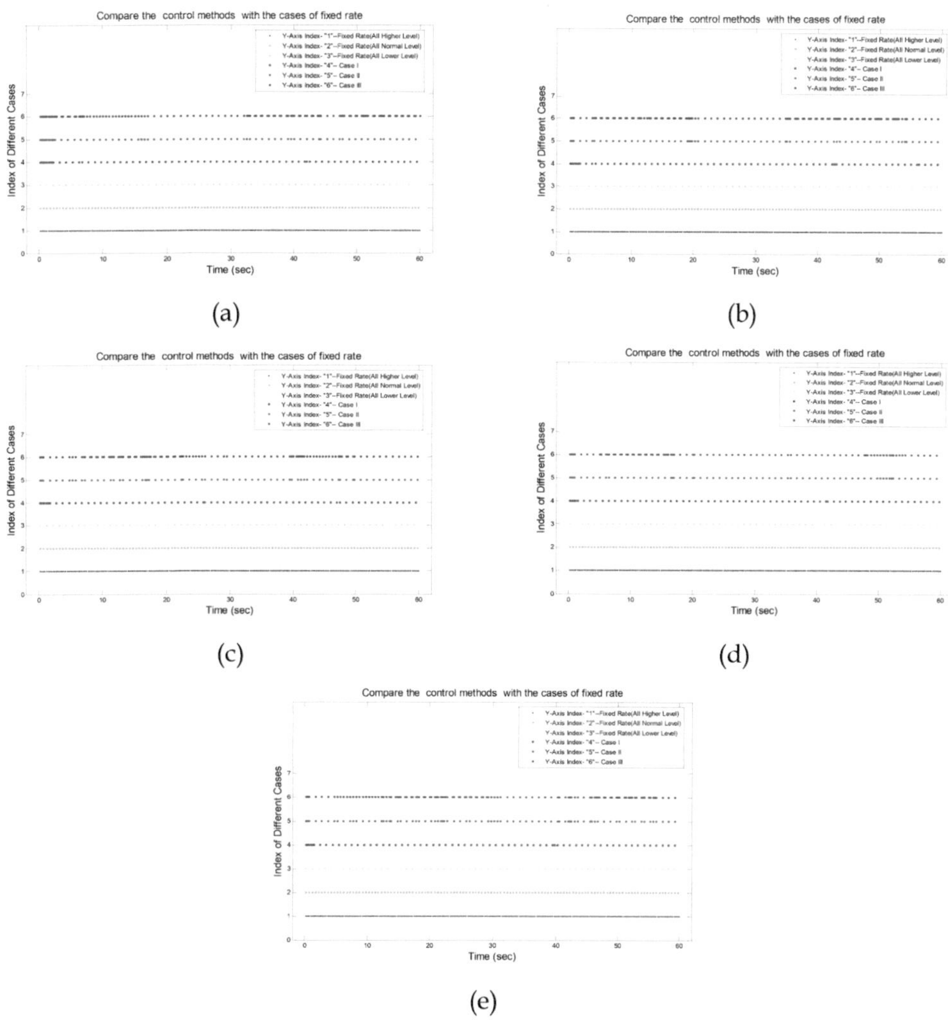

Fig. 13. The timing comparison for different image acquisition mechanisms by using the three control methods and the fixed rate cases. (a)-(e) The five experiments performed

5. Conclusions and future work

In this study, three methods for controlling image acquisition rate are designed and analyzed. In order to verify the control methods, the 3-D positioning of balls is used to compare the performance of the three control methods in terms of the percentage of saving images and the accuracy of the 3-D positioning results. Experimental results show that the calculating results for the percentage of saving images in Case C is smaller than that in Case A and Case B. However, since Case C adopts more images to predict the motion of the balls in the physical domain, the accuracy of the 3-D positioning result in Case C is better than that in Case A and Case B. The accuracy for the 3-D positioning result for Case B is worse than that in Case A and Case C. In order to compare the performance of the three cases, a performance criterion for judging these control methods is proposed. In practical applications, cameras should be placed or moved in an appropriate position to avoid the problem of getting too little object information from the images.

In the future, the following three tasks can be further performed. The first task is to use advanced mathematical methods for predicting the positions of the interested objects in the physical domain. The second task is to design more advanced control methods for better characterize the object states. The third task is to test the scenarios with more cameras and interested objects for testing the complexity achieved by the proposed control methods.

6. Acknowledgement

This work was supported in part by the National Science Council, Taiwan, ROC, under the grants: NSC 95-2221-E-002-303-MY3, and NSC 96-2218-E-002-030, and by DOIT/TDPA: 96-EC-17-A-04-S1-054.

7. References

Andrade, E.L.; Woods, J.C.; Khan, E. & Ghanbrai M. (2005) Region-Based Analysis and Retrieval for Tracking of Semantic Objects and Provision of Augmented Information in Interactive Sport Scenes, *IEEE Transactions on Multimedia*, Vol. 7, No. 6, (Dec. 2005) pp. 1084-1096, ISSN: 1520-9210

D'Orazio, T.; Ancona, N.; Cicirelli, G. & Nitti, M. (2002) A Ball Detection Algorithm for Real Soccer Image Sequences, *Proceedings of the 16th International Conference on Pattern Recognition*, pp. 210-213, ISBN: 0-7695-1685-x, Quebec, Canada, Aug. 2002, Institute of Electrical and Electronics Engineers, Piscataway

Hong, S.M. (2002) Steady-State Analysis of Computational Load in Correlation-Based Image Tracking, *IEE Proceedings on Vision, Image, and Signal Processing*, Vol. 149, No. 3, (June 2002) pp. 168-172, ISSN: 1350-245X

Iwase, H. & Murata A. (2001) Discussion on Skillful Baseball Pitch Using Three-Dimensional Cinematographic Analysis. Comparison of Baseball Pitch between Skilled and Unskilled Pitchers, *Proceedings of the IEEE International Conference on Systems, Man, and Cybernetics*, pp. 34-39, ISBN: 0-7803-7087-2, Tucson, AZ, USA, Oct. 2001, Institute of Electrical and Electronics Engineers, Piscataway

Ohno, Y.; Miura, J. & Shirai Y. (2000) Tracking Players and Estimation of the 3D Position of a Ball in Soccer Games, *Proceedings of the IEEE International Conference on Pattern Recognition*, pp. 145-148, ISBN: 0-7695-0750-6, Barcelona, Spain, Sep. 2000, Institute of Electrical and Electronics Engineers, Piscataway

Pingali, G.; Opalach, A.; Jean, Y. & Carlbom, I. (2001) Visualization of Sports Using Motion Trajectories: Providing Insights into Performance, Style, and Strategy, *Proceedings of the IEEE International Conference on Visualization*, pp. 75-82, ISBN: 0-7803-7200-x, San Diego, CA, USA, Oct. 2001, Institute of Electrical and Electronics Engineers, Piscataway

Pingali, G.; Opalach, A. & Jean, Y. (2000) Ball Tracking and Virtual Replays for Innovative Tennis Broadcasts, *Proceedings of the IEEE International Conference on Pattern Recognition*, pp. 152-156, ISBN: 0-695-0750-6, Barcelona, Spain, Sep. 2000, Institute of Electrical and Electronics Engineers, Piscataway

Ren, J.; Orwell, J.; Jones, G.A. & Xu, M. (2004) A General Framework for 3D Soccer Ball Estimation and Tracking, *Proceedings of the IEEE International Conference on Image Processing*, pp. 1935-1938, ISBN: 0-7803-8554-3, Genova, Italy, Oct. 2004, Institute of Electrical and Electronics Engineers, Piscataway

Shah, H. & Morrell, D. (2004) An Adaptive Zoom Algorithm for Tracking Targets Using Pan-Tilt-Zoom Cameras, *Proceedings of the IEEE International Conference on Acoustics, Speech, and Signal Processing*, pp. 17-21, ISBN: 0-7803-8484-9, Quebec, Canada, May 2004, Montreal, Institute of Electrical and Electronics Engineers, Piscataway

Shin, B.S. & Shin, Y.G. (1998) Fast 3D Solid Model Reconstruction from Orthographic Views, *Computer-Aided Design*, Vol. 30, No. 1, (Jan. 1998) pp. 63-76, ISSN: 0010-4485

Shum, H. & Komura, T. (2004) A Spatiotemporal Approach to Extract the 3D Trajectory of the Baseball from a Single View Video Sequence, *Proceedings of the IEEE International Conference on Multimedia and Expo*, pp. 1583-1586, ISBN: 0-7803-8603-5, Taipei, Taiwan, June 2004, Institute of Electrical and Electronics Engineers, Piscataway

Theobalt, C.; Albrecht, I.; Haber, J.; Magnor, M. & Seidel, H.P. (2004) Pitching a Baseball: Tracking High-Speed Motion with Multi-Exposure Images, *ACM Transactions on Graphics*, Vol. 23, No. 3, (Aug. 2004) pp. 540-547, ISSN: 0730-0301

Wang, C.K. ; Cheng, M.Y.; Liao, C.H.; Li, C.C.; Sun, C.Y. & Tsai, M.C. (2004) Design and Implementation of a Multi-Purpose Real-Time Pan-Tilt Visual Tracking System, *Proceedings of the IEEE International Conference on Control Applications*, pp. 1079-1084, ISBN: 0-7803-8633-7, Taipei, Taiwan, Sep. 2004, Institute of Electrical and Electronics Engineers, Piscataway

Yan, X.; Yu, X. & Hay, T.S. (2004) A 3D Reconstruction and Enrichment System for Broadcast Soccer Video, *Proceedings of the 12th ACM International Conference on Multimedia*, pp. 746-747, ISBN: 1-58113-893-8, New York, NY, USA, Oct. 2004, Institute of Electrical and Electronics Engineers, Piscataway

Yu, X.; Xu, C.; Tian, Q. & Leong, H.W. (2003a) A Ball Tracking Framework for Broadcast Soccer Video, *Proceedings of the IEEE International Conference on Multimedia and Expo*, pp. 273-276, ISBN: 0-7803-7965-9, Baltimore, MD, USA, July 2003, Institute of Electrical and Electronics Engineers, Piscataway

Yu, X.; Leong, H.W.; Lim, J.; Tian, Q. & Jiang, Z. (2003b) Team Possession Analysis for Broadcast Soccer Video Based on Ball Trajectory, *Proceedings of the IEEE International Conference on Information, Communications and Signal Processing*, pp. 1811-1815, ISBN: 0-7803-8185-8, Singapore, Dec. 2003, Institute of Electrical and Electronics Engineers, Piscataway

Yu, X.; Sim, C.H.; Wang, J.R. & Cheong, L.F. (2004) A Trajectory-Based Ball Detection and Tracking Algorithm in Broadcast Tennis Video, *Proceedings of the IEEE International Conference on Image Processing*, pp. 1049-1052, ISBN: 0-7803-8554-3, Genova, Italy, Oct. 2004, Institute of Electrical and Electronics Engineers, Piscataway

15

Active Tracking System with Rapid Eye Movement Involving Simultaneous Top-down and Bottom-up Attention Control

Masakazu Matsugu, Kan Torii and Yoshinori Ito
Canon Inc.
Japan

1. Introduction

Visual tracking of complex objects has been studied extensively in the field of robot vision, visual servoing, and surveillance. Detection of reliable low level visual features has been crucial, in the literature, for the stability of tracking in cluttered scene. However, using only low level features for tracking tends to be illusory for practical vision systems, and the selection of reliable visual features is still an important unsolved issue.

In recent studies it has been stressed the importance of high-level features in guiding control for long-duration tracking (Matsugu et al., 2006; Li et al., 2007; Yang et al., 2007), computer vision (Sun & Fisher, 2003), and visual search (Lee et al., 2005). Recent cognitive neuro-psychological as well as brain imaging studies also revealed a role of top-down attention in visual search task in human vision system (Patel & Sathian, 2000; Hopfinger et al., 2000; Corbetta & Shulman, 2002; Navalpakkam & Itti, 2006).

In this chapter, we present a new object tracking vision system that incorporates both top-down and bottom-up attention processes. Tracking a specific object using both low-level and high-level features is not new and was previously studied (Isard & Blake, 1998) in a stochastic framework. The proposed active vision system in this chapter is task-oriented and tracks a specific object (i.e., person). The tracking process is initiated by the top-down process which is activated by robust object detection module (Matsugu & Cardon, 2004; Matsugu et al., 2004). Subsequent feature selection for tracking involves simultaneous *consolidation* mechanism between higher level complex features (e.g., face) obtained from the top-down process and low level features from the bottom-up process (detailed description is in Section 3). The active vision system controls eye movement based on prediction of an attended object's location by the above processes.

Main contribution of this chapter is that we propose a stable object tracking algorithm involving selective attention together with FF and FB hybrid control that enable smooth and saccadic pursuit. Specifically, we introduce a coherency measure of tracking features. Tracking using such measure ensures stability and fast recovery from failure (missing the object to be tracked) by way of *consolidation* among bottom-up and top-down attention cues.

For the bottom-up feature-based prediction of tracked object, we use local color histogram, and histogram intersection (Swain & Ballard, 1991; Birchfield & Rangarajan, 2005) is used for feature matching. High-level, top-down feature for tracking is defined as detected face

location and its predicted location. The coherency measure is used also for feature selection resulting in switching in-between low-level and high-level tracking features, and the active vision system controls panning/tilting angle of camera module.
We demonstrate fast and stable tracking of a person moving rapidly with abrupt motion change, attaining maximum instantaneous panning speed of 6deg/40ms. This saccadic pursuit is roughly equivalent to tracking an object moving at 10m/sec at the distance of 3m. Persistent tracking with stability and robustness is demonstrated in a number of experiments under drastic illumination changes, background clutters, and occlusions.
The organization of this chapter is as follows. In Section 2, we review conventional active vision systems for object tracking. In Section 3, details about the proposed algorithms are given and we propose a new feature coherency measure for selecting useful features for tracking, followed by demonstration of robustness and stability of tracking as well as fast and smooth eye movement control in a number of human tracking experiments. In Section 4, details about hardware implementation are explained. Section 5 shows results and performance, followed by discussion and conclusions in Section 6 and 7.

2. Overview of attention control, object tracking, and active vision

A great many models for attention control have been proposed (e.g., Koch & Ullman, 1985; Itti & Koch, 2000). Most existing algorithms in machine vision, with a few exceptions (e.g., Culhane & Tsotsos, 1992; Yang et al., 2007), exploit a class of saliency map derived from low-level features (Koch & Ullman, 1985; Treisman & Gelade, 1980) and a spatial attention window operates on the saliency map. It is a map of scalar values that encodes locations of something conspicuous in the visual field to guide vision related tasks such as visual search and servoing. Most of saliency measure is described in terms of low-level features such as color cues (Swain et al. 1992) or motion cues (Cretual et al., 1998; Bur et al., 2007) that are *different and popped-out* from neighborhood surrounding features.
On the other hand, a limited number of methods have been proposed for attention control that involves both top-down and bottom-up processes (Giefing et al., 1992; Olshausen et al., 1995; Sun & Fisher, 2003; Lee et al., 2005; Yang et al., 2007). Interest map (Giefing et al., 1992) is a kind of saliency map which unifies maps of pre-attentive low-level features and attentive features indicating object hypothesis, which is used to induce top-down saccadic shift. Dynamic routing circuit (Olshausen et al., 1995) was introduced for top-down attention control in a hierarchical feed-forward neural network model for object detection. Late attentional selection mechanism (Yang et al., 2007) involves top-down, higher cognitive process to enhance robustness of tracking under occlusion and cluttering and also to ensure long duration tracking. In this model, low-level features are used for bottom-up fast process and high-level features for top-down, slow process. A slow attentional process using top-down, object cue (Sun & Fisher, 2003) was combined with a fast, bottom-up process. Biologically motivated attention control architecture (Mancas et al., 2007) is also proposed with three levels of units, namely, low-, mid-, and high-levels, as opposed to conventional two levels of pre-attentive and attentive systems.
Integration of multiple modalities has been proven to be helpful for enhancing robustness in tracking as they act complementary source of visual cues. In fact, a saliency map is a class of integral representation of multiple cues (Itti et al., 1998; Bur et al., 2007). In particular, the integration of different cues for tracking using stochastic framework has long been addressed in the literature (Isard & Blake, 1998; Rasmussen & Hager, 2001; Wu & Huang,

2001, Serby et al., 2004). For instance, multiple low-level features (e.g., edges, textures, interest points) can be integrated into a particle filter framework for tracking (Serby et al., 2004). Covariance tracking (Porikli et al., 2006) can also combine different modalities such as infrared and color cues in covariance matrix. Integration of detection and tracking has also been proven to be effective for enhanced reliability (Sigal et al., 2004; Matsugu et al., 2006; Li et al., 2007). Model-based cues and model-free cues are also integrated in the framework of Kalman filtering (Kyrki & Kragic, 2005).

Complex object tracking (Drummond & Cipolla, 2002) is another important issue in robot vision functionalities such as visual servoing (Clark & Ferrier, 1992; Cretual, et al. 1998; Fujita et al., 2007), random bin-picking in eye-in-hand system, and people tracking in surveillance (Comaniciu et al., 2000; Li et al., 2006; Yang et al., 2006; Matsugu et al., 2006). In the field of visual search strategy for traditional purposive vision (Garvey, 1976; Ballard & Brown, 1992), fixation or gaze control was realized as a manifestation of attention control. The task oriented visual search deals with selecting objects and order of fixation that result in the control of eye movement.

Active vision system with tracking functionality has been studied extensively in the literature. A number of methods on object tracking with camera motion have been proposed (Hunt & Sanderson, 1982; Aloimonos et al., 1987; Burt et al, 1989; Birchfield, 1997; Birchfield & Rangarajan, 2005; Blake & Yuille, 1992; Murray & Basu, 1994; Bradshaw et al, 1994; Castrillón-Santana et al., 1998; Comaniciu et al., 2000; Murao et al., 2006; Yang et al., 2006), however, only a few works addressed co-realization of saccadic, quick eye-movement and smooth pursuit in an active vision head with pan/tilt operation. A notable exemplary work is coarse and fine resolutions for saccadic and smooth pursuit (Bradshaw et al., 1994).

As regards feature selection in active tracking system that involves pan/tilt/zoom control, primitive features such as color and motion have been favorably used in the literature. A notable system for tracking specific object using color cue is mean shift method (Comaniciu et al., 2000) that relies on color histogram for camera control. On-line feature selection is also important for enhanced stability. In a face tracking active vision (Yang et al., 2006) dominant color feature was selected during tracking. Motion cue has also been used as major and important feature. For instance, majority tracking algorithm (Burt et al., 1989) used optical flow and was implemented on pyramid vision hardware. Motion energy and ego-motion compensation (Murray & Basu, 1994) was introduced for calculating pan/tilt angles about the lens center. As in attention control, there have been a limited number of works (Castrillón-Santana et al., 1998, Matsugu et al., 2006; Yang et al., 2007) on using both low level and high level cues in active vision systems.

3. Tracking with selective attention

3.1 Top-down process

Specific goal of our task oriented active vision system is *long duration tracking* of a person under drastic illumination change, in cluttered scene with lots of distracters. The top-down process which constitutes slow subsystem involves fast and robust object detection (Matsugu & Cardon, 2004) using modified convolutional neural networks (MCoNN). In Fig. 2, we show a schematic architecture of MCoNN which constitutes a subsystem for face detection. The top-down stream generates prediction data sequence of a specific object to be tracked.

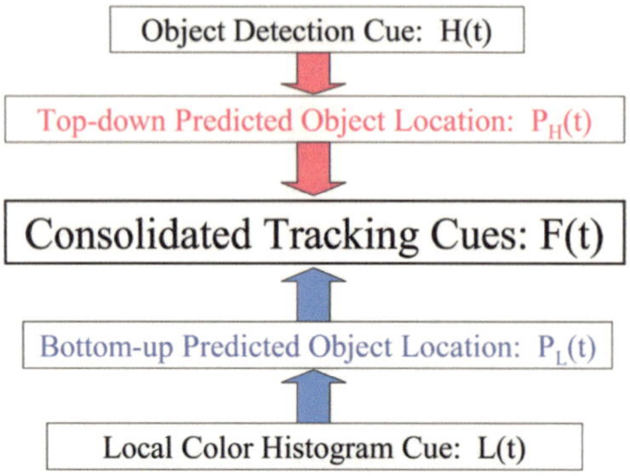

Fig. 1. Top-down and bottom-up attention cues are integrated as consolidated tracking cues

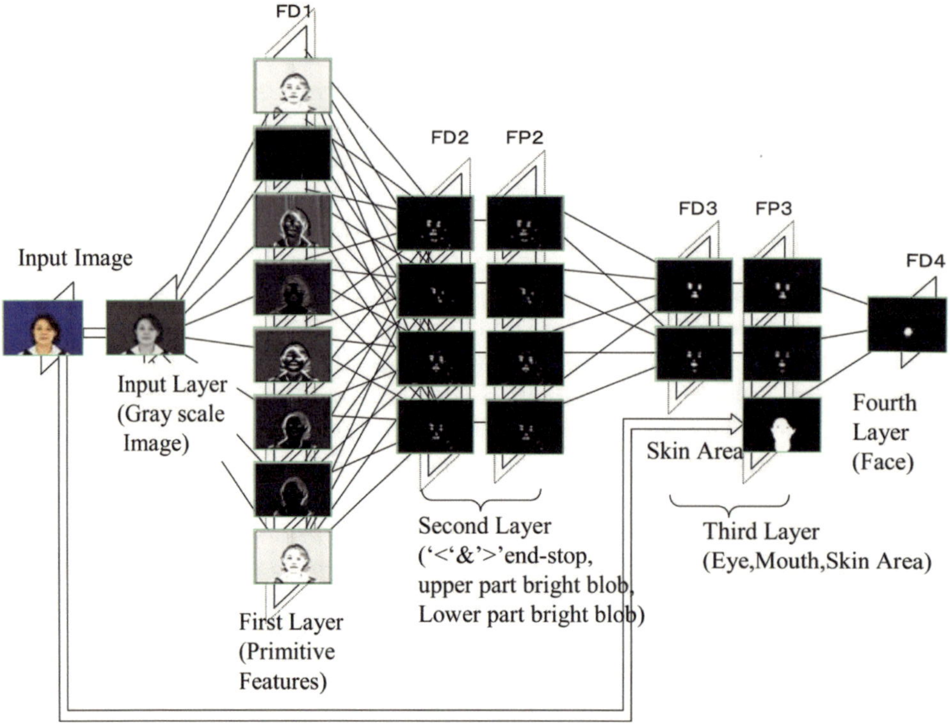

Fig. 2. Hierarchical architecture (MCoNN) for integrating predefined alphabetical local features (indicated in the second layer level) for object detection.

Fig. 3 shows a schematic diagram of object (face) detection algorithm as a whole. The algorithm is composed of two sub-modules. The first stage is a combination of modified cascaded filtering (Viola & Jones, 2001) system for fast and robust face detection, followed by MCoNN. The modified V&J (details will be published elsewhere) uses cascaded simple filters (e.g., rectangle filters extracting Haar-like features) and *integral image* representation (Crow, 1984; Viola & Jones, 2001). The second stage is composed of a set of MCoNNs each tuned to a specific rotation/size class of faces (Mitarai et al., 2003).

As indicated in Fig.1, sequence of locations of a particular object-to-be-tracked obtained from the top-down subsystem is stored and fed to an intermediate subsystem that evaluates coherency. The intermediate subsystem receives inputs from bottom-up stream as well, and it integrates those cues from the two streams to predict the location of the object in the upcoming frames as *consolidated* tracking cues.

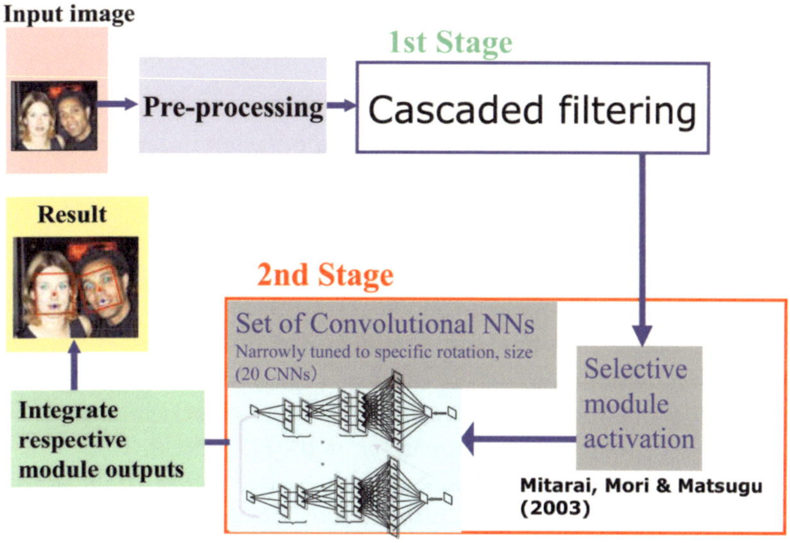

Fig. 3. Face detection process as a whole in the active vision system

3.2 Bottom-up process: integral feature description and matching using intersection

The bottom-up process involves extraction of local color cues inside attended region. In the proposed system, we used local color histogram as feature descriptor, since it potentially gives stable representation against noise without losing spatial information. We introduce a variant of integral representation of such features in order for fast computation of tracking features necessary for agility both in tracking (Porikli, 2005; Matsugu, et al., 2006) and in attention control (Frintrop et al., 2007). The integral representation of color histogram is given in (1).

$$H_{Y,I,Q}(x,y) = \sum_{x' \le x,\ y' \le y} b_{Y,I,Q}(x',y') \tag{1}$$

, where H(x, y) is the integral data at (x, y). Y, I, and Q are luminance and chrominance color coordinate value. The value of $b_{Y',I',Q'}(x, y)$ is 1, if the bin with representative value of (Y', I', Q') is not empty at (x, y), and otherwise, $b_{Y',I',Q'}(x, y)$ is zero. The local color histogram in a rectangle region can be computed with reference to integral data at four corner points of the region (Crow, 1984). Face location can be predicted using local histogram matching by using difference measure. In this paper, we use histogram intersection (Swain & Ballard, 1991; Birchfield & Rangarajan, 2005) between local image patch *I(R)* and *I(R')*, which is defined by (2).

$$\phi(I(R), I(R')) = \frac{\sum_{Y,I,Q} \min\left(\sum_{R} H_{Y,I,Q}(R), \sum_{R'} H_{Y,I,Q}(R')\right)}{\sum_{Y,I,Q}\sum_{R} H_{Y,I,Q}(R)} \tag{2}$$

, where R and R' are rectangle regions for local color histogram, and $H_{Y,I,Q}(R)$ is the area-summation (Crow, 1984) of local color histogram by using four H values given by (1) at respective corner points of the rectangle region R. Although the histogram intersection is not scale invariant, it is simple and effective for reliability and quick response of tracking even when the object moves with drastic appearance change in size (e.g., face, approaching the camera with much higher speed).

3.3 Feature coherency and autonomous switching between detection and tracking

The proposed system, without saliency map, *consolidates* respective streams of predicted object locations from bottom-up process by histogram matching (HM) and those from top-down process by face detection (FD). In the system, attention is covert, and attention shift is activated in an event driven manner so that tracking is maintained as long as possible. Once the system shall lose the sight of the tracked object, the top-down process (FD) dominates to search for the 'lost' object, and tracking is maintained by the bottom-up process (HM). Covert attention shift is activated when the lost object is detected inside the attention window in a way that attention window as well as camera pan/tilt angle is shifted to the predicted location (angle) of the object obtained from the FD process.

Control of pan/tilt camera head (details are given in Section 4) is accompanied by autonomous switching between two operation modes; detection mode and tracking mode. The duality and switching in between these two modes has also been explored in the literature (Chesi et al., 2003; Morioka et al., 2006; Yang et al., 2006). Distinct aspect of the present scheme as compared with similar past works (Sigal et al., 2004; Li et al., 2007) is the autonomous switching that results from integration of detection and tracking through a measure of coherence of top-down and bottom-up features. In view of preceding and current positional data (i.e., location queue of attention window), q, used for actual control, the coherency is given in (3).

$$C(p_{HM}, p_{FD}, q) = \min(dist(p_{HM}, q), dist(p_{FD}, q)) \tag{3}$$

, where $dist(p_s, q)$ is the distance between $\boldsymbol{p}_s$ (predicted position vector of object obtained from s process: FD or HM) and $\boldsymbol{q}$ (actual position vectors of preceding attention window). The coherency serves as tolerance parameter indicating whether or not hypothesized (predicted) location data are in accordance with previous control data. If p_{FD} for the current frame is not available due to occlusion or failure of object detection, p_{FD} is given as some fixed large value, C_0 (e.g., frame size) such that for any coherency value C, $C_0 > C$.

By using the above coherency measure, the consolidated tracking cue, $F(t)$, for the frame number t in Fig.1 for the pan/tilt control is drawn as follows.

$$F(t) = \begin{cases} p_{FD}(t-1) & \text{if top-down signal, } p_{FD}\text{, available and } C = dist\,(p_{FD}, F(t-1)) \\ p_{HM}(t-1) & \text{if } C = dist\,(p_{HM}, F(t-1)) \text{ or } |p_{HM}(t) - pred(F(t))| < |p_{HM}(t) - F(t-1)| \\ F(t-1) & \text{otherwise} \end{cases} \tag{4}$$

, where $pred(F)$ is the linear prediction obtained from the preceding data F for more than 250ms. For faster calculation, we will simply use absolute difference for $dist(\boldsymbol{p}, \boldsymbol{q}) = |\boldsymbol{p} - \boldsymbol{q}|$.

3.4 Adaptive search area

Size and location of attention window are updated based on averaged prediction error for a fixed time interval (e.g., 150ms). This adaptive scheme is effective for increasing stability of tracking and to facilitate recovery from face detection failure and prediction error. The prediction error is defined by distances in horizontal and vertical directions on image plane, between predicted face location and the image center when face is detected. In the case of missing object (face) to be tracked, the error is given by *arctan* of the last detected face size multiplied by a constant parameter. The size is gradually enlarged during the detection failure (missing the object to be tracked) inside the window. Fig. 4 illustrates how the attention window enlarges depending on the motion of the object and the difference between the center of window and object location. In the left side picture of Fig. 4, the attention window is enlarged in horizontal direction since the object is moving horizontally, whereas in the right picture, the window size is set larger due to missing (failure in the top-down process) of object in the previously set window.

Fig. 4. Variable attention window (rectangle region with pink line segments)

4. Hardware system

The prototype active vision system is composed of a small camera module, pan/tilt movement subsystem, DC motors, multi-rate hybrid control units. Most part of tracking control for each subsystem is implemented on FPGA board. Tracking and object detection algorithms run on PC as parallel tasks composed of multiple threads.
The best available instantaneous tracking speed was approximately 6 deg/40ms (pan) as shown in Fig. 5 (left). The result is equivalent to tracking a person running and switching motion direction approximately at 10m/sec with distance about 3m of the camera. By tuning control parameters to avoid overshooting, the result was obtained with estimated prediction data of face location given at every 10ms.
Fig. 6 shows the results of pan/tilt angle control and associated prediction, with the hybrid (feed-forward/feed-back) PD control system (details are given in Fig. 8). Linear prediction of face location based on observation sequence has resulted in noisy and unsteady sequence (pan and tilt prediction). Applying critical sensitivity analysis and appropriate tuning of gain parameters (i.e., P and D gain) of step response, the proposed hybrid control attained smoothness (stability) and agility of tracking as well. Observation period for prediction is over 250ms and more than three points of prior observations (e.g., predicted face locations or detected face locations) are utilized to obtain the linear prediction.

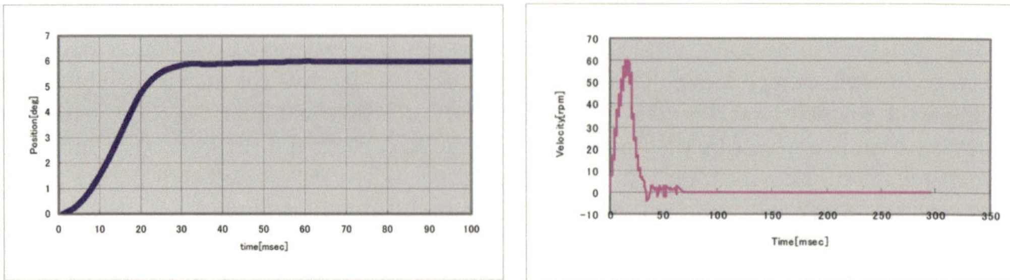

Fig. 5. Saccadic eyemovement without overshooting (left): angle-time, (right): vlocity-time

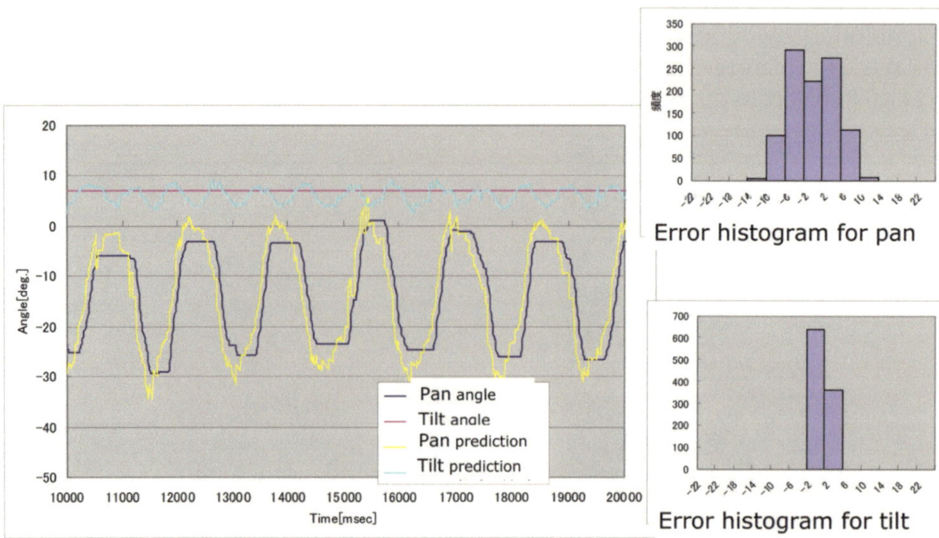

Fig. 6. Smooth and agile control with noisy prediction

The structure of pan/tilt system is a classic gimbal as shown in the middle and right side of Fig.7. Major component of the entire mechanical system with the time constant of 13ms are coreless DC motor (Maxon RE10), 1/40 reducer unit composed of three gears and a compact camera module (CK300: Keyence). Prototype picture of the vision head with display is given in the left of Fig. 7.

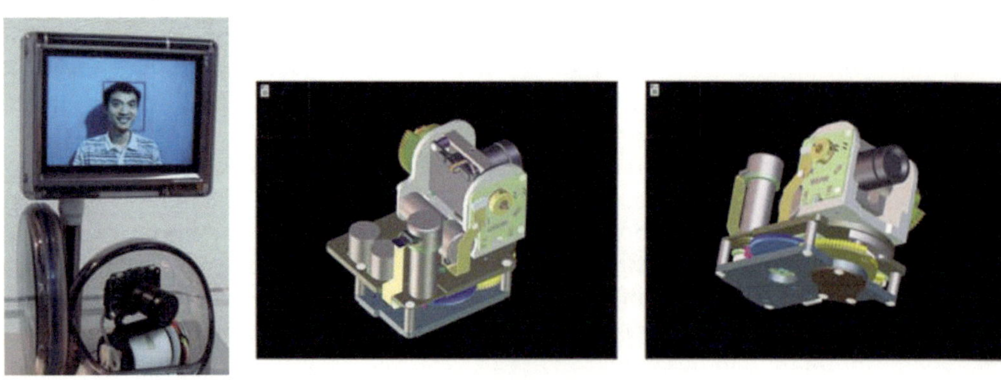

Fig. 7. Prototype active vision module with pan/tilt mechanical system

The maximum attainable pan/tilt speed is 900 deg/sec. The tilting mechanical unit is placed on top of panning unit, so that the panning has low inertia to realize quick response in horizontal direction. Thus, the tilting unit is accompanied by relatively larger inertia with gentler response as compared with the panning.
We employed a hybrid multi-rate control composed of FF based velocity control circuits and software operating at 100 Hz and FB based position control circuits operating at 5000Hz. The former helped realize smooth pursuit, and the latter contributed to the saccadic and quick response in our active tracking system. In Fig.8, most of components including camera controller and driver module, except for FF-velocity controller are implemented as hardware circuits on FPGA board (yellow block in Fig. 8).

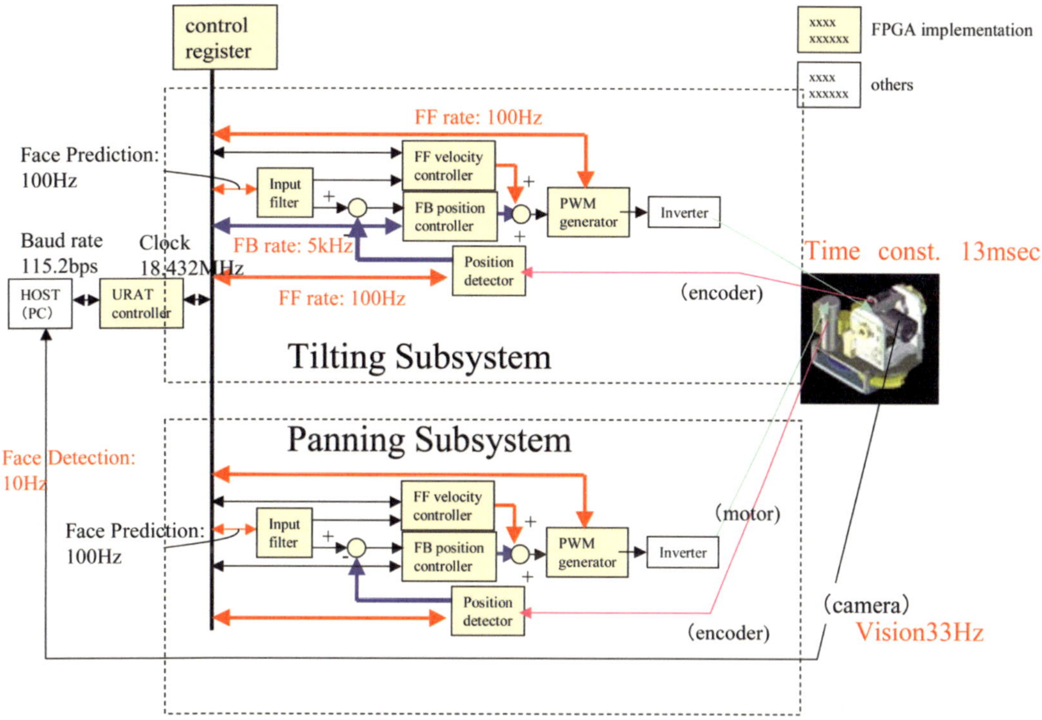

Fig. 8. Control system with fast feedback (5kHz) and slow feed-forward (100Hz) control signals

5. Results

Proposed system demonstrates remarkable response to track agile and nonlinear motion of object (person), as can be seen in Figs. 9, 10, and 11.
The minimum size of attention window is 3.7deg x 3.7deg and the maximum is 22.5deg x 22.5 deg. The system generated interpolated sequence of face locations for every 10ms. To suppress hopping from one subject to another during tracking in a scene where multiple faces present, maximum tracking speed of face motion is set as 0.1 deg/ms, leading to limitation of search window size.
Algorithms for detecting object to be tracked and prediction of the object location in our active vision system are implemented on PC (Pentium IV at 3.6 GHz). The system operates with five approximately concurrent processes: image capturing, object detection, object

prediction, camera control, and external output. As shown in Fig. 10, a person jumping with abrupt change in direction of motion can be tracked under the condition of heavy illumination change, and such tracking response can also be observed in panning sequence.

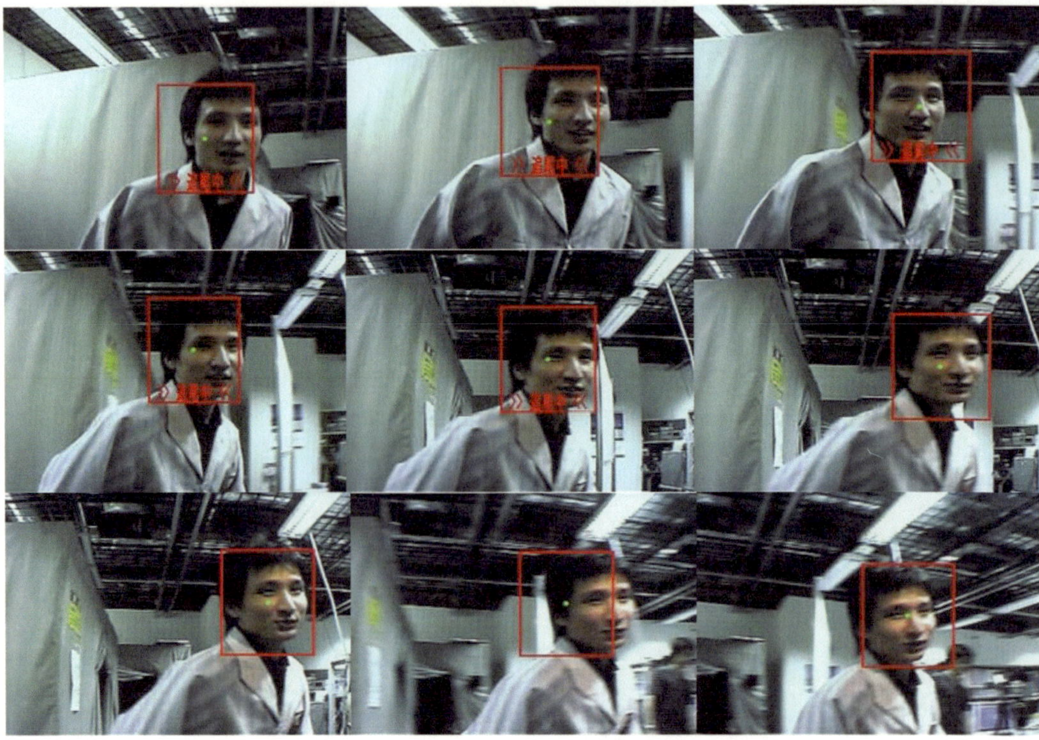

Fig. 9. Running sequence tracked with panning camera control.

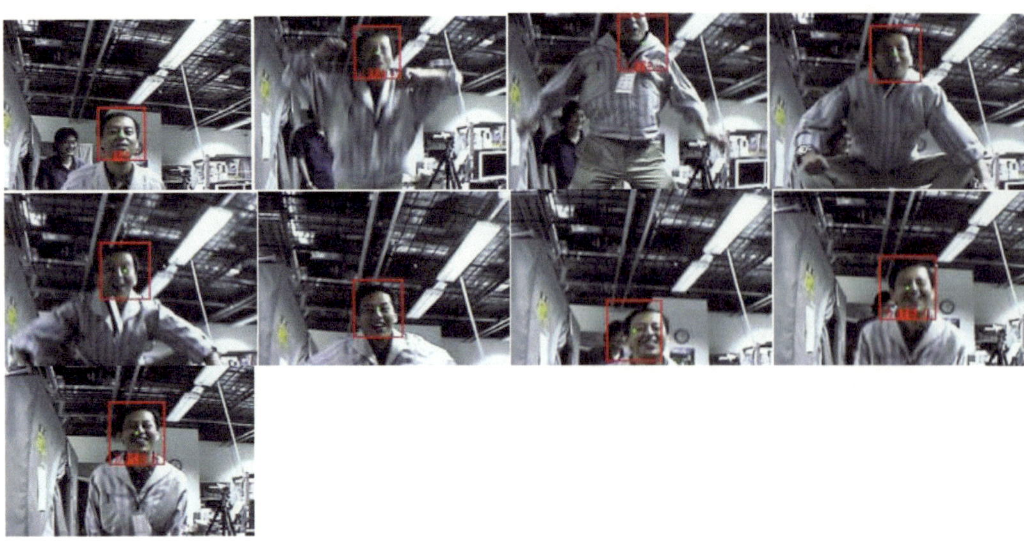

Fig. 10. Jumping sequence with motion blur, tracked with tilting camera control

Fig. 10 and Fig. 11 show tilting and panning control respectively for tracking sequences of jumping person with substantial motion blur. To further enhance the stability of tracking and to deal with temporary missing of tracked face due to occlusion or error in the top-down process, we introduced several heuristics; 1) inactivate pan/tilt control when located face is beyond the maximum speed of 0.1 deg/ms and no face location query is available in the time interval of 675ms, 2) use the last available object location obtained from the top-down process for pan/tilt control when the number of stored face location data that meet the coherency criterion (2) is less than four.

Fast recovery from error can be observed from these sequences. For example, the second picture in the top row of Fig. 11, the center of attention window is erroneous due to detection failure or prediction error, but in the next frame the center is correctly set. Such behavior results from the proposed attention control with feature consolidating mechanism proposed in Section 3, wherein both top-down and bottom-up processes are involved.

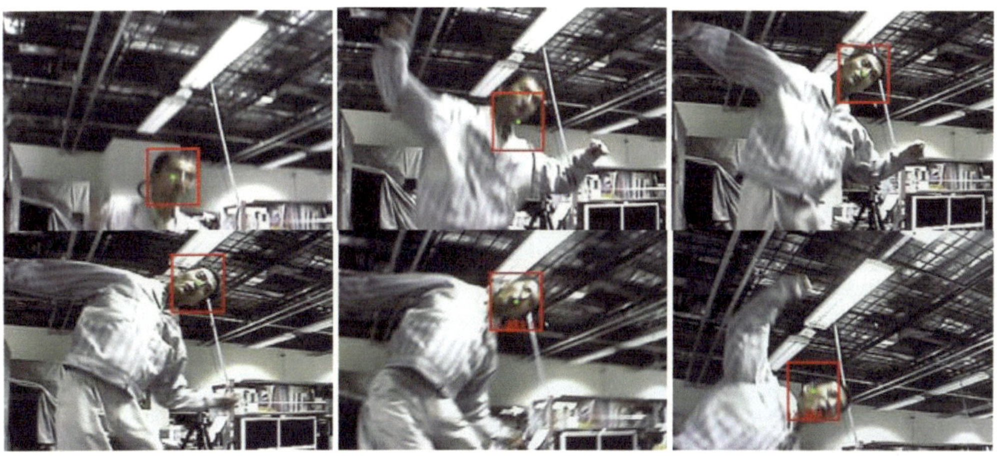

Fig. 11. Tracking a face of jumping person with rotation and motion blur

6. Discussion

Switching from detection (FD) mode to tracking mode with histogram matching (HM) is initiated typically when face detection is failed. Recovery from HM to FD mode is enforced when successful face detection inside the search window ensues. Stability in "visual servo" is thus realized by such covert attention shift and coherency based switching using top-down process. This event driven control turned out to be helpful for long-duration-tracking. Appropriate selection of control strategy is important to maximize performance (Papanikolopoulos et al., 1993), in terms of speed, stability, and robustness of active tracking systems. In this paper, we explored co-realization of saccadic and smooth pursuit using hybrid multi-rate control system (i.e., slow FF-velocity control and fast FB-position control). The proposed system integrated variety of modalities; fast processes (HM in bottom-up process and FB-position control) and slow processes (FD in top-down process and FF-velocity control). Such integrity of perception and control capable of long duration tracking is a distinct aspect in contrast to similar active vision system (Castrillón-Santana et al., 1998). Using rather classical control strategy combined with the fast object detection and reliable computation of object cues from the image sequence, we successfully demonstrated quick and smooth response in visual servo and also effectiveness of proposed coherency based attention shift during tracking.

One notable point of this attention shift is fast recovery from failure (error) and another is the balance between quick response and smoothness in tracking. The former aspect is manly due to the covert attention shift that utilizes robust object detection, which is accompanied with autonomous switching between FD mode and HM mode. Integral image representation of local color histogram was indispensable for quick computation of attention cues, and adaptive setting of search area based on linear prediction errors was also effective for ensuring the top-down attention shift.

Even if faced with nonlinear motion and abrupt change of moving direction of the tracked object, no sopshisticated nonlinear control strategies are required due to covert attention shift resulting from top-down process, while preserving agility in response. This result was obtained partly because fast computation and selection of reliable bottom-up cues. The multi-rate (i.e. slow FF velocity control and fast FB position control) control turned out to be simple and computationally inexpensive, in contrast to existing methods (Yang et al., 2006; Morioka et al., 2006), and it could also strike a balance between saccade and smooth pursuit.

7. Conclusion

In this study, the task oriented active vision with top-down and bottom-up attention control demonstrated long duration tracking under bad illumination conditions, fast recovery from tracking error and quick response to abrupt change in moving direction of the tracked object. Nonlinearity of the object motion is handled by the proposed attention control without recourse to state-of-the art nonlinear control strategy. The consolidating mechanism between top-down and bottom-up features through coherency measure can serve as substrate for stable tracking of specific object with covert attention shift.

8. Acknowledgements

We thank T. Osaka (Fig. 7), T. Hayashi (Figs. 5, 6, and 8), and Onodera (Fig. 7) for the implementation and design of the proposed system.

9. References

Aloimonos, J. Weiss, I. & Bandyopadhyay, A. (1987). Active Vision. *International Journal of Computer Vision*, Vol. 1, No. 4, 333-356

Ballard, D. H. & Brown, C. M. (1992). Principles of Animate Vision. *Computer Vision, Graphics and Image Processing*, Vol. 56, 3-21

Birchfield, S. (1997). An elliptic head tracker. Proceedings of 31st Asilomar Conference on Signals, Systems, and Computer, pp. 1710-1714

Birchfield, S. & Rangarajan, S. (2005). Spatiograms versus histograms for region-based tracking, *Proceedings of IEEE International Conference on Computer Vision Pattern Recognition CVPR'05*, pp. 1158-1163

Blake, A. & Yuille, A. (1992). *Active Vision*, MIT Press, ISBN: 978-0262023511, Cambridge

Bradshaw, K. J., McLauchlan, P. F., Reid, I. D. & Murray D. W. (1994). Saccade and Pursuit on an Active Head/Eye Platform. *Image and Vision Computing*, Vol. 12, 155-163

Bur, A., Wurtz, A., Müri, R. M. & Hügli. H. (2007). Dynamic visual attention: competitive and motion priority scheme. *Workshop on Computational Attention & Application in International Conference on Computer Vision Systems*

Burt, P.J., Bergen, J.R., Hingorani, R. & Kolczynski, R. (1989). Object tracking with a moving camera. *Proceeding of Workshop on Visual Motion*

Castrillón-Santana, M., Guerra-Artal, C., Hernández-Sosa, J., Domínguez-Brito, A., Isern-González, J., Cabrera-Gámez, J. & Hernández-Tejera, F.M. (1998). An Active Vision System Integrating Fast and Slow Processes. *Proceeding of the SPIE'98 Symposium on Intelligent Systems and Advanced Manufacturing*, pp. 487-496, Boston

Chesi, G., Hashimoto, K., Prattichizo, D. & Vicino, A. (2003). A switching control law for keeping features in the field of view in eye-in-hand visual servoing. *Proeedings of IEEE International Conference on Robotics and Automation* (Taipei, Taiwan), pp. 3929-3934

Clark, J. J. & Ferrier, N. J. (1992). Attentive Visual Servoing. *Active Vision*, Blake, A. & Yuille, A. (Eds.), 137-154, MIT Press, ISBN: 978-0262023511, Cambridge

Comaniciu, D., Ramesh, V. & Meer, P. (2000). Real-time tracking of non-rigid objects using mean shift. *Proceedings of International Conference on Computer Vision & Pattern Recognition*, pp. 142-149

Corbetta, M. & Shulman, G. L. (2002). Control of Goal-direct and Stimulus-driven Attention in the Brain. *Nature Neuroscience*, Vol. 3, 201-215

Cretual, A., Chaumette, F. & Bouthemy, P. (1998). Complex object tracking by visual servoing based on 2D image motion. *Proceedings of International Conference on Pattern Recognition*, pp. 1251-1254

Crow, F. (1984). Summed-Area Tables for Texture Mapping. *Computer Graphics*, Vol. 18, 207-211

Culhane, S. M. & Tsotsos, J. K. (1992). A Prototype for Data-Driven Visual Attention. *Proceedings of International Conference on Pattern Recognition*, pp.36-40

Drummond, T. & Cipolla, R. (2002). Real-Time Visual Tracking of Complex Objects. *IEEE Transactions on Pattern Analysis & Machine Intelligence, Vol. 24, No. 7, 932-946*

Frintrop, S., Klodt, M. & Rome, E. (2007). A Real-time Visual Attention System Using Integral Images, *Proceedings of International Conf. on Computer Vision Systems*

Fujita, M., Kawai, H. & Spong, M. W. (2007). Passivity-based dynamic visual feedback control for three dimensional target tracking: stability and L2-gain performance analysis. *IEEE Transactions on Control Systems Technology*, Vol. 15

Garvey, T. D. (1976). Perceptual strategies for purposive vision. *Technical Note* Vol. 117, SRI International

Giefing, G.-J., Janβen, H. & Mallot, H. (1992). Saccadic Object Recognition with an Active Vision System. *Proceedings of European Conference on Artificial Intelligence*, pp. 803-805

Hopfinger, J. B., Buonocore, M. H. & Mangun, G. R. (2000). The neural mechanisms of top-down attentional control. *Nature Neuroscience*, Vol. 3, 284-291

Hunt A. E. & Sanderson, A. C. (1982). Vision-based predictive robotic tracking of a moving targets. *Technical Report*, Carnegie Mellon University,

Isard, M. & Blake, A. (1998). ICondensation: Unifying Low-level and High-level Tracking in a Stochastic Framework. *Proceedings of European Conference on Computer Vision*, pp. 893-908

Itti, L., Koch, C. & Niebur, E. (1998). A Model of Saliency-Based Visual Attention for Rapid Scene Analysis. *IEEE Transactions on Pattern Analysis and Machine Intelligence*, Vol. 20, 1254-1259

Itti, L., & Koch, C. (2000). A saliency-based search mechanism for overt and covert shifts of visual attention, *Vision Research*, Vol. 40, 1489-1506

Koch, C. & Ullman, S. (1985). Shifts in selective visual attention: Towards the under-lying neural circuitry. *Human Neurobiology*, Vol. 4, 19-227

Kyrki, V. & Kragic, D. (2005). Integration of Model-based and Model-free Cues for Visual Object Tracking in 3D. *Proceedings of International Conference on Robotics and Automation*

Lee, K. W., Buxton, H. & Feng, J. (2005). Cue-Guided Search: A Computational Model of Selective Attention. *IEEE Transactions on Neural Networks*, Vol. 16, 910-924

Li, Y., Ai, H., Huang, C., & Lao, S. (2006). Robust head tracking based on a multi-state particle filter. *Proceedings of Automatic Face & Gesture Recognition*, pp.335-340

Li, Y., Ai, H., Yamashita, T., Lao, S. & Kawade, M. (2007). Tracking in Low Frame Rate Video; A Cascade Particle Filter with Discriminative Observers of Different Lifespans. *Proceedings of International Conference on Computer Vision & Pattern Recognition.*

Mancas, M.; Gosselin, B. & Macq, B. (2007). A Three-Level Computational Attention Model. *Workshop on Computational Attention & Application in International Conference on Computer Vision Systems.*

Matsugu, M. & Cardon, P. (2004). Unsupervised feature selection for multi-class object detection using convolutional neural networks. *Advances in Neural Networks – ISNN 2004 International Symposium on Neural Networks, LNCS 3173,* 864-869, Springer, ISBN: 978-3-540-22841-7, Berlin

Matsugu, M., Mori, K. & Mitarai, Y. (2004). Convolutional Spiking Neural Network for Robust Object Detection with Population Code Using Structured Pulse Packets. *Neural Information Processing: Research and Development*, Rajapakse, J.C. & Wang, L. (Eds.), 39-55, Springer, ISBN: 3-540-21123-3, Berlin

Matsugu, M., Torii, K., Ito, Y., Hayashi, T. & Osaka, T. (2006). Face Tracking Active Vision System with Saccadic and Smooth Pursuit. *Proceedings of IEEE International Conference on Robotics and Biomimetics.*

Mitarai, Y., Mori, K. & Matsugu, M. (2003). Robust face detection system based on convolutional neural networks using selective activation of modules (In Japanese), *Proceedings of Forum in Information Technology*, pp. 191-193

Morioka, K., Kuroda, Y., Lee, J.-H. & Hashimoto, H. (2006). Multiple objects tracking based on auto-selection of color image processing methods. (in Japanese) *IEEJ Trans. EIS*, Vol. 126, No.2, 210-219

Murao, T. , Yamada, T. & Fujita, M. (2006). Predictive visual feedback control with eye-in-hand system via stabilizing receding horizon approach. *Proceedings of the 45th IEEE Conference on Decision and Control*, pp. 1758-1763

Murray, D. & Basu, A. (1994). Motion tracking with active camera. *IEEE Transactions on Pattern Analysis and Machine Intelligence*, Vol. 16, 449-459

Navalpakkam, V. & Itti, L. (2006). Top-down attention selection is fine grained. *Journal of Vision*, Vol. 6, 1180-1193, ISSN: 1534-7362

Olshausen, B.; Anderson, C.H. & Van Essen, D.C. (1995). A Multiscale Dynamic Routing Circuit for Forming Size- and Position-Invariant Object Representations. *Journal of Computational Neuroscience*, Vol. 2, 45-62, ISSN: 0929-5313

Papanikolopoulos, N. P., Khosla, P. K., & Kanade, T. (1993). Visual tracking of a moving object by a camera mounted on a robot. *IEEE Transactions on Robotics and Automation*, Vol. 9, 14-35

Porikli, F. (2005). Integral histogram: a fast way to extract histograms in Cartesian spaces. *Proceedings of International Conference on Computer Vision ond Pattern Recognition*, pp. 829 - 836

Porikli, F., Tuzel, O. & Meer, P. (2006) Covariance Tracking Using Model Update Based on Lie Algebra. *Proceedings of International Conference on Computer Vision ond Pattern Recognition*.

Rasmussen, C. & Hager, G. D. (2001). Probabilistic Data Association Methods for Tracking Complex Visual Objects. *IEEE Transactions on Pattern Analysis and Machine Intelligence*, Vol. 23, 560-576

Ribraic, S., Adrineck, G. & Segvic, S. (2004). Real-time active visual tracking system. *Proceedings of IEEE Mediterranean Electrotechnical Conference on Pattern Recognition*, pp. 231-234

Sigal, L., Zhu, Y., Comaniciu, D. & Black, M. (2004). Tracking Complex Objects Using Graphical Object Models. *Proceedings of 1st International Workshop on Complex Motion*, Springer- Verlag, Vol. LNCS 3417, pp. 227-238

Serby, D., Koller-Meier, E. & Van Gool, L. (2004). Probabilistic Object Tracking Using Multiple Features. *Proceedings of International Conference on Pattern Recognition*, pp. 184-187

Sun, Y. & Fisher, R. (2003). Object-based Visual Attentions for Computer Vision. *Artificial Intelligence*, Vol. 146, 77-123

Swain, M.J. & Ballard, D.H. (1991). Color Indexing. *International Journal of Computer Vision*, Vol. 7, 11-32

Swain, M.J., Kahn, R. & Ballard, D.H. (1992). Low Resolution Cues for Guiding Saccadic Eye Movements. *Proceedings of International Conference on Computer Vision and Pattern Recognition*, pp. 737-740

Viola, P. & Jones, M. (2001). Rapid Object Detection Using a Boosted Cascade of Simple Features. *Proceedings of IEEE Computer Vision on Pattern Recognition*

Yang, S., Li, S. Z., Pan, Q., Li, J. & Zhao, C. (2006). Reliable and fast tracking of faces under varying pose. *Proceedings of Automatic Face and Gesture Recognition,* pp.421-426

Yang, M., Yuan, J. & Wu, Y. (2007). Spatial selection for attentional visual tracking. *Proceedings of International Conference on Computer Vision and Pattern Recognition*

16

Parallel Processing System for Sensory Information Controlled by Mathematical Activation-Input-Modulation Model

Masahiko Mikawa[1], Takeshi Tsujimura[2], and Kazuyo Tanaka[1]
[1]*University of Tsukuba*
[2]*Nippon Telegraph and Telephone Corporation*
Japan

1. Introduction

It is required for intelligent robots like humanoid robots (AIST) (Honda) (tmsuk) (Ogura et al., 2006) to be equipped with several and many kinds of sensors for executing variety tasks. Especially, audio and visual information is important for these intelligent robots. In recent years, personal computers and audio and visual and devices improve their performance and their costs become cheaper. In lots of audition and vision systems, however, perceptual information obtained by external sensors is processed by procedures designed previously depending on their tasks or purposes. These kinds of perceptual information processing system are not suitable to use in dynamical and complex environments. Moreover, perceptual information is processed at full power regardless of use or non use. This wastes computer resources and electric power.

On the other hand, human beings have external and internal information processing systems that are flexible about dynamical and complex environments. External information is obtained by external sensory organs, and internal one means memories stored in a brain. External and internal information processing systems of a human being are in parallel and multi-layered. In philosophy, Freud proposed that there were three levels of human mind, that are conscious, preconscious and unconsciousness (Solms, 2004). In the unconsciousness state, internal and external information processing modules are executed independent of human intentions in parallel. In the preconsciousness state, information is stored as memories, which can be easily summon into consciousness. In the consciousness state, particular information is processed intentionally in serial. In physiology, cycle models between rapid eye movement (REM) sleep and non-REM sleep have been proposed (Hobson et al., 1986) (McCarley et al., 1995), and these models are relative to the unconsciousness. Moreover, Hobson has proposed the Activation-Input-Modulation (AIM) model that is able to express several statuses like waking and sleeping of human beings (Hobson, 2000). In visual neuroscience, five visual areas related to low level vision have been identified in visual cortex. Primitive image features, edges, forms, colors or motions, are processed in these visual areas, V1, V2, V3, V4 and V5, independently from each other in parallel. In the consciousness, moreover, several complex processing related to high level vision are also executed.

Memories of human beings also have important role in information processing in his/her brain. Memories are used as knowledge for processing external information when waking, and also they are processed when dreaming. Plural external and internal information processings run in parallel regardless of waking or sleep, and human beings control behaviors of these processings consciously or unconsciously and can process important information as needed. It is important for processing external information intellectually that the external information is stored as internal information in a memory system. The internal information is utilized as knowledge. It is known that a human has two kinds of memories: a working memory (WM) and a long-term memory (LTM) (Baddeley, 1982) (Klatzky, 1984). And a short-term memory (STM) is included in a concept of WM.

In the robotics and computer science fields, several memory models have been proposed for intelligent systems equipped with external sensory devices. A collaborative development system equipped with WMs for an interactive robot has been proposed by Matsusaka and Kobayashi (Matsusaka & Kobayashi, 2001). Functional modules for the interactive robot have working memories, that are used in their self modules or referred by other modules. Zhang and Knoll have developed two manipulator control system based on human instructions for interactive assembly tasks (Zhang & Knoll, 2002). This system includes functions of scene recognition, dialog preparation and action. Knowledge stored in STM is used in these functions. Kawamura and et al. have developed the humanoid called Intelligent Soft-Arm Control (ISAC), whose memory architecture consists of STM, LTM and the Working Memory System (WMS) (Kawamura, 2005) (Ratanaswasd et al., 2006) used for a human-robot interaction.

The purpose of our study is to develop an intelligent perceptual information processing system equipped with plural external sensory devices, in which plural information processing runs in parallel. One feature of our perceptual information processing system is that the system is equipped with our proposed mathematical Activation-Input-Modulation (AIM) model (Mikawa & Tsujimura, 2005) (Mikawa et al., 2006), which can express consciousness states such as waking, relaxing, Rapid Eye Movement (REM) sleep or non-REM sleep. The mathematical AIM model, that is newly designed based on Hobson's AIM model as described before, can control each execution frequency of plural external and internal information processors independently and dynamically based on degrees of external stimuli detected by external sensors. For example, when external stimuli are detected by some of external sensors, information processing tasks related to the sensors should have a priority to be executed in real-time, and the stimuli are stored in a memory system. When no external stimulus is detected, the execution frequencies of almost external information processing decrease, and information stored in the memory system is organized by internal information processors. The other feature is that our system is equipped with the three kinds of memories: WM, STM and LTM. All perceptual information is stored in the WM for a few seconds at all times. When external stimuli are detected by some of external sensory devices, the contents of the WM included the stimulus information move into the STM temporarily. After no external stimulus is detected, all external information processors sleep, and internal information processors begin to organize information stored in the STM and move important information into the LTM and stored permanently. These behaviors are also controlled based on the state of the mathematical AIM model as well as the external processing. In this chapter, we use both a multi channel microphone a stereo vision system as the external sensory devices. Since auditory external stimuli are detected by using both amplitude and frequency characteristics, several audio information can be stored in the memory system. Some experimental results reveal the validity and effectiveness of our proposed perceptual information processing system.

2. AIM state-space model

We describe the Activation-Input-Modulation (AIM) state-space model that has been proposed by Hobson (Hobson, 2000 & 2001), that is the origin of our proposed mathematical AIM model, in this section. The AIM state-space model is able to express several states of human's consciousness in a three dimensional space as shown in Fig. 1. He describes that human's consciousness states are able to express by levels of three elements, Activation, Input and Modulation of which the AIM model consists. Activation controls an amount of information which is being processed. Input switches information sources. Where, External means that information is obtained from external sensory organs, and Internal means that it is obtained from internal sources such as a memory in a brain. Modulation switches external and internal processing modes. When an aminergic level becomes higher, external information is mainly processed. When a cholinergic level becomes higher, internal information is mainly processed.

For example, it is able to express normal states of waking, relaxing, rapid eye movement (REM) sleep and non-REM sleep in a three dimensional space as shown in Fig. 1. It can also express abnormal mental conditions such as coma, hallucination or deliration. In the waking, external information is processed actively. In the relaxing, processing power is less than that in the waking. In REM sleep, internal information stored in a memory is processed actively. In non-REM sleep, input and output gates are closed and the processing power declines totally. When a normal person falls asleep, at first the sleeper enters non-REM sleep, which is a deep sleep. After the first non-REM, he/she enters REM sleep and non-REM sleep alternately until he/she awakes naturally or large stimuli interrupt the sleep. As mentioned, a consciousness state of normal human moves along the gray line as shown in Fig. 1.

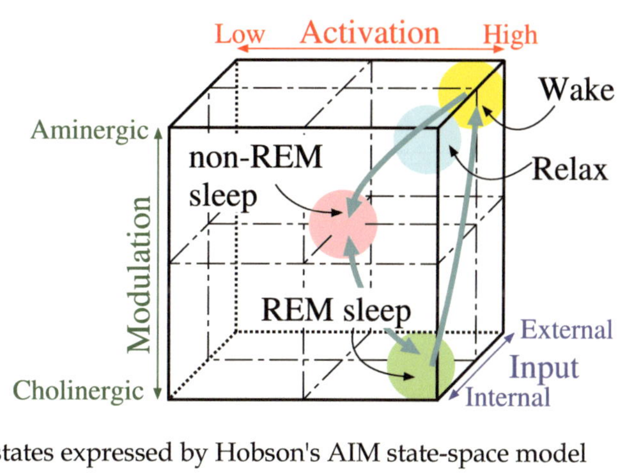

Fig. 1. Conscious states expressed by Hobson's AIM state-space model

3. Perceptual information processing system and mathematical AIM model

3.1 External and internal information processing systems

Figure 2 shows a relation among external and internal information processing systems, a mathematical AIM model and an internal memory system. One set of an external information processing system consists of an external sensor device, a data sampler and external information processors. It is important for the external information processing system that data obtained by the external sensor device is processed in real-time and translates to meaningful information as soon as possible. A number of the external information processing systems depends on a number of external sensor devices and required tasks.

An internal information processing system consists of memory storing processors, a data sampler and an internal information processor. In the internal information processing, following kinds of data are treated. One is a kind of data that it is difficult to process in real-time, because it takes much time to process it. Another is what it is not necessary to process in real-time. The third is lots of data such as time-series data that must be processed all together.

Information obtained by external sensors is stored by memory storing processors in an internal memory, and also utilized by the internal information processors. This internal memory system is described in the subsection 3.4.

Each execution interval of external and internal samplers or processors is controlled by the mathematical AIM model independently and dynamically. The details are described in the subsections 3.2 and 3.3.

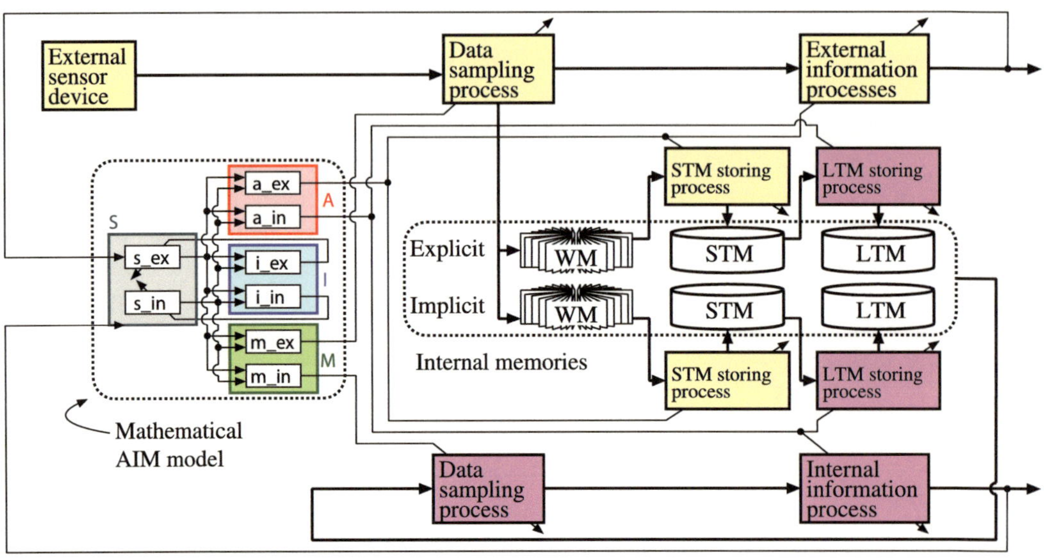

Fig. 2. Relation among external and internal information processing system, mathematical AIM model and internal memory system

3.2 Mathematical AIM model

We have designed the mathematical AIM model based on the AIM state-space model described in the section 2. As shown in Fig. 1, several conscious states of human beings are able to be expressed by levels of three elements: Activation, Input and Modulation. Activation controls an amount of information which is being processed. Input switches information sources. Modulation switches external and internal processing modes.

The mathematical AIM model controls each execution interval of the external and internal data samplers, the information processors and the memory storing processors. The AIM model consists of elements *S*, *A*, *I* and *M*. The element *S* calculates stimuli based on sampled data. The element *A* decides execution frequencies of external and internal information processing and memory storing processing. The element *I* decides parameters used for calculating stimuli in the element *S*. The element *M* decides an execution frequency of each data sampling. Each element consists of two sub-elements as shown in Fig. 2. The subscript *ex* or *in* of the sub-elements *a*, *i* and *m* means that each sub-element is related to the external or internal respectively.
Figure 3 shows an example of variations of the sub-elements with time. Statuses of each sub-element change depending on external stimulus. When the detected external stimulus *sm_ex* is larger than the threshold th_s ($sm\_ex \geq th_s$), the levels of the elements related to the external are higher than those related to the internal. After the external stimulus becomes lower than the threshold ($sm\_ex < th_s$) at t_0 , the state is shifted the relaxing. The relaxing is kept while the external stimuli are detected by the other processes run in parallel are larger than the threshold ($sm'\_ex \geq th'_s$). All the levels of the external stimuli become lower than the threshold ($sm\_ex < th_s$ and $sm'\_ex < th'_s$) at the time t_3 . After T_a [sec], all the levels become lower, then the state is shifted to the non-REM. Moreover after T_n [sec], each level increases and decreases periodically. In the REM, the levels of the elements related to the internal are higher than those related to the external. Once again the external stimulus *sm_ex* becomes larger than the threshold th_s at the time t_7 , the state is shifted to the waking.

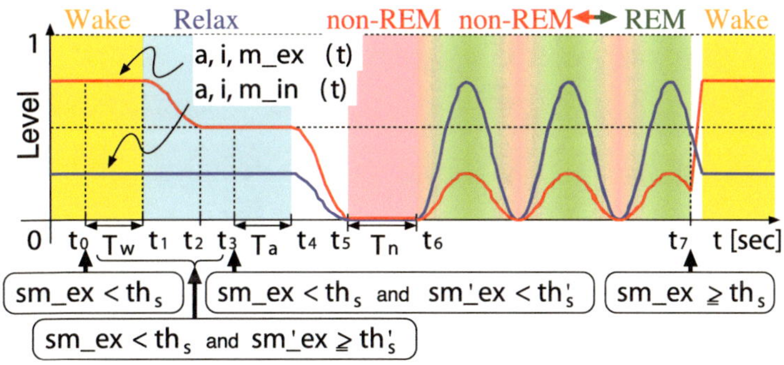

Fig. 3. Variations of sub-elements *A*, *I* and *M* with time

The sub-element *a_ex(t)* is given by the following equations.

$$a\_ex(t) = \begin{cases} L_w + b & (t < t_1) \\ \frac{L_w - L_a}{2}\left(1 + \cos(\frac{2\pi(t-t_1)}{f_w})\right) + L_a + b & (t_1 \leq t < t_2) \\ L_a + b & (t_2 \leq t < t_4) \\ \frac{L_a - L_n}{2}\left(1 + \cos(\frac{2\pi(t-t_4)}{f_a})\right) + L_n + b & (t_4 \leq t < t_5) \\ L_n + b & (t_5 \leq t < t_6) \\ \frac{o_r}{2}\left(1 - \cos(\frac{2\pi(t-t_6)}{f_r})\right) + L_n + b & (t \geq t_6) \end{cases} \quad (1)$$

Since it is able to express the other sub-elements in the same way, their equations are omitted here. The parameter T_w , T_a , T_n , L_w , L_a , L_n , f_w , f_a , f_r , o_r and b are constant and independent each other. It is able to design several sleep patterns by choosing these constant parameters properly depending on applications. For example, the sleep pattern shown in Fig. 3 was designed based on a human's normal sleep pattern by using the following values. In other words, it is designed that the state of the mathematical AIM model moves along the gray line as shown in Fig. 1.

$$L_w = 0.75, \quad L_a = 0.50, \quad o_r = 0.25, \quad L_n = b = 0.00 \tag{2}$$

Let the numbers of the external information processors, the internal information processors, the external sensory organs and the internal memories be *p_ex* , *p_in* , *q_ex* and *q_in* respectively, then the elements *A*, *I* and *M* are shown by the following equations. The AIM model shown in Fig. 1 can be expressed by these equations. Figure 4 shows the variations of these elements with time. This example was designed based on a human's normal sleep pattern.

$$\begin{aligned} A(t) &= \frac{1}{2p_{ex}}\sum_{i=1}^{p_{ex}} a\_ex_i(t) + \frac{1}{2p_{in}}\sum_{j=1}^{p_{in}} a\_in_j(t) \\ I(t) &= \frac{1}{p_{ex}}\sum_{i=1}^{p_{ex}} i\_ex_i(t) - \frac{1}{p_{in}}\sum_{j=1}^{p_{in}} i\_in_j(t) \\ M(t) &= \frac{1}{q_{ex}}\sum_{i=1}^{q_{ex}} m\_ex_i(t) - \frac{1}{q_{in}}\sum_{j=1}^{q_{in}} m\_in_j(t) \end{aligned} \tag{3}$$

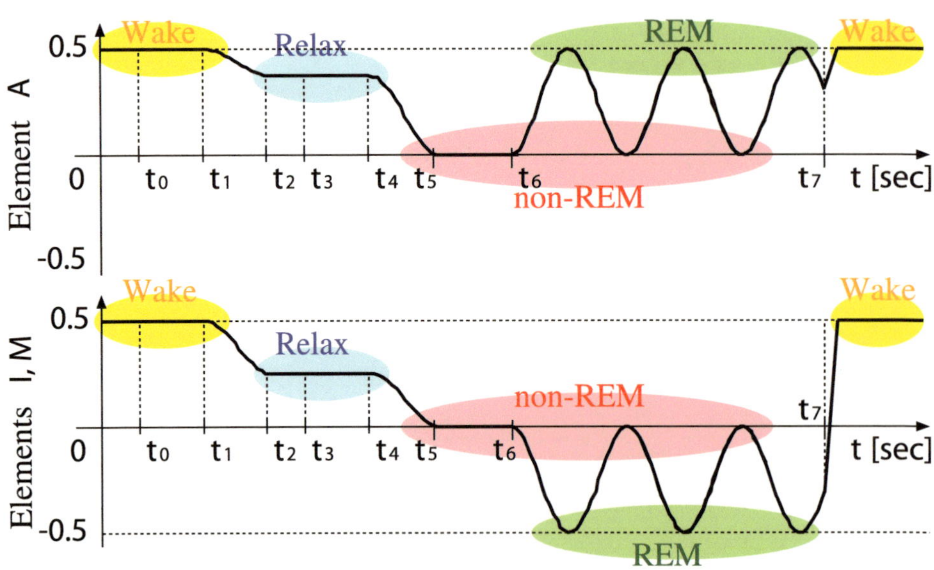

Fig. 4. Variations of elements *A*, *I* and *M* with time

3.3 Dynamic control of information processing systems by mathematical AIM model

Behaviors of the external and internal information processing systems and the memory system are controlled based on the states of the sub-elements of the AIM model as shown in Fig. 2.

The execution frequencies of the external and internal information processing are determined in proportion to each level of the sub-elements *a_ex* and *a_in*, respectively. For example, when *a_ex* becomes higher, the external information processing frequency increases. As a result, more external information is processed. When *a_in* becomes higher, the internal information processing frequency increases. In the same way, the external and internal data sampling frequencies are determined by the sub-elements of M. The element I decides the threshold th_s and the resolution rs_s in order for the element S to detect stimuli from the external sensors or the internal memories. Here, the thresholds th_s are values for determining whether stimuli are included in obtained information or not. And the resolution means a number of skipped data to be processed in a frame. These thresholds and resolutions vary in proportion to each level of the sub-elements *i_ex* and *i_in*. For example, when *i_ex* increases, th_s and rs_s increases. This means that the system becomes more sensitive about smaller changes.

The storing frequencies of the explicit and implicit WM are the same with the frequency of the external data sampling and depend on the level of the sub-element *m_ex*. When external stimuli are detected ($sm\_ex \geq th_s$), the explicit STM processor transfers information stored in the explicit WM to the explicit STM. Its execution frequency depends on *m_ex*. When no stimulus is detected ($sm\_ex < th_s$), the implicit STM processor transfers information stored in the implicit WM to the implicit STM periodically. When the state of the AIM model is in the REM sleep, the explicit and implicit LTM processors are executed.

3.4 Internal memory system

A memory system of human beings is so complex and not unrevealed yet completely. So we have designed a new internal memory system by rearranging a part of human's memory functions. As shown in Fig. 2, the internal memory system consists of an internal memory and memory storing processors. The internal memory consists of working memories (WMs), short-term memories (STMs) and long-term memories (LTMs). Each memory is classified into an explicit or implicit type respectively. When dynamic changes are detected as external stimuli by an external sensor, the changes are stored in the explicit memories. Gradual changes that are not detected by real-time information processing or static information are stored in the implicit ones. In the case of human beings, perceptual information is symbolized by high-order functions of a brain and stored in memories efficiently. In our system, however, let raw signals obtained by external sensory devices store in the internal memory.

All information obtained by external sensory devices are stored in these WMs in real-time. Let memory size of the WMs have an upper limit, old information is overwritten by newer one sequentially. Since an explicit STM is a memory in consciousness states, when external stimuli are detected by external sensory devices, all the contents of the explicit WM are transferred into the explicit STM. Since an implicit STM is a memory in unconsciousness states, when no external stimulus is detected, all the contents of the implicit WM are transferred into the implicit STM periodically. Human being's LTM is classified into a procedural or declarative type (Kellogg, 1995), and its functions are complex. Redundant or useless information are included in the STM. Then the contents of the STM are organized

and transferred into the LTM by the LTM storing processors. When no external stimulus is detected and the state of the mathematical AIM model is in REM sleep, the AIM model starts to execute these LTM storing processors. Since the explicit STM and LTM storing processes detect external stimuli, dynamical information is stored in the explicit memories. Since the implicit STM storing process stores information periodically while no external stimulus is detected, the implicit LTM storing process is able to detect static or gradual changes and store the changes in the implicit LTM by analyzing the implicit STM stored for long period.
Let the memory capacities of the explicit and implicit WMs be N_{wm} [frame] respectively. There is no limit to the capacity of the STMs and LTMs as far as the system permits.

4. Experimental system

4.1 System configuration

Figure 5 shows a configuration of an audition and vision system. This system is equipped with two CCD cameras and a stereo electret condenser microphone, that are fixed in an experimental room. Analog video signals are converted to digital video (DV) signals through media converters, and captured by a personal computer (PC) through an IEEE 1394 interface board. Audio signals are captured by the PC through a USB audio interface. The operation system (OS) of the PC is Fedora Core Linux, and the versions of the OS and the other libraries are also shown in Fig. 5.

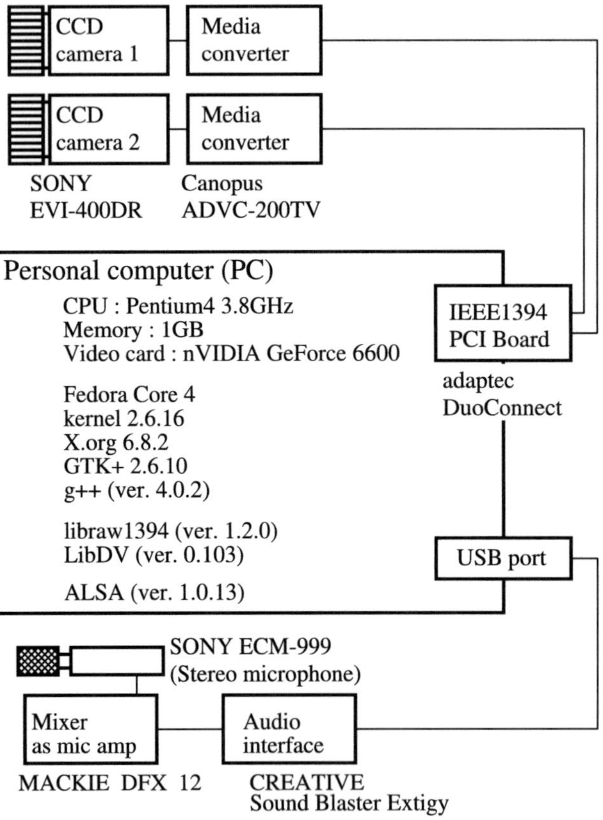

Fig. 5. Configuration of experimental audition and vision system

4.2 Multi-threaded application program

We made an application program to evaluate a validity of our proposed perceptual information processing system. The application programming interface (API) developed in (Mikawa, 2003) was used for implementing the program. It is able to capture audio and video signals from plural audition and vision devices in real-time. Color images were captured at a frequency of 1/30 [sec], and the resolution was 720 x 480 [pixel] with 8 [bit] per each color. A sampling rate of stereo audio signals was 44.1 [kHz], a bit depth was 16 [bit], and one frame length was 100 [msec]. Plural external and internal processes run in parallel are multi-threaded by using this API.

Figure 6 shows all the threads and their relations. As shown in Fig. 5, video capturing, DV decoding, image displaying and AIM state calculating processes, external and internal information processes were multi-threaded by using the API. The execution intervals of the video and audio capture threads are constant, their values are 1/30 and 1/10 [sec] respectively. These capture threads send commands to the other threads. The execution intervals of the decode threads are decided by the element M. The execution intervals of the external and internal information processing threads are decided by the element A.

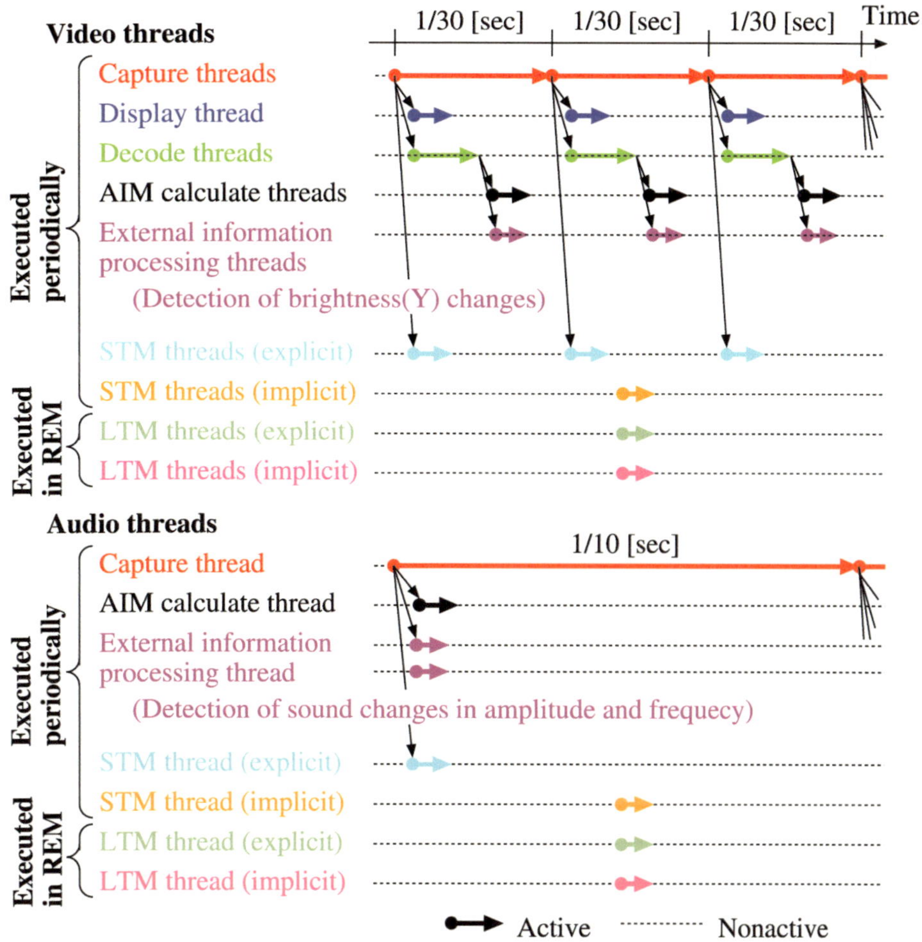

Fig. 6. Threads implemented in application program

Two kinds of the external stimuli are detected by the external information processing threads related to the vision and audio. One is brightness changes of captured image. Brightness is Y component of color images, and the changes are detected by comparing each pixel included in two time-series image frames. The other is magnitude of captured sound. The value of th_s related to images changes from 80 to 200 depending on the value of the sub-element i_ex. The value of th_s related to audio signals changes from 600 to 2000.
The explicit and implicit WMs storing processes are included in the audio and video capturing threads. The explicit STM storing processes are executed when brightness changes are detected. Let the capacities of the WMs related to vision be N_{wm} = 99 [frame]. The WMs can hold image frames for 3 [sec]. And let the capacities of the WMs related to audition be N_{wm} = 50 [frame]. The WMs can hold audio frames for 5 [sec]. The STMs related to vision are stored in DV format, of which size are 12000 [byte/frame], in a hard disk drive (HDD). The LTMs related to vision are converted by the LTM storing processes and stored in YUV format. The WMs, STMs and LTMs related to audio are stored in WAVE format.
The implicit STM storing threads are constantly executed at a frequency of 1 [sec] in all states of the AIM model, and store captured image in the HDD. When $sm\_ex \geq th_s$, the explicit STM storing process transfers all the explicit WMs to the HDD as the explicit STM. This means that the last 99 image frames can be stored. When $sm\_ex < th_s$, the implicit STM storing threads constantly stores captured frames in the HDD as the implicit STM. And the explicit and implicit LTM storing threads are executed in the REM sleep.When the system is in the REM sleep ($a\_in \geq 0.375$), the explicit and implicit LTM storing threads are executed, and store vision and audio frames, in which changes are detected by comparing each pixel included in two time-series STMs. This means that only images, that include dynamic changes for brief periods of time, are stored in the explicit LTM, and only images, that include gradual changes for long periods, are stored in the implicit LTM.
The following values and Eqs. (2) were used for the constant parameters included in the AIM model as shown by Eq. (1). Each unit is second. These values determine the pace of change from one state of the AIM model to another state.

$$T_w = T_a = T_n = 5, \quad f_w = f_a = 20, \quad f_r = 60 \tag{4}$$

Figure 7 shows a screen shot of the application program. The resolution of the display was 1600 x 1200 [pixel]. Since no external stimulus was detected by the camera 1, the conscious state related to the camera 1 was in the relaxing. Since some external stimuli indicated in purple were detected by the camera 2, the camera 2 was in the waking. It is determined whether brightness change is more than the threshold th_s or less at each green points. In this application, the resolution rs_s described in the subsection 3.3 means the distance among green points. In the waking, all pixels in the image function as sensors for detecting external stimuli, and every captured image frames are processed. Moreover, as the threshold th_s decreases, the sensitivity to stimuli increases. The distance among green points becomes largest in the non-REM, the process execution frequency becomes lowest, the threshold th_s increases, and as a result, the sensitivity to stimuli decreases. The audio threads are executed in the same manner.

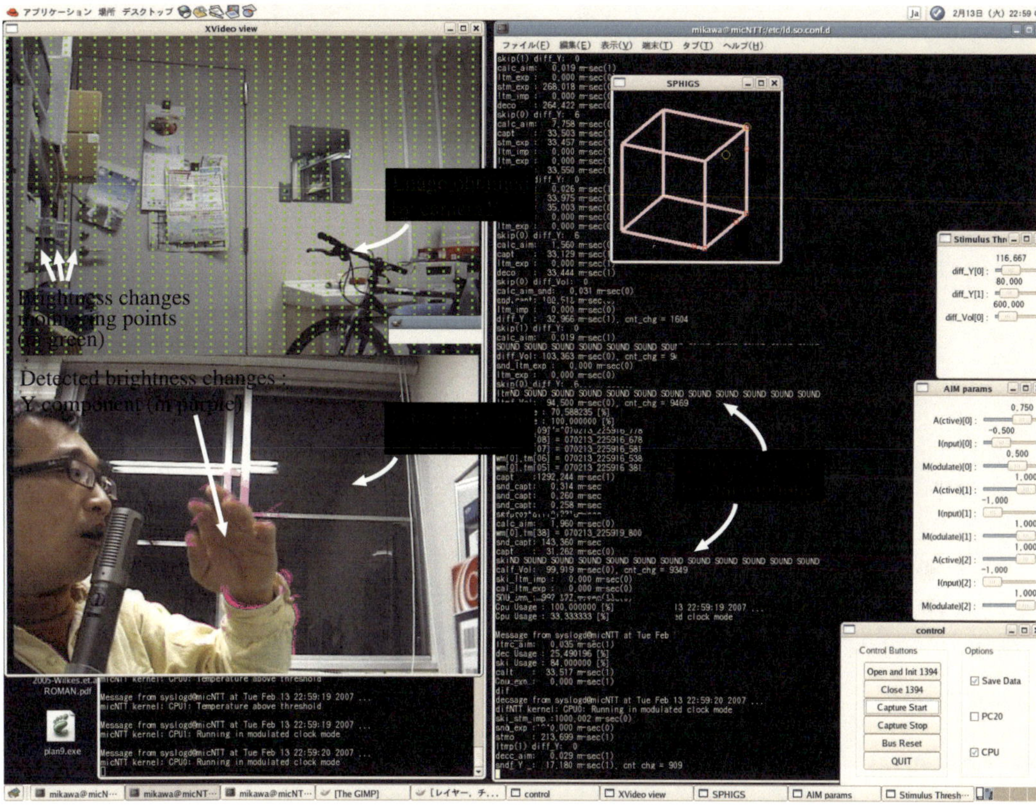

Fig. 7. Screen shot of sample application in waking & relaxing

5. Experimental results

5.1 Simplest application program processes only external information using monocular camera

We describe an expeiment result using a simplest application program to show the effectiveness of our proposed mathematical AIM model. This application program had the only external information processing using only one CCD camera, no internal information processing and no memory such as WMs, STMs and LTMs. Brightness changes were detected as external stimuli in an external information processing as shown in Fig. 8. Pentium 4 (2.4 [GHz]) and Red Hat Linux 9, that had no Hyper-Threading (HT) function, were used only in this experiment.

Figure 9 shows the variation of the CPU utilization with time while the program was running. In the waking, image data was processed in real-time (30 [frame/sec]), as the result, the CPU utilization was more than 90 [%]. After the change of image, in other words, stimuli from external information had disappeared at the time t_0, the CPU utilization fell around 15 [%] in the relaxing. After another T_n [sec], it fell below 10 [%] in the non-REM sleep. In the REM sleep, it became around 15 [%]. When the change of image was detected again at the time t_7, the external information processing began to be executed in real-time again. The function of the AIM model makes it possible to make a margin of the CPU power for other processing while no external stimulus is present.

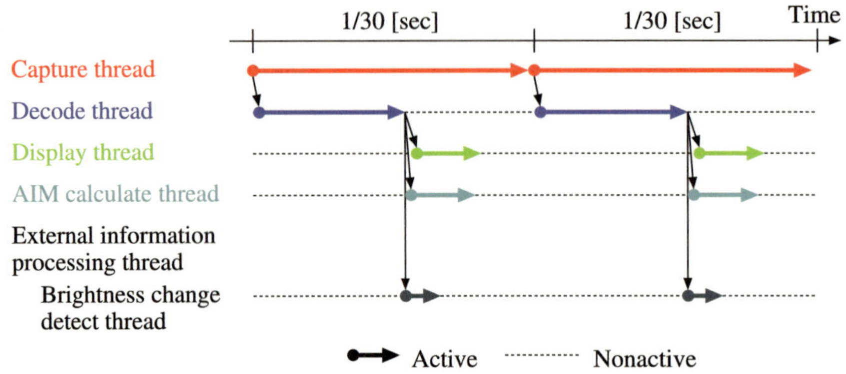

Fig. 8. Variation of CPU utilization with time

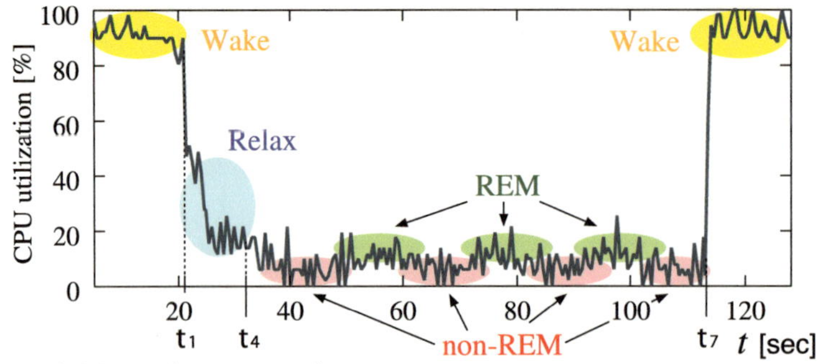

Fig. 9. Variation of CPU utilization with time

5.2 Execution of application program for brief period

In this experiment, the application program, that has several threads shown in Fig. 6, was executed for about 170 [sec] in order to confirm the behaviors of all threads run in parallel.

Figure 10 shows the variations of the execution intervals of all the threads related to the camera 1, the camera 2 and the microphone. The camera 2 detected external stimuli in a period of 0 ~ 25 [sec]. The states of the camera 1 and the microphone were shifted to the relaxing at 15 [sec]. When the microphone detected external stimuli at 35 [sec], the state of the microphone was shifted to the waking and the states of the camera 1 and 2 were shifted to the relaxing. After no external stimulus was detected at 40 [sec], the states of the both cameras and the microphone were shifted to the sleep state, that REM/non-REM cycle was repeated periodically, through the relaxing. In the REM sleep, the frequency of the external information processing became lower, and the explicit and implicit LTM storing processes were executed. Here, the explicit and implicit LTM are not executed periodically but depending on the status of the AIM model. When the execution intervals of the explicit and implicit LTMs indicate non 0 [sec] respectively, it just means that they are executed and the values mean nothing. And when the execution intervals indicate 0 [sec], it means that they are not executed. When the microphone detected external stimuli again at 145 [sec], the microphone was shifted to the waking, and the camera 1 and 2 were shifted to the relaxing.

Figure 11 shows the variation of the CPU utilization with time. Since a HT CPU was used, the numbers of the CPUs was two. Although changes of the CPU utilization were more complex than that using the non-HT CPU in the previous subsection 5.1, this result showed that the function of the AIM model could control plural threads run in parallel well, and make effective use of computer resources.

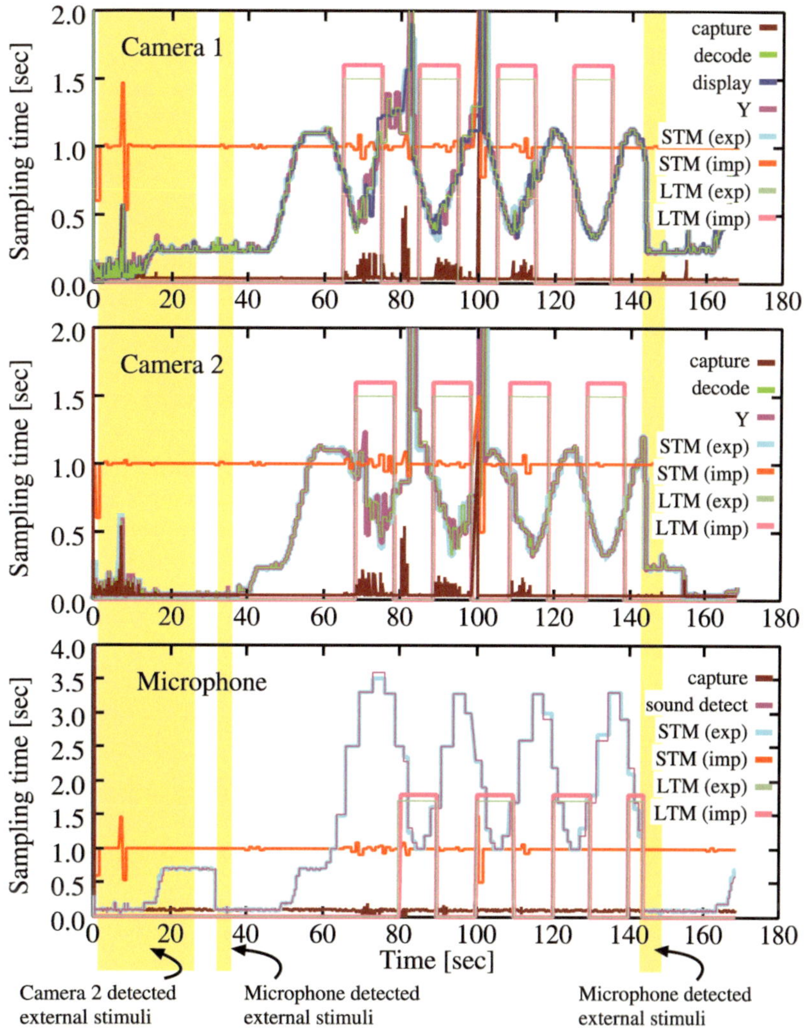

Fig. 10. Variation of execution interval of all threads with time

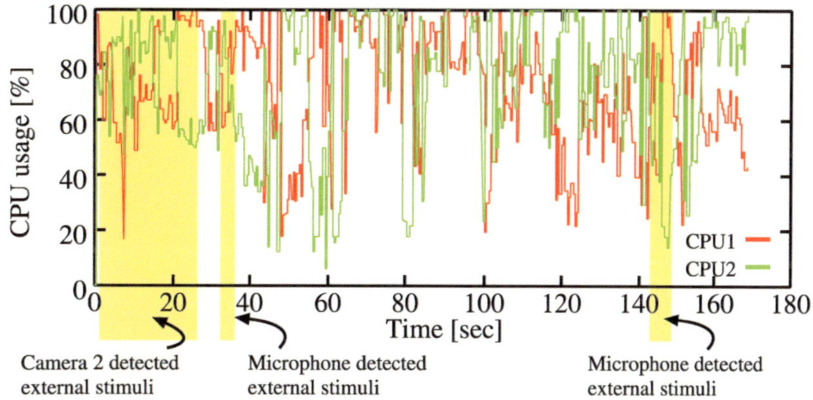

Fig. 11. Variation of CPU utilization with time

Table 1 shows the numbers of audio and image files stored as the memories while the application program was executed. These results mean that the memory system related to the camera 2 and the microphone can store dynamic stimuli detected for brief periods of time in the explicit memories, and that related to the camera 1 can store gradual changes over long periods of time in the implicit memories.

devices	STM		LTM	
	explicit	implicit	explicit	implicit
camera 1	14	168	7	1
camera 2	805	148	646	3
microphone	313	160	157	3

Table 1. Numbers of image and audio frames stored as STM and LTM

5.3 Execution of application program for long period of 12 hours

The application program was executed for about 12 [hour] in this experiment. The camera 1 was trained on a door in an experimental room in order to monitor person who came in and out. The camera 2 was trained on a window in the room in order to monitor gradual changes of outdoor conditions.

Figure 12 shows a part of the explicit LTM stored in the HDD. When these dynamical changes were detected as external stimuli, the system state was shifted to the waking, and the changes were stored in the explicit STM. When the system was shifted to the REM, the explicit STM was transferred to the explicit LTM while deleting redundant images.

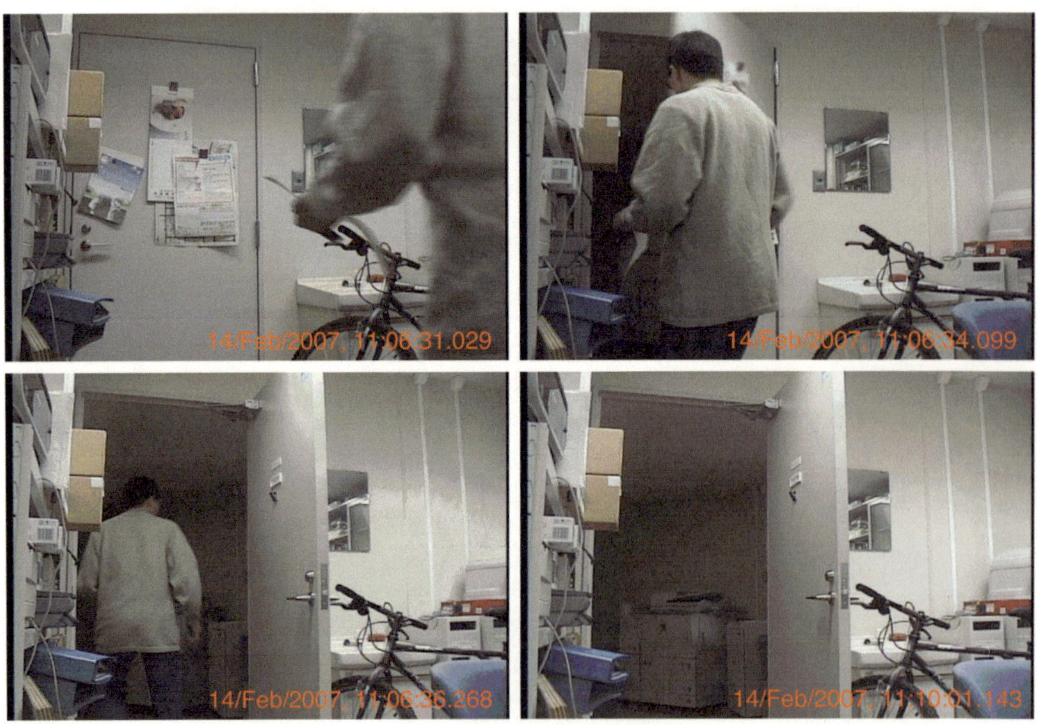

Fig. 12. Dynamic change for brief period detected by explicit LTM storing process

Figure 13 shows a part of the stored implicit LTM. Gradual changes of a sunset sky could by detected. Although it is difficult to detect these kinds of gradual changes by the explicit memories that is processed in real-time, it is easy to detect them by using the implicit memories. Since the explicit memories related to the microphone monitored amplitude of sound signals, large sound generated in the experimental room could be detected. Since the implicit memories monitored frequency characteristic changes of sound signals, not only amplitude changes but also changes of different kinds of small sounds, for example engine sound of a motorcycle or talking voice outside the experimental room, could be detected.

Fig. 13. Gradual brightness changes of sunset sky detected by implicit LTM storing process

These results also indicates that our perceptual system controlled by the AIM model works well.

6. Conclusion

We proposed a new architecture for an intelligent perceptual information processing system that has sleep and wake functions, and applied it to an audition and vision system. Plural perceptual information processes and storing processes run in parallel and these processes are controlled by the mathematical Activation-Input-Modulation (AIM) model. The memory architecture consists of a working memory (WM), a short-term memory (STM) and a long-term memory (LTM), that can store environment information in its memories efficiently. The advantage of our proposed architecture is that required processes are executed only when needed and only useful perceptual information are stored. As a result, the system is able to make effective use of computer resources.

The validity and effectiveness of our proposed system were confirmed with three kinds of experimental results using an application program equipped with a monocular vision system or a stereo vision and a stereo microphone system.

In future works, we will try to use more kinds and numbers of sensors and implement more kinds of information processing modules in this system.

7. References

Baddeley, A. (1982). Your Memory: A Users Guide, Macmillan Publishing Co..

Hobson, J. A.; Lydic, R. & Baghdoyan, H. (1986). Evolving Concepts of Sleep Cycle Generation: From Brain Centers to Neuronal Populations, Behavioral and Brain Sciences, Vol. 9, No. 3, pp. 371-448.

Hobson, J. A.; Pace-Schott, E. F. & Stickgold, R. (2000). Dreaming and the brain: Toward a cognitive neuroscience of conscious states, Behavioral and Brain Sciences, Vol. 23, No. 6, pp. 793-842.

Hobson, J. A. (2001). Consciousness, W. H. Freeman & Co..

Hobson, J. A. (2001). The Dream Drugstore, The MIT Press.

Honda Motor Co., Ltd., ASIMO, http://world.honda.com/ASIMO/index.html.

Klatzky, L. (1984). Memory and Awareness: An Information-Processing Perspective, W. H. Freeman & Co.

Kellogg, R. T. (1995). Cognitive Psychology, Sage Publications, Inc..

Kawamura, K. (2005). Cognitive approach to a human adaptive robot development, Proceedings of the 14th IEEE International Workshop on Robot and Human Interactive Communication, pp. 629-634, Aug 2005, Nashville.

Matsusaka, Y. & Kobayashi, T. (2001). System Software for Collaborative Development of Interactive Robot, Proceedings of the IEEE-RAS International Conference on Humanoid Robots, pp. 271-277, Nov 2001, Tokyo.

McCarley, R. W.; Greene, R. W.; Rainnie, D. & Portas, C. M. (1995). Brainstem Neuromodulation and REM Sleep, Seminars in The Neurosciences, Vol. 7, No. 5, pp. 341-354.

Mikawa, M. (2003). A Programming Interface for IEEE 1394 Video Device in Robot Vision, SICE Annual Conference 2003: Proceedings, pp. 2132-2137, Aug 2003, Fukui.

Mikawa, M. & Tsujimura, T. (2005). Sleep and Wake Control System Based On Mathematical AIM model, SICE Annual Conference 2005: Proceedings, pp. 2550-2555, Aug 2005, Okayama.

Mikawa, M.; Yoshikawa, M & Tsujimura, T. (2006). Memory System Controlled by Mathematical AIM Model for Robot Vision Equipped with Sleep and Wake Functions, SICE-ICASE International Joint Conference 2006, pp. 2272-2277, Oct 2006, Busan.

National Institute of Advanced Industrial Science and Technology (AIST), HRP-2, http://www.is.aist.go.jp/humanoid/index.html.

Ogura, Y.; Aikawa, H.; Shimomura, K.; Kondo, H.; Morishima, A.; Hun-ok Lim & Takanishi. (2006). Development of a new humanoid robot WABIAN-2, *Proceedings 2006 IEEE International Conference on Robotics and Automation*, pp. 76-81, ISBN 0-7803-9505-0, May 2006, Orlando.

Ratanaswasd, P.; Garber, C. and Lauf, A. (2006). Situation-Based Stimuli Response in a Humanoid Robot, Proceedings of the Fifth International Conference on Development and Learning, May 2006, Bloomington.

Solms, M. (2004). Freud Returns, *Scientific American*, Vol. 290, No. 5, pp. 56-63.

tmsuk Co., Ltd., KIYOMORI, http://kiyomori.jp/main.html.

Zhang, J. & Knoll, A. (2002). Control Architecture and Experiment of A Situated Robot System for Interactive Assembly, Proceedings of the 2002 IEEE International Conference on Robotics & Automation, pp. 3906-3911, May 2005, Washington DC.

17

Development of Pilot Assistance System with Stereo Vision for Robot Manipulation

Takeshi Nishida[1], Shuichi Kurogi[1], Koichi Yamanaka[1],
Wataru Kogushi[1] and Yuichi Arimura[2]
[1]*Kyushu Institute of Technology*
[2]*tmsuk co., LTD*
Japan

1. Introduction

Recently, the rescue robots called "T-52 Enryu" and "T-53 Enryu"(Fig. 1) that aimed at the rescue operation in danger zone such as disaster district etc. (Fig. 2) have been developed. The robots have two airms with eight DOFs for execution of various tasks, and it can be operated remotely in order to achieve the tasks such as removal, mining, and so on without sending the pilot to a dangerous place (Yokokohji, 2006). However, these operations were difficult at the beginning of development of the robot because there was not any pilot assistance system, and time for a great deal of training was necessary (Nishida et al. 2006). Namely, the pilot had to understand a situation of surrounding of the robot from a few monitors that display the images of the cameras installed in the robot. Thus, because an assistance system to help the understanding of the positions of target objects had been necessary to improve the efficiency of the remote operation of the robot, we have developed a vision system that assists the pilot by tracking multiple targets and intelligibly presenting them.

In the development of this pilot assistance system, we had to note following matters. Namely, we considered the simplicity of employment and maintenance, and the cost of devices. Moreover, since scenery consists of the achromatic color objects such as sand and rubble by many cases at place of the rescue operation, the measurement and the calibration of the system should be appropriately executed without the color information. Furthermore, since the vision system equipped on the gripper, the system should be robust to the vibration caused by the movement of the arm. Thus, we had developed a fast executable stereovision system robust against vibration of the arm without using the color information and easy to understand for the pilot. The system consists of a parallel stereo camera equipped on the gripper joint of the right arm and a laptop PC, and they were installed into the Enryus.

The remainder of this chapter is divided into the following topics: Section 2 describes the structure of the pilot assistance system. Section 3 describes a calibration method of the system robust for environmental change. Section 4 details interfaces of the system for displaying the results of target tracking and distance measurement, and finally Section 5 discusses the overall implementation and successful application of the robot.

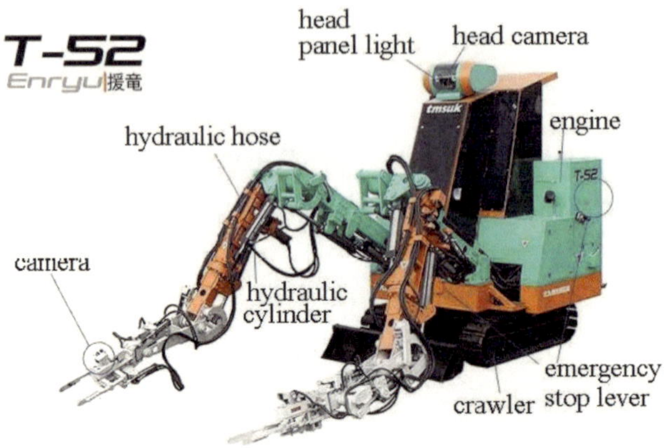

(a)

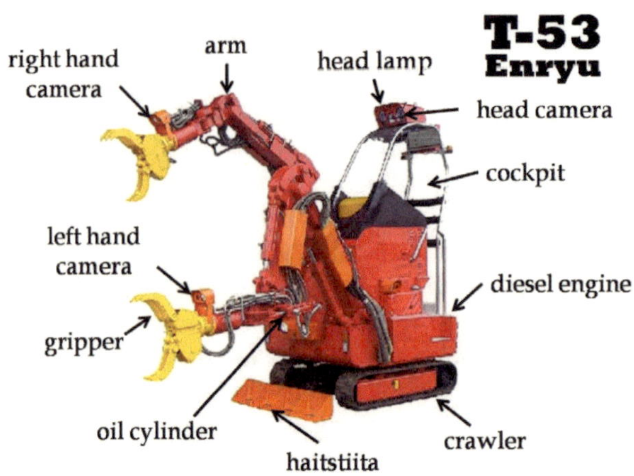

(b)

Fig. 1. Rescue robots: (a) T-52 Enryu, height: 3.45 [m], width: 2.4 [m], length: 3.5 [m] (maximum length: 10 [m]), weight: 5 [t]; and (b) T-53 Enryu, height: 2.3 [m], width: 1.4 [m] (maximum length: 7.23[m]), length: 2.32 [m], weight: 2.9 [t].

(a) T-52

(b) T-53

Fig. 2. Appearances of the activity of the robots in disaster district.

2. Parallel stereo camera system

Two kinds of camera systems and those applications were developed. One is a suite of fixed parallel cameras and a 3D motion sensor (Fig. 3(a)), and another is a suite of parallel cameras and a camera mount for adjusting the installation angles and positions of them (Fig. 3 (b)). The former called "A-system" was composed to verify what visual application is effective to support of the pilot; the latter called "B-system" was developed to examine installation position and effective calibration method on the actual robot arm.

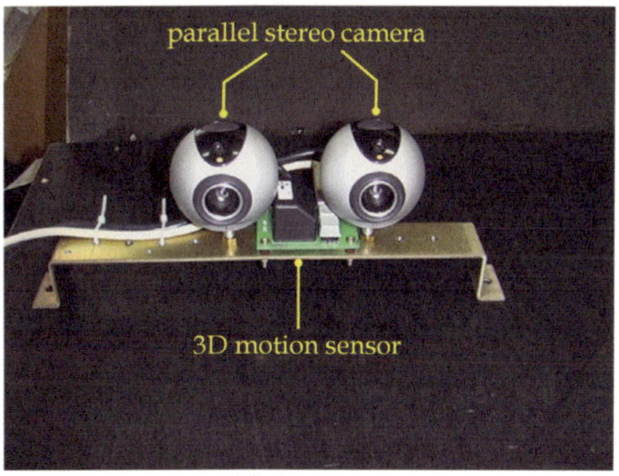

(a) A-system

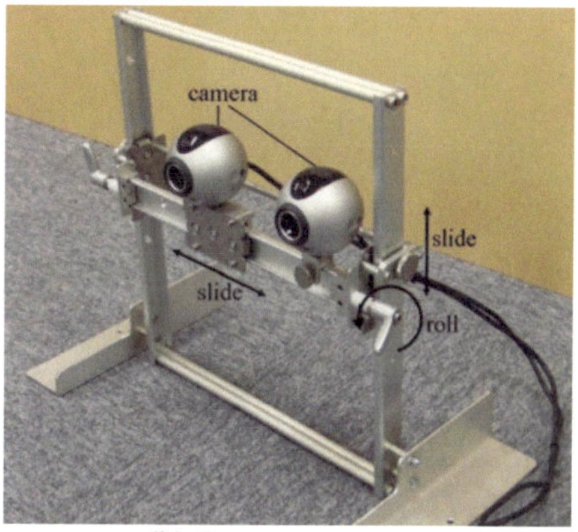

(b) B-system

Fig. 3. Developed parallel stereo camera systems: (a) A-system consists of fixed parallel USB cameras and a motion sensor; (b) B-system consists of parallel USB cameras and a camera mount for adjusting the installation angles and positions.

We selected the inexpensive USB cameras (QV-400R, USB CCD camera) and motion sensor in order to simplify the replacement of them even if breaking down by severe work in outdoor environment. This suite of camera system is mounted on a joint of gripper as shown in Fig. 4 (a) and (b), and they are connected to a laptop PC installed in the robot. The obtained images are transmitted to a remote control cockpit via wireless LAN for supplying the information around the right gripper and the image processing results (Fig. 5).

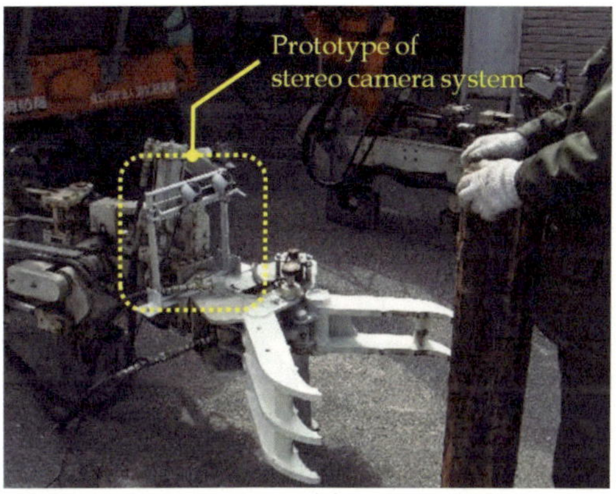

(a)

(b)

Fig. 4. Installation of the system: (a) the system mounted on the right gripper of T-52; (b) the system mounted on the right gripper of T-53.

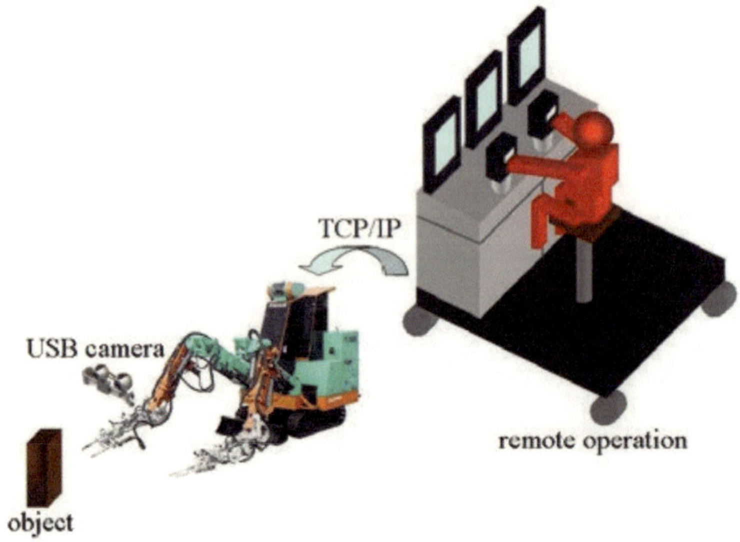

Fig. 5. Whole structure of the system. The pilot operates the robot remotely by watching plural monitors and using joysticks etc.

3. Calibration of the camera systems robust for environmental change

3.1 Camera model

The USB cameras are modeled by using the basic pinhole camera model (e.g. Tsai et al. 1987; Hartley et al. 2003) and the geometry is shown in Fig. 6. Let $\Sigma_w = \{X, Y, Z\}$ be the camera coordinate system, and $\Sigma_c = \{x, y\}$ be the image plane coordinate system. A mapping a point $\boldsymbol{X} = (X, Y, Z)^T \in \Sigma_w$ to a point $\boldsymbol{x} = (x, y)^T \in \Sigma_c$ is represented as

$$\tilde{\boldsymbol{x}} = \boldsymbol{K}\left[\boldsymbol{R}|\boldsymbol{t}\right]\tilde{\boldsymbol{X}} \triangleq \boldsymbol{P}\tilde{\boldsymbol{X}}, \quad (1)$$

where,

$$\tilde{\boldsymbol{x}} \triangleq \begin{bmatrix} \boldsymbol{x} \\ 1 \end{bmatrix}, \quad \tilde{\boldsymbol{X}} \triangleq \begin{bmatrix} \boldsymbol{X} \\ 1 \end{bmatrix}, \quad \boldsymbol{K} = \begin{bmatrix} \alpha & -\alpha\cot\theta & u_0 \\ 0 & \beta/\sin\theta & v_0 \\ 0 & 0 & 1 \end{bmatrix}, \quad \boldsymbol{R} = \begin{bmatrix} \boldsymbol{r}_1^T \\ \boldsymbol{r}_2^T \\ \boldsymbol{r}_3^T \end{bmatrix}, \quad \boldsymbol{t} = \begin{bmatrix} t_x \\ t_y \\ t_z \end{bmatrix}, \quad (2)$$

and $[u_0, v_0]^T$ is the camera center. The number of pixels per unit distance in image coordinates are m_x and m_y in the x and y directions, f is focal length, and $\alpha = fm_x$ and $\beta = fm_y$ represent the focal length of the camera in terms of pixel dimensions in x and y directions. Moreover the parameter θ is the angle between the vertical and horizontal axes in the image plane, namely it is referred to as the skew parameter.

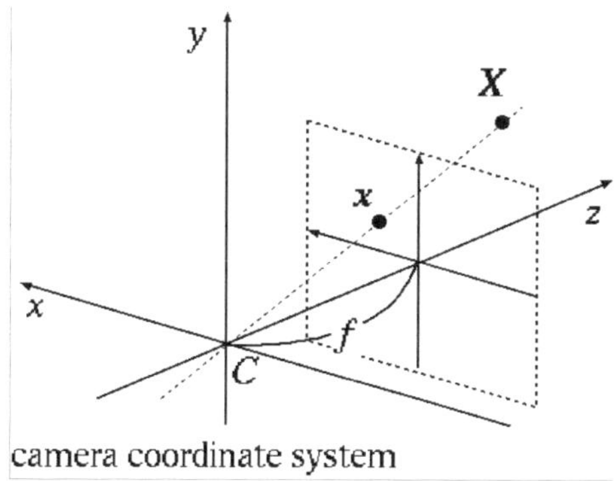

Fig. 6. Pinhole camera geometry.

3.2 Calculation of camera parameters

Next, in this research, Eqn. (1) is expanded to two linear equations as follows,

$$\begin{cases} \boldsymbol{p}_1^T\tilde{\mathbf{X}}_i - x_i\boldsymbol{p}_3^T\tilde{\mathbf{X}}_i + p_{14} - x_i p_{34} = 0, \\ \boldsymbol{p}_2^T\tilde{\mathbf{X}}_i - y_i\boldsymbol{p}_3^T\tilde{\mathbf{X}}_i + p_{24} - y_i p_{34} = 0, \end{cases} \tag{3}$$

where

$$\boldsymbol{P} \triangleq \begin{bmatrix} p_{11} & p_{12} & p_{13} & p_{14} \\ p_{21} & p_{22} & p_{23} & p_{24} \\ p_{31} & p_{32} & p_{33} & p_{34} \end{bmatrix} \triangleq \begin{bmatrix} \boldsymbol{p}_1^T & p_{14} \\ \boldsymbol{p}_2^T & p_{24} \\ \boldsymbol{p}_3^T & p_{34} \end{bmatrix}. \tag{4}$$

Combine the points $\tilde{\mathbf{X}}_i = [X_i, Y_i, Z_i, 1]^T$ $(i = 1, 2, \cdots, n)$ and the points $\boldsymbol{x}_i = [x_i, y_i]^T \in \Sigma_c$ correspond to them, it becomes

$$\boldsymbol{Ep} = \mathbf{0} \tag{5}$$

$$\boldsymbol{E} \triangleq \begin{bmatrix} X_1 & Y_1 & Z_1 & 1 & 0 & 0 & 0 & 0 & -x_1X_1 & -x_1Y_1 & -x_1Z_1 & -x_1 \\ 0 & 0 & 0 & 0 & X_1 & Y_1 & Z_1 & 1 & -y_1X_1 & -y_1Y_1 & -y_1Z_1 & -y_1 \\ \vdots & \vdots & \vdots & \vdots & \vdots & \vdots & \vdots & \vdots & \vdots & \vdots & \vdots & \vdots \\ X_n & Y_n & Z_n & 1 & 0 & 0 & 0 & 0 & -x_nX_n & -x_nY_n & -x_nZ_n & -x_n \\ 0 & 0 & 0 & 0 & X_n & Y_n & Z_n & 1 & -y_nX_n & -y_nY_n & -y_nZ_n & -y_n \end{bmatrix}, \tag{6}$$

$$\boldsymbol{p} \triangleq \left[\boldsymbol{p}_1^T, p_{14}, \boldsymbol{p}_2^T, p_{24}, \boldsymbol{p}_3^T, p_{34}\right]^T. \tag{7}$$

The projection matrix $\boldsymbol{E}$ is including 11 independent variables. In general, the solution of $\boldsymbol{p}$ in Eqn. (7) is obtained as an eigenvector corresponds to the minimum eigen value which derived by singular value decomposition of the covariance matrix $\boldsymbol{E}^T\boldsymbol{E}$. Here, the elements of $\boldsymbol{p}$ are normalized to be $\|p_{34}\| = 1$. Moreover,

$$\boldsymbol{P} = \begin{bmatrix} \boldsymbol{p}_1^T & p_{14} \\ \boldsymbol{p}_2^T & p_{24} \\ \boldsymbol{p}_3^T & p_{34} \end{bmatrix} = \begin{bmatrix} \alpha \boldsymbol{r}_1^T - \alpha(\cot\theta)\boldsymbol{r}_2^T + u_0\boldsymbol{r}_3^T & \alpha t_x - \alpha(\cot\theta)t_y + u_0 t_z \\ (\beta/\sin\theta)\boldsymbol{r}_2^T + v_0\boldsymbol{r}_3^T & (\beta/\sin\theta)t_y + v_0 t_z \\ \boldsymbol{r}_3^T & t_z \end{bmatrix}, \tag{8}$$

where,

$$\begin{aligned} u_0 &= \boldsymbol{p}_1^T \boldsymbol{p}_3, \\ v_0 &= \boldsymbol{p}_2^T \boldsymbol{p}_3, \\ \theta &= \cos^{-1}\left(-\frac{(\boldsymbol{p}_1 \times \boldsymbol{p}_3)^T (\boldsymbol{p}_2 \times \boldsymbol{p}_3)}{\|\boldsymbol{p}_1 \times \boldsymbol{p}_3\| \|\boldsymbol{p}_2 \times \boldsymbol{p}_3\|} \right), \\ \alpha &= \sqrt{\boldsymbol{p}_1^T \boldsymbol{p}_1 - u_0^2}\,\sin\theta, \\ \beta &= \sqrt{\boldsymbol{p}_2^T \boldsymbol{p}_2 - v_0^2}\,\sin\theta, \\ \boldsymbol{r}_1 &= \frac{1}{\alpha}\left(\boldsymbol{p}_1 + (\boldsymbol{p}_2 - v_0\boldsymbol{p}_3)\frac{\alpha}{\beta}\cos\theta - u_0\boldsymbol{p}_3 \right), \\ \boldsymbol{r}_2 &= \frac{\sin\theta}{\beta}(\boldsymbol{p}_2 - v_0\boldsymbol{p}_3), \\ \boldsymbol{r}_3 &= \boldsymbol{p}_3, \end{aligned} \tag{9}$$

$$\begin{aligned} t_x &= \frac{1}{\alpha}\left(p_{14} + (p_{24} - v_0 p_{34})\frac{\alpha}{\beta}\cos\theta - u_0 p_{34} \right), \\ t_y &= \frac{\sin\theta}{\beta}(p_{24} - v_0 p_{34}), \\ t_z &= p_{34}. \end{aligned} \tag{10}$$

3.3 measurement of 3D position

Next, let the projected points of $\boldsymbol{X} \in \Sigma_w$ on the left and the right camera image planes be $\boldsymbol{x}^{\text{left}} \triangleq \left[x^{\text{left}}, y^{\text{left}} \right]^T$ and $\boldsymbol{x}^{\text{right}} \triangleq \left[x^{\text{right}}, y^{\text{right}} \right]^T$. Moreover, let $\boldsymbol{P}^{\text{left}}$ and $\boldsymbol{P}^{\text{right}}$ be projection matrices, the following equations are derived,

$$\tilde{\boldsymbol{x}}^{\text{left}} = \boldsymbol{P}^{\text{left}} \tilde{\boldsymbol{X}}, \qquad \tilde{\boldsymbol{x}}^{\text{right}} = \boldsymbol{P}^{\text{right}} \tilde{\boldsymbol{X}}. \tag{11}$$

When the above mentioned expression are brought together about the variable $\boldsymbol{P}$, the following expression is obtained.

$$\boldsymbol{B}\tilde{\boldsymbol{X}} = \boldsymbol{b}, \tag{12}$$

where,

$$\boldsymbol{B} \triangleq \begin{bmatrix} x^{\text{left}} p_{31}^{\text{left}} - p_{11}^{\text{left}} & x^{\text{left}} p_{32}^{\text{left}} - p_{12}^{\text{left}} & x^{\text{left}} p_{33}^{\text{left}} - p_{13}^{\text{left}} \\ y^{\text{left}} p_{31}^{\text{left}} - p_{21}^{\text{left}} & y^{\text{left}} p_{32}^{\text{left}} - p_{22}^{\text{left}} & y^{\text{left}} p_{33}^{\text{left}} - p_{23}^{\text{left}} \\ x^{\text{right}} p_{31}^{\text{right}} - p_{11}^{\text{right}} & x^{\text{right}} p_{32}^{\text{right}} - p_{12}^{\text{right}} & x^{\text{right}} p_{33}^{\text{right}} - p_{13}^{\text{right}} \\ y^{\text{right}} p_{31}^{\text{right}} - p_{21}^{\text{right}} & y^{\text{right}} p_{32}^{\text{right}} - p_{22}^{\text{right}} & y^{\text{right}} p_{33}^{\text{right}} - p_{23}^{\text{right}} \end{bmatrix}, \tag{13}$$

$$\boldsymbol{b} \triangleq \left[p_{14}^{\text{left}} - x^{\text{left}} p_{34}^{\text{left}}, p_{24}^{\text{left}} - x^{\text{left}} p_{34}^{\text{left}}, p_{14}^{\text{right}} - y^{\text{right}} p_{34}^{\text{right}}, p_{24}^{\text{right}} - y^{\text{right}} p_{34}^{\text{right}} \right]^T. \tag{14}$$

The least squares solution $\tilde{\boldsymbol{X}}$ of Eqn. (12) is solved by the pseudo-inverse matrix $\boldsymbol{B}^+$ of $\boldsymbol{B}$ as follows,

$$\tilde{\boldsymbol{X}} = \boldsymbol{B}^+ \boldsymbol{b}. \tag{15}$$

3.4 procedure of actual camera calibration

The distance measurement with enough high accuracy is necessary in the range of motion of the arm. Namely, the important measurement distances are as follows: about 1500 [mm] for rough scene understanding; about 1000 [mm] for searching of grasping point on the target object; about 500 [mm] for judgment to hold the target object by the gripper. Therefore, we developed a calibration rig where 30 target patterns were arranged as shown in Fig. 7. This calibration rig is set up to become a constant position to the installed cameras on the robot arm by using several tripods, and when the robot starts, it is used according to the following procedures if calibration is necessary. A comparatively high accuracy calibration can be achieved in the depth direction by using this calibration rig.

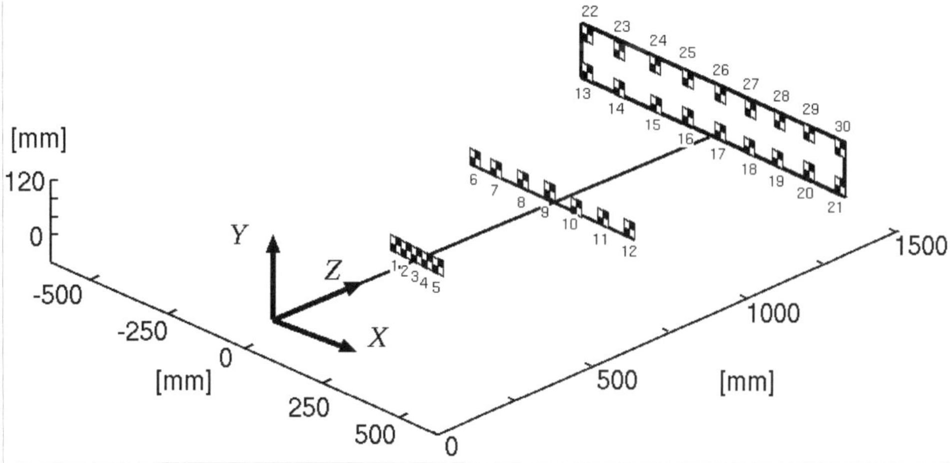

Fig. 7. Configuration of a calibration rig.

The camera calibration by using the rig might be executed in outdoor; therefore the detection of the target patterns by steady accuracy in the various outdoor environments is necessary. In this research, we employ the LoG (Laplacian of Gaussian) filter (Marr, 1982) to search for the position of the target patterns from camera images including noise, brightness change, geometric transformation, etc. with stability and fast computing. It is well known that the LoG filter is isotropic band pass filter capable of reducing low and high frequency noise and completely removing both constant and linear-varying intensity. The LoG filter is represented by

$$\nabla^2 G(\boldsymbol{u}) \triangleq \frac{-1}{\pi\sigma^4}\left(1-\frac{\|\boldsymbol{u}\|^2}{2\sigma^2}\right)e^{-\frac{\|\boldsymbol{u}\|^2}{2\sigma^2}}, \tag{16}$$

where $\boldsymbol{u} = (u^{(*)}, v^{(*)})^T$ (* is left or right) represents a unit vector on the projection plane. Namely, this filter eliminates high frequency noise and local brightness change by Gaussian, and eliminates low frequency brightness change by Laplacian. Fig. 8 shows the example of applying this filter to the image of the calibration rig. The target patterns are detected by the subpixel matching with template image after this filtering is applied in each, and the camera calibration is executed by the above mentioned procedure.

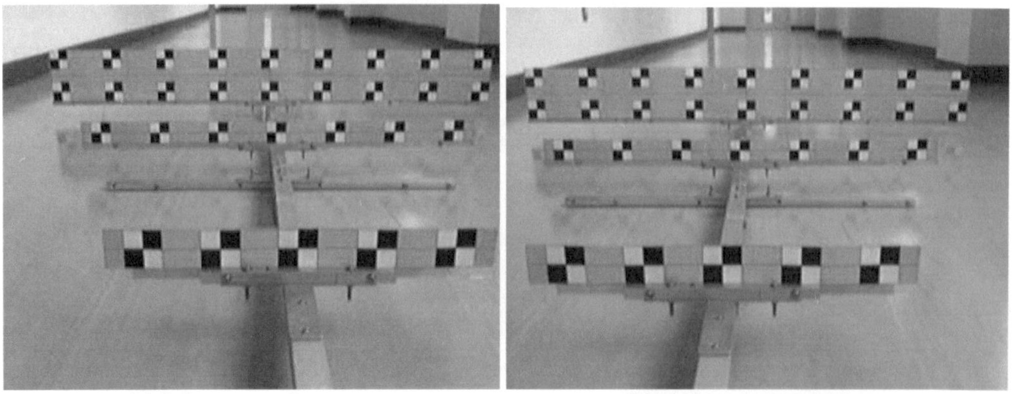

(a) left camera image (b) right camera image

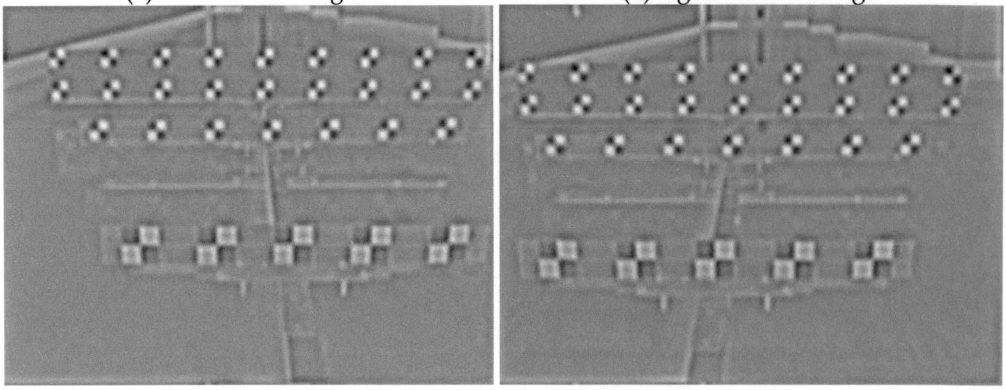

(c) LoG image of left camera image (d)LoG image of right camera image

Fig. 8. Captured images and LoG filtering images of the calibration rig.

The installation position and angles of the cameras were decided by the trial and error in consideration of the structure of the gripper of T-52, and then, the calibration accuracy according to the procedure is shown in Fig. 9. It is understand from this figure that the error of the calibration was within 100 [mm] in the range of motion of the arm, and this camera calibration procedure was able to decrease the error of the target pattern extraction and to achieve the highly accurate calibration under the outdoor environment. Here, these errors include the setting error of the rig. To cancel these errors, we are developing now the method of extraction of characteristic feature points of the gripper for automatic calibration. The camera parameters obtained by calibrations above are used to calculate the distance to the object in the following camera systems.

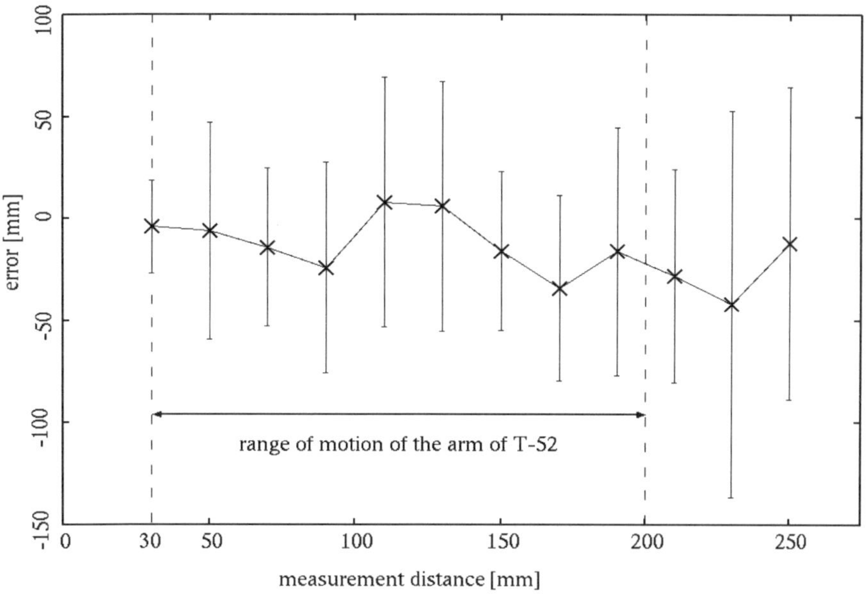

Fig. 9. Calibration accuracy vs. measurement distance.

4. System interfaces

Here, two kinds of developed interfaces are described: one is a monitor system that provides the sensor information efficiently for the pilot, and another is an interaction display system that tracks and displays the distances of the places that are set by the pilot. The image processing algorithms of them are different; the former is designed to present overall information of surroundings: the latter is designed to provide specific information desired by the pilot and to execute the processing in video rate. In the following, these systems are explained respectively.

4.1 Display of overall information on scene

The pilot understands a situation around the robot from information of the installed various sensors and operates it remotely. Although it is desirable that a lot of information is presented to the pilot, on the other hand, it is desirable for the system to be intuitive on the presentation of information, and to be designed not to accumulate tiredness in the pilot for efficiency operation. Therefore, we developed an intuitive interface system that indicates posture of the arm to the ground and distance surroundings of a target object. Fig. 10 shows an example of a monitor image presented to the pilot in the remote place by this system.

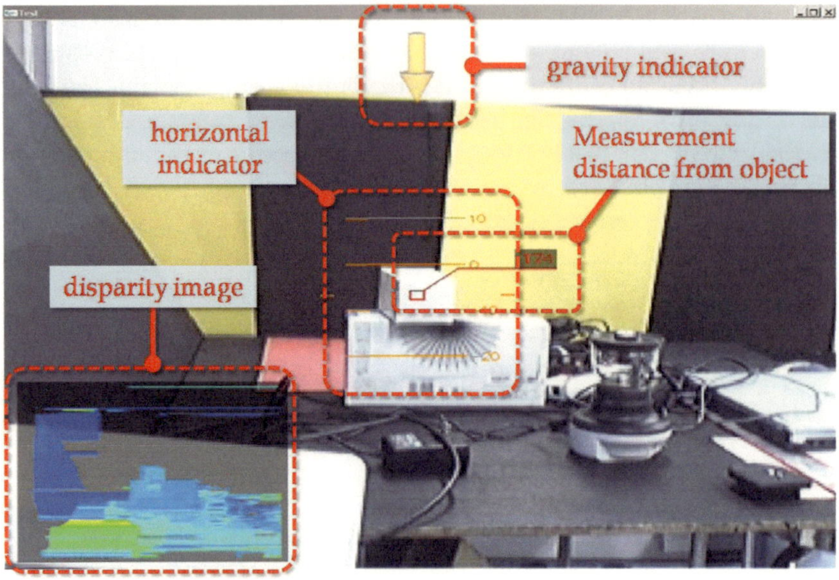

Fig. 10. Monitor image presented to the pilot. The system generates a gravity indicator, a horizontal indicator, a disparity image window, and a distance indicator.

4.1.1 Gravity indicator and disparity image

A gravity indicator that shows the direction of ground in the camera system was arranged at the upper part on the screen, and a horizontal indicator was arranged at the center part on the screen. These are displayed based on information obtained with the motion sensor: the rotation angles to the world coordinate system are calculated by integrating the acceleration x-y-z axes in the camera coordinate system, and they are re-displayed in the video rate, i.e. 30 [fps]. Moreover, a disparity image generated by a dynamic programming method (Birchfield et al. 1988) is displayed at the lower right of the screen, and the distance from the object is shown at the center part. Since the computational complexity of these processing based on the stereo vision is comparatively high, these indicators are re-displayed in the rate of 3-5 [fps]. The pilot can acquire various information by these displays without greatly changing the glance on the monitor. Examples of transition of display according to motion of the camera system are shown in Fig. 11. We see from Fig. 11 that the disparity images had been including the noise caused by matching error of the dynamic programming, and the property of the algorithm will be considered in the following.

4.1.2 Generation of disparity image in outdoor environments

The Birchfield's method is an algorithm to generate the disparity image efficiently by using a rectified parallel stereo camera (i.e. the image planes of two cameras are coplanar and their scanlines are parallel to the baseline). Moreover, the adjustments of five parameters, namely maximum disparity, occlusion penalty, match reward, reliability threshold, and reliability buffer factor are required for the execution of this algorithm. It is necessary to adjust these parameters in consideration of distance from target object, complexity of the scene, etc. by trial and error method after the installation of the camera system. Furthermore, the synchronization of the white balance and the shutter timing and the stable brightness images of the scene are needed for execution of this algorithm. The experimental results of this algorithm on some conditions are shown in Fig. 12. Although the disparity image was generable efficiently when a steady brightness images were able to be acquired in the indoor environment, much noise was caused in the disparity images generated from the images with "black outs or white outs" occurred due to shortages of dynamic range or with complex background. Namely, it has been understood that the condition concerning the environment might be limited for the use though this system efficiently provides the pilot various information.

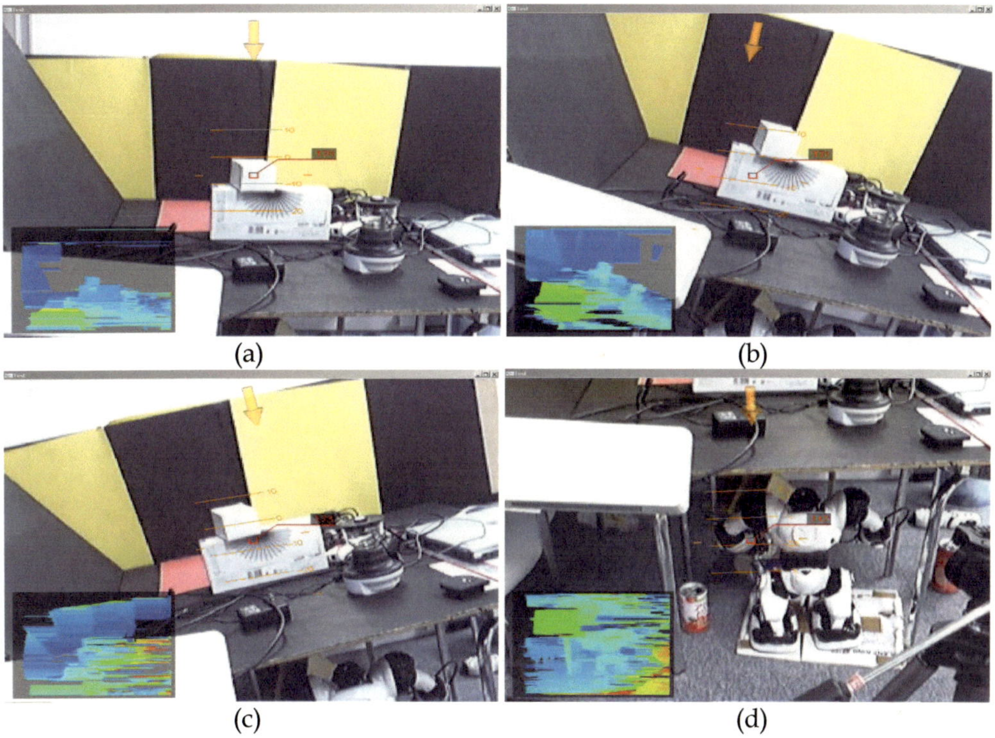

Fig. 11. Example of transition of display according to motion of the camera system.

4.2 Target tracker and distance indicator

Next we aimed to construct an interface executable at high speed and robust against the change of the environmental condition. The outline of an operating flow of the developed system is as follows. First of all, the pilot touches the monitor to specify the target points for tracking, and small windows (e.g. 9×9 pixels) are generated around the set positions on the monitor. Next, the tracking and the distance measurement of the set points are executed at once, and the results of them are reflected on the monitor in real time and the distance is displayed on the window frame. When the pilot touches the tracking window again, the set point is released. Moreover, the color of the window frame shows the following meanings: "green color" represents the success of the tracking and the measurement; "blue color" represents that the tracking point exists in the distance where it can be grasped by the gripper, i.e. the point exists near less than 1 [m]; "yellow color" represents the failure of the stereo matching and the displayed distance is untrustworthy. As mentioned above, this system can be used by an easy operation of the touch panel. The procedure of the processing of this system is described as follows.

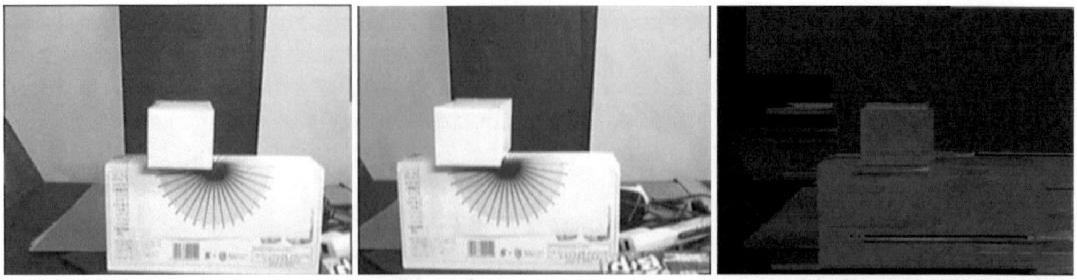

(a) left camera image (b) right camera image (c) disparity image

(d) left camera image (e) right camera image (f) disparity image

(g) left camera image (h) right camera image (i) disparity image

Fig. 12. Experimental results of generating of disparity images on several conditions: (a), (b), and (c) show results of an indoor environment; (d), (e), and (f) show results of an outdoor environment; and (g), (h), and (i) show results of a backlighting condition.

4.2.1 Detection algorithm

Considering of the following items is necessary for the tracking and the distance measurement of specified points under the outdoor environment.

- Keep the image processing speed at about 15-30 [fps].
- Ambient light changing.
- Camera shakes from vibration of the arms by oil pressure drive and mis-registration of the cameras.
- Achromatic color and complex scenes at the disaster scene.

Therefore, we developed an algorithm for simultaneous execution of the tracking and the stereo matching by using the Harris corner detector (Harris et al. 1988) and a fast feature tracking algorithm (Bouguet et al. 2000). The Bouguet's algorithm is a pyramidal implementation of the Lucas Kanade feature tracker description (Lucas et al. 1981), and it generates the optical flow between two images for the given set of points with sub-pixel accuracy. The proposed image processing algorithm is executed according to the following procedures.

4.2.2 Flow of target tracking and measurement

Let I_t and J_t be images captured by the left and the right camera at time t, and let $I_t(\boldsymbol{u})$ ($\boldsymbol{u} \equiv [x,y]^T$) be a pixel on I_t.

1. The pilot sets the target point $I_t(\boldsymbol{u}_n)$ on I_t, where n represents the index of target.
2. Generate a tracing window
$$W_{n,t}^I \triangleq \{I_t(\boldsymbol{u}_n)+\boldsymbol{w}\},$$
where, $\boldsymbol{w}=[\pm w,\pm w]^T$ (e.g. $w=4$[pixel]).
3. Find the corner points in $W_{n,t}^I$ by employing the Harris corner detector. If more than three points are not found around $I_t(\boldsymbol{u}_n)$, then the set point is canceled.
4. Generate a search window
$$S_{n,t}^J \triangleq \{J_t(\boldsymbol{u}_n+\boldsymbol{b})+\boldsymbol{s}\}$$
on J_t, where $\boldsymbol{b}=[b_x,\ 0]^T$, $b_x=\text{const.}$ is determined based on the camera parameters, and $\boldsymbol{s}=[\pm s,\ \pm s]^T$ (e.g. $s=10$[pixel]) represents the size of the search window.
5. Find
$$W_{n,t}^J \triangleq \left\{J_t(\boldsymbol{u}_n+\boldsymbol{d}^J)+\boldsymbol{w}\right\} \in S_{n,t}^J,$$
corresponding to $W_{n,t}^I$ on J_t by employing the Bouguet's algorithm (Fig. 13(b):(a-0)), where $\boldsymbol{d}^J \triangleq [d_x^J,\ d_y^J]^T$.
6. Calculate the distance to the point $I_t(\boldsymbol{u}_n)$ by using $\boldsymbol{d}^J$ and the calibrated camera parameters. If $d_y^J > d_{\text{threshold}}$, the result is judged as untrustworthy.
7. Find $I_{t+1}(\boldsymbol{u}_n+\boldsymbol{d}^I)$, i.e. the feature point in the next frame image corresponding to feature points of $I_t(\boldsymbol{u}_n)$ by employing the Bouguet's algorithm for the feature tracking (Fig. 13(b):(b-0)), and go to the 2nd step (Fig. 13(b):(a-1)).

The distance measurement and the target tracking are executed simultaneously by iteration of this procedure. Each window parameter is decided based on the range of motion of the arm and the camera parameters etc. beforehand. The experimental results of this algorithm implemented to the interface are shown in Fig. 14. Since this interface provides the pilot information only on the target points based on Bouguet's algorithm, it was possible to adapt to the tracking of fast movement object and the oscillation of the camera system.

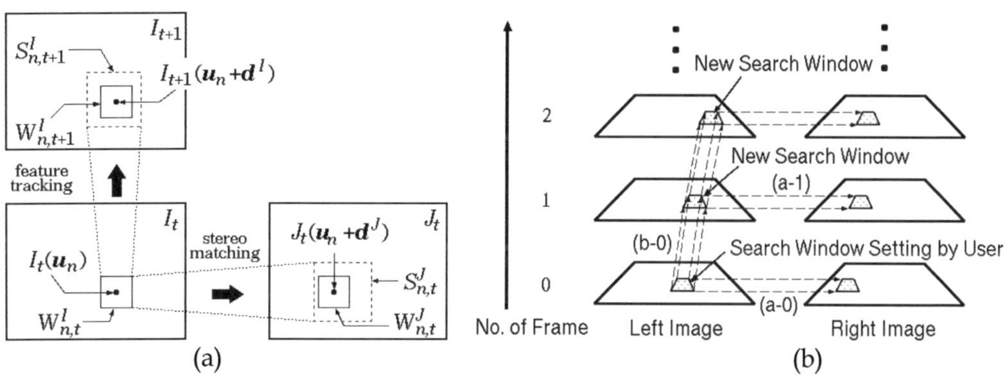

Fig. 13. Outline of the target tracking and the feature tracking: (a) relation of the target points, the tracking windows, and the search windows; (b) relation of the windows on the time flow.

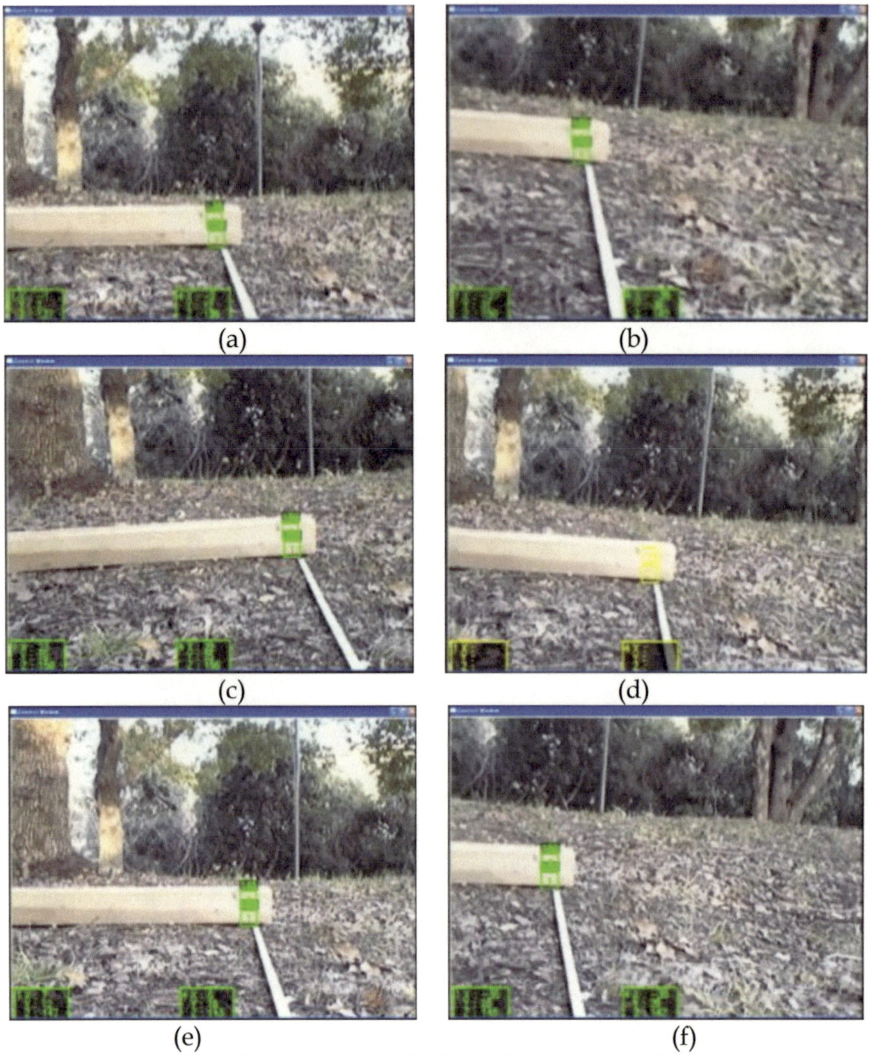

Fig. 14. Execution results of the proposed algorithm for simultaneous execution of the tracking and the stereo matching. Two small windows at the center part of images are shown the tracking windows, and the windows at the bottom of the images are shown parameters of the tracking points. The target points were not lost though the camera system was intensely shaken for five seconds. Although the stereo matching failed on two frames (the color of target window changed to yellow as shown in (d)), the distance measurement succeeded in almost all frames.

4.2.3 Experiment with robot

The result of the experiment conducted by installing the developed interface in the robot is shown in Fig. 15. These images were captured by the left camera of the B-system mounted on the joint of the gripper of T-52, and a rectangular lumber was set in front of the gripper. The tracking windows at the upper part of the image were specified by the pilot and a figure in the window shows the order of specifying the feature point (first and second points had been canceled). Moreover, the figure at upper part of the tracking window shows the measured distance, and the lower squares of the images and its inner figures show the order of the feature points and 3D position in a robot arm coordinate system, respectively. The color of the window changes according to the distance and the state of measurement as mentioned in **4.2**. It was found from the experiment that the interface was able to provide the pilot with the measurement distance of the tracking points with stability, and the operation to grasp the rectangular lumber was executed smoothly.

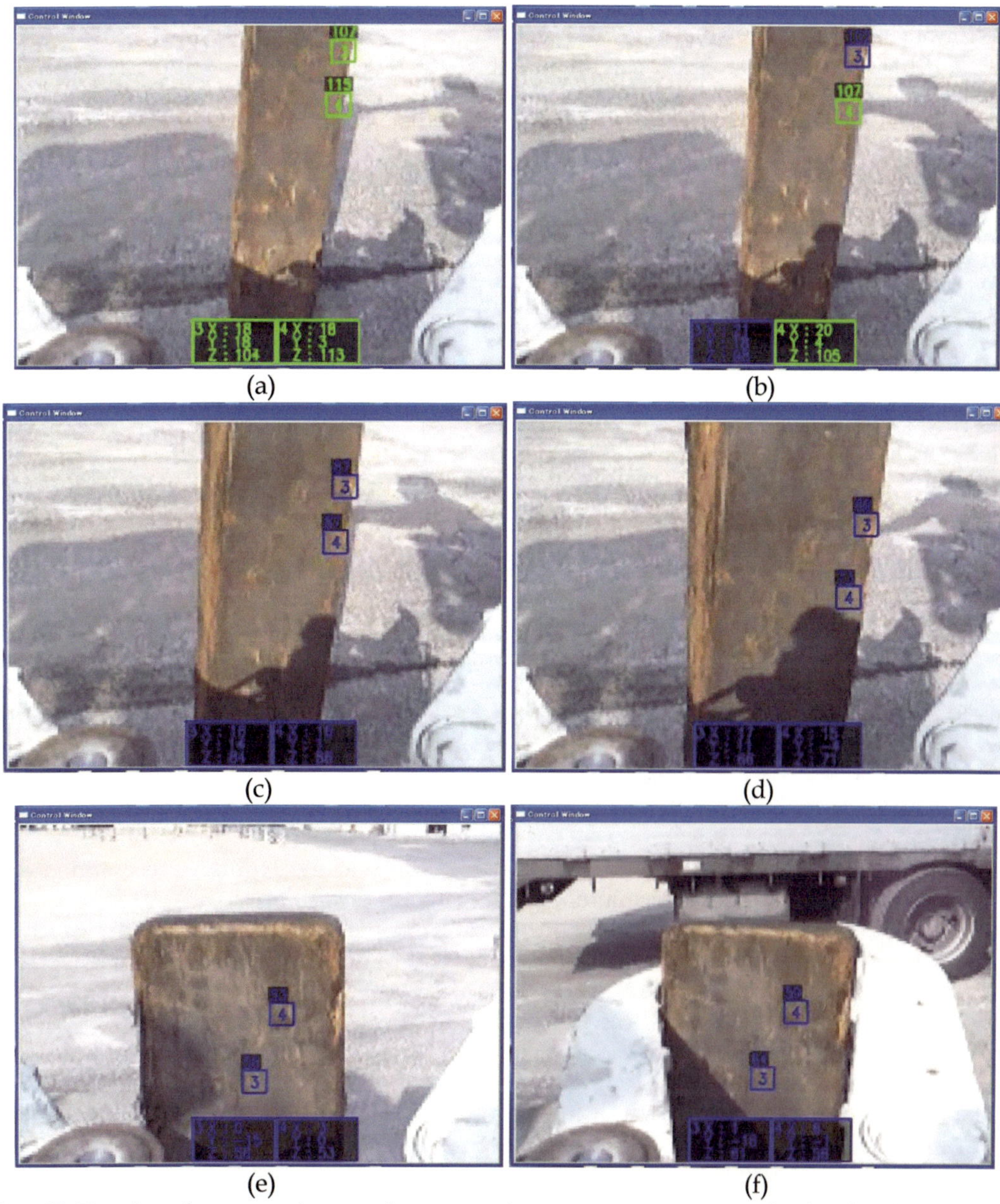

Fig. 15. Results of an experiment of an operation to grasp a rectangular lumber by using B-system installed in the joint of gripper of T-52. These images were captured by the left camera.

5. Conclusion

In this research, we developed two kinds of pilot assistance systems for T-52 and T-53 working in a disaster district. One is an interface that provides the information from several sensors efficiently for the pilot. Another is an interface that tracks and displays the distances of the points that are set by the pilot. This system can tell the pilot the distance by the change in the color that understands intuitively easily, and the processing speed is also fast enough. The pilot switches the two kinds of proposed interfaces according to the situation. The former is suitable for searching of a target object by the camera installed in the robot arm, and the latter is suitable for the operation that grasps a specific position of the target object by the arm. Then, the basic experiments for the construction of each system were conducted, and the effectiveness of them was confirmed.
From now on, a further various tests and examinations will be necessary to use of these system and interface efficiently in the disaster scene. Moreover, more interface development research according to disaster scene to achieve the many kinds of work by the rescue robot will be necessary. We are continuing the research for the solution of these research topics now, furthermore have started the development for automatic work system of the robots.

6. Acknowledgements

We would like to thank Yasuhiro Fuchikawa, Osamu Matsumoto, Hiroshi Koga, Yoichi Kitayama of Kyushu Institute of Technology.

7. References

Birchfield, S. & Tomasi C. (1988). Depth Discontinuities by Pixel-to-Pixel Stereo, *Proc. of the 6th IEEE International Conference on Computer Vision*, pp. 1073–1080.
Bouguet, J. Y. (2000). Pyramidal Implementation of the Lucas Kanade Feature Tracker: Description of the algorithm, *Technical Report, Intel Corporation, Microprocessor Research Labs 2000, OpenCV documentation*, 2680.
Harris, C. & Stephens., M. (1988). A Combined Corner and Edge Detector, *Proc. of Alvey Vision Conf.*, pp. 147–151.
Lucas, B. D. & Kanade, T. (1981). An Iterative Image Registration Technique with an Application to Stereo Vision, *Proc. of the 7th International Joint Conference on Artificial Intelligence*, pp. 674–679.
Marr, D. (1982). Vision: A Computational Investigation into the Human Presentation and Processing of Visual Information, *W. H. Freedman Company*.
Tsai, Y. Roger. (1987). Synopsis Recent Progress on Camera Calibration for 3D Machine Vision, The Robotcs Review 1, Oussama Khatib, John J. Craig and Tomas Lozano-Perez, pp.147–159, MIT Press.
Yokokohji, Y. (2006). ENRYU T-52 Advance -A Teleoperated Heavy-Duty Robot for Assisting Rescue Activities", *Journal of Robotics Society of Japan*, Vol.24, No.2, pp.113. (in Japanese)
Nishida, T., Koga, H., Fuchikawa, Y., Kitayama, Y., Kurogi, S., & Arimura, Y. (2006). Development of Pilot Assistance System with Stereo Vision for Robot Manipulation, *Proc. of SICE-ICCAS 2006*, pp. 2675-2680.
Hartley, R. & Zisserman, A. (2003). Multiple View Geometry in Computer Vision Second Edition, *Cambridge Univercity Press*.

18

Camera Modelling and Calibration - with Applications

Anders Ryberg, Anna-Karin Christiansson,
Bengt Lennartson and Kenneth Eriksson
University West
Sweden

1. Introduction

Methods for measuring/calculating positions and poses using vision and 2D images are presented in this chapter. In such calculations a calibrated camera model is needed, and a newly developed generic camera model (GCM) is proposed and presented together with calibration routines. A camera model is a mapping of a 3D object space to a 2D image space and/or vice versa. This new GCM is aimed to be more accurate, computationally efficient, flexible and general compared to conventional camera models. See Fig. 1 for an application. The new camera model was developed because measurements showed that a conventional camera model (CCM) did not have a high enough accuracy for some camera types and robot positioning applications.

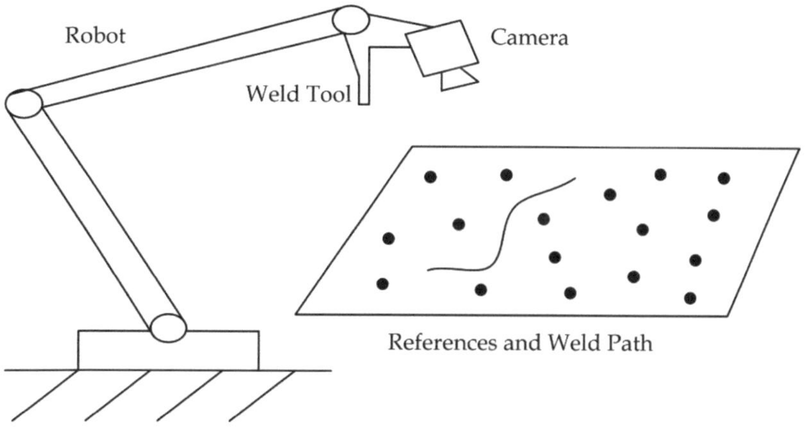

Fig. 1. A vision system can measure the pose of a robot if the camera can see references. It can also determine the geometry of a curve to be welded by the robot. In that case it needs to first see the path from at least two directions and use stereo vision.

The calibration calculates intrinsic and extrinsic camera parameters as well as positions of references from several images of these, using optimization methods. The extrinsic camera parameters are the 6D pose of the camera. The intrinsic camera parameters determine how the 2D image is formed in the camera given relative positions of the camera and the environment.

Methods for estimating the camera parameters and the reference positions are presented. These calculations are based on the position, size and shape of references in the images. Estimates of these parameters are needed as initial values in the calibration to assure convergence. A method of calculating the "centre point" of a reference in the image is developed for increased accuracy, since the centre of gravity of the reference in the image generally does not correspond to the centre of the reference. The GCM allows for variable focus and zoom. This fact and that it can be used for wide angle fisheye cameras (which can not be modelled by the CCM) as well as low distortion cameras makes the GCM very versatile.

Together with the GCM and the calibration, ambiguities or nontrivial null spaces are also discussed. Nontrivial null spaces occur when the same image can be obtained with different sets of camera parameters and camera poses. This can happen with the GCM, as well as the CMM to some extent, and is therefore important to consider in the calibration. Methods to handle these null spaces are described.

Image processing techniques are not explicitly described, except for methods of finding centre points of the references in the image. It is assumed that the image coordinates needed are found with some method.

Different kinds of distortions can be captured by a camera model. In a camera with no distortion, a collinear camera, a straight line in object space is mapped to a straight line in image space. A model of a collinear camera is called a pinhole camera model (PCM). Both the CCM and the GCM can model ordinary radial distortion, but in different ways, while other types of distortions are modelled by some CCMs and the GCM, e.g. variations in entrance pupil (as in (Gennery 2006)) and decentring distortion (more in (Heikkila 2000) and (Kannala & Brandt 2006)). The GCM has an efficient way of including varying entrance pupil in the model, and two methods for compensating for decentring distortion. The CCM, described by (Brown 1971), (Tsai 1987), (Heikkila 2000), (Motta & McMaster 2002), and the GCM, have been used in a laboratory experiment, where the accuracy of the vision systems were compared to a coordinate measuring machine (CMM). When only radial distortion is accounted for the GCM is better in accuracy. Then the other types of distortion can be added for further improvement of accuracy. Furthermore, the CCM is poor in handling cameras with a wide angle of view, such as fisheye cameras, which is why there are several other models developed, specialised for these (Basu & Licardie 1995), (Brauer-Burchardt & Voss 2001), (Bakstein & Pajdla 2002), (Shah & Aggarwal 1996). The GCM can be used for both fisheye and ordinary cameras, and at the same time it includes the undistorted PCM as the simplest meaningful special case. Therefore there is no longer a need to use different models for these different kinds of cameras.

Calibration methods using references which are a priori known can be found in (Brown 1971), (Tsai 1987) and (Heikkila 2000). If the positions of the references are not known the calibration procedure is called self-calibration. Both self-calibration and calibration with known references are presented in this chapter. Self calibration procedures can also be found in (Fraser 1997) and (Dornaika & Chung 2001). Other methods for self-calibration use modulus constraint (Pollefeys & Van Gool 1999) and Kruppa's equations (Olivier et al. 1992), the last two use only the undistorted PCM. Another calibration method that uses external measurements of the calibration camera poses is (Wei et al. 1998). Such a method is called active, while passive methods only use the information in the images for the calibration. Both passive and active methods are discussed below, and a method of improving the calibration by measuring camera positions after a passive calibration, is presented.

A calibrated camera can then be used for calculating a camera pose from an image, by using references with known positions. If a point or curve is seen from at least two directions its position can be calculated, using stereovision methods. A new general method for calculating positions from stereo vision is presented.
There are other models that can be considered generic, as in (Kannala & Brandt 2006) and (Gennery 2006). An advantage with the GCM compared to (Kannala & Brandt 2006) is that they do not include the undistorted PCM as a special case, and also do not have entrance pupil variations included. Advantages compared to (Gennery 2006) are that GCM is more simple and efficient, both to implement and to run. (Gennery 2006) needs several iterations to do one camera model mapping, while the GCM can do it in a single strike. Fast calculations are important for both calibration and the applications; in the calibration since it involves many camera model calculations, and in the applications if the result is to be used on-line.
To summarize the novelties of this contribution are as follows:

- Introduction of a generic camera model (GCM) and its different kinds of distortion compensations, as well as its relation to other camera models. A main benefit of the GCM is that it includes wide angle of view (fisheye) cameras as well as ordinary cameras within the same unified model structure.
- Methods for including variable zoom and focus in the model as well as procedures for how to include it in the calibration.
- Discussions on nontrivial null spaces and how to handle them.
- Algorithms for initial estimates of intrinsic and extrinsic camera parameters as well as reference positions.
- Methods for calculating image centre points of references.
- A new stereo vision calculation method.
- Experimental investigation where the accuracy of different camera model configurations are analysed.

The chapter is organised as follows; Section 2 presents camera models in more detail, both the CCM and especially the GCM. Section 3 describes calibration while Section 4 introduces vision pose calculations and stereo vision. Section 5 presents an accuracy investigation, and conclusions and future work are given in Section 6.

2. Camera models

A mathematical camera model consists of algorithms for conversion between the position of points in a 3D object world and their appearance as points in a 2D image plane. If the intrinsic and extrinsic camera parameters are known and an observed 3D object point position is known, the camera model can consequently be used to calculate where the object point ends up in the image. It can also be used the other way around; if an image point and the camera parameters are known the camera model can calculate all possible object points the image point could originate from.
Both the CCM and GCM are described here. First an image coordinate system is introduced, where the origin is in the intersection of the image plane with the optical axis, called the principal point. The scaling is the same in both image coordinate directions. A conversion to the detector pixel image coordinate plane is made in Section 2.3. First only radial distortion is considered and decentring distortion can be added afterwards. Vectors with a superscript

^{w} are coordinates in a world coordinate system, superscript ^{i} in a 2D image coordinate system, and superscript ^{c} in a 3D camera coordinate system. Indices $_1$, $_2$ and $_3$ denote x- y- and z- components of a vector respectively.

2.1 Conventional Camera Model (CCM)

In the simplest kind of camera model, the pinhole camera model (PCM), a point in 3D space is projected to the image plane through a straight line passing a point P inside the lens system on the optical axis, see image point x_p^i in Fig 2. This model is collinear and takes no distortion into consideration. To calculate an image coordinate point, x_p^i, corresponding to an observed object point, x_o^w, using this model, first the points coordinates in a 3D camera coordinate system, x_o^c, should be calculated, by rotating and translating the coordinates according to a camera pose. The pose is the position and orientation of the camera

$$x_o^c = Rx_o^w + T \tag{1}$$

R is a rotation matrix and T is a translation vector of the conversion defining the pose of the camera, that is rotation and translation between a world and a camera coordinate system. The camera coordinate system has its x- and y- axes parallel to the image coordinate axes, and its z-axis along the optical axis. Its origin is in a point P, in the centre of the lens system, so this point is defined as the camera position for PCM and CCM, see Fig. 2. Note that the definition of the camera position differs for the GCM in the next section. For the GCM the origin of the camera coordinate system is the principal point, that is the intersection between the optical axis and the image plane. The image coordinates for a PCM are now

$$x_{p1}^i = -f\, x_{o1}^c / x_{o3}^c \tag{2a}$$

$$x_{p2}^i = -f\, x_{o2}^c / x_{o3}^c \tag{2b}$$

where f (related to the focal length) is the distance from the detector to the pinhole point P. Sometimes a geometrical construction where the image is formed in front of the detector is used, and then the minus signs in (2) change to plus signs.

One way of modelling distortion is to use a conversion between an image point and where it would end up in a PCM, i.e. a conversion between a distorted and a non distorted image. A CCM models radial distortion by taking a PCM point x_p^i, and moving it in the radial direction to the point x_r^i where it would end up in a radially distorted image, see Fig 2. A polynomial in $r_p = \sqrt{{x_{p1}^i}^2 + {x_{p2}^i}^2}$, the distance in the image from the image point to the principal point, is used to adjust the position of the image point, according to

$$x_r^i = x_p^i f_p(r_p) \tag{3}$$

$$f_p(r_p) = (1 + k_{p1} r_p + k_{p2} r_p^2 + \ldots) \tag{4}$$

This polynomial adjusts the image point radially from or to the principal point. The constants k_{pi} are intrinsic camera parameters and the degree of the polynomial $f_p(r_p)$ can be adjusted according to the camera used and the accuracy needed. Other functions than polynomials can be used in (4), but a polynomial was chosen for simplicity. Sometimes only even powers of r_p are used. Note that from (3) it follows that

$$r_r(r_p) = r_p f_p(r_p) \tag{5}$$

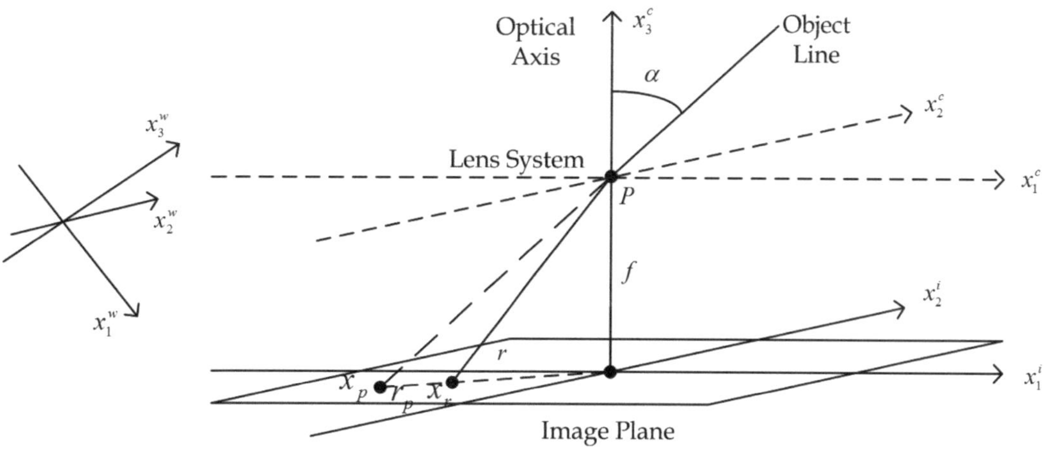

Fig. 2. Illustration of the CCM with the world, camera and image coordinate systems. Two points in the image are defined, one undistorted, x_p, and one radially distorted, x_r.

In (5) r is the distance to the principal point in the radially distorted image, $r_r = \sqrt{x_{r1}^{i\,2} + x_{r2}^{i\,2}}$. If every image point is moved radially according to (5) this is the same as (3). The points are moved radially if the ratio between x_1^i and x_2^i is the same before and after the transformation. The transformation (3) or (5) can be performed in the opposite direction, so that

$$x_p^i = x_r^i f_r(r_r) \tag{6}$$

where $f_r(r_r) = (1 + k_{r1}r_r + k_{r2}r_r^2 + ...)$. Also here, usually only even powers of r_r are used. These methods are described in (Brown 1971), (Tsai 1987), (Swaminathan & Nayar 1999), (Heikkila 2000), (Motta & McMaster 2002) and (Nowakowski & Skarbek 2007). If there is a need to calculate from the 2D image to 3D object space an equation for a straight line from the undistorted image coordinate converted to the 3D coordinate system through the pinhole point, P, is made. Then an image conversion from the distorted to non distorted image is needed. So whether (5) or (6) should be used depends mostly on the direction of the camera model transformation. When transforming to the image only the function value needs to be computed in (5), while in the other direction a polynomial equation has to be solved. With (6) it is on the contrary easier to convert from distorted to non-distorted image. The inclination angle α in Fig 2 is between the optical axis oaches 90 degrees, therefore large angles can not be modelled with the CCM. and the object line. One problem with the CCM is that r_p tends to infinity when α approaches 90 degrees, therefore large angles can not be modelled with the CCM.

2.2 The new Generic Camera Model (GCM)

The GCM handles radial distortion in a different way than the CCM, and can also include variation of the entrance pupil position and decentring distortion. Entrance pupil can be viewed as another kind of radial distortion than discussed in the previous section. To explain entrance pupil, think of an image point. That corresponds to a line in the 3D object space, corresponding to all points the image point can have originated from, the object line. The line crosses the optical axis, but it can cross it on different positions depending on the inclination angle. The crossing point is called the entrance pupil and is denoted x_{fo}, see Fig 3. The GCM and the different distortions are divided into steps where each step accounts for one type of distortion. All of these steps can be performed in two directions either adding or removing the distortion type. Adding distortion is done when converting from object space to image space. In converting from image to object space the distortions need to be removed. If the different distortions are compensated for in the right order they can be separated into different steps, except for radial distortion and entrance pupil, which are connected, so they have to be handled simultaneously. First a conversion between a 3D object world and an image with radial distortion and varying entrance pupil, x_r^i is introduced. Then a conversion between x_r^i, the radially distorted image point, to a decentring distorted point, x_d^i, is performed. Finally, a conversion between x_d^i and x_c^i, where, x_c^i is the measured chip pixel coordinates, is presented. The undistorted PCM coordinates x_p^i can also be computed using the GCM as in (28). In converting to the detector the calculations should be in this order. When converting to object space the calculations are done in reverse, i.e. from x_c^i to x_d^i, then from x_d^i to x_r^i and from x_r^i to the object line. Variable focus and zoom in the model is presented in the calibration section.

Radial Distortion and Entrance Pupil

Again we start by using a 2D image coordinate system where the origin is in the principal point. The 3D camera coordinate system has its origin in the same point, that is in x_{ca} in Fig 3, and not in P $(=x_{fo})$, as for the CCM. So x_{ca} is the position of the camera in the GCM. We start by converting from image to object space. In calculating with radial distortion and entrance pupil with the GCM first two points are defined on the optical axis, called x_{fi} and x_{fo}, see Fig 3, where x_{fo} already has been discussed. Both of these points can slide along the optical axis depending on the inclination angle, α, or depending on r which is a measure of α. The object line is parallel to a line from an image point, x_r, to x_{fi}, and it goes through x_{fo}. This geometrical construction defines the radial distortion and the entrance pupil of the GCM, see Fig 3.

The distance from the detector to the points x_{fi} and x_{fo} are called $f_{inner}(r)$ and $f_{outer}(r)$. r is the distance from the image point to the principal point as before. The dependence of r in f_{inner} and f_{outer} can be set to polynomials,

$$f_{inner}(r) = d_0 + d_1 r + d_2 r^2 + \ldots \tag{7}$$

$$f_{outer}(r) = e_0 + e_1 r + e_2 r^2 + \ldots \tag{8}$$

where d_i and e_i are intrinsic camera parameters. Here d_0 is the same as f in the CCM. The degrees of the polynomials can be chosen to get a good enough accuracy and a simple enough model. It might seem more natural to have f_{inner} and f_{outer} as functions of α instead of *r*, but since α is not directly known, that would give a more complicated and slower calculation. The reason that it is possible to use *r* instead of α is that for a given camera there is a one to one relationship between them and that we have the freedom to design an appropriate function dependence (by choosing polynomial coefficient values) between f_{inner} and f_{outer} and its variable. Compare with (Gennery 2006), which gives more complicated formulas for modelling the same phenomena.

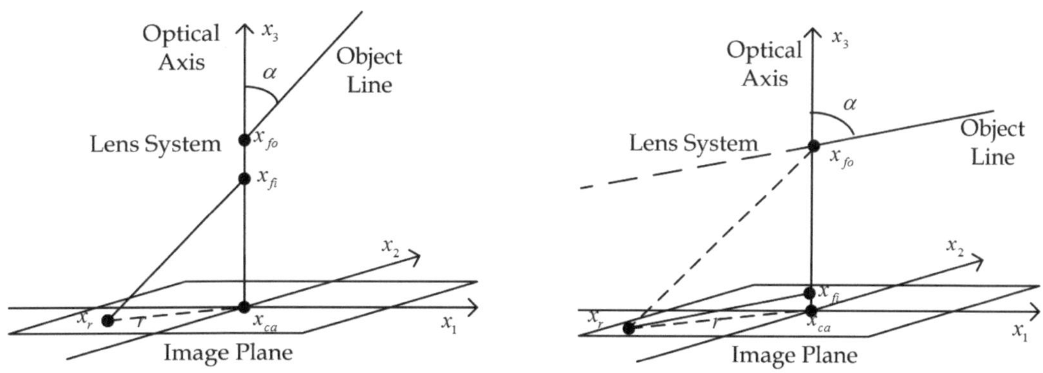

Fig. 3. Geometrical construction of the GCM, with different inclination angles. The points x_{fo} and x_{fi} can slide along the optical axis depending on *r*, the distance to the centre principal point. For large angles, α, the undistorted image point of the CCM would be far away from the centre of the image, causing problems for the CCM. The GCM solves that by having x_{fi} close to the detector (or even below it).

Let the unit vectors e_x, e_y and e_z span a 3D camera coordinate system. The *x*- and *y*- axes in this 3D camera coordinate system are the image *x*- and *y*- axes, and the *z*- axis is pointing along the optical axis. If the camera is rotated by angles θ, φ and γ compared to a world coordinate system, the unit vectors in the world coordinate system can be expressed as

$$e_z^w = \begin{bmatrix} \cos\theta\cos\varphi \\ \cos\theta\sin\varphi \\ \sin\theta \end{bmatrix}; \quad e_x^w = \begin{bmatrix} \cos\gamma\sin\varphi + \sin\gamma\sin\theta\cos\varphi \\ \cos\gamma\cos\varphi + \sin\gamma\sin\theta\sin\varphi \\ -\sin\gamma\cos\theta \end{bmatrix} \tag{9ab}$$

$$e_y^w = e_z^w \times e_x^w = \begin{bmatrix} \sin\gamma\sin\varphi + \cos\gamma\sin\theta\cos\varphi \\ -\sin\varphi\cos\varphi + \cos\gamma\sin\theta\sin\varphi \\ -\cos\gamma\cos\theta \end{bmatrix} \tag{9c}$$

Relations between the points in Fig 3 and the unit vectors and the polynomials (7,8) in a world coordinate system are

$$x_{fo}^w = x_{ca}^w + f_{outer}(r)e_z^w \tag{10}$$

$$x_{fi}^{w} = x_{ca}^{w} + f_{inner}(r)e_{z}^{w} \tag{11}$$

$$x_{r}^{w} = x_{ca}^{w} + x_{r1}^{i}e_{x}^{w} + x_{r2}^{i}e_{y}^{w} \tag{12}$$

The object line can now be expressed as

$$x_{fo}^{w} + a(x_{fi}^{w} - x_{r}^{w}) \tag{13}$$

where the parameter, a, can be varied to move along the object line. Using (10,11,12) the object line (13) can also be written

$$x_{ca}^{w} + f_{outer}(r)e_{z}^{w} + a(f_{inner}(r)e_{z}^{w} - x_{r1}^{i}e_{x}^{w} - x_{r2}^{i}e_{y}^{w}) \tag{14}$$

The terms inside the parenthesis after a defining the direction of the line should be measured in the same unit, where an image unit like pixels is convenient. The two first terms should be in the length unit of a world coordinate system, not necessarily the same as inside the parenthesis. Equations (7)-(14) represent the conversion from the 2D image to the 3D object world. Using this method it is also possible to go in the other direction, i.e. from the object space to the image space. Assume we have a point in the object space, x_{o}^{w}, with a certain position relative to the camera. First calculate the point's position in the 3D camera coordinate system, x_{o}^{c}, using (1). Then the following equation for r can be used, derived using similarity of triangles:

$$\frac{f_{inner}(r)}{r} = \frac{x_{o3}^{c} - f_{outer}(r)}{\sqrt{x_{o1}^{c\,2} + x_{o2}^{c\,2}}} \tag{15}$$

This is an equation that can be solved for r so the distance to the centre of the image is known. Then use the fact that if there is no decentring distortion the ratio between x_{r1}^{i} and x_{r2}^{i} in the image is the same as between x_{o1}^{c} and x_{o2}^{c}, but they have opposite signs (or the same signs if it is projected in front of the lens). This gives the following formulas for x_{r}^{i} based on the solution of (15) and the vector x_{o}^{c}

$$x_{r1}^{i} = -r\frac{x_{o1}^{c}}{\sqrt{x_{o1}^{c\,2} + x_{o2}^{c\,2}}} \tag{16a}$$

$$x_{r2}^{i} = \begin{cases} x_{r1}^{i}\dfrac{x_{o2}^{c}}{x_{o1}^{c}}, & x_{o1}^{c} \neq 0 \\ -\operatorname{sign}(x_{o2}^{c})r, & x_{o1}^{c} = 0 \end{cases} \tag{16b}$$

Since (15) can be transformed into a polynomial equation if $f_{inner}(r)$ and $f_{outer}(r)$ are polynomials it can have several solutions. If more than one is real a test has to be made to obtain the correct solution. r should have appropriate values in relation to the size of the detector. It can also be tested if the corresponding values of $f_{inner}(r)$ and $f_{outer}(r)$ are reasonable. The degree of the equation (15) is

$$\text{degree(eq 15)=max((degree } f_{inner}(r)\text{); (degree } f_{outer}(r)\text{)+1)} \quad (17)$$

Therefore, if conversion shall be done to the image, the degree of $f_{outer}(r)$ should usually be at least one lower than $f_{inner}(r)$ so that it does not contribute to give a higher degree of the polynomial equation. This is not a problem since it is more important to have an accurate $f_{inner}(r)$ than $f_{outer}(r)$. If $f_{outer}(r)$ is constant and a low order polynomial in (15) is wanted, in relation to the number of camera parameters, then a quotient between two polynomials can be used as $f_{inner}(r)$, where the degree of the denominator polynomial is one degree lower than the numerator.

Decentring Distortion

Decentring distortion can be caused by e.g. a leaning detector surface, badly aligned lens system and non constant refraction index in the lenses. These effects are usually larger for cheap cameras. A special method accounting for leaning detector is presented first, and then a more general method will be presented. Leaning detector is compensated for by using formulas defining a conversion between points in a leaning detector and a non-leaning detector. So now we convert between x_r and x_d. The compensation for leaning detector is such that a straight line between a point in the non-leaning and the corresponding point in the leaning detector crosses the optical axis at a distance $f_l(r)$ from non-leaning image plane, Fig 4.

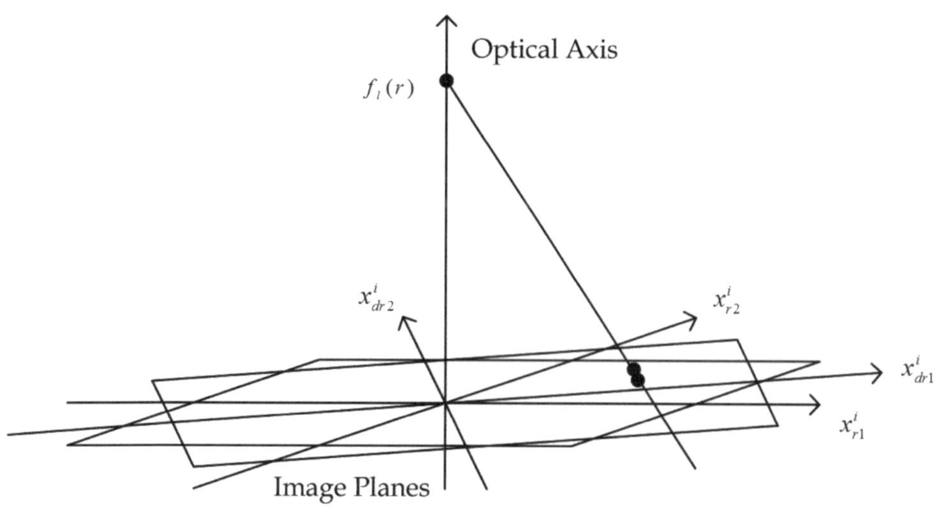

Fig. 4. The leaning image compensation converts between leaning and non-leaning detectors so that a line between the points on the two planes hits the optical axis at a point $f_l(r)$ units from the principal point.

First it is assumed that the image coordinate system is rotated, by an angle β, so that the x-axis is pointing in the direction of the steepest descent of the leaning detector, and the centre of the image is still in the principal point. The point x^i_r is called x^i_{rr} in the rotated image coordinate system. If δ is the leaning angle of the detector, the relations between the coordinates in the two planes are obtained from geometric analysis as

$$\frac{\cos(\arctan(x^{i}_{rr1}/f_{l}(r)))}{x^{i}_{dr1}}=\frac{\cos(\delta+\arctan(x^{i}_{rr1}/f_{l}(r)))}{x^{i}_{rr1}} \tag{18a}$$

$$\frac{\cos(\arctan(x^{i}_{rr2}/f_{l}(r)))}{x^{i}_{dr2}}=\frac{\cos(\arctan(x^{i}_{rr2}/f_{l}(r)+\arctan(x^{i}_{rr1}\tan\delta/x^{i}_{rr2}))}{x^{i}_{rr2}} \tag{18b}$$

Here $f_l(r)$ is a polynomial defining a point on the optical axis similar to $f_{inner}(r)$ and $f_{outer}(r)$. r is the distance to the principal point in the non-leaning image plane, just like before. x^{i}_{dr} is the image coordinates in the leaning image plane. This leaning image plane should be rotated back so that the orientation of the image plane coordinate is equivalent to the orientation before the leaning detector compensation. Since the plane is now leaning it is better to rotate back a slightly different value than β. If it is desirable to have the optical axis and images x- axes before and after the transformation in the same plane, a relation between the rotation angles is

$$\beta_{\delta}=\arctan(\cos\delta\tan\beta) \tag{19}$$

Here β is a rotation in the non leaning plane and β_δ is the corresponding rotation in the leaning plane. Note that this gives a relation between the rotation angles, but the rotations should be in opposite directions.

The result of the back rotation, called x^{i}_{d}, is then the coordinate in the leaning detector. With (18) it is easy to obtain a closed expression converting from non-leaning to leaning plane, but the other direction is more difficult, because then two equations have to be solved. One simplification conversing from leaning to non-leaning is obtained by using r in the leaning detector as approximation to r in the formulas. If this does not give an accurate enough result an iteration can be used, so that an r from the solution of the approximated equation is used, and solve the system again, giving a better and better value for r. This can be done any number of times, but it should converge quickly. If $f_l(r)$ is constant these iterations are not needed.

Another way of solving the equations (18) from leaning to non-leaning is to use vector algebra. Construct a line going from an image point in the leaning detector plane to a point on the optical axis defined by $f_l(r)$, and solve a linear equation of where this line crosses a non-leaning image plane. One difficulty here is again that r in the non-leaning plane is not known. Again it can be approximated by r in the leaning plane, and if necessary perform iterations to get a better r. So we have methods for converting in both directions.

Leaning detector compensation may also be useful for modelling inaccurately aligned lenses. Another method, taking decentring distortion into account, can be used if there is a combination of different kinds of decentring distortion, or if it is not known what causes the decentring distortion. The method uses a conversion between an image plane with no decentring distortion and an image with decentring distortion, or the other way around. ϕ is an image angle around the optical axis, and r is as before the distance to the principal point from the image point. e^{i}_{r} is a unit vector pointing radially away from the centre of the image to the image point. e^{i}_{t} is a unit vector perpendicular to that but still in the image plane. Formulas for converting from non-decentring distortion coordinates x^{i}_{r} to an image with decentring distortion x^{i}_{d} are then

$$d_r(r,\varphi)=(g_1r+g_2r^2+g_3r^3)(g_4\cos\varphi+g_5\sin\varphi)+(g_6r+g_7r^2)(g_8\cos(2\varphi)+g_9\sin(2\varphi)) \tag{20}$$

$$d_t(r,\varphi) = (h_1 r + h_2 r^2 + h_3 r^3)(h_4 \cos\varphi + h_5 \sin\varphi) + (h_6 r + h_7 r^2)(h_8 \cos(2\varphi) + h_9 \sin(2\varphi)) \quad (21)$$

$$d_{tot}(x_r^i) = d_r(r,\varphi)e_r^i(\varphi) + d_t(r,\varphi)e_t^r(\varphi) \quad (22)$$

$$x_d^i = x_r^i + d_{tot}(x_r^i) \quad (23)$$

Here d_r is a distortion in the radial direction and d_t is a distortion in the tangential direction. This is a bit similar to (Kannala & Brandt 2006), but r is used instead of α for the same reason as above, and also odd powers are included. Another difference is that the ϕ and r dependences are not separated here, as it is in (Kannala & Brandt 2006). More parameters can easily be added or removed, so it describes a family of decentring distortion compensation methods. If there is a need to go more efficiently in the direction from distorted to not distorted image a more suitable method can be achieved by just changing x_r^i and x_d^i in (20-23), and use unit vectors pointing radially and tangentially in the distorted image, then the values of the constants g_i and h_i in (20) and (21) will change. There are other ways to take care of decentring distortion (Brown 1971), (Swaminathan & Nayar 1999), (Heikkila 2000). These types of decentring distortion can also be combined with the GCM. One advantage of the calculations presented here is that the same behaviour can be achieved independently of the directions of the image coordinate axes.

To summarise, with decentring distortion we have methods that efficiently can go from either decentring distorted image plane to non-decentring distorted or vice versa. If there is a need to go in both directions one of the directions will be a bit slower and more complicated.

2.3 Image plane coordinate conversions

In the equations so far it has been assumed that the image coordinate system has its origin in the principal point. Also the same coordinate axis units are used in the two image directions. In a real camera however, this is usually not the case, but that problem is easily solved by having a conversion between the real camera detector chip coordinate system and the simplified ones used above. This is needed both for the CCM and the GCM. The transformation between the coordinate systems, i.e. from a point x_d^i to a detector chip coordinate, x_c^i, is

$$x_c^i = \begin{bmatrix} m_1 & s \\ 0 & m_2 \end{bmatrix} x_d^i + x_{c0}^i \quad (24)$$

Here m_1 and m_2 adjust the image unit scales in x- and y- direction of the detector. They are different if the pixel distances are different in the two image directions, the ratio between them is called the aspect ratio. x_{c0}^i is the detector pixel coordinates of the principal point. (24) shifts the origin of the coordinate systems, so that it is in the sensor coordinate system origin. If the detector image coordinate axes are not perpendicular to each other the parameter s is used, otherwise it is zero.

2.4 Comparison between the models

The models can be compared by looking at a simple version of the GCM, with constant entrance pupil and no decentring distortion. In that case the CCM and the GCM both model a camera with ordinary radial distortion. The relation between the angle α and r and f are, for PCM, CCM and the GCM respectively,

$$\text{Pinhole Model, PCM } \tan\alpha = \frac{r}{f} \tag{25}$$

$$\text{Conventional Camera Model, CCM } \tan\alpha = \frac{r_p(r)}{f} \tag{26}$$

$$\text{Generic Camera Model, GCM } \tan\alpha = \frac{r}{f_{inner}(r)} \tag{27}$$

Here it can be seen that if $r/p(r)$ where $p(r)$ is a polynomial in r was used in the CCM instead of $r_p(r)$, the same radial distortion model can be obtained as the GCM with constant entrance pupil. The other way around the GCM can be equivalent to a CCM if $f/p(r)$ is used as f_{inner}. A mix between the models can be constructed if a quotient between polynomials is used as $f_{inner}(r)$ or $r_p(r)$. That will also give polynomial equations for the projection to the image (15) for the GCM, (this is true even if also variation in entrance pupil is used in the model, if f_{outer} is a polynomial or quotient between polynomials).

The fact that $\tan\alpha$ is large or even goes to infinity as α approaches 90 degrees is a problem for the CCM, since that can not be modelled by its polynomial trying to compensate that. It is no problem for the GCM, since if $f_{inner}(r)$ is zero also the right hand side of (27) goes to infinity. If $f_{inner}(r)$ is small or even negative it is no problem for the object line of GCM to be directed in larger angles α.

Sometimes there is a need to know how the image would look without distortion. That can be done even if the camera is calibrated (see Section 3) with the GCM, if f_{outer} is constant. The undistorted image can be calculated from similarity of triangles according to:

$$r_p = \frac{f_0 r}{f_{inner}(r)} \tag{28}$$

Every point should be moved radially from the centre according to (28) to get the corresponding undistorted image. Any value of the constant f_0 gives an undistorted image, but if the image scaling in the centre of the image should be preserved, the first constant in the $f_{inner}(r)$ polynomial, d_0, should be used as f_0. Then the image scale will be the same as for the CCM after radial distortion compensation. If decentring distortion was used first the non decentring distorted image points should be calculated and then use (28) on the resulting image. If f_{outer} is not constant this formula will only be an approximation.

Entrance pupil variations are more important for cameras with a high angle of view. Also it is more important if the distance between the camera and the observed objects can vary. That is since, if the distance is not varying, a camera model with a slightly wrong position of

the entrance pupil can approximate an exact model in a good way, see Fig 7. Fisheye cameras have a large depth of focus. Therefore there are three reasons for using the GCM for fisheye cameras. The large viewing angle and the depth of focus makes entrance pupil important, and the way to handle ordinary radial distortion is suitable for fisheye cameras. Since the simplest meaningful special case of the GCM is the PCM, it is suitable for low distortion cameras as well. Therefore the GCM has the best of both worlds compared to the CCM and models specialised for fisheye lenses.
The GCM is also suitable for situations where the focus and/or zoom can vary, as will be described in Section 3.1.

3. Calibration

To use a camera model its intrinsic parameters have to be known, and these are determined in a calibration. That can be done by taking several images of reference points from different angles and distances, and perform a calibration calculation based on the images. In these calculations the positions of the references will be calculated, as well as the camera poses for the calibration images. The reference positions are also useful if there is a need to calculate camera poses based on images, described in Section 4.1. The calibration problem can be transformed into a least squares optimization problem. If the optimization is made in image space the function to minimize is obtained from the norm of a residual vector of distances between the measured image points x_c^i and the estimated points, $\hat{x}_c^i$ calculated based on (24) of the camera model and its partly unknown parameters:

$$\min \sum_j \sum_k \left| x_{cjk}^i - \hat{x}_{cjk}^i \right|^2 \tag{29}$$

The sum is taken over all calibration images with indices j and all reference points with indices k. It is an advantage if approximate initial values of reference positions, camera poses and intrinsic camera parameters are known. Otherwise the optimization procedure may not converge, see Section 3.3.
One optimization issue is that it has to be known which reference point in the object world corresponds to which point in the images, the correspondence problem. One way of solving that is to place unique groups of references in the environment, like star constellations. These can be matched with a matching algorithm. Actually the references together can be viewed as one large constellation, but then it takes a longer time to match. Another way of doing this is to manually instruct the system the identity of each point in the images. The same optimization criterion, (29), is used weather the reference positions are known or not, but if they are not known they are calculated by the optimization program, otherwise they are considered given constants.
In the calibration calculations there are a large number of unknown parameters. If the references are unknown there are six pose parameters for each calibration image, three for each reference position in addition to the intrinsic camera parameters. A residual vector containing all the optimization image errors can be sent to the optimizer. The optimizer can then square and sum if needed. Also a Jacobian matrix can be sent to the optimizer. This Jacobian contains all the partial derivatives of all the elements in the residual vector with respect to all the unknown parameters. Calculation time can be saved by using the fact that

most of the elements in this matrix are always zero. For example the derivative of a residual element corresponding to one image is zero with respect to a pose parameter of another image camera pose. The same is valid for the derivative of an image reference position with respect to the position of another 3D reference point. The derivative with respect to an unknown intrinsic camera parameter will in general not be zero though. These derivatives can be computed numerically, or analytically. The residual vector can have the double length if each image point difference is divided into individual difference in x and y direction.

The optimization can also be made in object space. By using a measured image reference coordinate, the camera model can be used to calculate the corresponding object line $x_{fo}^{w} + a(x_{fi}^{w} - x_{r}^{w})$. The shortest distance from this line to its corresponding 3D reference point position x_{o}^{w} can then be used as residual. An optimization criterion for this case is

$$\min \sum_{j} \sum_{k} \left(\frac{\left| (x_{fijk}^{w} - x_{rjk}^{w}) \times (x_{fojk}^{w} - x_{ok}^{w}) \right|}{\left| x_{fijk}^{w} - x_{rjk}^{w} \right|} \right)^2 \tag{30}$$

In the parenthesis is the formula for the shortest distance between a point and a line. Minimization can also be performed at any stage in between, for example the points can be converted to non-decentring distorted image coordinates and the residual vector is formulated accordingly. Yet another possibility is to use (28), and minimization can be done in a non distorted image plane, if f_{outer} is constant. There are calibration methods specialized in minimizing errors in a non distorted image plane, that uses the fact that there straight lines are mapped to straight lines in the images (Devernay & Faugeras 2001), and these can be applied also for the GCM if (28) is used. Reference points can be placed in the environment for that purpose, or natural points and corners can be used.

Another way of performing the calibration when camera poses can be measured independently, e.g. by a laser tracker, is to also include differences between the calculated calibration poses from vision and measured poses in the optimization criterion. If the calibration camera poses are measured, the calibration is called active. One thing to consider then is that if the systems measure in different coordinate systems, and it is not exactly known which point on the camera is measured transformation parameters will be added as variables in the optimization. Weights should be added to the least squares error components, to get the right importance of image pixel errors compared to position errors and orientation errors.

3.1 Variable Focus and Zoom

The geometry of the camera has been considered constant so far. It is possible to allow for variable focus and zoom in the system using the GCM if there is some kind of measure of how the camera is focused and zoomed. There are two reasons that the GCM is suitable for variable focus and zoom applications. One is that the position of the camera can be a point on the detector, and not in the lens system that can move when zooming and focusing. Another is that the entrance pupil can move considerably when changing the zoom.

The calibration procedure would be similar as for fixed geometry, but the calibration images must of course be taken with different focus and zoom. Some kind of interpolation or function dependency will be needed between different values of the focus and zoom parameters and the other intrinsic camera parameters. If f_{oc} is the focus and z_o is the zoom, one way is to let the intrinsic parameters depend on them in the following way

$$c(f_{oc}, z_o) = q_0 + q_1 f_{oc} + q_2 z_0 + q_3 f_{oc}^2 + q_4 z_o^2 + q_5 f_{oc} z_o \tag{31}$$

That is each camera parameter can be replaced by this kind of expression. This implies there will be six times as many camera parameters. These dependencies are in general different for different camera parameters though, e.g. m_1, m_2 and s for the image plane conversions do not depend on the focus and zoom and therefore do not imply more parameters. Another way of calculating with variable focus and zoom is to do a regular calibration for some fixed values of these parameters, and then use interpolation between them, like in Fig 5. Here a triangular net is constructed in the 2D space of f_{oc} and z_o values.

If the system is calibrated in the points of Fig 5, then if for some value of these parameters it can be determined which triangle we are in, e.g a linear interpolation between the corner points of the triangle can be done. If a projection to the image shall be done, first calculate the corresponding image coordinates for the triangle corners, and do the interpolation. A similar thing can be done in the other direction by calculating the vectors of the object line and do a linear interpolation. If it is important to have exactly the same transformation both from image to object space and vice versa, as in the method to be shown in the last part of Section 3.3, the following can be done. Make an interpolation of the different camera parameter values in the triangle corners, and use them to do the camera model projections. A rectangular net can also be used, then a bilinear interpolation should be used.

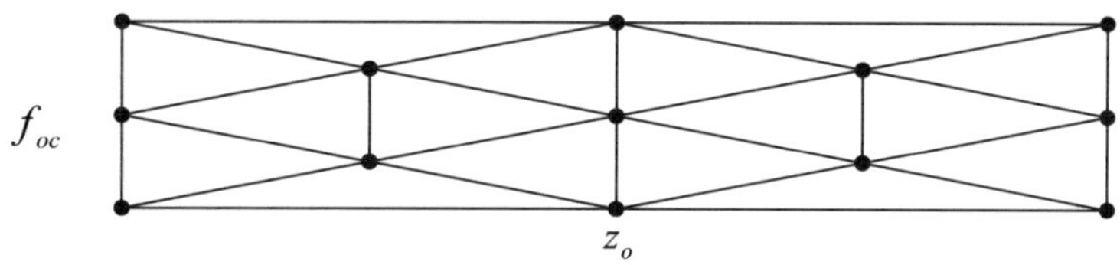

Fig. 5. Triangular net used for interpolation between points calibrated for different values of focus and zoom.

3.2 Nontrivial null spaces

Before the actual calibration calculations, we consider so called non trivial null spaces. These are ambiguities occurring when the same image can be formed with different parameter setups, such as camera parameters and camera poses. That can cause problems when the calibration is based on images. One obvious null space occurs when changing the world coordinate system. By redefining the world coordinate system or moving the complete system with camera and references the same images can be obtained. Therefore the coordinate system should be locked somehow before the calculations.

Seven parameters need to be locked for defining the world coordinate system, three for position, three for orientation and one for scaling.

First force the system to have the coordinate system origin, $(0,0,0)^T$, in one reference point. Let the x-axis be in the direction to one other reference point by measuring the distance, x, between these points and set the coordinates of this second reference to $(x,0,0)^T$.

Then the z- coordinate of a third point can be set to zero, defining the final rotation degree of freedom. These numbers should be constants, and hence not be changed during the calibration calculation. The length scales of the system will be defined by x. The more exact x is measured, the more accurate the length scales will be. This will define a 3D world coordinate system that the vision system relates to.

Another nontrivial null space occurs when determining the constant e_0 of f_{outer} in (8). If it is increased for a camera pose, the same image can be formed by in the same time moving the camera backwards the distance of change of e_0. To solve that e_0 should be set to a constant and not be changed during calibration, if focus and zoom are constant. As a matter of fact it is usually best to set that coefficient to zero. That will give a camera model that differs a bit from Fig 2, but mostly for pedagogical reasons it was first described it in that way. Instead in Fig 2 the point x_{f0} together with the object line will be moved down close to the image plane (or more correctly the image plane and x_{fi} moved up). This makes the position of the camera defined as a point in the centre of the optics, just as with the CCM, which is good. One exception of $e_0=0$ is if the camera is calibrated also with respect to varying focus and zoom. Then e_0 can be a function of these parameters, but to find that function dependency the calibration camera positions have to be measured with some other system, as in the last part of the calibration section, because of this null space. One way of determining the dependence of e_0 with respect to zoom is to look at the camera and see how much the front lens moves when zooming. That dependency can be used for that parameter and then optimize the rest with respect to images.

Another null space is in the values of the constants m_1 and m_2. Their ratio, the aspect ratio, is the ratio between the pixel distances in x- and y- on the detector. Though one of them can be set to any positive value. Therefore it is convenient to set one of them to one. Then the unit of f_{inner} will be a pixel distance unit. The unit of f_{outer} is the same as for an outer world coordinate system. The other of the two constants m_i can be seen as a camera parameter, to be determined in the calibration procedure. The calibration will then find it to be the mentioned ratio between the pixel distance in the image directions. With this method we actually don't have to know the actual pixel distances in the detector, in fact it can not be determined in this kind of calibration, and it is not needed, at least for the applications here.

Other nontrivial null spaces can occur when the detector surface is parallel to a planar reference plate. Consider, for simplicity, a PCM. Then if the camera is moved away from the reference plane and in the same time the focal distance is increased, with the same proportions as the movement distance from the plate. Then the same image would be obtained, see the left part of Fig 6. In the figure two "light beams" are shown but actually the whole image will be the same. This can cause problems if the calibration images are non-leaning enough compared to the reference plate, even in calibration with known references. Therefore images with leaning camera have to be included in the calibration, at least in passive calibration and the references are in a plane. This can occur also when the camera has distortion.

If the detector is not perpendicular to the optical axis, and again the references are in a plane another null space can occur. Think again of a PCM, but with leaning detector compensation. Then the detector can be kept parallel to the reference plane even though the optical axis is leaned, Fig 6. If this camera is moved to the side, and the lens system is held directed towards the same point on the reference plate (by leaning the detector surface), then the image will not change. Hence this is another nullspace. This is another reason to include calibration images with leaning camera poses.

In order to get a good calibration the calibration images have to be such that the references seen in the images cover the range of inclination angles, α, the system shall be used for. If the entrance pupil is not constant compared to the camera the calibration images have to vary both in distance and angle to the references. Otherwise the calibration calculation can make the system work accurately only for the particular distance of the calibration images, see Fig 7. The problem occurs if there is a large enough interval of α where the distance to the references does not vary. That is because of another null space. If somewhere in the α interval f_{outer} is e.g. too large that can be compensated by having f_{inner} a little too small, see Fig 7. Then the system will be accurate only for one distance in that direction, α .

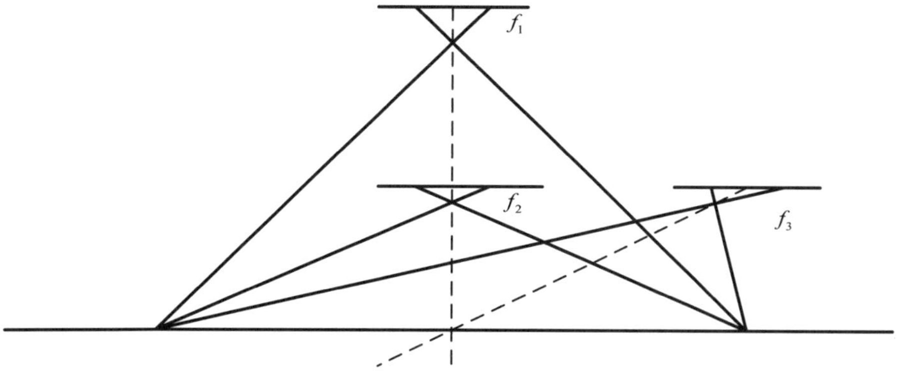

Fig. 6. If the detector surface is parallel to a reference plane nontrivial null spaces occur.

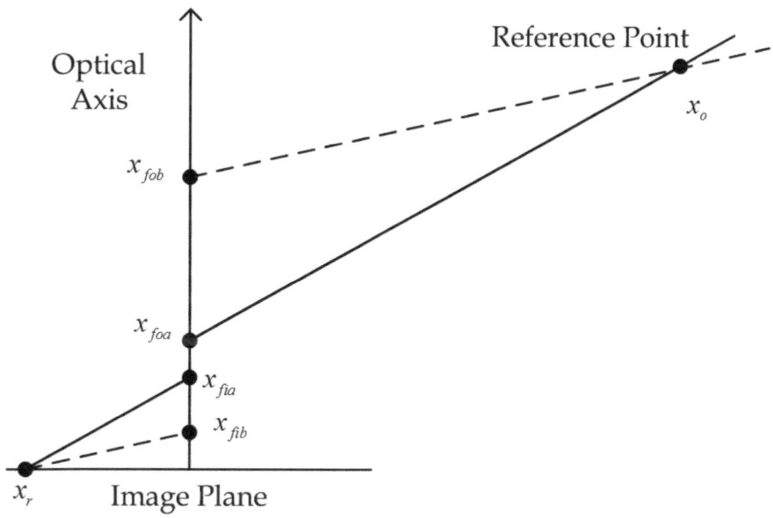

Fig. 7. If the distance to the reference does not vary two different sets of camera parameters *a* and *b* can both give a small error norm in both image and object space. The calibration can not determine if situation *a* or the dotted *b* in the figure is the right one.

3.3 Pre-processing algorithms

This section suggests means for improved calculation results, especially initial values for extrinsic and intrinsic camera parameters as well as reference positions to assure convergence, and estimation of the centre of a reference in the image. The centres of the references are important since the centre of gravity of a projected shape in the image does in general not reflect the centre of the object in object space. The calibration is a large calculation, and without estimations of the parameters it is hard for them to converge at all. For the methods in this section to be valid the references needs to be flat and with a known geometry.

Estimating Intrinsic Camera Parameters

Initial values of intrinsic camera parameters are estimated based on the shapes of images of reference points. For each reference in the image, extract image coordinates around its border on a sub pixel level by using greyscale intensities of the pixels. Use the camera model to convert these points to object space lines, see Fig 8, project them to a plane in object space, and then match the known real shape and size of the reference to these object lines using optimisation routines. The set of intrinsic parameters that give best match are used as initial estimates of the camera parameters.

This can be done to several or all of the references in the images. When a good match is achieved we have probably found good estimates of the intrinsic camera parameters.

Details in the problem formulation are now given, and to ease the work start the calculations in the camera coordinate system. The points used in the camera model to project to the object space is simplified to

$$x_{fi}^c = \begin{bmatrix} 0 \\ 0 \\ f_{inner}(r) \end{bmatrix}; \; x_{fo}^c = \begin{bmatrix} 0 \\ 0 \\ f_{outer}(r) \end{bmatrix}; \; x_r^c = \begin{bmatrix} x_{r1}^i \\ x_{r2}^i \\ 0 \end{bmatrix} \qquad (32\ \text{a,b,c})$$

The corresponding object line is then expressed by inserting (32) into (13). The equation of a plane through an estimated flat reference can be written

$$\text{Reference Plane: } \hat{x}_o + a_1 v_x + a_2 v_y \qquad (33)$$

The vectors $\hat{x}_o$, v_x and v_y define the location and angle of the estimated reference plane and a_1 and a_2 are parameters.

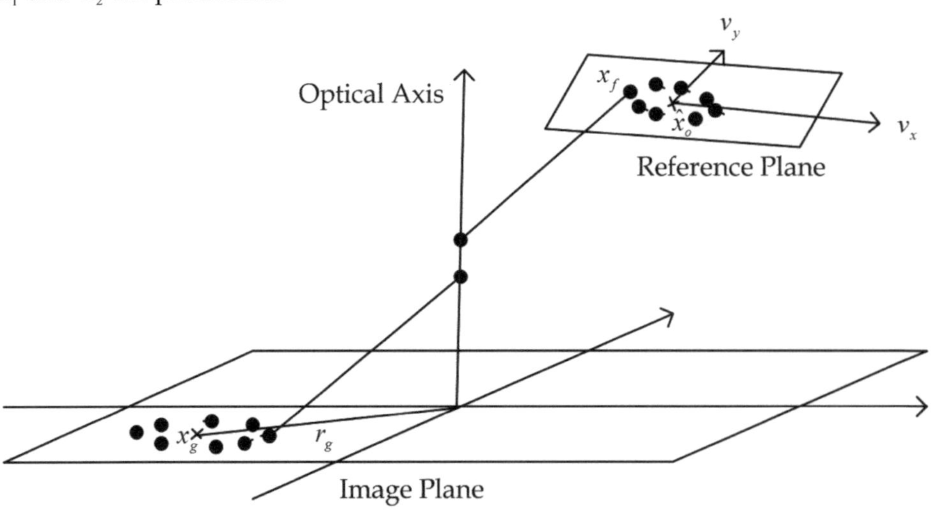

Fig. 8. For estimating calibration parameters, and also calculating reference image centre points, the boundary of the image of the reference is projected to a reference plane in object space, the results are points x_f. $\hat{x}_o$ is the centre of the points x_f. After optimization of (34), $\hat{x}_o^c$ will be estimations of reference positions x_o^c.

The vectors $\hat{x}_o$, v_x and v_y are first estimated roughly, see below, and then an optimization procedure can be used to adjust them more exactly. By setting the formula for the plane (33) equal to the object line expression, a system of equations is obtained where the solution, x_f, is their intersection. Without loss of generality $\hat{x}_o$ can be set as the centre, or some other well defined point on the reference, in the object world. v_x and v_y span the plane, and must not be parallel.

Now the least squares sum can be expressed. Index j represents the camera poses, index k the reference number and l is a numbering of the points around the image of a reference circle. The sum should be minimized with respect to the reference centre points and the plane angles ($\hat{x}_o$, v_x and v_y) and the intrinsic camera parameters. For circles this can be expressed as

$$\min \sum_j \sum_k \sum_l (|x^c_{fjkl} - \hat{x}^c_{ojk}| - r_k)^2 \tag{34}$$

This is a sum over squared differences between the distances from the out projected border points x^c_{fjkl} to the estimated reference circle centre points, $\hat{x}^c_{ojk}$, and the circle radius, r_k. The points x_{fjkl} are assumed to be in the projection planes, which they always are if they are calculated as the intersection between the plane and the lines described above. The radius r_k of the reference points should be measured before the calculations, so that they are known and inserted in the expression. If the radius is not correctly measured it will change the distance between the camera and the reference points in the calculations, but the values of the intrinsic camera parameters will be almost exactly the same. The calculations can also be performed in two steps so that an outer optimization of the camera parameters calls a plane matching optimization routine. This should give more stable calculations.

Since this is only an estimation calculation decentring distortion should probably be ignored, as well as the entrance pupil variations. As starting approximation of the principal point, the centre of the detector can be used. This coordinate can be further optimized if needed.

Computationally it is efficient to just start with a few references, and add more while the estimation is improved. When adding new references starting values of $\hat{x}_o$, v_x and v_y should be estimated for the reference. From the centre of gravity x^c_g of the image coordinates around the reference an object line can be computed that approximately should go through the reference x^c_o. But at first we don't know the distance from the camera. To determine the distance a test plane can be constructed somewhere on the object line that is orthogonal to it. Calculate object lines based on each image point around the reference, and calculate their intersections with the test plane. The test plane is obtained by setting the vectors (35) into (33).

$$\hat{x}^{c\,\prime}_o = x^c_{fi}(r_g) - x^i_{g1}e^c_x - x^i_{g2}e^c_y + x^c_{fo}(r_g) \tag{35a}$$

$$v^{c\,\prime}_x = e^c_z \times (x^i_{g1}e^c_x + x^i_{g2}e^c_y) \tag{35b}$$

$$v_y^c{}' = (\hat{x}_o^c{}' - x_{fo}^c(r_g)) \times v_x^c{}' \tag{35c}$$

The intersection can be calculated with linear equation systems, setting (33) equal to (13). The unit vectors in (35) in the camera coordinate system are simply $e_x^c = (1,0,0)^T$, $e_y^c = (0,1,0)^T$ and $e_{cz}^c = (0,0,1)^T$. From the out projected points not only the direction but also the distance and the angles can be compued. Calculate the out projected points centre of gravity, x_{gf}^c, in the plane defined by (35). Find the out projected point with the maximum distance to this centre of gravity. Call a vector from the centre of gravity x_{gf}^c to the point furthest away $R_{\max}$ and the corresponding distance $r_{\max}$. Find out the shortest distance to the centre of gravity, call the distance $r_{\min}$. Observe that $r_{\max}$ is the radius corresponding to a non-leaning direction of the circular reference. Therefore the ratio between r_k and $r_{\max}$ determines how far from $x_{fo}(r_g)$ the reference is, measured in units of $\left|x_{gf}^c - x_{fo}^c(r_g)\right|$. In the direction corresponding to $r_{\min}$ the reference plane leans the most corresponding to the test plane. The leaning angle in that direction is $\arccos(r_{\min}/r_{\max})$. Good starting values for $\hat{x}_o$, v_x and v_y in the optimization (34) can now be expressed as:

$$\hat{x}_o = x_{fo}^c(r_g) + \frac{r_k}{r_{\max}}(x_{gf}^c - x_{fo}^c(r_g)) \tag{36a}$$

$$v_x = v_{hc}\cos\chi + v_{ha}\sin\chi \tag{36b}$$

$$v_y = v_{ha}\cos\eta \pm v_{hb}\sin\eta \tag{36c}$$

where the vectors v_h are

$$v_{hb} = \frac{x_{gf}^c - x_{fo}^c(r_{cg})}{\left|x_{gf}^c - x_{fo}^c(r_g)\right|} \tag{37a}$$

$$v_{hc} = \frac{R_{\max} - x_{gf}^c}{\left|R_{\max} - x_{gf}^c\right|} \tag{37b}$$

$$v_{ha} = v_{hb} \times v_{hc} \tag{37c}$$

v_x and v_y contains angles. It is usually better to adjust these angles in the optimizations (34) than the vectors v_x and v_y directly. Starting values of the angles are then 0 for χ and $\arccos(r_{\min}/r_{\max})$ for η. There are two values of v_y because of the plus and minus signs. Both should be tried, and the one leading to the best fit is used. The calculation of starting values for intrinsic camera parameters here are not only used for that, but also as a starting values in the next two sections.

Approximate Reference Positions and Pose Calculations

In the above calculations not only the intrinsic camera parameters were estimated, but also the relative positions of the references and the camera poses, through the $\hat{x}_o^c$ vectors.

Therefore from the output of the optimization in (34) the relative positions of the reference positions, and also the different poses for the calibration images, can be approximately calculated also in the world coordinate system. These positions are valuable starting points for the calibration procedure.

The extrinsic camera parameters and reference positions are calculated by matching the reference positions that are now given in the camera coordinate systems for the different calibration poses. The idea is to transform the systems by rotation and translation so that the reference positions match each other as well as possible.

One way of making the coordinate transformations to calculate camera poses and reference positions, is again to optimize using a least squares expression.

The relative positions of the reference point to the camera positions are $\hat{x}^c_{ojk}$, calculated in the initial camera parameter estimation section above. These are transformed by a rotation and translation for each image, similar to (1) but this time from camera to world coordinates, to get the points

$$\hat{x}^w_{ojk} = R_j \hat{x}^c_{ojk} + T_j \tag{38}$$

Here $\hat{x}^w_{ojk}$ are approximations of the reference point positions x^w_{ok}. These are transformed for each image j so that the different approximations of the same point match each others as well as possible. R_j is a rotation matrix defining rotations by three angles around the three axes, T_j is a translation vector with three components. These are transformations from the different camera coordinate systems to the world coordinate system. The least squares expression should be optimized with respect to T_j and the three angles in R_j and can be expressed as:

$$\min \sum_k \sum_j \left| (\hat{x}^w_{ojk} - \frac{1}{n_k}(\sum_i \hat{x}^w_{oik})) \right|^2 \tag{39}$$

This is the sum of squares of the reference points distances to their average position based on all images. The sum over i is actually another sum over images where n_k is the number of images for each reference point.

Here some degrees of freedom need to be locked, to prevent the optimization from "drifting away". One way of doing that is to formulate a variation of (39). For the three references with fixed coordinates for the calibration (see Section 3.2), replace the aveage sum for these reference parameters with the known fixed values. The optimization in (39) now gives all the elements in every R_j and T_j which hold the information of the poses of the camera for the images j.

As approximation of the reference positions the last sum in the expression (39) can be used. If references are already known before the calibration calculation a similar method can be used to calculate the calibration camera poses R_j and T_j, but then the last averaging sum should be replaced by the known reference positions.

Image Reference Coordinates

Image points that correspond to certain points in the 3D object world are needed in the calculations. If we for simplicity assume circular references, it is natural to use the centre of

it in the 3D object world as the reference 3D position. To get a good accuracy we need to know a 2D point in the image that corresponds to that 3D point. It is not optimal to use the centre of gravity as the reference point in the image, not even if a simple PCM camera is used. What we want is an image point that as exactly as possible is "looking at" the reference centre point. The result of (34) is a good starting point also for calculating these image centre points. The image references are projected to planes in the object space in (34), and their 3D positions of their centers are calculated. Now we can just project these points back to the image using the camera model. We even know the reference points in the camera coordinate systems, giving even simpler projections, since equations (15,16) can be used right away without doing coordinate transformations first. The reference positions and camera parameters are only approximately known, but when projecting the centre point back the errors will cancel each other. That is since the error in projecting to the object space will be done in reverse when projecting the centre point back, giving good image points. Another method for centre points of circular references can be found in (Heikkila 2000).
These centre point calculations can be made both before the calibration and in pose calculations that will be explained in Section 4.1. Good values of the image reference positions are important for accuracy of calibration and pose calculations, and also give better defined optimums in the algorithms making them converge easier and faster. There is a trade off between calculation time and accuracy. If accuracy is important, new image reference coordinates can be calculated again using preliminary camera parameters, and then calibrate again. In that case, when the new centre points are calculated the camera parameters should be kept constant to the values from the previous calibration when calculating new centre points, but be optimized again in the new calibration.

3.4 Further improvements of calibration

The accuracy of this kind of vision system has been measured using a Coordinate Measuring Machine (CMM) as a reference. The system was calibrated, and then pose calculations were made based on the calibration, and finally the calculated poses were compared to CMM position data. The pose calculations will be described in Section 4.1.
After the camera was calibrated it was placed on the hand of the CMM. The CMM was programmed to move to different locations above a reference plate with reference IR-LEDs. Measurements with both the vision system and the CMM were done in the locations where the CMM stopped. The two systems measured in different coordinate systems. Therefore, to do the comparison the coordinate systems had to be matched, so the vision coordinates were transformed into the CMM coordinate system. The transformation was done with a matching procedure, where seven transformation parameters were determined. The parameters were three for rotation, three for translation and one for scaling. They were determined with an optimization program. One part of the CMM positions was scanning along a line vertically, away from the centre of the reference plate, stopping every centimetre along that line. A plot of the error in mm in the *z*- direction, the direction away from the reference plate, along that line can be seen in Fig 9. The left diagram is based on an ordinary calibration for the GCM as described above.
The curve is almost straight but leaning. A good result would be a curve close to the $y = 0$ line. It seems like some systematic error is involved. This behaviour occurs when the distance error in the direction to the reference plate is proportional to the distance to the reference plate. That is what happens when the focal distance is wrong, or the f_{inner}

polynomial is wrong in a way similar to multiplying it with a constant. That can happen because of the nulls pace shown in Fig 6. It shows that there were not enough leaning calibration poses. To correct that error, first the first constant in the f_{inner} polynomial was locked to a slightly lower value, but the rest was calibrated as before. The corresponding curve after that is the centre curve of Fig 9. The curve is better since the errors are smaller. It is not leaning much, but has been a little more bended. That the curve does not just lean down but gets bended indicates there are some systematic bias that wants to change f_{inner}.

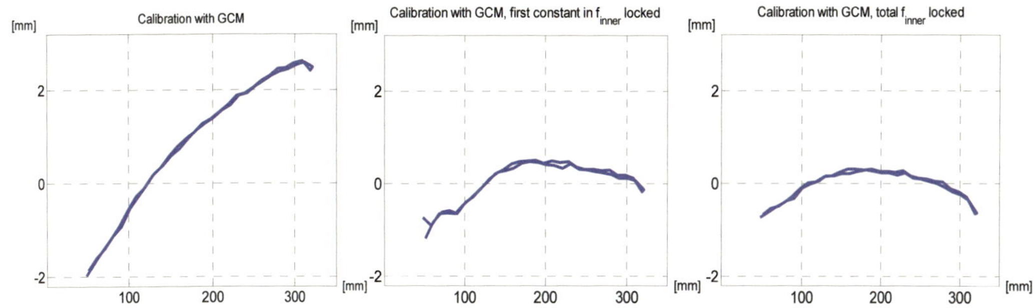

Fig 9. Error curves in mm from scanning a line in direction away from the reference plate. Only the errors in the direction away from the reference plate are shown. Four radial distortion parameters are used. Left, ordinary calibration from images using GCM. Centre, curve leaned down by adjusting the first constant in $f_{inner}(r)$. Right, the whole polynomial $f_{inner}(r)$ multiplied with a constant.

The residual is not only the same (as in the null-space) when changing f but it strives to be a slightly wrong value. The reason can be that because of how the diodes are mounted on the reference plate, leaning camera angles sometimes can not see the whole reference diode, a part of it is shadowed. Therefore the leaning images that should correct this error do not have perfect image coordinates. Also the light intensities from the diodes are lower for larger angles, making them harder to see from the side. Another way of trying to correct this is to not only change the first parameter in f_{inner}, but multiply the whole polynomial after calibration with a constant. That can be achieved by multiplying all the parameters in f_{inner} with a constant. So the system was calibrated as usual and then the f_{inner} parameters were multiplied by another constant, and then the system was calibrated again but with f_{inner} parameters fixed. Then the resulting diagram was the right one in Fig 9. This is a little better than the centre curve, and the procedure give a slightly smaller errors (smaller error norm in mm, see Section 5). The same calculations were done with the CCM. The result of ordinary calibration was almost the same as the left diagram in Fig 9 for the GCM. This can be corrected for the CCM in a similar way as the GCM was corrected.
Note that this behaviour of leaning *z*- curve would not be possible to see if only a line is scanned in the *z*-direction. That is since then the coordinate matching optimization would take that error away. The poses have to be spread parallel to the reference plate also, when the coordinate transformation between the vision coordinate system and the CMM coordinate system is done.

The procedure of including measured poses in the calibration could also correct this error. That procedure could not be done in a good way here because once the camera was placed on the CMM it could not rotate. The angle should vary for the different calibration images.
If enough non biased leaning calibration images are used this error should disappear. So this correction is not always necessary. It could sometimes be a good idea to do this control of comparing with another position system, like a CMM, to be sure that the calibration is correct.

4. Applications

Methods for using the calibrated camera model for calculating a camera pose based on an image is first shown here. Then a method of using stereo vision from calibrated cameras for calculating positions is described.

4.1 Pose calculations

The 6D pose of a calibrated camera taking an image can be calculated using a single image. That is done in a similar way as the calibration, but both the camera parameters as well as reference positions have to be known, as they are after the calibration. Project the reference points to the image using the camera model, and calculate the difference to the detected image points. In that way an optimization criterion can be formulated to be solved by an optimization program. Also, the references need to be recognized somehow, to know which reference in the object world is which in the image. The same error criterion can be used as in the calibration, but the camera parameters and the reference positions are known constants. The only things to adjust by the optimization program are the six pose parameters. Since only one image is used there is no summing over images here. To calculate the pose from an image it needs to see at least four references. There will be the same number of unknowns as equations for three references, but there will still be many solution points, so at least four should be used. A better accuracy can be achieved with more references. Just like in the calibration an object space minimization criterion can be used instead.
These methods can also be used if there is a need to know the relative pose between a camera and an object with known geometry, known from e.g. a CAD model. First extract corners and edges of the object in the image. Then try to match it with the CAD model by projecting it to the image with the camera model. An optimization program can find the relative pose that best matches the image.
A similar procedure can be used in object recognition. If a set of known 3D geometries can appear in the image, then try to match the image with a mathematically projected image calculated with the camera model and the known geometry. If an optimization can find a good match the object is found.

4.2 Stereo vision and other 3D vision methods

To find the position of a point using vision normally at least two viewing angles are needed in order to find depth, if there is no other known geometrical information about the viewed point. To use stereovision, take images of the point or points of interest from (at least) two directions. Then find the same point in both of the 2D images. The camera poses need to be known e.g. with the method in Section 4.1, and the camera needs to be calibrated. Then calculate the two corresponding object lines using the camera model. The crossing of these lines is then the position of the observed point. Since the system is not exact the two lines will probably not cross each other exactly. But the closest points of the two lines can be calculated. Assume we have two object lines, one for each camera view, calculated from (13) or (14)

$$\text{Line 1: } x_{0a} + av_a\text{; Line 2: } x_{0b} + bv_b \tag{40a,b}$$

An equation for the points closest to each other on the two lines are

$$\begin{bmatrix} v_a^T v_a & -v_a^T v_b \\ v_a^T v_b & -v_b^T v_b \end{bmatrix} \begin{bmatrix} a \\ b \end{bmatrix} = \begin{bmatrix} -v_a^T x_{0b} + v_a^T x_{0a} \\ -v_b^T x_{0b} + v_b^T x_{0a} \end{bmatrix} \tag{41}$$

This equation can be derived from the fact that a straight line between the points on the lines closest to each other is perpendicular to both of the lines. The equation can be solved for the parameters a and b. When these are inserted into (40) the points on the lines that are closest to each other are obtained. The centre point between these points can be used as the 3D position searched for. The distance between these points on the lines can give a hint of the accuracy, especially if several points are calculated or if a similar procedure is done from more than two images of the same point. If a point is found in one of the images of which the 3D coordinates are wanted, then its object line from that point can be computed and projected to the other image(s), for different values of the parameter. Then a line in the other image is obtained where the point should lie. This makes it easier to find the point in the other image(s).

If there is a known constraint on the point, e.g. the point is on a known surface, then the coordinates of the point can be calculated from only one image. The coordinates of the point will be the intersection between the object line and the known plane or line.

Structured light is another method to determine 3D coordinates (Zhou & Zhang 2005). If a point is illuminated with structured light and the position of a light line is known the position of the point is the intersection of the object line and the light line. Another way of using structured light is to have a light source that projects a line, that is the structured light is in a plane. If the geometry of the plane is known the 3D geometry of a line can be calculated. First find the 2D line in the image corresponding to where the light plane hits an object. Then several object lines can be calculated, one for each image pixel of the line in the image. Points following the 3D curve can be calculated as the intersections between the object lines and the structured light plane. This method to find the curve will not work if the camera is in the same plane as or too close to the structured light plane.

Stereovision can also be used for determining the 3D geometry of a curve. Take images of the curve from two different directions. Find the curve in both of the 2D images. Sort the points according to position along the curve. Then go through the points of one of the images and calculate the "object line" for the point. By going through the points of the other image find which of their object lines are closest "above" and "below" the first object line, using (40-41). In that procedure the following expression is useful

$$(x_a - x_b)^T (v_a \times v_b) \tag{42}$$

where x_a and x_b are the points on the lines (40) obtained by using (41). (42) will have a different sign for points "above" and "below" the first object line (40a), so it can be used for determining the closest "object lines" (if v_a and v_b always points in the directions from the

camera to what is observed or always in the opposite direction, which is the case in practice). Once the closest object lines from the other image are found use their closest points on the first object line and determine their average position. The average should be weighted inversely proportional to the distance to the lines from the other image. The result can be used as a 3D point that is on the 3D curve searched for. By repeating this with the image points along the curve in the image a sequence of 3D points will be obtained along the 3D curve. Some method of smoothing the curve can be used if needed. An alternative here is to make a plane of the object line closest "above" and "below", and determine the planes intersection with the first object line (calculated by setting the object line equal to the parameterised plane). The plane is well defined if the object lines are determined from a camera with constant f_{outer}. The fact that the distance between object lines is given in a straightforward way with this method (40-41), and also on which sides the lines are compared to each other (42), is useful here. Therefore the method is suitable for determining curves as well as points.
In doing these stereo calculations, as mentioned, the two different camera positions needs to differ to get a good accuracy, and to be able to do this at all. When the geometry of a curve is determined in this way the camera poses have to differ in a way that the cross product of unit vectors along the object lines has as big component along the observed 3D curve as possible. If the component of this cross product along the curve is zero it is not possible to use this procedure, without being able to distinguish each individual point along the curve. That is, then it is not enough to know that the two curves correspond to each other but also which point corresponds to each other.
Sometimes there is a need to know relative positions between points or curves both seen in the stereovision images. Then if one of them is already known there could still be a good idea to determine the positions of both of them with the vision system. Then the difference between the points calculated with vision, from the same images, can be used as their relative positions. This can increase accuracy since approximately the same errors can occur for both points, so when the difference is calculated, this error will almost cancel each other out. This is for example the case if stereovision errors originate from not exactly known camera poses.

5. Accuracy

To compare accuracy the calibration and pose calculations were implemented in MatLab. The calculated poses were compared with data from a Coordinate Measurement Machine (CMM). Both the GCM and a CCM were used, with the ability to choose the number of and combination of camera parameters, and hence different kinds of distortion accounted for in the model. Both the residual vector and Jacobian were calculated and sent to the optimization program. The Jacobian was calculated numerically, but the components that are always zero were not updated in the program, to increase the calculation speed. Calibration images and images taken with the camera placed on the CMM together with corresponding position data from the CMM were input data to the calculations. The calibration images were photos of a reference plate from different positions and angles. As mentioned in section 3.4, the vision coordinate system was transformed into the CMM coordinate system before the poses were compared. The seven parameters of this transformation were calculated with an optimization program. Only position errors were compared and not orientation errors.

As references, IR-LEDs were used, mounted on the reference plate. These references were grouped into twenty unique patterns of six diodes, to solve the correspondence problem. To make the calculations faster only one reference per pattern were used in the calibrations and pose calculations, except for two of the patterns where two diodes were used. They helped defining the coordinate system. The calibrations, with the different variations of models and distortion parameters, calculated intrinsic and extrinsic camera parameters as well as the reference positions. An image space minimization criterion was used in the calibration, as well as in the pose calculations. The CMM scanned two lines parallel to the reference plate, at height five and nine centimetres, and one line perpendicular to the reference plate, above the centre of it. Each scanning stopped at every centimetre along the line, and each line were scanned twice. To analyse the accuracy, average differences between the vision system positions and the CMM positions were used, together with a residual vector error norm after the calibration optimization. The residual vector contains image errors measured in pixel units. The camera had 640*480 pixels. The angle of view was 60 degrees in the x-direction and a bit less in y. 526 calibration images were used, the same images for every calibration. In comparison with the CMM, poses calculated from seven or more references were used. The focus and zoom are the same for all the images.

Errors results can be shown with error diagrams, similar to Fig 9. To compare different combinations of camera parameters and the different models, bar charts of error norms are made in Fig. 10 and 11. First a bar chart for the GCM with only radial distortion and constant entrance pupil is shown, with different degrees of the f_{inner} polynomial (7). The principal point and the aspect ratio are held constant. The parameter s is zero. The average error in mm in 3D is shown for the three lines scanned above the reference plate. The improvement in Section 3.4 is used for the errors in mm. Also the error residual norm from the calibration is shown, this is an image pixel error norm, and this is based on an optimization not using the procedure in 3.4. In the table it can be seen how much is gained from adding more parameters for radial distortion. The error is around 0,35mm in 3D position or 3 pixels in the 2D image when two or more distortion parameters are used. Possible error sources when many radial distortion parameters are used could be bad quality of calibration images, as discussed above, not regular detector pixel coordinate system, bad focus, not exact centre points of the image of the references. Another source of error could be that the object line is not exactly straight especially for close ranges.

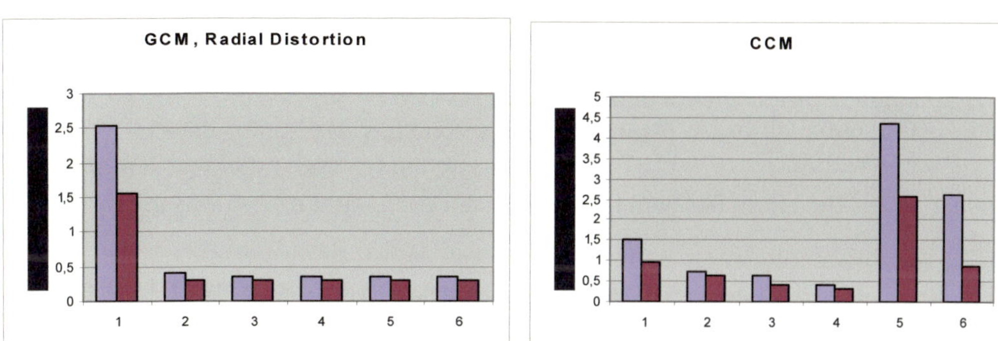

Fig 10. Bar charts over error norms. Left bar chart shows GCM with only radial distortion. The x- axis shows the number of distortion parameters. The first of the double charts shows

average position error in mm in 3D for the calculated poses, the second is an image pixel error norm after calibration. The pixel errors are divided by ten to be able to use one scale in the *y*- axis. The right bar chart shows errors with the CCM. In the first four bar pairs the x-axis shows number of radial distortion parameters. The second last pair has one quadratic distortion term, k_{p2} in (3c), and the last has one quadratic, k_{p2}, and one with power four, k_{p4}.

For a PCM, i.e. the GCM model with only one parameter in f_{inner} and no distortion parameter, the errors are about 13 mm and 6,6*10 pixels. It is not shown since it would give a too small scale in the diagram. If the procedure in Section 3.4 was not used the error norm in mm would be 1.14 instead of 0.35 for four radial distortion parameters with the GCM. A similar gain was achieved for the CCM.
The corresponding bar chart for the CCM is shown in the right bar chart of Fig 10, for one to four radial distortion parameters. First both odd and even powers in the radial distortion of CCM were used. Then it was investigated what happens when only even powers are used. The procedure of Section 3.4 was used to improve the accuracy in mm, even though it can be viewed as a method for the GCM. If that was not used the errors in mm would be considerably larger, see above. Since image minimization is done it is easier to use the type of CCM conversion in (5) instead of (6), so (5) is chosen.
By comparing error norms between the GCM and the CCM with the same number of distortion parameters, it can be seen that with only one distortion parameter the accuracy is better with the CCM, but when more parameters are included the GCM has a better performance. It can also be seen that a better result is actually achieved when including also odd powers in the polynomial (5), even though most of the CCM papers suggest only even powers. This is perhaps not true if the polynomial is used in the other direction as in (6), in that case it can be an advantage to use only even powers.

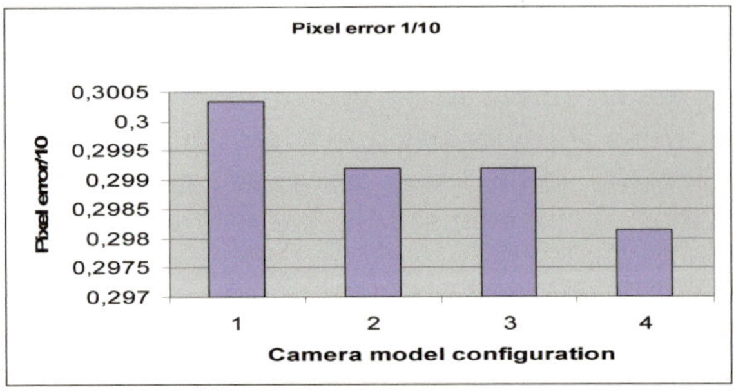

Fig 11. Calibration residual norm in pixels, again divided by ten. Results for the GCM, all four have four radial distortion parameters. The second has also leaning detector compensation with constant $f_l(r)$. The third has varying entrance pupil with a second degree $f_{outer}(r)$. The fourth has both leaning detector compensation and varying entrance pupil.

When adding the additional distortion types the results can be seen in Fig 11. Here the GCM is used for the ordinary radial distortion and then other distortions are added. For ordinary radial distortion four parameters were used. Here only the calibration error residual norm was used for comparison. This is because for the camera used, the improvements of more parameters were small. Therefore since a "manual part" described in Section 3.4 is included

this does not give an exact enough comparison. So the residual vector norm is probably a more exact measure for how much can be gained with the additional types of distortion in case better leaning calibration images were included in the calibration. Here it can be seen that with this camera very little was gained when using decentring distortion and varying entrance pupil. Decentring distortion was not important because the particular camera used did not have much decentring distortion, probably it can be important for other cameras. Also entrance pupil variations did not give a much higher accuracy with the camera used. If it had a larger viewing angle and also a larger lens, that could be more important.
For decentring distortion only the leaning detector formula (18) was used and not (20-23). Since the leaning detector angle was very small (as well as the gain in residual norm), probably no other decentring distortion methods would give large differences in behaviour either with the camera used. The leaning angle for the detector was calculated to 0.07 degrees with this camera.

6. Conclusions and future work

The general GCM model introduced in this chapter includes the best features from conventional camera models CCMs and models specialized for wide angle fisheye cameras in one unified model structure. Therefore there is no longer a need to use different models for these camera types. The GCM may also handle varying entrance pupil and decentring distortion as well as variations in focus and zoom.
In an experimental investigation it was concluded that the accuracy using the new radial distortion compensation in GCM performed better compared to the CCM model tested when few camera parameters were used. The additional distortions in GCM can be added for increased accuracy depending on the camera used. The decentring distortion is usually more important to include in models of cheap cameras, while "entrance pupil" variation can be important even for high precision cameras and mostly if it has a large viewing angle, and is more important for variable zoom and focus applications.
For future research we recommend to perform the accuracy investigation for different kinds of cameras, especially fisheye cameras. With a larger angle of view the advantage of the GCM should be bigger. These experiments should also be done with better leaning calibration images, so the compensation in Section 3.4 is not needed. Investigations on which kind of decentring distortion compensation is the best to use in practice should be done in such an investigation. It would be interesting to try the different "pre processing algorithms" e.g. with circular references, both for analysing how good parameter estimations can be achieved and also the accuracy of the "centre points" and calculation time. Another topic is to use natural corners in the environment as references. Also work on calculating analytical derivatives in the Jacobian for one or both of the transformation directions can be useful. To make calibrations with variable focus and zoom can also be of interest when the focus and zoom can be measured.

7. References

Bakstein, H. and T. Pajdla (2002). Panoramic mosaicing with a 180/spl deg/ field of view lens. *Proceedings of Third Workshop on Omnidirectional Vision, 2002.*

Basu, A. and S. Licardie (1995). Alternative models for fish-eye lenses. *Pattern Recognition Letters* 16(4): 433-441.

Brauer-Burchardt, C. and K. Voss (2001). A new algorithm to correct fish-eye- and strong wide-angle-lens-distortion from single images. *Proceedings of IEEE International Conference on Image Processing (ICIP)* Oct 7-10 2001, Thessaloniki, Institute of Electrical and Electronics Engineers Computer Society.

Brown, D. C. (1971). Close- range camera calibration. *Photogramm. Eng.* 37(8): 855-66.

Devernay, F. and O. Faugeras (2001). Straight lines have to be straight. *Machine Vision and Applications* 13(1): 14-24.

Dornaika, F. and R. Chung (2001). An algebraic approach to camera self-calibration. *Computer Vision and Image Understanding* 83(3): 195-215.

Fraser, C. S. (1997). Digital camera self-calibration. *ISPRS Journal of Photogrammetry and Remote Sensing* 52(4): 149-159.

Gennery, D. B. (2006). Generalized camera calibration including fish-eye lenses. *International Journal of Computer Vision* 68(3): 239-266.

Heikkila, J. (2000). Geometric camera calibration using circular control points. *Pattern Analysis and Machine Intelligence, IEEE Transactions on* 22(10): 1066-1077. 0162-8828.

Kannala, J. and S. S. Brandt (2006). A generic camera model and calibration method for conventional, wide-angle, and fish-eye lenses. *IEEE Transactions on Pattern Analysis and Machine Intelligence* 28(8): 1335-1340.

Motta, J. M. S. T. and R. S. McMaster (2002). Experimental validation of a 3-D vision-based measurement system applied to robot calibration. *Revista Brasileira de Ciencias Mecanicas/Journal of the Brazilian Society of Mechanical Sciences* 24(3): 220-225. 0100-7386.

Nowakowski, A. and W. Skarbek (2007). Lens Radial Distortion Calibration Using Homography of Central Points. *Proceedings of EUROCON, 2007. The International Conference on "Computer as a Tool"*.

Olivier, D. F., L. Quang-Tuan, et al. (1992). Camera Self-Calibration: Theory and Experiments. *Proceedings of the Second European Conference on Computer Vision*, Springer-Verlag.

Pollefeys, M. and L. Van Gool (1999). Stratified self-calibration with the modulus constraint. *IEEE Transactions on Pattern Analysis and Machine Intelligence* 21(8): 707-724.

Shah, S. and J. K. Aggarwal (1996). Intrinsic parameter calibration procedure for a (high-distortion) fish-eye lens camera with distortion model and accuracy estimation. *Pattern Recognition* 29(11): 1775-1788.

Swaminathan, R. and S. K. Nayar (1999). Non-Metric Calibration of Wide-Angle Lenses and Polycameras. *Department of Computer Science, Columbia University, New York.*

Tsai, R. (1987). A versatile camera calibration technique for high-accuracy 3D machine vision metrology using off-the-shelf TV cameras and lenses. *Robotics and Automation.* 3(4): 323 - 344.

van Albada, G. D., J. M. Lagerberg, et al. (1995). A low-cost pose-measuring system for robot calibration. *Robotics and Autonomous Systems* 15(3): 207-227. 0921-8890.

Wei, G.-Q., K. Arbter, et al. (1998). Active self-calibration of robotic eyes and hand-eye relationships with model identification. *Robotics and Automation, IEEE Transactions on* 14(1): 158-166.

Zhou, F. and G. Zhang (2005). Complete calibration of a structured light stripe vision sensor through planar target of unknown orientations. *Image and Vision Computing* 23(1): 59-67.

19

Algorithms of Digital Processing and the Analysis of Underwater Sonar Images

S.V. Sai[1], A.G. Shoberg[1] and L.A. Naumov[2]
[1]*Pacific national university*
[2]*Institute of Marine Technology Problems FEB RUS*
Russia

1. Introduction

At the present time in many countries the great attention is given to the problems of research of Ocean and development of underwater robotics. The vision system is one of the basic systems of "intellectual" autonomous unmanned underwater vehicle (AUV). Modern AUV vision systems can be equipped by various detectors including acoustic sensors, photo and video cameras. The side-scanning sonar or sector- scanning sonar is acoustic sensors. The given device is usually connected to a separate computer for the analysis, processing, recording and transmission of sonar images signals. The present chapter covers actual problems of computer processing and the analysis of the images received from a side-looking sonar (SSS).

At the beginning the main principles (Ageev et al., 2005) of sonar image signals creation are contemplated. The principle of scanning of a sea-bottom surface by narrow angle acoustic beam which is moved in the water environment by progressive motion of SSS antenna is assumed as basis of AUV action. The antenna has the harp diagram directivity, wide (up to 40-60 degrees) in a vertical plane and narrow (no more than 1-2 degrees) in horizontal. The parameter in horizontal plane determines angular resolution of SSS. An acoustic echo signal reflected from a sea-bottom surface, is formed with the help of two antennas located on the left and the right side of the underwater vehicle. During the presentation of information the sonar image is formed in such a manner that the distribution of probing pulses to space corresponds to the image deflection by lines. Thus in the process of device movement an echo signals of each probing cycle represent a separate line. As the result of n cycles of probing the image of a sea-bottom surface will be generated. During movement of AUV, an analog echo signal of every sonar image line will be transformed to the digital form and further can be exposed to preliminary processing, saved in the onboard computer memory and, also, can be transmitted by a communication channel.

The primary goals of preliminary processing of sonar images are the following: a filtration of signals from noise and time automatic gain control (TAGC).

Necessity of a signals filtration is caused by the fact that during the reception of hydro acoustic signals there is always noise on the background. Generally noise in the hydro acoustic channel can be divided into external and inherent (Olyshevsky, 1983). On the point of interaction the noise can be classified into additive and multiplicative. Additive noise according to its structure can be fluctuation noise, pulse and harmonious noise. The most frequent noise is fluctuation, representing the infinite sum of radiations from different noise sources which are not connected to a useful signal. Impulsive noise includes such noise as single impulses originating, for example, during work of the radiating antenna. Noise action results in noise pollution of images and, hence, in impairment of its visual perception while solving analysis problems and recognition of underwater objects by the person - operator.

The peak signal-to-noise ratio (PSNR) is considered nowadays the most popular criterion of noisy images (Gonzalez & Woods, 2002). According to this criterion the normalized root-mean-square deviation of brightness coordinates of the test image pixels without noise and noisy images is calculated. Thus averaging is carried out at all square of the image. The ratio of the maximal value of brightness to a root-mean-square deviation in logarithmic scale defines PSNR value. Accordingly, if the closer the noisy image to the original, the bigger the PSNR value, the better its quality. However this and other similar metrics allow estimating only root-mean-square difference between images, therefore the best results from the metrics point of view is not always correspond to the best visual perception. For instance, the noisy image at which there are fine details with low contrast can have high PSNR value even in that case when the details are not visible on the noise background.

In the first part of the chapter the alternative criterion of the analysis of noisy sonar images in which properties of visual perception of fine details contrast are taken into account is offered. Results of the comparative analysis base algorithms of a filtration of images by objective criterion of an estimation of quality of reproduction of fine details and on peak PSNR value are resulted. The new filtration algorithm allowing effectively to filter a pulse noise and to keep at it image sharpness is offered.

Necessity of application time automatic gain control is caused by the following features (Ageev et al., 2005) of received an echo signals. The amplitude of acoustic echo signal depends on range of reception of a signal in each point of the antenna diagram. Thus the amplitude of the reflected signal in a distant zone of reception will be essentially lower, than in a near zone. Hence, alignment of sonar image contrast along a line needs automatic gain control of a signal depending on time (spatial) position of each pixel. Such control is usually carried out by TAGC device (Kravhenko, 2007). However at a finishing stage of computer processing, with the purpose of improvement of the image quality, manual contrast control of the image on its local segments usually is required.

The following actual task of digital processing of the underwater image is its compression. Compression algorithms are applied to more compact storage of the information on a hard disk or for transfer of the digital data on narrow-band communication channel. Use of compression algorithms with losses usually results in impairment of image quality. The traditional objective criterion of images quality considers root-mean-square criterion (MSE) or the PSNR. That they are integrated concerns to lacks of such criteria and not always correspond to the best visual perception of fine underwater details. In work (Sai, 2007) objective algorithms and criteria of the quality analysis of fine details reproduction of a photo and video images are described. In the second part of the chapter questions of the sonar images compression in real time are investigated. Results of the comparative analysis of compression efficiency and images quality on a basis of discrete cosine transformations, Haar transformations and wavelet transformations are resulted.

Now there are various variants of computer editors of sonar images. With the help of such editors the user can carry out: filtering of the image from noise; to change contrast and brightness of separate segments of the image; to scale the image; to measure and analyze navigating parameters, etc. In the third part of the chapter the description of the developed computer editor of images is resulted. Its functions and features are described, examples of real images processing are resulted.

2. Filtering of the sonar image

Algorithms of images filtering are well enough investigated and submitted in references (Pratt, 2001). Known filtering algorithms usually specialize on suppression of any particular kind of noise. Meanwhile there are no universal filters which could detect and suppress all kinds of noise. However many noise can be approached rather well model Gaussian noise, therefore the majority of algorithms is focused on suppression of this kind of noise. The basic problem at noise filtering consists in not spoiling sharpness of details borders of the image, and also do not lose fine details, comparability on amplitude with noise.
One more complexity is the rating of noise suppression quality. As a rule, quality is estimated as follows: on the original image artificial noise is imposed, then the received image is filtered with the help of the chosen algorithm and compared to the initial image with the help of the chosen metrics. More often for this purpose use PSNR metrics which for gray-scale images is determined by the formula:

$$PSNR = 20 log_{10} \frac{255}{\sqrt{\frac{1}{N}\sum_{i=1}^{N}\left(Y_i - \widetilde{Y}_i\right)^2}} \tag{1}$$

where Y_i and $\widetilde{Y}_i$ is the brightness values of *i-th* pixels of two compared images, N is the common of pixels number in the image. Accordingly, the closer the filtered image to original, there is more value PSNR, and it is above considered that quality of the work of algorithm. As it has been marked above, value PSNR allows to estimate only root-mean-square difference between images, therefore the best results from the point of view of the metrics do not always correspond to the best visual perception.
An alternative analysis algorithm and criterion of noisy images in which properties of visual perception of fine details contrast are taken into account.
With the purpose of the analysis the following preliminary processing of the original image is carried out. At the first stage search of fragments of the image as blocks with a size 3×3 a pixel which contrast corresponds to the established limits is carried out. Thus contrast of each block is calculated in normalized equal color space (Sai, 2007) in which thresholds of visual perception of fine details on brightness index are taken into account.

$$\Delta K = \Delta W^* / \Delta W^*_{th}, \tag{2}$$

where $\Delta W^* = 3(W^*_{max} - W^*_{min})$ is the contrast of the original image block, determined by number of the minimum perceptible color difference (MPCD); ΔW^*_{th} is the threshold value of contrast at which fine details differ with an eye. Value of a brightness index of in equal color space (Wyszecki, 1975) for everyone *i-th* pixel it is calculated as $W^*_i = 25\ Y_i^{1/3} - 17$.
Further for the analysis fragments with the contrast satisfying a condition ($1 \le \Delta K \le 4$) get out and recognition of the image blocks to the following attributes is carried out: «dot object», a «thin line», a «structure fragment». The recognition algorithm is submitted in work (Sai & Sorokin, 2008).

At the second stage, the noise adds in the test image where model of the noise at model Gaussian noise is chosen. Further the maximal brightness deviation of original and noisy image for everyone *k-th* the block is calculated:

$$\Delta_k = max_{i,j,k}\sqrt{\left(\frac{W^*_{i,j,k} - \widetilde{W}^*_{i,j,k}}{\Delta W^*_{th}}\right)^2} \quad (3)$$

and average value of brightness deviation for all fragments of the image:

$$\overline{\Delta}_k = \frac{1}{M}\sum_{k=1}^{M}\Delta_k \, , \quad (4)$$

where M is the amount of fragments with low contrast fine details.

Finally on deviation value ($\overline{\Delta}_k$) and, hence, on value of contrast reduction of fine details it is made a decision on a noisy degree of images. As criterion the rule is chosen simple: if contrast decrease does not exceed one normalized threshold

$$\overline{\Delta}_k \leq 1 \, , \quad (5)$$

that is made a decision that fine details differ with an eye on a noise level and definition of noisy images essentially is not reduced.

With the purpose of research of noise influence on quality of reproduction of fine details of images, authors have developed the computer analyzer. The user interface of the analyzer is shown on Fig. 1.

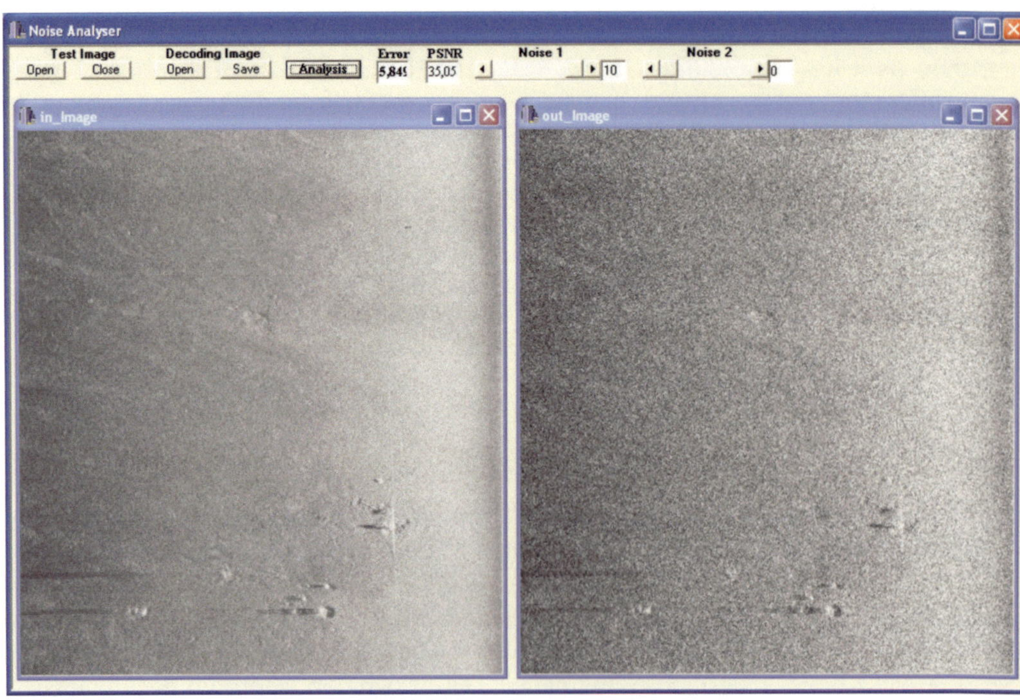

Fig. 1. Computer Noise Analyzer

Let's consider the basic functions of the analyzer. Before the beginning of the analysis the user opens in the first window original image ("Test Image" - "Open").
In the second window on the original image additive noise is imposed. As model of noise gets out fluctuation noise with Gaussian the law of distribution (Noise 1) or pulse noise (Noise 2). The noise level is set in percentage terms to the maximal amplitude of a signal.
By pressing button "Analysis" the program analyzes two images and carries out algorithm of calculation of value $\overline{\Delta}_k$ (4). Thus, the result appears in window "Error". Also, in window "PSNR" there is a calculated value of the peak signal-to-noise ratio (1). Thus, by results of the analysis of value ($\overline{\Delta}_k$) the user makes a decision about a degree of image noisy.

As an example in table 1. experimental dependences ($\overline{\Delta}_k$) and PSNR from root-mean-square value (σ) of the additive Gaussian noise in the brightness channel for a test fragment of sonar images are resulted.

σ %	0,5	1,0	1,5	2,0	2,5	3,0	3,5	4,0	4,5	5,0
$\overline{\Delta}_k$	0,30	0,57	0,84	1,08	1,40	1,68	1,96	2,24	2,54	2,82
PSNR	47,8	44,9	43,3	42,0	41,0	40,3	39,6	39,0	38,5	38,1

Table 1. Dependences of $\overline{\Delta}_k$ and PSNR from root-mean-square deviation σ

On Fig. 2. fragments of sonar image with a various noise level are shown. The analysis of images quality shows that at value of noise in the brightness channel ($\sigma \leq 2\%$), the condition (5) is carried out. At performance of this condition, reduction of contrast of fine details invisibility for an eye and influence of noise does not reduce quality of visual perception of the image. Thus, the developed criterion, as against metrics PSNR, allows estimating objectively influence of noise on reduction in clearness of fine details of images.
It is obvious, that the computer analyzer also can be used for an estimation of the efficiency of filtration algorithms. In this case in the second window it is necessary to open the filtered image and to analyze.
From known filtration algorithms images it is possible to allocate the following base algorithms (Gonzalez & Woods, 2002) 1. Linear pixels averaging; 2. Median filtration; 3. Gaussian diffusion. The features of formation of sonar image concerns that in real time it is formed line-by-line. Hence, filtration algorithms should process pixels of the image also line-by-line.
The authors research influence of base filtration algorithms into efficiency of noise suppression and into quality of reproduction of fine details of sonar image.
The elementary idea of a noise filtration consists in averaging values of pixels in a spatial vicinity. For each pixel the next pixels for it which settle down in a window at the left and to the right of this pixel are analyzed. Then the size of a window is more taken, the there is an averaging more strongly. The simplest variant of a filtration is when as new value of the central pixel average gets out arithmetic all pixels in a window.
Median filtration is a standard way of pulse noise suppression. For each pixel in a window it is searched median value and it is given to this pixel. Definition median values: if a massive of pixels in a window to sort on their value, a median will be an average element of this massive.

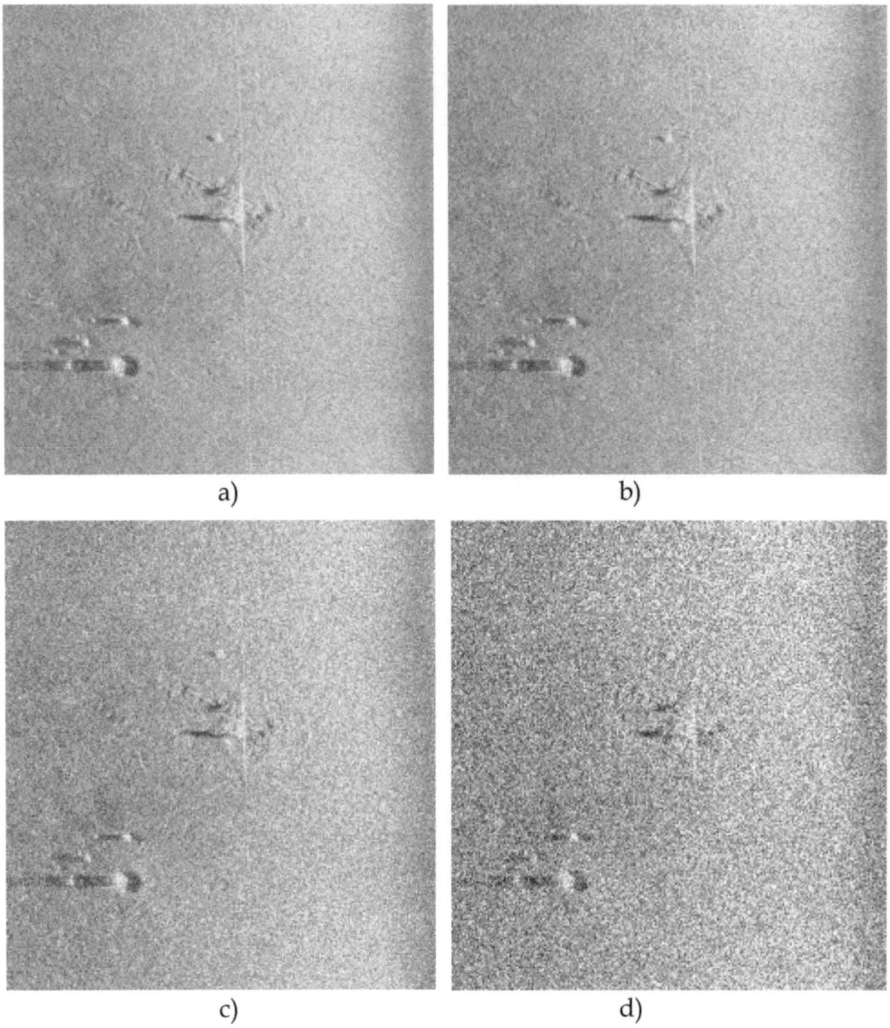

Fig. 2. Fragments of the test image:

a) σ =0%, $\overline{\Delta}_k$ =0 ; b) σ =2%, $\overline{\Delta}_k$ =1,08; c) σ =5%, $\overline{\Delta}_k$ =2,82; d) σ =10%, $\overline{\Delta}_k$ =5,85.

Gaussian diffusion is a convolution of the image with function $g(x) = A \cdot exp\left[-x^2 / \delta^2\right]$, where the parameter ($\delta$) sets a diffusion degree, and parameter A provides normalization. Actually, this same averaging, only pixel mixes up with associates under the certain law set by Gaussian function.

With the purpose of the analysis of efficiency of noise suppression by base algorithms of a filtration we shall take advantage of the computer analyzer (Fig. 1). For this purpose at the first stage of processing it is execute two variants of noisy a test fragment of sonar images: fluctuation and pulse noise with the following parameters. For fluctuation noise it is installed σ =10%, thus an average deviation of fine details contrast equally $\overline{\Delta}_k$ =5,85 and value PSNR = 35,04 дБ. For pulse noise it is installed σ =80% and probability of its appearance P = 0,2, thus an average deviation of fine details contrast equally $\overline{\Delta}_k$ =11,3 and value PSNR = 41,6 дБ.

At the second stage the filtration of noisy images is carried out and quality of noise suppression on value $\overline{\Delta}_k$ is estimated.

In table 2. results of the analysis of quality of noise suppression for three base algorithms where the size of a window of filters is set by three pixels are resulted.

Filter	**Average**	**Median**	**Gaussian**	Noise
$\overline{\Delta}_k$	3,25	3,74	3,02	Fluctuation
PSNR	36,94	36,35	37,26	
$\overline{\Delta}_k$	3,23	2,07	3,41	Impulse
PSNR	38,44	41,15	39,39	

Table 2. Dependences of $\overline{\Delta}_k$ and PSNR from type of Filter

The analysis of the received results allows doing the following conclusions.

1. The best characteristics at a filtration of fluctuation noise has Gaussian filter.
2. The best characteristics at a filtration of pulse noise has median filter.
3. For the set noise parameters in the brightness channel, the condition (5) after a filtration of images is not carried out. Hence, for improvement of quality of fine details reproduction it is required to increase the signal–to-noise ratio in the initial image or to use more optimum filtration method.

In the present work the original method of a filtration of pulse noise of sonar images, based on probability methods of detection and recognition of a pulse noise, and also on a method of a prediction is offered.

The essence of a method consists in the following.

At the first stage average value M and a root-mean-square deviation σ of a S signal in a line of the image are calculated:

$$M_s = \frac{1}{N}\sum_{n=1}^{N} S_n \; ; \; \sigma_s = \frac{1}{N}\sqrt{\sum_{n=1}^{N}(S_n - M_s)} \, , \tag{6}$$

where N is the number of elements in line.

At the second stage, the condition is checked

$$\left|S_{n+2} - S_n\right| > a_1 \cdot \sigma_s \quad and \quad \left|S_{n+2} - M_s\right| > a_2 \cdot \sigma_s \, , \tag{7}$$

where n = 1...(N-2); a_1 and a_2 is the constant factors.

If the condition (7) is carried out, we count, that the element of a image line the with number (n+2) is a noise pulse, and it is replaced with the help of the following equation:

$$S_{n+2} = (S_{n+1} + S_n)/2 \, . \tag{8}$$

If the condition (7) is not carried out, the element of the image line S_{n+2} does not change. Factors a_1 and a_2 are picked up experimentally on the basis of the analysis of real signals of the sonar images.

On Fig. 3. fragments of noisy sonar images are shown: b) up to a filtration; c) after median filtrations; d) after a filtration a new method.
As have shown results of experiments, as against known filtration methods of the pulse noise (Mastin, 1985) , the offered method has such advantages as preservation of quality of fine structures reproduction of underwater images with a high degree of pulse noises suppression.

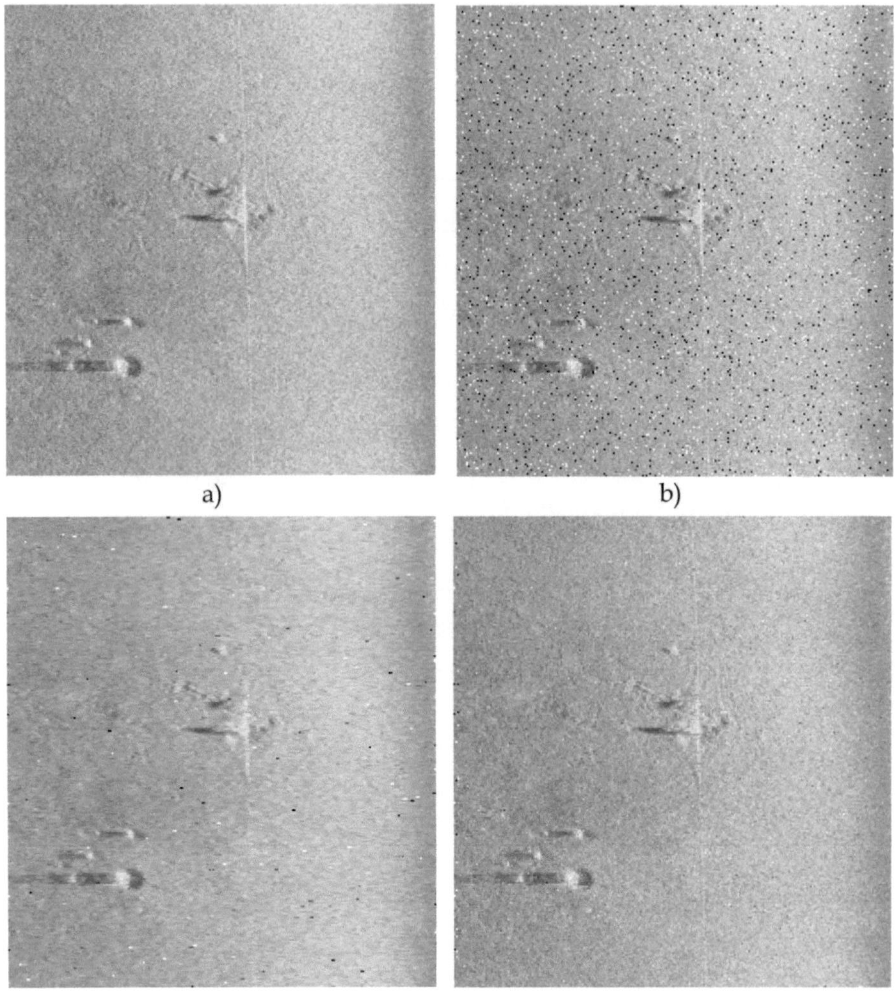

Fig. 3. Fragments of the test image:
a) Test image; b) σ =80%, $\overline{\Delta}_k$ =11,3; c) σ =80%, $\overline{\Delta}_k$ =2,07. d) σ =80%, $\overline{\Delta}_k$ =1,06.

3. Sonar image compression

The basic complexity in design of vision system of AUV in real time is restriction of a pass band of a communication channel. In particular (Ageev et al., 2005), speed of transfer of the information on existing hydro acoustic communication channels can not exceed 3 ... 4 KBit/s.

As an example we shall consider the following characteristics of sonar images signals. We believe, that the period of probing pulses is equal 0,5 seconds and digitization frequency of the analog signals received from antenna of left and right board of AUV is equal 3,2 KHz. In this case we have on 1600 pixels for every line transmitted image. Believing, that each pixel has byte structure, we shall receive, that digital stream speed of the entrance data is equal 3,2 Kb\ss. Thus, for signals transmission on a hydro acoustic channel it is necessary to provide compression of a digital stream approximately in 8 … 10 times and thus to keep enough high quality of the image.

Now standards JPEG and JPEG 2000, based on discrete cosine transformation (DCT) and on wavelet transformation (DWT) are considered as the most effective methods of compression of photo images. It is known, that in comparison with other types of orthogonal transformations, DCT and DWT have the best results of images coding on value of an root-mean-square (MSR) or on value PSNR, i.e. on global quality measures. Therefore, other types of transformations practically are not used for compression of images. In work (Sai & Gerasimenko, 2007) for compression of images as an alternative variant Haar transformation (DHT) is investigated. Results of the comparative analysis of coding efficiency of sonar image signals for three types of transformations below are resulted — DCT, DHT and DWT.

Let's consider algorithm of sonar images compression on basis DCT and DHT in real time.

During AUV movement digital image signals go line by line on an input of the coding block where its record in a buffer memory (RAM) in 16 lines capacity. After record of first eight lines, block process of transformation is beginning, where the size of the block is equal 8×8 pixels. During same time the data consistently record in second half RAM.

Realization of DCT or DHT is realized with the help of sequence matrix multiplying. Direct discrete cosine transformation or Haar transformation are described by the following expressions

$$P_{DCT} = M_{DCT} * P * M^{T}_{DCT};$$

$$P_{DHT} = M_{DHT} * P * M^{T}_{DHT},$$

where P – the block in the size 8×8 pixels; P_{DCT} and P_{DHT} is the blocks of factors DCT or DHT; M is the direct transformation matrix; M^T is the transposed matrix.

After transformation, factors of transformation, which value less than threshold Q size, are nulled. Further, for each block compression by the modified method RLE is carried out. It is obvious, that efficiency of compression and image quality in the big degree depends on Q size.

Let's consider of wavelet-transformation algorithm in real time.

As against two-dimensional block transformation one-dimensional transformation of a line sonar images here is used. Thus, capacity RAM is equal to two lines of the image.

For the first iteration of wavelet-transformation of a line of the image it is calculated (Mallat, 1999):

$$H_j^{(i)} = \sum_{k \in Z} X_{2j+k}^{(i+1)} h_k; \quad G_j^{(i)} = \sum_{k \in Z} X_{2j+k}^{(i+1)} g_k,$$

where $H_j^{(i)}$ is the low-frequency wavelet-factors, $G_j^{(i)}$ is the high-frequency wavelet-factors, X_j is the pixels entrance sequence, h_k and g_k is the low-frequency and high-frequency components of wavelet parent.

Further the wavelet-factors calculated on the previous step of transformation, are compared to values of threshold factors. If the value of wavelet-factors appears smaller value of corresponding threshold factors their values transform in a zero.
After threshold quantization the received values of wavelet-factors are kept in out massive of transformation, and massive of LF components, which size twice less initial, is an entrance signal for the following iteration of wavelet-transformation

$$H_j^{(i)} = \sum_{k \in Z} H_{2j+k}^{(i+1)} h_k; \quad G_j^{(i)} = \sum_{k \in Z} H_{2j+k}^{(i+1)} g_k .$$

The quantity of transformation iterations can be varied, from one and up to such quantity that after last iteration the number of wavelet-factors and LF components of a signal will be less size of a window of the synthesizing filter. Optimum number of wavelet-transformation iterations - from 3 up to 5. After performance of transformation the line of wavelet-factors was coded by modified RLE method.
Factors of threshold quantization for each iteration of transformation were selected by practical consideration, by criterion of achievement of the best quality of the restored image at the maximal factor of compression. We shall note, that the velum of threshold factors decreases in process of increase in a level of wavelet-transformation, i.e. in process of increase in their influence at result of reconstruction of the image.
In work (Sai & Gerasimenko, 2007) influence on efficiency of compression of the following types parent wavelet - Daubechies (2, 4, 6, 8, 10, 12, 20) (Mertins A., 1999) is investigated. As a result of experiments it is received, that the optimum circuit for sonar images compression with sufficient quality is the circuit, realizable by four iterations of filter Daubechies 4.
Let's execute the comparative analysis of efficiency of signals sonar images coding on basis DCT, DHT or DWT. With this purpose we shall take advantage of the computer analyzer shown on Fig. 1. In the second window of the analyzer interface it is opened the decoded image after chosen transformations. Further it is carried out calculations (1-4) and the estimation of images quality on value ($\overline{\Delta}_k$) is put.

In table 3 experimental dependences of compression factor *Cf* test sonar images from threshold factors for three transformations are shown. For the analysis the test fragment of the image of a sea-bottom in the size 1600×500 pixels has been chosen. Here, values ($\overline{\Delta}_k$) and PSNR are resulted. On Fig. 4. examples of fragments (260×280) of the test image before compression and after decoding for approximately identical values of quality parameter ($\overline{\Delta}_k \approx 2{,}1$) are shown. In the table the given line of parameters is allocated by grey color.

DCT				DHT				DWT			
Q	*Cf*	$\overline{\Delta}_k$	PSNR	*Q*	*Cf*	$\overline{\Delta}_k$	PSNR	*Q*	*Cf*	$\overline{\Delta}_k$	PSNR
1	3,44	1,69	40,89	1	3,49	1,72	40,79	6-3-2-1	3,06	1,39	40,80
2	6,14	1,98	40,23	2	6,31	2,02	40,14	12-6-4-1	5,17	1,84	39,87
3	9,16	2,14	39,92	3	9,51	2,16	39,84	18-9-6-1	6,89	2,06	39,50
4	12,22	2,23	39,73	4	12,73	2,27	39,66	24-12-8-1	8,00	2,31	39,17
5	15,04	2,29	39,61	5	15,71	2,32	39,55	30-15-10-1	8,17	2,42	38,99

Table 3. Test image compression factors from *Q*

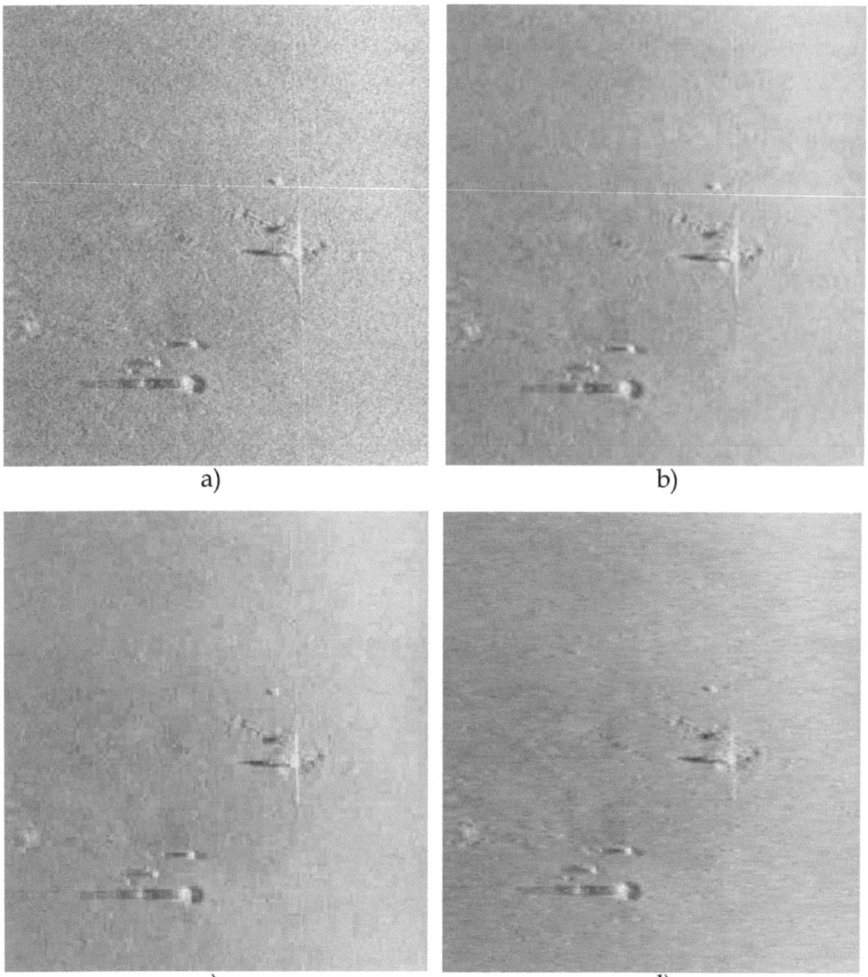

a) b) c) d)

Fig. 4. Fragments of the test image:

a) Test image; b) **DCT**, *Cf* = 9,16; c) **DHT**, *Cf* = 9,51; d) **DWT**, *Cf* = 6,8.

The analysis of the received results allows doing the following conclusions.

Factors of compression of the sonar images after processing DCT or DHT are approximately identical. Visual comparison of images quality also gives approximately identical result. Wavelet-transformation concedes both on efficiency, and on visual quality of images that explain speaks first of all application of one-dimensional transformation and the feature of sonar images in which granular structures prevail and practically there are no brightness smooth fluctuations.

Thus, Haar transformation is competitive DCT and is more preferable at processing of sonar images signals, both on compression efficiency, and on images quality.

4. The computer editor of the sonar images

At the present time there are different variants of computer editors of underwater sonar images. With the help of such editors the user can carry out various functions of processing and the analysis of the hydro location information. The description of the computer editor of the sonar images has been developed in a research laboratory at the Institute of Marine Technology Problems FEB RAS and at the Pacific National University which is shown below.

The program of the sonar editor works with the files with expansion *.gbo, where echo signals of sonar images (digitized and compressed up to word length 8 bit) are registered, and with the additional files with expansion *.idx where the auxiliary information (time, signals from navigating gauges, etc.) is registered. The program is realized in language C ++ in application C ++ Builder 6.

Sonar files are formed in the process of AUV movement and are recorded on a hard disk of an onboard computer. For towed fastened AUV the mode line transfers sonar information through the modem on a conducting rope is provide with the purpose of sonar images supervision in a real time.

User interface

The program represents itself as a multiwindows viewer (Fig. 5), it is allows to open some files (the quantity is limited to computer memory) and to place them on the screen as convenient for the analysis (the cascade, vertically, horizontal). The tools panel and a condition line can be disconnected.

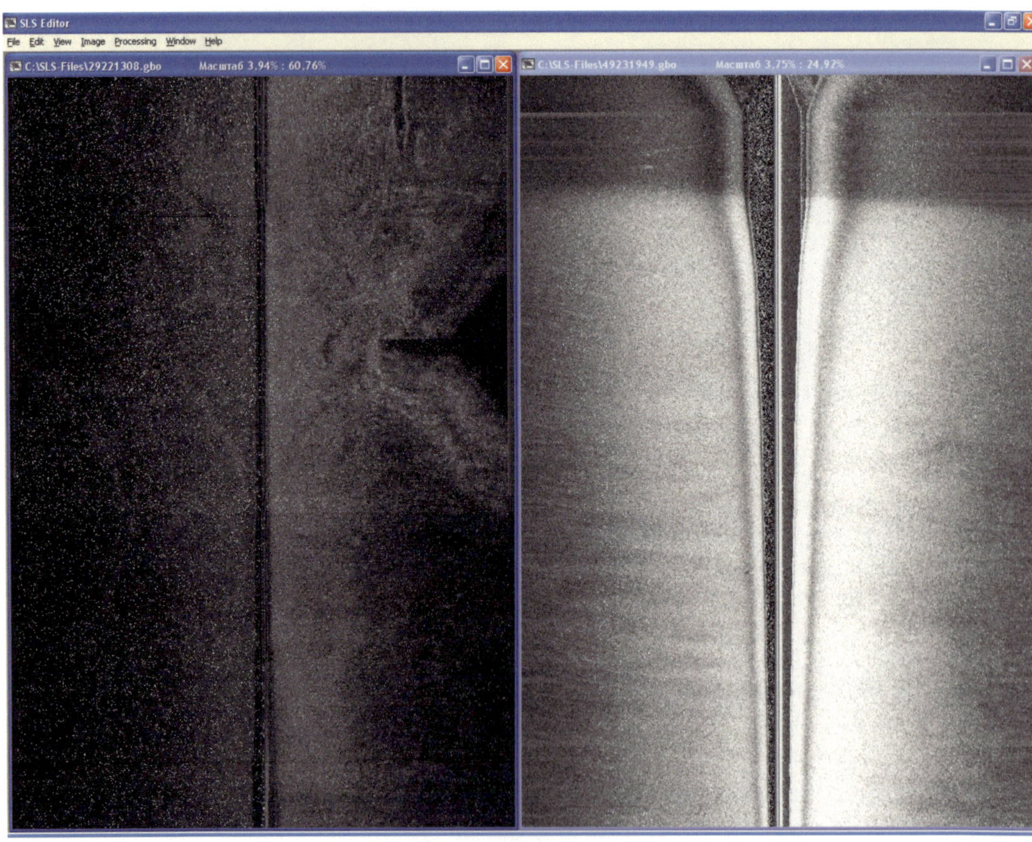

Fig. 5. User interface

In the top part of each window with the image there is the information about the file name with the indication of folders where it is.

In a mode "Editing", the user can allocate a rectangular fragment of the image with the purpose of its more detailed viewing.

To save of the processed file with the purpose of prevention of deleting of the initial information there is the option « Save As … ». In this case the user with the help of the mouse allocates completely or a rectangular fragment (the size of lines does not change) and in a window there is a table with the counted navigating parameters about a tack (the description is shown below). Further by pressing button "OK " the processed file can be saved with an arbitrary name.

Scaling

Scale (the panel of tools: "View" - "Scale") can be chosen arbitrarily up to 100 % on width and height without saving of proportions.

In the window "Scale" the user can choose the following types of scaling: "On width of the screen", "Proportionally", "Without of proportions", "On all screens".

The type of scaling "Proportionally" allows viewing images with a real ratio of the sizes on width and height, for the decimation pixels across with the purpose of alignment of spatial inter elements intervals along a line and between lines of probing.

Application of a preliminary low-frequency filtration of the image lines concerns to features of scaling in a case reduction of its size. Thus, the size of a window averaged the filter is chosen as a quantity of the ratio of the initial image size to the size of its reduced copy.

Modes of the image processing

Images processing is submitted by the following known methods (Shoberg, 2007):

- Inversion;
- Adjustment of brightness – linear increasing and reduction, automatic adjustment under the image and separately on the left and right board;
- Change of a palette on grayscale and on color "Sepia";
- Median filtration (on lines and on column with the any odd of a window sizes);
- Low-frequency filtration (one-dimensional, two-dimensional, Gaussian filtration).

In additional with well- known methods, in the program the new method of a pulse noise filtration is realized. Its description is shown in the second part of the chapter. The panel of tools: "Image" - "Filters" – "New Filter".

In the program the original method of time automatic gain control (TAGC) of sonar images signals is realized. Fig. 6 illustrates the example of TAGC window which is called through the tools panel ("Image" - "TAGC").

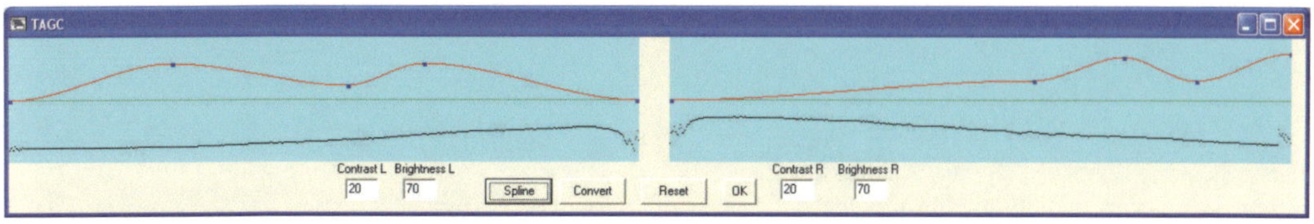

Fig. 6. TAGC window

At initialization diagrams of signal amplitudes distribution along lines for each side are appeared. Each point on the diagram is submitted as average value of brightness of all lines.

In "windows" for the left and right side the brightness and contrast in percentage terms to half of maximal amplitude of signal are shown.
After initialization of TAGC mode, the user can operate the following functions:

1. To install brightness and contrast of the image separately on each board. After installation of values the user can press "Convert" and look result. If the result does not settle the user should press the "Reset" button, thus reset of all options is carried out and the image is restored to an initial kind. Further it is possible to install the new parameters.
2. To adjust contrast on the chosen sites of the image with the help of construction of TAGC diagram. By pressing "Spline" button the horizontal axes of TAGC diagram are appeared. By pressing of the mouse button in any point of the left or right panel the third point of TAGC diagram is appeared, by the following pressing the fourth, etc. (up to 100 points). The diagram is drawn on a cubic spline. After diagram construction, "Convert" button is pressed and for everyone *n-th* pixel of a line for left or for the right board the following transformation is carried out

$$\widetilde{S}(n) = SPF(n) \cdot S(n) \cdot K_C + K_Y ,$$

where $SPF(n)$ is the spline - function; K_C and K_Y is the established factors of contrast and brightness.

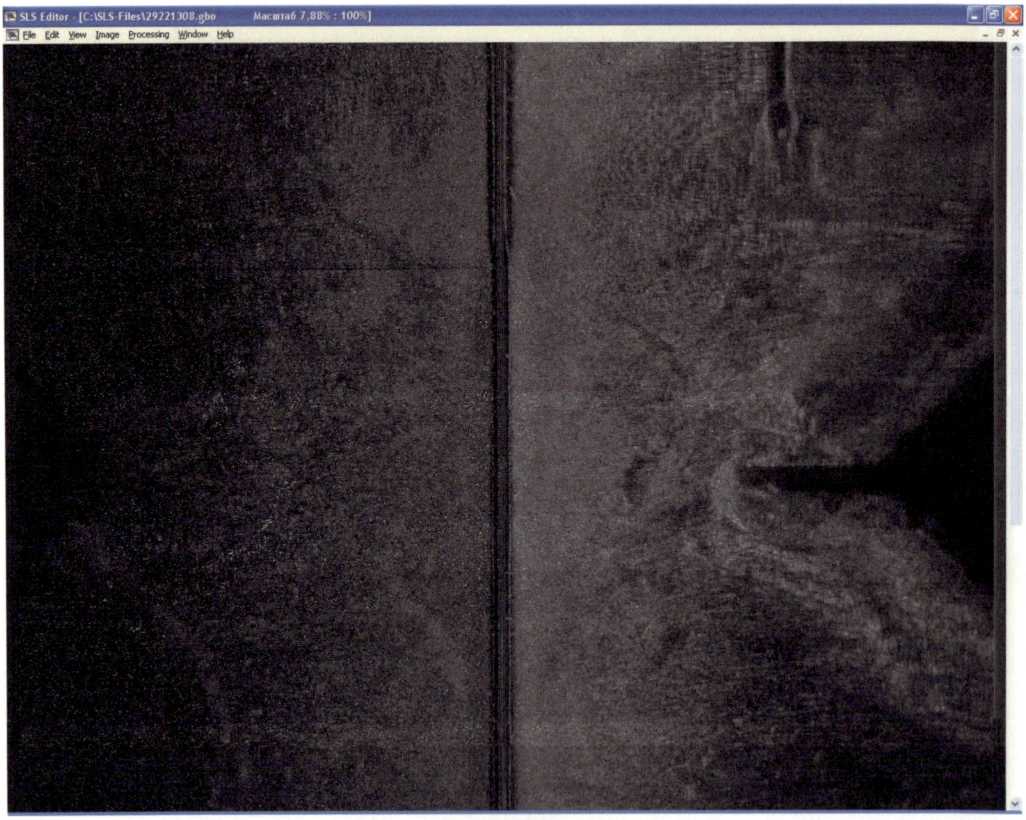

Fig. 7. The examples of the image before processing

The following advantages of developed TAGC program should be noted.

- Points of the diagram can be arbitrary moved in any direction. For this purpose it is enough to place the cursor in the chosen point and keeping the left key of the mouse operate the removing.
- For avoiding signal saturation in the program for every line (separately on each board) average value and an average deviation are calculated. If at tuning brightness, contrast and TAGC parameters the signal moves into saturation, the gain factor of amplification or brightness for each point of a line is automatically reduced.

Fig. 7 and Fig. 8 illustrates the examples of the sonar images before processing (Fig. 7) and after processing: filtrations of pulse noise ("New Filter") and TAGC adjustments (Fig. 8).

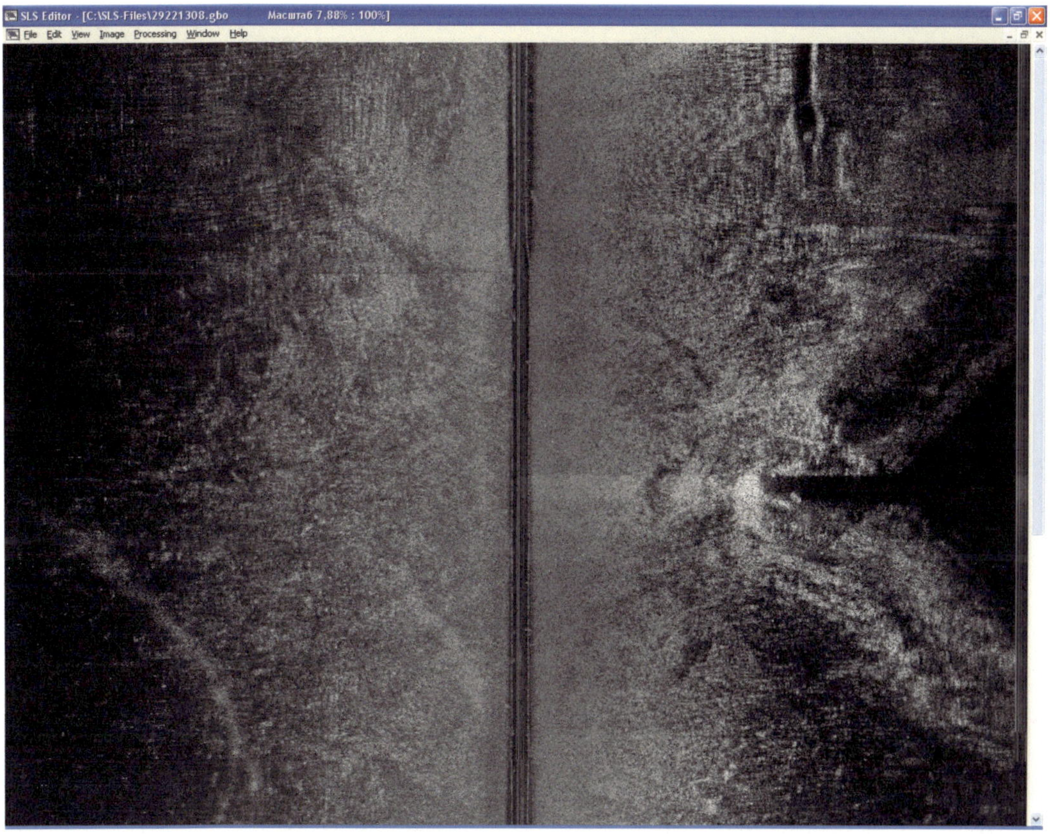

Fig. 8. The examples of the image after TAGC processing

Modes of the analysis and measurement of navigating parameters

The analysis of navigating parameters is made on the basis of additional *.idx file. The most important parameters are the periods of the beginning and the ending of a tack; latitude and longitudes of the beginning and the end of a tack; the probing period, etc. On their basis: average speed, tack length, traveling discreteness, discreteness (in meters) along a line and other parameters are calculated.

The table of parameters with the received information on a tack can be looked using the tools panel: "Processing" - "Tack". The user can find more detailed navigating information

on a tack heading ("Processing" - "IDX-file" - "Header") and on each line ("Processing" - "IDX-file" - "Data"). Observing the data on each line the user has the opportunity to choose the lines with the help of buttons " Step " and « Next line number ».
For calculation of navigating parameters in the fixed points of the sonar images the following ratio is used.
Angular coordinates of the sonar targets ($\varphi_{T,i}$, $\lambda_{T,i}$), fixed on SLS echograms are determined on the basis of formulas (Zolotarev & Kosarev, 2007):

$$\varphi_{T,i} = \varphi_{A,i} + sin(-\kappa)\cdot\left(\frac{D}{R}\right), \tag{9}$$

$$\lambda_{T,i} = \lambda_{A,i} + cos(\kappa)\cdot\left(\frac{D}{R\cdot cos\,\varphi}\right), \tag{10}$$

where $\varphi_{A,i}$, $\lambda_{A,i}$ is the coordinates of SSS antenna in *i-th* time moment received from a IDX-file; κ — the current course values for *i-th* lines; R is the value of Earth radius of the at average latitude φ ; D is the distance up to the target.
In case of the towed device the correction between coordinates of SSS and GPS antenna's is entered.
As the current course values (κ) at shooting from AUV board are not always contained in data of a IDX-file, in this case the program uses the approximate calculations, where instead of course value in expressions (9) - (10) quantity ($k = \eta_T + \delta_K$) is substituted, where η_T is the current value of a traveling angle average on some interval, and quantity δ_K is the angular additive to the current traveling angle, describing lateral AUV drift way. The quantity (δ_K) is entered manually.
The current value of a traveling angle in *i-th* point is estimated under the approximate formula:

$$\eta_{Ti} = a\,tan2\left(\left(\lambda_i - \lambda_{i-m}\right)\cdot cos\,\varphi, \left(\varphi_i - \varphi_{i-m}\right)\right), \tag{11}$$

where φ_i and λ_i is the latitude and longitudes of SLS antenna in *i-th* moment of time, φ_{i-m} and λ_{i-m} is the latitude and longitudes of SSS antenna in *i-m -th* moment of time.
Value *m* for the towed device is calculated on the basis of a preset value δL of horizontal position of a cable (i.e. on the basis of the set distance between SSS and GPS antenna), and for AUV (in case of absence of course values *k* in each scan-line, it is set manually).
Calculation *m* on the basis of a preset value of cable horizontal position is made as follows. Under the formula

$$\delta L = R\cdot\sqrt{(\varphi_i - \varphi_{i-m})^2 + (\lambda_i - \lambda_{i-m})^2\cdot cos^2(\varphi)} \tag{12}$$

in a cycle with increasing *m* the length of a segment δL between points with coordinates (φ_i , λ_i) and (φ_{i-m} , λ_{i-m}) is calculated. The length of this segment is being constantly compared with the entered value of horizontal position. As soon as δL exceeds the parameter of horizontal position, a cycle on *m* is stopped and under the formula (11) the value η_{Ti} for received *m* is calculated.

Further, substituting ($k = \eta_T + \delta_K$) in formulas (9) - (10), the corrected coordinates of SLS targets having taken into account the horizontal position of a cable will be received:

$$\varphi_{T,i} = \varphi_{A,i-m} + sin(-(\eta_{Ti} + \kappa)) \cdot \left(\frac{D}{R}\right), \quad (13)$$

$$\lambda_{T,i} = \lambda_{A,i-m} + cos(\eta_{Ti} + \kappa) \cdot \left(\frac{D}{R \cdot cos\,\varphi}\right). \quad (14)$$

Before the beginning of measurements the user establishes the initial parameters in a window of adjustment ("Processing" - "Option"). Further parameters of initial installation are used at calculation of target coordinates.

During measurements ("Processing" - "Measurement") the index point is fixed with the help of the mouse and further after removing to the following point. In the table navigating parameters are displayed. The program allows allocating any area and, thus, its navigating parameters are fixed in the table. It should be noted, that at drawing a contour, last point connects to the first point with the help of pressing of the right key of the mouse.

As a whole, the developed program is effective for the analysis and processing of sonar images of a sea-bottom, includes original decisions and represents the competitive product in a comparison with analogues.

5. Conclusion

In the present work the brief description of the following basic algorithms of computer processing and the analysis of underwater sonar images is submitted: *Filtration, Compression, Time automatic gain control, Editing, Measurement of navigating parameters.* The given algorithms are realized as the computer program - editor of sonar images. The developed program has passed successful tests on research expeditions on studying World Ocean which were carried out by the Institute of Marine Technology Problems FEB RAS.

The basic results of scientific researches include the following.

1. The alternative criteria of the analysis of noisy sonar images is developed taking into account the properties of visual perception of fine details contrast.
2. The new filtration algorithm allowing to filter a pulse noise effectively and to keep the image sharpness is developed.
3. Results of the comparative analysis of compression efficiency of sonar images in real time on a basis of discrete cosine transformations, Haar transformations and wavelet transformations are received.
4. The original algorithm of time automatic gain control (TAGC) of sonar images signals is developed.
5. The original program - editor, allowing to increase the efficiency of processing and analyzing of underwater images is developed.

It should be noted, that the results of the quality analysis of underwater sonar images are received on the basis of the developed algorithms and criteria of the analysis of fine details quality of a photo and video images the description of which was submitted in the previous author article (Sai, 2007).

The received results do not limit the development of vision systems of the autonomous unmanned underwater devices. At the present time in joint research laboratory of the

Institute of Marine Technology Problems FEB RAS and the Pacific National University perspective researches are carried out in areas: transmission of underwater images signals on a hydro acoustic communication channel; noise proof coding; 3-D processing of images; recognition of underwater objects, etc.

6. References

Ageev, M.D., Kiselev L.V., & Matvienko Yu.V. (2005). *Autonomous underwater robots : systems and technology,* Nauka, ISBN 5-02-033526-6, Moscow, Russia.

Gonzalez, R.S., Woods, R.E. (2002). *Digital Image Processing*. Prentice Hall. New Jersey, ISBN 0-201-18075-8

Krivosheev, M.I. & Kustarev, A.K. (1990). *Color Measurements*. Energoatom, Moscow, ISBN 5-283-00545-3.

Kravhenko, A.P. (2007). Sonar System of Time Automatic Gain Control, *Proceedings of the Scientific and Technical Conference on Technical Problems of Development of the World Ocean*, pp. 348-352, ISBN 978-5-8044-0794-1, Vladivostok, October 2007, Dalnauka, Russia.

Mallat, S. (1999). *A Wavelet Tour of Signal Processing.* 2nd Edition. ISBN 0-12-466606-X, Academic Press, London, UK.

Mastin, G.A. (1985). Adaptive filters for digital image noise smoothing: an evaluation, *Computer Vision, Graphics and Image Processing*, No. 31, 103-121.

Mertins A. (1999). *Signal Analysis: Wavelets, Filter Banks, Time-Frequency Transforms and Applications*, John Wiley & Sons Ltd., ISBN 0-471-98627-7, Baffins Lane, Chichester, West Sussex, England.

Olyshevsky, V.V. (1983) *Statistical methods in a hydrolocation.* Shipbuilding, Leningrad, Russia.

Pratt, W.K. (2001) *Digital Image Processing*. Wiley, ISBN 0471374075.

Sai, S.V., (2007). *Methods of the Definition Analysis of Fine Details of Images.* Chapter in the book: Vision Systems: Applications, G. Obinata and A. Dutta (eds.), pp. 279-296, Advanced Robotic Systems, ISBN 978-3-902613-01-1, Vienna, Austria.

Sai, S.V. & Gerasimenko K.A. (2007). Efficiency Analysis of Compression Algorithms of Underwater Sonar Images, *Proceedings of the Scientific and Technical Conference on Technical Problems of Development of the World Ocean*, pp. 287-290, ISBN 978-5-8044-0794-1, Vladivostok, October 2007, Dalnauka, Russia.

Sai, S.V. & Sorokin, N.Yu. (2008). Search Algorithm and the Distortion analysis of Fine Details of Real Images, *Proceedings of the 1st International Workshop on Image Mining Theory and Applications IMTA 2008*, pp. 58-64, ISBN 978-989-8111-25-8, Madeira, Portugal, January 2008, INTTICC, Funchal, Portugal.

Shoberg, A.G. (2007). Use of Algorithms of Images Processing in Work with SSS Files, *Proceedings of the Scientific and Technical Conference on Technical Problems of Development of the World Ocean*, pp. 291-295, ISBN 978-5-8044-0794-1, Vladivostok, Octorber 2007, Dalnauka, Russia.

Wyszecki, G. (1975). Uniform Color Scales: CIE 1964 U*V*W* Conversion of OSA Committee Selection. *JOSA*, Vol. 65, pp. 456-460.

Zolotarev, V.V. & Kosarev, G.V. (2007). Dialogue Program Complex for a Coordinate Fixation of the Sonar Targets, *Proceedings of the Scientific and Technical Conference on Technical Problems of Development of the World Ocean*, pp. 354-359, ISBN 978-5-8044-0794-1, Vladivostok, October 2007, Dalnauka, Russia.

20

Indoor Mobile Robot Navigation by Center Following based on Monocular Vision

Takeshi Saitoh, Naoya Tada and Ryosuke Konishi
Tottori University
Japan

1. Introduction

We address the problem of indoor mobile robot navigation by center following without prior environmental information based on visual information provided by a single camera.
Recently, the research on the mobile robot of the automatic moving type works actively (DeSouza & Kak, 2002). It is an important problem to acquire moving environment information to move automatically. Various sensors such as the ultrasonic sensor, the position sensing device (PSD) sensor, the laser rangefinder, radar, and camera are used to acquire moving environmental information. The ultrasonic sensor is cheap but suffers from specular reflections and usually from poor angular resolution. The laser rangefinder and radar provide better resolution but is more complex and more expensive. These range-based sensors have difficulty detecting small or flat object on the ground. These sensors are also unable to distinguish between difference types of ground surfaces. While small objects and different types of ground are difficult to detect with range-based sensors, they can in many cases be easily detected with color vision. Though the obtained accuracy of distance using the camera decrease compared with the range-based sensors, various methods for acquiring the moving environment with one or more cameras are proposed.
The stereo vision can measure distance information with two or more cameras as well as the ultrasonic sensor and the PSD sensor (Herath et al., 2006). However, the processing cost becomes complex with two or more cameras. The omni-directional camera has an advantage to obtain all surrounding environments of the robot at one time (Gaspar et al, 2000; Joochim & Chamnongthai, 2002; Argyros et al., 2002). However, the omni-directional camera is a special camera, and should mount it on the top of the robot to take all round view. This causes the limitation in appearance. Since the detection of obstacle region or the wall is difficult with the acquisition image, it is necessary to convert to the panoramic image. A lot of mobile robots with only one camera are proposed (Vassallo et al., 2000; Ebner & Zell, 2000; Tomono & Yuta, 2004; Aider et al., 2005; Hayashi, 2007; Bellotto et al., 2008). Using a single camera, only forward information can be acquired, and information is less than the stereo vision and omni-directional camera. However, if the robot moves to the forward, the means to supplement with other sensors, such as the ultrasonic sensor and PSD sensor is considered, even if the accurate intelligence is not acquired. Moreover, it has the advantage that the processing cost decreases compared with two or more cameras.

There are various moving methods where the indoor mobile robot moves by using the landmark while estimating the self-localization using the camera image (Tomono & Yuta, 2004; Rous et al., 2005; Doki et al., 2008). The method of setting up the artificial landmark in the wall and ceiling, and using the natural landmark, such as on the corner of the door are proposed. However, it is necessary to give environmental information to use the landmark beforehand, and it is difficult to move in the unknown environment. There is other method that the route is generated from the map prepared beforehand, and the robot follows the generated route (Tomono & Yuta, 2004). But this method is also need the environmental information in advance. In addition, the methods for detecting the wall and door that is an indoors common object are proposed (Moradi et al., 2006; Liu et al., 2006; Murillo et al., 2008). For the robot navigation, it is a mainstream method to follow the robot generated the route with the prior environmental information. When the environmental information is unknown, the wall following and the center following methods are proposed (Joochim & Chamnongthai, 2002; Vassallo et al., 2000; Ebner & Zell, 2000).
The purpose of this research is development of the indoor mobile robot that can move even in unknown environment. Then, the center following type mobile robot is targeted the use of neither the landmark nor map information. Furthermore, the collision avoidance of the obstacle and wall is a big problem in the automatic moving in an unknown environment. Then, we develop the robot which moves at the center of the corridor when the obstacle does not exist. When the obstacle exists forward, the avoidance or stop movement is worked according to the size and position of the obstacle.

2. Approach

We develop the powered wheelchair based mobile robot. Our mobile robot is consisted of a general USB camera and a laptop, as shown in Fig. 1. The dimension of our robot is L = 116 cm, W = 56 cm. The camera is mounted in front of the mobile robot. The position C_L of the camera is from the center of rear axle forward to 87 cm, its ground height is C_H = 40 cm, and the elevation downward angle is C_φ = 15 degrees. The acquired image size from the camera is 320 times 240 pixels. Two obtained images are shown in Fig. 2. The bottom of the image is about 60 cm forward of the robot, and top of the image is about 20 m forward. The moving speed of the robot is 0.823 km/h.

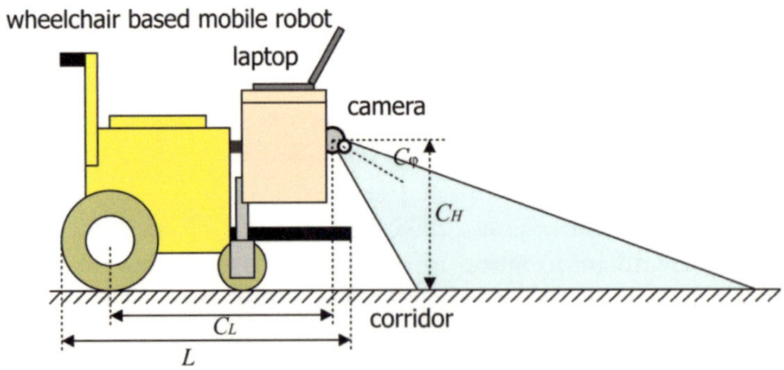

Fig. 1. Overview of mobile robot.

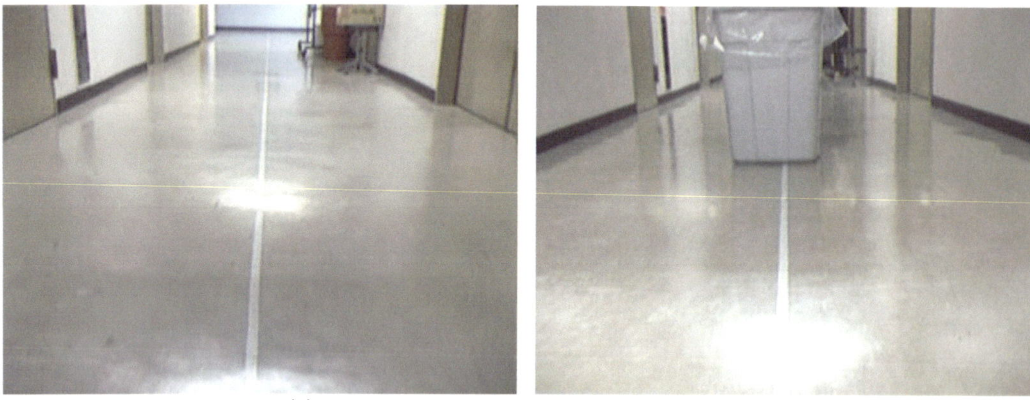

(a) (b)

Fig. 2. Original images.

The developed mobile robot in this research has the following characteristics.

- The prior landmark or map information of the moving environment is not needed.
- A special device is not needed, and the moving environment is recognized in real time with only one general camera.
- The robot moves at the center of the corridor when the obstacle does not exist. The avoidance or stop movement is worked according to the size and position of the obstacle when the obstacle exists forward.

The process flow of our mobile robot is as follows roughly. The frontal view information is obtained by using the color imaging camera which is mounted in front of the robot. Then two boundary lines between the wall and corridor are detected. To detect these lines, we apply not a normal Hough transform but a piece wise linear Hough transform to reduce the processing time. As the space between two boundary lines, namely, the detected corridor region, we apply the proposed appearance based obstacle detection method which is improved the method proposed by Ulrich and Nourbakhsh (Ulrich & Nourbakhsh, 2000). When an obstacle exists, the size and place of obstacle is computed, and then, the robot works the avoidance or stop movement according to the information of obstacle. Otherwise, it moves toward the center of the corridor automatically. Figure 3 shows the process flow of the above mentioned. Here, in this research, the mobile robot is assumed to be moved on the indoor corridor, and human or the plant is targeted to the obstacle.

3. Appearance based moving environment recognition

Ulrich and Nourbakhsh proposed the appearance based obstacle region detection method (called Ulrich's method). They apply their method to the whole image. In this research, because our robot is the indoor mobile robot, not only the corridor region but also the wall and doors are observed as shown in Fig. 2. Moreover, in general, it is a straight line though the corridor in a university, a hospital, and a general building, has a little concavity and convexity by the pillar. Then, two boundary lines between the wall and corridor are detected first, different from the Ulrich's method, and the corridor region is extracted. The reduction of the processing cost is designed by applying the obstacle detection method only to the detected corridor region. The moving direction of the robot is decided by using the detected boundary line.

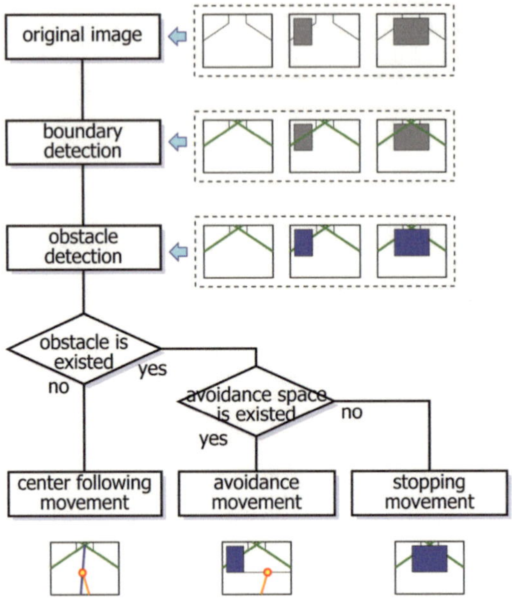

Fig. 3. Flowchart of proposed algorithm.

3.1 Corridor boundary detection

3.1.1 Line detection method

The left and right boundary lines of the corridor are almost considered to be a straight line. To detect a straight line, we use a well-known Hough transform. In general Hough transform, one point of the image space (x - y space) corresponds to one sine curve of the θ - ρ space. This relational expressed as $\rho = x \cos\theta + y \sin\theta$. When some points on one straight line of the x - y space shown in Fig. 4(a) are transformed onto the θ – ρ space, sine curves on the θ – ρ space intersects by one point Q_1 as shown in Fig. 4(b). The Hough transform is an effective method to detect straight line, however, it has the problem with a lot of calculation costs.

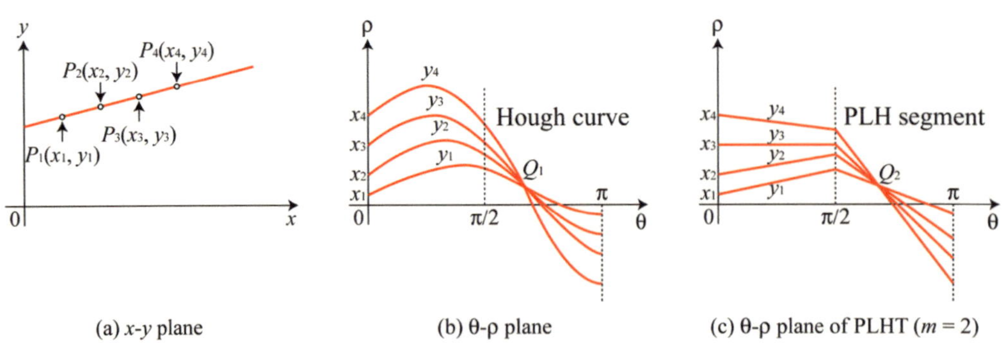

Fig. 4. Overview of Hough transform and PLHT.

Then, in this research, to reduce the processing time, we apply not a normal Hough transform but a piece wise linear Hough transform (PLHT) (Koshimizu & Numada, 1989).

This method was proposed by Koshimizu and Numada, and this method achieves the high speed processing by representing the Hough curve as piece wise linear approximation in Hough plane. PLHT is divided into m of θ axis ($0 <= \theta < \pi$) of Hough plane, and divided points denote θ_k, $k = 1, 2, ..., m$ as shown in Fig. 4(c). This method considers m line segments which connect a section (θ_{k-1}, ρ_{k-1}) - (θ_k, ρ_k), and a piece wise line is called as PLH segment. This segment is obtained from following equation.

$$\rho - (x\cos\theta_{k-1} + y\sin\theta_{k-1}) = \frac{x(\cos\theta_k - \cos\theta_{k-1}) + y(\sin\theta_k - \sin\theta_{k-1})}{\theta_k - \theta_{k-1}}(\theta - \theta_{k-1})$$

3.1.2 Boundary pixel detection

To apply PLHT, we first detect two boundary lines from original image. In general, there is a baseboard which color is darker than that of the wall and corridor, at the bottom side of wall, namely, the boundary between the wall and corridor as shown in Fig. 2. Thus, we detect the boundary pixel using the characteristics of this baseboard.

There is edge detection method for detecting the boundary pixel. Figure 5(a) shows the applied result of well-known method of Sobel vertical edge detector to Fig. 2(a). The height of the baseboard is about 7.5 cm, and two edges, one is the edge between the wall and baseboard, and the other is the edge between the baseboard and corridor, are detected. As for the general corridor, because wax is coating, reflectivity of the corridor is higher than wall, and the baseboard, the door, and the lighting reflect to the corridor region. Especially, a part of the corridor near the boundary is unclear because the baseboard reflects. On the other hand, the edge between the wall and baseboard is clear. Then, this paper detects this edge as the boundary pixel.

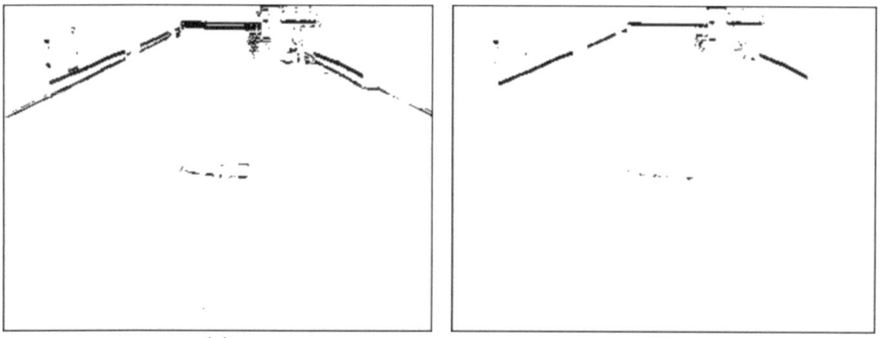

(a) (b)

Fig. 5. Binary edge images. (a) Applied result of Sobel vertical edge detector. (b) Applied result of the proposed edge detection method between the wall and boundary.

The binary vertical edge pixel (called the temporary edge pixel) is detected by applying Sobel edge detector from the original image. Only when the density value of the temporary edge pixel is lower than the density value of the upside pixel, it is assumed that is an edge pixel. This uses the characteristic whose density value of the wall is higher than the density value of the baseboard. Figure 5(b) shows the applied result of our boundary pixel detection method to Fig. 2(a). Only the edge in the upper part of the baseboard has been detected. In addition, the detected edge pixel is fewer, and it causes the reduction of the processing cost to apply PLHT described in the next section.

Here, the boundary pixel detection method using Sobel edge detector is called edge 1, the proposed method is called edge 2.

3.1.3 Boundary detection by PLHT

Right and left two straight lines are detected as a boundary line by applying PLHT based on the boundary pixel detected by the previous section. Here, the boundary line may occlude by the obstacle. In this case, the obtained boundary pixel decreases, and a wrong boundary line is detected. To avoid this problem, the information of the past boundary line is used. The computed two parameters at frame f of PLHT denote θ_f and ρ_f. If either $|\theta_f - \theta_{f\text{-}1}| > 3$ or $|\rho_f - \rho_{f\text{-}1}| > 10$ is satisfied, we consider that the wrong boundary line is detected, and we set $\theta_f = \theta_{f\text{-}1}$, $\rho_f = \rho_{f\text{-}1}$. Figure 6 shows the applied result of our method to Fig. 2.

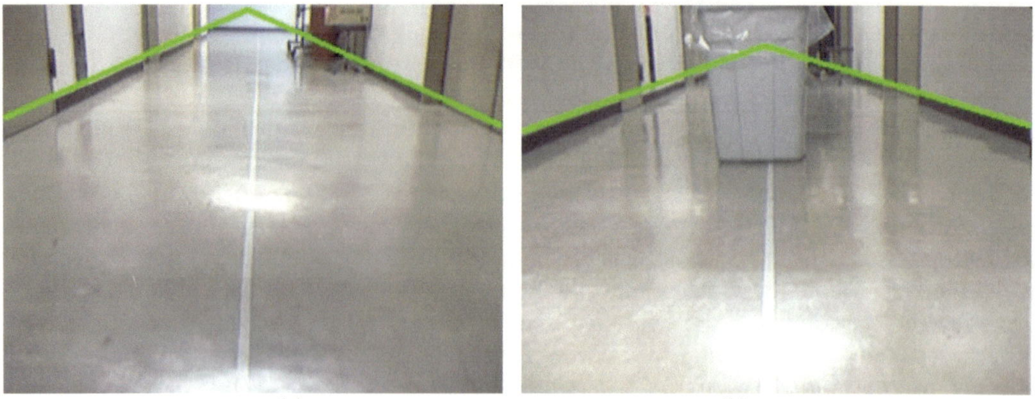

(a) (b)

Fig. 6. Detected boundary lines of Fig. 2.

3.2 Obstacle detection

3.2.1 Ulrich's method

The corridor region is between two boundary lines detected in the previous section, and the obstacle detection method is applied in this region. Ulrich and Nourbakhsh proposed the appearance based obstacle detection method using the histogram (Ulrich & Nourbakhsh, 2000). Their method generates the histogram of the reference region set in the image. In their method, a trapezoid region (called the reference region) is set at the bottom side of the image as shown at the left of Fig. 7. This method assumes that the color of obstacle differs from this reference region. Then, any pixel that differs in appearance from this region is classified as an obstacle. Concretely, the bin value of histogram which each pixel belongs is computed, and when this value is lower than the threshold value, it considers that this color differs from the reference region, and this pixel is classified as the obstacle region, otherwise, it is classified as the corridor region. As a result, the pixel whose color not included in the reference region is detected as the obstacle. This method is based on three assumptions that are reasonable for a variety of indoor environments:

1. obstacles differ in appearance from the corridor,
2. the corridor is relatively flat,
3. there are no overhanging obstacles.

In this research, we first applied their method. The original image is converted from RGB (red-green-blue) color space into HLS (hue-lightness-saturation) color space (Foley et al. 1993). Then, the histogram of L value is generated with the reference region. The bin value Hist($L(x, y)$) of generated histogram and threshold value T_L are compared, where $L(x, y)$ is the L value at pixel (x, y). When Hist($L(x, y)$) > T_L then the pixel (x, y) is classified into the corridor region, when Hist($L(x, y)$) <= T_L then it classified into the obstacle region. The applied result of their method is shown in the second row of Fig. 7. The wrong region, such as the lighting by fluorescent or sunlight, the shadow of the person or other obstacle, are detected, though such regions does not existed in the reference region.

3.2.2 Proposed method

The false detection of the obstacle is caused by the influence of the lighting by Ulrich's method. Then, we proposed the improved detection method to solve above problems.

To remove reflected region by lighting, the high luminance color is removed. In particular, if $L(x, y) > 0.7$ then the pixel is classified into corridor region even if its color does not include in the reference region. The result is shown in the third row of Fig. 7. Observing Fig. 7(a)(b), it can be confirmed that the lighting region has been removed compared with Ulrich's method of the second row.

The pixel which luminance has intermediate value remains as an obstacle only by removing high luminance region as shown in Fig. 7(b)-(d). Then, two characteristics are used to solve this problem. The pixel of the intermediate value as shown in Fig. 7(b)-(d), remains as obstacle region only by removing high luminance. Then, to solve this problem, we use two characteristics. One is that the edge appears between the obstacle and corridor. Because there is roundness in a part of the edge, the object whose surface is almost flat, such as shoes and box, put on the corridor is detected as edge. On the other hand, as long as the corridor is not all-reflective material such as mirror, the reflected edge is blurred. Then, we use binary edge image described in **3.1.2**. The other is the false detection is occurred easily to the dark color obstacle, which is not removed with edge information. Then, we pay attention not the edge but the color of object, and even if the edge is not detected, the darker pixel is classified into the obstacle region.

The process flow of proposed method is as follows. At first, Ulrich's method is applied to detect temporary obstacle. Next, when the pixel detected as the temporary obstacle is not an edge or a dark pixel, it classifies into the corridor region. This classification process is scanned from the bottom side of the image in the temporary obstacle to the upper side. The target line changes to the next line without scanning when the obstacle is detected. The processing time is shortened though it is a little because all temporary obstacle pixels are not scanned. The applied result of proposed method is shown in the fourth row of Fig. 7. It can be confirmed that the obstacle is detected accurately compared with the result of the second and the third rows of Fig. 7.

3.3 Target obstacle region detection

The obstacle region is detected to the corridor region by the proposed method as shown in the fourth row of Fig. 7. The obstacle in the distance may not work the collision avoidance movement though it needs to work the collision avoidance movement when the obstacle exists near the robot. Then, the area S_O of the obstacle region within the search range $[D_n, D_f]$ where $D_n < D_f$, is measured. If $S_O > T_O$ then the avoidance movement is worked, otherwise center following movement is worked. Here, T_O [pixel] is the threshold value.

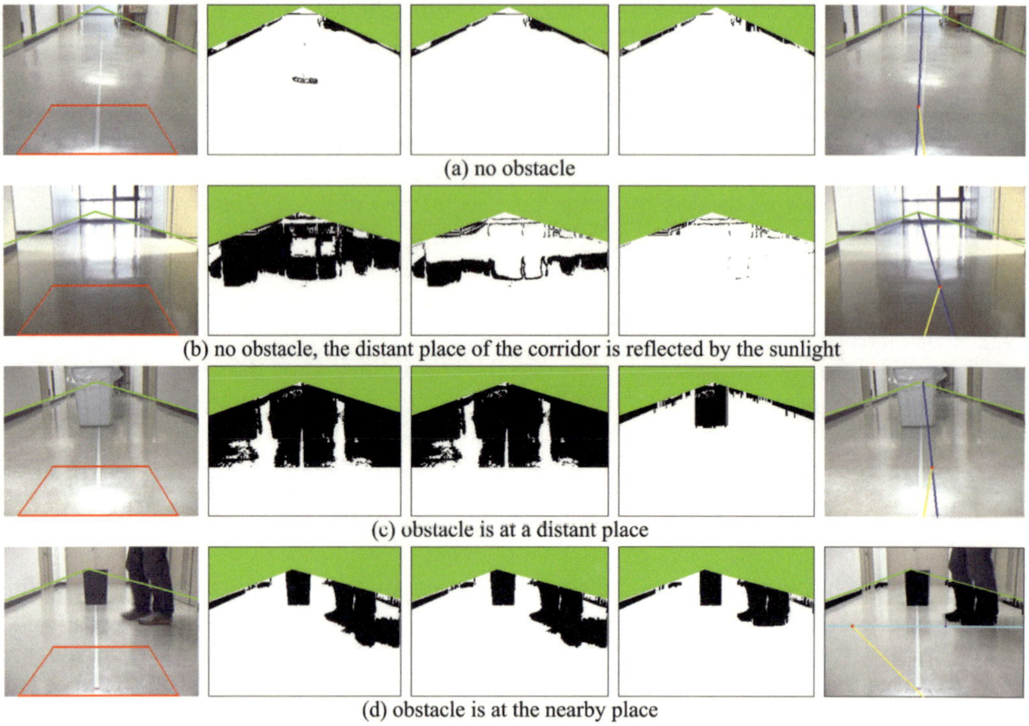

Fig. 7. Obstacle detection and moving direction detection.

4. Movement of mobile robot

4.1 Correspondence of image space and real space

In this research, the search range $[D_n, D_f]$ is given to detect the obstacle region described in the previous section. Moreover, in order to work the center following movement, stop movement, and avoidance movement, the distance from the mobile robot to the obstacle and the width of the corridor are needed. Here, the position of the camera mounted in the robot is fixed. At this time, the position (X, Y) of a real space at the arbitrary position (x, y) in the image can be estimated. Then, to obtain the correspondence of image space and the real space, we develop two expressions for the conversion with the real space and image space of the horizontal axis and vertical axis.

The vertical position Iy [pixel] in the image space is corresponding to the distance Ry [cm] from the robot in a real space. We put several markers on the corridor. We measure the position of the image space at each marker, and calculate the conversion function. Figure 8(a) shows the measurement point of the marker and the conversion function curve. The conversion function is the fourth polynomials derived by the least square method as follow.

$$Ry = 9.19\times10^{2} - 1.55\times10^{-1} Iy + 1.19\times10^{-1} Iy^{2} - 4.44\times10^{-4} Iy^{3} + 6.37\times10^{-7} Iy^{4}$$

The conversion between the horizontal position Ix [pixel] in the image space and distance Rx [cm] in the real space is calculated as well as the above mentioned. Here, the marker was put from the robot to three kinds of distances of 1 m, 2 m, and 3 m. Figure 8(b) shows the measurement point of the marker and the conversion function lines. These functions are the first polynomial derived by the least square method. Moreover, we set the center of the image $Ix = 0$. The calculated functions are as follows.

$$Rx^{(1m)} = 0.757 + 0.347Ix$$
$$Rx^{(2m)} = 1.540 + 0.585Ix$$
$$Rx^{(3m)} = 2.515 + 0.825Ix$$

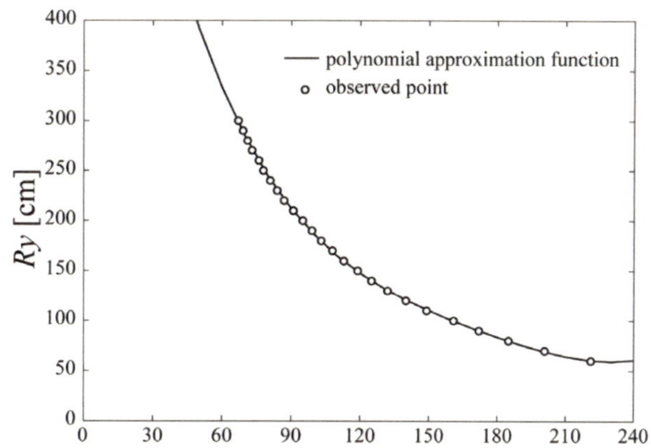

(a) *Iy* - *Ry*

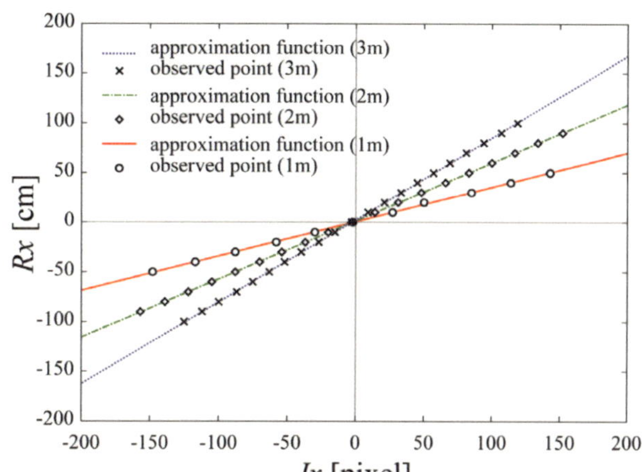

(b) *Ix* - *Rx*

Fig. 8. Conversion function of image space and real space.

4.2 Center following movement

When the vanishing point obtained as an intersection of two boundary lines is assumed to be a moving direction, a location about 20 m or more away from the mobile robot should be assumed to be the destination. In this case, when the mobile robot is located at wall side, it

does not immediately return to the central position. It returns gradually spending long time in the position of the center. Then, a central position of the corridor of 1 m forward is assumed to be the destination.
The right of Fig. 7(a)-(c) shows the detected moving direction of the center following movement. The blue line is the center line of the corridor, the red point in the terminal of yellow line is the target position. In Fig. 7(c), though the obstacle is detected forward, the center following movement is worked because it is in the distance.

4.3 Stopping movement and avoidance movement

About the stopping movement and avoidance movement, we present these movements by using Fig. 9. In our system, the collision avoidance movement avoids the obstacle so as not to collide with the obstacle according to the size and the position of the obstacle. It moves again at the center of the corridor after it avoids. In this case, the strategy to avoid the obstacle by a smooth route is considered. However, the main point of this research is to move the mobile robot in real time frontal environment recognition of the robot using monocular vision. Then, the robot is moved in a polygonal line route with a few parameters as shown in Fig. 9. The avoidance angle θ and avoidance distance d_1 toward from point P to point Q are computed, and the robot rotates θ in point P, and goes straight d_1 and moves to point Q. The robot rotates -θ in point Q and it stands in parallel direction to the wall. Afterwards, the robot goes straight d_2 and moves to point R. Next, the robot rotates θ in point R, and goes straight d_1 and moves to point S. The robot returns to the center of the corridor again by rotating -θ at the end. Afterwards, the center following movement is restarted again. In a word, it returns to the center of the corridor by four turn movement. Here, the target obstacle is a person or a plant described in **2**, and we set d_2 = 1 m. Point Q is a central position of the open space in corridor region. QR is parallel to PS.
When the robot reaches point P, and the obstacle is detected forward d_0, two widths of two free spaces w_R and w_L on right and left both sides of the obstacle are measured. The stopping movement or avoidance movement is worked according to following condition (1)-(3).

$$(w_L > W + a) \cap (w_L > w_R) \tag{1}$$

$$(w_R > W + a) \cap (w_L \le w_R) \tag{2}$$

$$otherwise \tag{3}$$

Where, W and L are the total width and total length of the mobile robot. a is a margin distance in which the robot avoid colliding with the wall and obstacle.
When the condition (1) is satisfied, the mobile robot works the avoidance movement in the direction of the left side as shown in Fig. 9. Oppositely, when the condition (2) is satisfied, the avoidance movement is worked in the direction of the right side. When the condition (3) is satisfied, there is no free space where the mobile robot can move to right and left both sides. The stopping movement keeps until the obstacle goes some place.
Fig. 7(d) shows the moving direction that is judged the avoidance movement. The light blue line means the bottom of the detected obstacle region. A red point which is the tip of yellow line is a target direction.

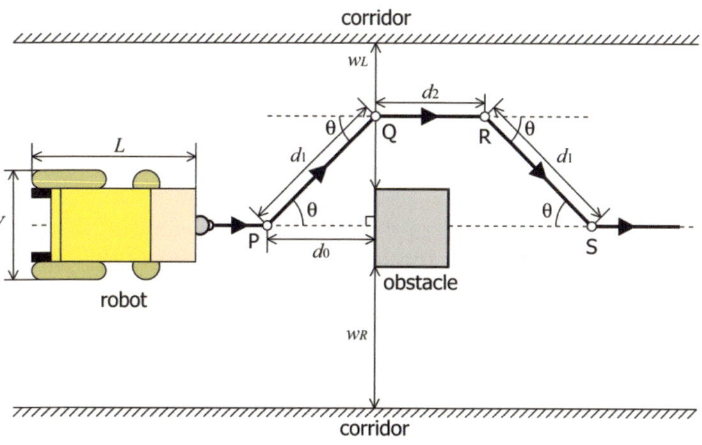

Fig. 9. Avoidance movement.

5. Evaluation experiments

5.1 Boundary detection estimation

The boundary detection was applied to four kinds of method that combined Hough transform, PLHT where the number of division is $m = 9$, and two boundary pixel detection methods (edge 1 and edge 2) for ten scenes taken beforehand. To evaluate the detection accuracy, the angle error of the detected boundary is computed with visual observation. The error angle and processing time per a frame are shown in Table 1. The number of average frame of ten scenes is 557 frames. We used a laptop (CPU: Core2 Duo T7300 2.00GHz, main memory: 2GB), and an USB camera Logicool Pro 3000.

	edge 1		edge 2	
	Hough	PLHT	Hough	PLHT
error [deg]	2.30	2.31	1.45	1.52
processing time [ms/frame]	116.4	30.7	57.7	26.6

Table. 1. Boundary line detected result.

The detection accuracy of PLHT is lower than that of the Hough transform in the both boundary pixel methods edge 1 and edge 2 from Table 1. However, it is greatly improved the processing time, the processing time is shorten 1/4 and 1/2 with edge 1 and edge 2, respectively. In addition, by applying proposed boundary pixel detection method edge 2, the error angle of 1.52 degrees, and the processing time of 26.6 ms/frame was obtained. Thus, we were able to prove the improvement of both the detection accuracy and processing time.

5.2 Stopping experiment

The proposed method was implemented on the mobile robot, and the recognition system of the moving environment in real time was constructed. Six obstacles shown in Fig. 10 at the position of 3 m forward of the mobile robot were put respectively, and the stopping movement was carried out five times per each obstacle on the corridor which width is 2 m. Table 2 shows the distance d_0' where the mobile robot actually stopped, the distance d_0 where the robot detected the obstacle. Here, we set the threshold area T_O = 1800 pixel to work the stopping movement. We set the search range D_n = 1 m and D_f = 2 m in

consideration of the moving speed of the robot. It stopped surely within the search range that the distance from the robot to the obstacle had given with D_n and D_f though it differed depending on the size of the obstacle. As a result, it can be confirmed that the proposed method can correctly detect the obstacle. Moreover, the difference between d_0 and d_0' was occured, and alway $d_0 > d_0'$ is satisfied is the braking distance of the mobile robot. Though, the proposed mobile robot is worked either the stopping movement or avoidance movement according to the size and position of the obstacle, this experiment was to verify the accuracy of the stopping movement, and whenever the obstacle was detected, it was stopped.
Stopped distance d_0' = 155 cm is short though the width 57 cm of the chair is the largest of six obstacles. Since, the open space under the chair was existed due to the legs and casters, S_O of the chair was small. As for this case, the comparable result was seen in the person on the front and the side.
Moreover, the processing time was 9.7 fps using the same camera and a laptop of previous experiment. It was confirmed to be able to recognize a running environment forward in real time.

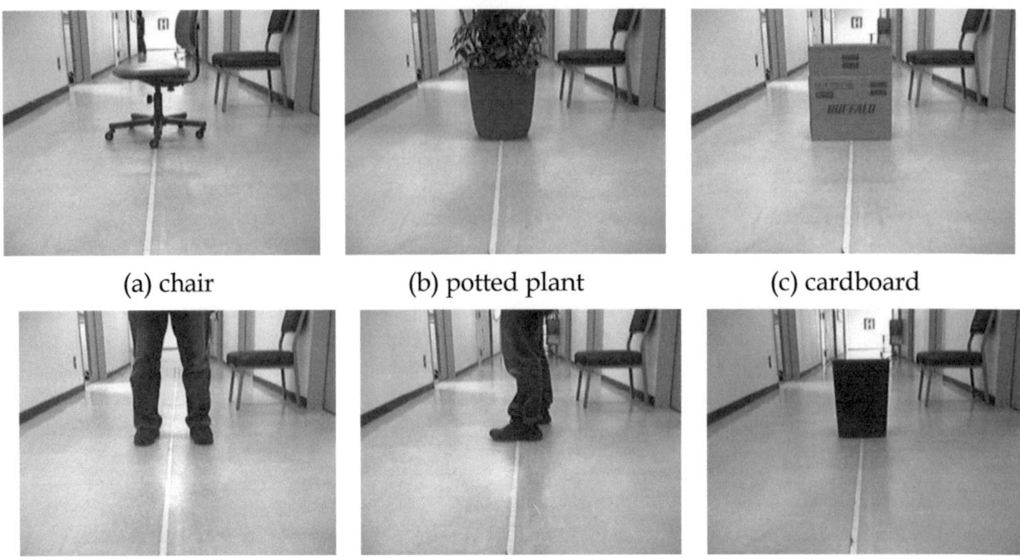

(a) chair (b) potted plant (c) cardboard

(d) person (front) (e) person (side) (f) trash can

Fig. 10. Six obstacles for stopping experiment.

object	width [cm]	d_0 [cm]	d_0' [cm]	braking distance [cm]
chair	57	159.8	155.0	4.8
potted plant	45	173.2	168.8	4.8
cardboard	44	174.2	169.4	4.8
person (front)	44	166.6	161.2	5.4
person (side)	30	171.6	167.0	4.6
trash can	28	174.4	169.6	4.4

Table 2. Result of stopping experiment.

5.3 Moving experiment

The moving experiment of the mobile robot in five scenes that changed the location of the obstacle was carried out. The target route and result route of the mobile robot at an axle center, and the location of the obstacle is shown in Fig. 11. The start point of the robot was (0, 0), and the goal point G was (1000, 0). In Fig.11(a)-(d), the obstacle was the potted plant which diameter was 45 cm, and the center location of each scene was, (500, 0) at (a), (500, 45) at (b), (500, -45) at (c), and (500, 105) at (d). In Fig. 11(e), we put the potted plant at (500, 105) and two persons were stood at location of (500, 0) and (500, -105), respectively.

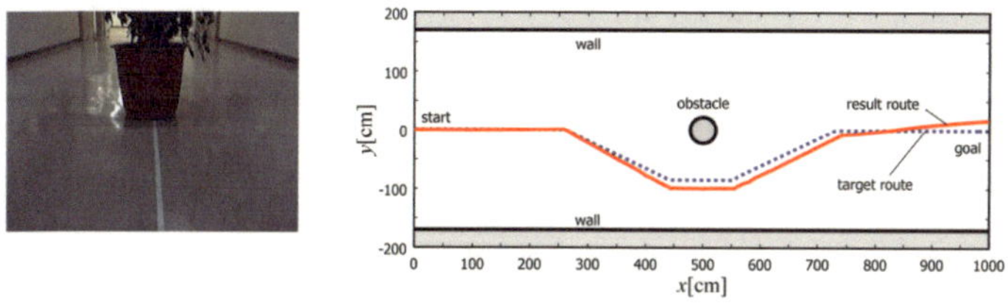

(a) obstacle = (500, 0)

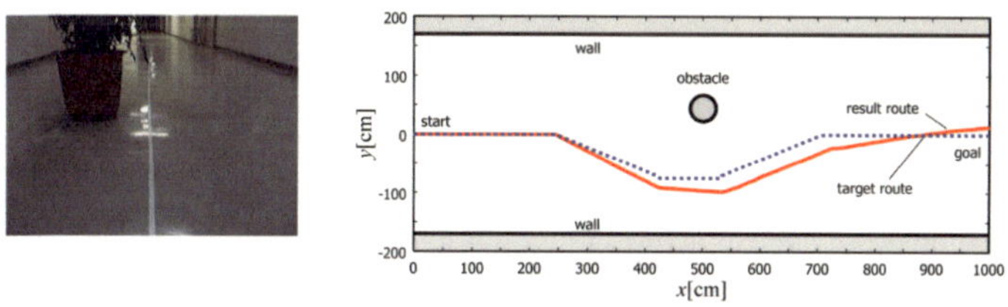

(b) obstacle = (500, 45)

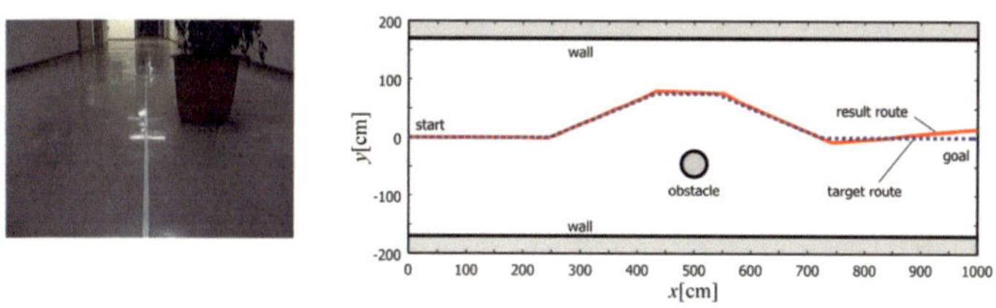

(c) obstacle = (500, -45)

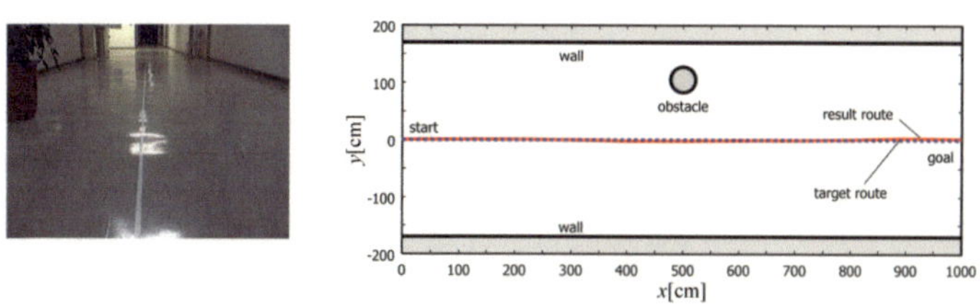

(d) obstacle = (500, 100)

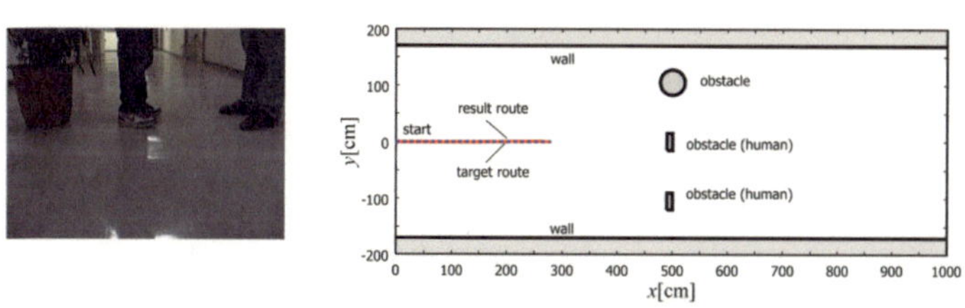

(e) obstacles = {(500, 105), (500, 0), (500, -105)}

Fig. 11. The resulting route of the moving experiment.

Table 3 shows the computed distance d_O, and avoidance angle θ, and four error values, Δx_S, Δy_S, $\Delta\theta_S$, these are in point S, and Δy_G in point G. When there was avoidance space like Fig. 11(a)-(c) even when the obstacle exists forward, the robot avoided correctly and returned the center of the corridor again. Moreover, the robot moved straight without working the avoidance movement when not colliding by driving straight ahead even if the obstacle existed forward like Fig. 11(d), and it stopped when there was no avoidance space like Fig. 11(e). The maximum error distance in point S was 22.5 cm and 30.8 cm of x and y axes, respectively. The maximum error distance in point G was 17.0 cm. It is thought that the width of the corridor is narrow in the distance, and it caused the error easily in a positive direction.

scene	d_O [cm]	θ [deg]	Δx_S [cm]	Δy_S [cm]	$\Delta\theta_S$ [deg]	Δy_G [cm]
(a)	183	-25	17.2	-7.5	5.0	17.0
(b)	181	-22	17.5	-22.5	5.4	13.6
(c)	184	22	30.8	-7.5	5.2	14.5
(d)	—	—	—	—	—	2.0
(e)	186	—	—	—	—	—

Table 3. Result of traveling experiment.

5.4 Face-to-face experiment

The previous experiment was the moving experiment with the stationary obstacle. In this experiment, we use two mobile robots with the same function as a moving obstacle. Two center following robots R_1 and R_2 were made to coexist in the same environment, and face-to-face moving experiment was carried out. R_1 is a robot that has used by the previous experiment, and R_2 is a newly developed robot whose total length is 107 cm and the width is 60 cm. The experiment place is on the corridor which width is 340 cm, and this width is enough to work the avoidance movement. Two robots were put face-to-face on both sides of 10 m away. Figure 12 and Fig. 13 show the experiment scenes taken by video camera and camera mounted on R_1, respectively. In these figures, R_1 moved from the far side to the near side, and R_2 moved from the near side to the far side. In Fig. 12(a) and Fig. 13(a), these are the initial scenes. In Fig. 12(b) and Fig. 13(b), R_1 was stopped to detect R_2 as the obstacle, at point P, and R_2 was also stopped to detect R_1. In Fig. 12(c) and Fig. 13(c), R_1 was rotated θ to work avoidance movement. In Fig. 12(d) and Fig. 13(d), R_1 was at point Q after second rotation. In this time, R_2 moved again at the center of the corridor when R_1 moved outside the view of the camera of R_2. In Fig. 12(e) and Fig. 13(e), R_1 was stopped at point S, and Fig. 12(f) and Fig. 13(f) are scenes when R_1 was worked four rotation. After that, R_1 moved again at the center of the corridor after having correctly worked the avoidance movement. It was confirmed that two robots were able to coexist under the same environment.

6. Conclusions and future works

This paper proposed the appearance based method for detecting two boundary lines between the wall and corridor and the obstacle region through the image processing based on monocular vision. Moreover, the proposed method was implemented in the wheelchair based indoor mobile robot. The developed robot moved at the center of the corridor, and it worked the stopping or avoidance movement according to the size and position of the obstacle even in the moving environmental information was unknown.
There is a problem only that our robot is possible to go straight though it can move at the center of the corridor while avoiding the obstacle. Then the future work is the corner

detection to turn the corridor. Furthermore, our robot is only allowed to move automatically with center following. Thus, we give the destination of the robot, and it moves to the destination automatically.

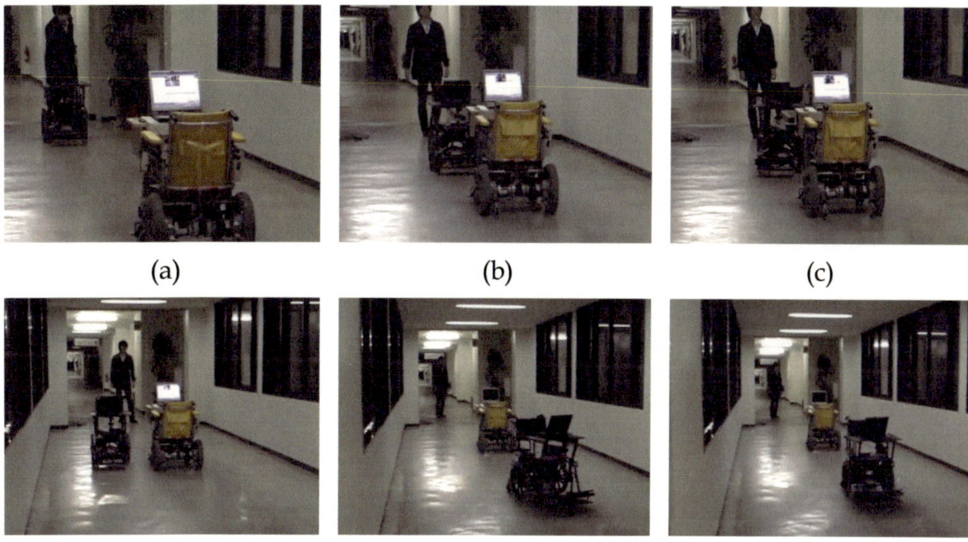

(a) (b) (c)

(d) (e) (f)

Fig. 12. Face-to-face moving experiment taken by video camera.

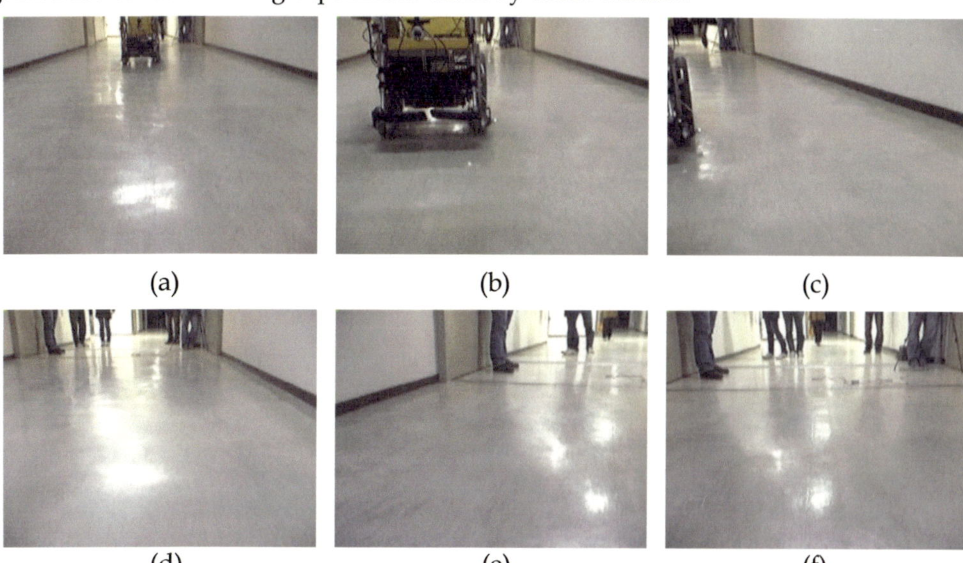

(a) (b) (c)

(d) (e) (f)

Fig. 13. Face-to-face moving experiment taken by R_1 camera.

7. References

Argyros, A. & Georgiadis, P.; Trahanias, P. & Tsakiris, D. (2002). Semi-autonomous navigation of a robotic wheelchair. *Journal of Intelligent and Robotic Systems,* Vol.34, 2002, pp.315-329.

Murillo, A. C.; Kosecka, J.; Guerrero, J. J. & Sagues, C. (2008). Visual door detection integrating appearance and shape cues. *Robotics and Autonomous Systems,* Vol.56, 2008, pp.512-521.

Herath, D. C.; Kodagoda, S. & Dissanayake, G. (2006). Simultaneous localisation and mapping: a stereo vision based approach, *Proceedings of IEEE/RSJ International Conference on Intelligent Robots and Systems*, pp. 922-927.

Hayashi, E. (2007). A navigation system with a self-drive control for an autonomous robot in an indoor environment, *Proceedings of IEEE International Conference on Robot and Human Interactive Communication*, pp. 246-251.

DeSouza, G. N. & Kak, A. C. (2002). Vision for mobile robot navigation: a survey. *IEEE trans. on Pattern Analysis and Machine Intelligence,* Vol.24, No.2, 2002, pp.237-267.

Koshimizu, H. & Numada, M. (1989). On a fast Hough transform method PLHT based on piece-wise linear Hough function. *IEICE trans. on Information and Systems,* Vol.J72-D-II, No.1, 1989, pp.56-65.

Liu, H.; Zhang, Z.; Song, W.; Mae, Y.; Minami, M. & Seiji, A. (2006). Evolutionary recognition of corridor and turning using adaptive model with 3D structure, *Proceedings of SICE-ICASE International Joint Conference*, pp. 2840-2845, Jeju, Korea.

Moradi, H.; Choi, J.; Kim, E. & Lee, S. (2006). A real-time wall detection method for indoor environments, *Proceedings of IEEE/RSJ International Conference on Intelligent Robots and Systems*, pp. 4551-4557.

Ulrich, I & Nourbakhsh, I. (2000). Appearance-based obstacle detection with monocular color vision, *Proceedings of AAAI National Conference on Artificial Intelligence*, pp. 403-408.

Foley, J. D.; Hughes, J. F.; Dam, A. & Feiner, K. (1993) *Computer graphics principles and practice,* Addison-Wesley.

Gaspar, J.; Winters, N. & Santos-Victor, J. (2000). Vision-based navigation and environmental representations with an omni-directional camera. *IEEE trans. on Robotics and Automation,* Vol.16, No.6, 2000, pp.890-898.

Doki, K.; Isetani, N.; Torii, A.; Ueda, A. & Tsutsumi, H. (2008). Self-position estimation of an autonomous mobile robot with variable processing time. *IEE trans. on Electronics, Information and Systems,* Vol.128, No.6, 2008, pp.976-985.

Ebner, M. & Zell, A. (2000). Centering behavior with a mobile robot using monocular foveated vision. *Robotics and Autonomous Systems,* Vol.32, No.4, 2000, pp.207-218.

Rous, M.; Lupschen, H. & Kraiss, K.-F. (2005). Vision-based indoor scene analysis for natural landmark detection, *Proceedings of IEEE International Conference on Robotics and Automation*, pp. 4642-4647.

Tomono, M. & Yuta, S. (2004). Indoor navigation based on an inaccurate map using object recognition. *Journal of Robotics Society of Japan,* Vol.22, No.1, 2004, pp.83-92.

Bellotto, N.; Burn, K. & Wermter, S. (2008). Appearance-based localization for mobile robots using digital zoom and visual compass. *Robotics and Autonomous Systems,* Vol.56, 2008, pp.143-156.

Aider, O. A.; Hoppenot, P. & Colle, E. (2005). A model-based method for indoor mobile robot localization using monocular vision and straight-line correspondences. *Robotics and Autonomous Systems,* Vol.52, 2005, pp.229-246.

Vassallo, R. F.; Schneebeli, H. J. & Santos-Victor, J. (2000). Visual servoing and appearance for navigation. *Robotics and Autonomous Systems,* Vol.31, No.1-2, 2000, pp.87-97.

Joochim, T. & Chamnongthai, K. (2002). Mobile robot navigation by wall following using polar coordinate image from omni-directional image sensor. *IEICE trans. on Information and Systems,* Vol.E85-D, No.1, 2002, pp.264-274.

21

Temporal Coordination among Two Vision-Guided Vehicles: A Nonlinear Dynamical Systems Approach

Cristina P Santos and Manuel João Ferreira
Industrial Electronics Department, University of Minho, Guimarães Portugal

1. Introduction

The field of multiple autonomous robots cooperating is emerging as a key technology in mobile robots and is currently under intense effort. The use of multi-robots synchronized, coordinated or cooperating in production processes where there is a high requirement on flexibility and manoeuvrability is highly desirable. This is an option to be considered in complex and integrated production processes including assembling, transporting, painting and welding tasks.

Broadly, the applied general approaches for controlling and coordinating the movement of several robots that cooperatively perform a task illustrate the major trade-off in the control and coordination of multi-robots: between precision and feasibility and between the necessity of global information and communication capacity. Further, multiple robot systems working in external synchronization, e.g master-slave and coordinated schemes or mutual synchronization, e.g. cooperative schemes, imply the design of suitable controllers to achieve the required synchronous motion.

The work presented in this paper, combines insights of computer vision, dynamical systems theory, computational neuroscience and robotics. We aim at generating online flexible timed behavior stably adapted to changing online visual, infrared and proprioceptive sensory information, such that different entities may achieve autonomous timed and flexible cooperative/coordinated behavior. As a first attempt, we do not take into account communication issues. We apply an attractor based dynamics as recent studies have shown that this theory helps synchronize systems and reduces the computational requirements for determining identical movement parameters across different coupled entities. The inherent advantages from an engineering viewpoint are huge, since the control system is released from the task of recalculating the movement parameters of the different entities.

The main motivation is that once solutions for this problem are found, they can be applied in search and rescue operations, landing removal, remote terrain and space exploration, and also to the control of satellites and unmanned aerial vehicles. In this domain, the achievement of robots able to exhibit intelligent and flexible cooperative behaviour is a first issue.

The approach is demonstrated in the cooperation among two vision-guided mobile robots such that they are able to reach a visually acquired goal, while avoiding obstacles, without

prior knowledge of the non-structured and complex environment. Both systems have to deal with time constraints, such that vehicles have to reach the goal location within a certain time independently of the environment configuration or the distance to the target. Goal position is acquired by a camera mounted on the top of the robot and facing in the direction of the driving speed.
The results illustrate the robustness of the proposed decision-making mechanism and show that the two vehicles are temporal coordinated: if a robot movement is affected by the environment configuration such that it will take longer to reach the target, the control level coordinates the two robots such that they terminate approximately simultaneously.
To the best of our knowledge, temporal coordination among robots able to deal with both space and time constraints, has not been addressed in the framework of dynamical systems except from our previous work. The system is novel because coordination (to synchronize or to sequentialize) autonomously results from the current sensorial context through an adaptive process that is embedded in the dynamical systems controller. Online modification of the parameters is used to steer action and feedback loops enable to do online trajectory modulation. We also attempt to demonstrate that the approach can be extended for a larger number of vehicles.
In the rest of the article, we will first give a brief review of the state of the art of trajectory planning considering time control. A brief discussion of the proposed method and its advantages is done in this section. In section 3 we present the dynamical systems approach used to generate timed trajectories, formulate the proposed controller and discuss its intrinsic properties. In the next section, we describe the problem we try to solve in this chapter. The overall architecture is presented. We also describe the dynamical systems that act at the level of heading direction, the vision system, the behavioural specifications and control of forward velocity. and the other controlling the robot's velocities. In this section, it is also described the vision system. We then describe the simulation environment for the application, we present two simulations and our results and discuss the properties of the system. We conclude by presenting the conclusions and presenting future directions for the work (section 6).

2. State-of-the-art

Trajectory planning has been extensively studied over the last few years, ranging from the addition of the time dimension to the robot's configuration space (Erdmann & Lozano-Perez, 1987), visibility graph (Reif & Sharir, 1985), cell decomposition (Fujimura & Samet, 1989) or neural networks (Glasius et al., 1994). There are several results for time-optimal trajectory planning (Fraichard, 1999).
Despite the efficient planning algorithms that have been developed and the advances in the control domain which validated dynamic, robust and adaptive control techniques, the path planning problem in autonomous robotics remains separated in theory from perception and control. This separation implies that space and time constraints on robot motion must be known before hand with the high degree of precision typically required for non-autonomous robot operation. In order to develop autonomous robot systems capable of operating in changing and uncertain environments it is required a tight coupling of planning, sensing and execution.
However, timing is more difficult to control when it must be compatible with the requirement of continuous coupling to sensory information. Some approaches have addressed this issue (Buhler & Kindlmann, 1994), but timing was not fully explored.

In this article, we propose an approach fully formulated in terms of nonlinear dynamical systems which lead to a flexible timed behaviour stably adapted to changing online sensory information. Dynamical systems have various desirable properties which makes them interesting and powerful for trajectory generation. See (Schoner & Dose, 1992; Tani et al., 2004; Schaal et al., 2001; Schoner & Santos, 2001; Fukuoka et al., 2003; Ijspeert et al., 2001) for related work. First, the structural robustness of the solutions implies intrinsic robustness against small perturbations and noise and the possibility to fuse new inputs into the system without completely destroying its properties. Second, the low computation cost is well-suited for real time. Other properties are the smooth online modulation of the trajectories through changes in the parameters of the dynamical systems; the possibility to synchronize with external signals and to add sensory feedback pathways. The dynamics of the system globally encode a task (i.e. the whole attractor landscape) with the goal state as the point attractor. This is a "always online" property, i.e., once a task is encoded into a dynamical system (e.g. learning) it will be always active, and no discrete trials are needed. Once properly designed, the dynamical system can be robust enough against perturbations and able to smoothly recover from perturbations by means of coupling terms in the dynamics. Another particularity is that these systems produce coordinated multidimensional rhythms of motor activity, under the control of simple input signals. Such systems are deemed to strongly reduce the dimensionality of the control problem.

We build on previous work (Santos, 2004; Schoner & Santos, 2001; Schoner, 1994), where we proposed a dynamical system architecture that generated timed trajectories, including rhythmic and discrete movement, movement sequences and temporally coordinated movements. The model consists of a dynamical system composed of stable fixed points and a stable limit cycle (an Hopf oscillator). Trajectories are generated through the sequencing of these primitives, in which the limit cycle is activated over limited time intervals. This sequencing is controlled by a "neural" competitive dynamics. By controlling the timing of a limit cycle, the system performs well tasks with complex timing constraints. The online linkage to noisy sensorial information, was achieved through the coupling of these dynamical systems to time-varying sensory information (Schoner, 1994; Santos, 2004). In (Santos, 2004), this architecture was implemented in a real vehicle and integrated with other dynamical architectures which do not explicitly parameterize timing requirements. In (Schoner & Santos, 2001), we have generated temporally coordinated movements among two PUMA arms by coupling two such dynamical systems.

In this work, coordination is modeled through mutual coupling of such dynamical systems. This coupling enables to achieve temporal coordination and synchronization of the different systems, providing an independency relatively to the specification of their individual parameters. Specifically, we address the following questions: Can the temporal coordination among different degrees-of-freedom (dofs) be applied to the robotics domain such that a tendency to synchronize among two vehicles is achieved? Can the applied dynamical systems approach provide a theoretically based way of tuning the movement parameters such that it is possible to account for relationships among these?

These questions are positively answered and shown in exemplary simulations in which two low-level vehicles must navigate in a simulated non-structured environment while being capable of reaching a target in an approximately constant time. For each robot, target position is internally acquired by a visual system mounted over the robot and robot velocity is controlled such that the vehicle has a fixed time to reach the target while continuously avoiding sensed obstacles in its path. The two robot movements are coupled in time such that if the two movements onsets are not perfectly simultaneous or if their time trajectories are evolving differently (one is going faster/slower than the other), leading to different movement times (time it takes to reach the target), this coupling coordinates the two movements such that they terminate approximately simultaneously.

Interesting properties of the system include: 1) the possibility to include feedback loops in order to do online trajectory modulation and take external perturbations into account, such that the environmental changes adjust the dynamics of trajectory generation; 2) online modulation of the trajectories with respect to the amplitude, frequency and the midpoint of the rhythmic patterns (discrete movements goal), while keeping the general features of the original movements, and 3) the coordination and synchronization among the robots, achieved through the coupling among the dynamics of each robot, that provides for a smooth and an adaptive behaviour of the complete system in face perturbations in the sensed environment. This type of control scheme has a wide range of applications in multi-dimensional control problems.

It is our belief that planning in terms of autonomous nonlinear attractor landscapes promises more general movement behaviours than traditional approaches using time-indexed trajectory planning. Further, by removing the explicit time dependency one can avoid complicated 'clocking' and 'reset clock' mechanisms.

3. The dynamical systems trajectory generator

Our aim is to propose a controller architecture that is able to generate temporally coordinated trajectories for two wheeled vehicles such that they reach in time a visually acquired target, independently of the environment configuration or the distance to the target. These trajectories should be smoothly modulated both individually and in coordination when simple control parameters change.

We build on a previously proposed solution in which timed trajectories were generated as attractor solutions of dynamical systems (Santos, 2004). The controller is modelled by a dynamical system that can generate trajectories that have both discrete and rhythmic components. The system starts at an initial time in an initial discrete position, and moves to a new final discrete position, within a desired movement time, and keeping that time stable under variable conditions. The final discrete position and movement initiation change and depend on the visually detected target, on the environment configuration and its perception, on proprioceptive data and on the robot internal model. Thus, trajectories generated by this architecture are modulated by sensory feedback.

The overall controller architecture is depicted in Fig. 1.

In this section we describe the dynamical system architecture that generates timed trajectories. First, we describe the dynamical systems composed of stable fixed points and a stable limit cycle (an Hopf oscillator). The solutions of these dynamical systems are temporally coordinated through the coupling of these architectures. Second, the "neural" dynamics that control the sequencial activation of these dynamic primitives is described. Finally, we discuss some relevant properties of the overall system that enables to achieve generation and temporal coordination of complex movements.

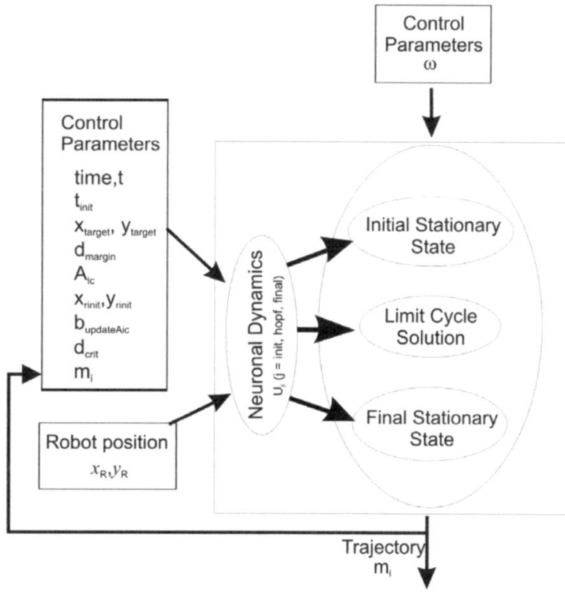

Fig. 1. Controller architecture for timed trajectory generator. Timed movement for x and y spatial coordinates are generated through the sequencing of stable fixed points and a stable limit cycle. This sequencing is controlled by a neural competitive dynamics according to sensorial context and logical conditions. Trajectories are modulated according to the A_{ic} parameter.

3.1 Fixed points an limit cycle solutions generator

The developed controller is divided in three subsystems, one generating the initial discrete part of movement, another generating the oscillatory part and another generating the final discrete part of movement. A dynamical system for a pair of behavioral variables *(m,n)* is defined to generate the timed movement (Santos, 2004; Schoner & Santos, 2001). Although only the variable, *m*, will be used to set the robotic variable, a second auxiliary variable, *n*, is needed to enable the system to undergo periodic motion.

This dynamical system can operate in three dynamic regimes that correspond to the stable solutions of the individual dynamical systems: two discrete states (stationary states) and a stable oscillation (a limit cycle solution). We set two spatially fixed coordinates systems each centered on the initial robot position: one for the x and the other for the y spatial coordinates of robot movement. A dynamical system is defined for each of these fixed coordinate systems as follows:

$$\begin{pmatrix} \dot{m}_i \\ \dot{n}_i \end{pmatrix} = 5|u_{init,i}|\begin{pmatrix} m_i \\ n_i \end{pmatrix} + |u_{hopf,i}| f_{hopf,i} + 5|u_{final,i}|\begin{pmatrix} m_i - A_{ic} \\ n_i \end{pmatrix} + gwn, \tag{1}$$

where the index $i = x,\ y$ refers to x and y spatial fixed coordinate systems of robot movement.

The "init" and "final" contributions describe a discrete motion whose solutions converge asymptotically to a globally attractive point at $m_i = 0$ for "init" and A_{ic} for "final" with $n_i = 0$ for both. Speed of convergence is controlled by $\sigma = 1/5 = 0.2.$ time units. If only the final

contribution is active ($u_{hopf} = u_{init} = 0;\ |u_{final}| = 1$), each time A_{ic} is changed, the system will be attracted by the new A_{ic} value, generating a discrete movement towards A_{ic}.
The "Hopf" term describes an Hopf oscillator, that generates the limit cycle solution (as defined in (Santos, 2004; Schoner & Santos, 2001) and is given by:

$$f_{hopf,i} = \begin{pmatrix} \alpha & -\omega \\ \omega & \alpha \end{pmatrix} \begin{pmatrix} m_i - \frac{A_{ic}}{2} \\ n_i \end{pmatrix} - \gamma_i \left((m_i - \frac{A_{ic}}{2})^2 + n_i^2\right) \begin{pmatrix} m_i - \frac{A_{ic}}{2} \\ n_i \end{pmatrix} \quad (2)$$

where $\gamma_i = 4\ \alpha / A_{ic}^2$ controls the amplitude of the oscillations, ω is the oscillator intrinsic frequency and α controls the speed of convergence to the limit cycle. This oscillator in isolation ($u_{init} = u_{final} = 0;\ |u_{hopf}| = 1$) , contains a bifurcation from a fixed point (when $\alpha < 0$) to a structurally stable, harmonic limit cycle with radius $A_{ic} = sqr(\alpha/\gamma_i)$ cycle time $\Gamma = 2\ \pi/\omega = 20$ time units and relaxation to the limit cycle given by $1/(2\ \alpha\ \gamma_i) = 0.2$ time units, for $\alpha > 0$. Thus, it provides a stable periodic solution (limit cycle attractor)

$$m_i(t) = \frac{A_{ic}}{2} + \frac{A_{ic}}{2} \sin(\omega\, t). \quad (3)$$

The fixed point m has an offset given by $A_{ic} / 2$. For $\alpha < 0$ the system exhibits a stable fixed point at $m = A_{ic} / 2$.
Because the system is analytically treatable to a large extent, it facilitates the smooth modulation of the generated trajectories according to changes in the frequency, amplitude or offset parameters. This is interesting for trajectory generation in a robot.
Basically, this Hopf oscillator describes a rhythmic motion which amplitude of movement is specified by A_{ic} and its frequency by ω.
The dynamics of (Eq. 1) are augmented by a Gaussian white noise term, *gwn*, that guarantees escape from unstable states and assures robustness to the system.
The system is able to cope with fluctuations in amplitude A_{ic} because quantities that depend on sensory information are included in the vector field. Lets consider the dynamical systems defined for the x spatial coordinate. The periodic motion's amplitude, A_{xc}, is updated during periodic movement each time step as follows,

$$A_{xc} = (x_{target} - x_{Rinit}) - \left((x_R - x_{Rinit}) - m_x\right), \quad (4)$$

where x_{target} is x target position, x_R is x robot position, x_{Rinit} is initial x robot position previously to movement initiation and m_x is the dynamical variable. We always consider movement is relative to the origin of an allocentric reference frame, which is coincident with x_{Rinit}. Online trajectory modulation is achieved through the inclusion of this feedback loop that enables to take robot movement and environment configuration into account, such that when a change occurs, the system online adjusts the dynamics of trajectory generation. The same behavior applies for the dynamical systems defined for the y spatial coordinate.
Here an approach is defined to achieve temporal coordination among the two robots, by coupling these two architectures in a way that generates phase-locking (synchronization) in the oscillation regime. This was achieved by modifying the *Hopf* contribution that generates the limit cycle solution (Eq. 2) as follows:

$$f_{hopf,i} = \ldots + c\,|u_{hopf,j}| \begin{pmatrix} \cos\theta_{ij} & -\sin\theta_{ij} \\ \sin\theta_{ij} & \cos\theta_{ij} \end{pmatrix} \begin{pmatrix} m_j \\ n_j \end{pmatrix} \quad (5)$$

where index j refers to index i time courses of the coupled dynamical system (the other robot) and θ_{ij} is the desired relative phase among oscillators i and j ($-\theta_{ij}$ among oscillators j and i). For instance, (m_x, n_x) of robot 1 is coupled with (m_x, n_x) of robot 2. The coupling term is multiplied with the neuronal activation of the other system's Hopf state so that coupling is effective only when both components are in the oscillation regime. Because we want both coupled dynamical systems to be in-phase we set $\theta_{ij} = 0$ degrees.
A neural dynamics controls the switching between the 3 possible modes of movement through three "neurons" $u_{j,i}$ (j =*init, hopf, final*). This switch is controlled by several parameters including calculated target position, acquired by the vision system. Moreover, the amplitude A_{ic} of movement depends on the calculated target position and this provides for online trajectory modulation. By modifying on the fly these parameters, one can easily generate different stable trajectories.

3.2 Neural dynamics

The "neuronal"' dynamics of $u_{j,i} \in [-1,1]$ (j = *init, final, hopf;* $i = x,y$ refers to x and y spatial fixed coordinate systems of robot movement) switches the dynamics from the initial and final stationary states into the oscillatory regime and back. Thus, a single discrete movement act is generated by starting out with neuron $|u_{init,i}| = 1$ activated, the other neurons deactivated ($|u_{final,i}| = |u_{hopf,i}| = 0$), so that the system is in the initial stationary state (m_i=0). Then, neuron $|u_{init,i}| = 0$ is deactivated and neuron $|u_{hopf,i}| = 1$ activated and the system evolves along the oscillatory solution. After approximately a half-cycle of the oscillation, this oscillatory solution is deactivated again turning on the final postural state instead ($|u_{final,i}| = |u_{hopf,i}| = 1$). Temporally discrete movement is autonomously generated through a sequence of neural switches such that an oscillatory state exists during an appropriate time interval of about a half-cycle. This approximately half-cycle is movement time (*MT*).
These switches are controlled by the following competitive dynamics

$$\alpha_u \dot{u}_{j,i} = \mu_{j,i} u_{j,i} - |\mu_{j,i}| u_{j,i}^3 - 2.1 \sum_{a,b \neq j} \left(u_{a,i}^2 + u_{b,i}^2 \right) u_{j,i} + gwn \tag{6}$$

where "neurons", $u_{j,i}$, can go "on" (=1) or "off" (=0). The first two terms of the equation represent the normal form of a degenerate pitchfork bifurcation: A single attractor at $u_{j,i} = 0$ for negative $\mu_{j,i}$ becomes unstable for positive $\mu_{j,i}$, and two new attractors at $u_{j,i} = 1$ and $u_{j,i} = -1$ form. We use the absolute value of $u_{j,i}$ as a weight factor in (Eq 1).
The third term is a competitive term, which destabilizes any attractors in which more than one neuron is "on". For positive $\mu_{j,i}$ all attractors of this competitive dynamics have one neuron in an "on" state, and the other two neurons in the "off" state (Schoner & Dose, 1992; Large et al., 1999). The dynamics of (Eq. 6) are augmented by the Gaussian white noise term, *gwn*, that guarantees escape from unstable states and assures robustness to the system.
Fig. 2 presents a schematic illustrating this dynamics. This dynamics enforces competition among task constraints depending on the neural *competitive advantages* parameters, $\mu_{j,i}$. As the environmental situation changes, the competitive parameters reflect by design these changes causing bifurcations in the competitive dynamics. The neuron, $u_{j,i}$, with the largest competitive advantage, $\mu_{j,i} > 0$, is likely to win the competition, although for sufficiently small differences between the different $\mu_{j,i}$ values multiple outcomes are possible (the system is multistable) (Large et al., 1999).

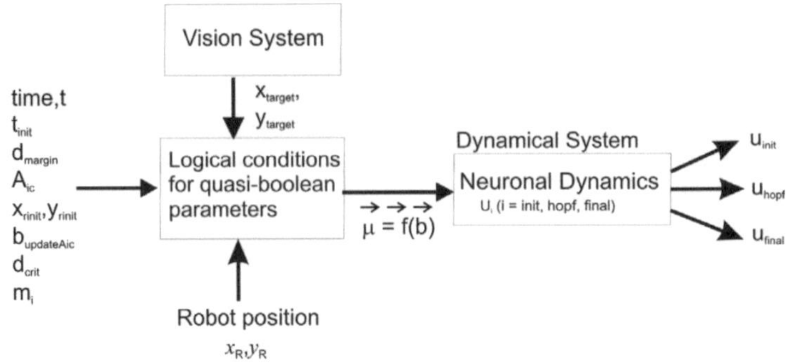

Fig. 2. Schematic representation of the neural dynamics. Current sensorial context and global constraints change as the environmental situation changes. By design, the $\mu_{j,i}$ parameters reflect these changes causing bifurcations in the neural dynamics and activation of a neuron $u_{j,i} \in [-1,1]$. These neurons enable the system to appropriately control sequencing of movement primitives.

In order to control switching, the $\mu_{j,i}$ parameters are explicitly designed such that their functions reflect the current sensorial context and the global constraints expressing which states are more applicable to the current situation. They are defined as functions of robot position, parameters returned by the visual system, information from the other robot and internal states and control the sequential activation of the different neurons (see (Steinhage & Schoner, 1998)), for a general framework for sequence generation based on these ideas and (Schoner & Santos, 2001) for a description). Herein, we vary the μ-parameters between the values 1.5 and 3.5: $\mu_{j,i} = 1.5 + 2\, b_{j,i}$, where $b_{j,i}$ are "quasi-boolean" factors taking on values between 0 and 1 (with a tendency to have values either close to 0 or close to 1). Hence, we assure that one neuron is always "on".

The time scale of the neuronal dynamics is set to a relaxation time of $\sigma_{uj,i} = 1 / \alpha_u = 0.02$, ten times faster than the relaxation time of the (m_i, n_i) dynamical variables. This difference in time scale guarantees that the analysis of the attractor structure of the neural dynamics is unaffected by the dependence of its parameters, $\mu_{j,i}$ on the dynamical variable, m_i, which is a dynamical variable as well. Strictly speaking, the neural and timing dynamics are thus mutually coupled. The difference in time scale makes it possible to treat m_i as a parameter in the neural dynamics (adiabatic variables). Conversely, the neural weights can be assumed to have relaxed to their corresponding fixed points when analyzing the timing dynamics (adiabatic elimination). The adiabatic elimination of fast behavioral variables reduces the complexity of a complicated behavioral system built up by coupling many dynamical systems (Santos, 2005; Steinhage & Schoner, 1998). By using different time scales one can design the several dynamical systems separately.

3.3 Intrinsic properties of the overall dynamics

The fact that timed movement is generated from attractor solutions of nonlinear dynamical systems leads to a number of desirable properties for trajectory generation. The system is able to make decisions such that it flexibly responds to the demands of any given situation while keeping timing stable. Intrinsic stability properties are inherent to the Hopf oscillator, which has a structurally stable limit cycle. Thus, the generated trajectories are robust to the presence of noise and stable to perturbations. This property is specially useful for adding feedback pathways because sensory information is forgotten as soon as it disappears from the environment. This structural robustness of solutions further guarantees the stability and controllability of the overall system if the time scale separation principle is obeyed. These intrinsic properties, including bifurcation and hysteresis, enable planning decisions to be made and carried out in a flexible, yet stable way, even if unreliable sensory information is used to steer action. These properties are explained in more detail in (Santos, 2004).

An advantage of this approach is that it is possible to parameterize the system by analytic approximation, which facilitates the specification of parameters. Not only we have generated discrete movement as well as we provide a theoretically based way of tuning the dynamical parameters to fix a specific movement time or extent. Smooth trajectory online modulation of the trajectories with respect to the goal, amplitude and frequency is now possible, while keeping the general features of the original movements. Trajectories are thus modulated according to the environmental changes, such that action is steered by online modulation of the parameters. A simple modulation of the parameters can generate an infinite variation of stable trajectories.

Moreover, we showed that it was easy to couple two dynamical systems to generate coordinated multidimensional trajectories. The extension to a more enlarged number of dynamical systems is feasible and brings no added complications. The coordination and synchronization among the generated trajectories, achieved through the coupling of their dynamical systems, provides for a smooth and an adaptive behavior of the complete system in face of perturbations in the sensed environment. The coupling of nonlinear oscillators offers multiple interesting properties which enable smooth integration of their parameters and makes them interesting and powerful for trajectory generation.

In the next section, we show the application of this dynamical architecture to the generation of timed trajectories for two vision-guided vehicles.

4. Problem statement

In this article we try to solve a robotic problem applying an attractor based dynamics to timing and coordination. Fig. 3 depicts the problem setup: two low-level vehicles must navigate in a simulated non-structured environment while being capable of reaching a

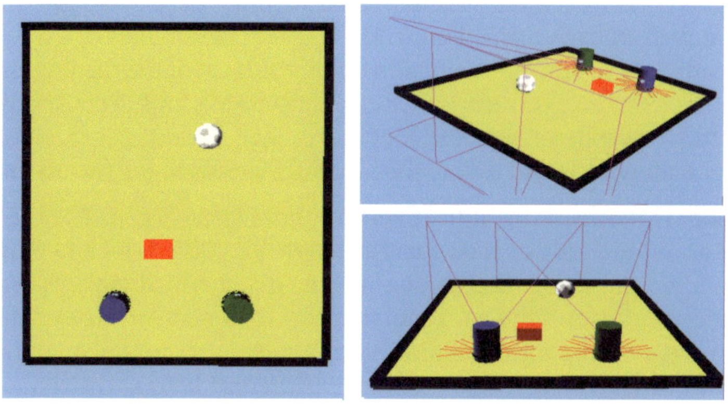

Fig. 3. Three views of a same scenario where two low-level vehicles navigate in a simulated non-structured environment. Each robot moves, senses obstacles and acquires target information through online visual sensory information. Each robot movement is controlled such that target locations are reached in a certain fixed time while avoiding obstacles in its path. The robot controllers are coupled such that their movements are temporally coordinated.

target within a certain time independently of the environment configuration or the distance to the target. Each robot moves, senses obstacles and acquires target information through online visual sensory information. Each robot movement is controlled such that target locations are reached in a certain fixed time while avoiding obstacles in its path. Thus, if the vehicle takes longer to arrive at the target because it needed to circumnavigate an obstacle, this change of timing must be compensated for by accelerating the vehicle along its path.
The task is to temporally coordinate the timed movements of both robots, meaning that if one robot movement is affected by the environment configuration such that it will take longer to reach the target, this robot has to be accelerated and the other robot de-accelerated such that they terminate approximately simultaneously.

4.1 Overall architecture

The overall system architecture is depicted in fig. 4.

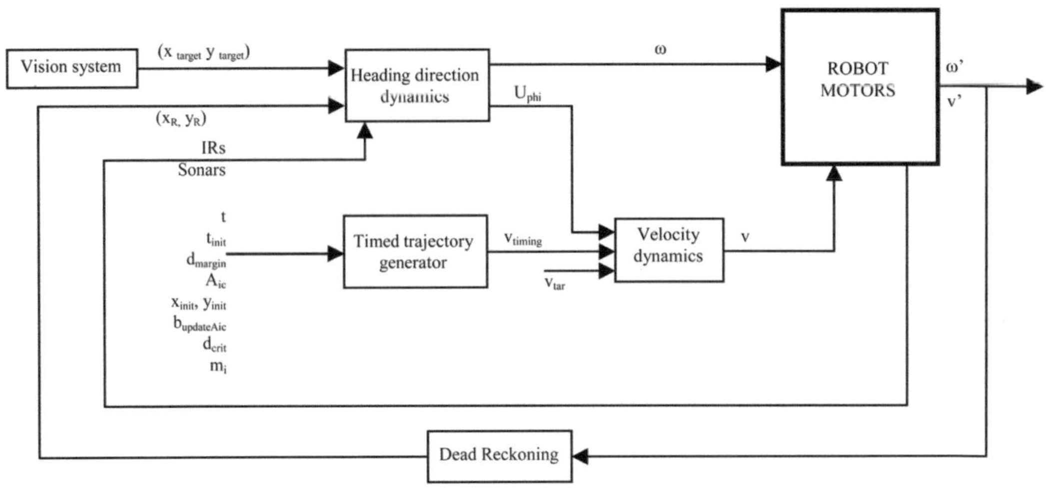

Fig. 4. The overall architecture of the system. Visual acquired target position, robot position and other internal data are transformed onto time-varying parameters of a trajectory controller. An heading direction dynamics acts out at the level of the turning rate and generates angular velocity, ω. Forward velocity, v, considering timing constraints is generated by a timed trajectory controller. A forward kinematics model translates these velocities into the rotation speeds of both wheels and sent to the velocities servos of the two motors.

At $t = 0$ s, the robot is resting at its initial fixed position, (x_{Rinit}, y_{Rinit}). The robot rotates in the spot in order to orient towards or look for the target direction, which is internally acquired by a visual system mounted over each robot. At time t_{init}, forward movement is initiated.
Forward movement in real time is generated by a controller formulated in terms of nonlinear dynamical systems for dynamical variables $(\phi_h, (m_i, n_i))$. The controller is divided onto two integrated architectures which act out at different levels. The dynamics of heading direction act out at the level of the turning rate (ϕ_h). The dynamics of driving speed (forward velocity) express time constraints and generate timed movement (m_i, n_i). Movement is obtained by integrating these dynamical systems.
Each robot forward velocity is controlled such that the vehicle has a fixed time to reach the target. The time courses of the m_i dynamical variables evolve from an initial to a final value,

yielding a timed movement with amplitude A_{ic}. The state of the movement is represented by the dynamical variable, m_i, which is not directly related to the spatial position of robot, but rather represents its temporal position. At each instant of time, the current robot position, calculated by dead-reckoning, is compared to the position each robot should have if no obstacle had been avoided. The robot velocity is dynamically controlled based on the results of this comparison: if the robot is farther from the target than what it should be, the robot is accelerated. Conversely, if the robot is closer to the target than what it should be, the robot is de-accelerated.

Target and robot position are transformed onto time-varying parameters that control the parameters of the (m_i, n_i) dynamical systems that generate timed movement in real time. More precisely, these parameters specify the amplitude A_{ic} of the movement, given by the visually detected target, current motor values and robot internal model. The inclusion of these feedback-loops enables online trajectory modulation.

The two robot movements are coupled in time such that if the two movements onsets are not perfectly simultaneous or if their time trajectories are evolving differently (one is going faster/slower than the other), leading to different movement times (time it takes to reach the target), this coupling coordinates the two movements such that they terminate approximately simultaneously.

Another velocity dynamical system assures that the system is in a stable state at all times and controls the forward robot velocity depending whether obstacles were detected or not.

The rotation speeds of both wheels are computed from the angular velocity, ω, and the forward velocity, v, of the robot. The former is obtained from the dynamics of heading direction. The later, is given by the velocity dynamics. By simple kinematics, these velocities are translated into the rotation speeds of both wheels and sent to the velocity servos of the two motors.

4.2 Attractor dynamics of heading direction

The robot action of turning is generated by letting the robot's heading direction, ϕ_h, measured relative to some allocentric reference frame, vary by making ϕ_h the behavioral variable of a dynamical system (for a full discussion see (Schoner & Dose, 1992). This behavioral variable is governed by a nonlinear vector field in which task constraints contribute independently by modelling desired behaviors (*target acquisition*) as attractors and undesired behaviours (*obstacle avoidance*) as repellers of the overall behavioural dynamics.

The direction ϕ_{tar} points towards the target location from the current vehicle position relative to the allocentric reference frame (Fig. 5). This task is expressed by a specific value of ϕ_h ($\phi_h = \phi_{tar}$). The direction ϕ_{obs} points towards the obstacle locations from the current vehicle position relative to the allocentric reference frame. The task of avoiding collisions with obstacles is expressed by the undesired behavioral state $\phi_h = \phi_{obs}$.

The specified values ϕ_{tar} and ϕ_{obs}, expressing either desired or to be avoided values for the heading direction, ϕ_h, are independent of ϕ_h since they are both measured within an allocentric reference frame. This invariance enables the design of individual behaviors independently from each other.

Integration of the *target acquisition*, $F_{tar}(\phi_h)$ and *obstacle avoidance* , $F_{obs}(\phi_h)$ contributions is achieved by adding each of them to the vector field that governs heading direction dynamics (Fig. 6)

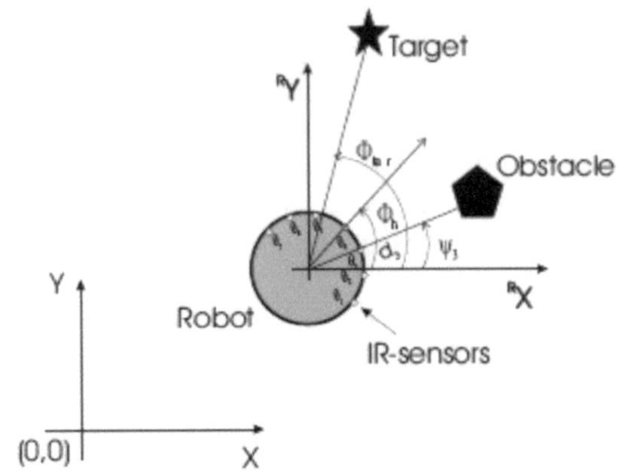

Fig. 5. The task of moving in the *(x, y)* plane toward a target while avoiding obstacles. The heading direction, ϕ_h, relative to the *x-axis* of the allocentric reference frame, is the behavioral variable which controls vehicle motion. Constraints for the dynamics of heading direction, ϕ_h, are parameterized as particular values, ϕ_{tar} and ϕ_{obs} of heading direction. These specify the directions at which target and obstacles lie from the current position of the robot. Seven Infra-red sensors are mounted on the robot's periphery at an angle θ_i relative to the robot reference frame. These sensors measure the distance d_i to objects in the direction $\psi_i = \phi_h + \theta_i$ relatively to the allocentric reference frame.

$$\frac{d(\phi_h)}{dt} = F_{obs}(\phi_h) + f_{tar}(\phi_h) + f_{stoch}(\phi_h) \tag{7}$$

We add a stochastic component force, F_{stoch}, to ensure escape from unstable states within a limited time. The complete behavioral dynamics for heading direction has been implemented and evaluated in detail on a physical mobile robot (Bicho et al., 2000; Santos, 2004).

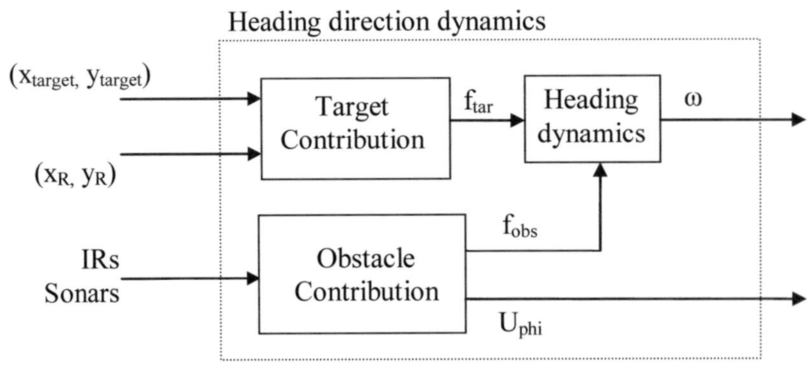

Fig. 6. Heading direction dynamics results from the sum of target and obstacle contributions. This dynamics specifies the angular velocity, ω, of the robot. By simple kinematics, angular velocity and forward velocity are translated into the rotation speeds of both wheels and sent to the velocity servos of the two motors.

4.2.1 Target acquisition

Target location, (x_{target}, y_{target}), is continuously extracted from visual segmented information acquired from the camera mounted on the top of the robot and facing in the direction of the driving speed. The angle ϕ_{tar} of the target's direction as "seen" from the robot is:

$$\phi_{tar} = \arctan\frac{y_{target} - y_R}{x_{target} - x_R} \Leftrightarrow \phi_{tar} = \arctan\frac{{}^R y_{target}}{{}^R x_{target}} \quad (8)$$

where (x_{target}, y_{target}) and (x_R, y_R) are the target location and current robot position respectively, in the allocentric coordinate system. The latter is given by the dead-reckoning mechanism. $({}^R x_{target}, {}^R y_{target})$ is the target location relatively to the robot. In a real implementation the integrated value for robot position and heading direction has some error. This error comes from the fact that motor commands are not correctly executed and the robot does not move has much as it thinks it did. Moreover, this error is cumulative during time. Thus, the position estimated for the robot as well as the estimate of the heading direction should be calibrated with respect to the external reference frame such that the robot is capable of accurately reaching the target position.

An attractive force-let is erected at the direction $\phi_h = \phi_{tar}$, specifying the position of an attractor in the heading direction dynamics:

$$f_{tar}(\phi_h) = -\lambda_{tar}\sin(\phi_h - \phi_{tar}) \quad (9)$$

This contribution is sinusoidal such as to reflect the requirement that the dynamics is the same again after the robot has made a full 360 degrees, leading to a repellor in the direction $\pi + \phi_{tar}$ opposite to ϕ_{tar}. This range expresses the fact that target acquisition behavior is desired from any starting orientation of the robot.

4.2.2 Obstacle avoidance

The robot measures distance to nearby surfaces through seven infra-red sensors mounted on a ring centred on the robot's rotation axis. Each sensor is mounted at an angle θ_i relative to the frontal direction in a reference frame fixed to the robot. Hence, relatively to the allocentric reference frame, each sensor looks into a direction, $\psi_i = \phi_h + \theta_i$ (Fig. 5).

The used strategy says that if an obstruction is detected in the direction, ϕ_i, read by each of these sensors ($i = 1, ..., 7$), a virtual object was detected in that direction. A repulsive-force, $F_{obs,i}$, centred at ϕ_i is erected for each virtual object detected and summed up for the overall obstacle avoidance dynamics

$$f_{obs}(\phi_h) = \sum_{i=1}^{7} f_{obs,i}(\phi_h) = \sum_{i=1}^{7} \lambda_i(\phi_h - \psi_i)e^{\left(\frac{-(\phi_h-\psi_i)^2}{2\sigma_i^2}\right)} \quad (10)$$

Note that the obstacle avoidance term does not depend on the current heading direction, ϕ_h. Only the position of the IR sensors relative to the robot's reference frame, which is fixed and known ($\phi_h - \psi_i = -\theta_i$), is required for the heading direction dynamics. Thus, calibration of the robot is not important within this module. In fact, as described and discussed in previous work (Schoner et al., 1995; Steinhage & Schoner, 1998) using an external reference frame for the behavior variables does not always imply a calibration of the planning coordinate system.

The two parameters within this equation that have to be mathematically defined are: the strength of repulsion of each repellor, λ_i, and the angular range, θ_i.
The former is a decreased function of the sensed distance, *di*:

$$\lambda_i = \beta_1 e^{(\frac{-d_i}{\beta_2})} \tag{11}$$

Objects farther than β_2 are repelled weakly than objects closer. The maximum repulsion strength of this contribution is controlled by β_1 (tuned later).
The latter, σ_i, determines the angular range over which the force-let exerts its repulsive effect:

$$\sigma_i = \arctan\left[\tan\left(\frac{\Delta\theta}{2}\right) + \frac{R_{robot}}{R_{robot} + d_i}\right] \tag{12}$$

The first term reflects the fact that infra-red sensors cannot determine the exact position of an obstacle within their angular range: an obstacle is assumed to cover the entire sensor sector, $\Delta\theta$ (= 30 degrees).
The second term expresses the fact that a bigger robot needs a larger distance to turn away from an obstacle that occupies maximally the entire sensor range than a smaller robot.

4.3 Coupling to sensorial information

Object tracking is a crucial research issue in robot vision, especially for the applications where the environment is in continuous changing, like mobile robot navigation, and in applications that must deal with unstable grasps (Pressigout & Marchand, 2005; Taylor & Kleeman 2003).
The most common approaches for object tracking are based on the detection of one of these three cues: edges, color and texture (Pressigout & Marchand, 2005; Taylor & Kleeman 2003) Everingham & Thomas, 2001; Zhao & Tao, 2005; Yilmaz et al., 2004).
The first concerns the extraction of a number of features of the object, like points, lines, distances and models of the contours. These features allow to have fast tracking process and also to estimate the pose of the object. Therefore, this approach is also used in visual servoing systems (Pressigout & Marchand, 2005; Armstrong & Zisserman, 1995). The fact that this is generally based on the analysis of the gradients intensity, other approaches are necessary for applications with highly textured environments or objects Pressigout & Marchand, 2005; Shahrokni et al., 2004; Yilmaz et al., 2004). For applications where the light conditions are not stable or its interaction with the objects produces shadows, the edge based techniques are not suitable as well.
When color is the main different characteristic of the object in relation with the environment, than the most suitable approaches are based on this feature. Several works can be found in the literature regarding the extraction of several characteristics based on different color spaces (Zhao & Tao, 2005; Yilmaz et al., 2004; Bradski,1998) Some works have been proved to be efficient for situations where the light conditions are not uniform and are changing during the tracking procedure (Yilmaz et al., 2004; Bradski,1998). Nevertheless, the majority of these algorithms are too computationally complex due to the use of color correlation, blob analysis and region growing.
In the presence of highly textured objects and clutter, which produce too many irrelevant edges, texture segmentation techniques are recently been used. However, because texture

segmentation techniques require computing statistics over image patches, they tend to be computationally intensive and have therefore not been felt to be suitable for such purposes (Giebel et al., 2004; Shahrokni et al., 2004; Everingham & Thomas, 2001).
However, robots cannot rely on the regular presence of distinctive colours, high contrast backgrounds or easily detected textures when tracking arbitrary objects in an unstructured domestic environment. As a result, individual cues only provide robust tracking under limited conditions as they fail to catch variations like changes of orientation and shape. Nevertheless, if flexibility and/or simplicity, speed and robustness are required they are a good option.
In this particular application the goal is to robustly detect a color target in an unstructured, complex environment. Target position is acquired by simulating a camera mounted on the top of the robot and facing in the direction of the driving speed. We have assumed that target size is known and can be measured in the image.
In our application, we have to deal with the following main computer-vision problems: (1) a clutter environment, including non-uniform light conditions and different objects with the same color pattern (distractors); (2) irregular object motion due to perspective-induced motion irregularities; (3) image noise and (4) a real-time performance application with high processing time. Some of these constraints may not be a problem in a simulated environment, but they will be as soon as we move on to a real application.
The overall vision module showing outputs and information flow is depicted in fig. 7.

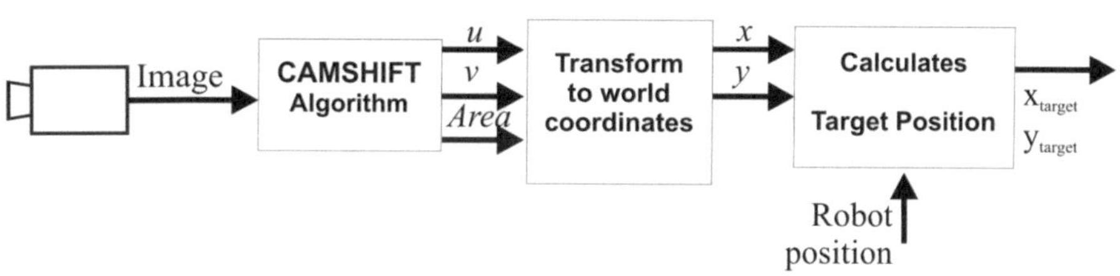

Fig. 7. Vision module.

Since the application demands a fast algorithm for color tracking, we have chosen a color based real-time tracker, Continuously Adaptive Mean Shift (CAMSHIFT) algorithm (Bradski, 1998). This algorithm deals with the described computer-vision application problems during its operation and has low computational cost.
CAMSHIFT algorithm uses a search window to track the moving object, ignoring objects outside this search window. Also scales the search window to object size thus allowing different distances between the object and the camera. The color space used is the HSV, which is less sensitive to lighting changes. The color model is mainly based on the hue histogram. The block diagram of the CAMSHIFT algorithm is presented in fig. 8 and tracks the u, v coordinates and Area of the color blob representing the target.
The CAMSHIFT tracks objects using a probability distribution image of the desired color. To do this, first, a model of the desired hue (H of the target) must be created using a 1D color histogram. During tracking, this H histogram is used as a lookup table to convert the pixels of a new image to a corresponding probability of target image. The centre and size of the color object are found via the convergence algorithm operating on the color probability image. The current size and location of the tracked object are reported and used to set the size and location of the search window in the next video image. The process is then repeated for continuous tracking. The calculus of color probability distribution for the new image will

be restricted to a smaller image region surrounding the current CAMSHIFT window. This results in large computational savings.

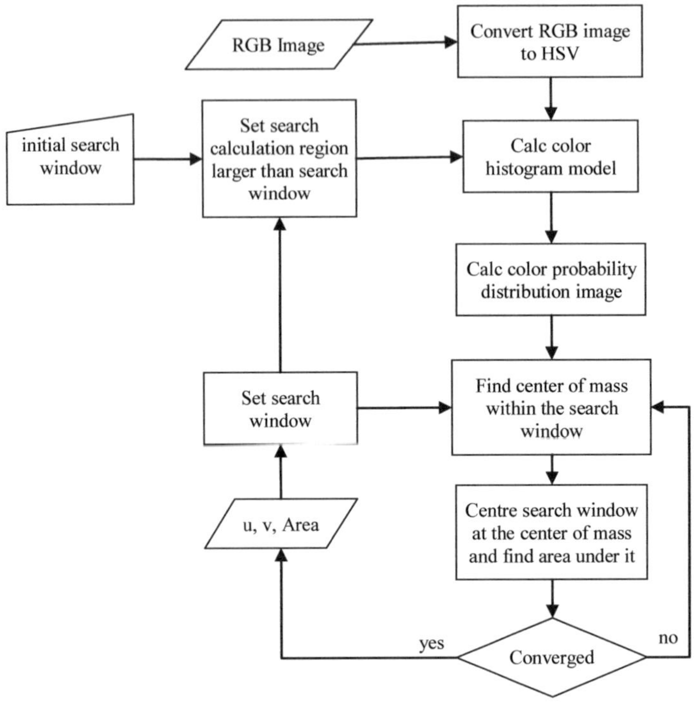

Fig. 8. Block diagram of CAMSHIFT algorithm.

The HSV color space presents some problems, specifically when brightness is low. In this case, saturation is also low and then hue values become instable. To overcome this problem, hue that has very low corresponding brightness values must be ignored. For very low saturation values, hue is not defined and the corresponding pixels must be ignored.
CAMSHIFT tracks the u, v image coordinates and the area of the color blob representing the object. To convert the blob coordinates in pixels to camera coordinates, the camera Pinhole model was used, which estimates the rays going from point C (projection center) through the image point $m=(u,v)$ and through the world point M=(X,Y,Z), fig 9.
In this model, for a still image, a world point (X,Y,Z) in the camera frame is projected to an image point (u,v), which can be obtained using the perspective transformation as follows:

$$\begin{bmatrix} u \\ v \\ 1 \end{bmatrix} = \begin{bmatrix} f_x & s & c_x \\ 0 & f_y & c_y \\ 0 & 0 & 1 \end{bmatrix} \times \begin{bmatrix} x' \\ y' \\ 1 \end{bmatrix} \tag{13}$$

where $x' = X/Z$, $y' = Y/Z$; (c_x, c_y) are the u and v coordinates of the principal point C in pixel units (optical center of the image, fig. 9) and f_x, f_y are focal lengths expressed in pixel units. $f_x = f/P_x$ and $fy = f/P_y$, where P_x and P_y are the width and height of the pixels. s factor reflects the pixel drift of the rectangular form. For most cameras the pixels are almost perfectly rectangular and thus s is very close to zero.

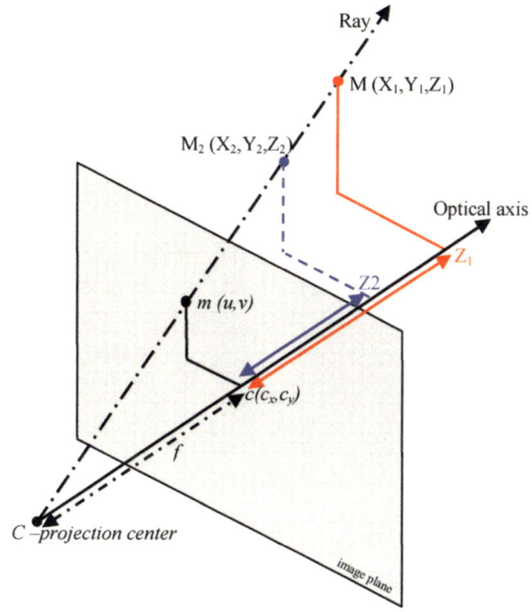

Fig. 9. Camera Pinhole representation, to estimates the rays going from point C (projection center) through the image point m=(u,v) and through the world point M=(X,Y,Z).

The matrix defined by these parameters is called the camera matrix, or the matrix of intrinsic parameters. In order to have in consideration the radial and tangential distortion of the real lens, the model is extended as follows:

$$x'' = x'(1 + k_1 r^2 + k_2 r^4 + k_3 r^6) + 2p_1 x' y' + p_2(r^2 + 2x'^2) \tag{14}$$

$$y'' = y'(1 + k_1 r^2 + k_2 r^4 + k_3 r^6) + p_1(r^2 + 2y'^2) + 2p_2 x' y' \tag{15}$$

$$r^2 = x'^2 + y'^2 \tag{16}$$

$$u = f_x x'' + s y'' + c_x \tag{17}$$

$$v = f_y y'' + c_y \tag{18}$$

where k_1, k_2 and k_3 are radial distortion coefficients and p_1, p_2 are tangential distortion coefficients. These coefficients do not depend on the scene viewed, thus they are also considered as intrinsic camera parameters.

The Vision module calculates the world X and Y coordinates in the camera frame in mm for image points of the target centre using the distance of Z value, which is proportional to the Area given by the CAMSHIFT algorithm. The coordinates in the camera frame are transformed to the allocentric reference frame by a simple rotation around the X axis.

The same camera model was used for the simulation in Webots (Michel, 2004), but with different intrinsic parameters. In Webots, an ideal camera was considered.

Herein, we illustrate two real applications of this algorithm to a real, clutter environment. Fig.10a shows the result of this algorithm in the presence of a distractor element. In Fig. 10b the incident illumination as been increased by a factor of 1.5. In both situations, the algorithm is able to track the target.

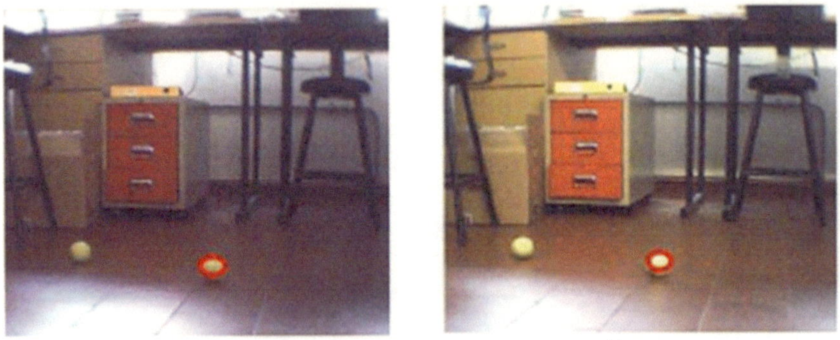

a) b)

Fig. 10. Application of the CAMSHIFT algorithm to real, clutter environment. a) Presence of a distractor element. b) variations in lighting conditions.

To simulate sensor noise (which can be substantial if such optical measures are extracted from image sequences), we added either white or colored noise to the image coordinates. Here we show simulations that used coloured noise, ζ, generated from

$$\dot{\varsigma} = -\frac{1}{\tau_{corr}}\varsigma + \sqrt{Q}gwn \tag{19}$$

where gwn is gaussian white noise with zero mean and unit variance, so that $Q = 5$ is the effective variance. The correlation time, τ_{corr}, was chosen as $0.2\ s$.

4.4 Behavior specifications

Herein, the time, t, visual acquired sensory information, proprioceptive data and the robot internal model, fully control the neural dynamics through the quasi-boolean parameters. The sequence of neural switches is generated by translating sensory conditions and logical constraints into values for these parameters.

The competitive advantage of the initial postural state is controlled by the parameter b_{init}. This parameter must be "on" (= 1) when either of the following is true: (1) time, t, is bellow the initial time, t_{init}, set by the user ($t < t_{init}$); (2) dynamical variable m_i is close to the initial state 0 ($b_{m_i colosem_{init}}(m_i)$ and time exceeds t_{init} ($t > t_{init}$) and target has not been reached.

We consider that the target has not been reached when the distance, d_{tar}, from the actual robot position (as internally calculated through dead-reckoning) and the (x_{target}, y_{target}) position is higher than a specified value, d_{margin}. This logical condition is expressed by the quasi-boolean factor, $b_{m_i hasnotreachedtarget}(d_{tar}) = \sigma(d_{tar} - d_{margin})$, where $\sigma(.)$ is a sigmoid function that ranges from 0 for negative argument to 1 for positive argument, chosen here as

$$\sigma(x) = [\tanh(10x) + 1]/2 \tag{20}$$

although any other functional form will work as well. Note that this switch is driven from the sensed actual position of the robot.

The factor $b_{m_i colosem_{init}}(m_i) = \sigma(0.15A_{ic} - m_i)$ has values close to one while the dynamical variable m_i is bellow $0.15A_{ic}$ and switches to values close to zero elsewhere. A_{ic} is the final postural state, but it is also the periodic motion amplitude which is updated based on the robot internal model, visual sensory information and the system internal state.

An additional problem arises here, however. Consider that the target position in i coordinate system (x or y) is close to robot position previous to movement initiation. In such case, a small amplitude for the corresponding periodic motion results and is dominated by $((x_R - x_{Rinit}) - m_x)$, meaning that the attractor shifts randomly. This is specially notorious when the system is in the initial postural state. The main drawback is that the periodic motion is not deactivated since the logical condition to do it is dependent on the percentage of a small value. The proposed solution is to algorithmically turn off the i periodic motion update, A_{ic}, once this changes sign relatively to the previous update and the corresponding dynamical system is in the initial postural state. Another possible solution is to replace the criterion used on $b_{m_i colosem_{init}}$ logical condition by a criterion based on absolute distances to the initial postural state.

These logical conditions are expressed through the mathematical function:

$$b_{init} = 1 - \{(t \geq t_{init})[1 - (b_{m_i\ close\ m_{init}}(m_i)(t \geq t_{init})b_{m_i\ has\ not\ reached\ target}(d_{tar}))]\} \quad (21)$$

A similar analysis derives the b_{hopf} parameter which controls the competitive advantage of the oscillatory state. b_{hopf} parameter must be on (= 1) when none of the following is false: (1) time, t, exceeds t_{init} ($t \geq t_{init}$); (2.) dynamical variable m_i is not close to the final postural state $A_{ic}.(b_{m_i notcolosem_{final}}(m_i))$; and target has not been reached ($b_{m_i hasnotreachedtarget}(d)$); and the update of the i periodic motion has not been algorithmically turned off $(b_{updateA_{ic}})$.

The factor $b_{m_i notcolosem_{final}}(m_i) = \sigma(d_{switch} - d_{crit})$ is specified based on absolute values, where d_{switch} represents the distance between m_i and the final postural state, A_{ic}. If the distance, d_{switch}, is bellow a specified value, d_{crit}, which is tuned empirically, this factor has values close to one. If this factor was not specified based on an absolute distance to the final postural state but rather was defined based on a percentage of this state, such as $0.95\ A_{ic}$, the same error as that described in factor $b_{m_i colosem_{init}}(m_i)$ would apply.

The mathematical equation that yields these results is:

$$b_{hopf} = (t \geq t_{init})b_{m_i\ not\ close\ m_{final}}(m_i)b_{m_i\ has\ not\ reached\ target}(d_{tar})\sigma(b_{update\ A_{ic}}) \quad (22)$$

Analogously, b_{final}, which controls the competitive advantage of the final postural state, can be derived from a similar analysis. b_{final} parameter must be "on" (= 1) when time, t, exceeds t_{init} (t ≥ t_{init}) and either of the following is true: (1) dynamical variable m_i is close to the final postural state $(A_{ic}.(b_{m_i notcolosem_{final}}(m_i)))$; (2) target has been reached $(b_{m_i reachedtarget}(d))$; (3) m_i is not close to the initial postural state zero $(b_{m_i notcolosem_{final}}(m_i))$ and (4) the update of the i periodic motion has been algorithmically turned off.

$$b_{final} = (t \geq t_{init})[b_{m_i\ not\ close\ m_{final}}(m_i) + b_{m_i\ reached\ target}(d_{tar}) + b_{m_i\ not\ close\ m_{final}}(m_i) + (1 - \sigma(b_{update\ A_{ic}}))] \quad (23)$$

4.5 Velocity

The system is designed such that the planning variable is in or near a resulting attractor of the dynamical system most of the time. If we control the driving velocity, v, of the vehicle, the system is able to track the moving attractor. Robot velocity must depend on the behaviour exhibited by the robot, depending whether or not obstacles are detected for the current heading direction value.

In case an obstacle has been detected, velocity is set as V_{obs}, which is computed as a function of the current distance to the obstacle (Bicho et al., 2000) such that good tracking of the attractor's movement is achieved:

$$V_{obs} = d\,\dot{\psi}_{\max}, \tag{24}$$

where $\dot{\psi}_{\max}$ represents the maximal rate of shift of the fixed points and is a design parameter. In case no obstacle has been detected, velocity is set as V_{timing}:

$$V_{timing} = \sqrt{\dot{m}_x^2 + \dot{m}_y^2} \tag{25}$$

where m_x, m_y are given by (Eq. 1). The path velocity, V_{timing}, of the vehicle is thus controlled through the described dynamical system architecture that generates timed trajectories.

Velocity is imposed by a dynamics equal to that described by (Bicho et al., 2000).

$$\frac{dv}{dt} = -c_{obs}\left(v - V_{obs}\right)\exp\left(-\frac{(v - V_{obs})^2}{2\sigma_v^2}\right) - c_{timing}\left(v - V_{timing}\right)\exp\left(-\frac{(v - V_{timing})^2}{2\sigma_v^2}\right) \tag{26}$$

If heading direction, ϕ_h, is currently in a repulsion zone of sufficient strength, λ_i, a strong obstacle contribution is present: $c_{obs} > 0$ and $c_{timing} = 0$ is required. In such case, this potential functional has positive values. If no obstacles are present or repulsion is weak for the current heading direction value, the above potential has negative values and $c_{obs} = 0$, $c_{timing} > 0$ is required. For further details regarding this dynamics or the above equations refer to (Bicho et al., 2000).

In the following, we briefly explain the dynamic architecture behavior of each robot that generates a timed movement from the robot resting position to a target location. At $t = 0$ s the robot is resting at its initial fixed position, (x_{Rinit}, y_{Rinit}). The robot rotates in the spot in order to orient towards or look for the target direction. At time t_{init}, the quasi-boolean for motion, b_{hopf}, becomes one, triggering activation of the corresponding neuron, u_{hopf}, and timed forward movement initiation. Amplitude of periodic motion is set as the distance between the origin of the fixed frame (same as robot position before movement initiation) and target location.

During periodic movement and at each instant of time, amplitude of i periodic motion is set as the difference between the target location and the error term between the calculated robot position and the dynamical m_i variable. If positive, this error term means the robot is ahead the position it should be if no obstacle had been circumnavigated, and the vehicle must be de-accelerated. If negative, this error term means the robot is behind the position it should be if no obstacle had been circumnavigated, and the vehicle must be accelerated. Robot i velocity is controlled according to this update. However, in the presence of obstacle contributions, the obstacle term dominates and velocity is set according to the distance to the obstacle (the maximal rate of shift of the fixed point is a design parameter).

The periodic solution is deactivated again when the x vehicle position comes into the vicinity of A_{ic}, and the final postural state (which equals A_{ic}) is turned on instead (neurons $|u_{hopf,i}| = 0$; $|u_{final,i}| = 1$). At this moment in time, the i periodic motion is no longer updated. The same behavior applies for the dynamical systems defined for the y spatial coordinate.
We want to assure that the velocity is already with the desired values, (V_{timing} or V_{obs}), before the fixed points, (ϕ_{tar}, ϕ_{obs}), change again. The desired velocity, V_{obs} or V_{timing}, must be constant from the velocity dynamics point of view. Thus, the velocity dynamics must be faster than each of the individual contributions of the heading direction dynamics. Note that the velocity variable is also coupled to the timing dynamics since V_{timing} is set dependent on the current m_i dynamical variable which is in turn dependent on the heading direction variable.
The following hierarchy of relaxation rates ensures that the system relaxes to the stable solutions, obstacle avoidance has precedence over target acquisition and target achievement is performed in time

$$\tau_{v,obs} << \tau_{v,obs}, \tau_{v,timing} << \tau_{tar}, \tau_{obs} << \tau_{tar} \qquad (27)$$

5. Experimental results

The dynamic architecture was simulated in Matlab/Simulink (product of the MATHWORKS company) and in webots (Michel, 2004). This simulator is based on ODE, an open source physics engine for simulating 3D rigid body dynamics. Each vehicle has seven infrared sensors equidistantly mounted on a ring on the robot's periphery, used to measure distance to surfaces at the height of the ring. The model of the robots are as close to the real robots as the simulation enable us to be. Thus, we simulate the exact kinematic equations, mass distributions, infra-red sensor and the visual system. The dynamics of heading direction, timing, competitive neural, path velocity and dead-reckoning equations are numerically integrated using the Euler method with fixed time step. The cycle time is 70 ms and MT is 10s.
The initial heading direction is 90 degrees. Forward movement initiation is triggered by an initial time set by the user, t_{init} = 3s, and not from sensed sensorial information. Sensed obstacles do not block vision. In case the target is not currently in the limited viewing angle of the camera but has been previously seen, we algorithmically update the previous target location based on dead-reckoning information.
The rotation speeds of both wheels are computed from the angular velocity, w, and the path velocity, v of the robot. The former is obtained from the dynamics of heading direction. The later, as obtained from the velocity dynamics is specified either by obstacle avoidance contribution or by V_{timing} (eq. 25). By simple kinematics, these velocities are translated into the rotation speeds of both wheels and sent to the velocity servos of the two motors.
In order to verify if temporal coordination among the two robot movements is achieved we have performed several simulations. Herein, due to space constraints, we illustrate two exemplary simulations.
During its path towards the target, robot 2 is faced with an obstacle which it must circumnavigate (Fig. 11). This obstacle does not interfere with the robot 1 movement towards the target. Fig. 12 illustrates the robot motions and time stamps of these trajectories. The target (ball) is depicted by a light circle. Small crosses around ball position indicate ball

position as acquired by the vision systems. The robot paths are indicated by lines formed by crosses. The interval between two consecutive crosses indicates the robot's path velocity since the time acquisition interval is constant: the smaller the velocity the closer the points. When the obstacle is no longer detected for the current heading direction, at $t = 9.1s$, robot 2 is strongly accelerated in order to compensate for the object circumnavigation.

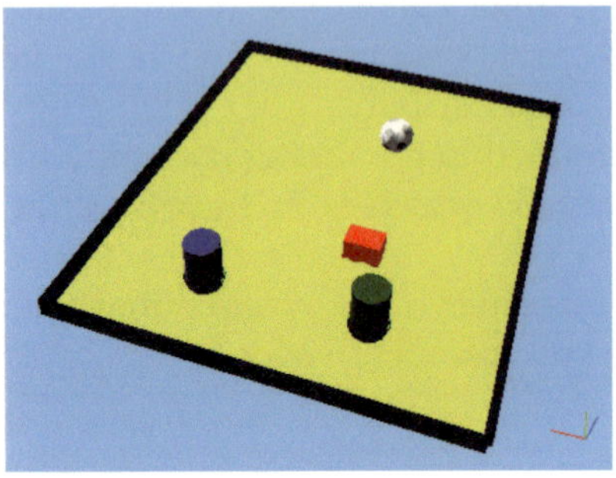

Fig. 11. Webots scenario of experiment 1.

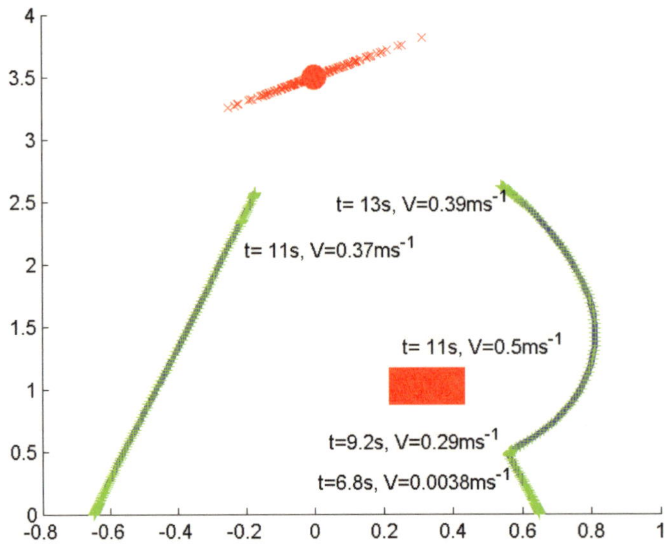

Fig. 12. The simulated robot timed trajectories for reaching the ball.

Robot velocities are depicted in Fig. 13. v represents forward velocity of the robot. v_{timing} and v_{obs} represent velocity imposed by the discussed dynamical architecture and velocity imposed in case an obstacle is detected, respectively.
The proposed dynamic architecture without coupling ($c = 0$ in eq. 2) is similar to work presented in (Santos, 2004), where results have shown that robot velocity is controlled such that the target is reached in an approximately constant time ($MT = 10s$) independently of the environment configuration and of the distance to the target.
The introduction of a coupling of this form tends to synchronize movement in the two robots. Thus, when x and/or y movement of robot 2 is affected by the environment configuration such that its periodic motion amplitude is increased, robot 1 movement is coordinated through coupling such that movements of both robots terminate

simultaneously. This results in delayed simultaneous switch, around $t = 12.8$ s, among Hopf and final contributions for x and y dynamical systems of both robots (see Fig. 14). Note that synchronization only exists when both dynamical systems exhibit periodic motion.

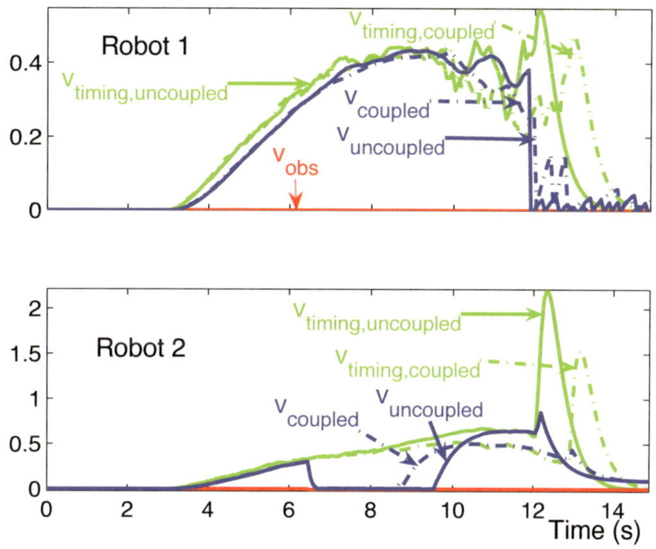

Fig. 13. Velocity variables for robot 1 and 2 for the simulation run depicted in Fig.12.

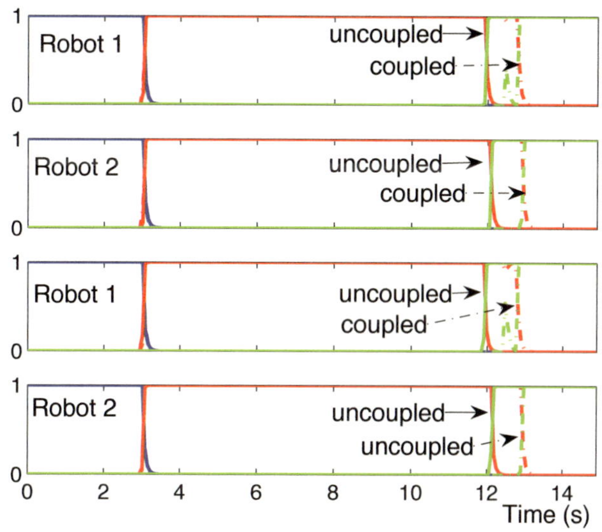

Fig. 14. u neural variables for x (top) and y (bottom) coordinate dynamical systems of both robots.

Coupling two such dynamical systems removes the need to compute exactly identical movement times for two robot movements that must be temporally coordinated. Even if there is a discrepancy in the movement time programmed by the parameter, ω, of the Hopf dynamics (which corresponds to larger *MT*s due to complex environment configurations), coupling generates identical effective movement times.

One interesting aspect is that since the velocities applied to the robots are different depending if there is coupling or not, this results in slightly different qualitative paths followed by the robot.

Fig. 15 represents the Webots scenario and fig. 16 illustrates the robot motions and time stamps of these trajectories towards the target, when both robots are faced with obstacles which they must circumnavigate. These circumnavigations lead to different movement times for both robots. Further, movements on-sets are set differently: robot 1 starts its movement at t_{init} = 3 s and robot 2 starts its movement at t_{init} = 1.5s.

The coupling coordinates the two movements such that they terminate approximately simultaneously (see Fig. 17).

Fig. 15. Webots scenario of experiment 2.

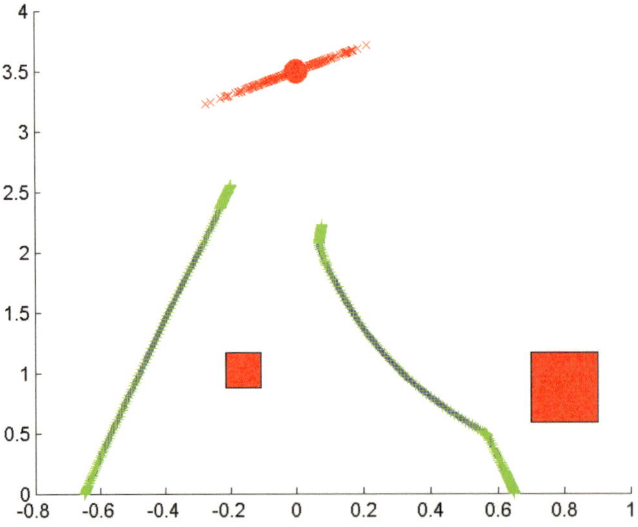

Fig. 16. A simulation run when movement on-sets are set differently for each robot. Object circumnavigation leads to different movement times for each robot.

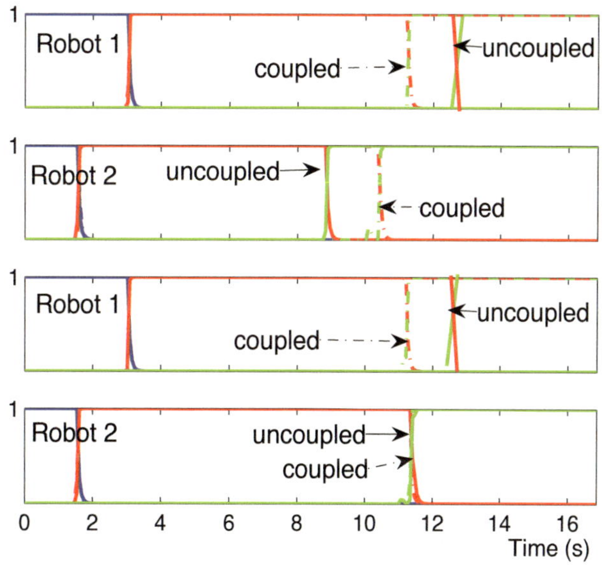

Fig. 17. u neural variables for simulation run depicted in Fig. 16.

6. Conclusion/ outlook

In this article, an attractor based dynamics autonomously generated temporally discrete and coordinated movements. The task was to temporally coordinate the timed movements of two low-level vehicles, which must navigate in a simulated non-structured environment while being capable of reaching a target within a certain time independently of the environment configuration. Movement termination was entirely sensor driven and autonomous sequence generation was stably adapted to changing unreliable simulated visual sensory information. We applied autonomous differential equations to formulate two integrated dynamical architectures which act out at the heading direction and driving speed levels of each robot. Each robot velocity is controlled by a dynamical systems architecture based on previous work (Santos, 2004), which generates timed trajectories. Temporal coordination of the two robots is enabled through the coupling among these architectures.

Results enable to positively answer to the two questions addressed in the introduction. The former asked if synchronization among two vehicles can be achieved when we apply temporal coordination among dofs. Results illustrate the dynamic architecture robustness and show that such a coupling tends to synchronize movement in the two robots, a tendency captured in terms of relative timing of robots movements.

The later question asked if the applied approach provides a theoretically based way of tuning the movement parameters such that it is possible to account for relationships among these. Results show that the coupled dynamics enable synchronization of the robots providing an independence relatively to the specification of their individual movement parameters, such as movement time, movement extent, etc. This synchronization reduces computational requirements for determining identical movement parameters across robots.

From the view point of engineering applications, the inherent advantages are huge, since the control system is released from the task of recalculating the movement parameters of the different components.
Currently, we are implementing this approach in two real wheeled vehicles which will allow to validate the proposed approach to coordination. We believe that due to the controller intrinsic properties communication issues such as delay will not be a major problem. Further, we are developing an higher dynamical system level which will implement the turning off and on of the timing control.

7. References

Armstrong, M. & Zisserman, A. (1995). Robust Object Tracking, *Proceedings of the Asian Conference on Computer Vision* , (1995).

Bicho, E.; Mallet P. & Sch¨oner,G. (2000). Target representation on an autonomous vehicle with low-level sensors, *The Int. Journal of Robotics Research,* Vol. 19, No. 5, May 2000, (424–447).

Bradski, G.R. (1998). Computer vision face tracking as a component of a perceptual user interface. *Workshop on Applications of Computer Vision,* pp. 214–219, Princeton, NJ, Oct. 1998.

Buhler, D. K. M & Kindlmann, (1994). Planning and control of a juggling robot, *International Journal of Robotics Research,* Vol. 13, No. 2, (101–118).

Erdmann, M. & Lozano-Perez, T. (1987). On multiple moving objects, *Algorithmica,* Vol. 2, (477–521).

Everingham, M. & Thomas, B. (2001). Supervised Segmentation and Tracking of Non-rigid Objects using a "Mixture of Histograms" Model. *Proceedings of the 8th IEEE International Conference on Image Processing (ICIP 2001),* pp. 62-65, October 2001, IEEE.

Fraichard, T. (1999). Trajectory planning in a dynamic workspace: A "statetime space" approach, *Advanced Robotics,* Vol. 13, No. 1, (75–94).

Fujimura, K. & Samet, H. (1989). A hierarchical strategy for path planning among moving obstacles, *IEEE Transaction on Robotics and Automation,* Vol. 5, No. 1, February 1989, (61–69).

Fukuoka, Y.; Kimura, H. & Cohen A. (2003). Adaptive dynamic walking of a quadruped robot on irregular terrain based on biological concepts, *The International Journal of Robotics Research,* Vol. 3–4, (187–202).

Giebel, J.; Gavrila, D. M. & Schnörr, C. (2004). A Bayesian Framework for Multi-Cue 3D Object Tracking, *Proc. of the European Conference on Computer Vision,* Prague, Czech Republic, 2004.

Glasius, R.; Komoda, A. & Gielen, S. (1994). Population coding in a neural net for trajectory formation, *Network: Computation in Neural Systems,* Vol. 5, July 1994, (549–563).

Ijspeert, A. J.; Nakanishi, J. & Schaal, S. (2001). Learning control policies for movement imitation and movement recognition, *Neural Information Processing System (NIPS2001),* 2001.

Large,E.; Christensen, H. & Bajcsy,R. (1999). Scaling the dynamic approach to path planning and control: Competition amoung behavioral constrains, *International Journal of Robotics Research,* Vol. 18, No. 1, (101-118).

Michel, O. (2004). Webots: Professional mobile robot simulation, *International Journal of Advanced Robotic Systems,* Vol. 1, No. 1, (39–42).

Pressigout, M. & Marchand, E. (2005). Real-time planar structure tracking for visual servoing: a contour and texture approach. *IEEE/RSJ Int. Conf. on Intelligent Robots and Systems, IROS'05,* August, 2005.

Reif, J. & Sharir, M. (1985). Motion planning in the presence of moving obstacles, *Proceedings of the 25th IEEE Symposium on the Foundation of Computer Science,* pp. 144–153, Portland, OR (USA), October 1985.

Santos, C. (2005). Generating Timed Trajectories for Autonomous Robotic Platforms. A Non-Linear Dynamical Systems Approach, *Cutting edge robotics, in: Navigation Section.* (255-278).

Santos, C. (2004). Generating timed trajectories for an autonomous vehicle: A non-linear dynamical systems approach, *IEEE Int. Conf. On Robotics and Automation.* pp. 3741–3746, New Orleans, April-May 2004.

Schaal, S.; Kotosaka S. & Sternad, D. (2001). Nonlinear dynamical systems as movement primitives, *International Conference on Humanoid Robotics,* pp. 117–124, Cambridge, MA, Sept, 2001. Springer.

Schoner, G. & Santos,C. (2001). Control of movement time and sequential action through attractor dynamics: A simulation study demonstrating object interception and coordination, *9th Intelligent Symp. On Intelligent Robotic Systems,* pp. 18-20, Toulouse, France, July 2001.

Schoner, G. (1994). Dynamic theory of action- perception patterns: The timebefore-contact-paradigm, *Human Mov. Science,* Vol. 3, (415–439).

Schoner, G. & Dose, M. (1992). A dynamical systems approach to tasklevel system integration used to plan and control autonomous vehicle motion, *Robotics and Autonomous Systems,* Vol. 10, (253–267).

Schoner, G.; Dose, M. and Engels, C. (1995). Dynamics of behaviour: Theory and applications for autonomous robot architecture, *Robotics and Autonomous Systems,* Vol. 16, (213–245).

Shahrokni, A.; Drummond, T. & Fua, P.(2004). Texture Boundary Detection for Real-Time Tracking, *Eur. Conf. on Computer Vision,* Prague, Czech Republic, May 2004.

Steinhage, A. & Schoner, G. (1998). Dynamical system for the behavioral organization of autonomous robot navigation, *Spie-Intelligent Sys. Manufactors,* pp. 169-180, 1998.

Taylor, G. & Kleeman,L. (2003). Fusion of multimodal visual cues for model-based object tracking, *2003 Australasian Conference on Robotics and Automation,* pp. 1-3, Brisbane, December 2003.

Tani, J.; Ito, Y. & Sugita, Y. (2004). Self-organization of distributedly represented multiple behavior schemata in a mirror system: reviews of robot experiments using rnnpb, *Neural Networls,* Vol. 17, (1273–1289). [Online]. Available: http://www.bdc.brain.riken.go.jp/ tani/publications.htm

Yilmaz, A.; Xin, L. & Shah, M. (2004). Contour-based object tracking with occlusion handling in video acquired using mobile cameras, *IEEE Transactions on Pattern Analysis and Machine Intelligence,* Vol. 26, No. 11, (1531- 1536).

Zhao, Qi & Tao, H. (2005). Object tracking using color correlogram, *IEEE Workshop on VS-PETS,* October 2005, IEEE.

Machine Vision: Approaches and Limitations

Moisés Rivas López, Oleg Sergiyenko and Vera Tyrsa
Engineering Institute of Autonomous University of Baja California, Polytechnic University of Baja California
Mexicali, BC, México

1. Introduction

Machine vision in its common definition is a possibility of a machine (by sensing means and computer mathematic processing consecutively) to obtain an information about surrounding environment for further analytical treatment.

According to this common definition we can unite in a general classification various, sometimes quite different by its principle, technical systems.

These classification tables can be represented on the base of two different approaches: 1) practical causes (Soini, 2001) for necessity to "see surrounding environment", and 2) technical principle and means using for this task solution.

According to the common definition any complete Machine vision system combines two components: technical means (or hardware) and information processing mathematics and algorithm (or software). However, the various software analyses is not expedient in view of variety of mathematical methods and their object focused applications in each case (Mordohai & Medioni, 2006); and finally can't give clearer problem understanding.

We are now observing a rapid growth of 3D software and hardware capabilities for mainstream PCs, and 3D graphics accelerator boards with processing capabilities of roughly millions polygons per second are becoming commonplace (Petrov et al., 1998). At the same time, dynamic level-of-detail algorithms—built into standard 3D software packages— offer considerable acceleration of model viewing and progressive loading and transmission of 3D models. Despite the fast growth of computer 3D visualization capabilities, until recently data input technology has remained unchanged.

So, in our research for better understanding what is Machine vision, what is its modern state, which practical and technical tasks it decide, and which objective limitations and open problems recently it have, we'll based on the two mentioned above approaches.

In a part of practical reasons, which caused for necessity to develop Machine (or computer) vision concept, can be mentioned:

- security problems in static/dynamic image analysis in perimeter/volume protection (motion/dangerous object detection); (Chellappa et al., 2005), (Itti & Baldi, 2005)
- analysis of short/long term deformation of important engineering structures (more commonly known as 'structural health monitoring' or SHM); (Athavale et al., 1990), (Allen et al., 2005), (Mallet et al., 2004), (Tyrsa et al., 2004), (Ohno et al., 2002), (Benedetti et al., 2004), (Slob & Hack, 2004), (Stewart & Tsakiri, 2002), (Liwen Dai et al., 2002)

- surface digital mapping and micro-surface analysis; (Winkelbach et al., 2006), (Slob & Hack, 2004), (Tunstel, 1995), (Vang et al., 2000), (Peng-Hsiang Weng & Fu-Jen Kao, 2004)
- automatic navigation of robot in unknown scene (Tunstel, 1995), (Diosi & Kleeman, 2005), (França et al, 2005), (Ibeanusi et al, 1999), (Chaumette & Hutchinson, 2006), (Surmann et al, 2003), (Kee et al, 2008), (Hada & Takase, 2001)

In a part of technical principle and means Machine vision system can be classified to:

- camera (or "stereo camera") principle with further image analysis algorithms; (Chellappa et al., 2005), (Itti & Baldi, 2005), (Selectes papers on CCD and CMOS imadges, 2003), (Lavelle et al., 2004)
- 2D-3D image reconstruction techniques (most frequently - 3D laser scanning on triangulation principle); (Tyrsa et al., 2004), (Peng-Hsiang Weng & Fu-Jen Kao, 2004), (França et al, 2005), (Surmann et al, 2003), (Lavelle et al., 2004), (*Handbook of Optical and Laser Scanning,* (2004), (Forman & Parry, 2001), (Pierce et al., 1992), (Lichti et al., 2000), (Petrov et al., 1998)
- terrestrial laser total stations, or airborne laser scanners; (Slob & Hack, 2004), (Baltsavias, b, 1999), (Baltsavias, a, 1999), (Wehr & Lohr U, 1999)
- obstacle detection y description techniques, based on signal "time-of-flight"(radar, lidar, sonar, rangefinders or UWB technologies); (Vang et al, 2000), (Pierce et al., 1992), (Yu et al., 2008)
- GPS-based systems for objects surface reconstruction; (Kee et al., 2008), (Stewart, & Tsakiri, 2002), (Hada & Takase, 2001), (Liwen Dai et al., 2002)
- combined systems, which use a certain combination of mentioned above basic means for increase total system resolution and noise robustness (Ohno et al., 2002), (Benedetti et al., 2004), (Lavelle et al., 2004), (Retscher, 2007), (Liu et al., 2006).

The goal of our work is to compare several of mentioned approaches to Machine vision design, compare their advantages over each other, and the most principal limitations for practical application.

In general, variety of practical applications which strongly requires the technical vision device it is just a confirmation of an actuality and high importance of a new technical vision methods development.

However, sometimes very different practical tasks use very similar techniques for practical task solution. And it has a different level of success. Because of various practical limitation and specific requirements which appears in each unique case. So, the key parameter for to analyze different technical principle for machine vision system design is a basic technical device for task solution.

2. Approaches to machine vision design

More attentive analysis of the mentioned above technical principle and means list permit us to make a simplified conclusion. There are four completely distinct technical approaches to technical vision device design. More truly, if to be rigorous in definitions, three relatively independent methods, and the fourth group which cannot be an independent basis for creation of the device, but possesses such important advantages, that at use of other methods it is not to forget about them, and it is desirable to use actively them as auxiliary means.

These four groups are:

- camera methods;
- laser scanning systems;
- GPS-based methods;
- numerous rangefinder devices (radar-, sonar- , laser-principle, etc.)

As evident the last one cannot be an independent basis for creation of the complete Machine vision system. Because of its physical nature this system it is only capable to estimate the distance to "averaged object", but not reconstruct its surface point-by-point.
Let us carefully review all mentioned principles of Machine vision design for establish their strong and weak points.

2.1 Camera based machine vision

The machine vision system includes (Selectes papers on CCD and CMOS images, 2003) a stereo TV camera assembly and a processing unit. It detects obstacles in real time within its field of view in a range from 5 m to 50 m ahead of the vehicle with a viewing angle of 40 degrees. The cameras are arranged vertically at the front part of the vehicle. The system locates obstacles in the trapezoidal field of view. The scanning of each camera is synchronized and the processing unit uses hard-wired logic instead of a programmable device in order to realize high speed processing of video signals from the cameras. The principle of the obstacle detection is parallax. When two images from both of the cameras are compared, the two images of an obstacle are identical except the positions in the frames. On the other hand each image of figures on the ground differs due to the positions of the cameras. Fig. 1 illustrates the principle of the obstacle detection.

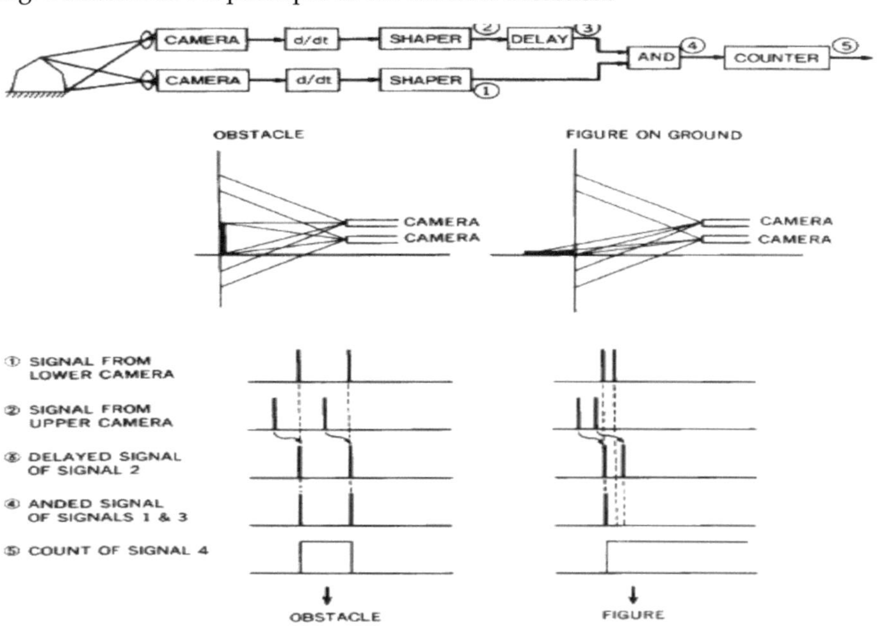

Fig. 1. The principle of the real time obstacle detection

The video signals are differentiated regarding time and the signals are shaped to obtain pulses that correspond to edges in the images. Each time interval of the pulses from each cameras, (*signal* 1 and *signal* 2 in Fig. l), discriminates an obstacle from a figure on a road.

An obstacle generates same time intervals, but a figure on a road generates different time intervals. The cameras have to be, thus, synchronized with each other, and have to employ vertical and progressive scanning techniques. The position of a scanning line corresponds to the direction to the obstacle, and the point where the optical axes of the cameras are crossing indicates the distance to the obstacle. Delaying of one of the signals from the TV cameras is equivalent IO rotation of the optical axis of the camera. Thus, varying the delay time enables us to detect obstacles at other locations. For enlargement of the field of view and detection of obstacle:; in the two-dimensional field of view during one scanning period, parallel processing with 16 kinds of delay time is employed, which yields the field of view of 16 zones arranged longitudinally at intervals of **1** m. Time required to detect obstacles is 35.6 ms, which consists of 33.3 ms of scanning OF one frame and 2.3 ms of processing to detect and locate obstacles. Fig. 2 shows an example of the obstacle detection. The guardrail is identified as a series of obstacles that are indicated by black elements in the figure at the bottom. Since the system had no measures against brightness, shadows, and shades, the operating condition was restricted.

Fig. 2. The obstacle detection: a road scene (top) and obstacles in the scene (bottom) (Sadayuki Tsugawa, 1994)

In a basis of any camera method it is the principle of the human volumetric vision, capable to reconstruct a 3-dimensional picture and approximately estimate distances up to the objects within scene. That is in other words, stereovision.

Any stereovision technical system is approach to a multicamera system. In the elementary case under consideration it is two cameras system. If a stereovision system (Chaumette & Hutchinson, 2006) is used, and a 3-D point is visible in both left and right images (see Figure 3), it is possible to use as visual features s (vector s contains the desired values of the scene/features):

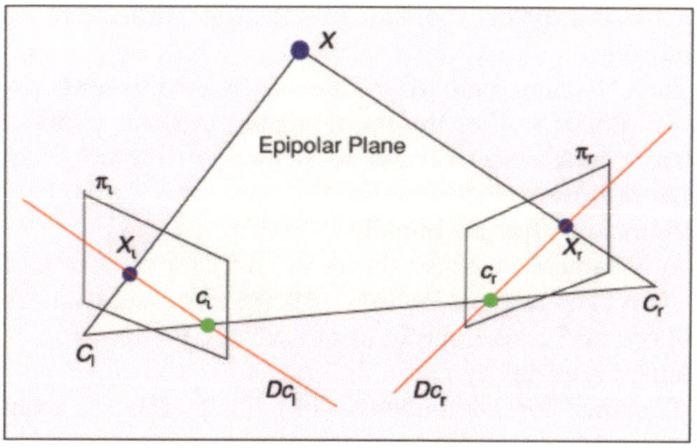

Fig. 3. A stereovision system

$$\mathbf{s} = \mathbf{x}s = (\mathbf{x}l, \mathbf{x}r) = (xl, y\,l, xr, yr),$$

i.e., to represent the point by just stacking in **s** the x and y coordinates of the observed point in the left and right images.

For a 3-D point with coordinates $X = (X,Y,Z)$ in the camera frame, which projects in two images as a 2-D point with coordinates $\mathbf{x} = (x, y)$, we have (Chaumette & Hutchinson, 2006):

$$\begin{cases} x = X/Z = (u - c_u)/f\alpha \\ y = Y/Z = (v - c_v)/f, \end{cases} \tag{1}$$

where image measurements matrix $\mathbf{m} = (u, v)$ gives the coordinates of the image point expressed in pixel units, and $\mathbf{a} = (c\,u, c\,v, f, \alpha)$ is the set of camera intrinsic parameters: $c\,u$ and $c\,v$ are the coordinates of the principal point, f is the focal length, and α is the ratio of the pixel dimensions. In this case, we take $\mathbf{s} = \mathbf{x} = (x, y)$, the image plane coordinates of the point.

Taking the time derivative of the projection equations (1), we obtain the result which can be written in general form

$$\mathbf{X} = \mathbf{L}_x \mathbf{V}_c, \tag{2}$$

where $\mathbf{V}_c$ is a spatial velocity of the camera be denoted by $\mathbf{v}_c = (v_c, \omega_c)$, (with v_c the instantaneous linear velocity of the origin of the camera frame and ω_c the instantaneous angular velocity of the camera frame) and the interaction matrix $\mathbf{L}_x$ (we consider here the case of controlling the motion of a camera with six degrees of freedom) related to **x** is

$$L_x = \begin{bmatrix} \frac{-1}{Z} & 0 & \frac{x}{Z} & xy & -(1+x^2) & y \\ 0 & \frac{-1}{Z} & \frac{y}{Z} & 1+y^2 & -xy & -x \end{bmatrix} \tag{3}$$

L_x is an interaction matrix related to s, *or* feature Jacobian. In the matrix $\mathbf{L}_x$, the value Z is the depth of the point relative to the camera frame. Therefore, any control scheme that uses this form of the interaction matrix must estimate or approximate the value of Z. Similarly

(Chaumette & Hutchinson, 2006), the camera intrinsic parameters are involved in the computation of x and y.

Let us analyze this basic "camera method" parameters regard to equations (1)-(3).

1. Focal distance f in (1), as well as the set of camera intrinsic parameters, shows us that camera uncertainty is strongly related to fabrication imperfections for each unique camera. And, hence the absolute value of this camera uncertainty is rising sufficiently with scene depth increase (proportionally to $1f$, $2f \dots nf$).
2. $\mathbf{V}c$ in (2), which is camera velocity, shows us that any camera method error strongly related to any own camera motions. And, taking to account an arbitrary character of camera self-motions and consequently instant vector $\mathbf{V}c$ direction, it is very difficult to estimate real camera uncertainty.
3. Depth Z in (3) shows for components (1;1), (2;2) (2;3) for example, that method resolution and reasonable operating rate are strongly limited by own theory.

These reasons permits us to understand exactly clear a principal limitations for any practical application of camera based technical vision method. They are very critical for practical using in any application with self-moving camera positioning, are extremely sensible to any vibration and dynamic shocks. Moreover, in spite of significant achievements of camera technologies in last ten years, it still exist a possibility of "camera error", i.e. when one typical object image is assigned with typical properties of another. And this possibility is proportionally increased with distance growth. Finally, camera methods application is naturally limited with distances up to 50 m.

2.2 Laser principle based machine vision systems

Modern laser sensor technologies have made fast and accurate 3-D data acquisition possible as evidence by several commercialized 3-D laser sensors (Tyrsa et al., 2004), (Peng-Hsiang Weng & Fu-Jen Kao, 2004), (Diosi & Kleeman, 2005), (França et al., 2005), (Surmann et al., 2003), (Lavelle et al., 2004), (Handbook of Optical and Laser Scanning, 2004), (Forman & Parry, 2001), (Pierce et al., 1992), (Lichti et al., 2000), (Petrov et al., 1998). Other than some existing 3-D technologies based on CCD 2-D image reconstruction, these 3-D sensors are based on laser scanning and geometric methodologies such as triangulation (Petrov et al., 1998), (Tyrsa et al., 2006, a), (Tyrsa et al., 2006, b), (Rivas et al., 2008) and have achieved more and more attentions in machine vision application due to its robustness and simplicity. However, to expand functional application of these laser sensors, powerful algorithm add-on is still needed to effectively process measured data from them, normally depending on individual application case.

Laser triangulation principle (Handbook of Optical and Laser Scanning, 2004) in general can be based on two schemes represented in Fig 4 (a and b). The first one uses a fixed angle of emission and variable distance; the second one, on the contrary, fixed triangulation base and variable scanning angle.

The first one works as follows.

A laser beam is projected onto the measurement surface (Fig. 4, a), where it is scattered from the surface and its image is detected by an optical detector, usually a CCD camera. By using a suitable angular arrangement between the laser and sensor positions, the detected location of the laser spot on the image plane produces an accurate measurement of the distance between the sensor and the surface. Therefore, the profile of a surface can be measured by using laser triangulation. The laser beam is made to scan across the surface of the object. The range data at each location is calculated according to its position within the image plane so that the whole 3-dimensional profile of the surface can be obtained. The positioning of the laser beam is normally controlled by an adjustable mirror system, which is able to change the angular direction of the laser beam over a 2-dimensional plane.

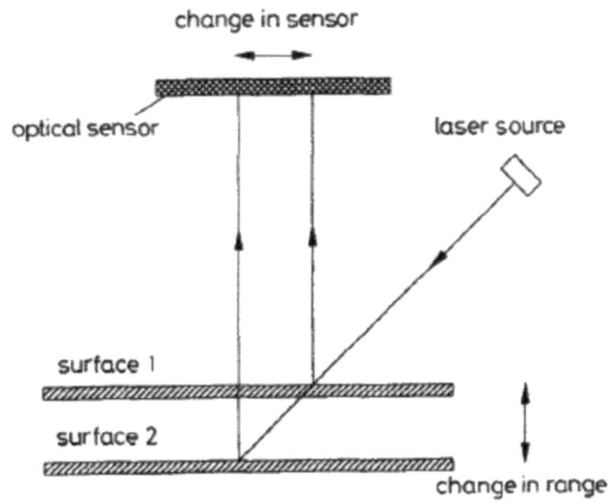

a)

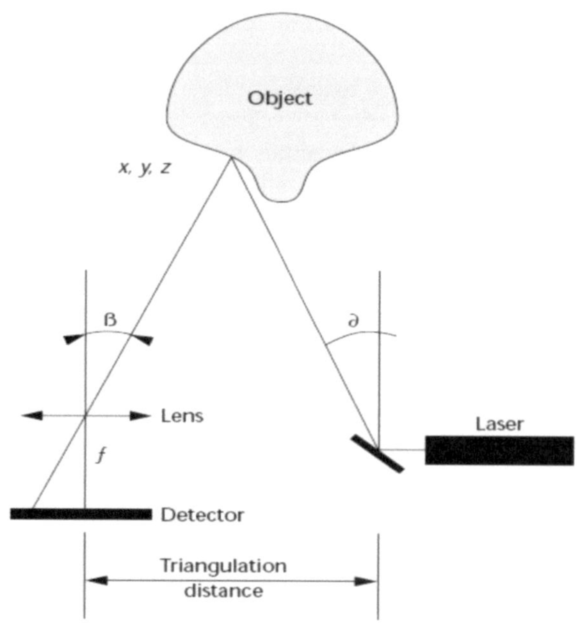

b)

Fig. 4. Two principles of laser triangulation (a – "with fixed angle of emission"; b - "with fixed triangulation distance", consists of a laser dot or line generator and a 1D or 2D sensor located at a triangulation distance from the light source (Petrov et al., 1998). Optionally, the laser light can be steered by a motor)

A second one basic triangulation scheme (Fig. 4, b) is an active optical triangulation 3D digitizing systems, which visualize real-life objects. These active optical systems provide photorealistic representations of shapes and textures with reasonable speed. Figure 4,b shows a simple diagram of a triangulation scanner. The laser beam—reflected from a mirror—is projected on the object. The diffusely reflected light is collected by the sensor, which is a linear array if a laser dot is projected or a 2D matrix (typically a charge coupled device camera) if laser stripes are projected.

The laser positioning circuitry controls the angle α and is known. The angle β is determined in the sensor measurements if the focal length f and the detector pixel size are given. The triangulation distance—the distance between the sensor and the mirror—is also known.

As Figure 4, b shows, since all geometric parameters are known, the x, y, z coordinates of the point on the object can be computed in a trigonometric fashion. If a single laser dot is projected, the system measures the coordinates of just one point of the object. When a laser stripe is projected, all points along the stripe are digitized. The basic triangulation scheme can be enhanced to improve the optical quality and depth of field (see www.vit.iit.nrc.ca for several good examples). The modifications, however, require custom-manufactured components and are relevant mostly for scanners used in high-accuracy reverse engineering tasks. In general, any other kind of structured light can replace the laser dot or stripe. For example, several dots or laser stripes can be projected. However, if the system projects multiple patterns, it's difficult to identify individual elements. If, say, two stripes are projected, then the image processing software must separate the first and second lines. Solutions to the identification problem include using a sequence of different colored stripes. Such schemes typically become sensitive to ambient light, as we'll discuss later.

The most well-known optical triangulation 3D scanner is the one developed by Cyberware of Monterey, California. This legendary scanner was used by a generation of computer scientists. The company has maintained essentially the same product line for more than 10 years. Cyberware products can capture photorealistic images of a range of objects—from apple-size models to fullsize human bodies. The scanner head contains a laserline generator, a system of mirrors, and black-and-white and color video cameras. Scanning occurs by moving the object on a rotation and translation platform, or by moving the sensor around the object in a circular motion. In the basic Cyberware scanner model, a system of mirrors collects laser light from left and right triangulation paths relative to the laser. This scheme helps avoid shadows in the scans caused by the triangulation angle. However, it imposes strict requirements on the optical assembly's quality and the system's calibration, and increases the scanner's size. The scanners are complex, not portable, and prohibitively expensive for many applications. One version, the full-body scanner, digitizes a complete human body as a combination of four scans in about 17 seconds. Each scan has 250 × 1000 points of resolution. The four scans can be glued using commercial software packages (Petrov et al., 1998).

Another typical method for laser scanners is a Circular laser scanning vision sensor for detecting position of singular points (Tao Dai et al., 2005). Usually it called data acquisition device-circular scanning sensor (CSS). By singular point in this case we mean small convex or concave points deviated from smooth surface manifold, caused by either faulty or normal production/machining. The platform for this devise features a three degree of freedom (hence, accommodate 3-D) motion control through a processor, three servo motors and a circular scanning sensor (CSS), as well as a computing system. An emulated head is attached rigidly with CSS to indicate the tracking and focusing actions. The circular scanning sensor (CSS) (Figure 5), with embedded data acquisition device, is a laser scanning multi-axis machine vision device which produces 3-D data sequences of a target work piece for reconstruction of geometry characteristics.

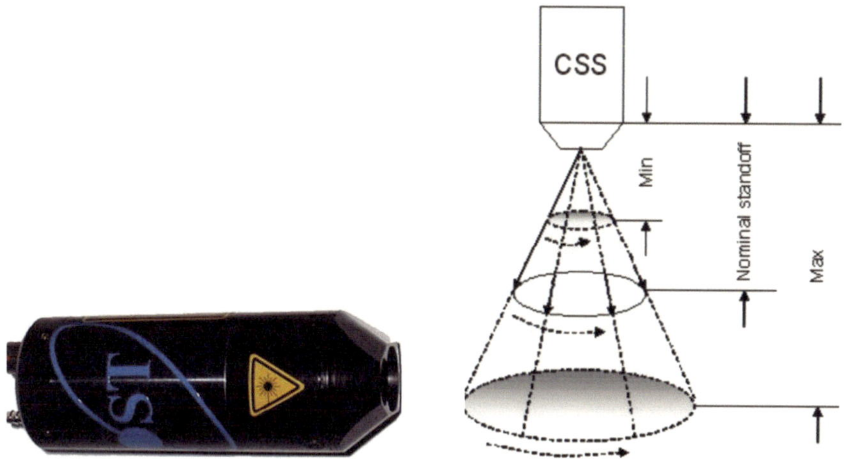

Fig.5. A Laser Circular Scanning Sensor and illustration of Circular Scanning Principle

The CSS and the emulated head are driven by three servo motors to generate 3-D (*x*, *y*, *z*-axis) motion: arbitrary planar scanning route, up and down motion. The main emulated head could track any 3-d singular point on the surface of the work piece while conducting scanning and concentrate on it at specified focusing distance.
The motors are controlled by a central processor which receives location information of singular points from a PC system. The loop is then closed by feedbacking 3-D geometric data of target points acquired by the CSS to the PC system which processes the data sequence continuously using DMA based algorithm (Fig. 6.) to return the location information of singular points, if any, on the surface of work pieces.

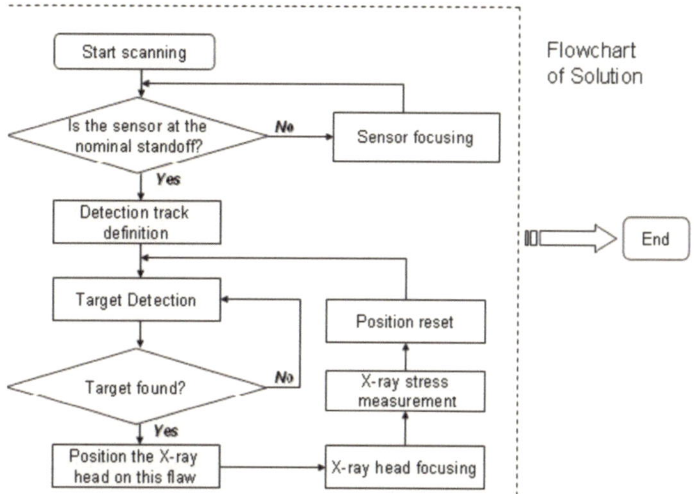

Fig. 6. Flow-Chart of DMA Based Operating Algorithm

For central laser scanning sensor, scanned data is obtained in sequence:

$$Xi = [x_0, x_2, \cdots, x_{N-1}], i= 1, 2, \cdots, \tag{4}$$

where Xi indicates the $i - th$ data sequence captured and N is the number of scanning times called the depth of the data sequence. This data sequence could represent data piece acquired by one sensor in different pre-set time period or by multiple sensors at same time. For example, a line or circular scanning laser sensor generates a geometric data sequence of objects in one scanning cycle. For circular scanned data is considered, hence the depth N is also the scanning cycle period. An example of a 1-D real circular scanning data cycle is illustrated in Figure 7, which is conducted, for example, on a horizontally flat iron plate placed on a table.

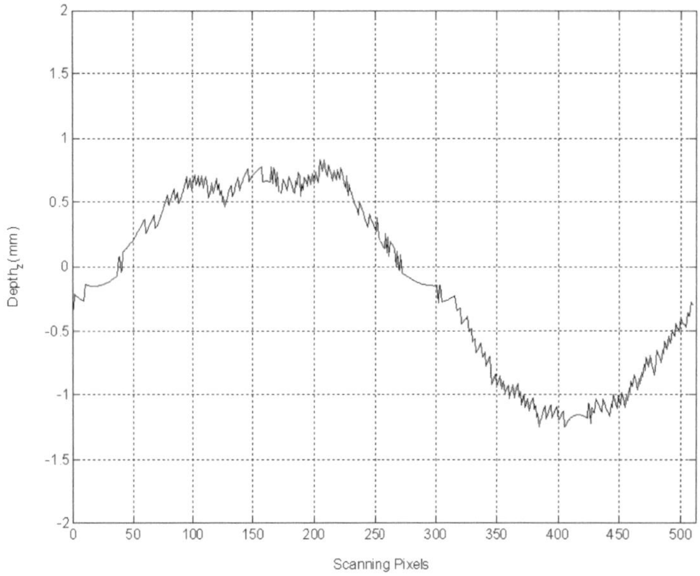

Fig. 7. A 1-D Circular Scanning Data Cycle

In ideal case, one would expect scanned data yields a horizontal line. However, this hardly happens in reality. Instead, as Figure 7 shows, a pseudo-sinusoid shape is presented reflecting either unevenness of plate surface or table leaning, or both. In the case that there is a hole-like singular point, caused by either normal or faulty machining, on the surface, the scanned data would normally reflect that point with a peak significantly deviated from the profile, unlike small peaks around the profile induced by noise. Such an example with a hole of depth 0.4 mm at the 100th pixel is shown in Figure 8 (1-D circular scanning data).

From these two examples, it is clear that two major tasks have to be performed in order for us to obtain accurate information of targets from laser scanned data: reduction of effect of noise on the measurement and detection of singular peak.

This method even it is a laser scanner practically is similar to 3-D technologies based on 2-D image reconstruction and posses all weak points, which are mentioned for these group of methods.

For static object shape monitoring also possible to use a multi-beam laser triangulation (Noll & Krauhausen, 2003) up to more than 120 laser beams are used to simultaneously measure geometric features of moving products such as e.g. the thickness, profile or surface topology. The laser beams form a series of measuring points or lines on the object surface.

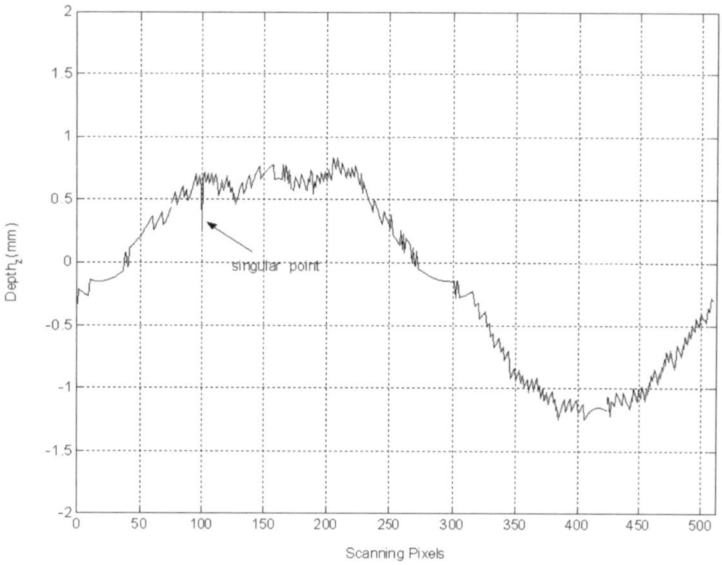

Fig. 8. A 1-D Circular Scanning Data Cycle with a Singular Point

By temporal modulation of the pulse width of the laser diodes and control of the exposure time of the CCD or CMOS detectors **a** dynamic range of more than $1 \div 10^4$(without considering the dynamic range of the detector elements itself is realized enabling the measurement of object surfaces ranging from black to metallic bright. The use of different laser wavelengths allows suppressing cross-talking originating from overlapping laser projections on the surface of the specimen. However, this method is a good tool for dynamic surface control, but it is unsuitable for high-grade image reconstruction. It cannot be related to pure "camera methods" because CCD or CMOS devices are used only like "light 1/0 detectors", also for incident ray preliminary positioning. This example highlights those sometimes optical sensors matrixes are the better detectors because of their good sensitivity/resolution.

Another laser tools for static perimeter control is Laser radar (LADAR) (Sahba et al., 2006), (Stutz, 2005). LADAR scanning is far advanced over conventional active infrared (AIR) sensing. The transmitter and receiver units are usually coaxially located, making the installation less prone to misalignment or tremors than traditional opposed or retro-reflective sensor posts. Laser scanning also has much finer resolution that RADAR and microwave-RADAR, allowing the definition of the intruding target size. Time of flight pulse detection or continuous wave phase shift methods are used to derive range measurements. According to tests conducted to determine the feasibility of using laser scanning for perimeter protection (Sahba et al., 2006), it has been confirmed the capability of detecting humans and vehicles, with a maximum range of 25m and 80m respectively. The testing demonstrated large area coverage, the ability to determine intruder size, the definition of multiple detection zones, a good detection rate and low false alarm rate (Hosmer, 2004). It has also been claimed that camouflage and other methods for masking an object can deceive near infrared devices, but it is impossible to mask a physical volume moving through space, thereby implying that by scanning a plane at high speed and resolution, any object moving through this plane will be detected (Hancock et al., 1998). Riza, et. al. propose generic criteria for an ideal optical scanner including a wide scanning range, no moving parts, high resolution, high speed and low power consumption. Additionally, they place significance on reconfiguration (Riza & Muzammil, 2003). By projecting many spots, a laser curtain is produced and multiple range measurements from a dense array of laser spots provide a 3D contour of the perimeter. In current LADAR scanners, a laser beam is deflected by rotating mirrors as show in Fig. 9 where D is the incident beam diameter, a is the beam-feed angle, θ is the active scan angle and L is the scan length.

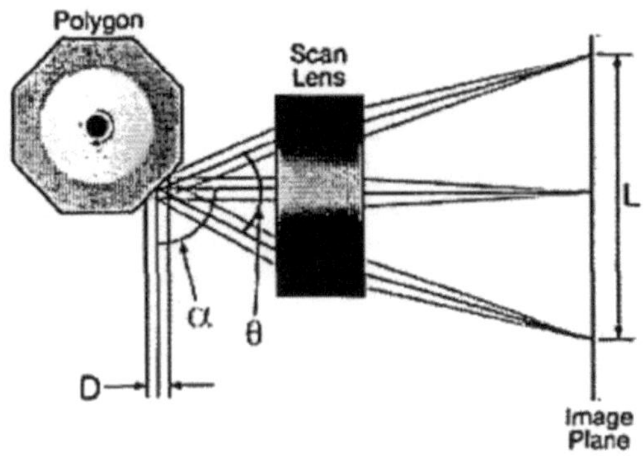

Fig. 9. Principal of laser beam deflection using a rotating mirror (Stutz, 2005)

As we can observe, commonly static object monitoring methods strongly related to basic optical property of focal distance and its practical consequence of a sharp image in a focal plane. From the other hand, it makes these technical solutions initially (apriori) unsuitable for such dynamic task like a mobile robot vision.

In applications where information from more than one physical point of an object needs to be derived, a scanning mechanism must be employed to deflect the light beam from the laser source, towards the desired point of interest on the object surface. This deflection is usually driven in two or three dimensions electro-mechanically. Laser scanning mechanisms have been used in a large variety of applications ranging from photo and document scanners to airborne topographic mapping, surveying of buildings and plants, counting and collision prevention. Approximately over the past ten years laser scanning has found new applications in photoelectric security sensing. Some common uses include providing light curtains in front of assets on a wall display or over the facade of a building. More commonly, laser scanners are employed to provide high resolution range measurements to the outer perimeter (e.g. fencing, walls) of a building and detect a change in range values when beams are intersected by an intruder.

To date, driving the deflection mirror in the desired direction has been accomplished using different devices such as electro-mechanics, rotating polygon shaped mirrors and galvanometers. Figs. 10. (c) and (d) show the layout of a typical commercially available laser scanner and its mirror driving mechanics. Typically, the whole optical head is rotated by a servo motor head around the azimuth in the order of a 1000 rpm, and the mirror rotates in elevation at the same time. This dual movement deflects the beam in the desired directions. However, the intrinsic motion of the mirror causes scanning problems which are the hardest to quantify and correct. Acceleration time taken to reach the constant scanning speed from a stationary position can result in range measurements being stored at the wrong corresponding points in the scanned image. Additionally, all mirrors and measurement components must be synchronized exactly. In general, laser scanning is much more sensitive to vibration than a multi-beam stationary optic approach. In particular, mirror device scanners are slow, bulky and expensive and being inherently mechanical they wear out as a result of acceleration, cause deflection errors and require regular calibration. Stutz in (Stutz, 2005) explains that the performance of polygonal scanners, especially with respect to maintaining an accurate deflection beam path, is prone to manufacturing tolerances.

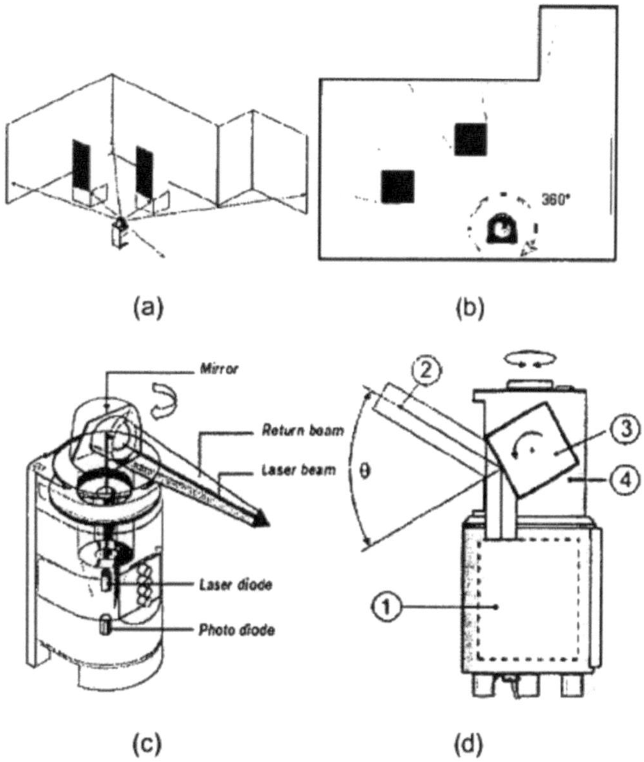

Fig. 10. (a) and (b) indoor room surveillance scanning, (c) scanner with mirror mounted on motor, (d) scanner with rotating mirror where 1 contains the range finding electronics, 2 is the deflected beam, 3 is the rotating mirror and 4 is the complete optical head which also rotates (Sahba et al., 2006)

Dynamic track and jitter errors are caused by tolerances for:

- Polygon machining errors
- Mounting errors
- Mounting-hub errors
- Random wobble caused by ball bearings
- Motor cogging
- Torque variations
- Noisy start of scan circuit

Machining and mounting errors directly cause the deviation of the deflection beam from the desired path of propagation towards the correct point at the image plane. Errors can range from 1 to 60 arc-seconds in angular deviation. Cogging, torque and facet flatness variations cause errors in the actual scan line.

Other problems listed with rotational scanners are as follows (Stutz, 2005):

- Synchronization with other time-dependent elements in the system is rather difficult.
- Motor stability and durability at higher rotation speeds also present problems.
- There is an upper limit to the rotation speed due to the tensile strength of the mirror material. The mirror must not disintegrate at the maximum rotation speed.

Another strong tool for 3D spatial data acquisition is terrestrial laser scanning (Slob & Hack, 2004), (Baltsavias, 1999, a), (Baltsavias, 1999, b). These are active scanners based on laser signals for measurement of slant distances to acquire information about the surface of the Earth and objects on it. As mentioned above, there are several laser scanning systems being operational. Concerning the measurement principle two different methods had been realized: *runtime* measurement using pulsed laser signals and *phase difference* measurement using continuous-wave lasers. Because most systems are based on the first mode, it will be described in more detail in the next section. A good overview on both topics can be found in (Wehr & Lohr, 1999). The pulsed mode laser scanner emits pulsed laser light in exactly determined time intervals. The system measures the runtime of these laser pulses, i.e. the elapsed time between emitting a signal and receiving it after reflection on the surface of the Earth or objects on it. Therefore, slant distances can be derived from these time differences by the wellknown formula v = Ds / Dt or Ds = v / Dt. By means of the exterior orientation of the sensor (recorded by differential GPS (dGPS) and INS systems) 3D co-ordinates of the illuminated surface points can be determined.

Laser systems need to be designed mainly regarding two components: the *emitting and receiving unit* and the *positioning unit*. Both will be described as the example by means of the operational system TopoSys (Wehr & Lohr, 1999) which was used to acquire the data sets about terrestrial landscape.

In this system, the emitting and receiving unit is realized by means of a glass fiber optic. The laser light is emitted on a nutating mirror, i.e. a rotating mirror which deflects it on a glass fiber bunch. The ends of the glass fibers are connected to a row-shaped optic, so the resulting measuring pattern on the surface of the Earth is a single scanning line. In addition to the movement of the airplane this results in a strip-wise data acquisition as shown in Figure 11.

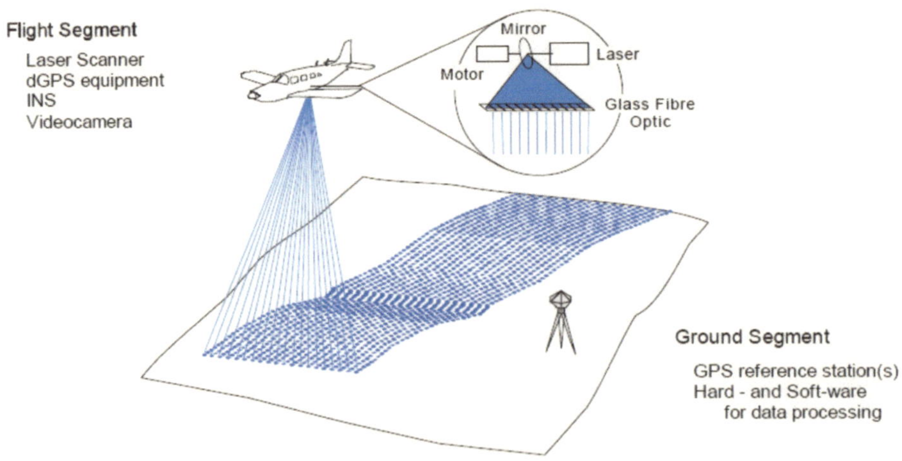

Fig. 11. Laser scanner system TopoSys (Wehr & Lohr, 1999)

The positioning component of the system consists of several elements. As navigation principle differential Global Positioning System (dGPS) is chosen. Therefore, GPS antennas are mounted on the airplane, as well as on reference stations on the ground. Although this positioning strategy yields to good results concerning the accuracy of the obtained coordinates (in the range of some few centimeters), the measurement rate is lower than the one of the laser scanner. Therefore, additionally Inertial Navigation Systems (INS) are used, i.e. navigation units register the rotations of the airplane based on gyros. These are capable to determine a position with a higher temporal resolution.

In Table 1 the performance parameters of this system are listed. It should be mentioned that the system is capable of acquiring up to 5 points per m^2. This results in data sets of high point density and suitable accuracy in position as well as in elevation.

sensor type	pulse modulated laser Radar	range	< 1000 m
scanning principle	fibre optic line scanner	transmitter	solid state at 1.5 μm
measurement principle	run-time measurement	scan frequency	300 Hz (adjustable)
field of view	+/- 7°	number of pixels per scan	127
swath width (1000m flight height)	250 m	accuracy of a single distance measurement	< 0.3 m
accuracies of point coordinates x,y,z	~ 0.3, 0.3, 0.1 m	resolution of a distance measurement	< 0.1 m

Table 1. Performance parameters of TopoSys laser system (Steinle & Vogtle, 2000)

It is relatively more expensive method over another laser application. Hence the principle limitation of it is the practical importance of the task. However, terrestrial laser scanning have a significant flexibility of provided practical use acts. For example, terrestrial scanning lidar (light detection and ranging) is applied to outcrop stratigraphic mapping enables researchers to capture laser range data at a rate of thousands of individual X, Y, Z and laser-intensity points per second (Bellian et al., 2005).

Fig. 12. A typical field setup in Patagonia in early 2002. All equipment was transported in a backpack by a single person (picture courtesy of Jeremy Willson, Shell Oil). Lithium Ion batteries have helped reduce battery weight to 1,540 grams (3.4 pounds) per approximately 2 hours of continuous scan time (Bellian et al., 2005)

Research group of (Bellian et al., 2005) store the 3D coordinates data set with an Optech Laser Imaging ILRIS 3D terrestrial (ground-based) scanning lidar (Fig.12). This instrument was chosen for its 1 km range, palm-type interface, and light weight. All data from the ground-based lidar surveys were processed on a standard laptop computer with at least a gigahertz processor speed, 1 gigabyte of RAM and Innovmetric Incorporated's Polyworks CAD (Computer Aided Design) software. The principal result of (Bellian et al., 2005) was: high-resolution lidar (approx. 1cm point spacing) is far more accurate in three dimensions than nearly all GPS currently available to the public.

2.3 GPS-based and combined machine vision principles

GPS-based solutions sometimes also are acceptable for machine vision, especially for navigation tasks. The good example of such system is presented in (Vang et al., 2000).
GPS based navigation for autonomous land vehicles has the capabilities of GPS to determine the locations of vehicles, as far as static objects, basing on satellites (Kee et al., 2008), (Stewart & Tsakiri, 2002).
GPS measurements consist of biased and noisy estimates of ranges to the orbiting satellites. The principal source of bias is the unknown receiver clock offset, whereas the remaining errors arise from:

- ' modelling of the satellite clock and ephemeris.
- ' modelling of the ionospheric and tropospheric delay.
- ' measurement of the code and carrier phase influenced by both receiver noise and multipath.

DGPS is a technique that improves the user's position accuracy by measuring the infinitesimal changes in variables in order to provide satellite positioning corrections. It should contain a reference station, a data-link, and user applications. The reference station generates corrections by means of a measured pseudo-range or carrier-range, a calculated distance from the reference station to each satellite, and a satellite clock bias as well as an estimated receiver clock bias, and broadcasts them to the user application. The correction messages contain a Pseudo Range Correction (PRC) for DGPS, a Carrier Phase Correction (CPC) for CDGPS, and their time rates, Range Rate Correction (RRC) (Kee et al., 2008):

$$PRC = -(-b + I + T + \delta R) = d - \rho + \widehat{B} \quad (5)$$

$$CPC = -(-b - I + T + \delta R + N\lambda) = d - \varphi + \widehat{B} \quad (6)$$

Where:

ρ:	pseudo range measurement
φ:	carrier phase measurement
λ:	wavelength of the carrier phase
N:	integer ambiguity
d:	distance from the reference station to the satellite
b:	satellite clock bias error
$\widehat{B}$:	estimated clock bias of the receiver
I :	ionospheric delay
T:	tropospheric delay
δR:	orbit error

Unfortunately, the available accuracy for civilian applications is very poor because of all basic components in (5, 6). First of all, because of objective atmospheric delays (ionospheric and tropospheric). Although commercial DGPS (Differential GPS) service increases the accuracy up to several meters, it is still not sufficient for autonomous driving. Hence it is possible use an image processing to compensate this error. In spite of the fact that it is difficult to use image processing for recognition of a complex environment, it is possible to use it to determine some specified objects that haw obviously simple features. For example, lane tracking in highway, forward car tracking have been reported in (Vang et al., 2000). In this study, information about some specified objects is provided by a 3D map which is synthesized based on a real environment. The autonomous land vehicle uses these features to identify the indicated objects from the complex environments so as to position the vehicle's location. Because image processing consumes long time and positioning accuracy cannot satisfy the autonomous driving in many cases, environmental sensors, such as a 3D scanning laser rangefinder: ultrasonic environmental sensors, are also used.
Fig. 13 depicts the autonomous land vehicle used in the experiments (Vang et al., 2000). This vehicle was equipped with a color CCD camera, a GPS unit, a 3D scanning laser rangefinder, ultrasonic sensors, etc.

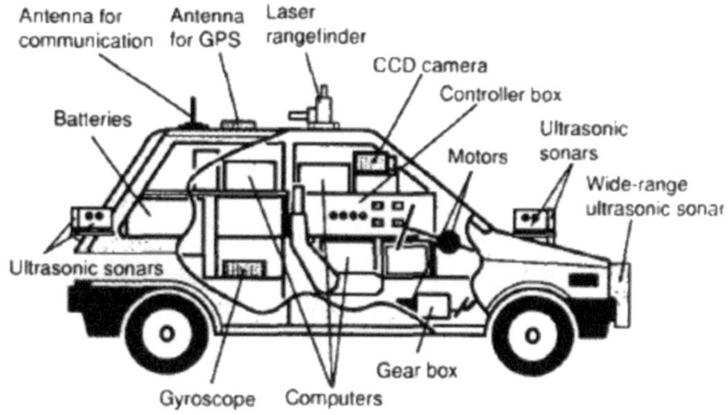

Fig. 13. The autonomous land vehicle used in the experiments (Vang et al., 2000)

Pedals and steering wheel are controlled with servomotors. The environmental sensing and control system is multitools. The position information from DGPS is used to retrieve environmental data from the 3D map. The 3D map provides the information about landmarks and features of some targets. Based the target features, the image processing system identify the landmarks by which the position of the vehicle is determined. An encoder attached to the wheel of a tire and a gyroscope are used for determination of the vehicle position and attitude. Because draft error may become unallowably large, these sensors are only for short distance measurement. A 3D scanning laser rangefinder is employed for compensation of the image processing system. The computers control the steering based on the information from the environmental recognition.
Positioning of GPS uses satellites. The resolution of the GPS used in the experiments is about 0.18m. However, the accuracy available for civilian applications is very poor. Even though DGPS makes the accuracy improved greatly, the positioning error is still insufficient for automatic driving. The positioning accuracy is not so good to navigate a vehicle, but enough to indicate the vehicle t o search some landmarks around the location. The synthesized 3D map provides geographic information that is referred by DGPS for positioning the vehicle's location. Because of the error of DGPS, some other information has

to be given for the vehicle to compensate the positioning error of GPS. In study (Vang et al., 2000) the information about landmarks and their geometry and features is contained in the 3D map. The vehicle locates itself position by referring to the landmarks. The 3D map was synthesized by using OpenGL[1]. In the scene some objects are specified as landmarks for the image processing system to recognize as well to correct the positioning error caused by GPS. For the sake of simplicity of the image processing, some obvious features of the indicated objects are provided. The image processing identifies some objects indicated by the 3D map. By detecting the relative position to the indicated objects, the vehicle can determine itself position. Image processing is not always effective in any situation. In such case, **a** 3D scanning laser rangefinder is used. A laser rangefinder measures distance using time-of-flight method. It has advantages in positioning accuracy, detection speed in comparison with image processing. By horizontal and vertical scanning 2D or 3D maps can be obtained. The above discussed environmental sensors are effective for long range detection. To guarantee a safe driving the near surroundings of the vehicle have to be monitored. For this purpose, ultrasonic sensors were used. 8 ultrasonic sensors that have detection range of several meters are arranged around the vehicle. A no-scanning wide-range ultrasonic sensor was also developed and mounted in the front, of the vehicle. The experimental results of (Vang et al., 2000) demonstrated a higher performance in comparison with a video camera only.

But, if we'll analyze presented system, it can be classified more like combined system, than GPS-based as declared by authors. It shows one more again that robust and secure systems nowadays more and more became combined system, which shares strong skills of mentioned above classical approaches.

It is important to note, that, in our opinion, the GPS have a strong potential in a field of future machine vision design. Because in last ten years there is a lot of financial and intellectual investments to GPS and GPS-based technologies application. But this branch still can not be adopted as an independent base for machine vision, because of impossibility to scan nearby environment, to detect an arbitrary object in the scene. We are consider, that with years comes detailed GPS-maps with marked details in landscape. It will give a possibility to navigate a mobile object using dead reckoning principle (Ibeanusi et al., 1999), (Sadayuki Tsugawa, 1994). In this case a quantity of arbitrary objects in the scene will be minimized, and their location it is possible to fix by simple locator or UWB (Yu et al., 2008). But recently it is problematic use GPS as an independent vision tool. Another principle limitation of GPS is a nonlinear uncertainty growth for such dynamic application like mobile robot navigation for example.

Also it is essential to note that in present time any GPS application still have a fundamental problem of the method. The GPS technology cannot be used outside the radio signals receiving zone such as tunnels, mines, complex indoor spaces, up to that sometimes can not functioning correctly at dense cloudiness or overcast, etc.

A good example of "combined system" design is presented in (Petrov et al., p. 32, 1998). It is given the detailed consideration to the optical 3D scanner developed by company MetaCreations Real-Time Geometry Lab (www.metacreations.com/products/rtgeom). The principal design goals are portability, low cost, fast scanning speed, and photorealistic quality of models. To fulfill these requirements, a scanner is built mostly from off-the-shelf components. Also a set of rather complex software algorithms to help facilitate the scanning process is developed. The basic image processing algorithms were implemented in hardware. The scanning resolution is better than 1 mm, while the acquisition time is sufficient. In the hardware design we avoided using complex optical schemes, instead transferring the complexity of the problem to algorithm development. This software-oriented approach allowed us to use simple components in an easy-to-manufacture design. Figure 14 shows a block diagram of Galatea scanner.

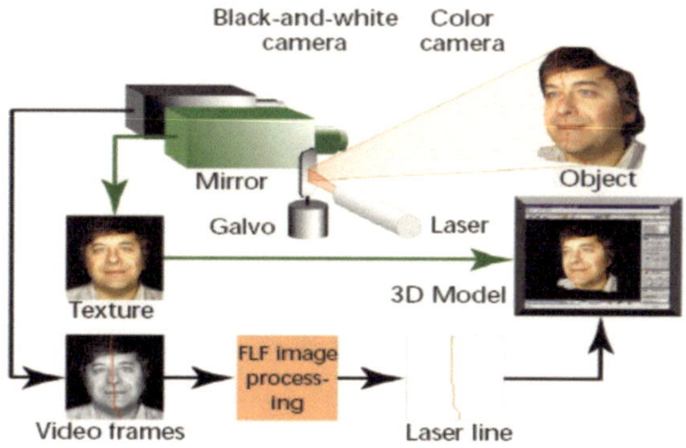

Fig. 14. Galatea scanner block-diagram. A galvanometric motor steers the laser stripe. The Fast Laser Finder (FLF) image processor processes the black-and-white camera's video stream. Merging the texture image of the color camera with the geometric model generates the final 3D model

The optical part consists of a laser-line generator, a galvanometric scanner, and black-and-white and color cameras. It's quite natural to use a laser as the light source in a triangulation system. Diode lasers are compact and inexpensive, and can be easily focused down to their diffraction limit. The depth of field is considerably larger than the sensor camera's depth of field. For this reason, the laser does not require focusing during normal operation. In general, a properly designed scanner is eye safe, so that the system can be certified as a Class 1 laser according to the CDRH (Center for Devices and Radiological Health, Food and Drug Administration) classification. One of the major advantages of a laser source is that it can be easily filtered out from the ambient illumination using a narrow-bandpass filter. This allows laser-based digitizers to be operated in daylight conditions. Also, the laser signal can be easily filtered out from the color camera data, allowing the color texture and geometry to be captured simultaneously. The laser projection system consists of a laser-line generator and an ultrafast galvanometric scanner. The repeatability of average galvanometric scanners is about 20 microradians, while the nonlinearities are small enough to be calibrated for, if necessary. The positioning speed of such a motor exceeds 1,000 angles per second. An NTSC formatted high resolution black-and-white camera senses the geometry. A color CCD camera—installed between the laser projection system and the black-and-white camera—captures the texture map. The scanning speed of 3D laser digitizers is limited by the rate of video cameras, typically 60 frames per second. Acquiring a 200-stripe resolution image would take about 3.3 seconds in a traditionally built digitizer. For many applications, including scanning the human body, this speed is not satisfactory. Using faster cameras provides a straightforward solution to increase speed. However, fast cameras tend to be rather expensive. To avoid using fast cameras, several solutions have been proposed.
Meanwhile, this system - as far as mentioned by authors collective - is designed as low cost solution for practical application where not necessary a high resolution. This example highlights the next fact. Any combined design always have larger coordinates error because a generalized system uncertainty is caused by complex cross-action of all components error sources and their interaction in this case is almost impossible to estimate by classic metrological methods.

3. Synthetic approach to machine vision system design

The first principle conclusion from the methods overview is the next. The machine vision can be divided in a two general groups of methods:

- relatively fast, but rough form estimation methods of scene analysis (with significant uncertainty of form reconstruction);
- metrological methods based on the precise coordinates measurement. These methods requires for insignificant form reconstruction uncertainty a lot operating time and gives a enormous data set for memory storage. Practically it is almost impossible to use this group in real time for any dynamic system.

The second principle conclusion from the methods overview is the next. Competitive machine vision can not be based on any of these two bases. It must to share the main advantages of them: fast operability of the first one and precise 3D coordinates accuracy of the second one.

The third conclusion. Many modern scanners use "time of flight" to measure distance on the basis of the average speed of light in air. This measurement varies with air density, but because the speed of light is so great, these perturbations are very small for distances less than several kilometers. Other instruments use phase recognition to augment this technique for increased precision; however, this method is associated with an increase in data volume, which is undesirable.

The fourth conclusion from the methods overview: laser shows the high competitive ability over other scanning tools. It gives higher resolution, reasonable range and operation velocity. The weak point of laser technology is a limited power source of continuous scan time.

The key solution of this problem we are considering in a carefully thought over algorithm of information processing, very closely tied to each practical application. It must be flexibly used similar to human brain estimation: combine a very rough scene analysis in general, with furthering "zoom"-possibility for most problematic points surrounding (i.e. singular points). For this final fine stage it is only acceptable to provide a metrological accuracy method.

System optimized design according to open problem requirements will be explained on example of 3D laser Machine vision system, based on (Tyrsa et al., 2006, a), (Tyrsa et al., 2006, b), (Rivas et al., 2008).

4. Multipurpose scanning vision system design

It is considered in this paper a system with several characteristics previously referred; such as a high resolution, speed and versatility, can be used by our system in low cost.

In the most of fully autonomous navigation systems is used a vision system like this, our prototype can stand out among the other systems because has a very low cost; other advantage is the versatility, has a wide range of vision that can change to increase precision; and large sight depending of laser power.

This vision of environment is very similar to the human sight, has wide range of view, but can focus a specific area to get a high resolution and detailed image, so to make this task is not necessary modify hardware in prototype, just adjust some parameters in software

4.1 Original principle of 3D spatial coordinates measurement

On fig.15, basic elements of machine vision system (MVS), placed as example on mobile robot (MR), are shown.

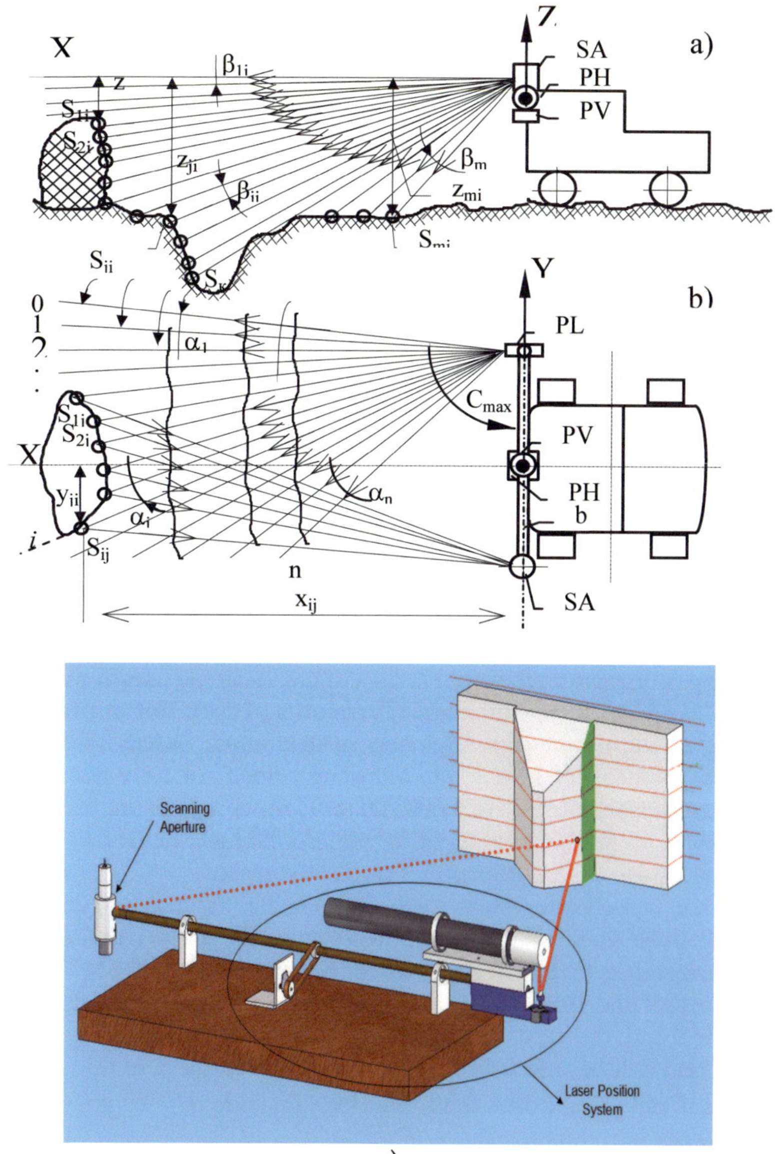

c)

Fig. 15. General principle of MVS functioning (a – lateral view; b - top view; c - laser scanner prototype view)

MVS represents laser angle-distance-measuring system located in the upper forward part of MR. MVS contains a rather high-power laser with a collimator. The laser and the collimator are installed in own laser positioning system (PL) (fig.15, b). PL has its step drive, which on a command from the onboard computer can turn PL in a horizontal plane at each for one

angle pitch. PL is on one end of a horizontal bar b. On the other end of the bar is located a scanning aperture (SA), shown separately on fig.16. The SA axle is perpendicular to a bar and plane XOY. The bar b is installed by its middle part in its own positioning system, containing horizontal (PH) and vertical (PV) step drives (fig.1).
MVS works in the next way (Tyrsa et al., 2006, a). By the command from the computer the bar is installed so that the SA rotation axis becomes perpendicular to plane XOY of MVS reference system (fig. 15). PL puts the laser with the collimator, for example, in an extreme right position. The axis of the collimator (with the help of PV-step drive) then takes extreme top position (above the horizon). The laser and the SA are switched on. SA is rotated by the electromotor EM. At each SA turn a laser ray should hit an obstacle, is reflected difusely by it (point Sij) and returns to mirror M (fig.16). At the moment when three objects: the point of reflection Sij, the perpendicular to mirror M and the vertical axis of SA - takes their common plane, perpendicular to plane XOY while SA is rotating, an optical signal, having trevelled a path "Sij - mirror M - objective O - optical channel OC - photoreceiver PR ". It makes an electrical stop signal. A start signal is previously formed by SA by means of a zero-sensor (installed on a bar b axis).
Filling in a time interval $t_{B1} = B_1/\omega$, (where: B_1 - angle between the bar axis (zero-sensor direction) and direction SA – Sij (fig.3); ω - SA rotation rate) with pulses of reference frequency f_0, we shall receive a code $N_{B1} = t_{B1} \cdot f_0$. Rotation of SA cycle time $T_{2\pi 1} = 2\pi/\omega$ is simultaneously filled with same impulses of reference frequency f_0. The code $N_{2\pi 1} = T_{2\pi 1} f_0$ is formed. The angle $B_1 = 2\pi \cdot N_{B1}/N_{2\pi 1}$ is stored.
It is essentially to note, that this SA, or properly PSA (passive SA) as independent node have a very precise angle coordinates measurement accuracy. It can be used for navigation task as well as the static coordinates measurement (Tyrsa et al., 2004), for example for structural health monitoring of important civil engineering structures. Exactly, for inferior limit of stabilized reference oscillator of 1 MHz and scanning velocity of 1 rev per sec, consequently we have an exact measurement scale of 1,000,000 units for complete angle of 360°. Even such resolution (0.00036° of angle) is an excellent for mentioned task. But it can be increased easy by reference frequency increase or scanner's velocity decrease.
When mirror SA has passed a direction towards point Sij, the laser is switched off to save power. The electric pulse goes to PL, the step-drive turns the laser with the collimator on an angle α_1 along horizon (fig.15, b). By approach of SA mirror M to the MR 'view sector' the laser is switched on. If the laser ray in its new position hits an obstacle, a new point of reflection is formed and the measurement is re-cycled. If the laser ray does not hit an obstacle, no reflection will be, and a new point will not be formed. In this case, as well as in case when a point of reflection exists, the formation of a code $N_{в2}$ begins with the signal of zero-sensor start pulse.
As soon as this code reaches some pre-determined value overlapping a range of possible code values corresponding to an operative sector, the counter, where codes N_{Bi} are formed, is installed on zero, and the laser is switched off. PL step-drive turns the laser on an angle α_2. Cycles with measurements of angles on reflection points, if these are formed by obstacles, or single cycles of scanning, when the obstacle is not present, are repeated in the same order. Values of angles Bi, in a cycle where reflection points took place, are stored. When the system PL stands in an extreme position *n*, stipulated by a minimum distance and

a maximum angle of view, the bar positioning system step drive turns it round a horizontal axes by an angle β_1 (fig.15,a). The cycles with measurements of angles B_i are recurred. Angles α_i are fulfilled in the back order from a position n up to a position 0.

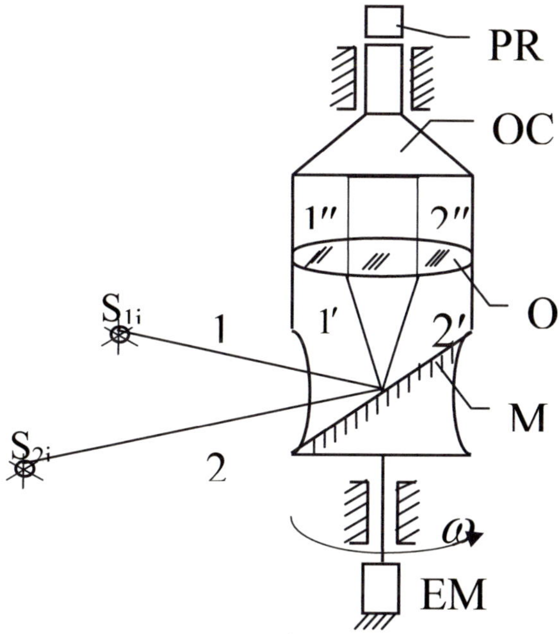

a)

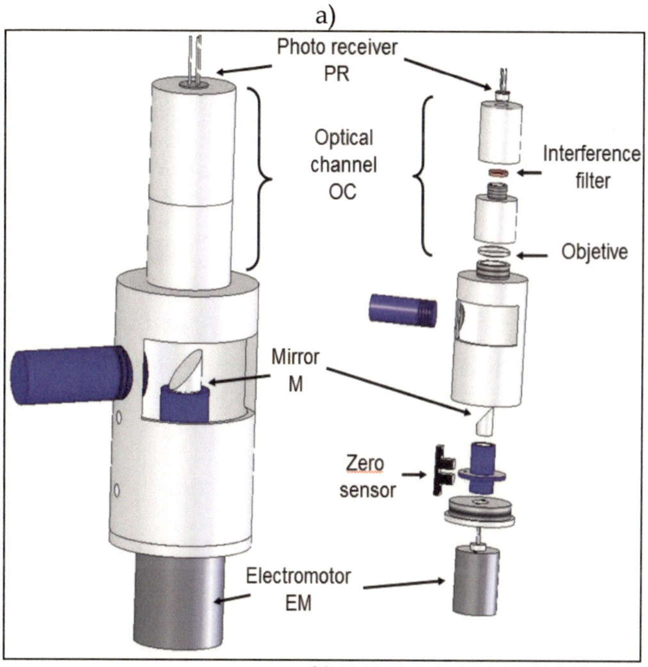

b)

Figure 16. Scanning aperture functioning principle (a), general design (b)

After some position of a plane, where the laser ray moves in the plan from the right to the left or reverse, all fixed laser rays hit a surface under research, making points of reflection S_{ij}. If in this case laser emission power and distance to points of reflection as well as sensitivity of the photoreceiver are sufficient for formation of stop pulses, empty cycles of SA scanning will not exist. The measurement cycles are repeated until the plane, formed by a horizontal axes of a bar b and the last point S_{ij}, deviates from a plane XOY by angle $\sum_{j=1}^{m}\beta_j$.

As mentioned above, data on angles B_{ij} measured will be accumulated in computer memory. One of these angles is shown on Fig.3. A related angle $C_{ij} = C_{\max} - \sum_{i=1}^{i}\alpha_i$, where $C_{\max}$ – is an initial angle of PL position. Angles C_{ij}, as well as angles $\sum_{j=1}^{j}\beta_j$, are fixed in memory simultaneously with the measured angles B_{ij} during each cycle.
Using the theorem of sines as well as correlation between the sides and the height in a triangle represented on Fig.17.

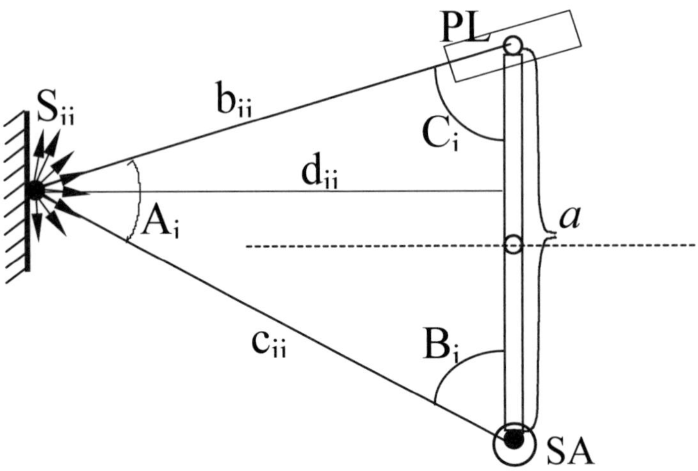

Fig. 17. Triangulation scheme for precise coordinates measurement

It is possible to find the formula for calculating sloping distances d_{ij} from basis *b* up to points highlighted by the laser

$$d_{ij} = a\frac{SinB_{ij} \cdot SinC_{ij}}{Sin\left[180^{\circ} - \left(B_{ij} + C_{ij}\right)\right]}, \tag{7}$$

where *a* - is basic distance between rotation axes of PL and SA. It is accurately enough pre-measured.

Using value of angles B_{ij} , C_{ij}, $\sum_{j=1}^{j}\beta_j$, and basis *a*, it is possible to calculate the Cartesian coordinates by each of the laser-highlighted points, in reference system OXYZ of MVS by the following formulas

$$x_{ij} = a \cdot \frac{SinB_{ij} \cdot SinC_{ij} Cos \sum_{j=1}^{j} \beta_j}{Sin\left[180^\circ - \left(B_{ij} + C_{ij}\right)\right]}, \tag{8}$$

$$y_{ij} = a \cdot \left(\frac{1}{2} - \frac{SinB_{ij} \cdot CosC_{ij}}{Sin\left[180^\circ - \left(B_{ij} + C_{ij}\right)\right]} \right) \text{at } B_{ij} \le 90^\circ, \tag{9}$$

$$y_{ij} = -a \cdot \left(\frac{1}{2} + \frac{SinB_{ij} \cdot CosC_{ij}}{Sin\left[180^\circ - \left(B_{ij} + C_{ij}\right)\right]} \right) \text{ at } B_{ij} > 90^\circ, \tag{10}$$

$$z_{ij} = a \cdot \frac{SinB_{ij} \cdot SinC_{ij} Sin \sum_{j=1}^{j} \beta_j}{Sin\left[180^\circ - \left(B_{ij} + C_{ij}\right)\right]}. \tag{11}$$

Thus, the onboard computer with the help of TVS provides digital map-description of the terrain in a MR sector of view in an actual time scale. If in a direction of observation any obstacles shaped as a dredging or as a big item above a surface (in these places points Sij are heaped), MR, with the help of vertical step drive PV, turns TVS by an angle $\sum_{i=1}^{n} \alpha_i$ To the left or to the right depending on a position of obstacles in relation with axis OX, and "searches" a new sector.

Fig. 18. Prototype parts (Scanning aperture; Emisor part (laser positioning system); and Software screen in function, taking epperimental data on obstacles

4.2 Prototype construction and experimentations

This prototype (Figs. 18 and 19) can be fabricated in very simple way using low-cost elements. A prototype was made with the follows elements: an aluminum base bar with 1m of length, step motors to make vertical and horizontal scanning, source of light in this case a laser, a pair of mirrors with 45 degrees cut to redirection the light beam, in laser emisor part and scanning aperture (Fig.18), a photo receiver to convert light signal to electrical signal, a lens in the aperture part to get a fine convergence of light in photo receiver, a sensor (start) in the aperture part to detect and count revolutions of mirror2, and a interference filter to get only the selected source of light; this hardware is controlled by a laptop IBM Pentium II using "turbo c" program in MS-DOS where the measurement distances is stored (Fig.18), the connection to transfer data between hardware and software is by parallel port. The complete prototype (Rivas et al., 2008) is no longer than 1m, data can be stored in another system, and the prototype fabricated with all elements is shown in Fig.19 in action.

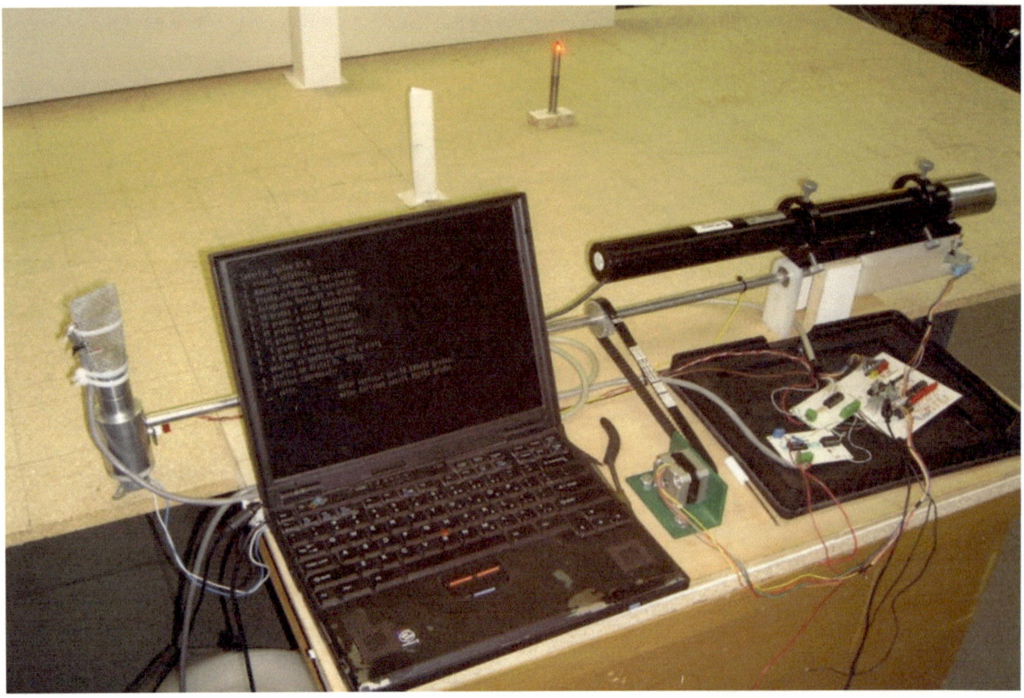

Fig. 19. Complete prototype system testing view.

This prototype was tested 100 times in different locations in grid nodes (see Figure 20) to verify accuracy on vision by different angles in 2D, making tests on reflective and absorptive objects; in Table 2 are partially shown the measurement values by the prototype on a plane surface with grid-scale.

The values in the table 2 are shown graphically in (Figure 20). The violet points are distance values taken by the prototype working usual way; the yellow points are distances measured by the prototype but using an independent source of light in each point to measure (without prototype laser), finally the real distances can be shown by squares in the table base.

As it is evident, the range of error is very small in the center of the table, this center is the center of the prototype sight, and near both sides of the prototype sight angle the error is minimal. This prototype is very similar to human sight, at front the image view is very detailed and precise, both borders of angle of view have no much accuracy, this can be resolved rotating the vision of focus of the prototype exactly humans sight do.

Analyzing the measurement results (Fig.20) and its numerical values (Table 2), it is possible to say that all the experiments were carried out not less at 95% confidence level. And measurement uncertainty, especially its offset error, not overcomes a 5% threshold in any point, even in extended angle of sight where such accuracy is not obligatory.

Test Point	Theoric Value				Measured Value			
	X (m)	Y (m)	B (°)	C (°)	*x(m)*	*y(m)*	*B (°)*	*C (°)*
B	120	120	120,26	35,22	124,21	128,68	123,43	34,8
D	100	100	116,57	33,69	99,83	104,48	118,46	32,87
F	100	80	106,70	37,57	95,3	76,86	106,4	36,91
H	120	60	94,76	47,49	122,92	63,49	96,38	47,28
J	80	60	97,13	36,03	77	58,62	96,57	35,33
L	80	40	82,87	41,63	79,99	42,15	84	40,95
N	120	40	85,24	53,13	119,86	40,04	84,48	53,08
O	120	20	75,96	59,74	119,22	19,48	76,01	59,76
P	100	20	73,30	55,01	97,6	19,15	72,94	54,67
Q	80	20	69,44	48,81	79,11	18,7	68,39	49,04
R	60	20	63,43	40,60	60,33	21,7	64,3	40,07
S	40	20	53,13	29,74	39,14	19,59	52,07	29,35
T	40	0	38,66	38,66	36,52	1,06	36,52	36,73
U	60	0	50,19	50,19	59,8	0,9	49,39	50,625
V	80	0	57,99	57,99	80,93	3,49	56,7	60,11
W	100	0	63,43	63,43	103,58	1,51	63,45	64,68
X	120	0	67,38	67,38	120,72	-4,7	66,23	69,43
Y	120	-20	59,74	75,96	118,54	-18,36	59,95	75,05
Z	100	-20	55,01	73,30	96,72	-18,37	54,7	71,9
A1	80	-20	48,81	69,44	75,79	-18,33	48,03	67,32
B1	60	-20	40,60	63,43	58	-18,53	39,5	61,52
C1	40	-20	29,74	53,13	36,17	-20,31	27,3	50,62
D1	60	-40	33,69	80,54	58,05	-38,63	33,6	78,92
E1	80	-40	41,63	82,87	77,46	-38,26	40,46	81,38
F1	100	-40	48,01	84,29	97,1	-38,02	46,94	82,96
H1	120	-60	47,49	94,76	123,68	-61,03	48,21	95,09
J1	80	-60	36,03	97,13	78,9	-59,73	35,37	97,03
L1	80	-80	31,61	110,56	80,52	-80,21	31,81	110,56
N1	120	-80	42,71	104,04	121,01	-78,73	43,34	103,35
P1	100	-100	33,69	116,57	101,65	-96,18	35,06	114,43
R1	100	-120	30,47	124,99	111,73	-126,15	32,09	124,27

Table 2. Experimental results of point-coordinates measurement (Rivas et al., 2008)

Fig. 20. Experimental graphic of 2D points measurement and obstacle positioning

Also detailed analyzis of scanning aperture original construction (Fig. 16, 18) and principle deduce us to conclusion that it is possible to obtain measurement results with the same uncertainty from highlighted points of the different attitudes inside precertain angle of view. It is significant advantage of the presented device over other known laser triangulation scanners (Forman & Parry, 2001), (Pierce et al., 1992), (Surmann et al., 2003). In general behavior of uncertainty repeats graphic presented on Figure 6 in (Pierce et al., p. 1765, 1992), however accuracy nearby edge in our system is more advanced. Also accuracy (coordinate measurement offset) in a central part of scanner's angle of view is 2-7 times better in a different checked points respect to (Pierce et al., 1992) for example.

4.3 Prototype application for static monitoring

The above-described passive scanning aperture (Figs. 16 and 18) (PSA) independently can be able for static object deformation monitoring (Tyrsa et al., 2004). PSA, or POS (passive optical scanner), using the vertical axis of rotation is destined for the measurement of the horizontal angles. Let's call it a vertical POS. The vertical angles between the "emissive beacons"(EBs) are measured by the POS with the horizontal axis of the rotation. This POS is the horizontal POS. The system, which consists of the vertical and horizontal POSs, permits to measure the displacement of the EB in horizontal and vertical planes.
Fig.2 shows the adoption of the horizontal POS for the realization of the bridge points monitoring in a vertical plane.

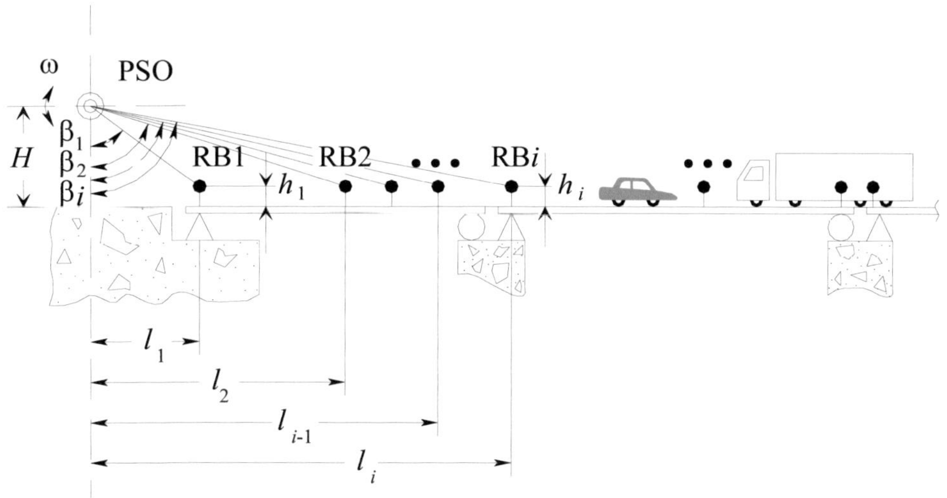

Fig. 21. Horizontal POS placement for bridge monitoring

The POS is placed outside the bridge and measures the vertical angles β_i. The EBs are installed with the same height h_i above the bridge surface. As EB it is possible to use any sufficiently cheap light source, for example mentioned above lamp HRQ3010-5071. The distances l_i are measured during the installation of the EB.
In the absence of a deformation, for each EB_i, the following expression is valid:

$$\frac{H-h}{l_i} = \tan\left(\frac{\pi}{2} - \beta_i\right) \tag{12}$$

For the bridge deformation with the magnitude Δh_i in the placement point of the beacon EBi, the angle β_i, measured by the POS, will change on the magnitude $\Delta\beta_i$. As a result the expression (13) will receive the form:

$$\frac{H - h \pm \Delta h}{l_i} = \tan(\frac{\pi}{2} - \beta_i \pm \Delta\beta_i) \tag{13}$$

Therefore:

$$\Delta h_i = (H - h) - l_i \tan(\frac{\pi}{2} - \beta_i \pm \Delta\beta_i)\,. \tag{14}$$

In a similar manner the POS for tunnel monitoring is installed. In extended tunnels several functionally connected POS can be placed along its axis.

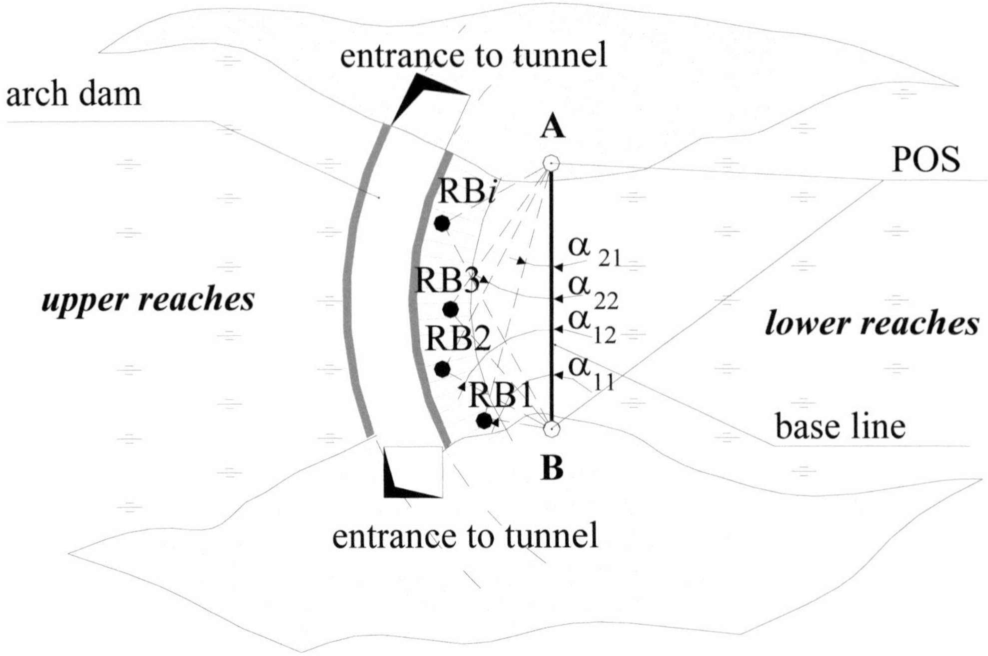

Fig. 22. Placement of two vertical POSs for arch dam monitoring.

Fig. 22 shows the placement of two vertical POSs for the arch dam monitoring of a hydroelectric power station. The POSs measure in pairs the horizontal angles α_{1i} and α_{2i} between the base line AB and the EBi. The length of the base line D and the Cartesian coordinates of the POS are determined beforehand by known geodetic methods. The angles ∠EBi are found by the formula:

$$\angle RB_i = 180^\circ - (\alpha_{1i} + \alpha_{2i})\,. \tag{15}$$

According the sine theorem we find the triangles sides, which have the vertex A, B, EB_i ; and the coordinates x_i, y_i of the points EB_i, in the national system or conditional Cartesian coordinate system. The change of coordinates of the points RB_i in the repeated measurements of the angles α_{1i} and α_{2i} reveal the dam deformation.

5. Conclusions

Presented research was provided with a general goal to design simple and secure method for 3D laser scanning of any unknown surface placed on a variable distance from scanner location. Other advantage of a present system over other laser triangulation system is a higher in principle order of exactitude in a part of 3D coordinates calculation. Preliminary prototype testing is shown

- This theoretical principle can be realized with modern electronic and electromechanic devices in low cost;
- With completely acceptable operation velocity this device can detect an obstacle and to cover it with digital 3D map of n points on it's surface;
- This factor n is easy possible to change as only one variable in software; such way provide basic principle "more points - less uncertainty, but more operating time". This task must be solved carefully for each practical application;
- Coordinates calculation uncertainty is less than any known laser triangulation with electronic scanning because of exact surveying techniques principle using;
- This system in a closest way simulates the human binocular vision; as shown, the best exactitude can be achieved in a center of angle of view, and nearby both edges the picture is not has so sharpness. It possible to overcome by base bar rotation;
- These techniques can be implemented with insignificant changes for various practical applications, such as large engineering structures Structural Health Monitoring, mobile robot navigation, microsurface inspections, etc.

6. References

Allen, D.; Park, G.; & Farrar, C. (2005). Overview of Wireless Active Sensing Systems for Structural Health Monitoring, In *Structural health monitoring*, Fu-Kuo Chang, page numbers (1578-1585), DEStech Publications, ISBN: 1-932078-51-7

Athavale, N.; Ragade, R.; Cassaro M.; & Fenske, T. (1990). *A prototype for KYBAS: the Kentucky Bridge Analysis System.* Proceedings of the 3rd international conference on Industrial and engineering applications of artificial intelligence and expert systems, pp. 781-789, Vol. 2, 1990

Baltsavias, E. P. (1999), a. A comparison between photogrammetry and laser scanning. *ISPRS Journal of Photogrammetry & Remote Sensing*, Elsevier, Vol. 54, (July 1999) page numbers (83–94)

Baltsavias, E. P. (1999), b. Airborne laser scanning: basic relations and formulas. *ISPRS Journal of Photogrammetry & Remote Sensing,* Elsevier, Vol. 54, (July 1999) page numbers (199–214)

Bellian, J. A.; Kerans, C. & Jennettem, D. C. (2005). Digital outcrop models: applications of terrestrial scanning lidar technology in stratigraphic modeling. *Journal of sedimentary research*, SEPM , Vol. 75, No. 2, pp. 166–176, ISBN 1527-1404/05/075-166, march, 2005

Benedetti, M.; Donelli, M.; Massa, A. & Rosani. A. (2004). *An innovative microwave imaging technique for non destructive evaluation: applications to civil structures monitoring and biological bodies inspection. IEEE Proceedings of International "Imaging Systems and Techniques, (IST-2004)"*,(may 2004) page numbers (91 – 94)

Chaumette, F. & Hutchinson, S. (2006). Visual servo control PART I: basic approaches. *IEEE Robotics & Automation Magazine*, December 2006, pp.82-90.

Chellappa, R.; Roy-Chowdhury, A. K. & Zhou, Sh. K. (2005). *Recognition of humans and their activities using video.* Morgan & Claypool Publishers, ISBN 1598290061

Diosi, A. & Kleeman, L. (2005). Laser scan matching in polar coordinates with application to SLAM. *Proceedings of IEEE/RSJ International Conference on Intelligent Robots and Systems (IROS 2005)*, pp. 3317- 3322, ISBN: 0-7803-8912-3, august 2005

França, J.; Gazziro, M.; Ide, A. & Saito, J. (2005). A 3D scanning system based on laser triangulation an variable field of view, *Proceedings of the 2005 International Conference on Image Processing (ICIP 2005)*, pp. 425-428, IEEE Volume 1, Italy, 2005, Genoa

Forman, P. & Parry, I. (2001). Rapid Data Collection at Major Incident Scenes using Three Dimensional Laser Scanning Techniques. *2001 IEEE 35th International Carnahan Conference on Security Technology*, pp. 60-67, october 2001

Hada, Y. & Takase, K. (2001). Multiple Mobile Robot Navigation Using The Indoor Global Positioning System (iGPS). *Proceedings of IEEE/RSJ International Conference on Intelligent Robots and Systems*, Vol. 2, pp. 1005-1010, ISBN: 0-7803-6612-3, USA, Maui, HI, 10/29/2001 - 11/03/2001

Hancock, J. ; Langer, D.; Hebert, M.; Sullivan, R.; Ingimarson, D.; Hoffman, E.; Mettenleiter, M. & Fredlich, C. (1998). Active Laser Radar For High-Performance Measurements, *IEEE International Conference on Robotics & Automation*, pp 1465-1470, Belgium, Leuven, 1998

Handbook of Optical and Laser Scanning. (2004).Edited by Gerald F. Marshall, 769 p., ISBN: 0-8247-5569-3, Marcel Dekker, Inc., New York – Basel, 2004

Hosmer, P. (2004). Use of Laser Scanning Technology for Perimeter Protection. *IEEE Aerospace and Electronic Systems Magazine*, vol. 19, page numbers (13-17), 2004

Ibeanusi, U.; Lafond-Favieres, V. ; McLawhorn, L. & Anderson, S. (1999). Understanding robot navigation and control, Proceedings of the 37th annual *ACM Southeast Regional Conference*, 7p, CD version, 1999

Itti, L. & Baldi, P. (2005). A principled approach to detecting surprising events in video. *Proceedings of IEEE CVPR2005*, pp. 631- 637, vol. 1, International Conference on Computer Vision and Pattern Recognition, 20-25 June 2005

Kee, C.; Park, B.; Kim, J.; Cleveland, A.; Parsons, M. & Wolfe, D. (2008). A Guideline to Establish DGPS Reference Station Requirements. *The journal of navigation. Royal Institute of Navigation-Cambridge Journals* (2008), 61, page numbers (99–114)

Lavelle, J. P. ; Schuet, S. R. & Schuet, D. J. (2004). High Speed 3D Scanner with Real-Time 3D Processing. *Proceedings of ISA/IEEE Sensors for Industry Conference*, pp.102- 108, ISBN: 0-7803-8143-2, 2004

Lichti, D. D. ; Stewart, M. P.; Tsakiri, M. & Snow, A. J. (2000). Benchmark tests on a Three-Dimensional Laser Scanning system. Department of Spatial Sciences of Curtin University of Technology, Geomatics Research Australasia, 23 p., 2000

Liu, F.; Bhakar, S.; Fevens, T. & Mudur, S. (2006). Environment Lighting for Point Sampled Geometry. *Proceedings of International Conference on Computer Graphics, Imaging and Visualisation (CGIV'06)*, pp. 522-527, 2006

Liwen Dai, Jinling Wang, Rizos, C. & Shaowei Han. (2002). Pseudo-satellite applications in deformation monitoring. *GPS Solutions Journal, Springer Berlin / Heidelberg*, Vol. 5, No 3, (January, 2002), page numbers (80-87), ISSN: 1080-5370 (Print) 1521-1886 (Online)

Mallet, L.; Lee, B.; Staszewski, W. & Scarpa, F. (2004). Structural health monitoring using scanning laser vibrometry: II. Lamb waves for damage detection. *IOP electronic journals; Smart Mater. & Struct.*, 13, (2004), page numbers (261-269)

Mordohai, P. & Medioni, G. (2006). *Tensor Voting: A Perceptual Organization Approach to Computer Vision and Machine Learning*, Morgan & Claypool Publishers, ISBN: 1598291009

Noll, R. & Krauhausen, M. (2003). Multibeam laser triangulation for the measurement of geometric features of moving objects in production lines. *Conference on Lasers and Electro-Optics Europe CLEO/Europe*, p. 468, ISBN: 0-7803-7734-6, 22-27 June 2003

Ohno, H.; Naruse, H.; Kurashima, T.; Nobiki, A.; Uchiyama, Y. & Kusakabe, Y. (2002). Application of Brillouin Scattering-Based Distributed Optical Fiber Strain Sensor to Actual Concrete Piles. *IEICE TRANSACTIONS on Electronics*, Vol. E85-C, No.4, (2002), page numbers (945-951)

Peng-Hsiang Weng & Fu-Jen Kao. (2004). Modulation Based Time Resolved Laser Scanning Microscopy. *The Second Asian and Pacific Rim Symposium on Biophotonics, APBP 2004*, pp.97- 98, ISBN: 0-7803-8676-0, december 2004

Petrov, M.; Talapov, A.; Robertson, T. Lebedev, A.; Zhilyaev, A. & Polonskiy, L. (1998). Optical 3D Digitizers: Bringing Life to the Virtual World. *IEEE Computer Graphics and Applications*, Vol., 18, (May/Jun 1998), page numbers (28-37). Issue: 3, ISSN: 0272-1716

Pierce, D.S.; Ng, T.S. & Morrison, B.R. (1992). A Novel Laser Triangulation Technique for High Precision Distance Measurement, *Proceeding of IEEE Industry Aplications Society Annual Meeting*, vol.2, pp. 1762-1769, USA, october, 1992, Houston

Retscher, G. (2007). Test and Integration of Location Sensors for a Multi-sensor Personal Navigator. *The Journal of Navigation*, 60 (1), page numbers (107–117)

Rivas, M.; Sergiyenko, O.; Aguirre, M.; Devia, L.; Tyrsa, V. & Rendón, I. (2008). Spatial data acquisition by laser scanning for robot or SHM task. *Proceeding of IEEE/IES International Conference ISIE-2008 pp.*1458-1463, ISBN 978-1-4244-1666-0, UK, Cambridge, 30June - 2 July, 2008

Riza N. A. & Muzammil, A. A. (2003). Code-multiplexed optical scanner, In: *Applied Optics*, vol. 42, pp. 1493-1501, 2003

Sadayuki Tsugawa. (1994). Vision-Based Vehicles in Japan: Machine Vision Systems and Driving Control Systems. *IEEE Transactions on industrial electronics*, Vol. 41, No. 4, pp.398-405, august, 1994

Sahba, K.; Alameh, K. E. & Smith, C. (2006). A Proposed Motionless Laser Scanning Architecture for Perimeter Security. *Proceedings of 40th ICCST2006*, pp. 9-16, ISBN: 1-4244-0174-7, Lexington, KY, October 17, 2006

Slob, S. & Hack., R. (2004). 3D Terrestrial Laser Scanning as a New Field Measurement and Monitoring Technique, In: *Engineering Geology for Infrastructure Planning in Europe, Springer Berlin*, page numbers (179-189), Heidelberg

Selectes papers on CCD and CMOS imadges. (2003). SPIE Press Bellingham, editor Moon Gi Kang, General editor Brian J.Thompson,Vol. MS177, 636p., ISBN 0-8194-5114-2 USA, Washington, 2003

Soini, A. (2001). Machine vision technology take-up in industrial application. *Proceedings of the 2nd International Symposium on Image and Signal Processing and Analysis ISPA,* pp. 332-338, ISBN: 953-96769-4-0, Pula, Croatia

Steinle, E. & Vogtle, T. (2000). Effects of different laser scanning modes on the results of building recognition and reconstruction. *International Archives of Photogrammetry and Remote Sensing*, 2000 - www-ipf.bau-verm.uni-karlsruhe.de. 8p.

Stewart, M. P. & Tsakiri, M. (2002). The Application of GPS to Dam Surface Monitoring. *Journal of Geospatial Engineering*, Vol.3, No.1, page numbers (45-57)

Stutz, G. (2005). Guiding Light, *SPIE's magazine*, vol. 5, page nnumbers (25-27), 2005

Surmann, H.; Lingemann, K.; Nuchter, A. & Hertzberg, J. (2003). A 3D laser range finder for autonomous mobile robots. *Robotics and Autonomous Systems, Issues 3-4,* vol. 45, pp. 181-198, december 2003

Tao Dai; Xiang Chen; Drake, R. & Jun Yang. (2005). Vision Sensor Based Tracking and Focusing of 3-D Singular Points. *Proceedings of 2005 IEEE International Conference on Mechatronics and Automation,* Vol. 3, pp. 1312-1317, ISBN: 0-7803-9044-X, Canada, 2005, Niagara Falls, Ont.

Tunstel, E. (1995). *Fuzzy spatial map representation for mobile robot navigation.* Proceedings of the 1995 ACM symposium on Applied computing, pp. 586 – 589, ISBN:0-89791-658-1, USA, (1995), Nashville, Tennessee

Tyrsa, V.E.; Burtseva, L.; Rivas Lopez, M.; & Tyrsa, V.V. (2004) Monitoring of civil engineering structures. *Proc. of SPIE Int. Conf. Health monitoring and smart nondestructive evaluation of structural and biological systems III, 5394,* pp. 485-492, USA, 2004, San-Diego

Tyrsa, V. Ye.; Sergiyenko, O.; Burtseva, L.; Bravo-Zanoguera, M.; Devia, L.; Rendon, I. & Tyrsa, V. V. (2006), a. Mobile Transport object control by technical vision means. *Proceeding of IEEE International Conference CERMA2006*, Vol. II, p.74-79, ISBN: 0-7695-2569-5/ ISBN13 978-0-7695-2569-3, Mexico, Cuernavaca, September 2006

Tyrsa, V.Ye.; Sergiyenko, O.Yu.; Tyrsa, V.V.; Bravo, M.; Devia, L. & Rendon, I. (2006), b. Mobile Robot navigation by Laser Scanning Means. *Proceeding of 3rd International "Conference on Cybernetics and Information Technologies, Systems and Applications CITSA – 2006"*, Vol. I, p. 340-345, ISBN: 980-6560-82-5 (collection)/ 980-6560-83-3 (volume I), USA, July 20-23, 2006, Orlando, Florida

Vang, L.; Emura, T. & Ushiwata, T. (2000). Automatic Guidance of a Vehicle Based on DGPS and a 3D Map, *Proceedings of IEEE Intelligent Transportation Systems,* pp.131-136, ISBN: 0-7803-5971-2, USA, october 2000, Dearborn, MI

Wehr, A. & Lohr, U. (1999). Airborne laser scanning—an introduction and overview. *ISPRS Journal of Photogrammetry and Remote Sensing,* Elsevier, Vol. 54, Issues 2-3, (July 1999) page numbers (68-82) et al.,

Winkelbach, S.; Molkenstruck, S. & Wahl, F. (2006). Low-cost Laser Range Scanner and Fast Surface Registration Approach. *Proceedings of DAGM 2006, Springer Berlin Heidelberg,* (2006) page numbers (718-728)

Yu, H.; Aguado, E.; Brodin, G.; Cooper, J. ; Walsh D. & Strangeways H. (2008). UWB Positioning System Design: Selection of Modulation and Multiple Access Schemes. *The Journal of Navigation*, 61, page numbers (45–62)

Image Processing for Next-Generation Robots

Gabor Sziebig[1], Bjørn Solvang[1] and Peter Korondi[2]
[1]*Narvik University College,*
[2]*Budapest University of Technology and Economics,*
[1]*Norway*
[2]*Hungary*

1. Introduction

During the 21st century rapid progress in computer communication and technologies influences robot systems: becoming larger and more complicated than ever previously. To manage the rapidly growing sensor data the single robot systems transformed to networked systems, facing new challenges. The demand of low-cost mass production of robots (industrial or service type), the rising number of elderly people, who needs support of their everyday life, called forth of middleware technology in robot technologies (Brugali & Reggiani, 2005). The middleware technologies provide the heterogenic environment that hides low level functions (hardware specific implementations) and provides the required flexibility for robot system developers. In the beginning of the middleware developments it was doubtful, that the technology causes retardation in speed, but after benchmarks of Christopher D. Gill and William D. Smart (Gill & Smart, 2002) it showed that it has more advantages then disadvantages. They strongly believe that Common Object Request Broker Architecture (CORBA)-based middleware offers great advantages in robotics and embedded sensor applications. The urgent need of middleware forced the robot programmers create their own middleware's that meets best their need. Unfortunately, most of the pioneering initiatives are developed independently of the others, driven by specific applications and objectives (Kotoku & Mizukawa, 2006).

In conventional robot system development, the different robot parts (sensors, processing elements and actuators) are combined together in a compact, self contained system. Both type of robot system (industrial or service type) faces challenges in the sense of flexibility, reusability and new part integration. In case of industrial robots, the end-user has very limited intervention to the control system itself (Brogårdh, 2007) and in case of the service robots, the human - robot co-existence demands an extreme flexibility to care take all of human ever changing needs. Robot systems usually consist of sensors that provide information about the environment, computational units that process information about the environment and actuators that are controlled according to the decisions made by the computational units. In recent robot systems one of the most important sensors are image sensors that provide visual information about the environment. Effective robot system design requires that image sensors and image processing functionalities can as easily be integrated with robot systems as any other component. The vision related components of a robot system should thus be integrated using the same middleware as the robot system

itself. Thus, development of new robot systems (industrial and service type) should be addressed with great concern of the user demand for flexible solutions.
In Japan the basics of Next-Generation Robots are being developed with the purpose of improving the efficiency of robot design. The development was started in 2004 at the International Robot Fair, Fukuoka, Japan. The following three expectations were defined for the Next-Generation Robots (IRF, 2004):

1. Be partners that coexist with human beings.
2. Assist human beings both physically and psychologically.
3. Contribute to the realization of a safe and peaceful society.

To achieve these expectations new technologies are being promoted and spread in wider areas. To satisfy every user's individual needs, robot systems must be constructed more flexibly. Creation of new functions is made easy by using RT (Robot Technology) - Middleware (Ando et al., 2005 b), which is a modularized software supporting robot program development for Next-Generation Robots (Ikezoe et al., 2006). RT-Middleware was chosen as the platform also in the proposed work, because it is the only middleware solution that is under standardization (Object Management Group, 2007). This solution has proved to be industry ready and used by many industrial partners (Toshiba (different system components), Honda (ASIMO humanoid robot), AIST (OpenHRP humanoid robot), etc.) and also many research institutes (Ando et al., 2005 a).
In this chapter the Distributed Image Analyzer and one example application of the framework will be introduced. Distributed Image Analyzer is a distributed image processing framework for RT-Middleware. Originally it was designed to be grid computing like distributed image processing framework (with own communication interfaces), which was developed to increase processing speed by applying distributed computational resources. The modules created for the grid type version can be utilized without any change in the RT-Middleware based. As the system is modular, the high computational costs of image processing can be shared with different components; on board the robot or the environment can be utilized to execute the computation.
The rest of this chapter is organized as follows: in Section 2 the idea and basic structure of the RT-Middleware is presented. In Section 3 the Distributed Image Analyzer framework is presented. In Section 4 example application of vision system in industrial environment is introduced.

2. RT-Middleware

This section is intended to give an overview about the RT-Middleware. The proposed distributed image processing framework is built upon this middleware and will be introduced in the next section.
In 2002 the Japanese Ministry of Economy, Trade and Industry (METI) in collaboration with the Japan Robot Association (JARA) and National Institute of Advanced Industrial Science and Technology (AIST) started a 3 year-national project "Consolidation of Software Infrastructure for Robot Development". With the purpose of implementing robot systems to meet diversified users' needs, this project has pursued R&D of technologies to make up robots and their functional parts in modular structure at the software level and to allow system designers or integrators building versatile robots or systems with relative ease by simply combining selected modular parts (Ando et al., 2005 b).
To realize the proposed robot architecture, a robot technology middleware was developed, named "OpenRTM-aist", where OpenRTM stands for Open Robot Technology Middleware.

The concept of RT-middleware can be seen in Fig. 1. Not only thousands of hours of robot programming could be saved, but even more the interoperability between simulation and real applications in robots is solved.

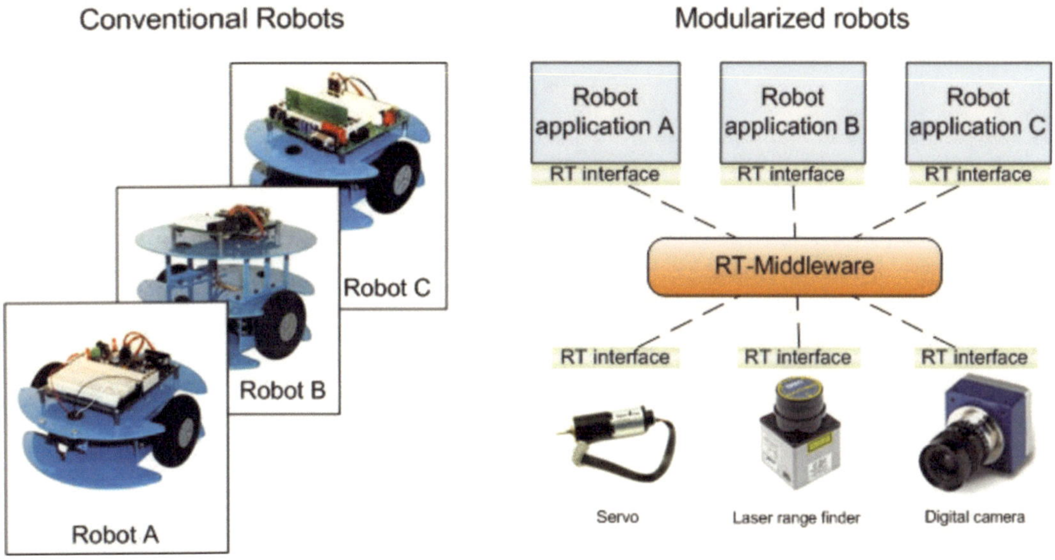

Fig. 1. Difference between the conventional and modularized robot concepts

Two prototype systems have been made to ascertain the effectiveness of the developed RT-middleware (Ando et al., 2005 a).

1. A robot arm control system based on real time control.
2. A life supporting robot system (also known as iSpace (Lee & Hashimoto, 2002)), one of the promising applications.

2.1 Architecture

The framework's basic functional unit is the RT-Component. Modularization is achieved by utilizing the RT-Components. The necessary functions, structure and a realization method based on distributed objects are defined within this component. Fig. 2. shows the architecture block diagram of the RT-Component.

For reasons of platform independency, the RT-Components are modelled using CORBA as a distributed object middleware. An RT-Component consists of the following objects and interfaces (items not listed here are mainly for administrative functions and description can be found at (Ando et al., 2005 a)):

- Component object (Describes the component itself (e.g. name))
- Activity (Core logic, this must be implemented separately in every component)
- InPort as input port object (Data is received here)
- OutPort as output port object (Data is sent from here)
- Command interfaces (Management of Component object)

In general the distributed object model can be described as some interfaces that contain operations with parameters and a return value. Every single component has the same structure (contains the same interfaces) and the only difference is inside the core logic (Activity) and the number of the InPort and OutPort. This allows system transparency, creating a "black-box" of all components. Every RT-Component has an activity which is responsible for data processing with the purpose of device control, such as controlling a motor drive, speech recognition, video processing, etc. The life-cycle of an RT-Component can be observer in Fig. 3.

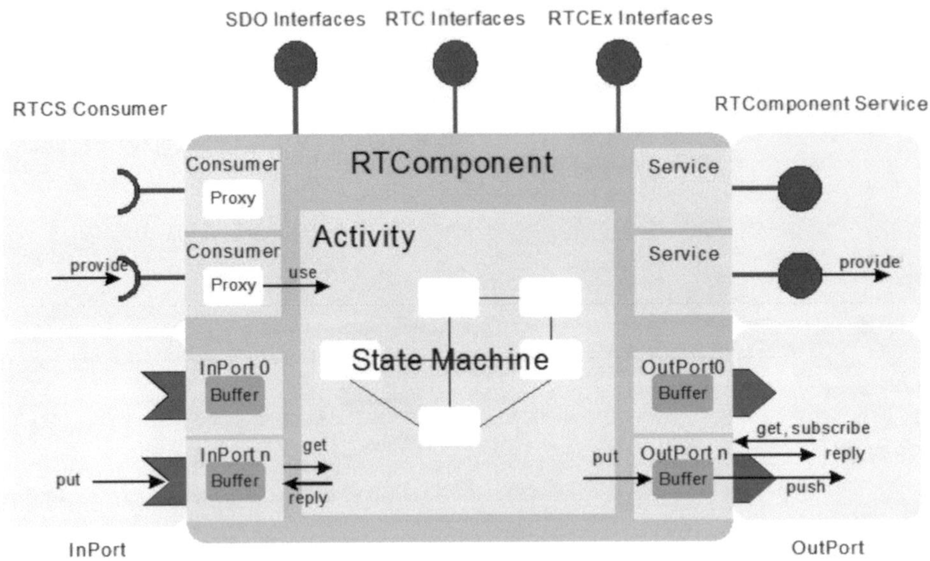

Fig. 2. RT-Component architecture (OpenRTM-aist, 2007)

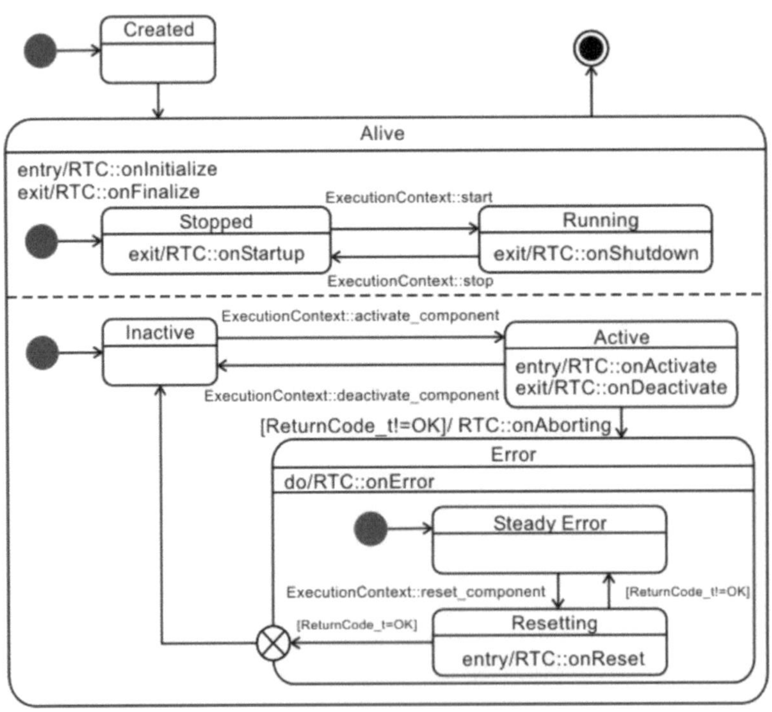

Fig. 3. RT-Component life-cycle (OpenRTM-aist, 2007)

Once the RT-Components are filled up with content and ready to be used, they have to be integrated to form a robot system. The assembly of a system is helped by a Graphical User Interface (GUI) tool that manages a connection of InPort/OutPort between RT-Components like a control block diagram and performs activation/deactivation of an RT-Component. This GUI can be seen in Fig. 4.

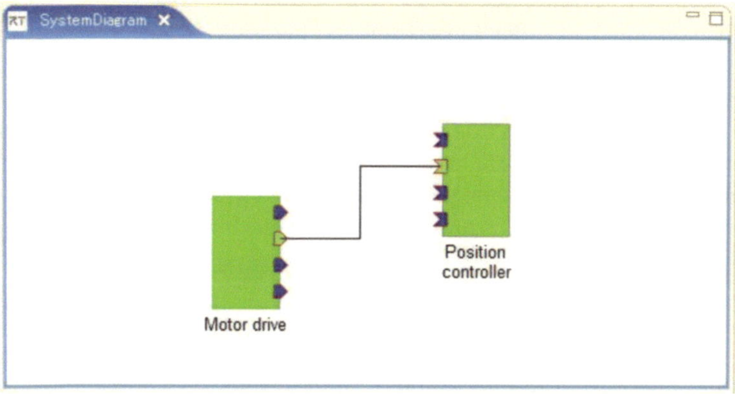

Fig. 4. User interface for system construction

The scope of this chapter is narrow to involve further details about RT-Middleware and its evaluation. More can be found in references (Ando et al., 2005 a), (Ando et al., 2005 b).

3. Distributed image analyzer

This section presents the Distributed Image Analyzer, which is a framework for distributed information processing, with a special respect on image processing. It was designed to overcome the heavy computational load of image processing and vision related operations. Image processing tasks are packed in modules and are distributed on several computers, forming a grid computing system. Also it provides a high level of modularity so that modules can easily be connected with each other. Another consideration is that the display of visual data can be done on any of the participating computers. This allows simultaneous supervision of many steps of an image processing algorithm on many screens connected to the computers participating in the framework. This feature is usually unavailable with most of the grid computing systems. The framework can accommodate several modules that are processing nodes of a dataflow-like module graph.

New modules can easily be constructed and added to the framework; only the information processing function has to be implemented. The modules represent the operators for information processing in the framework. They are designed to cooperate as a distributed network of modules, allowing a higher level of complexity. A module provides standard interfaces for communication through a container. Every module can be treated the same way, as a "black-box". The development of a new module is very efficient. A new module is derived from the same class (*CoreModule*). This holds the communication interfaces and the Application Programming Interface (API), only the data processing part of the module has to be implemented.

The modularized system architecture is not only achieved by standardized communication, in Distributed Image Analyzer framework the Dynamically-Loadable Library (DLL) technology is also used, which is a basic technology in Microsoft Windows environment. Every module is isolated in one DLL file and can easily be distributed over the network. There is no need for setup or installation, the DLL containing a certain module is copied to a specified directory and can be immediately used. This becomes possible by introducing a parent class (*CoreModule*) for the modules, where the basic interfaces are specified as virtual functions. When a new module is created, it is derived from *CoreModule*, and the virtual functions are implemented in order to perform the necessary data processing functions. The framework handles the modules through the interfaces defined in *CoreModule*, and has no specific information about the inside of any module. A DLL containing a module is loaded into memory and treated as a *CoreModule* type. The communication between modules is based on events: there is an event for data receiving (called *IncomingDataEvent*) and data sending (called *OutgoingDataEvent*). The management of each module and connection establishment between modules are done by the framework. This architecture can be seen in Fig. 5.

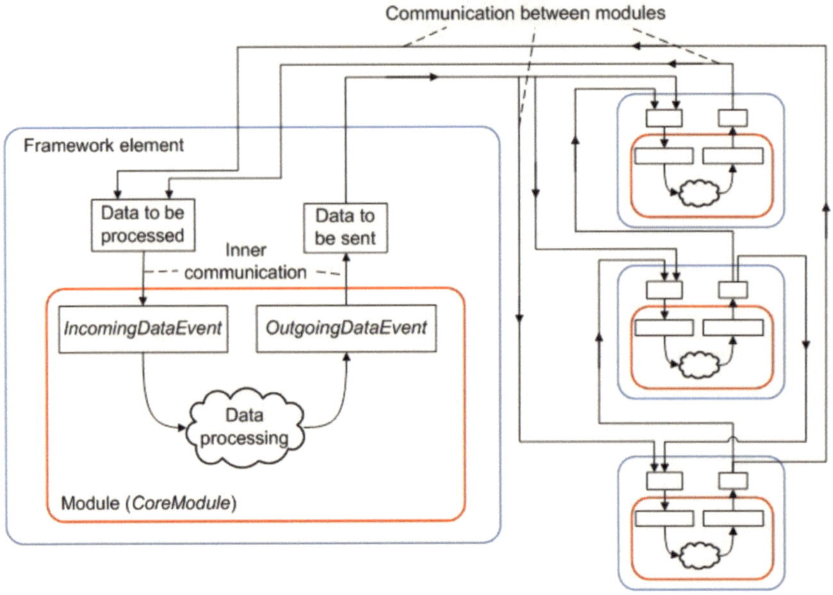

Fig. 5. Architecture of Distributed Image Analyzer

As a reference the following modules are implemented:

- Camera Module, to simulate an eye of a robot
- Edge Detector Module, to detect edges
- Motion Detector Module, to demonstrate an application of image processing
- Colour Mode Converter Module, conversion between colour spaces
- 2D-3D Converter Module, 3D stereo calculations
- Display Module, to display the result of image processing

The similarity between the architecture of the Distributed Image Analyzer framework and the RT-Middleware, which can be noticed from the previous paragraph, makes the module integration to RT-Middleware easy. Only an interface conversion is needed between the modules used in Distributed Image Analyzer framework and RT-Middleware. This allows new image processing algorithms to be tested without involving a robot and after successful test, seamless integration to real environment is possible. This is demonstrated in Fig. 6.

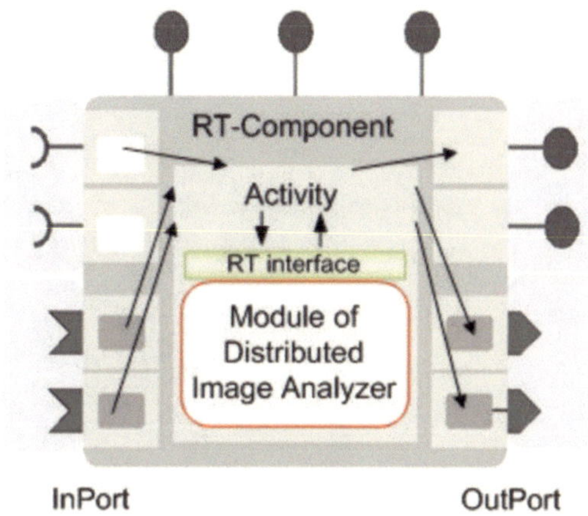

Fig. 6. Integration of an image processing module to RT-Component

After the introduction of the basics of a vision system for robots, in the next section one of its applications is shown.

4. Vision system for old Numerical Control (NC) machines

One example of vision systems in industrial environment is a supervisory system of old NC machines; these machines are usually manufactured before 1980s and lacks capability of Input/Output communication. In that time, these were produced to be as user friendly as possible and only had output through low quality monitors. Even though some might be able to communicate with Personal Computers (PC), it was only one way communication and can only be used from program uploading/downloading. In order to monitor the state of manufacturing process an operator should always observe the screen of NC machine and decisions made by the operator are mainly based on the information shown on the screen.

Based on this idea the operator can be replaced with a vision system, which can detect changes in the screen of machines and can also provide input for other elements in flexible manufacturing systems, also an industrial robot that is used for feeding the NC machine with raw material can be utilized to "operate" the machine by pushing buttons on the operator console. Full remote control of old NC machines can be achieved by this solution.

Fig. 7. shows a flexible manufacturing system with an industrial robot and an NC machines.

In this case the vision system is constructed of a digital camera and a PC, which uses image processing tools for Optical Character Recognition (OCR). From the image acquired by the camera, numerous data can be extracted (position, distance to go, current line of the running program, operator messages, etc.). These data describes the current state of the NC machine. For OCR artificial neural networks are trained and used for character recognition. This makes the system robust and self learning. The novelty of the system is not the technology behind (OCR is used for over 20 years now), but the application of it in such an industrial environment. OCR is mainly used in industry for tracking objects (serial number recognition, container localization (Elovic, 2003)), but in this case utilized as a supervisory system.

In the following section after a small introduction of neural networks, the structure and realization of the vision system will be introduced.

Fig. 7. Example setup of flexible manufacturing system, where the operator is replaced by a camera system and an industrial robot

4.1 Artificial neural network

Modeling functions and systems with neural networks (Gurney, 2003) is a developing science in computer technologies. This special field derives basis from biology, especially from brain of humans. It is well known, that human brain is constructed from neurons and interconnections among neurons, which are called synapses. One neuron can be connected to thousands of other neurons, which results a complex system and provides high level of parallelism. So thus, makes the human brain capable of recognition, perception of objects, human beings, animals, speech, etc. Also this is the explanation for the damage recovery capabilities of the brain.

On the other hand the computers used in everyday life are working in serial mode, which means that only one instruction is processed at a time. Measuring the reaction time of a human brain would result millisecond response, and would result nanoseconds in case of an average computer. Despite of this speed difference, until now, computer technology has not reached the level of the understanding of human brain. This inspired researchers to use the speed of modern computers and the parallel model of the human brain to create artificial intelligence. The combination of the speed and parallel computation model resulted mega leap in solving complex problems, which were previously believed to be impossible to solve.

Power of the neural networks is the fact, that they are nonlinear, which make them capable of solving nonlinear problems, while observing the limits in dimensions. It is easy to apply to any kind of problem and there is no need to know the exact data representation, unlike traditional statistical nonlinear methods. A neural network learns by examples, the more provided the better network is created, which is the same as how children learn.

4.2 Multi-layer perceptron neural network model

Nonlinear functions, such as Optical Character Recognition (OCR) (Bhagat, 2005), cannot be learned by single-layer neural networks. Hence use of multi-layer neural network is a must. A multi-layer neural network is constructed from one input layer, one or more hidden layers and one output layer. In Fig. 8 this structure is introduced. Each layer has a predefined amount of artificial neurons (perceptons). The Multi-Layer Perceptron Neural Network (Haykin, 1998) is a feed-forward network, where the layers are in distinct topology. Every artificial neuron is connected to each of artificial neuron in preceding layer. The artificial neuron receives number of inputs. Input can be either original data (in case of input layer) or from the output of other neurons in the network. Each connection has strength, called weight, which corresponds to synaptic efficiency of biological neuron. Every artificial neuron also has a threshold value, which is subtracted from the sum of incoming weights. This forms the activation of neuron. Activation signal is passed through the activation (transfer) function, called sigmoid function. The result of the activation function is the output of the artificial neuron.

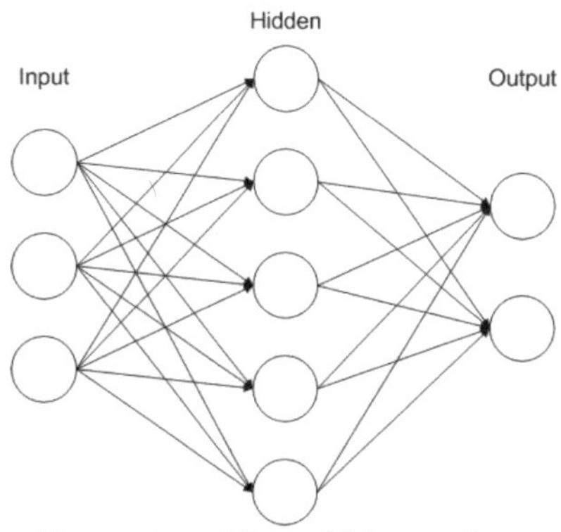

Fig. 8. Example of Multi-Layer Perceptron Neural Network

4.3 Structure

The vision system structure can be observed in Fig. 9. The image acquired by a digital camera is transferred to a PC, where the OCR is executed. The result of the OCR is the information shown on the operator screen. Based on this, different tasks can be carried out: instruct industrial robot to push a button, change I/O levels, stop NC machine, program upload, etc. The system is constructed from modular parts. Every component can be replaced to machine (where is the needed information on the screen) and camera (connection type) specific module. In the setup phase also the neural network (layer and neuron number, weights and learning rate) can be customized.

4.4 Realization

The Multi-Layer Perceptron Neural Network is trained with back propagation learning algorithm (Rojas & Feldman, 1996) and for the activation function bipolar sigmoid function is used (1):

$$f(x) = \frac{2}{1+e^{-\alpha * x}} - 1$$
$$f(x)' = \frac{2 * \alpha * e^{-\alpha * x}}{(1+e^{-\alpha * x})^2} = \alpha * \frac{1-f(x)^2}{2} \qquad (1)$$

where α is the parameter that decides the gradient of the function and x is the sum of the outputs of the previous layer.

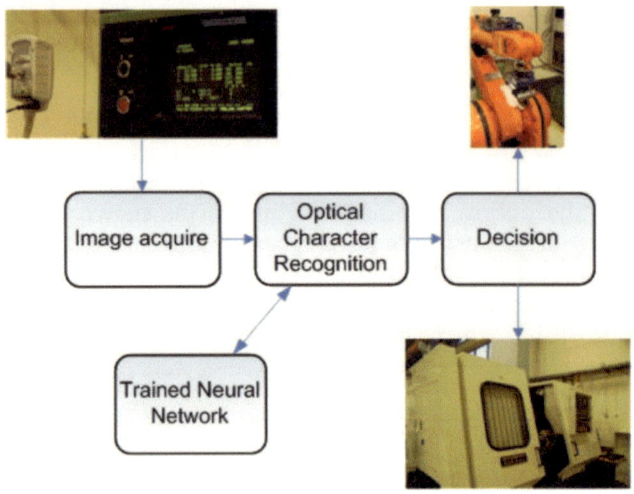

Fig. 9. Vision system structure

The training uses two inputs: the well formatted input image, captured by the digital camera, and the desired output. Both inputs are represented as binary values (0 or 1) and the process is shown in Fig. 10.

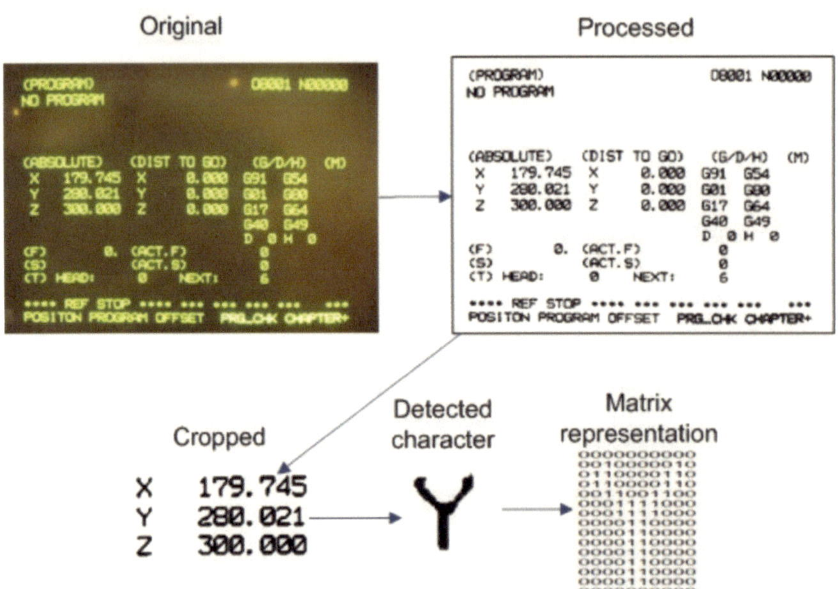

Fig. 10. Processing of input image

In order to get a well formatted image the following steps are executed:

1. Screen colour extraction (usually the old NC machines use one colour), the goal is to achieve higher contrast
2. Threshold filtering

With these steps an image will only contain black and white pixels. The black pixels are representing the binary value 1 and the white pixels represent 0. When only a specific region (Region of Interest) is needed, the image is cropped after this stage to specific dimension.

1. Characters are detected
2. Characters are converted to matrix representation (binary values of pixels)

These matrixes form the first input of the training.
The second input is the desired output: the 16bit Unicode representation of the detectable character (e.g. X = 0000000001011000).
The training is using character sets, which are machine specific (images and binary value of the characters).

4.5 Results

The neural networks weakest point is the training. Experiments were carried out to define the layer number, neuron numbers in each layer, best learning rate and sigmoid function alpha value. The goal with the experiments was to achieve 100% character detection in a 30 minute video stream of the operator screen. The character is stored as a 10*15 matrix, which results 150 neurons in the input layer and the output layer is composed of 16, because of the Unicode characters. Table 1. concludes the experimental results.

Parameter name	Parameter value
Layer number	3
Neurons in 1. layer	150
Neurons in 2. layer	300
Neurons in 3. layer	16
Maximum learning iteration	300
Maximum average error	0.0002
Initializing weight	30
Learning rate	120
Sigmoid function alpha value	0.014

Table 1. Results of experimental trials for neural network

5. Conclusion

In this chapter an image processing framework (Distributed Image Analyzer) and its integration into RT-Middleware as RT-Components is introduced. The integration becomes possible by introducing a simple conversion between interfaces. By this interface, image processing modules can easily be loaded to RT-Middleware and provides an image processing and vision toolbox for building complex robot systems.
If a simple image processing system is designed and implemented using the Distributed Image Analyzer toolbox in RT-Middleware, its advantages become apparent. Until now, vision components in robots were highly integrated to robot systems, without the possibility of reuse and easy adjustment.
As a special kind of vision system, vision based observation of old NC machines is introduced. This supervisory system replaces an operator with a camera and an industrial robot.
In the future the proposed image processing framework will be implemented and tested on a humanoid robot.

6. References

Ando, N.; Suehiro, T.; Kitagaki, K. & Kotoku, T. (2005 a). RT-middleware: distributed component middleware for RT (robot technology), *Proceedings of IEEE/RSJ International Conference on Intelligent Robots and Systems (IROS 2005)*, pp. 3933- 3938, ISBN 0-7803-8912-3, Aug. 2005.

Ando, N.; Suehiro, T.; Kitagaki, K.; Kotoku, T. & Yoon, W.-K. (2005 b). RT-Component Object Model in RT-Middleware: Distributed Component Middleware for RT (Robot Technology), *Proceedings of IEEE International Symposium on Computational Intelligence in Robotics and Automation (CIRA 2005)*, pp. 457-462, ISBN 0-7803-9355-4, Jun. 2005.

Bhagat, P. (2005). *Pattern Recognition in Industry*, Elsevier Science, ISBN 0-0804-4538-1, USA

Brogårdh T. (2007). Present and future robot control development—An industrial perspective. Annual Reviews in Control, Vol. 31, No. 1, 2007, pp. 69-79, ISSN 1367-5788

Brugali, D. & Reggiani, M. (2005). A Roadmap to crafting modular and interoperable robotic software systems, *Proceedings of IEEE ICRA 2005 Workshop on Software Development and Integration in Robotics*, pp. 1-4, Apr. 2005, IEEE Robotics and Automation Society, Barcelona

Elovic, P. (2003). Implementation of Gate and Crane OCR Systems for Container Terminal Automation and Security, *Proceedings of Terminal Operations Conference ASIA (TOC ASIA 2003)*, pp. 1-7, Feb. 2003.

Gill, C.D. & Smart, W.D. (2002). Middleware for Robots?, *Proceedings of AAAI Spring Symposium on Intelligent Distributed and Embedded Systems*, pp. 1-5, 2002.

Gurney, K. (2003). *An Introduction to Neural Networks*, CRC Press, ISBN 1-8572-8503-4, United Kingdom

Haykin, S. (1998). *Neural Networks: A Comprehensive Foundation*, Prentice-Hall, ISBN 0-1390-8385-5, USA

Ikezoe, A.; Nakamoto, H. & Nagase, M. (2006). Development of RT-Middleware for Image Recognition Module, *Proceedings of SICE-ICASE International Joint Conference, pp. 2036-2041*, ISBN 89-950038-5-5, Oct. 2006.

International Robot Fair (IRF) Organizing Office (2004). *World Robot Declaration*, press release, 25. Feb. 2004.

Kotoku, T. & Mizukawa, M. (2006). Robot Middleware and its Standardization in OMG - Report on OMG Technical Meetings in St. Louis and Boston, *Proceedings of SICE-ICASE International Joint Conference*, pp. 2028-2031, ISBN 89-950038-5-5, Oct. 2006.

Lee, J. H. & Hashimoto, H. (2002). Intelligent Space—concept and contents. *Advanced Robotics*, Vol. 16, No. 3, 2002, pp 265-280, ISSN 0169-1864

Object Management Group (OMG) Robotics DTF (2007). *Robotic Technology Component Specification [Online]*, http://www.omg.org/docs/ptc/07-08-18.pdf, 1.0 beta 2, Aug. 2007.

OpenRTM-aist project team (2007). *OpenRTM-aist [Online]*, http://www.openrtm.org/, 2007.

Rojas, R. & Feldman, J. (1996). *Neural Networks: A Systematic Introduction*, Springer, ISBN 3-5406-0505-3, Germany

Projective Reconstruction and Its Application in Object Recognition for Robot Vision System

Ferenc Tél and Béla Lantos
Budapest University of Technology and Economics
Hungary

1. Introduction

More and more applications (path planning of a robot, collision avoidance methods) require 3D description of the surround world. This chapter describes a 3D projective reconstruction method and its application in an object recognition algorithm.
The described system uses 2D (color or grayscale) images about the scene taken by uncalibrated cameras, tries to localize known object(s) and determine the (relative) position and orientation between them. The scene reconstruction algorithm uses simple 2D geometric entities (points, lines) produced by a low-level feature detector as the images of the 3D vertices and edges of the objects. The features are matched across views (Tél & Tóth, 2000). During the projective reconstruction the 3D description is recovered. The developed system uses uncalibrated cameras, therefore only projective 3D structure can be detected defined up to a collineation. Using the Euclidean information about a known set of predefined objects stored in database and the results of the recognition algorithm, the description could be updated to a metric one.

Projective reconstruction methods

There are many known solutions to the projective reconstruction problem. Most of the developed methods use point features (e.g. vertices), but there are extensions to use higher order features, such as lines and curves (Kaminski & Shashua, 2004). The existing methods can be separated into three main groups. The *view tensors* describe the algebraic relationships amongst coordinates of features in multiple images that must be satisfied in order to represent the same spatial feature in 3D scene (Faugeras & Mourrain, 1995). These methods estimate fundamental matrix from two views (Armangué et al., 2001) or trifocal tensor from three views (Torr & Zisserman, 1997). The *factorization based methods* use the fact that collecting the weighted homogeneous (point) projection vectors into a large matrix (measurement matrix), the rank must be four, because it is a product of two rank four matrices. An iterative solution to solve this problem can be found in (Han & Kanade 2000). In *bundle adjustment methods* the reprojection errors between original image feature locations and an estimated projection of spatial feature locations are minimized. The solution for the problem can be found applying e.g. nonlinear least squares algorithm (Levenberg-Marquardt).

Object recognition methods

The aim of object recognition methods is to recognize objects in the scene from a *known* set of objects, hence some *a-priori* information is required about the objects. These types of methods are called *model based* object recognition methods, where predefined object databases are used to store the required information about the objects. There are many classification types of the applied (and stored) object models, such as object-centered or viewer-centered models, physical or geometrical models, rigid or deformable models, etc. The dimensionality of the used information is also changed in different recognition systems, there are 2D only, mixed and 3D only systems. The developed algorithms are usually evaluated against set of different criteria, such as search complexity, discriminative power and robustness. The *appearance based methods* use 2D images as object representations. Using multiple views, the stored information can be reduced to a minimal set. Here the intensity distribution of the images is used as the basis of the comparison of the similarity of the projected intensity image among views. The two different strategies are global ones, e.g. eigenface (Belhumeur et al., 1997) or local approach, where local properties of the images (neighborhood of edges or corner points) are used to improve the discriminative power, e.g. GLOH (Mikolajczyk & Schmid, 2005)).

The *aspect graph methods* use the changes in the projected geometry of the objects and group views bounded by transitions of the geometry (Schiffenbauer, 2001). The information reduction is based on the determination of general views, which are equivalent with each other.

The *indexing based methods* use those properties of the data that are invariant against a selected group of transformations. In this case the transformation describes the relationship between the object data as stored in the database and scene information, therefore the transformations could be rigid (translation and rotation), similarity (rigid and scaling), etc., up to the most general projective one (collineation). The most widely used methods are based on the geometric hashing (Wolfson & Rigoutsos, 1997). In this case subsets of features (points) are selected that can be used to form a basis and define local coordinate system with that basis. Calculating the coordinates of all of the remaining features in this coordinate system and quantizing the calculated coordinates a hash table is constructed. During the query a similar method is applied and vote is generated into the respecting entry of the hash table.

Euclidean update methods

The last step of the reconstruction is (if the robot control application requires) the update of the reconstructed data from projective to a metric one. There are several algorithms that address this issue. One group of applications uses known a-priori information to recover metric information. In (Boufama et al., 1993) e.g. the coordinates of known points, points laying on the plane of the given (reference) frame, known alignment of points on vertical or horizontal line and known distance between points are used to involve metrical information into the reconstruction. In (Faugeras, 1995) an update sequence is described, that converts the reconstruction from projective to affine, then from affine to Euclidean. The proposed a-priori information is either the known motion of the camera, parallelity of lines (for affine) or angle between lines (for Euclidean) reconstruction.

The other type of methods uses the hypothesis of fixed (but unknown) intrinsic camera parameters. These algorithms are known camera self-calibration methods. This yields the intrinsic parameters of the cameras using only imaging information. (Hartley, 1993) supposes that the cameras have common calibration matrices and uses nonlinear minimizations to calculate camera matrices. A huge nonlinear minimization is achieved to get the final description.

The chapter is divided in sections as follows. Section 2 gives an overview of the most important methods of projective reconstruction. The main part of the chapter is section 3 dealing with object recognition based on a new indexing method. Section 4 presents a method of Euclidean reconstruction assuming uncalibrated cameras for robot applications if the goal is to find the relative position and orientation between the gripper and the recognized object. Section 6 contains the conclusions and some directions of future developments. Section 7 is the Appendix summarizing the basic results of projective geometry and notations used in the chapter.

2. Projective reconstruction

The developed system uses two types of reconstruction algorithms, the first uses point features only and the other uses point and line features together.

2.1 Cost function for points

Using the pinhole camera model the projection equation for points can be written into linear form $\rho_{ij}\mathbf{q}_{ij} = \mathbf{P}_i\mathbf{Q}_j$. In this case the scale factor ρ_{ij} denotes the projective depth of the given point. If there are m cameras and n_P points in the scene, then the number of projected image points (and scale factors) are $m \times n_P$. But only $m + n_P$ are independent amongst them, therefore the projective depths should be decomposed into camera dependent and feature dependent parts. The decomposition equation can be written as a product of two other quantities: $\rho_{ij} = \pi_i\gamma_j$. Using this decomposition, the projection of a point is described by $\pi_i\gamma_j\mathbf{q}_{ij} = \mathbf{P}_i\mathbf{Q}_j$. This decomposition has some advantages: i) the system is described with the minimum number of parameters, therefore the parameterization is consistent. ii) the number of unknowns is greatly reduced. E.g. $m = 3, n_P = 40 \rightarrow N(\pi_i, \gamma_j) \leq 43 << N(\rho_{ij}) = 120$.
If the ρ_{ij} projection depths were known, the joint projection matrices $\mathbf{P}_i$ and the projective shape $\mathbf{Q}_j$ could be determined by using a rank 4 decomposition method, this is the base of the factorization methods.
In order to minimize a physically meaningful quantity, the weighted reprojection error used in the cost function has the form

$$E_P(\cdot) = \sum_{i=1}^{m}\sum_{j=1}^{n_P} \omega_{ij}^2 \left\| \pi_i\gamma_j\mathbf{q}_{ij} - \mathbf{P}_i\mathbf{Q}_j \right\|^2 \tag{1}$$

where the unknowns are $\pi_i, \gamma_j, \mathbf{P}_i, \mathbf{Q}_j$.

2.2 Cost function for points and lines

At first sight it seems a natural choice to extend the decomposition algorithm to lines simply writing the line projection equations into similar form as in the points-only case using the line projection matrix $\mathbf{G}_i$, see (A7) in Appendix:

$$E_L(\cdot) = \sum_{i=1}^{m}\sum_{j=1}^{n_L} \omega_{ij}^2 \left\| \pi_i\lambda_j\mathbf{l}_{ij} - \mathbf{G}_i\mathbf{\Lambda}_j \right\|^2$$

But unfortunately i) the projective depth could not directly be interpreted for lines, ii) the mapping between elements of the point and the line projection matrices is a non-linear function, iii) there exists no distance metric that can easily (linearly) be expressed with the terms of 2D line.

Therefore the original error function (1) was modified. The calculation of projective depths was eliminated using a cross product instead of difference, namely $\mathbf{q}_{ij} \sim \mathbf{P}_i\mathbf{Q}_j \rightarrow \mathbf{q}_{ij} \times (\mathbf{P}_i\mathbf{Q}_j) = 0$. This error is an algebraic distance, it describes the incidence relation between the true (2D feature point) and the projected point. For lines, similar error metric (geometric configurations) was defined:

- The incidence relation of 2D line feature and a projected 3D point is $\mathbf{l}_{ik}\mathbf{P}_i\mathbf{Q}_k(\mathbf{\Lambda},t) = 0$, where $\mathbf{Q}_k(\mathbf{\Lambda},t)$ is the t'th point on the $\mathbf{\Lambda}$ 3D line in Plücker representation (A3). The points can be extracted from Plücker matrix using SVD, see (A5) and (A25). This form can be used during the calculation of $\mathbf{P}$ matrices (resection phase).
- The identity relation of the 2D line feature and a projected 3D line is $\mathbf{l}_{ik} \times (\mathbf{G}_i\mathbf{\Lambda}_k) = 0$. This form can be used during the calculation of $\mathbf{\Lambda}$ vectors (intersection phase).
- The containment relation of 3D line and a plane. The plane can be determined as a backprojected 2D line: $\mathbf{S}_{ik} = \mathbf{P}_i^T\mathbf{l}_{ik}$. The line $\mathbf{\Lambda}_k$ lies on the plane if $\mathbf{U}(\mathbf{S}_{ik})\mathbf{\Lambda}_k = 0$, where $\mathbf{U}(\mathbf{S}_{ik})$ is defined by (A10) in Appendix. This form can be used during the calculation of $\mathbf{\Lambda}$ vectors (intersection phase).

2.3 Minimization of the cost functions

It can be seen, that the cost functions $E_P(\cdot)$ and $E_L(\cdot)$ are nonlinear in the unknowns and their minimization is similar. A possible solution could be the use of the Levenberg-Marquardt method and general initial values to directly minimize this cost function. But fortunately the parameters to be estimated can be separated into different groups, because they are "independent" from each other (e.g. 3D features are independent from each other, because they depend only on the objects in the scene and they are not influenced by the projections). This is the well-known resection-intersection method that holds every group of parameters fixed, except those, that are currently minimized. Therefore the minimization of $E_P(\cdot)$ can be achieved in repeated steps. After every iteration the revaluation of the ω_{ij} weighting factors are achieved and the actual value of the cost function is calculated. If the cost is less than a desired threshold (or maximum allowed number of iterations is reached), the algorithm terminates. The estimation of the given entity can be calculated by making the derivative of $E_P(\cdot)$ by the respecting entity to zero and the solution can be found in closed form for each of the features, see (Tél & Lantos, 2007) for details.

For the more general mixed case the detailed calculations are as follows. The error function for the *intersection phase* is

$$E_I(\cdot) = \sum_{i=1}^{m}\sum_{j=1}^{n_P}\omega_{Q,ij}^2\left\|\mathbf{q}_{ij} \times (\mathbf{P}_i\mathbf{Q}_j)\right\|^2 + \sum_{i=1}^{m}\sum_{k=1}^{n_L}\omega_{\Lambda,ik}^2\left\|f(\mathbf{P}_i,\mathbf{l}_{ik})\right\|^2$$

where $f(\mathbf{P}_i,\mathbf{l}_{ik}) = \mathbf{l}_{ik} \times (\mathbf{G}_i\mathbf{\Lambda}_k)$ or $f(\mathbf{P}_i,\mathbf{l}_{ik}) = \mathbf{U}(\mathbf{S}_{ik})\mathbf{\Lambda}_k$.

During this phase, the $\mathbf{P}_i$ (therefore the $\mathbf{G}_i$) projection matrices are held fixed. After some manipulation the $E_I(\cdot)$ can be written into the following form:

$$E_I(\cdot)=\sum_{j=1}^{n_P}\sum_{i=1}^{m}\omega_{Q,ij}^2\mathbf{Q}_j^T\mathbf{A}_{I,ij}^T\mathbf{A}_{I,ij}\mathbf{Q}_j+\sum_{k=1}^{n_L}\sum_{i=1}^{m}\omega_{\Lambda,ik}^2\mathbf{\Lambda}_k^T\mathbf{B}_{I,ik}^T\mathbf{B}_{I,ik}\mathbf{\Lambda}_k$$

where $\mathbf{A}_{I,ij}=[\mathbf{q}_{ij}]_\times\mathbf{P}_i$ and $\mathbf{B}_{I,ik}=[\mathbf{l}_{ik}]_\times\mathbf{G}_i$ or $\mathbf{B}_{I,ik}=\mathbf{U}(\mathbf{S}_{ik})$. The estimation for the j'th feature can be calculated by making the derivative of $E_I(\cdot)$ by $\mathbf{Q}_j$ and $\mathbf{\Lambda}_k$ to zero, respectively. After the differentiation the solution for each $\mathbf{Q}_i$ and $\mathbf{\Lambda}_k$ can be found in closed form. During the calculation of $\mathbf{Q}_j$ an additional constraint must be introduced, in order to eliminate trivial all zero case. The solution of the problem for $\mathbf{Q}_j$ is the normalized eigenvector corresponding to the smallest eigenvalue of the matrix $\mathbf{C}_{R,ij}=\sum_{i=1}^{m}\omega_{Q,ij}^2\mathbf{A}_{I,ij}^T\mathbf{A}_{I,ij}$

During the calculation of $\mathbf{\Lambda}_k$ lines, two additional constraints must be fulfilled. The first one is the elimination of the trivial (all zero) case, the second one is the Plücker constraint for vector $\mathbf{\Lambda}_k$, see (A3). The measurement error part is similar to the point-case but here the matrix is $\mathbf{D}_{I,ik}=\sum_{i=1}^{m}\omega_{\Lambda,ik}^2\mathbf{B}_{I,ik}^T\mathbf{B}_{I,ik}$. The error function with the constraint can be written into the matrix equation $\mathbf{\Lambda}_k^T(\mathbf{D}_{I,ik}+\alpha\mathbf{\Delta})\mathbf{\Lambda}_k=0$. Taking the derivative by $\mathbf{\Lambda}_k$ and rearranging the terms yields $(\alpha:=-\alpha)$ $\mathbf{D}_{I,ik}\mathbf{\Lambda}_k=\alpha\mathbf{\Delta}\mathbf{\Lambda}_k$. The matrix $\mathbf{\Delta}$ in (A4) is invertible and $\mathbf{\Delta}^{-1}=\mathbf{\Delta}$, therefore the (approximate) solution of the problem for $\mathbf{\Lambda}_k$ is the vector corresponding to the smallest singular value of the matrix $\mathbf{D}_\Delta=\mathbf{\Delta}\mathbf{D}_{I,ik}$.

The error function for the *resection phase* is

$$E_R(\cdot)-\sum_{i=1}^{m}\sum_{j=1}^{n_P}\omega_{Q,ij}^2\left\|\mathbf{q}_{ij}\times(\mathbf{P}_i\mathbf{Q}_j)\right\|^2+\sum_{i=1}^{m}\sum_{k=1}^{n_L}\omega_{\Lambda,ik}^2(\mathbf{l}_{ik}\mathbf{P}_i\mathbf{Q}_k(\Lambda,t))^2$$

During this phase the $\mathbf{Q}_\mathrm{j}$ and $\mathbf{\Lambda}_\mathrm{j}$ entries are held fixed. Again the cameras are independent from each other. After some manipulation $E_R(\cdot)$ can be rewritten into the form

$$E_R(\cdot)=\sum_{i=1}^{m}\mathbf{p}_i^T\left(\sum_{i=1}^{n_P}\omega_{Q,ij}^2\mathbf{A}_{R,ij}^T\mathbf{A}_{R,ij}+\sum_{k=1}^{n_L}\omega_{\Lambda,ik}^2\mathbf{g}(t)_{R,ik}\mathbf{g}(t)_{R,ik}^T\right)\mathbf{p}_i$$

where $\mathbf{A}_{R,ij}=\begin{pmatrix}\mathbf{0}_4^T & -w_{ij}\mathbf{Q}_{ij}^T & v_{ij}\mathbf{Q}_{ij}^T\\ w_{ij}\mathbf{Q}_{ij}^T & \mathbf{0}_4^T & -u_{ij}\mathbf{Q}_{ij}^T\\ -v_{ij}\mathbf{Q}_{ij}^T & u_{ij}\mathbf{Q}_{ij}^T & \mathbf{0}_4^T\end{pmatrix}$ and $\mathbf{g}_{R,ij}=\left(a\mathbf{Q}_j^T(L,t)\;\; b\mathbf{Q}_j^T(L,t)\;\; c\mathbf{Q}_j^T(L,t)\right)^T$.

The estimation for the i'th camera can be calculated by making the derivative of $E_R(\cdot)$ by $\mathbf{P}_i$ to zero. Note, that in this case the error function contains only the "point-form" $\mathbf{P}$ of the projection matrices. An additional constraint must be introduced, in order to eliminate trivial $\mathbf{p}=\mathbf{0}$ case. The solution of the problem is the normalized eigenvector corresponding to the smallest eigenvalue of the matrix

$$\mathbf{C}_{R,i}=\sum_{i=1}^{n_P}\omega_{Q,ij}^2\mathbf{A}_{R,ij}^T\mathbf{A}_{R,ij}+\sum_{k=1}^{n_L}\omega_{\Lambda,ik}^2\mathbf{g}(t)_{R,ik}\mathbf{g}(t)_{R,ik}^T$$

2.4 Initialization of the entities

The parameters of the cost function are estimated using an iterative method, therefore an initial estimation for its values is required. The developed initialization algorithm:

1. Choosing a subset (pair) of views and subset of points that can be seen on all of the selected images (note: the developed algorithm chooses the views that have the largest number of point correspondences). Using these points a rank 4 factorization method is achieved. This gives initial estimation for the given projection matrices and for selected points.
2. Calculate the projection matrix of a new (not yet processed) view using the points detected on that view and have the spatial coordinates already determined. This can be achieved in closed form using SVD.
3. Calculate the spatial coordinates of the not-yet initialized points, that have projection on the images with determined projection matrix, by using triangulation-like method (Hartley & Sturm, 1997). This means the determination of a point which has minimal distance from the rays connecting the image points and the camera focal points in least squares sense. The solution can be found using SVD.
4. In order to initialize the line features, the algorithm uses the fact that $\mathbf{M}_{\mathrm{ij}} = \mathbf{P}_{\mathrm{i}}^{\mathrm{T}} \mathbf{l}_{\mathrm{ij}}$ yields a plane that goes through the optical center of the camera and the projected image of the line. Theoretically these planes intersect in the spatial line. Taking more than two views, the solution can be found using SVD. The matrix $\mathbf{A} = \left(\mathbf{M}_{ij} \quad \cdots \quad \mathbf{M}_{mj}\right)^T$ is a rank 2 matrix, therefore the two left null vectors yield two points whose join yields the desired line equation.

The algorithm repeats steps 2 and 3 until all of the projection matrices are calculated.

2.5 Minimization remarks

The two developed algorithms have some common properties.

- Handling of missing data (features having no projection on the given view) during the minimization is simple, the algorithms skip those entries in the error function that do not have valid $\mathbf{q}_{ij}$, $\mathbf{l}_{ik}$ respectively.
- In order to eliminate the effect of the outliers (caused by badly matched feature projections), the camera matrices are estimated only from some subsets of the features in each iteration cycle. These features are selected in a random way and the projection matrix yielding the smallest reprojection error is used in the further steps. The ω_{ij} weights can be used to make the algorithm more robust, e.g. decrease the influence of features with larger error.

3. Object recognition

The developed object recognition method uses permutation and projective invariant based indexing to recognize known object(s) in the scene. A verification step is achieved to finalize the results.

3.1 Invariants

During the recognition process two sets of entities are used. The first one is the feature sets of the object as stored in the object database. The second one is the features of the recovered

scene. Some elements (a subset) represent the same entity in different context (e.g. two representations of the geometric primitives in different coordinate systems). In order to determine the pairing of the two representations of the same entities the process requires the usage of those properties which are not changing (invariant) between representations.
Formally this can be written into the following form. Let $\mathbf{T} \in T$ denote the (linear) transformation between representations and G denote the geometric structure that describes the configuration. The number of functionally independent invariants can be calculated as

$$N_I = \dim(G) - \dim(T) + \dim(T_G), \tag{2}$$

where T_G denotes the isotropy subgroup (if exists), that leaves G unaffected using $\mathbf{T}$ and $\dim(\cdot)$ denotes the dimension of the given entity.
In case of projective invariants the relation between the two representations (Euclidean object database vs. output of the projective reconstruction) can be described with a 3D projective transformation (collineation). The number of parameters which describe the used entities are as follows.

- 3D point can be described with a 4-vector determined up to a scale. The degree of freedom is 3.
- 3D line can be described with a 6-vector determined up to a scale and a constraint (Plücker). The degree of freedom is 4.
- 3D projective transformation can be described with a 4x4 matrix determined up to a scale. The degree of freedom is 15.

Using these values the minimum number of entities to determine the invariant(s) is:

- 6 points yield $6 \times 3 - 15 + 0 = 3$ independent invariant
- 4 points and a line yield $(4 \times 3 + 4) - 15 + 0 = 1$ independent invariant
- 2 points and 3 lines yield $(2 \times 3 + 3 \times 4) - 15 + 0 = 3$ independent invariants
- 3 points and 2 lines yield $(3 \times 3 + 2 \times 4) - 15 + 0 = 2$ independent invariants
- 4 lines yield $4 \times 4 - 15 + 1 = 2$ independent invariants

The basic element of the projective invariants is the cross ratio and its generalizations for higher dimensions, see (A12), (A14) and (A15). In the following, using the different geometric configurations to calculate invariants, it is supposed that the elements are in general positions. Apart from the trivial degenerate cases, the nontrivial configurations will be determined.
An invariant could be undetermined, if one or more determinants are zero. This means coincident point(s) and/or lines. All of these cases are eliminated from further investigation.

Invariants of 6 points

As shown in (2) and also e.g. in (Quan, 1995), the number of independent solutions is 3. Using the ratio of product of determinants, a possible combination of independent invariants are:

$$I_1 = \frac{|\mathbf{Q}_1\mathbf{Q}_2\mathbf{Q}_3\mathbf{Q}_5| \cdot |\mathbf{Q}_1\mathbf{Q}_2\mathbf{Q}_4\mathbf{Q}_6|}{|\mathbf{Q}_1\mathbf{Q}_2\mathbf{Q}_3\mathbf{Q}_6| \cdot |\mathbf{Q}_1\mathbf{Q}_2\mathbf{Q}_4\mathbf{Q}_5|}, I_2 = \frac{|\mathbf{Q}_1\mathbf{Q}_2\mathbf{Q}_3\mathbf{Q}_5| \cdot |\mathbf{Q}_1\mathbf{Q}_3\mathbf{Q}_4\mathbf{Q}_6|}{|\mathbf{Q}_1\mathbf{Q}_2\mathbf{Q}_3\mathbf{Q}_6| \cdot |\mathbf{Q}_1\mathbf{Q}_3\mathbf{Q}_4\mathbf{Q}_5|}$$

$$I_3 = \frac{|\mathbf{Q}_1\mathbf{Q}_2\mathbf{Q}_3\mathbf{Q}_5| \cdot |\mathbf{Q}_2\mathbf{Q}_3\mathbf{Q}_4\mathbf{Q}_6|}{|\mathbf{Q}_1\mathbf{Q}_2\mathbf{Q}_3\mathbf{Q}_6| \cdot |\mathbf{Q}_2\mathbf{Q}_3\mathbf{Q}_4\mathbf{Q}_5|}$$

There are many ways to create a geometric configuration to represent the situation from which it is possible to calculate the cross ratio. Taking two points $\mathbf{Q}_1$ and $\mathbf{Q}_2$ as the axis, and using the remaining points $\mathbf{Q}_i, i=3,4,5,6$, four planes (pencil of planes) can be formed. The cross ratio of these planes can be determined as the cross ratio of points created as the intersection of these planes with an arbitrary line not intersecting the axis.

Invariant of 4 points and a line

Let $\mathbf{Q}_{L,i}, i=1,2$ denote two arbitrary distinct points on the line. In this case the invariant in the determinant form is:

$$I = \frac{|\mathbf{Q}_{L,1}\mathbf{Q}_{L,2}\mathbf{Q}_1\mathbf{Q}_3| \cdot |\mathbf{Q}_{L,1}\mathbf{Q}_{L,2}\mathbf{Q}_2\mathbf{Q}_4|}{|\mathbf{Q}_{L,1}\mathbf{Q}_{L,2}\mathbf{Q}_1\mathbf{Q}_4| \cdot |\mathbf{Q}_{L,1}\mathbf{Q}_{L,2}\mathbf{Q}_2\mathbf{Q}_3|}$$

The geometrical situation is similar to the 6 point case, but the axis of the pencil of planes is the line.

Invariants of 3 points and 2 lines

Let the two lines be denoted by $\mathbf{L}$ and $\mathbf{K}$, and $\mathbf{Q}_{L,i}, \mathbf{Q}_{K,i}, i=1,2$ are two points on these lines, respectively. As shown above, there must be two independent invariants for this configuration.

$$I_1 = \frac{|\mathbf{Q}_{L,1}\mathbf{Q}_{L,2}\mathbf{Q}_1\mathbf{Q}_2| \cdot |\mathbf{Q}_{K,1}\mathbf{Q}_{K,2}\mathbf{Q}_1\mathbf{Q}_3|}{|\mathbf{Q}_{L,1}\mathbf{Q}_{L,2}\mathbf{Q}_1\mathbf{Q}_3| \cdot |\mathbf{Q}_{K,1}\mathbf{Q}_{K,2}\mathbf{Q}_1\mathbf{Q}_2|}, \quad I_2 = \frac{|\mathbf{Q}_{L,1}\mathbf{Q}_{L,2}\mathbf{Q}_1\mathbf{Q}_2| \cdot |\mathbf{Q}_{K,1}\mathbf{Q}_{K,2}\mathbf{Q}_2\mathbf{Q}_3|}{|\mathbf{Q}_{L,1}\mathbf{Q}_{L,2}\mathbf{Q}_2\mathbf{Q}_3| \cdot |\mathbf{Q}_{K,1}\mathbf{Q}_{K,2}\mathbf{Q}_1\mathbf{Q}_2|}$$

A possible geometric configuration to determine the cross ratio is the three planes formed by $\mathbf{L}$ and points $\mathbf{Q}_i, i=1,2,3$, and the plane generated by the three points. Using the line $\mathbf{K}$ to cut through these planes, the intersection of the line and the planes gives four points. The other invariant can be determined by interchanging the role of the lines.

Invariants of 2 points and 3 lines

Let $\mathbf{L}_i, i=1,2,3$ and $\mathbf{Q}_j, j=1,2$, be the three lines and two points, respectively. Geometrically, four planes could be defined from a pair of a point and a line. For example, let the four planes: $(\mathbf{L}_1,\mathbf{Q}_1)$, $(\mathbf{L}_1,\mathbf{Q}_2)$, $(\mathbf{L}_2,\mathbf{Q}_1)$ and $(\mathbf{L}_2,\mathbf{Q}_2)$. The remaining line $\mathbf{L}_3$ intersects these planes and the four intersection points on the line determine the cross ratio. The other two invariants could be calculated using lines 1,3 and 2,3 in plane definition.

Invariants of 4 lines

Let $\mathbf{L}_i, i=1,2,3,4$ be the four lines. This configuration has $4\times4-15+1=2$ projective invariants, because there is an isotropy subgroup of any collineation of 3D projective space that leaves the four lines in place (Hartley, 1992). Algebraically the invariants can be written as:

$$I_1 = \frac{|\mathbf{Q}_{1,1}\mathbf{Q}_{1,2}\mathbf{Q}_{2,1}\mathbf{Q}_{2,2}| \cdot |\mathbf{Q}_{3,1}\mathbf{Q}_{3,2}\mathbf{Q}_{4,1}\mathbf{Q}_{4,2}|}{|\mathbf{Q}_{1,1}\mathbf{Q}_{1,2}\mathbf{Q}_{3,1}\mathbf{Q}_{3,2}| \cdot |\mathbf{Q}_{2,1}\mathbf{Q}_{2,2}\mathbf{Q}_{4,1}\mathbf{Q}_{4,2}|} \quad I_2 = \frac{|\mathbf{Q}_{1,1}\mathbf{Q}_{1,2}\mathbf{Q}_{2,1}\mathbf{Q}_{2,2}| \cdot |\mathbf{Q}_{3,1}\mathbf{Q}_{3,2}\mathbf{Q}_{4,1}\mathbf{Q}_{4,2}|}{|\mathbf{Q}_{1,1}\mathbf{Q}_{1,2}\mathbf{Q}_{3,1}\mathbf{Q}_{3,2}| \cdot |\mathbf{Q}_{2,1}\mathbf{Q}_{2,2}\mathbf{Q}_{4,1}\mathbf{Q}_{4,2}|}$$

where $\mathbf{Q}_{i,j}$ denotes the j'th point on the line $\mathbf{L}_i$.

3.2 Projective and permutation Invariants

It is shown in (A13), that there are six possible values for the cross ratio for four collinear points. Using higher dimensional configurations, the situation is worse, 6 points has 6!=720 possible labeling. Therefore in order to use the invariants for indexing in the object database, the complexity of the query must be reduced. This means that the effect of labeling (permutations of the geometric entities) must be eliminated.

As it was shown previously, the invariants of different geometric configurations of points and lines can be written as the ratio of product of determinants. According to the simplest generalization of the form, at least $N+3$ points required in an N -dimensional space, thus

$$I(\mathbf{Q}_1,\mathbf{Q}_2,\ldots,\mathbf{Q}_N,\mathbf{Q}_{N+1},\mathbf{Q}_{N+2},\mathbf{Q}_{N+3})=\frac{|\mathbf{Q}_1\mathbf{Q}_2\cdots\mathbf{Q}_N\mathbf{Q}_{N+2}|\cdot|\mathbf{Q}_1\mathbf{Q}_2\cdots\mathbf{Q}_{N+1}\mathbf{Q}_{N+3}|}{|\mathbf{Q}_1\mathbf{Q}_2\cdots\mathbf{Q}_N\mathbf{Q}_{N+3}|\cdot|\mathbf{Q}_1\mathbf{Q}_2\cdots\mathbf{Q}_{N+1}\mathbf{Q}_{N+2}|}.$$

It can be seen, that in this case the changing of the labeling of the first $N-1$ points leaves the value of the invariant intact (the sign changes of the four determinants cancel each other), the permutation of the last four points yields the six different values. Therefore the permutations inside the invariant can be separated as

$$I(\pi(\mathbf{Q}_1,\ldots,\mathbf{Q}_N,\mathbf{Q}_{N+1},\mathbf{Q}_{N+2},\mathbf{Q}_{N+3}))=I(\pi_1(\mathbf{Q}_1,\ldots,\mathbf{Q}_{N-1})\pi_2(\mathbf{Q}_N,\mathbf{Q}_{N+1},\mathbf{Q}_{N+2},\mathbf{Q}_{N+3}))$$

where π denotes the permutations of the elements. Interchanging the elements between π_1 and π_2 yields other invariants. Putting together, the projective and permutation invariants must fulfill two requirements:

- *Problem 1*: Eliminate the effect of the six possible values of the cross ratio. This can be accomplished using algebraic or stereographic permutation invariants.
- *Problem 2*: Eliminate the effect of interchanging the elements between π_1 and π_2.

Permutation invariants for cross ratio

In the solutions proposed by (Meer et al, 1998), (Csurka & Faugeras, 1999), the elimination of the effect of the different labeling inside the cross ratio is achieved in an algebraic way using higher order symmetric polynomials. The developed method follows a different method, applies a stereographic projection and a periodic function to give a solution for *Problem 1*.

Stereographic permutation invariants for cross ratio

As it can be seen in Fig. 1 (left), the plot of the six possible permutations of the cross ratio is symmetrical to the value 0.5 and (projectively) ∞. By pairs equating the three basic functions (occurs in cross-ratio) $\{x,1/x,1-x\}$ yields $x=1/x\rightarrow x=\pm1$ and $x=1-x\rightarrow x=0.5$, the mapping of these values could be calculated. (Note that the third possible combination $1/x=1-x$ does not give real solution.)

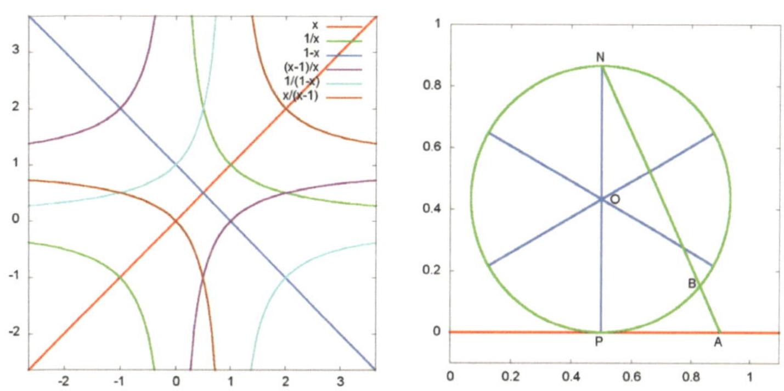

Fig. 1. Effect of permutations inside cross ratio (left), stereographic projection (right)

Considering Table 1 (note, that in projective manner the values ∞ and $-\infty$ represents the same) it can be concluded, that the key values of the six mappings are $(-1,0,0.5,1,2,\infty)$, because they form a closed set respecting to these mappings. In order to generate permutation invariants, application of such periodic function(s) is required that gives same value to the six possible combinations of the basic functions. This could be achieved in a two step process.

X	-1	0	0.5	1	2	∞
1/x	-1	∞	2	1	0.5	0
1-x	2	1	0.5	0	-1	∞

Table 1. Key values mappings inside cross ratio

Stereographic projection

In order to define a periodic function, the mapping of the infinite line (possible values of cross ratios) onto a circle is required. This could be achieved with the stereographic projection (used in the developed system, Fig. 1, right) or gnomonic projection. The parameters of the circle can be determined from the following constraints

- The values in the same pair must be mapped on the opposite side of the circle
- The infinity on the line must be mapped into the "north pole". Therefore the value 0.5 must be on the "south pole" (at point P).
- The arrangement of the (six) key values must be symmetrical.
- The mapping is continuous.

This yields, that the values $(0.5,1,2,\infty,-1,0)$ are mapped onto the angles $\sphericalangle(POB)=(0,\pi/3,2\pi/3,\pi,4\pi/3,5\pi/3)$, respectively. Note, that the $2\times\sphericalangle(PNB)=\sphericalangle(POB)$, because $\sphericalangle(POB)$ is the central angle and $\sphericalangle(PNB)$ is the respecting inscribed angle. The radius of the circle can be determined as $\tan(\sphericalangle(PNA))=\dfrac{A-P}{2r}\rightarrow r=\dfrac{A-P}{2\tan(\sphericalangle(PNA))}$.

Substituting the values $(A=1, P=0.5,\quad \sphericalangle(PNB)=\pi/6, \tan(\sphericalangle(PNB))=1/\sqrt{3})$ gives $r=\sqrt{3}/4$. The PDF (probability density function) of the stereographic permutation invariants is shown in Fig. 2.

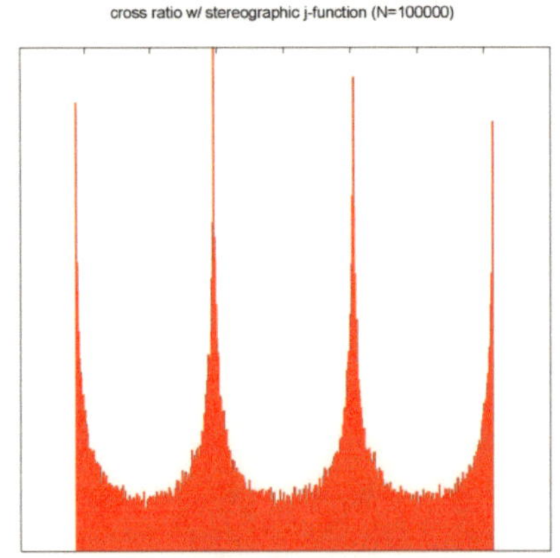

Fig. 2. Probability density function of stereographic permutation invariants

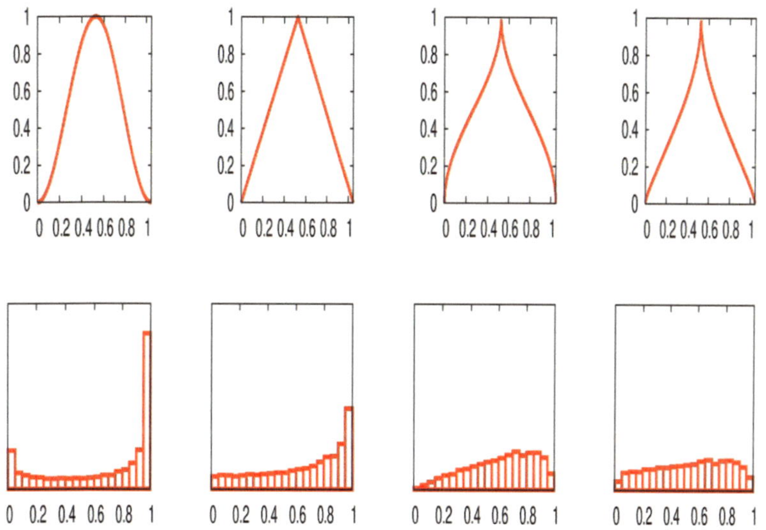

Fig. 3. The effect of nonlinear periodic functions (upper line) to the approximations of uniformly distributed PDF (lower line)

Application of a periodic function

Using the output of the stereographic mapping, the aim is to define a periodic function that fulfills the $J_p(I) = J_p(I + (k\pi/6)),\ k = 0,\ldots,5$ requirement. From the practical point of view, the outputs of the tested functions are mapped into [0,1] interval. In order to apply a simple (Euclidean) distance function during the indexing, a nonlinear transformation must be defined such a way, that the output density must be close to the uniform one. Amongst the several possibilities, the following functions (whose period is $\pi/6$, against $\arcsin(\sin(x)) = x$ whose period is 2π) are tested (see Fig. 3 and note, the first row shows only one period of functions):

- $J_{p1} = \sin^2(3I)$
- $J_{p2} = (2/\pi)\,|\arcsin(\sin(3I))|$
- $J_{p3} = (2/\pi)\arcsin(\sqrt{(2/\pi)\,|\arcsin(\sin(3I))|})$
- $J_{p4} = 0.57(J_{pb}(I) - 6J_{pb}(I - (\pi/6))) + 0.86$, where

  $J_{pb} = (1/\pi)\arcsin(\sqrt{(1/\pi)\,|\arcsin(\sin(3I))|})$

Examining the PDF of the invariants applying the different functions, it can be seen that the J_{p4} gives the PDF closest (most similar) to the uniform distribution.

The output of the periodic function gives the solution to the *Problem 1*.

Elimination of the effect of element interchanges

The next step is to eliminate the effect of interchanging the elements between two permutation groups (giving solution to the *Problem 2*). The number of possible combinations is $\binom{N+3}{4}$. Therefore the permutation invariant is not a single value but a vector $\mathbf{J}$. In order to remove the effect of the initial labeling of $N+3$ points, the vector must be sorted. The applicability of the following configurations is checked: 6 points, 1 line + 4 points, 2 lines + 3 points, 3 lines + 2 points, 4 lines, 5 lines.

Configuration: 6 points

In case of six points, interchanging the elements between the permutation groups yields the invariant vector

$$\mathbf{J} = \mathrm{S}\left(\mathrm{J}(\mathrm{I}_1), \mathrm{J}(\mathrm{I}_2), \mathrm{J}\left(\frac{\mathrm{I}_1}{\mathrm{I}_2}\right), \mathrm{J}\left(\frac{\mathrm{I}_1-1}{\mathrm{I}_2-1}\right), \mathrm{J}\left(\frac{\mathrm{I}_2(\mathrm{I}_1-1)}{\mathrm{I}_1(\mathrm{I}_2-1)}\right), \mathrm{J}(\mathrm{I}_3), \mathrm{J}\left(\frac{\mathrm{I}_1}{\mathrm{I}_3}\right), \mathrm{J}\left(\frac{\mathrm{I}_1-1}{\mathrm{I}_3-1}\right), \mathrm{J}\left(\frac{\mathrm{I}_3(\mathrm{I}_1-1)}{\mathrm{I}_1(\mathrm{I}_3-1)}\right), \right.$$
$$\left. \mathrm{J}\left(\frac{\mathrm{I}_2}{\mathrm{I}_3}\right), \mathrm{J}\left(\frac{\mathrm{I}_2-1}{\mathrm{I}_3-1}\right), \mathrm{J}\left(\frac{\mathrm{I}_3(\mathrm{I}_2-1)}{\mathrm{I}_2(\mathrm{I}_3-1)}\right), \mathrm{J}\left(\frac{\mathrm{I}_3-\mathrm{I}_1}{\mathrm{I}_3-\mathrm{I}_2}\right), \mathrm{J}\left(\frac{\mathrm{I}_2(\mathrm{I}_3-\mathrm{I}_1)}{\mathrm{I}_1(\mathrm{I}_3-\mathrm{I}_2)}\right), \mathrm{J}\left(\frac{(\mathrm{I}_2-1)(\mathrm{I}_3-\mathrm{I}_1)}{(\mathrm{I}_1-1)(\mathrm{I}_3-\mathrm{I}_2)}\right)\right) \quad (3)$$

where I_1, I_2 and I_3 are the invariants belonging to the permutation group $\pi_1(1,2)\pi_2(3,4,5,6)$ of points, $S(\cdot)$ denotes the sorting operator. The number of points in the configuration is six but the vector $\mathbf{J}$ has 15 elements. Therefore no one-to-one mapping exists between the points and the elements of the vector. Instead, the mapping exists between pairs of points and the respecting vector element. The first five elements in (3) depend on $(\mathbf{Q}_1\mathbf{Q}_i), i=2,\ldots,6$, the next four depend on $(\mathbf{Q}_2\mathbf{Q}_i), i=3,\ldots,6$, and so on. Finally the last element depends on $(\mathbf{Q}_5\mathbf{Q}_6)$. This means, that building a 6x6 table, according to the indexing with $\mathbf{J}$, the ordering of the points between two sets of respecting six point configurations can be determined in the following way.

We describe our concept for the 6-point case. Similar technique can be used for other feature combinations. The object database contains objects and the objects contain also points, from which different subsets containing 6 points can be built. The database contains Euclidean information belonging to the subset of points. From this information using the the homogeneous coordinates of the points the invariants can be computed. By using the nonlinear function J_{p4} the 15 (normalized) components of the vector $\mathbf{J}$ can be computed and sorted and the permutation $\mathbf{p}$ after sorting can be determined. This pair of $\mathbf{J}$ and $\mathbf{p}$ are precomputed and stored in the database before application. In the scene we can choose 6 point features and from their 3D projective coordinates we can determine another pair of $\mathbf{J}$ and $\mathbf{p}$ in a similar way during application. The basis for finding corresponding sets of points are the $\mathbf{J}$'s both in object database and scene. The $\mathbf{J}$'s are compared using Euclidean distance and a tolerance. Corresponding sets of points are marked and the collineation mapping points from scene into points from database is determined. This collineation makes it possible to map further points from the scene into database and check for correspondence. Thus the set of corresponding points belonging to the same object can be enlarged. In the success indices a and b identify the sets in database and scene, respectively. The main problem is that the order of the points in database and scene may be different. The details are as follows.

After sorting of the vectors $\mathbf{J}_a$ and $\mathbf{J}_b$, let $\mathbf{p}_a$ and $\mathbf{p}_b$ contain the permutation indices of the elements, therefore if $\mathbf{J}_a(i)=\mathbf{J}_b(i), i=1,\ldots,15$, then element indexed by $\mathbf{p}_a(i)$ corresponds to $\mathbf{p}_b(i)$. Defining the vector $\mathbf{V}$ according to Table 2 yields that the pair $\mathbf{V}(\mathbf{p}_a(i))$ corresponds to $\mathbf{V}(\mathbf{p}_b(i))$, e.g. $\mathbf{V}(\mathbf{p}_a(1))=\mathbf{V}(6)=\{2,3\}$ corresponds to

$\mathbf{V}(\mathbf{p}_b(1)) = \mathbf{V}(13) = \{4,5\}$. Let $\mathbf{A}$ be a 6×6 (symmetric) table, where $\mathbf{A}(\mathbf{V}(\mathbf{p}_b(i))) = \mathbf{V}(\mathbf{p}_a(i))$. The i'th point in the set 'a' corresponds to j'th point in the set 'b', iff every element in the i'th row of $\mathbf{A}$ contains the index j.
For example a query from the scene into the database contains the sorted vector and permutation:

$$J_a = (0.0075 \quad 0.0247 \quad 0.0322 \quad 0.0344 \quad 0.0420 \quad 0.0667 \quad 0.3196 \quad 0.3269 \quad \cdots \quad 0.4270 \quad 0.4341 \quad 0.7054 \quad 0.7185 \quad 0.7257 \quad 0.9517 \quad 0.9739)$$

$$p_a = (6 \quad 12 \quad 10 \quad 7 \quad 9 \quad 14 \quad 1 \quad 8 \quad 11 \quad 2 \quad 5 \quad 4 \quad 15 \quad 3 \quad 13)$$

The resulted entry from the database gives:

$$J_b = (0.0103 \quad 0.0338 \quad 0.0441 \quad 0.0468 \quad 0.0572 \quad 0.0909 \quad 0.3209 \quad 0.3309 \quad \cdots \quad 0.4270 \quad 0.4367 \quad 0.7037 \quad 0.7219 \quad 0.7315 \quad 0.9513 \quad 0.9816)$$

$$p_b = (13 \quad 3 \quad 14 \quad 15 \quad 4 \quad 5 \quad 11 \quad 8 \quad 7 \quad 10 \quad 2 \quad 6 \quad 1 \quad 12 \quad 9)$$

The vector **V** is given in detailed form in Table 2.

I	1	2	3	4	5	6	7	8	9	10	11	12	13	14	15
V	1,2	1,3	1,4	1,5	1,6	2,3	2,4	2,5	2,6	3,4	3,5	3,6	4,5	4,6	5,6

Table 2. Possible pairings in the six points configuration

Using the permutation vectors $\mathbf{p}_a(1) = 6$ corresponds to $\mathbf{p}_b(1) = 13$, yields that pair 2,3 corresponds to pair 4,5. Write 2,3 into the position 4,5 (and 5,4) of the 6×6 table and continuing the process gives the results in Table 3.

	1	2	3	4	5	6
1	*	5,6	1,6	3,6	2,6	4,6
2	5,6	*	1,5	3,5	2,5	4,5
3	1,6	1,5	*	1,3	1,2	1,4
4	3,6	3,5	1,3	*	2,3	3,4
5	2,6	2,5	1,2	2,3	*	2,4
6	4,6	4,5	1,4	3,4	2,4	*

Table 3. Determine correspondences in six points configuration

Searching for the common elements row-wise (e.g. 6 in the first row in Table 3) gives the final pairings of the features: 1-6, 2-5, 3-1, 4-3, 5-2, 6-4.
A fault tolerant method is also developed. For example some numerically close elements in the corresponding vectors are swapped by sorting process, hence the table does not yield a valid solution, see the cells underlined in Table 4.
The solution to the problem is the following. Fill another 6x6 table from the original one such that the element in (*i,j*) contains the number of occurrences of *j*'th value in *i*'th row of the original table. Then repeat the following process:

1. Search for a maximum value in this new table. The row-column index gives the pairing.
2. Fill the row and the column with zeros of the pair already found. If the current maximum value is less than the desired parameter (tipically 4, tolerating only one mis-match), the pairing is not possible.

	1	2	3	4	5	6
1	*	5,6	1,5	3,5	4,5	2,5
2	5,6	*	1,6	3,6	4,6	2,6
3	1,5	1,6	*	**2,3**	1,4	1,2
4	3,5	3,6	2,3	*	3,4	1,3
5	4,5	4,6	1,4	3,4	*	2,4
6	2,5	2,6	1,2	**1,3**	2,4	*

1	2	3	4	5	6
1	1	1	1	5	1
1	1	1	1	1	5
4	2	1	1	1	1
1	1	5	1	1	1
1	1	1	5	1	1
2	4	1	1	1	1

Table 4. Determine correspondences in six points configuration (fault tolerant version)

Configuration: 1 line, 4 points

The calculation of the permutation invariant from the projective one is very simple, applying the function $\mathbf{J}(\cdot)$ to the only one projective invariant. But no method is currently known to determine pairings from permutation and projective invariants, therefore this type of configuration is *not used during indexing*.

Configuration: 2 lines, 3 points

As mentioned earlier, the geometric configuration for this case could be traced back to the five coplanar points case. Therefore the results of (Meer et al, 1998) could be used, namely interchanging the elements between the permutation groups yields the vector

$$\mathbf{J}_{2D} = S\left(J(I_1), J(I_2), J\left(\frac{I_1}{I_2}\right), J\left(\frac{I_1 - 1}{I_2 - 1}\right), J\left(\frac{I_2(I_1 - 1)}{I_1(I_2 - 1)}\right) \right) \quad (4)$$

The elements of the vector can be determined by exchanging the first element with the elements at $2,\ldots,5$, respectively.

But this is unnecessary, because the lines and points can be clearly distinguished, therefore the first element should only be exchanged with the second and the third one. Interchanging the two lines means applying $I \to 1/I$ mapping of the invariant (see the algebraic form). This means, that the permutation invariant vector should contain only

$$\mathbf{J} = S\left(J(I_1), J(I_2), J\left(\frac{I_1}{I_2}\right) \right).$$

If the pairing of the points and lines between two sets is required, the simplest solution is to calculate the vector defined in (4), because there is a one-to-one mapping between the five points and the five elements of $\mathbf{J}_{2D}$. A possible additional check is to pair points generated by line intersection with a similar one.

Configuration: 3 lines, 2 points

This configuration yields six planes, because a plane can be formed from a line and a point, where the point and the line are not coincident. In the projective 3D space the points and planes are dual to each other (principle of duality), therefore the results of the six points case can be used.

Configuration: 4 lines

The calculation of the permutation invariant from the projective one is simple, applying the appropriate function to the projective invariants. But no method is currently known to determine pairings from permutation and projective invariants, therefore this type of configuration is *not used during indexing*.

Configuration: 5 lines

In order to be able to use line only configuration, from which the pairing can be determined, compound configuration must be used. The simplest one is 5 lines in general position. From 5 lines five different 4-lines configuration can be extracted. A 4-lines configuration gives two independent invariants. Applying a function $f(J_{i,1}, J_{i,2}) \rightarrow J_i, i = 1,\ldots,5$ yields five different invariants. From these invariants the pairing could be determined.

Let the i'th configuration be the one from which the i'th line is excluded (1st configuration is built from lines 2,3,4,5, etc.). Let the unsorted 5-vectors be $\mathbf{J}_a$ and $\mathbf{J}_b$. Let the permutation vectors containing the output of the sorting be $\mathbf{p}_a, \mathbf{p}_b$, respectively. This means that the $\mathbf{J}_a(\mathbf{p}_a(i))$ invariant equals to $\mathbf{J}_b(\mathbf{p}_b(i))$, therefore the (eliminated) lines $\mathbf{p}_a(i)$, $\mathbf{p}_b(i)$ correspond to each other.

3.3 Object database

The aim of the application of the object database is to recognize known, predefined (previously stored) object(s) in the scene. The stored information in the database is the invariant vectors computed from *the 3D Euclidean description of the objects* represented by homogeneous coordinates as described in the previous section. During the query the input is computed from the output of the projective reconstruction of the scene. The two sets of invariants must be paired (matched) in order to determine the corresponding feature configurations. Some additional attributes also stored that is required during verification. The developed system uses different tables for each of the possible configurations (six points, etc.). The attributes are the name of the candidate object, type and id of the stored features and the permutation of the features. These values will be used in a later processing step (verification).

Metric definition and feature transformation

The usage of the database algorithms (indexing) requires the definition of a metric that describes the similarity of the feature combinations. A definition of a metric uses a distance function $d(\cdot)$ that describes the (dis)similarity of the elements between two sets, where $d = 0$ denotes identical configurations and the dissimilarity is larger as d increasing. Therefore d forms a metric, because i) d is a non-negative (real) number, ii) the relation is symmetrical, iii) fulfills the triangle inequality. In order to be able to compare the two feature sets, application of a feature transformation is required. This feature transformation maps the configuration properties into a D-dimensional vector space, where the distance between the vectors is defined. The distance between feature vectors must somehow correspond to the original (theoretical) distance between the features from them it was derived (eliminating false positives). Usually this means, that the distance between vectors is the lower bound of the original distance (this means that the small vector distance may yield dissimilar feature distance, but similar feature combinations always yield small vector distance). The properties used in the feature transformation are task dependent, in this case the feature configuration is described by an invariant vector defined in previous section. Therefore the feature transformation maps from features (described by its coordinates) into (vector)space of invariants. Many distance function can be created that fulfill the requirement of the definition. The most widely used functions can be described as

$$L(\cdot) = \left(\sum_{i=1}^{D} (a_i - b_i)^p \right)^{1/p} .$$

Using the different values of p yields the Manhattan metric $(p=1)$, Euclidean metric $(p=2)$ and maximum metric $(p=\infty)$. In the developed system the Euclidean metric is used.

Query into the database

The query process extracts those elements from the database that are closest to the querying element (exact matching is not probable due to noise during feature detection). This is the well-known nearest neighbors (kNN) problem. In our case the invariants are higher dimensional vector valued entities. The standard R-tree algorithm is very inefficient for higher dimensions (Moenne-Loccoz, 2005), due to the *curse of dimensionality*. The developed method uses X-tree (Berchtold et al., 1996). The query into the database extracts the closest candidates to the query vector (typically 2-5 are used). A tolerance is applied to eliminate the truly false matches. The remaining candidates are further processed in the verification step.

3.4 Verification

Because of the feature transformation the query eliminates only the false positives (those configurations, that are surely do not yield a valid answer to the query), the remaining candidates must be post-processed with a verification process. (Note: the query process should yield sufficiently small number of candidates in order to prevent the post-processing of the whole database.)

Collineation between 3D feature sets

Denote $\mathbf{H}$ the 4×4 matrix of the invertible linear transformation (collineation), $\mathbf{X}_i, \mathbf{Y}_i$ the 4-length coordinate vector of corresponding 3D homogeneous points. Let the corresponding line pair be $\mathbf{L}_i$ and $\mathbf{K}_i$, described by 4×4 $\mathbf{L}_i, \mathbf{K}_i$ skew-symmetric Plücker matrices, see (A5). Let $\mathbf{X}_{\mathbf{L}_i,r}$ be points on the line $\mathbf{L}_i$ and $\mathbf{Y}_{\mathbf{K}_i,s}$ be points on the line $\mathbf{K}_i$, respectively. Let $\mathbf{\Omega}_{\mathbf{K}_i,p}$ be planes that contains $\mathbf{K}_i$. If the $\mathbf{X}_i$ and $\mathbf{Y}_i$, $\mathbf{L}_i$ and $\mathbf{K}_i$ represent the same entities in different coordinate frames (related by $\mathbf{H}$), then the relation between them can be written into the form $\mathbf{Y}_i \sim \mathbf{H}\mathbf{X}_i$ and $\mathbf{K}_i \sim \mathbf{H}\mathbf{L}_i\mathbf{H}^T$, or using the entity-dependent scaling factors with equality $\mu_i \mathbf{Y}_i = \mathbf{H}\mathbf{X}_i$, $\nu_i \mathbf{K}_i = \mathbf{H}\mathbf{L}_i\mathbf{H}^T$. The aim is to determine $\mathbf{H}$ from a given set of point and line pairs in a noisy environment (LS solution is preferable), in a closed form. The solution must handle any number of combinations of points and lines. The unknowns are the 16 elements of the $\mathbf{H}$ matrix (and optionally the μ_i $(i=1,\ldots,n_P)$ scaling factors for points and the ν_i $(i=1,\ldots,n_L)$ scaling factors for lines).

Geometric solution

Using point and line pairs together, the equations contain the unknowns in quadratic or mixed form. Therefore the direct applications of these functions are not advisable. Instead geometric constraints are introduced in order to calculate the desired collineation. Let $\mathbf{H}$ be assumed in vector form

$$\mathbf{h}_{16\times1} = \begin{pmatrix} H(1,1) & \cdots & H(1,4) & \cdots & H(4,4) \end{pmatrix}^T = \begin{pmatrix} \mathbf{h}_1^T & \mathbf{h}_2^T & \mathbf{h}_3^T & \mathbf{h}_4^T \end{pmatrix}^T$$

Point-point relations

For points, the constraint equation is the scaling factor free algebraic distances

$$Y_i(a)\mathbf{X}_i\mathbf{h}_b^T - Y_i(b)\mathbf{X}_i\mathbf{h}_a^T = 0$$

where the pairs $\{a,b\} = \{4,1\},\{4,2\},\{4,3\},\{2,3\},\{3,1\},\{1,2\}$.
The part of the coefficient matrix belonging to this point pair is

$$\begin{pmatrix} \vdots & \vdots & \vdots & \vdots \\ -Y_i(4)\mathbf{X}_i & 0_4 & 0_4 & Y_i(1)\mathbf{X}_i \\ 0_4 & -Y_i(4)\mathbf{X}_i & 0_4 & Y_i(2)\mathbf{X}_i \\ 0_4 & 0_4 & -Y_i(4)\mathbf{X}_i & Y_i(3)\mathbf{X}_i \\ 0_4 & Y_i(2)\mathbf{X}_i & -Y_i(3)\mathbf{X}_i & 0_4 \\ -Y_i(1)\mathbf{X}_i & 0_4 & Y_i(3)\mathbf{X}_i & 0_4 \\ Y_i(1)\mathbf{X}_i & -Y_i(2)\mathbf{X}_i & 0_4 & 0_4 \\ \vdots & \vdots & \vdots & \vdots \end{pmatrix} \quad (5)$$

Line-line relations

In order to eliminate the higher order members of the cost function, the line-type entities should be eliminated, points and planes relations must be used. The points on the line and planes, whose intersection is the given line can be extracted from the Plücker matrix of the line using SVD, see (A5) and (A25). Any linear combination of two points and two lines can be used as pairs instead of the original ones (resulted from SVD).

The two possible constraint types are:

- The transformed points $\mathbf{X}_{\mathbf{L}_i,r}$ should lie on the plane $\mathbf{\Omega}_{\mathbf{K}_i,s}$. Algebraically this means $\left(\mathbf{H}\mathbf{X}_{\mathbf{L}_i,r}\right)^T \mathbf{\Omega}_{\mathbf{K}_i,s} = 0$ where $r,s = 1,2$. The part of the coefficient matrix belongs to this configuration is

$$\begin{pmatrix} \vdots & \vdots & \vdots & \vdots \\ \mathbf{\Omega}_{\mathbf{K}_i,s}(1)\mathbf{X}_{\mathbf{L}_i,r} & \mathbf{\Omega}_{\mathbf{K}_i,s}(2)\mathbf{X}_{\mathbf{L}_i,r} & \mathbf{\Omega}_{\mathbf{K}_i,s}(3)\mathbf{X}_{\mathbf{L}_i,r} & \mathbf{\Omega}_{\mathbf{K}_i,s}(4)\mathbf{X}_{\mathbf{L}_i,r} \\ \vdots & \vdots & \vdots & \vdots \end{pmatrix} \quad (6)$$

A plane can be constructed from a transformed point $\mathbf{X}_{\mathbf{L}_i,r}$ and the line $\mathbf{\Omega}_{\mathbf{K}_i,s}$. If the point lies on the line, the plane equation must be invalid, $\mathbf{\Omega} = \mathbf{0}$. Using the representation in (A5), let $\mathbf{K}_i^T = \left(\mathbf{K}_{D,i}^T \quad \mathbf{K}_{O,i}^T\right)$, where $\mathbf{K}_{D,i}$ and $\mathbf{K}_{O,i}$ are 3-vectors. The plane can be generated using the matrix $\mathbf{\Lambda}_{\mathbf{K}_i} = \begin{pmatrix} [\mathbf{K}_{D,i}]_\times & \mathbf{K}_{O,i} \\ -\mathbf{K}_{O,i} & \mathbf{0} \end{pmatrix}$. Applying to the transformed point, the plane equation becomes $\mathbf{\Omega}_{\mathbf{K}_i,r} = \mathbf{\Lambda}_{\mathbf{K}_i}\left(\mathbf{H}\mathbf{X}_{\mathbf{L}_i,r}\right)$ where $r = 1,2$. The part of the coefficient matrix belongs to this configuration is

$$\begin{pmatrix} \vdots & \vdots & \vdots & \vdots \\ \mathbf{\Lambda}_{\mathbf{K}_i}(1,1)\mathbf{X}_{\mathbf{L}_i,r} & \mathbf{\Lambda}_{\mathbf{K}_i}(1,2)\mathbf{X}_{\mathbf{L}_i,r} & \mathbf{\Lambda}_{\mathbf{K}_i}(1,3)\mathbf{X}_{\mathbf{L}_i,r} & \mathbf{\Lambda}_{\mathbf{K}_i}(1,4)\mathbf{X}_{\mathbf{L}_i,r} \\ \vdots & \vdots & \vdots & \vdots \end{pmatrix} \quad (7)$$

Estimation of H

The equations (4), (5) and (6) yield linear constraints for the elements of the collineation $\mathbf{H}$. Collecting these coefficients into a matrix $\mathbf{A}$, the equations can be written into the form $\mathbf{Ah} = \mathbf{0}$. Applying an additional constraint $\|\mathbf{h}\| = 1$ in order to avoid the trivial solution $\mathbf{h} = \mathbf{0}$, the problem can be solved in a closed form, using SVD, as the vector corresponding to the smallest singular value.

An optional step is a nonlinear refinement. This uses nonlinear Euclidean distance-like values, therefore it can be used only if the destination frame is a metric frame. For points, the error function is the Euclidean distance

$$E_{point}(\cdot)=\left|\frac{Y_i(j)}{Y_i(4)}-\frac{\mathbf{h}_j^T\mathbf{X}_i}{\mathbf{h}_4^T\mathbf{X}_i}\right|^2 \quad \text{where } j=1,2,3 .$$

For lines, the error function uses the direction difference between the orientation of the lines and the distance between lines. Let $\mathbf{K}_{D,i},\mathbf{L}_{D,i}$ be the direction vector of the lines $\mathbf{K}_i$, $\mathbf{L}_i$, respectively. Similarly, let $\mathbf{K}_{P,i},\mathbf{L}_{P,i}$ be a point of the lines $\mathbf{K}_i,\mathbf{L}_i$, respectively. Using the notations and the results of (A17) and (A18), the distance between lines yields:

$$E_{line}(\cdot)=\left\|\mathbf{K}_{P,i}(j)-\mathbf{L}_{P,i}(j))+\frac{(be-cd)\mathbf{K}_{D,i}(j)-(ae-bd)\mathbf{L}_{D,i}(j)}{ac-b^2}\right\|^2$$

where $j=1,2,3$. The direction error can be calculated as the angle between direction vectors of the lines

$$E_{angle}(\cdot)=\arccos^2\left(\frac{\mathbf{K}_{D,i}^T\mathbf{L}_{D,i}}{\left\|\mathbf{K}_{D,i}\right\|\left\|\mathbf{L}_{D,i}\right\|}\right)$$

The suitably weighted sum of these error functions are minimized with a Levenberg-Marquardt nonlinear least squared optimizer.

Verification with collineation

In the developed object recognition system the output of the query is an ordered (matched) feature set (corresponding configurations). Initially these configurations contain only as many (minimum number) of features as required by indexing. During the verification process a 3D homogeneous transformation (collineation) is calculated (as described previously), that maps projective coordinates of the scene features into the Euclidean space of the candidate object. Checking those remaining object features that are not yet on the candidate list, corresponding scene features are searched (closest mapped scene feature, within a given distance threshold). If a sufficient pair is found, it is appended onto the support list of the given configuration. If the number of supports is above a limit, the whole transformation is stored for final consolidation processing.

3.5 Consolidation

Taking the space of the **h** vectors produced from the calculated collineation matrices in the verification case, the values are different due to the following effects.

- Numerical differences between the calculated values of the same object-scene transformation caused by noise and other disturbance effects. This causes (small) variations around the true value of the transformation.
- Object-scene transformation using different objects: the collineation that describes the mapping between the Euclidean frame attached to the object in database and the common projective frame in the scene is object specific. This could yield significantly different transformations. Note, that searching for a given collineation, other valid collineation data behaves as outlier (pseudo-outlier, see: (Wang & Suter, 2004))

- Outliers yielded by invalid object-scene matching (real outliers). This effect can cause
  - significantly different values scattered randomly in the space
  - accidentally occurrence nearby a valid transformation

Therefore the consolidation of the collineations is required. This could be achieved using a clustering. The requirements for this method are:

- Determine the valid collineations from the voting space (determination of the cluster centers). Note, that regarding to the experiments the form of the clusters are not (hyper)spherical.
- Detect the valid (possible more than one) collineation(s) in the voting space. This requires that the method be able to handle multiple structures.
- Eliminate or tolerate the effect of outliers. Note that in extreme cases the total percentage of real and pseudo outliers could be above 50%.
- Must be able to handle higher dimensional data (the 3D collineation yields 16-dimensional vectors).

Usually the clustering problems are solved with k-means clustering method, but the application of this method in the consolidation phase in not possible, because the number of clusters (valid object-scene transformations) is not known in advance. There are many clustering algorithms that can solve this problem, for example MUSE (Miller & Stewart, 1996), MDPE (Wang & Suter, 2004), FAMS (Georgescu et al., 2003), NDD clustering (Zhang et al., 2007).

In the developed system two nonparametric clustering methods have been used, FAMS and NDD clustering. The FAMS is an iterative clustering method that estimates the densest regions (modes) of the multivariate space. The NDD clustering method is a noniterative algorithm that is capable to estimate shape free clusters based on the normalized density derivative of the multivariate space. The output of both algorithms is the clusterized data space formed from the collineations. The individual collineation estimates are extracted from each cluster by checking the errors of the collineations to the support feature pairs (original object and transformed scene features). After the determination of the clusters (the valid member collineations of each cluster), the transformations are upgraded using the data of the members only (refinement).

4. Euclidean reconstruction

In a typical robot control system metrical information (e.g. distance between the gripper and the object) is required, hence the Euclidean update of the projective reconstruction must be achieved. Taking the projection equation for points (without indices) $\rho\mathbf{q} = \mathbf{PQ}$ it can be seen, that the result remains the same, if a collineation and its inverse is applied to this equation, namely $\rho\mathbf{q} = \left(\mathbf{PH}^{-1}\right)\left(\mathbf{HQ}\right)$. The same is true for lines. In order to select the metric information ($\mathbf{Q}$ contains Euclidean coordinates) from the many possible projective solutions, the value of $\mathbf{H}$ must be fixed. The method must avoid the sensitive camera calibration during the reconstruction of scene.

The developed method uses a-priori information, namely known 3D Euclidean data from object database that can be used together with the projective reconstruction to determine relative position and orientation between recognized objects.

As described earlier, in order to achieve the object recognition tasks, the used information about objects are stored in object database. The entries in the database consist of indices (created from invariants) and attributes. These attributes contain the coordinates of the 3D features of the objects, stored in object dependent (attached) metric coordinate system. There could be many source of information, for example CAD systems, processed range images (acquired by calibrated laser range sensors) or the applied stereo camera system itself is also capable to produce metric 3D information for object database using calibrated reconstruction. In this latter case, unlike during the free scene reconstruction, the cameras are calibrated and fixed, the objects are shown in prepared environment one-by-one.

4.1 Transformation decomposition

The coordinates of the features of the recognized objects are known in two coordinate systems, see Fig. 4:

- Common projective frame of the scene, in this coordinate system every feature is described with its projective coordinates. This system is common for every object in the scene though it contains no Euclidean information. The projective information of the features is the output of the projective reconstruction.
- Euclidean frame of an object (attached to the object) as stored in the object database. This information is object dependent and contains metrical data. Every object has its own Euclidean frame.

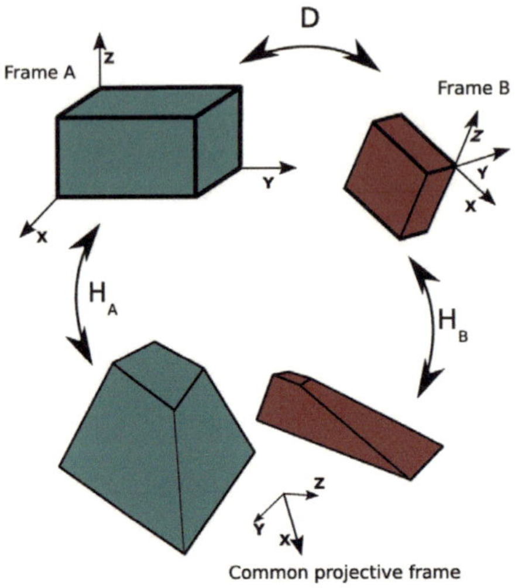

Fig. 4. Coordinate frames used during the calculation of the Euclidean transformation

Using this twofold description of the recognized features makes it possible to determine the relative Euclidean transformation (position, orientation) between object frames as occurs in the scene. If one of the frames is absolute (known in world reference frame), then it is possible to describe the scene in the absolute Euclidean coordinate frame.
The candidate collineations between the common projective frame of the scene and the local frame of the recognized objects are already determined as the output of verification step of the object recognition. From the members of the given cluster in consolidation the collineation is updated from the candidates, therefore this is the most accurate estimation that is available. But there exists no internal constraint that could be applied to the elements

of the collineation during projective reconstruction. This means that the elements depend only on the data from which they are estimated, there is no inter-dependency between elements.
However the calculation of the Euclidean transformation between objects allows introducing such additional constraints. Let the collineations of two recognized objects be $\mathbf{H}_A$ and $\mathbf{H}_B$, respectively. Let us suppose, that the collineations describe the mapping from scene frame into Euclidean object frames. In this case the displacement that describes the mapping from metric frame of the object *A* into metric frame of object *B*, can be calculated as $\mathbf{D} = \left(\mathbf{H}_B^{-1}\right)\mathbf{H}_A$. But matrix $\mathbf{D}_{4\times 4} = s\begin{pmatrix} \mathbf{\Omega} & \mathbf{t} \\ \mathbf{z}^T & 1 \end{pmatrix}$ describes a metric (Euclidean) transformation, therefore there are some constraints that must be fulfilled:

- $\mathbf{\Omega}$ should be a rotation matrix
  - Orthogonality condition: $\mathbf{\Omega}\mathbf{\Omega}^T = \mathbf{\Omega}^T\mathbf{\Omega} = \mathbf{I}$
  - Non-reflection condition: $|\mathbf{\Omega}| = +1$
- The $\left\|\mathbf{z}^T\right\|^2 = 0$
- The value of s should not be too small or too large (valid scaling)

Due to noise and other disturbances the matrix $\mathbf{\Omega}$ is not a rotation matrix. The aim is to determine the "closest" rotation matrix $\mathbf{R}$ to matrix $\mathbf{\Omega}$. Find $\mathbf{R}$ minimizing $\|\mathbf{R} - \mathbf{\Omega}\|_F^2$ such that $\mathbf{R}^T\mathbf{R} - \mathbf{I} = \mathbf{0}$ and $|\mathbf{R}| = +1$, where $\|\cdot\|_F$ denotes the vector compatible Frobenius norm of the matrix.
The solution can be found factorizing the matrix $\mathbf{\Omega}$. The possible (most commonly used) matrix factorization algorithms that yield orthogonal matrix are the following:

- Singular Value Decomposition (SVD) gives $\mathbf{\Omega} = \mathbf{U}\mathbf{\Lambda}\mathbf{V}^{\mathrm{T}}$ where $\mathbf{U}$ and $\mathbf{V}$ are orthogonal matrices. The drawbacks of the algorithm are:
  - Small perturbation could yield very different orthogonal factorization (though the singular values remain stable).
  - Theoretically there are infinite many ways as a rotation matrix can be composed from two other rotations.
- QR decomposition gives $\mathbf{\Omega} = \mathbf{Q}\mathbf{R}$, where $\mathbf{Q}$ is an orthogonal and $\mathbf{R}$ is a lower-triangular matrix, respectively. The drawback is that the given orthogonal matrix is basis-dependent.
- Polar decomposition gives $\mathbf{\Omega} = \mathbf{R}\mathbf{S}$, where $\mathbf{R}$ is an orthogonal and $\mathbf{S}$ is a symmetric positive definite matrix, see (A21) and (A22) in Appendix. If $|\mathbf{R}| = -1$ (reflection included), then the decomposition can be written into the form: $\mathbf{\Omega} = (-\mathbf{R})(-\mathbf{I})\mathbf{S}$

Using the polar decomposition let the original displacement matrix be factorized into the form:

$$\mathbf{D}_{4\times 4} = s\underbrace{\begin{pmatrix} \mathbf{I} & \mathbf{0} \\ \mathbf{x}^T & 1 \end{pmatrix}}_{\mathbf{P}}\underbrace{\begin{pmatrix} \mathbf{I} & \mathbf{t} \\ \mathbf{0}^T & 1 \end{pmatrix}}_{\mathbf{T}}\underbrace{\begin{pmatrix} \mathbf{R} & \mathbf{0} \\ \mathbf{0}^T & 1 \end{pmatrix}}_{\mathbf{\Theta}}\underbrace{\begin{pmatrix} \mathbf{V} & \mathbf{0} \\ \mathbf{0}^T & 1 \end{pmatrix}}_{\mathbf{\Delta}}\underbrace{\begin{pmatrix} \mathbf{S} & \mathbf{0} \\ \mathbf{0}^T & 1 \end{pmatrix}}_{\mathbf{\Sigma}}$$

where s is a scale, the matrices are responsible for perspectivity $(\mathbf{P})$, translation $(\mathbf{T})$, rotation $(\mathbf{\Theta})$, mirroring $(\mathbf{\Delta})$ and stretch (transformed shear, $\mathbf{\Sigma}$), respectively.

Using the above decomposition the constraints can be expressed as the limit on physically meaningful quantities.

- The perspectivity must be an identity matrix, this means that $\left\| \mathbf{x}^T \right\|^2 = 0$.
- The mirroring must be an identity matrix: $\mathbf{V} = \mathbf{I}$.
- The stretch must be an identity matrix: $\mathbf{S} = \mathbf{I}$ or in a more general case a diagonal matrix, yielding isotropically or anisotropically scaled Euclidean transformation.
- The value of s should not be too small or too large (valid scaling).

The translational part $\mathbf{t}$ is unconstrained.

The output of the algorithm is the Euclidean (metric) transformation between the two reference frames of the objects A and B, that describes the relative position and orientation between two recognized objects. This information can be directly used in a robot control system.

5. Results

The developed system was tested against simulated and real data. The accuracy of the algorithm was tested with simple simulated scenes, where the precise value of the data is known. In the reconstrcution part, the base of the evaluation criteria is the reprojection error. For points this is the distance between the true (original) and the reprojected 2D coordinates. In case of lines, the reprojection error consists of two parts, the angle between the original 2D line and the reprojected line, and a distance as the maximum of distances of the endpoints of the original line segments from reprojected line. Result of the simulations shows that the accuracy of the reconstruction depends approximately linearly on the noise added to position of the detected 2D features, Fig. 5.

A sample image from the sequence overlaid with reconstructed features can be seen in Fig. 6. The original images are 1024x1024 in size, the images of the reconstructed points are denoted with dark crosses, the lines are drawn with white.

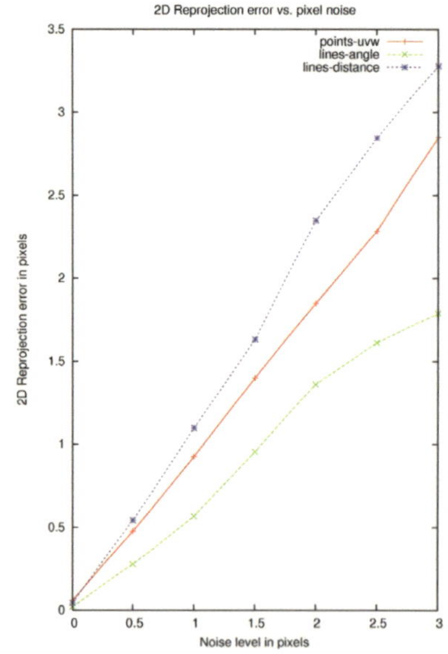

Fig. 5. Reprojection error of projective reconstruction as the function of noise level

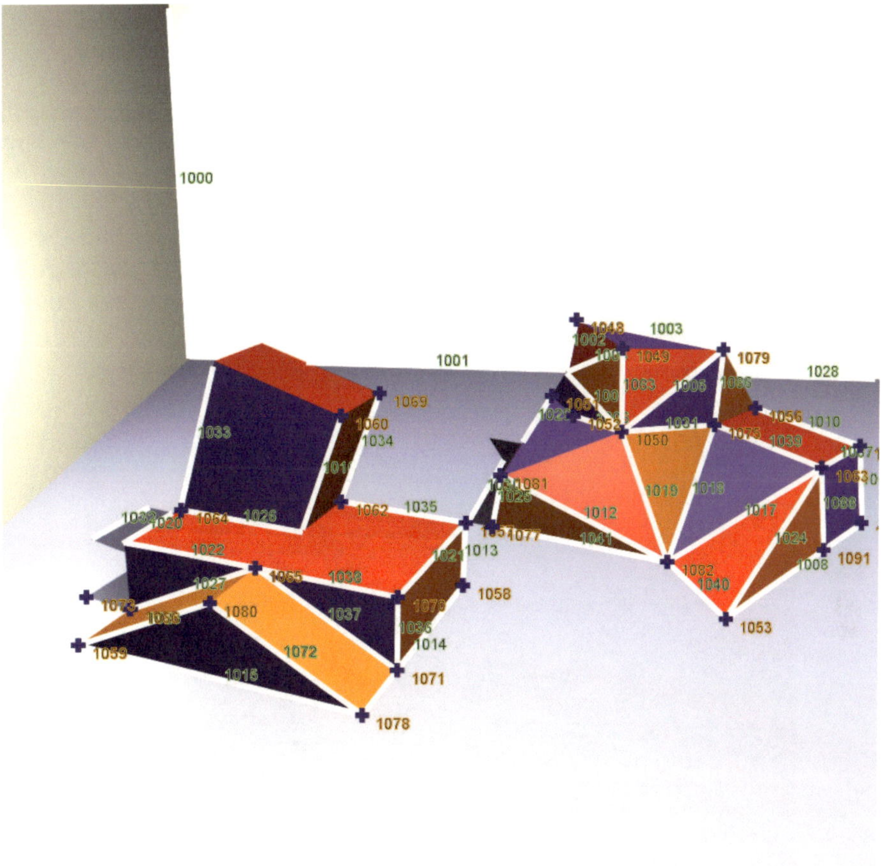

Fig. 6. A sample image of the simulated scene used during the numerical experiments

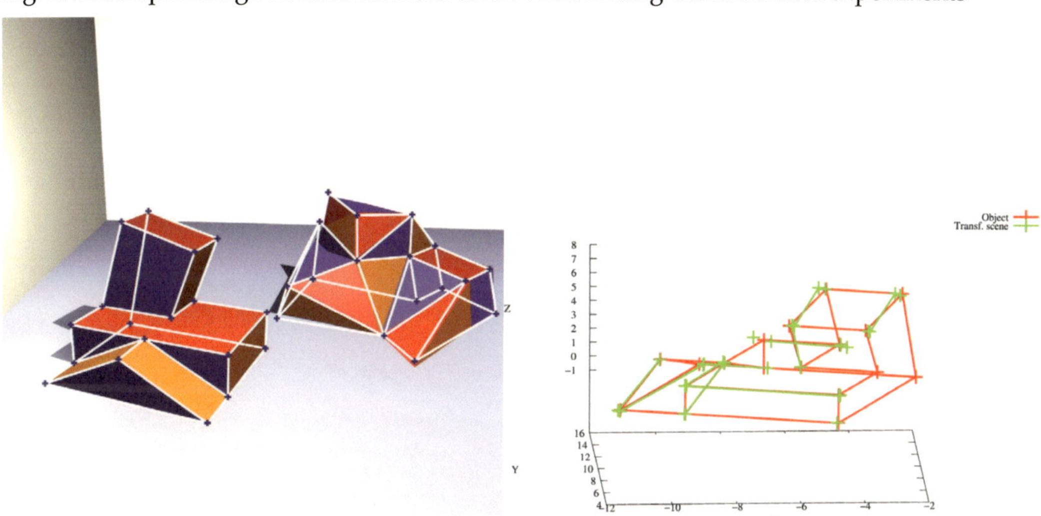

Fig. 7. Result of the object recognition using simulated scene

Checking the numerical results, the errors between the original (detected by a feature detector) and the reprojected (estimated) image features are in the range 0…3 pixels for points, the angle error between lines are in the range 0..5 degree.
The quality of the reconstruction depends on i) the accuracy of the matching algorithm, but outliers produced by false matches are eliminated using the robust version of the reconstruction; ii) the relative placement of the cameras, e.g. image sequence taken by cameras moving linearly away from the scene yields poor results.
Fig. 7 shows the result of the recognition of the simple scene. On the left side, the features stored in the database are overlaid onto one of the image used in the reconstruction. The right side shows (from a new viewpoint) the alignment of the object features (red) as stored in the database and the transformed scene features (green).

Fig. 8. Result of the projective reconstruction overlaid onto a real scene image

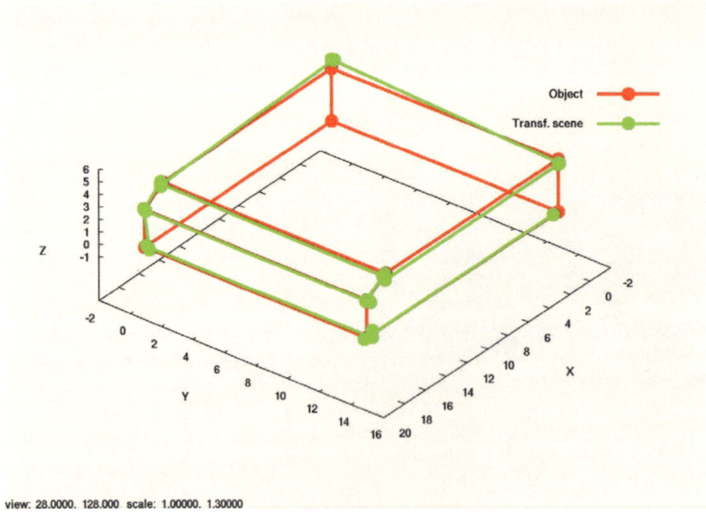

Fig. 9. Feature alignment on the recognized object from real scene

The accuracy of the displacement calculation is also checked during simulations. The experiments show, that the translation error remains within 3% range of the original scene size, the rotation error (in Euler form) is within -3…3 degree.
The algorithm was also tested with real data in order to demonstrate its applicability. Fig. 8 shows the features from the projective reconstruction. The alignment of the features on the recognized object is presented in Fig. 9.

6. Conclusion

The chapter describes a 3D projective reconstruction algorithm and its application in an object recognition system. The process first recovers the projective structure of the scene from 2D feature correspondences between images, then uses projective invariants to recognize known object(s) in the scene. Using the metric information attached to the objects in the database the system is able to determine the Euclidean structure of the scene and calculate the relative position and orientation between recognized objects.
The novelties of the presented system appear on three levels. First, both of the reconstruction methods are iterative, but the calculation can be achieved in closed form inside every iteration step because of separation of the unknown parameters. In order to handle point and line features together, geometric constraints are used in the error function to be minimized. Both of the algorithms can handle missing features (one or more features cannot be seen on one or more views). The output of the projective reconstruction is 3D projective information about the scene, namely homogeneous coordinates of point and line features.
Second, the object recognition method uses indexing based on permutation and projection invariants. For different combinations of point and line features the generalized (higher dimensional) cross ratios (invariants against projective transformations) are determined. These values are mapped with a novel, stereographic based transformation and a periodic function to eliminate the effect of permutation of features inside the cross ratios. A new collineation based verification process was developed to eliminate false positive object candidates.
As a final step, the system determines closest Euclidean transformation decomposing the nearly metric collineation between the recognized objects. This transformation is calculated from the collineations describing the mapping from the projective scene into the metric coordinate system attached to each of the object.
The further development of the system can be the inclusion of 2D imaging information beside projective invariants into the object recognition. This could reduce the computational complexity by selecting a region of interest and supporting feature selection used in the indexing. This also improves the selectivity of the recognition algorithm and eliminates false matches. The current implementation needs the choice of a large number of parameters. Another research direction is the automatisation of their selection for typical application in robotics.

7. Appendix

Points, lines, planes and transformations in projective spaces

A *point* in projective n-space P^n is given by a $(n+1)$-vector of coordinates $\mathbf{x}=(x_1,\dots,x_{n+1})^T$. At least one of these coordinates should differ from zero. These coordinates are called *homogeneous* coordinates. Two points represented by the vectors $\mathbf{x}$ and $\mathbf{y}$ are equal iff there exists a nonzero scalar λ such that $x_i = \lambda y_i$, for every i $(1 \le i \le n+1)$. This will be indicated by $\mathbf{x} \sim \mathbf{y}$.

A *collineation* from P^m to P^n is a mapping represented by a $(m+1)\times(n+1)$ matrix $\mathbf{H}$ by which points are transformed linearly: $\mathbf{x} \mapsto \mathbf{x}' \sim \mathbf{Hx}$.

In the projective plane P^2 points are denoted by the 3-vector $\mathbf{q} = (x, y, w)^T$. A *line* $\mathbf{l}$ is also denoted by a 3-vector. A point $\mathbf{q}$ is on the line $\mathbf{l}$ iff $\mathbf{l}^T\mathbf{q} = 0$. In this sense points and lines in P^2 are dual entities. A line $\mathbf{l}$ passing through the points $\mathbf{q}_1$ and $\mathbf{q}_2$ is given by $\mathbf{l} \sim \mathbf{q}_1 \times \mathbf{q}_2$.

In the 3D projective space P^3 *points* are denoted by the 4-vector $\mathbf{Q} = (X, Y, Z, W)^T$. In P^3 the dual entity of the point is the *plane*, which is also denoted by a 4-vector. A point $\mathbf{Q}$ is located on the plane $\mathbf{\Pi}$ iff $\mathbf{\Pi}^T\mathbf{Q} = 0$. A 3D line $\mathbf{L}$ can be given by the linear combination of two points $\lambda_1\mathbf{Q}_1 + \lambda_2\mathbf{Q}_2$ or by the intersection of two planes $\mathbf{\Pi}_1 \cap \mathbf{\Pi}_2$.

Transformations in the images are represented by *homographies* of $P^2 \to P^2$. A homography is represented by a 3×3 matrix $\mathbf{H}$. Again $\mathbf{H}$ and $\lambda\mathbf{H}$ represents the same homography. A point is transformed as $\mathbf{q} \mapsto \mathbf{q}' \sim \mathbf{Hq}$. Points and lines are transformed according to

$$\mathbf{q} \mapsto \mathbf{q}' \sim \mathbf{Hq} \text{ and } \mathbf{l} \mapsto \mathbf{l}' \sim \mathbf{H}^{-T}\mathbf{l}. \tag{A1}$$

Similar reasoning gives in 3D space P^3 the following equations for transformations of points and planes by a 4×4 matrix:

$$\mathbf{T} : \mathbf{Q} \mapsto \mathbf{Q}' \sim \mathbf{TQ} \text{ and } \mathbf{\Pi} \mapsto \mathbf{\Pi}' \sim \mathbf{T}^{-T}\mathbf{\Pi}. \tag{A2}$$

Plücker representation of lines

Let the points $\mathbf{Q}_1 = (X_1, Y_1, Z_1, W_1)^T = (\mathbf{X}_1, W_1)^T$ and $\mathbf{Q}_2 = (X_2, Y_2, Z_2, W_2)^T = (\mathbf{X}_2, W_2)^T$ define the line $\mathbf{L}$ in 3D projective space P^3. The *Plücker representation* of the line is given by the direction of the line $W_1\mathbf{X}_2 - W_2\mathbf{X}_1 =: \mathbf{L}_D$ and the normal of the plane spanned by the vectors $\mathbf{X}_1 \times \mathbf{X}_2 =: \mathbf{L}_O$. The Plücker representation is a 6-vector satisfying

$$\mathbf{L} := (\mathbf{L}_D^T, \mathbf{L}_O^T)^T =: (L_1, L_2, L_3, L_4, L_5, L_6)^T \tag{A3}$$

$$\mathbf{L}_D^T \cdot \mathbf{L}_O = L_1L_4 + L_2L_5 + L_3L_6 = \frac{1}{2}(\mathbf{L}_D^T, \mathbf{L}_O^T)\begin{pmatrix} \mathbf{0}_{3\times 3} & \mathbf{I}_{3\times 3} \\ \mathbf{I}_{3\times 3} & \mathbf{0}_{3\times 3} \end{pmatrix}\begin{pmatrix} \mathbf{L}_D \\ \mathbf{L}_O \end{pmatrix} =: \frac{1}{2}\mathbf{L}^T\mathbf{\Delta}\mathbf{L} = 0. \tag{A4}$$

The *Plücker matrix* $\mathbf{\Lambda}$ of the line is the skew-symmetric matrix

$$\mathbf{\Lambda} := \mathbf{Q}_1\mathbf{Q}_2^T - \mathbf{Q}_2\mathbf{Q}_1^T \sim \begin{pmatrix} [\mathbf{L}_O]_\times & \mathbf{L}_D \\ -\mathbf{L}_D^T & \mathbf{0} \end{pmatrix} \tag{A5}$$

Point and line projection matrices
The projection matrix for points is given as $\mathbf{q} \sim \mathbf{PQ}$ where

$$\mathbf{P}_{3\times4} = \left(\mathbf{\Pi}_{3\times3}\ \mathbf{p}_{3\times1}\right). \tag{A6}$$

Let $\mathbf{l}$ be the projection of the 3D line $\mathbf{L}$ and $\mathbf{q}_1,\mathbf{q}_2$ be the projections of the points $\mathbf{Q}_1 = (\mathbf{X}_1^T, W_1)^T$, $\mathbf{Q}_2 = (\mathbf{X}_2^T, W_2)^T$ defining the 3D line. Then $\mathbf{l} \sim \mathbf{q}_1 \times \mathbf{q}_2 \sim (\mathbf{PQ}_1)\times(\mathbf{PQ}_2)$ and the projection of the line can be written as $\mathbf{l} \sim \mathbf{q}_1 \times \mathbf{q}_2 = \mathbf{GL}$ and

$$\mathbf{G} = \left([\mathbf{p}]_\times \mathbf{\Pi} \quad |\mathbf{\Pi}|\mathbf{\Pi}^{-T}\right) \tag{A7}$$

is the line projection matrix.
Line on a plane in 3D
Plane:

$$Ax + By + Cz + D = 0 \rightarrow \mathbf{S} = (A,B,C,D)^T = (\mathbf{A}^T\ D)^T \tag{A8}$$

Line in Plücker representation:

$$\mathbf{L} := (\mathbf{L}_D^T, \mathbf{L}_O^T)^T \tag{A9}$$

Intersection point:

$$\underbrace{\begin{pmatrix} -D\mathbf{I}_{3\times3} & [\mathbf{A}]_\times \\ \mathbf{A}^T & \mathbf{0}_{1\times3} \end{pmatrix}}_{\mathbf{U(S)}} \underbrace{\begin{pmatrix} \mathbf{L}_D \\ \mathbf{L}_O \end{pmatrix}}_{\mathbf{L}} =: \mathbf{U(S)L} \tag{A10}$$

Line on the plain:

$$\mathbf{L} \subset \mathbf{S} \Leftrightarrow \mathbf{U(S)L} = 0 \tag{A11}$$

Cross ratio and generalizations
Let $\mathbf{M}$ and $\mathbf{N}$ be two distinct points in n-dimensional projective space P^n. Any point on the line spanned by $\mathbf{M}$ and $\mathbf{N}$ can be parametrized as $\mathbf{Q} = \mu\mathbf{M} + \nu\mathbf{N}$ where (μ,ν) are the homogeneous coordinates of the point $\mathbf{Q}$ on the line. Let $\mathbf{Q}_i$, $i = 1,2,3,4$ be four ponts on the line spanned by $\mathbf{M}$ and $\mathbf{N}$ having homogeneous coordinates (μ_i,ν_i), $i = 1,2,3,4$, on the line. With the notation $\lambda_i = \mu_i / \nu_i$ the *cross ratio* of the four points on the line is defined as

$$\{\mathbf{Q}_1,\mathbf{Q}_2;\mathbf{Q}_3,\mathbf{Q}_4\} = \frac{\lambda_1-\lambda_3}{\lambda_1-\lambda_4} : \frac{\lambda_2-\lambda_3}{\lambda_2-\lambda_4} = \frac{\left(\frac{\mu_1}{\nu_1}-\frac{\mu_3}{\nu_3}\right)\left(\frac{\mu_2}{\nu_2}-\frac{\mu_4}{\nu_4}\right)}{\left(\frac{\mu_1}{\nu_1}-\frac{\mu_4}{\nu_4}\right)\left(\frac{\mu_2}{\nu_2}-\frac{\mu_3}{\nu_3}\right)} = \frac{\begin{vmatrix}\mu_1 & \mu_3 \\ \nu_1 & \nu_3\end{vmatrix}.\begin{vmatrix}\mu_2 & \mu_4 \\ \nu_2 & \nu_4\end{vmatrix}}{\begin{vmatrix}\mu_1 & \mu_4 \\ \nu_1 & \nu_4\end{vmatrix}.\begin{vmatrix}\mu_2 & \mu_3 \\ \nu_2 & \nu_3\end{vmatrix}} \tag{A12}$$

Since there are $4! = 24$ possible permutations of four points hence the six different values of the cross ratios are

$$\lambda_1 =: \lambda,\ \lambda_2 = 1-\lambda,\ \lambda_3 = 1/\lambda,\ \lambda_4 = 1/(1-\lambda),\ \lambda_5 = \lambda/(\lambda-1),\ \lambda_6 = (\lambda-1)/\lambda \tag{A13}$$

The concept of cross ratio in determinant form makes it possible to introduce higher dimensional invariants based on the properties of determinants:
Multiplication with a scalar:

$$\left|\mathbf{Q}_1 \ldots \alpha\mathbf{Q}_2 \ldots \mathbf{Q}_n\right| = \alpha\left|\mathbf{Q}_1 \ldots \mathbf{Q}_2 \ldots \mathbf{Q}_n\right| \tag{A14}$$

Multiplication with a matrix:

$$\left|\mathbf{T}\mathbf{Q}_1 \ldots \mathbf{T}\mathbf{Q}_2 \ldots \mathbf{T}\mathbf{Q}_n\right| = \left|\mathbf{T}\right| \cdot \left|\mathbf{Q}_1 \ldots \mathbf{Q}_2 \ldots \mathbf{Q}_n\right| \tag{A15}$$

Similarly to the 1D case, the ratio of products of determinants is invariant to projective transformation (multiplication with a nonzero scalar and/or matrix), if each $\mathbf{Q}_i$ occures as often in the numerator as in the denominator, because the effect of α's and $\mathbf{T}$'s cancels each other, respectively.

Distance between 3D lines

Let $\mathbf{P}(s) = \mathbf{K}_0 + s\mathbf{u}$ and $\mathbf{Q}(t) = \mathbf{L}_0 + t\mathbf{v}$ be two 3D lines in general situation then their transversal $\mathbf{D}(s,t) = \mathbf{D}_0 + s\mathbf{u} - t\mathbf{v}$ is orthoganal to both lines, where $\mathbf{D}_0 = \mathbf{K}_0 - \mathbf{L}_0$, and is the solution of the constrained optimum problem

$$\min_{s,t} \left\|\mathbf{D}(s,t)\right\|_2^2, \; <\mathbf{u}, \mathbf{D}(s,t)> = 0, \; <\mathbf{v}, \mathbf{D}(s,t)> = 0 \tag{A16}$$

Let $a = <\mathbf{u},\mathbf{u}>, b = <\mathbf{u},\mathbf{v}>, c = <\mathbf{v},\mathbf{v}>, d = <\mathbf{D}_0,\mathbf{u}>, e = <\mathbf{D}_0,\mathbf{v}>$, then the solution is

$$\begin{pmatrix} s_{\min} \\ t_{\min} \end{pmatrix} = \frac{1}{ac - b^2}\begin{pmatrix} c & b \\ b & a \end{pmatrix}\begin{pmatrix} -d \\ e \end{pmatrix} = \frac{1}{ac - b^2}\begin{pmatrix} be - cd \\ ae - bd \end{pmatrix} \tag{A17}$$

$$\min\left\|\mathbf{D}(s,t)\right\| = \left\|\mathbf{D}(s_{\min}, t_{\min})\right\| = \left\|\mathbf{D}_0 + \frac{(be - cd)\mathbf{u} - (ae - bd)\mathbf{v}}{ac - b^2}\right\| \tag{A18}$$

Polar decomposition

The polar decomposition problem can be formulated as given $\mathbf{Q}$ find $\mathbf{R}$ such that

$$\min_{\mathbf{R}} \left\|\mathbf{R} - \mathbf{Q}\right\|_F^2, \; \mathbf{R}^T\mathbf{R} - \mathbf{I} = 0 \tag{A19}$$

where F denotes Frobenius norm $\mathbf{A} = (a_{ik}) \rightarrow \left\|\mathbf{A}\right\|_F^2 = \sum_i \sum_k a_{ik}^2 = trace(\mathbf{A}^T\mathbf{A})$. With the notations $\mathbf{R} = (\mathbf{r}_1 \; \mathbf{r}_2 \; \mathbf{r}_3)$ the constraint is equivalent to $\mathbf{r}_1^T\mathbf{r}_1 = 1$, $\mathbf{r}_1^T\mathbf{r}_2 = 0$, $\mathbf{r}_1^T\mathbf{r}_3 = 0$, $\mathbf{r}_2^T\mathbf{r}_2 = 1$, $\mathbf{r}_2^T\mathbf{r}_3 = 0$, $\mathbf{r}_3^T\mathbf{r}_3 = 1$, therefore six Lagrange multiplicators $\lambda_{11}, \lambda_{12}, \lambda_{13}, \lambda_{22}, \lambda_{23}, \lambda_{33}$ are needed which can be collected in a *symmetric* matrix $\mathbf{\Lambda}$. Thus the solution yields:

$$\mathbf{R} - \mathbf{Q} + \mathbf{R}\mathbf{\Lambda} = 0 \Rightarrow \mathbf{R}\underbrace{(\mathbf{I} + \mathbf{\Lambda})}_{symmetric} = \mathbf{Q} = \mathbf{R}\mathbf{S} \Rightarrow \mathbf{R} = \mathbf{Q}\mathbf{S}^{-1} \tag{A20}$$

$$\mathbf{Q}^T\mathbf{Q} \xrightarrow{SVD} \mathbf{U}\mathbf{\Sigma}\mathbf{U}^T \longrightarrow \mathbf{S} = \mathbf{U}\mathbf{\Sigma}^{1/2}\mathbf{U}^T \longrightarrow \mathbf{R} = \mathbf{Q}\mathbf{S}^{-1} = \mathbf{Q}\mathbf{U}\mathbf{\Sigma}^{-1/2}\mathbf{U}^T \tag{A21}$$

$$\mathbf{Q} \xrightarrow{SVD} \mathbf{U\Sigma V}^T \longrightarrow \mathbf{Q} = (\mathbf{UV}^T)(\mathbf{V\Sigma V}^T) = \mathbf{RS} \quad \text{(A22)}$$

Norm square minimization under constraint
The problem to be solved is given by

$$\min_{\mathbf{x}} \|\mathbf{Ax}\|_2^2 \text{ subject to } \|\mathbf{x}\|^2 = 1 \quad \text{(A23)}$$

and its solution can be determined using eigenvalue technique or SVD:

$$\lambda \text{ is the minimal eigenvalue of } \mathbf{A}^T\mathbf{A}\text{, } \mathbf{x} \text{ is the unit norm eigenvector to } \lambda \quad \text{(A24)}$$

$$\mathbf{A} \xrightarrow{SVD} \mathbf{A} = \mathbf{U\Sigma V}^T \rightarrow \text{ first column } \mathbf{v}_1 \text{ of } \mathbf{V} \rightarrow \mathbf{x} = \mathbf{v}_1 / \|\mathbf{v}_1\|, \ \min\|\mathbf{Ax}\|_2^2 = \sigma_1^2 \quad \text{(A25)}$$

8. Acknowledgement

Support for the research was provided by the Hungarian National Research Programs under grant No. OTKA K 71762 and NKTH RET 04/2004, and by the Control Systems Research Group of the Hungarian Academy of Sciences.

9. References

Armangué, X.; Pagés, J.; Salvi, J. & Batlle, J. (2001). Comparative Survey on Fundamental Matrix Estimation. *Simposium Nacional de Reconocimiento de Formas y Anáalisis de Imágenes*, Castellon (Spain)

Belhumeur, P.N.; Hespanha, J. & Kriegman, D.J. (1997). Eigenfaces vs. Fisherfaces: Recognition Using Class Specific Linear Projection. *IEEE Transactions on Pattern Analysis and Machine Intelligence*, Vol. 19, No. 7, pp. 711-720

Berchtold, S.; Keim, D.A. & Kriegel, H. (1996). The X-tree: An Index Structure for High-Dimensional Data. *VLDB96*, Bombay, India, pp. 28-39

Boufama, B.; Mohr, R. & Veillon, F. (1993). Euclidean Constraints for Uncalibrated Reconstruction. *Proceedings of the 4 the International Conference on Computer Vision*, Berlin Germany), pp. 466-470, May 1993

Csurka, G. & Faugeras, O.D. (1999). Algebraic and Geometric Tools to Compute Projective and Permutation Invariants. *IEEE Transactions on Pattern Analysis and Machine Intelligence*, Vol. 21, No. 1., pp. 58-65

Faugeras, O.D. & Mourrain, B. (1995). On the Geometry and Algebra of the Point and Line Correspondences Between N Images. *Rapport de recherche 2665*, INRIA, Sophia-Antipolis

Faugeras, O. (1995). Stratification of 3-D vision: Projective, Affine and Metric Representations. *Journal of the Optical Society of America, A*, Vol. 12, No. 3, pp. 465-484

Georgescu, B.; Shimshoni, I. & Meer, P. (2003). Mean shift based clustering in high dimensions: a texture classification example. *Proceedings 9th IEEE Int. Conf. on Computer Vision*, Vol. 1, pp. 456-463

Han, M. & Kanade, T. (2000). Creating 3D Models with Uncalibrated Cameras. *Proceeding of IEEE Computer Society Workshop on the Application of Computer Vision WACV2000*, December 2000.

Hartley, R.I. (1992). Invariants of points seen in multiple images. *Technical Report, G.E. CRD*, Schenectady, http://users.rsise.anu.edu.au/~hartley/Papers/invariant/inv2.pdf

Hartley, R.I. (1993). Euclidean reconstruction from uncalibrated views, *In J. Mundy, A. Zisserman (Eds.), Applications of Invariance in Computer Vision, Lecture Notes in Computer Science, 825*, Springer, Berlin, pp. 237-256

Hartley R.I. & Sturm P. (1997). Triangulation. *Computer Vision and Image Understanding*, Vol. 68, No. 2, pp. 146-157

Kaminski J.Y. & Shashua A. (2004) Multiple view geometry of general algebraic curves. *International Journal of Computer Vision*, Vol. 56. pp 195-219, February 2004

Meer, P.; Lenz, R. & Ramakrishna, S. (1998). Efficient Invariant Representations. *Int. J. of Computer Vision*, Vol. 26, Issue 2., pp 137-152

Mikolajczyk, K. & Schmid, C. (2005). A performance evaluation of local descriptors. *IEEE Transactions on Pattern Analysis and Machine Intelligence*, Vol. 27, No. 10, pp. 1615-1630

Miller, J.V. & Stewart, C.V. (1996). MUSE: Robust surface fitting using unbiased scale estimates. *Proceedings IEEE Conference on Computer Vision and Pattern Recognition*, pp. 300-306

Moenne-Loccoz, N. (2005). High-Dimensional Access Methods for Efficient Similarity Queries. *Technical Report, Computer Vision Group, Computing Science Center, University of Geneva*, Switzerland, http://vision.unige.ch/~moennen/publi/moennen_tech0505.pdf

Quan, L. (1995). Invariants of Six Points and Projective Reconstruction From Three Uncalibrated Images. *IEEE Trans. on Pattern Analysis and Machine Intelligence*, Vol. 17, No. 1. pp. 34-46

Schiffenbauer, R.D. (2001). A Survey of Aspect Graphs. *Technical Report*, 2001 http://cis.poly.edu/tr/tr-cis-2001-01.htm

Tél, F. & Tóth, E. (2000). Stereo image processing and virtual reality in an intelligent robot control system. *Journal of Intelligent Robotic Systems*, Kluwer Academic Publishers, Vol. 27, pp. 113-134

Tél, F. & Lantos, B. (2007). Projective reconstruction for robot vision system. *Proceedings IEEE 3rd International Conference on Mechatronics (ICM)*, Budapest (Hungary), pp. 357-362, ISBN 1-4244-9712-6

Torr, P. & Zisserman, A. (1997). Robust parameterization and computation of the trifocal tensor. *Image and Vision Computing*, Vol. 15, pp. 591-605

Zhang, C.; Zhang, X.; Zhang, M.Q. & Li, Y. (2007). Neighbor Number, Valley Seeking and Clustering. *Pattern Recognition Letters*, Vol. 28, pp. 173-180

Wang, H. & Suter, D. (2004). MDPE: A Very Robust Estimator for Model Fitting and Range Image Segmentation. *International Journal of Computer Vision (IJCV)*, Vol. 59, No. 2, pp. 139-166

Wolfson, H.J. & Rigoutsos, I. (1997). Geometric Hashing: An Overview. *IEEE Computational Science & Engineering*, Vol. 4, No. 4, pp. 10-21

25

Vision-based Augmented Reality Applications

Yuko Uematsu and Hideo Saito
Keio University
Japan

1. Introduction

Augmented Reality (AR) is a technique for overlaying virtual objects onto the real world. AR has recently been applied to many kinds of entertainment applications by using visionbased tracking technique, such as [Klein & Drummond, 2004, Henrysson et al., 2005, Haller et al. 2005, Schmalstieg & Wagner, 2007, Looser et al. 2007]. AR can provide users with immersive feeling by allowing the interaction between the real and virtual world.
In the AR entertainment applications, virtual objects (world) generated with Computer Graphics are overlaid onto the real world. This means that the real 3D world is captured by a camera, and then the virtual objects are superimposed onto the captured images. By seeing the real world through some sort of displays, the users find that the virtual world is mixed with the real world. In such AR applications, the users carry a camera and move around the real world in order to change their view points. Therefore the pose and the position of the moving user's camera should be obtained so that the virtual objects can be overlaid at correct position in the real world according to the camera motion. Such camera tracking should also be performed in real-time for interactive operations of the AR applications.
Vision-based camera tracking for AR is one of the popular research areas because the visionbased method does not require any special device except cameras, in contrast with sensorbased approaches. And also, marker-based approach is a quite easy solution to make the vision-based tracking robust and running in real-time.
This chapter focuses on marker-based approach. Especially, "AR-Toolkit" [H. Kato & M. Billinghurst, 1999] is a very popular tool for implementing simple on-line AR applications. ARToolkit is a kind of planar square marker for the camera tracking and estimates the camera position and pose with respect to the marker. By using the camera position and pose, virtual objects are overlaid onto the images as if the objects exist in the real world where the marker is placed. Since the user only has to place the marker, this kind of marker-base registration is very easy to implement AR systems. If only one marker is utilized, however, the camera's movable area is limited so that the camera (user) can see the marker. Moreover, when the marker cannot be recognized properly because of a change in its visibility, the registration of the virtual objects is getting unstable. In order to solve such problems, using multiple markers is a popular way.
When multiple markers are utilized in a vision-based method, it is necessary to know the geometrical arrangement information of the marker such as their position and pose in advance. For example, the method in [Umlauf et al., 2002] requires the position and pose of a square marker. The method in [Kato et al., 2000] also needs the position of a point marker in advance. In [Genc et al., 2002], they proposed two-step approach; learning process and

marker-less registration method. In the learning process, the geometrical information of the markers is required for learning the markers. As shown in these methods, the task of measuring the marker arrangement information in advance is necessary for AR applications using a vision-based registration.

In most cases, multiple markers are usually aligned with ordered arrangement as shown in Fig. 1 because the users manually measure the geometrical arrangement of the markers. However such a measuring task is very time-consuming. Moreover, if the markers can not be distributed on the same plane, manual measuring becomes more difficult. Kotake et al. proposed a marker-calibration method which is a hybrid method combining the bundle adjustment method with some constraints on the marker arrangement obtained a priori (e.g. the multiple markers are located on a single plane) [Kotake et al., 2004]. Although a precise measurement of the markers is not required, a priori knowledge of the markers is necessary.

Fig. 1. Multiple markers aligned with ordered arrangement

In this chapter, a vision-based registration method using multiple planar markers placed at arbitrary positions and poses is introduced [Uematsu & Saito, 2005-b]. This method is extended from the method using multiple planar structures in the real world without geometrical arrangement information [Uematsu & Saito, 2005-a].

In the previous method using multiple markers, a projection matrix from the marker to the input image is computed from each marker and then all the matrices are merged by using the marker arrangement information. However, such prior knowledge about the arrangement is not utilized in this method. In order to merge the projection matrices computed from the markers, this method introduces "Projective Space" which is defined by projective reconstruction of two reference images. Since the Projective Space is defined by 2D coordinate systems of the images, the coordinate system of the Projective Space is independent of every marker's coordinate system. Therefore by estimating the marker arrangement through the Projective Space, the projection matrices computed from the marker are merged. This method allows the markers to be distributed at arbitrary positions and pose, since the marker arrangement can be estimated by captured images.

This chapter also introduces two AR applications for entertainment; AR Baseball Presentation System [Uematsu & Saito, 2006]; Interactive AR Bowling System [Uematsu & Saito, 2007]. These applications are used on the tabletop with a handheld monitor and a web-camera connected to a general PC. Since any special device is not required such as high-speed cameras, high-performance PC or physical sensors, these applications are available for home users.

In Section 2, the registration method using multiple planar markers with Projective Space is explained. In Section 3 and Section 4, AR Baseball Presentation System and Interactive AR Bowling System are introduced.

2. Multiple markers based AR via 3D projective space

2.1 Definition of coordinate systems

In this section, three kinds of coordinate systems and transformation matrices used in this method are explained. In the typical registration method, two coordinate systems are utilized, which represent the real world and the input image, respectively. On the other hand, this method uses three kinds of coordinate systems; marker's coordinate system defined for each marker, Projective Space and the input image as shown in Fig. 2.

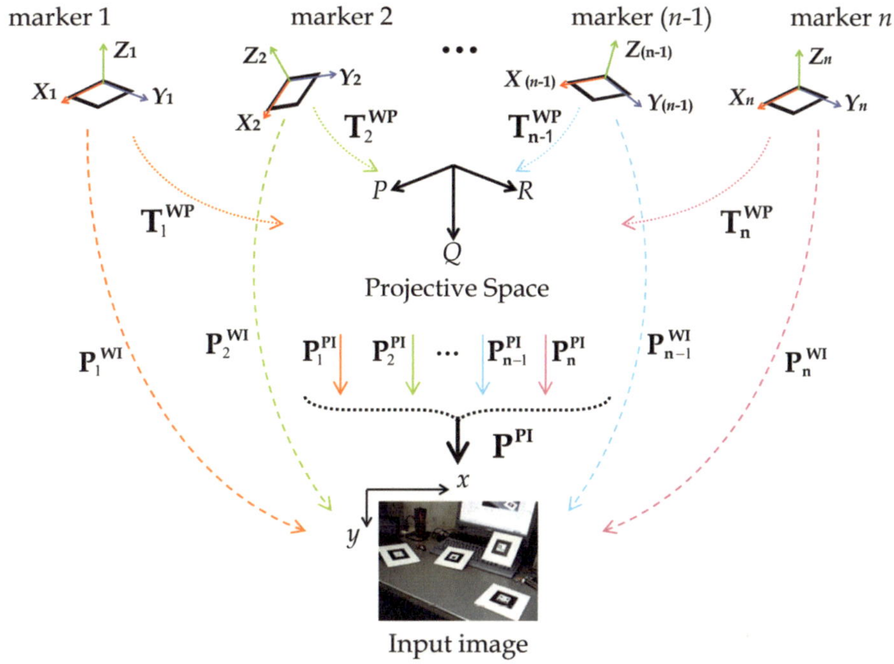

Fig. 2. Three kinds of coordinate systems in this method

(X_i-Y_i-Z_i) is a 3D coordinate system independently assigned to each marker plane *i*. (x-y) is a 2D coordinate system of the input image. Since the multiple markers are distributed in arbitrary positions and poses in the real world, the relationship among (X_i-Y_i-Z_i) is unknown. In order to estimate the relationship, we introduce "Projective Space" (*P*-*Q*-*R*) which is a kind of 3D non-Euclidean coordinate system defined by projective reconstruction [Hartley & Zisserman, 2000] of two images called "reference images". The reference images are captured from two different viewpoints.

As for transformation matrices, a transformation matrix $\mathbf{T}_i^{WP}$ which relates each marker *i* to the Projective Space is computed by corresponding points between each marker's coordinate system and the Projective Space. This matrix indirectly represents the geometrical relationship of the markers. A projection matrix $\mathbf{P}_i^{WI}$ which relates each marker *i* to the input image represents the camera's position and pose with respect to the marker. Therefore, it can be computed by marker tracking algorithm [H. Kato & M. Billinghurst, 1999] at every frame. Then a projection matrix $\mathbf{P}_i^{PI}$ which relates the Projective Space to the input image can be written as following equation.

$$\begin{bmatrix} x \\ y \\ 1 \end{bmatrix} \cong \mathbf{P}_{\mathrm{i}}^{\mathrm{WI}} \left(\mathbf{T}_{\mathrm{i}}^{\mathrm{WP}}\right)^{-1} \begin{bmatrix} P \\ Q \\ R \\ 1 \end{bmatrix} \cong \mathbf{P}_{\mathrm{i}}^{\mathrm{PI}} \begin{bmatrix} P \\ Q \\ R \\ 1 \end{bmatrix} \tag{1}$$

By using these coordinate systems, the geometrical relationship of the multiple markers is estimated, so that virtual objects can be overlaid onto the input image even though specific marker is not continuously detected in the input image sequence.

2.2 Registration algorithm of virtual objects with 3D projective space

For registration of virtual objects onto the real world, the virtual objects need to be defined in the 3D coordinate system of the real world. By computing the projection matrix from the real world to the input image at every frame, then, the virtual objects are projected onto the input image. In this way, the virtual objects are overlaid onto the real world.

In this method, the 3D coordinate system representing the real world corresponds to a marker's coordinate system. Therefore we select one marker plane as a base plane to define the virtual objects in the base marker's coordinate system. Then a projection matrix which relates the base marker to the input image has to be computed at every frame for overlaying the virtual objects.

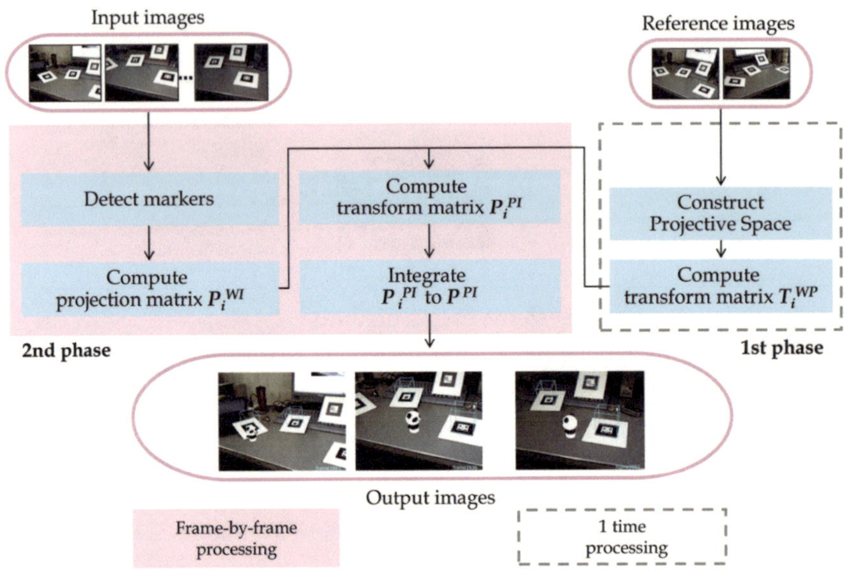

Fig. 3. Flowchart of this method

Fig. 3 shows the flowchart of this method. This method is divided into two phases. At the first phase, the projective space is constructed by two reference images. Then the transformation matrix $\mathbf{T}_{\mathrm{i}}^{\mathrm{WP}}$ of each marker i is computed by using corresponding points between each marker's coordinate system and the Projective Space. The first phase is performed just one time.

At the second phase, the projection matrix $\mathbf{P}_{\mathrm{i}}^{\mathrm{WI}}$ of each marker i is computed at every frame. Then the projection matrix $\mathbf{P}_{\mathrm{i}}^{\mathrm{PI}}$ for each marker is computed by eq. (1). Since all the matrices

$\mathbf{P}_i^{PI}$ represent the relationship between the Projective Space and the input image, all $\mathbf{P}_i^{PI}$ should coincide with each other and can be easily merged into one matrix in order to include the camera's position and pose from all the markers. However each $\mathbf{P}_i^{PI}$ may include computation errors. Therefore these matrices are merged into one projection matrix $\mathbf{P}^{PI}$ by least-square-method. By using the merged matrix $\mathbf{P}^{PI}$ and the transformation matrix $\mathbf{T}_i^{WP}$ of the base marker plane, the projection matrix from the base marker, in which the virtual objects are defined, to the input image is computed as following equation.

$$\mathbf{P}_{\text{base}} = \mathbf{P}^{PI}\mathbf{T}_{\text{base}}^{WP} \tag{2}$$

Finally, the virtual objects are overlaid onto the input image by $\mathbf{P}_{\text{base}}$. This matrix $\mathbf{P}_{\text{base}}$ includes the information from all the markers detected in the input image. Therefore as long as one marker is detected in the input image, the virtual objects can be overlaid onto the input image.

2.3 Constructing 3D projective space

3D Projective Space is used to estimate the geometrical relationship among the multiple planar markers which are distributed in arbitrary positions and poses. The Projective Space is defined by projective reconstruction of two reference images.

As shown in Fig. 6, the object scene is captured from two viewpoints. These captured images are called the reference image A and B, respectively. By using 2D coordinates (u_A, v_A) and (u_B, v_B) on the reference images, a 3D coordinate system (P-Q-R) is defined so that it has the following projective relationships with each of the reference images. This 3D coordinate system is called 3D Projective Space.

$$[u_A, v_A, 1]^T \cong \mathbf{P_A}[P, Q, R, 1]^T, \qquad [u_B, v_B, 1]^T \cong \mathbf{P_B}[P, Q, R, 1]^T \tag{3}$$

$$\mathbf{P_A} = [\mathbf{I} \mid \mathbf{0}]; \qquad \mathbf{P_B} = \left[-\frac{[\mathbf{e_B}]_\times \mathbf{F_{AB}}}{\|\mathbf{e_B}\|^2} \mid \mathbf{e_B} \right] \tag{4}$$

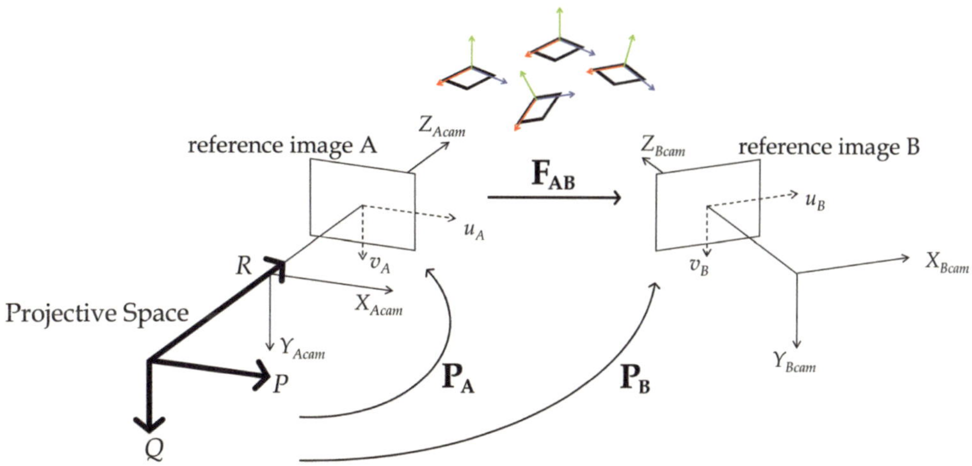

Fig. 4. Projective Space defined by two reference images

$\mathbf{F_{AB}}$ is a fundamental matrix from the image A to image B as shown in Fig. 4. $\mathbf{e_B}$ is an epipole on the image B, and $[\mathbf{e_B}]_\times$ is the skew-symmetric matrix of $\mathbf{e_B}$ [Hartley & Zisserman, 2000]. In this method, $\mathbf{F_{AB}}$ and $\mathbf{e_B}$ are computed by eight or more corresponding points between the reference images, which are detected by each marker. $\mathbf{P_A}$ and $\mathbf{P_B}$ are defined by eq. (4). Then 3D coordinates (P-Q-R) are computed by $\mathbf{P_A}$, $\mathbf{P_B}$ and 2D coordinates in the reference images when computing $\mathbf{T}_i^{\mathbf{WP}}$. The detail is described in the next section.

2.4 Computing $\mathbf{T}_i^{\mathbf{WP}}$

Since both of the marker's coordinate system (X_i-Y_i-Z_i) and the Projective Space (P-Q-R) are 3D coordinate systems, the transformation matrix $\mathbf{T}_i^{\mathbf{WP}}$ is a 4×4 matrix, which can be computed from five or more corresponding points between (X_i-Y_i-Z_i) and (P-Q-R).

We assume that a 3D point (X_i-Y_i-Z_i) is projected onto the reference image A and B as a 2D points (u_A, v_A) and (u_B, v_B), respectively. When these 2D points are projected into the Projective Space as a 3D point (P-Q-R), the relationship is as follows,

$$\begin{bmatrix} \mathbf{p}_\mathbf{A}^1 - u_A \mathbf{p}_\mathbf{A}^3 \\ \mathbf{p}_\mathbf{A}^2 - v_A \mathbf{p}_\mathbf{A}^3 \\ \mathbf{p}_\mathbf{B}^1 - u_B \mathbf{p}_\mathbf{B}^3 \\ \mathbf{p}_\mathbf{B}^2 - v_B \mathbf{p}_\mathbf{B}^3 \end{bmatrix} \begin{bmatrix} P \\ Q \\ R \\ 1 \end{bmatrix} = 0 \tag{5}$$

where, $\mathbf{p}_\mathbf{A}^k$ and $\mathbf{p}_\mathbf{B}^k$ are the kth row vectors of $\mathbf{P_A}$ and $\mathbf{P_B}$ in eq. (4). Then (P-Q-R) is computed by Singular Value Decomposition of the 4×4 matrix on the left-hand side of eq. (5). Therefore, the corresponding points (X_i-Y_i-Z_i) and (P-Q-R) are obtained through the 2D points (u_A, v_A) and (u_B, v_B) on the reference images.

As described before, five or more corresponding points are required to compute $\mathbf{T}_i^{\mathbf{WP}}$. In order to obtain the corresponding points, a cube is drawn on each marker in the reference image A and B as shown in Fig. 5. Since the size of the cube is already known, 3D coordinates (X_i-Y_i-Z_i) of the cube's vertices are known. By using (u_A, v_A) and (u_B, v_B) which are 2D coordinates of the vertices of the cube in the reference image A and B, eight corresponding 3D coordinates (P-Q-R) are computed by eq. (5).

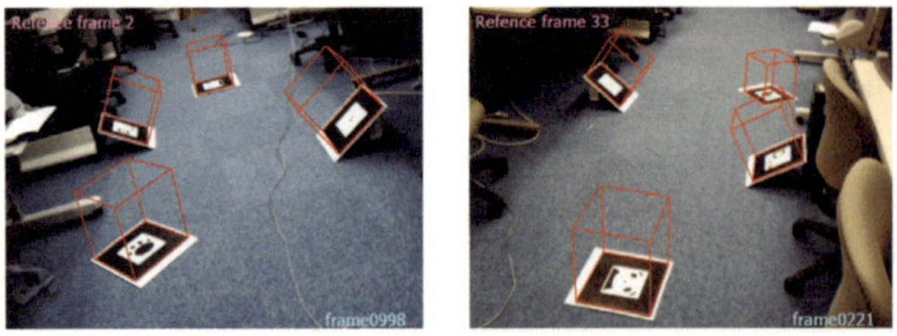

Fig. 5. Projected cubes on the reference images to obtain corresponding points

After obtaining the corresponding points in the coordinate system of each marker i, $\mathbf{T}_i^{\mathbf{WP}}$ is computed. When corresponding points between (X_i-Y_i-Z_i) in the coordinate system of the marker i and (P-Q-R) are obtained, the relationship between each marker i and the Projective Space is expressed by the following equation.

$$[X_{i\_j}, Y_{i\_j}, Z_{i\_j}, 1]^{\mathrm{T}} \cong \mathbf{T}_{\mathbf{i}}^{\mathbf{WP}}[P_j, Q_j, R_j, 1]^{\mathrm{T}} \quad (j > 0) \tag{6}$$

$$\mathbf{T}_{\mathbf{i}}^{\mathbf{WP}} = \begin{bmatrix} t_{11} & t_{12} & t_{13} & t_{14} \\ t_{21} & t_{22} & t_{23} & t_{24} \\ t_{31} & t_{32} & t_{33} & t_{34} \\ t_{41} & t_{42} & t_{43} & 1 \end{bmatrix} \tag{7}$$

By the following equation, the elements of $\mathbf{T}_{\mathrm{i}}^{\mathbf{WP}}$ are obtained.

$$\mathbf{M}_{\mathrm{j}}\mathbf{t} = \mathbf{b}_{\mathrm{j}} \tag{8}$$

where,

$$\mathbf{M}_{\mathrm{j}} = \begin{bmatrix} X_{i\_j} & Y_{i\_j} & Z_{i\_j} & 1 & 0 & 0 & 0 & 0 & 0 & 0 & 0 & 0 & -X_{i\_j}P_j & -Y_{i\_j}P_j \\ 0 & 0 & 0 & 0 & X_{i\_j} & Y_{i\_j} & Z_{i\_j} & 1 & 0 & 0 & 0 & 0 & -X_{i\_j}Q_j & -Y_{i\_j}Q_j \\ 0 & 0 & 0 & 0 & 0 & 0 & 0 & 0 & X_{i\_j} & Y_{i\_j} & Z_{i\_j} & 1 & -X_{i\_j}R_j & -Y_{i\_j}R_j \end{bmatrix} \tag{9}$$

$$\mathbf{t} = \begin{bmatrix} t_{11} & t_{12} & t_{13} & \cdots & t_{41} & t_{42} & t_{43} \end{bmatrix}^{\mathrm{T}}$$

$$\mathbf{b}_{\mathrm{j}} = \begin{bmatrix} P_j & Q_j & R_j \end{bmatrix}^{\mathrm{T}}$$

If m corresponding points are obtained, following equation is derived by eq. (8).

$$\begin{bmatrix} \mathbf{M}_1 \\ \vdots \\ \mathbf{M}_{\mathrm{m}} \end{bmatrix} \mathbf{t} = \begin{bmatrix} \mathbf{b}_1 \\ \vdots \\ \mathbf{b}_{\mathrm{m}} \end{bmatrix} \tag{10}$$

Then $\mathbf{t}$ (the elements of $\mathbf{T}_{\mathrm{i}}^{\mathbf{WP}}$) is obtained by least-square-method. In this method, the corresponding points are obtained by the cube's vertices. Therefore m=8.

2.5 Computing $\mathbf{P}_{\mathrm{i}}^{\mathbf{PI}}$

As described in Sec. 2.1, $\mathbf{P}_{\mathrm{i}}^{\mathbf{PI}}$ is the projection matrix which relates the Projective Space to the input image and is computed by $\mathbf{T}_{\mathrm{i}}^{\mathbf{WP}}$ and $\mathbf{P}_{\mathrm{i}}^{\mathbf{WI}}$. $\mathbf{T}_{\mathrm{i}}^{\mathbf{WP}}$ is computed in the first phase just one time. $\mathbf{P}_{\mathrm{i}}^{\mathbf{WI}}$ is computed by marker tracking at every frame in the second phase. As shown in eq. (1), $\mathbf{P}_{\mathrm{i}}^{\mathbf{PI}}$ is computed as follows.

$$\mathbf{P}_{\mathrm{i}}^{\mathrm{PI}} = \mathbf{P}_{\mathrm{i}}^{\mathrm{WI}} \cdot \left(\mathbf{T}_{\mathrm{i}}^{\mathrm{WP}}\right)^{-1} \tag{11}$$

2.6 Merging $\mathbf{P}_{\mathrm{i}}^{\mathbf{PI}}$ into $\mathbf{P}^{\mathbf{PI}}$

As described in Sec. 2.2, all $\mathbf{P}_{\mathrm{i}}^{\mathbf{PI}}$ should coincide with each other because they represent a common geometrical projection between the Projective Space and the input image. Therefore, all $\mathbf{P}_{\mathrm{i}}^{\mathbf{PI}}$ are merged into one matrix $\mathbf{P}^{\mathbf{PI}}$. The details are as follows.

When $\mathbf{P}_i^{PI}$ is computed from each marker *i*, corresponding points between (*P*-*Q*-*R*) in the Projective Space and (*x*-*y*) in the input image can be obtained by following equation.

$$[x, y, 1]^T \cong \mathbf{P}_i^{PI}[P, Q, R, 1]^T \tag{12}$$

In this method, by using (P_j-Q_j-R_j) obtained in computing $\mathbf{T}_i^{WP}$, corresponding points (x_j-y_j) in the input image is computed by eq. (12). Therefore *m* corresponding points are obtained for each marker.

If *n* markers are detected in the input image, the relationship between the corresponding points is as follows.

$$\begin{bmatrix} \mathbf{M}_1 \\ \vdots \\ \mathbf{M}_n \end{bmatrix} \mathbf{p} = \begin{bmatrix} \mathbf{b}_1 \\ \vdots \\ \mathbf{b}_n \end{bmatrix} \tag{13}$$

where,

$$\mathbf{p} = \begin{bmatrix} p_{11} & p_{12} & p_{13} & p_{14} & \cdots & p_{33} \end{bmatrix}^T \quad \mathbf{P}^{PI} = \begin{bmatrix} p_{11} & p_{12} & p_{13} & p_{14} \\ p_{21} & p_{22} & p_{23} & p_{24} \\ p_{31} & p_{32} & p_{33} & 1 \end{bmatrix} \tag{14}$$

$$\mathbf{M}_i = \begin{bmatrix} P_1 & Q_1 & R_1 & 1 & 0 & 0 & 0 & 0 & -P_1x_1 & -Q_1x_1 & -R_1x_1 \\ 0 & 0 & 0 & 0 & P_1 & Q_1 & R_1 & 1 & -P_1y_1 & -Q_1y_1 & -R_1y_1 \\ \vdots \\ P_m & Q_m & R_m & 1 & 0 & 0 & 0 & 0 & -P_mx_m & -Q_mx_m & -R_mx_m \\ 0 & 0 & 0 & 0 & P_m & Q_m & R_m & 1 & -P_my_m & -Q_my_m & -R_my_m \end{bmatrix} \tag{15}$$

$$\mathbf{b}_i = \begin{bmatrix} x_1, & y_1, & \cdots & x_m, & y_m \end{bmatrix}^T \tag{16}$$

Then $\mathbf{p}$ (the elements of $\mathbf{P}^{PI}$) is obtained by least-square-method.

By using this merged projection matrix $\mathbf{P}^{PI}$, the projection matrix from the base marker's coordinate system, in which the virtual objects are defined, to the input image is computed by eq. (2). Then, the virtual objects are overlaid onto the input image by $\mathbf{P}_{\mathbf{base}}$.

2.7 Automatic selection of reference images

As described in Sec. 2.3, the Projective Space is defined by projective reconstruction of two reference images. In projective reconstruction, a fundamental matrix between the two reference images is used for defining the Projective Space. This means that it is very important issue to compute an accurate fundamental matrix between the reference images. In this method, therefore, a reasonable pair of images as the reference images should be selected.

This method introduces automatic selection algorithm of the reference images. The overview is shown in Fig. 6. First, the object scene where multiple markers are distributed is captured for a few seconds by a moving camera. This image sequence in which all the markers should be included becomes the candidates of the reference image. From the candidate images, a pair of images is sequentially selected as temporal reference image A and B. Then a good pair is decided by evaluating the accuracy of the Projective Space which defined by the temporal reference images.

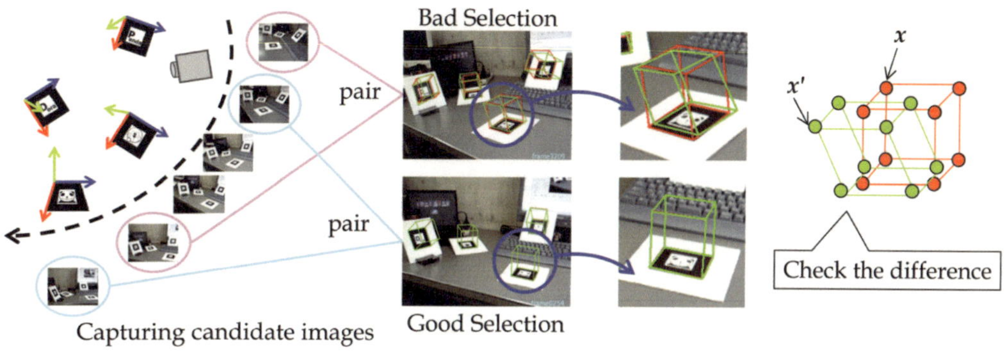

Fig. 6. Overview of automatic selection of reference images

For evaluating the temporal reference images, first, a fundamental matrix is obtained by projection matrices computed from every marker in the temporal reference images using ARToolkit algorithm [H. Kato & M. Billinghurst, 1999]. Where $\mathbf{P}_{\mathbf{Ai}}$ and $\mathbf{P}_{\mathbf{Bi}}$ are the projection matrix computed from marker i in the temporal reference image A and B, respectively. Then a fundamental matrix based on marker i is computed as following equation.

$$\mathbf{F}_{\mathbf{ABi}} = [\mathbf{e}_{\mathbf{Bi}}]_{\times} \mathbf{P}_{\mathbf{Bi}} \mathbf{P}_{\mathbf{Ai}}^{-} \tag{17}$$

where $\mathbf{P}_{\mathbf{Ai}}^{-}$ represents the pseudo inverse matrix of $\mathbf{P}_{\mathbf{Ai}}$ [Hartley & Zisserman, 2000]. By computing $\mathbf{F}_{\mathbf{ABi}}$ based on every marker, one matrix which has the smallest projection error *error* is selected as FAB which is the fundamental matrix between the temporal reference images.

$$error = [u_B \quad v_B \quad 1]\, \mathbf{F}_{\mathbf{ABi}} [u_A, \quad v_A, \quad 1]^{\mathrm{T}} \tag{18}$$

where, (u_A, v_A) and (u_B, v_B) are corresponding points in the temporal reference image A and B, respectively. In the same way as computing $\mathbf{T}_{\mathrm{i}}^{\mathbf{WP}}$ in Sec. 2.4, these corresponding points are obtained by vertices of a cube drawn on each marker as shown in Fig. 5.

After selecting the best fundamental matrix as $\mathbf{F}_{\mathbf{AB}}$, a Projective Space is defined by eq. (4). using $\mathbf{F}_{\mathbf{AB}}$. $\mathbf{T}_{\mathrm{i}}^{\mathbf{WP}}$ and $\mathbf{P}_{\mathrm{i}}^{\mathbf{PI}}$ are also computed and merged into $\mathbf{P}^{\mathbf{PI}}$. Then two projected coordinates (x_i, y_i) and (x'_i, y'_i) are compared as follows,

$$[x_i, y_i, 1]^{\mathrm{T}} \cong \mathbf{P}_{\mathbf{Bi}}[X, Y, Z, 1]^{\mathrm{T}}, \qquad [x'_i, y'_i, 1]^{\mathrm{T}} \cong (\mathbf{P}^{\mathbf{PI}} \mathbf{T}_{\mathrm{i}}^{\mathbf{WP}})[X, Y, Z, 1]^{\mathrm{T}} \tag{19}$$

(x_i, y_i) and (x'_i, y'_i) are corresponding to a red cube and a green cube in Fig. 6, respectively. Although these cubes should coincide with each other, these matrices in eq. may include computational error of computing $\mathbf{F}_{\mathbf{AB}}$. Therefore, the temporal pair of images which has smaller difference between two cubes than threshold value is selected as a good pair of reference images. If no temporal pair of images has smaller error than threshold value, the candidate image sequence is captured again. In the experiment described in the next section, threshold value is defined as 3 pixels.

2.8 Demonstrations

In this section, registration of a virtual object is demonstrated by using our method. In the real world, 4 planar markers distributed at arbitrary positions and poses as shown in Fig. 7. Of course, the relationship between the markers is unknown. This method is implemented by a PC (OS: Windows XP, CPU: Intel Pentium IV 3.6GHz) and a web camera (ELECOM UCAM-E130HWH). The captured image's resolution is 640x480 pixels and graphical views of virtual objects are rendered using OpenGL.

Fig. 7. Object scenes where multiple markers are distributed at arbitrary positions and poses

First, a user captures the object scene for 100 frames and waits about 1 minute for the automatic selection of the reference images from the captured sequence. After that, a virtual object is overlaid onto the input images as if the virtual object exists in the real world. The user can move the camera around the object scene for watching the virtual object from favorite view point.

The resulting images are shown in Fig. 8~11. In Fig. 8, a virtual object is overlaid onto one position in the real world. Even though specific marker is not continuously detected in all over the input image sequence, the virtual object is stably overlaid onto the same position. This result shows that the relationship of the markers can be estimated successfully. And also, the moving camera's position and pose with respect to the virtual object can be computed by introducing the detected markers via the Projective Space. Therefore, the registration of virtual object is achieved without prior knowledge about the geometrical relationship of the markers.

Fig. 8. Static object is overlaid on the real world.

In Fig. 9, the virtual object is walking on the tabletop. The user's camera moves according to the virtual object. Therefore, it is impossible that specific marker is always detected in the input image. Moreover, a planar marker is not detected depending on the camera's angle with respect to the marker plane. In Fig. 10, even though the marker indicated by the red circle is captured in the image, it cannot be detected. Therefore, if all the markers are placed in the same plane, no marker is detected depending on the camera's angle. In that case, it fails in the registration. On the other hand, since this method allows the markers to be distributed at arbitrary positions and poses, the registration of the virtual object can be continued.

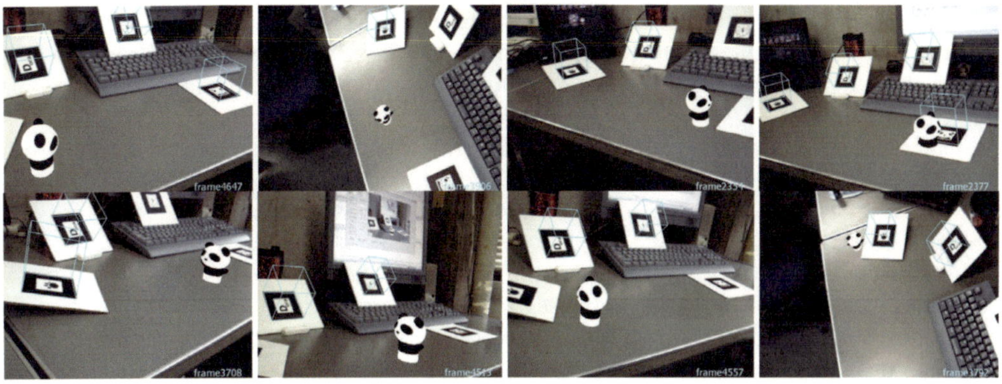

Fig. 9. Moving object is overlaid on the real world.

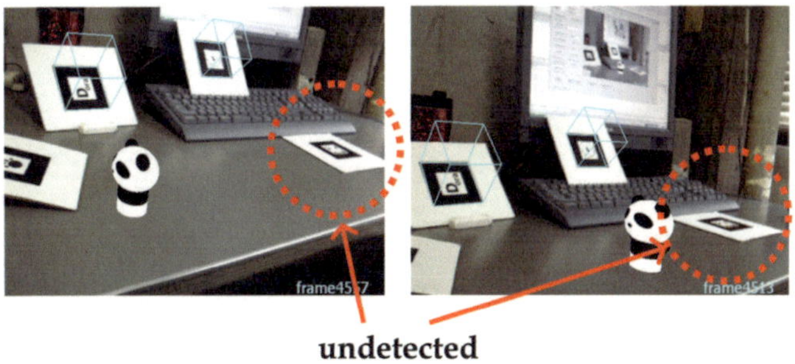

Fig. 10. Failure of marker detection even though it is captured in the image

In Fig. 11, the human-sized virtual object is overlaid onto the large space instead of the tabletop. For applying multiple markers based registration in such a large space, it becomes more difficult to manually measure the arrangement of the markers. Therefore this method is useful because of estimating the arrangement only by capturing the object scene.

Fig. 11. Moving object as large as a human is overlaid on the real world.

3. AR baseball presentation system

AR Baseball Presentation System is an observation system of a virtual baseball game. The overview of the system is shown in Fig. 12. Users place a real baseball field model on the tabletop and input a baseball game history (scorebook) that they want to watch into the system. Then they can watch the game by replaying with 3D virtual baseball players on the field model in front of them. On the field model, 2D markers are placed for registration of the virtual players. Therefore the users can watch the game from their favorite viewpoints around the field.
This sytem visually replays the baseball game which was previously played in the other place. In contrast with the usual way to know the game history, such as watching the captured video or reading the recorded scorebook, this AR system can provide the users with much realistic sensation as an entertainment application.
This sytem visually replays the baseball game which was previously played in the other place. In contrast with the usual way to know the game history, such as watching the captured video or reading the recorded scorebook, this AR system can provide the users with much realistic sensation as an entertainment application.

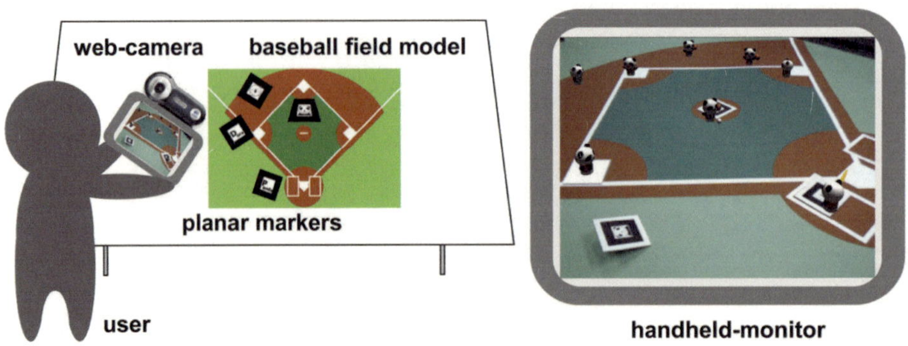

Fig. 12. AR Baseball Presentation System

3.1 Input scorebook data file

This system visually replays the baseball game which was previously played in the other place by a scorebook data, in which the game history they want to know is described. The input data file is called "Scorebook Data File" (SDF).
As shown in Fig. 13, the game history is described play-by-play in the SDF. "1 play" means the actions of the players and the ball from the time the pitcher throws the ball until the ball

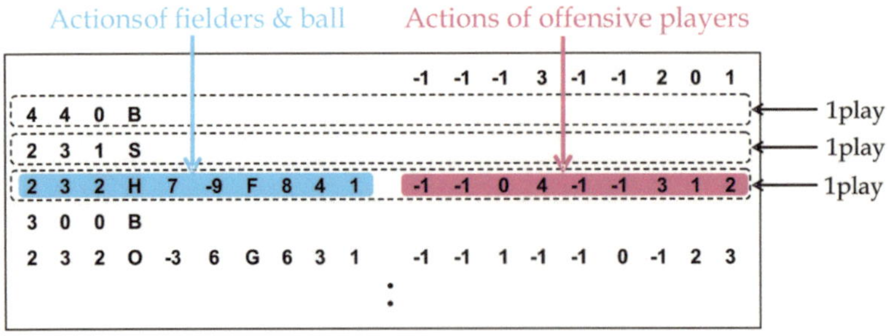

Fig. 13. Scorebook Data File (SDF)

returns to the pitcher again. It is about for 15 to 30 seconds. The actions of the players and the ball in 1 play are described on one line in the SDF. The former part of the line represents the actions of the fielders and the ball, while the latter part describes the actions of the offensive players. This file is loaded in starting the system and is sequentially read out lineby- line at every 1 play.

3.2 Actions of offensive players

Offensive players indicate a batter, runners, and players who are waiting in the bench. Each player belongs to one of the six states as shown in Fig. 14(a). The batter is in the batter's box, so its state is "0", third runner is "3", and the waiting players are "-1". In SDF, the destination state to which every player changes in each play is sequentially recorded. When one line of the file is read out, the destination of each player is decided according to the data like Fig. 14(b). Then the game scene that 3D players are moving from the present state to the destination state while 1 play is created with CG.

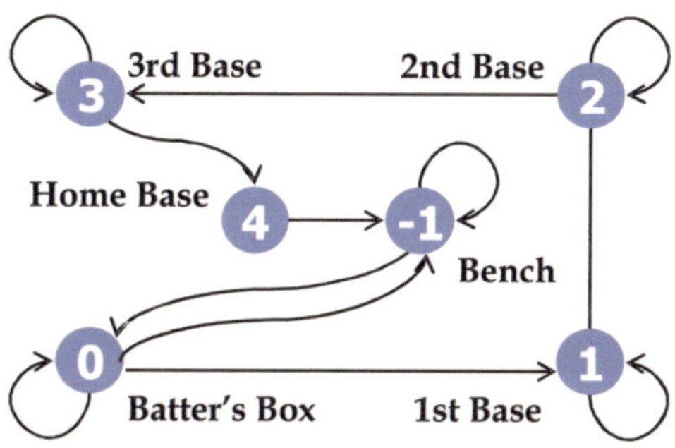

(a) State transition of offensive players

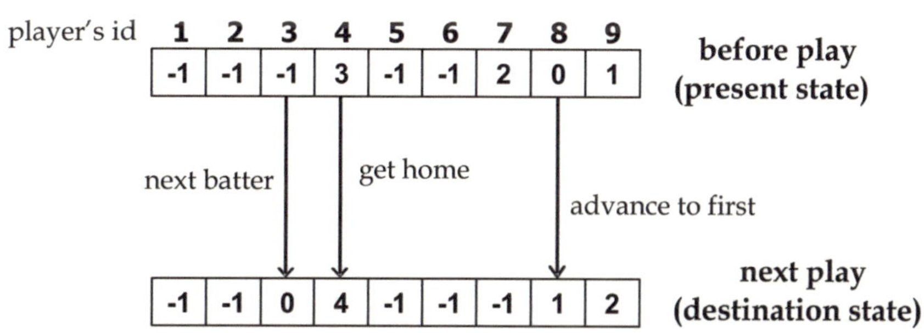

(b) Example of Scorebook Data File for offensive players

Fig. 14. Actions of the offensive players

3.3 Actions of fielders and ball

In contrast to the offensive players who are just moving from present state to destination while 1 play, the fielders are doing some actions while 1 play, such as moving around the field and throwing and catching the ball, etc. Therefore only the action of the ball is described in the SDF. Fielders move to catch the ball according to the action of the ball. The action of the ball while 1 play is described as shown in Fig. 15.

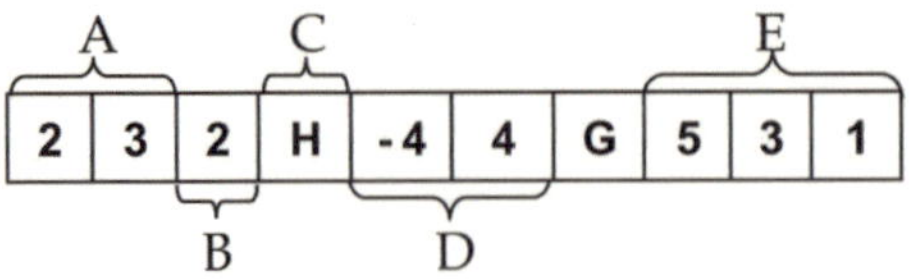

A: pitching position of strike zone
B: through / swing out / hit
C: ball / strike / out / hit
D: flying position on field model
E: fielders' No. who catch the ball

Fig. 15. Scorebook Data File of the fielders and the ball

In this system, the fielders basically stay own positions. First, the ball is thrown by the pitcher and hit to the position which is described in part D of Fig. 15. Then the player whose position number is described in the fist of part E moves to the position of part D to catch the ball. After catching the ball, the player throws the ball to the next player whose position number is described next. The next player moves to the nearest base and catches the ball. After the same iterations, finally, the ball is thrown to the pitcher.

3.4 Demonstrations

This section shows the demonstration results of this system. This demonstration is performed with a web-camera (ELECOM UCAM-E130HWH) attached to a handheld monitor connected a PC (OS: Windows XP, CPU: Intel Pentium IV 3.2GHz). The resolution of the captured image is 640x480 pixels. Multiple planar markers are distributed inside and outside the field model. In this system, one of the markers must be put on one of the bases in order to determine relationship between the field model and the markers. The other markers can be placed at arbitrary positions and poses. In this demonstration, 4 markers are utilized and one of them is placed on the third base. Fig. 16 shows the actual experimental environment of this system. A Scorebook Data File of a baseball game is manually prepared in accordance with Sec. 3.1. 3D models of virtual objects, such as players and a ball, are rendered with OpenGL.

Fig. 16. Experimental environment of AR Baseball Presentation System

Fig. 17 shows an example scene of a baseball game: team RED vs. team WHITE. In this situation, team WHITE is in the field and team RED is at bat. The bases are loaded and 4th batter of team RED is in the batter's box (frame 0~15). The pitcher throws the ball (frame

15~29). The batter hits safely to left (frame 29~35), and then all runners move up a base (frame 50~89). In the result, team RED gets a score. In this experiment, frame rate of AR presentation is about 30 fps. The user can see the baseball game at video-rate.

In Fig. 18, the angle of the camera with respect to the tabletop is too small to detect the markers lying on the tabletop plane as same as Fig. 10. Therefore one marker placed near the home base cannot be detected. Since another marker is placed at different pose from the ground plane, the registration of the virtual players can be continued. This is quite useful for observation system so that the user can watch the object scene from various view points.

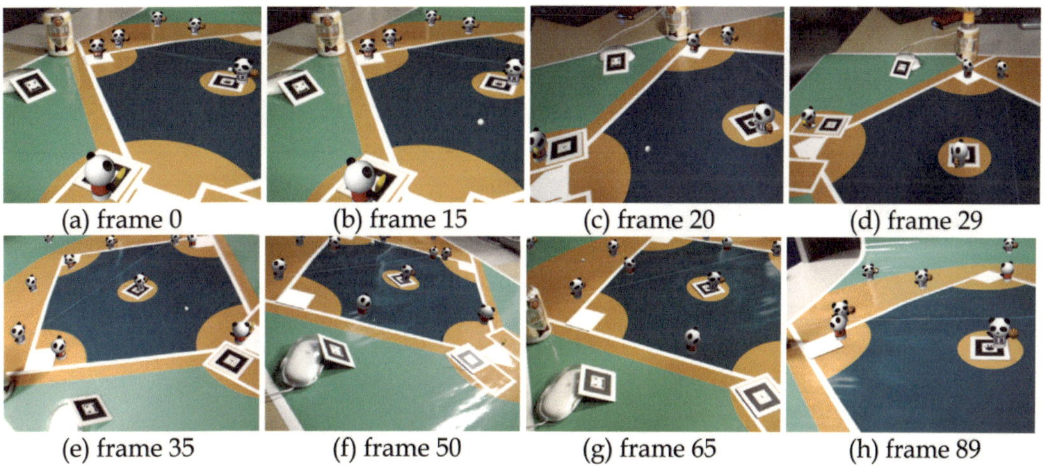

(a) frame 0 (b) frame 15 (c) frame 20 (d) frame 29
(e) frame 35 (f) frame 50 (g) frame 65 (h) frame 89

Fig. 17. Example scene of play: 4th batter of team RED sends a hit to left with the bases loaded, and then 3rd runner gets home

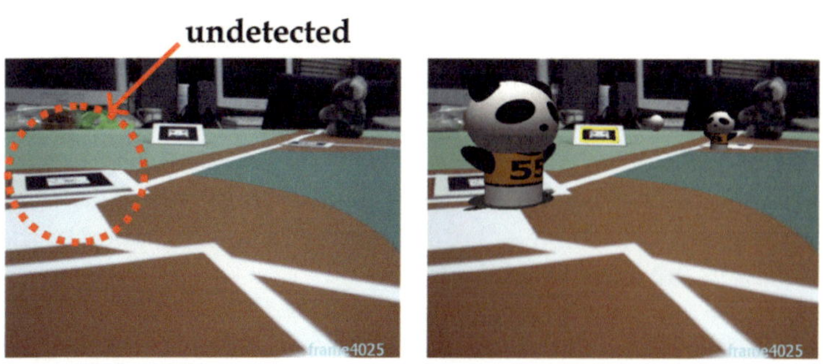

Fig. 18. Failure of marker detection even though it is captured in the image

Fig. 19 shows the resulting images which are watched from various view points. By using this system, the user can watch the baseball game from favorite view points, such as catcher's view point. For changing view points from (a) to (b), from (b) to (c), from (c) to (d), 15 users spend an average of about 7 seconds in this system. In contrast with using a typical CG viewer in which a keyboard is used for changing view points, the users spend an average of about 43 seconds. This is because the users only have to move around the field model for changing the view points in this system. Such simple way for watching the Cgrepresented event using the AR system is very useful and can provide immersive feeling as an entertainment tool.

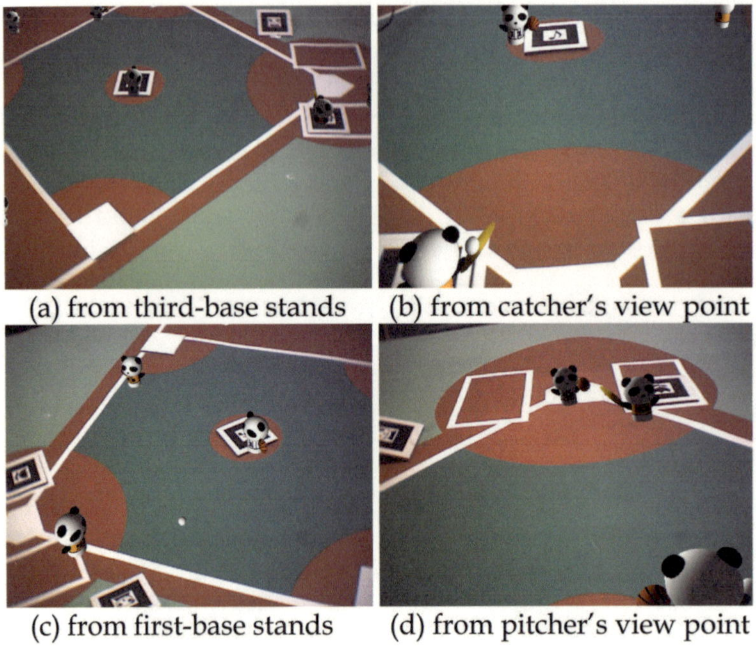

Fig. 19. Example resulting images watched from various view points

4. Interactive AR bowling system

With Interactive AR Bowling System, users can enjoy the bowling game by rolling a real ball down a real bowling lane model placed on a tabletop in the real world. Fig. 20 shows the overview of this system. On the lane model, there are virtual pins generated with CG. They knock down the virtual pins by rolling the real ball.
Touching and rolling the real ball provide a sort of tangible feeling in this system. It is wellknown that a tangible interface enhances the reality of communication [Ishii et al., 1999, Zigelbaum et al. 2006]. Moreover, because of placing some planar markers on the lane model, the users can watch the lane and pins from free view points. For registration of virtual objects such as the virtual players or the virtual pins, the motion of the user's camera is estimated by multiple 2D markers.

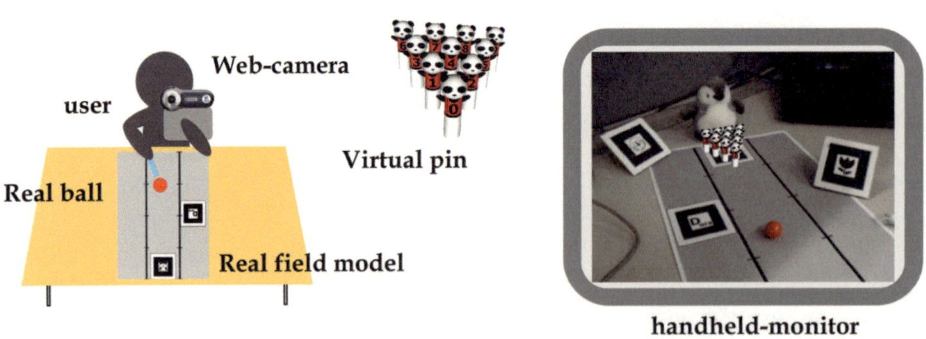

Fig. 20. Interactive AR Bowling System

4.1 Ball tracking

In this system, we assume that the color of the ball should be quite different from the lane model. In this paper, we use a red ball on a gray lane model as shown in Fig. 21(a). For detection of the ball, first, red regions are detected from the input image by dividing it into R, G, B channel images. Fig. 21(b) shows the image after dilation and erosion a few times. Finding the minimal circumscribed circle (contour) for the detected region, the center of the circle is considered as the 2D ball's position in the input image as shown in Fig. 21(c).

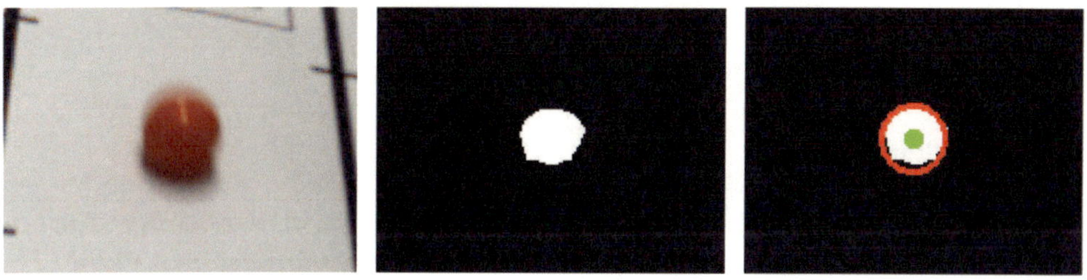

(a) Original image (b) Ball's region (c) Detected ball

Fig. 21. Ball detection

4.2 Transformation to top view image

Using homography **H** computed at the marker tracking process, the ball's position on the input image is transformed onto the top view image that provides a geometrical relationship between the ball and the pins on the lane model. As shown in Fig. 22, the trajectory of the ball can be obtained. This trajectory is used to detect the collision between the ball and the pins, and compute the directions which the pins are knocked down.

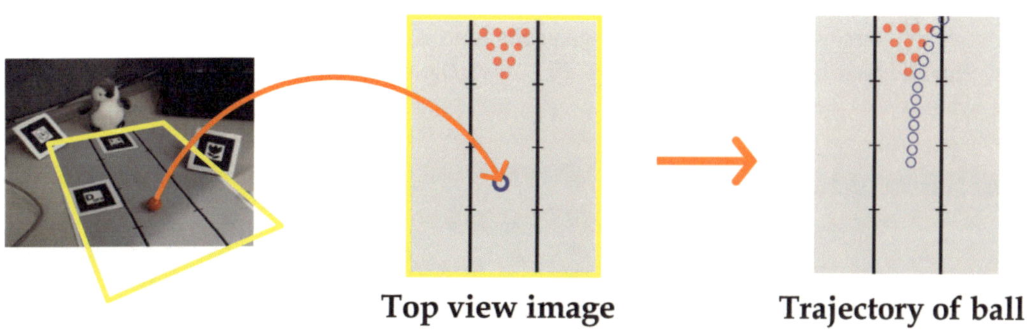

Fig. 22. Transform the ball's position to top-view image

4.3 Collision detection of ball and pins

We assume that radii of the ball and the pins are r_b and r_p, respectively, and define the distance between the ball and each pin as dis. For detecting a collision between the ball and the pins, the distance *dis* is computed from the top view image at every frame. The collision is detected by comparing distance and radius as following equations and Fig. 23.

$$(r_b + r_p) \le dis \Rightarrow \text{Not hit}; \qquad (r_b + r_p) > dis \Rightarrow \text{Hit} \tag{20}$$

Fig. 23. Collision detection by trajectory of the ball

4.4 Overlay virtual pins

After the collision detection, the pins are generated with CG and overlaid onto the image. If the collision is detected, the pins are gradually inclined and knocked down. The direction of knocking down is defined by trajectory of the ball. As shown in Fig. 24, the direction is computed by a motion vector of the ball, which is decided by ball's positions in previous and current frames, and a vector from the ball to each pin. The generated pins are superimposed onto the image by the extrinsic parameters computed by 2D markers. The user can see the virtual pins according to the motion of the camera and the rolling ball.

4.5 Demonstration

This section shows the demonstration results of this system. This demonstration is also performed with a web-camera (ELECOM UCAM-E130HWH) attached to a handheld monitor connected a PC (OS: Windows XP, CPU: Intel Pentium IV 3.2GHz). The resolution of the captured image is 640x480 pixels. On the table top, a real bowling lane model is placed and 4 planar markers are distributed inside and outside the lane model. In order to determine relationship between the lane and the markers, one marker is placed between the two lines of the lane. Fig. 25 shows the actual experimental environment of this system.

Fig. 24. Direction of knocking down of pins

Fig. 25. Experimental environment of Interactive AR Bowling System

Fig. 26 shows the detected lane and ball's trajectory. Both of the lane and the ball can be correctly detected and tracked all over the frames according to the camera motion. The ball's position is also successfully transformed onto the top view image by the homography computed by the markers. Since a real ball is used in this system, the marker placed on the lane can be occluded by the ball. However, this method can estimate the relationship of the markers and compute the homography successfully, even if some of markers are occluded.

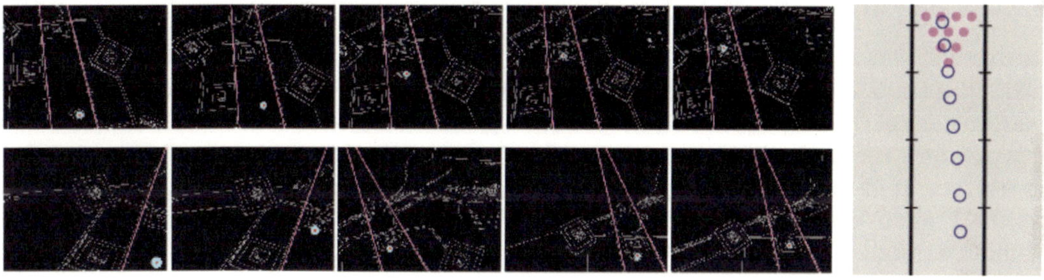

Fig. 26. Detected lane and ball, and trajectory of ball

Fig. 27 shows example scenes of playing this system. The virtual pins are overlaid on the lane model according to the camera motion. As described before, the virtual pins can b overlaid onto the lane model, even when the ball is rolling over the marker. The collision of the real ball and the virtual pins is successfully detected. Therefore some pins are knocking down by the real ball. The pins existing behind the hit pins are also knocked down as a chain reaction of the front pins by computing the direction of knocking down from the trajectory. In this experiment, this system also runs about 30 fps. The advantage of this system is that the user can physically touch and roll the real ball without special hardware such as physical sensors or special gloves in contrast with the previous application in [Matysczok et al. 2004]. Therefore this system achieves a real bowling style. If the ball and lane are also generated by CG, the user cannot freely control the ball. On the other hand, there are various ways to roll the ball in this system, the game is not too simple to complete; ex. inclining the lane, changing the material of the lane, or rolling the ball by a pen instead of a hand. Therefore this system can be challenging for the users.

Fig. 27. Example scene of playing Interactive AR Bowling System

5. Conclusion

In this chapter, we introduced a vision-based registration method using multiple planar markers placed at arbitrary positions and poses is introduced. We also demonstrate the performance of the proposed method by applying it to two AR applications. In contrast with the previous methods using multiple markers, this method requires no time-consuming measurement of the marker arrangement. Since the marker arrangement can be estimated by the Projective Space, the markers can be distributed at arbitrary positions and poses without a prior knowledge. This method can be applied not only for on the tabletop but also inside the room.

Both of the baseball system and bowling system can be enjoyed on the tabletop in the real world only with a web-camera and a handheld monitor connected a general PC. It is a big advantage for home users that these applications do not require any special device. Users can interactively change their view points by moving around the tabletop because of this registration method with multiple markers. In contrast with usual CG viewers in which a mouse or a keyboard is used for changing view points, changing view points by moving of the users is very intuitive and easy. By visualising 3D objects in front of the users, these applications will be future-oriented 3D game.

6. References

Y. Genc; S. Riedel; F. Souvannavong; C. Akinlar & N. Navab (2002). Marker-less Tracking for AR: A learning-Based Approach, *Proceedings of IEEE and ACM International Symposium on Mixed and Augmented Reality (ISMAR2002)*, pp. 295-304, ISBN: 0-7695-1781-1.

M. Haller; M. Billinghurst; J. Leithinger; D. Leitner & T. Seifried (2005). Coeno-enhancing face-to-face collaboration. *Proceedings of International Conference on Augmented Tele-existence (ICAT2005)*, pp. 40–47, ISBN:0-473-10657-4.

R. Hartley & A. Zisserman (2000). In: *Multiple View Geometry in Computer Vision*, CAMBRIDGE UNIVERSITY PRESS, ISBN: 0521540518.

A. Henrysson; M. Billinghurst & M. Ollila (2005). Virtual Object Manipulation Using a Mobile Phone, *Proceedings of International Conference on Augmented Tele-existence (ICAT2005)*, pp. 164–171, ISBN:0-473-10657-4.

A. Henrysson; M. Billinghurst & M. Ollila (2006). AR Tennis, *Proceedings of ACM SIGGRAPH Emerging technologies*, Article No. 1, ISBN: 1-59593-364-6, Boston, Aug.

H. Ishii; C. Wisneski; J. Orbanes; B. Chun & J. Paradiso (1999). curlybot: designing a new class of computational toys. *Proceedings of the SIGCHI conference on Human factors in computing systems*, pp. 129–136, ISBN: 1-58113-216-6.

H. Kato & M. Billinghurst (1999). Marker Tracking and HMD Calibration for a video-based Augmented Reality Conferencing System, *Proceedings of the 2nd International Workshop on Augmented Reality (IWAR 99)*, pp. 85-94, ISBN: 0-7695-0359-4.

H. Kato; M. Billinghurst; I. Poupyrev; K. Imamoto & K. Tachibana (2000). Virtual object manipulation on a table-top AR environment, *Proceedings of IEEE and ACM International Symposium on Augmented Reality (ISAR2000)*, pp. 111–119, ISBN: 0- 7695-0846-4.

K. Klein & T. Drummond (2004). Sensor fusion and occlusion refinement for tablet-based AR, *Proceedings of Third IEEE and ACM International Symposium on Mixed and Augmented Reality (ISMAR2004)*, pp. 38–47, ISBN: 0-7695-2191-6.

D. Kotake; S. Uchiyama & H. Yamamoto (2004). A Marker Calibration Method Utilizing A Priori Knowledge on Marker Arrangement, *Proceedings of IEEE and ACM International Symposium on Mixed and Augmented Reality (ISMAR2004)*, pp. 89–98, ISBN: 0-7695-2191-6.

J. Looser; R. Grasset & M. Billinghurst (2007). A 3D Flexible and Tangible Magic Lens in Augmented Reality, *Proceedings of IEEE and ACM International Symposium on Mixed and Augmented Reality (ISMAR2007)*, pp. 51–54, ISBN: 978-1-4244-1749-0.

C. Matysczok; R. Radkowski & H. Nixdorf (2004). AR-bowling: immersive and realistic game play in real environments using augmented reality. *Proceedings of the ACM SIGCHI International Conference on Advances in computer entertainment technology (ACE2004)*, pp. 269–274, ISBN: 1-58113-882-2.

D. Schmalstieg & D. Wagner (2007) Experiences with Handheld Augmented Reality, *Proceedings of IEEE and ACM International Symposium on Mixed and Augmented Reality (ISMAR2007)*, pp. 3–18, ISBN: 0-7695-1781-1.

Y. Uematsu & H. Saito (2005). Vision-based Registration for Augmented Reality with Integration of Arbitrary Multiple planes, *Proceedings of International Conference on Image Analysis and Processing (ICIAP2005), LNCS 3617*, pp. 155–162, ISBN: 978-3-540- 28869-5.

Y. Uematsu & H. Saito (2005). AR Registration by Merging Multiple Planar Markers at Arbitrary Positions and Poses via Projective Space, *Proceedings of International Conference on Augmented Tele-existence (ICAT2005)*, pp. 48–55, ISBN: 0-473-10657-4.

Y. Uematsu & H. Saito (2006). AR Baseball Presentation System with Integrating Multiple *Planar Markers, Proceedings of International Conference on Augmented Tele-existence (ICAT2006), LNCS 4282, pp. 163-174, ISBN: 978-3-540-49776-9.*

Y. Uematsu & H. Saito (2007). Interactive AR Bowling System by Vision-based Tracking, *Proceedings of the international conference on Advances in computer entertainment technology(ACE2007)*, pp. 236-237, ISBN: 978-1-59593-640-0.

E. J. Umlauf; H. Piringer; G. Reitmayr & D. Schmalstieg (2002). ARLib: The Augmented Library, *Proceedings of International Workshop on ARToolkit (ART02).*

J. Zigelbaum; A. Millner; B. Desai & H. Ishii (2006). Bodybeats: Wholebody, Musical Interfaces for Children. *Proceedings of Conference on Human Factors in Computing Systems (CHI '06), pp. 1595–1600, ISBN: 1-59593-298-4.*

26

Catadioptric Omni-directional Stereo Vision and Its Applications in Moving Objects Detection

Xiong Zhihui, Chen Wang and Zhang Maojun
College of Information System and Management, National University of Defense Technology
Changsha, P.R. China

1. Introduction

Catadioptric Omni-Directional Stereo Vision (ODSV) technology is the combination of omni-directional imaging and stereo vision, which has wide application potentials on robot vision and large-scale video surveillance [1-4]. Fig.1 gives the framework of ODSV technology, which includes four major parts: the design of omni-directional stereo vision imaging system, unwarping of omni-directional stereo images, rectification of omni-directional stereo images, stereo matching and depth estimation of omni-directional stereo vision.

Among these four parts, the imaging system can be used to capture omni-directional stereo image pair(s), which is the input of omni-directional stereo vision. An omni-directional stereo vision imaging system is typically composed of catadioptric mirrors, imaging sensors and fasteners.

The purpose of unwarping the omni-directional stereo images is to convert the circularity shaped omni-directional images into perspective projection images, which are suitable for human watching. Generally, we call the circularity shaped images captured by catadioptric omni-directional imaging system as omni-directional images, and we call the unwarped images that are suitable for human watching as panoramic images.

Rectification of omni-directional stereo images can be regarded as the pretreatment before stereo matching. In many cases, there are horizontal errors and vertical errors in the omni-directional images and panoramic images, these errors result in large searching space and mismatching when performing stereo matching. The rectification of omni-directional stereo images uses epipolar geometry to transform the images, which makes the matching points lie on a horizontal scan line, and reduce the searching space from two-dimension to one-dimension, so as to improve the stereo matching efficiency.

Stereo matching and depth estimation of omni-directional stereo vision are key problems in catadioptric omni-directional stereo vision, whose main function is to find correspondences between pixels among a pair of or more reference images, i.e. to estimate relative disparity for each pixel in reference images. Given pixel correspondence and calibrated camera, it is easy to figure out the depth information via triangulation for the determinate relationship between disparity and depth.

Taking its advantages of large FOV (Field of View) and depth information, catadioptric omni-directional stereo vision can be widely used in robot vision and video surveillance. For example, in robot football games, we can use this technology to make robots to "see" the football whenever it is at any direction. Furthermore, since the depth information is not sensitive to the surrounding disturbance, this depth information can be used to detect the football position.

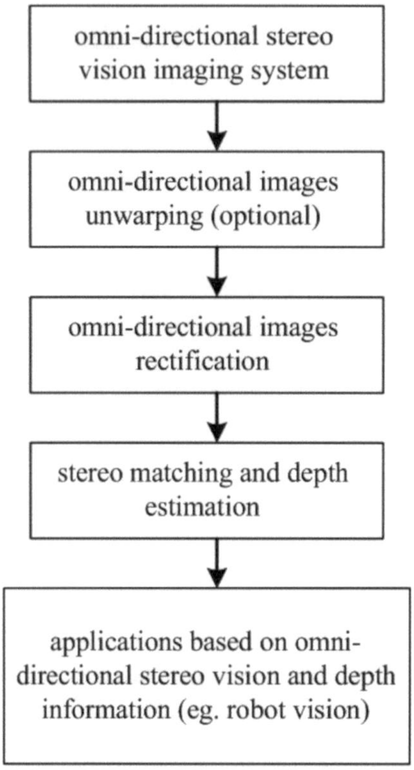

Fig. 1. Framework of catadioptric omni-directional stereo vision

2. Omni-directional stereo vision imaging system

2.1 Principle of catadioptric omni-directional imaging

The principle of the catadioptric omni-directional imaging is following: in the 3D space environment, rays from all the 360 degree FOV (Field of View) objects are collected and reflected by curve faced reflecting mirrors (such as paraboloid, hyperboloid, etc.); these reflected rays are captured by imaging systems and omni-directional images are obtained [5].
Taking the PROIS (Paraboloid Reflective Omni-directional Imaging System) [5] s an example, Fig.2 illustrates the principle and process of the catadiopric omni-directional imaging: 1) Incident rays from the scene are reflected by the paraboloid mirror. 2) Reflex rays run into the optics imaging system and forms an omni-directional image on the image sensor (such as CCD of a digital camera). 3) Finally, the omni-directional image is unwarped into panoramic image.

2.2 Omni-directional stereo imaging system

At present, there are three ways to construct the catadioptric omni-directional imaging systems [6], shown in Fig.3:

1. The pairs of omni-directional imaging systems are installed horizontally, and the axes of the pairs of imaging systems are vertical with the horizontal plane as shown in Fig. 3(a). However, there are occlusions between these two systems, which limit the FOV of the stereo vision system.
2. The pairs of omni-directional imaging systems are installed vertically on the same vertical axes, as shown in Fig. 3(b). Using this type of design, there exist no occlusions between these two systems, and it ensures that there exists parallax on 360 degree FOV. In this type of systems, the mirror can be reflecting mirrors (such as paraboloid, hyperboloid, etc.). When the system uses paraboloid as the reflecting mirrors, it requires using expensive telecentric lens.
3. Use two reflecting mirrors and a camera to construct an omni-directional stereo vision system, as shown in Fig. 3(c). This type of stereo imaging system requires that the two images of stereo vision are captured with a single camera, which limits the imaging resolution much. According to the principle of Fig. 3(c), Fig. 4 presents the design of a realistic omni-directional imaging system and its picture. As shown in Fig. 4(a), this system installs an *expensive telecentric* camera on vertical axes, and the upper mirror and nether mirror are also installed on the same axe. Fig.4(b) shows the practical picture of this system.

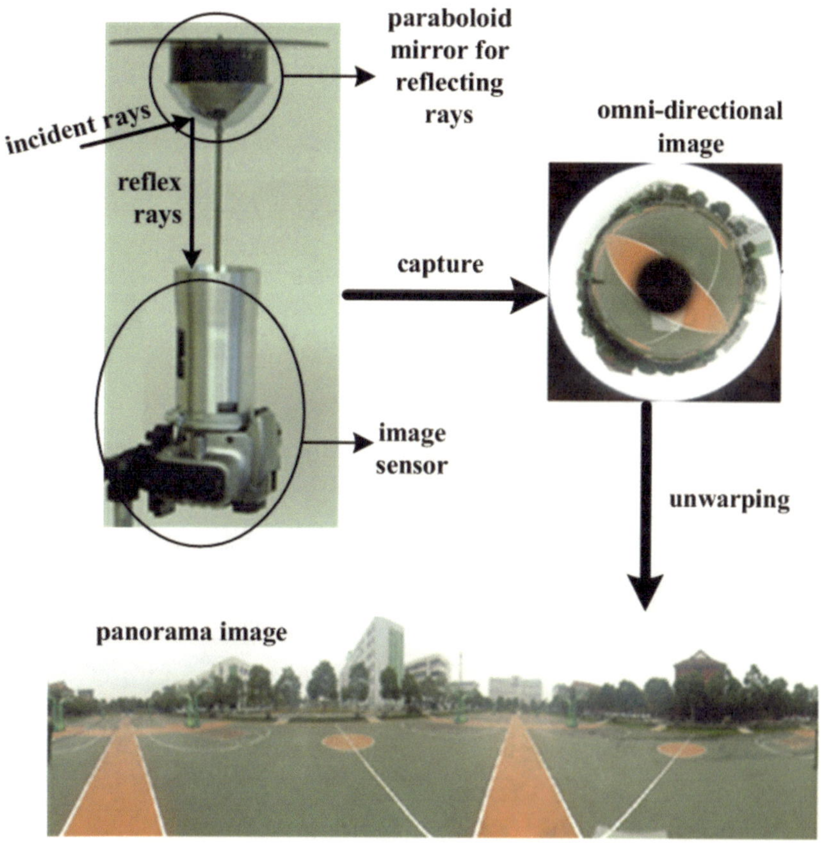

Fig. 2. Principle of catadioptric omni-directional imaging and its unwarping

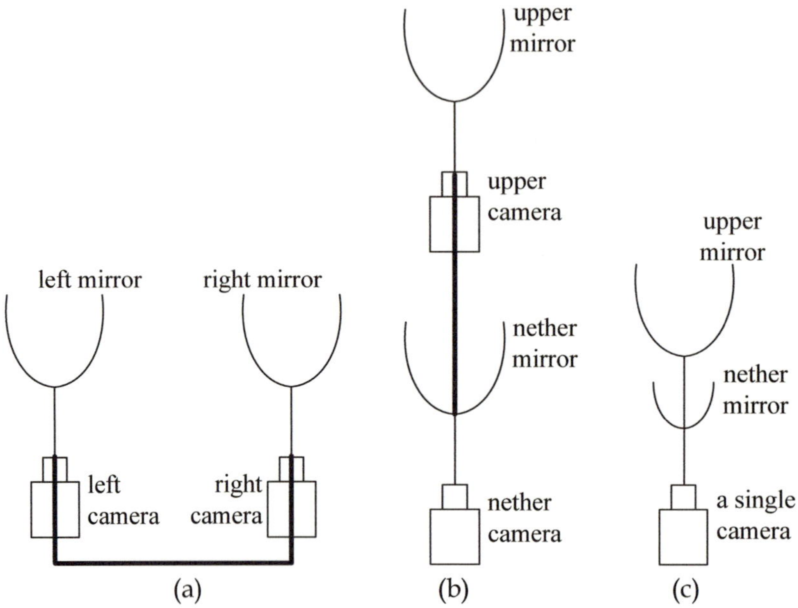

Fig. 3. Three ways to construct omni-directional stereo vision imaging system.
(a)horizontal cameras; (b)vertical cameras; (c)vertical and single camera.

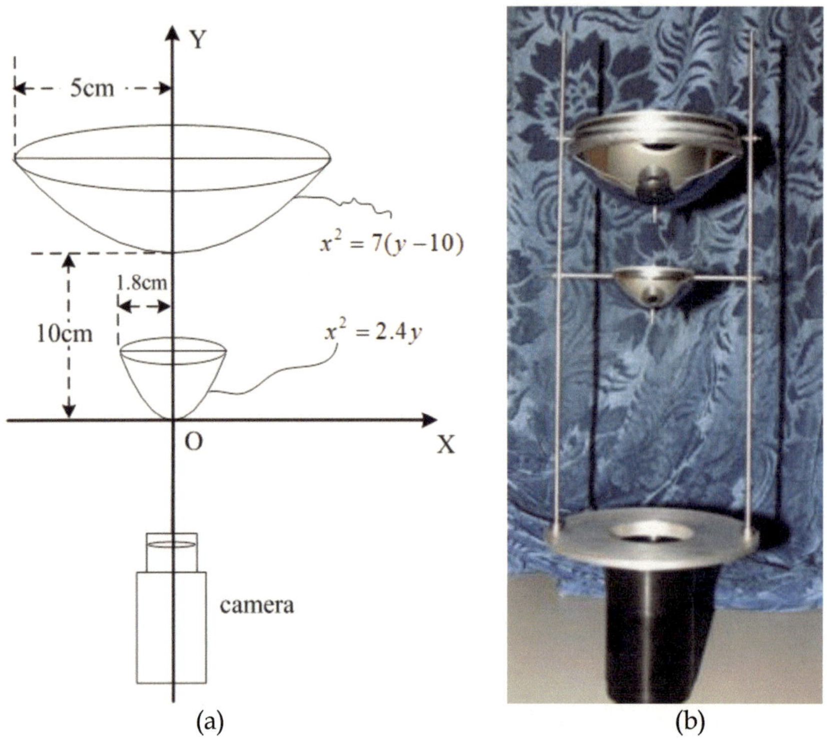

Fig. 4. Design and practical picture of single camera omni-directional stereo imaging system.
(a)design size; (b) practical picture.

3. Unwarping of omni-directional stereo vision images

There are two methods to perform stereo matching in omni-directional stereo vision. The first method is to perform stereo matching on the original images captured by the omni-directional imaging systems. When we use this method, we need to research and put forward new matching algorithms for omni-directional images. Another method is to unwarp the original captured omni-directional images into panoramic images, and then uses traditional stereo matching algorithms to finish the stereo matching on the panoramic images. When we use the second method, we need to unwarp the omni-directional images into panoramic images, as shown in Fig.5 (Note: the omni-directional image is captured with a virtual imaging system using 3D MAX).

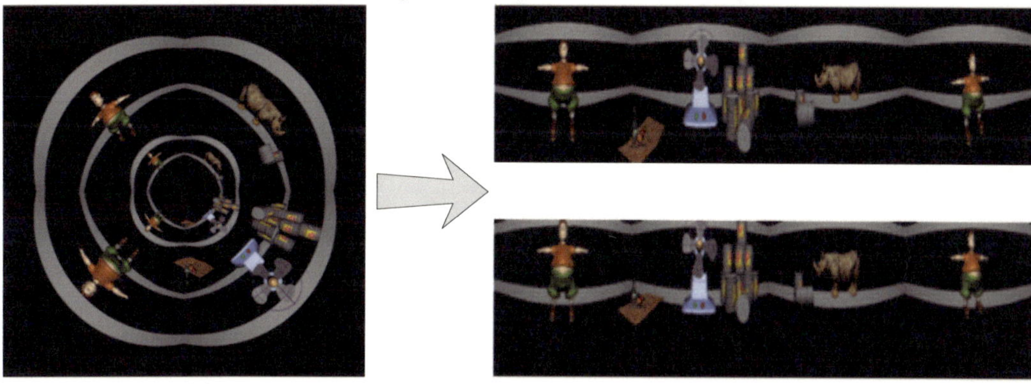

(a) (b)

Fig. 5. Omni-directional stereo vision image is unwarped into panoramic stereo vision image pair.(a)Omni-directional stereo vision image;(b)Panoramic stereo vision image pair.

For simplicity, we take the unwarping of a single omni-directional image into panoramic image as an example to describe the unwarping of omni-directional image. Presently, some general approaches for omni-directional image unwarping include ray-trace coordinate mapping, concentric circle approximate unwarping and look-up table unwarping [7].

Among these approaches, the ray-trace coordinate mapping method tracks and analyzes the propagation trace according to principles of light propagation and reflection, and draws a pixel coordinate mapping between the original omni-directional images and the unwarped panoramic images. This method unwarps panoramic images with both high precision and less distortions. The disadvantage is that this method needs heavy computation for coordinate mapping, which slows down the unwarping speed.

On the other hand, the concentric circle approximate unwarping method treats the omni-directional image as a series of concentric circles, and these circles are pulled straight and extended or compressed to the same length. This method needs lower computation time. But this method unwarps omni-directional images with bad visual effect because of its lower precision and higher distortions.

3.1 Concentric circle approximate method for omni-directional image unwarping

Fig.6 depicts the principle of concentric circle approximate unwarping. Fig.6(a) denotes a circular omni-directional image with inner radius r and outer radius R. The region between r and R is valid region. Fig.6(b) shows the corresponding unwarped panoramic image. For a pixel $P_0^{'}(X_0^{'},Y_0^{'})$ in the unwarped panoramic image, the coordinate of the corresponding pixel $P_0\ (X_0,Y_0\ )$ in the original omni-directional image (Fig.6(a)) can be determined by the following equation.

$$\begin{cases} X_0 = (r+Y_0^{'})*\sin\theta \\ Y_0 = (r+Y_0^{'})*\cos\theta \end{cases} \qquad (1)$$

Where $\theta = X_0^{'}/(r+Y_0^{'})$.

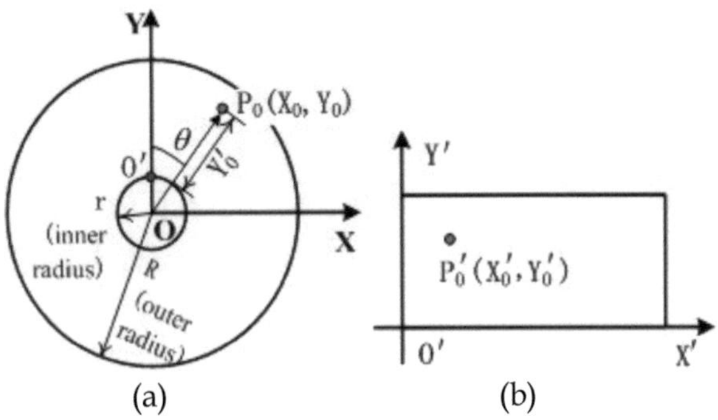

Fig. 6. Principle of unwarping the omni-directional image into panoramic image. (a)omni-directional image;(b)panoramic image.

3.2 Look-up table method for omni-directional image unwarping

Fig.7 describes the principle of look-up table method for omni-directional image unwarping. First of all, this method calculates the pixel coordinate mapping relationship between the omni-directional image and panoramic image (e.g. using the ray-trace coordinate mapping method), and saves the mapping relationship into a loop-up table. After that, when performing the omni-directional image unwarping, for each pixel in the unwarped panoramic image, what we need to do is to get the mapping from the look-up table, and then get the corresponding pixel from the omni-directional image.

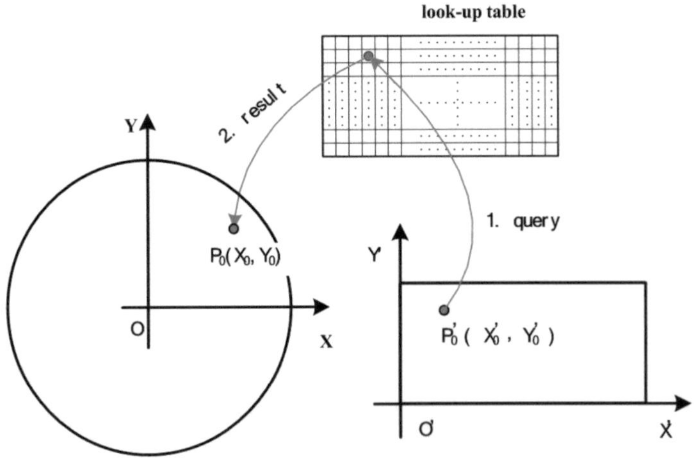

Fig. 7. Principle of look-up table method for omni-directional images unwarping

Advantages of the look-up table method including: this method unwarps omni-directional images with high precision (because this method generates the look-up table according to the results of ray-trace coordinate mapping); on the other hand, this method unwarps omni-directional images with high speed (since this method performs unwarping only by querying the look-up table and fetches the coordinate). Disadvantage of the look-up table method is: this method takes large storage space to store all the coordinate mappings (since we need to maintain an item for each pixel of the unwarped panoramic image).

3.3 Eight direction symmetry reuse algorithm for look-up table unwarping

In order to decrease the storage space needed for storing look-up table in the look-up table method for unwarping omni-directional images, we can use the eight direction symmetry reuse algorithm [7].

Eight direction symmetry reuse algorithm includes three steps: First of all, we sector the original omni-directional image into eight symmetrical regions and partition the target panorama image into eight rectangular regions (each corresponds to a sector). Secondly, based on any one of these sectors, compute the coordinate transform equation according to the principle of symmetrical transform. Finally, impose the ray-trace coordinate mapping function on only one sector, and perform symmetrical reusing process on the other seven sectors.

3.3.1 Eight direction symmetrical partition of omni-directional images

In order to reduce the storage space required to store the coordinate mappings, we reuse the coordinate mappings of the first sector using symmetrical principle. The strategy is to partition both the omni-directional image and cylinder panoramic images into eight symmetrical regions and find out the symmetrical relationship between them, and then reuse these relations.

Fig.8 indicates the principle of eight symmetrical partitions and eight direction symmetry reuse. In Fig.8(a), the coordinate system XOY is constructed at the centre of the omni-directional image O. The omni-directional image is divided into eight symmetrical regions named A_0 , A_1 ,……, A_7 . In Fig.8(b), we construct the coordinate system $X'O'Y'$ at point O' and partition the target panorama into eight equal regions named A_0' , A_1' , ……, A_7' .

After partitioning, the sectors A_0 , A_1 , ……., A_7 in Fig.8(a) are mapped to the rectangular regions A_0' , A_1' , ……, A_7' in Fig.8(b) respectively. We define the sector A_0 and the rectangular region A_0' as storing region, on which the coordinate mapping relationship need to be stored. The rest sectors A_1 , A_2 ,……, A_7 and the reset rectangular regions A_1' , A_2' ,……, A_7' are defined as reusing regions, on which the coordinate mapping relationship can be obtained by symmetrical transform reusing the computation result of storing region(A_0 and A_0').

3.3.2 Eight direction symmetry coordinate transform

For the point P_0 (X_0, Y_0) in storing region in Fig.8(a), its symmetrical points in the seven reusing regions A_i (i=1,2,3,...,7)are P_i (i=1,2,3,...,7). At the same time, the seven points P_i (i=1,2,3,...,7) in Fig.8(a) map to the seven points P_i' (i=1,2,3,...,7). Supposing the coordinates

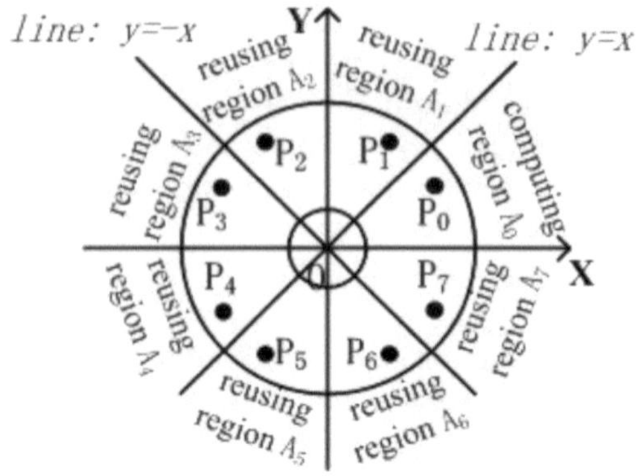

(a) Eight direction symmetry points in omni-directional image

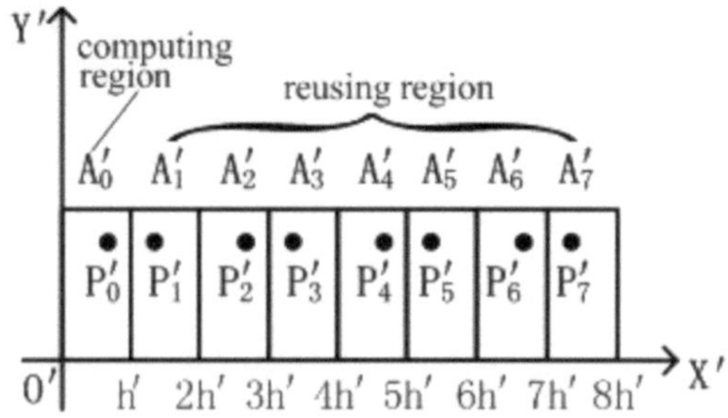

(b) Eight direction symmetry points in panorama

Fig. 8. Eight symmetrical partition and symmetry reuse

of point P_0 is (X_0, Y_0), owing to the symmetry of P_1 and P_0 at line $y = x$, the coordinates of point P_1 is (Y_0, X_0). By the same token, P_2 and P_1 are symmetric with respect to y-axis and the coordinates of P_2 is $(-Y_0, X_0)$. The rest may be deduced by analogy, finally we get:

$$\begin{cases} P_1 = (\ y_0,\ x_0),\ P_2 = (-y_0,\ x_0) \\ P_3 = (-x_0,\ y_0), P_4 = (-x_0, -y_0) \\ P_5 = (-y_0, -x_0), P_6 = (\ y_0, -x_0) \\ P_7 = (\ x_0, -y_0) \end{cases} \tag{2}$$

In Fig.8(b), suppose the coordinates of point $P_0^{'}$ is $(x_0^{'}, y_0^{'})$, the length of each rectangular region is $h^{'}$, and the seven points $P_i^{'}$ are the correspondences of the points P_i (i=1,2,3,...,7) in Fig.8(a). From Eq.(2) we can see that points P_i (i=1,2,3,...,7) relocated on the same concentric circle, thus they are of the same vertical coordinate value $y_0^{'}$ (equal to the vertical coordinate of $P_0^{'}$). In addition, their horizontal coordinates $x_i^{'}$ satisfies the following expression:

$$x_i^{'} = \begin{cases} i * h^{'} + x_0^{'} & \text{if } i = 0 \quad 2 \quad 4 \quad 6 \\ (i+1) * h^{'} - x_0^{'} - 1 & \text{if } i = 1 \quad 3 \quad 5 \quad 7 \end{cases} \tag{3}$$

Therefore, if the coordinates $(x_0^{'}, y_0^{'})$ of point $P_0^{'}$ are known, the coordinates of the rest seven reusing points $P_i^{'}$ (i=1,2,3,...,7)are:

$$P_i^{'} = \begin{cases} (i*h^{'} + x_0^{'},\ \ y_0^{'}) & \text{if } i = 2,\ 4,\ 6 \\ ((i+1)*h^{'} - x_0^{'} - 1,\ \ y_0^{'}) & \text{if } i = 1,\ 3,\ 5,\ 7 \end{cases} \quad (4)$$

3.3.3 The eight direction symmetry reuse algorithm

The algorithm includes three steps: preprocessing, coordinate mapping and coordinate reusing.

// preprocessing

Step1. Define the centre of the omni-directional image, the inner and outer radius of the valid region;

Step2. Define the resolution (height and width) of the unwarped panoramic image;

Step3. Define parameters in the ray-trace coordinate mapping;

//perform coordinates mapping and coordinate reusing

Step4. For each pixel $P_0^{'}(x_0^{'}, y_0^{'})$ in the rectangular region $A_0^{'}$ of the unwarped panoramic image, implement step 5 to step 9;

// coordinate mapping

Step5. Fetch the coordinates of point from the look-up table as (X_0, Y_0), in region A_0 of the omni-directional image, where point P_0 is correspondent with point $P_0^{'}(x_0^{'}, y_0^{'})$;

Step6. Copy the pixel value of point P_0 (X_0, Y_0) as that of $P_0^{'}$;

// coordinate reusing

Step7. Adopting Eq.(2), compute the coordinates (X_i, Y_i) of points P_i in the seven reusing region A_i of the omni-directional image respectively, and guarantee that P_i is the symmetrical point of P_0, where i=1,2,3,...,7;

Step8. Adopting Eq.(4), compute the coordinates $(x_0^{'}, y_0^{'})$ of points $P_i^{'}$ in seven reusing region $A_i^{'}$ of the unwarped panoramic image respectively, and guarantee that P_i is the symmetrical point of $P_0^{'}$, where i=1,2,3,...,7;

Step9. Copy the pixel values of symmetrical points P_i (x_i, y_i) in the seven reusing regions A_i of omni-directional image in step 7 as that of points $P_i^{'}(x_i^{'}, y_i^{'})$ in the seven reusing regions $A_i^{'}$ of unwarped panoramic image in step 8.

// complete the algorithm

Step10. When the implement traverses all the pixels in unwarped panoramic image, every pixel in other seven reusing regions of the unwarped panoramic image will get its correct pixel value.

4. Omni-directional stereo image rectification

After omni-directional images capturing and unwarping, we obtain cylindrical panoramic image pairs from the same scene. But it is not appropriate to carry out the stereo matching and depth estimation directly on the obtained cylindrical images for randomicity of imaging positions between panorama image pairs, and a rectification process should be done first (imaging systems in Fig.3(b), 3(c) are special cases of omni-directional imaging system, i.e. in which the relationship between imaging position of image pairs is particular, and unwarped panoramic pairs need no rectification). There is only horizontal disparity within rectified image pairs, therefore, we can search the corresponding points just along image scan line direction, which is a faster and more accurate approach.

The principle of rectification for cylindrical image pairs and for ordinary perspective image pairs is similar, both based on epipolar geometry. But because of particularity of cylindrical imaging model, there is biggish difference between the two rectification processes. Some related work has been done. [8-10] studied the epipolar geometry of cylindrical image and relevant mathematical formula was given. [9-12] discussed image rectification and corresponding matching problem in plenoptic modeling, range estimation and 3D reconstruction based on cylindrical image, but did not mention how to rectify image pair and to search corresponding points. [13-14]proposed a particular panoramic camera fix for range estimation and investigated the rectification problem, however, they didn't discuss about rectification on arbitrary pose of cylindrical camera pairs. While [15] firstly segmented panoramic image into several parts along axes direction, then projected every part on to plane tangent to the cylinder, and at last rectified image with proposed method for planar image. When working with approach in [15], the homographic and perspective project transformation (HPPT in short) is necessary and therefore inevitable result in pixel information losing and image distortion [16-18], and eventually reduces the correctness of the corresponding matching. Although [17] proposed a method, which transformed a line in planar image into a vertical line of cylindrical image, to minimize by-effect of HPPT, this method, in view of particularity of cylindrical imaging, can not apply to cylindrical image directly.

According to recent study literatures, the normal approach for rectifying cylindrical image pairs is the way via epiline-sampling based on epipolar geometry. It samples reference images as much as possible to obtain better pixel-maintain-rate and effective-pixel-rate by analyzing the epipolar constrain of cylindrical image pairs, and has a fair rectification result for unwarped omni-directional images. Compared with approach of HPPT, this method can reduce image distortion and pixel information losing obviously and maintain the scene information better.

4.1 Epipolar geometry of cylindrical panoramic image pairs

Epipolar geometry is an important constraint for stereo images from camera pairs, it reveals the inner relationship of the pixel positions of special scene projected onto the two cameras. As illustrated in Fig.9, let V_1, V_2 denote two viewpoints with origin v_1, v_2, and $Clind_1$, $Clind_2$ are two cylindrical panoramic images, p means a scene point with coordinates $p_1=(x_1,y_1,z_1)^T$ in V_1, $p_2=(x_2,y_2,z_2)^T$ in V_2. For generality, we assume coordinates V_1 is coincide with world coordinates. The plane spanned by v_1, v_2 and p is so-called epipolar plane, and its intersection lines (Epiline$_1$, Epiline$_2$) with $Clind_1$, $Clind_2$ are named epiline. Epipolar geometry of two views can be formalized as follows. Let p_{v1}, p_{v2} denote positions of a scene point in viewpoint coordinate of V_1 and V_2. The transformation between them is given by

$p_{v2}=Rp_{v1}+T$, where R is a (3x3) rotation matrix and T is a (3x1) translation vector. Then the normal of plane spanned by T and p_1 is $N_{TP1}=T\text{x}p_1$ where x denotes outer product. And the normal of plane spanned by T, p_2 is $N_{TP2}=RN_{TP1}=R(T\text{x}p_1)$. Since p_2 belongs to the intersection line between epipolar plane and $Clind_2$, Eq.(5) can be established by $N_{TP2}\cdot p_2=0$, i.e.

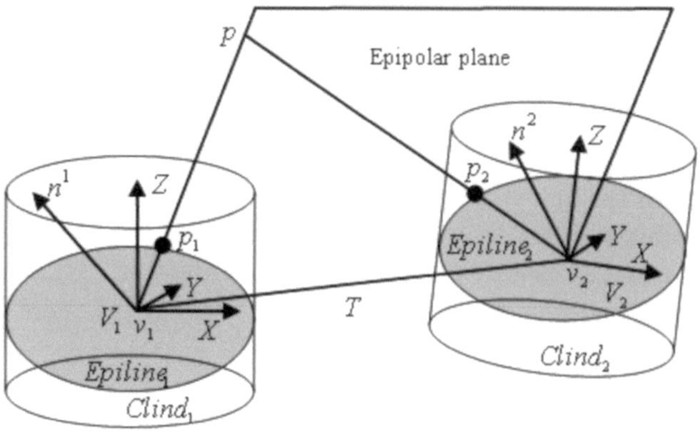

Fig. 9. Epipolar geometry of cylindrical image pairs

$$R(T\times p_1)\cdot p_2=0 \tag{5}$$

let $T=[t_x,t_y,t_z]^T$, and $[T]_\times=\begin{bmatrix}0 & -t_z & t_y\\ t_z & 0 & -t_x\\ -t_y & t_x & 0\end{bmatrix}$, then Eq.(5) can be expressed as

$$(R[T]_\times p_1)\cdot p_2=(Mp_1)\cdot p_2=p_2^TMp_1=0 \tag{6}$$

Where $M=R[T]_\times$ is a (3×3, rank 2) matrix. Eq.(5,6) presents the epipolar geometry of cylindrical panoramic image pairs.

4.2 Coordinate transformation

For what we actually get is the pixel coordinate of image, a transformation from pixel coordinates to camera coordinates is necessary. The transforming equation is:

$$p_1=(x_1,y_1,z_1)^T=\begin{cases}x_1=f\cos\alpha\\ y_1=f\sin a\\ z_1=(v_c-v_1)PixelSize\end{cases} \tag{7}$$

Where $\alpha=u_1\text{x}2\pi/ColNum$, f denotes camera focus, i.e. the radius of cylinder, (u_1,v_1) is pixel coordinates of p_1 on unrolling cylindrical image, v_c means the row index of center point on unwarped cylindrical image, $ColNum$ denotes width of unrolling cylindrical image, $PixelSize$ denotes the size of pixel. Obviously, the same transformation can by applied to p_2. Let $Mp_1=(k_{ij})_{3\text{x}1}=K$, according to Eq.(6,7), there is

$K \cdot \begin{bmatrix} f\cos\alpha_2 \\ f\sin\alpha_2 \\ (v_c - v_2)PixelSize \end{bmatrix} = 0$ where $\alpha_2 = u_2 \times 2\pi / ColNum$. Without subscript components of α_2 and v_2, we have $v = v_c + \dfrac{k_{11} f\cos\alpha + k_{21} f\sin\alpha}{k_{31} PixelSize}$, $\alpha = u \times 2\pi / ColNum$.

4.3 Epiline equation solving

When omni-directional image unwarping, it is obvious that: f can be fixed, and v_c, PixelSize is known (for the size of camera film is known). Therefore, we can only consider solving epipolar geometry equation under the following two cases:

1. Cylindrical camera has been calibrated, i.e. the values of $R, T, f, v_c, PixelSize$ are known. Then Eq.(6) will be a group of linear equations about p_2 if coordinates of p_1 (u_1, v_1) is known. And vice versa.
2. Cylindrical camera has not been calibrated. Thereby, we should firstly estimate fundamental matrix M. Let $M = (m_{ij})_{3\times 3}$, Eq.(6) can be expressed as

$$m_{11}x_1x_2 + m_{12}y_1x_2 + m_{13}z_1x_2 + m_{21}x_1y_2 + m_{22}y_1y_2 + m_{23}z_1y_2 + m_{31}x_1z_2 + m_{32}y_1z_2 + m_{33}z_1z_2 = 0 \quad (8)$$

If coordinates of (x_1, y_1, z_1) and (x_2, y_2, z_2) are known, Eq.(8) will be a nine variables linear equation with constrain of $\det(M) = 0$. Referring to 8-points algorithm of estimating fundamental matrix, we can get M similarly and then the corresponding epiline equation of every point.

4.4 Rectification via epiline sampling

To reduce distortions and pixel-information-losing of rectified images, it should sample the reference image maximum according to epipolar geometry.

For generality, assume the radius and height of $Clind_1, Clind_2$ is f_1, f_2, h_1, h_2, where $f_1 = f_2, h_1 = h_2$) f and h can be fixed when omni-directional unwarping), V_1, V_2 denote two viewpoints with origin v_1, v_2, X axes sets along $\overrightarrow{v_1v_2}$,and the coordinates V_1 is coincide with the world coordinates (see Fig. 10). For simplicity, we study the epiline sampling algorithm on *Part*$_1$and *Part*$_2$, parts of the cylindrical images.

Let $e_1 = (e_x^1, e_y^1, e_z^1)$, $e_2 = (e_x^2, e_y^2, e_z^2)$ be the two epipolars which have minimal distance among the four epipolars on *Clind*$_1$, *Clind*$_2$, since e_1,e_2 must be on all of the epipolar planes, i.e. all of the epipolar planes are composed of the plane cluster which intersect at $\overrightarrow{e_1e_2}$. Let the angle between epipolar plane and PH which is a plane spanned by $\overrightarrow{e_1e_2}$ and point p_f ($p_f = (-me_y^1, me_x^1, 0)$, $m = \dfrac{f}{\sqrt{e_y^{1\,2} + e_x^{1\,2}}}$) on $Clind_1$ be β. In order to sample pixel information on *Part*$_1$, *Part*$_2$ as much as possible, the value region ofs should be as large as possible, that is to say, epipolar plane should intersect *Part*$_1$, *Part*$_2$ maximally.

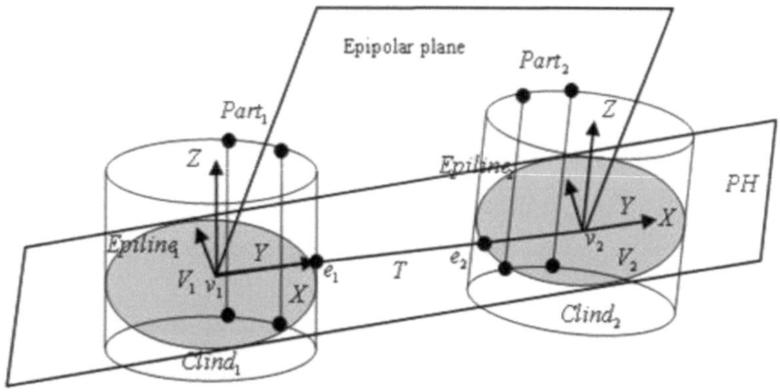

Fig. 10. Principle of epiline-sampling on cylindrical images

To calculate the largest value range of β, vertexes coordinates of $Part_1, Part_2$ should be taken into consideration. Let the coordinates of vertexes of $Part_1, Part_2$ be (x_i^j, y_i^j, z_i^j) where $i = 1,2,3,4$ and $j = 1,2$ (when $i = 1,2$, (x_i^j, y_i^j, z_i^j) denotes vertexes above PH, otherwise, denotes vertexes below PH), the normal of plane spanned by $(x_i^j, y_i^j, z_i^j), v_1, v_2$ is n_i^j, and the normal of PH is n_{ph}, then the angle between these two planes is $\beta_i^j = \arccos \frac{n_i^j \cdot n_{ph}}{|n_i^j||n_{ph}|}$. Thereby when the value region of cut angle β between PH and epipolar plane intersecting $Part_j$ is $[0, \max(\beta_{i=3,4}^j)]$ below PH, and $[0, \max(\beta_{i=3,4}^j)]$ above PH, the intersection line between epipolar plane and $Clind_1, Clind_2$ can sample the pixel information of $Part_1, Part_2$ as much as possible.

Following is the algorithm of calculating epilines on $Part_1, Part_2$. Let $\max(\beta_{i=1,2}^j) = \beta_m^l$, $\max(\beta_{i=3,4}^j) = \beta_n^k$, $m,l,k \in \{1,2\}, n \in \{3,4\}$, the Z coordinate of intersection point between line defined by $\begin{cases} x = x_m^l \\ y = y_m^l \end{cases}$ and plane spanned by $(x_m^l, y_m^l, z_m^l), e_1, e_2$ be $z_{\max}$, and Z coordinate of intersection point between the same line and plane spanned by $(x_n^k, y_n^k, z_n^k), e_1, e_2$ be $z_{\min}$, then for any point on

$$\begin{cases} x = x_m^l \\ y = y_m^l \\ z_{\min} \le z \le z_{\max} \end{cases} \tag{9}$$

we can figure out the corresponding epiline equation on $Clind_2$ referring to $(Mp_k) \cdot (x, y, z)^T = 0$, and corresponding epiline on $Clind_1$ as the intersection of cylinder and epipolar plane where the cylinder is defined as

$$\begin{cases} x^2 + y^2 = f^2 \\ 0 \le z \le h \end{cases} \tag{10}$$

and the epipolar plane is defined as

$$[(p_k - e_1)[(p_k - e_2)]_\times]\cdot[p_k - (x, y, z)] = 0 \tag{11}$$

With Eq.(10,11), epiline corresponding to p_k on $Clind_1$ can be solved. When set the value of z_k from z_{min} to z_{max}, we can sample $Part_1$, $Part_2$ by pairs of epilines as many as $(z_{max} - z_{min})$.

4.5 Rectification experiments

Corresponding rectifying experiments on part of the cylindrical image (Fig.11(a),Fig.12(a)) via algorithm of HPPT[15] and epiline-sampling are shown in Fig.11(b,c) and Fig.12(b,c). As experiments illustrated, rectifying with HPPT resulted in worse image distortions and resolution losing, while the approach based on epiline-sampling shows a better result, for it keeps the length of epiline and height and width of the image unchanged and reduced pixel information losing, as shown in Fig.11(c) and Fig.12(c).

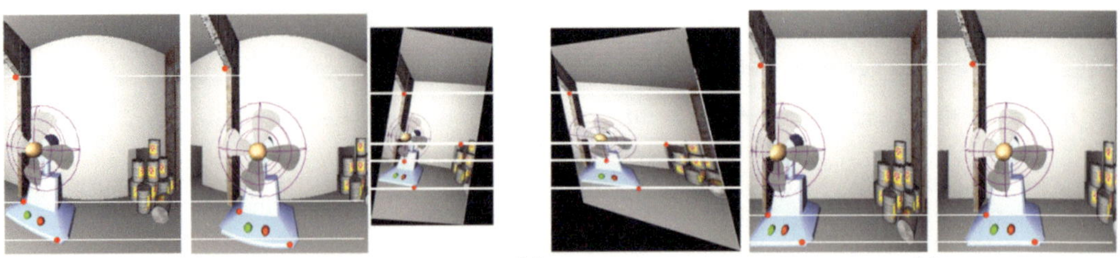

(a) (b) (c)

Fig.11 (a): Uncalibrated image pair of part of synthesized cylindrical images (corresponding points are not in the same scan line); (b): Rectified image pairs corresponding to images in (a) using the method [15] (corresponding points are in the same scan line); (c): Rectified image pairs corresponding to images in (a) using the proposed method (corresponding points are in the same scan line)

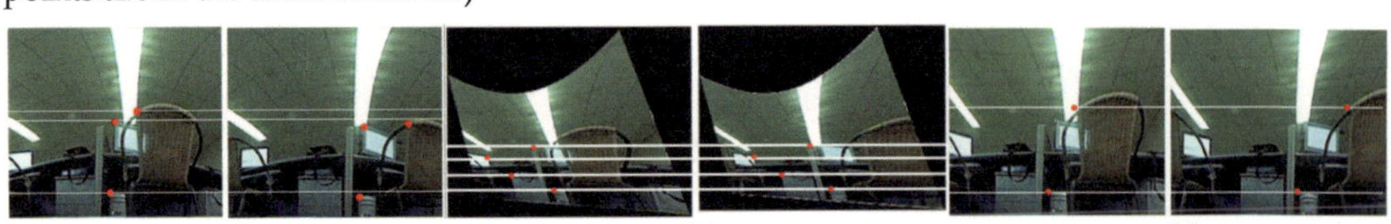

(a) (b) (c)

Fig. 12. (a): Uncalibrated image pair of part of real cylindrical images (corresponding points are not in the same scan line); (b): Rectified image pairs corresponding to images in (a) using the method [15] (corresponding points are in the same scan line); (c): Rectified image pairs corresponding to images in (a) using the proposed method (corresponding points are in the same scan line)

5. Stereo matching and depth estimation

After rectification of omni-directional image pairs, stereo matching should be done on rectified images to recovery depth information. Given camera calibrated, it is easy to figure out depth information from disparity via triangulation because of correspondence between disparity and depth. In this way, the problem of depth recovery is equal to finding correspondence within image pairs or series of images, i.e. stereo matching. However, stereo matching is a hard work for the reasons of noises, occlusion and perspective distortion.

At present, researches in this field mainly differ in problem modeling and solving, they can be categorized into algorithms based on feature information, region information, and local or global approaches based on pixel information. Each method has their own advantage and disadvantage, for example, algorithms based on feature information is robust against noise, but can only obtain sparse disparity image; algorithms based on region matching although can get dense disparity map, but its reliability is poor and result is incorrect in the region of untextured, occluded and discontinuity; algorithm based on local information is faster compared to other ones but more sensitive to image local features and apt to produce wrong result.

However, approaches with global graph cuts (GC) optimization are widely studied and showing strong performance in last few years. [19-21] utilized GC optimization in stereo matching decade ago; Yuri Boykov and Vladimir Kolmogorov developed new faster GC algorithm[23-27] on the basis of[19,21-22], which coped smoothness problem of resultant disparity map in the depth-jump area. Meanwhile, [28, 29, 31] adopted occlusion restriction in GC optimization, but occlusion itself is still too complex to deal with. [29-32] firstly initialized a disparity map and segmented it, then fitting each segment with a planar equation and labeling them via GC optimization, , therefore, a better result can be obtained.

In this section, methodology and processes of stereo matching via GC optimization will be introduced in the first instance, and then a stereo matching algorithm based on region restriction and GC optimization will be illustrated in detail. This algorithm assumes disparity jumps only at the region of color discontinuity, and constructs energy function subjected to restriction between region boundaries. In this way, not only the global solution of energy function can be work out, but also that the solution has the feature of discontinuity-preserving, meanwhile embodies occlusion restriction, ordering restriction and uniqueness restriction. Additional, for energy function is only constructed based on boundary pixels, the number of graph vertex in GC optimization should certainly reduce significantly and results in great efficient performance.

5.1 Energy minimization presentation of stereo matching

Stereo matching between image pair can be compared to a problem of carbonization optimization. For a scene of limit depth, the corresponding discrete integral disparity is also a limit set, and our goal is to find (according to some rules) an optimal combinatorial configuration of disparity for each pixel in stereo images. Energy minimization is a common solution for this issue, which is usually presented as:

$$\min\ E(f) = \sum_{p\in I} D_p(f_p) + \sum_{\{p,q\}\in N} V_{p,q}(f_p, f_q) \tag{12}$$

Where p , q denote pixels with neighborhood system N in image I , f is the combinatorial configuration of disparity for every image pixel. $D_p(f_p)$ (called data term) expresses color consistency of pixel p when its disparity is f_p . $V_{p,q}(f_p, f_q)$ (called smoothness term) means smoothness between pixels p with disparity f_q and q with disparity f_q .

5.2 GC optimization

To solve Eq.(12), there are many approaches such as simulating anneal, dynamic programming and neural network, but these methods are either fit for high dimension dataset or hard to converge, and usually are inefficient in terms of computation. Recent researches prove that algorithms based on min cuts are very appropriate for problem of combinatorial optimization. They can be categorized mainly into two sets:

1. GC algorithms obtaining global optimal solution

[20,21,33] regard combinatorial optimization as a labeling problem, and solving the problem via constructing a special graph whose min cuts/max flow just corresponds to optimal solution of energy function. To ensure a given energy function can be presented with graph, it demands smoothness term of energy function must be convex, therefore, result in bigger punish and over-smooth at boundary of disparity jump. Additional, for the convexity of smoothness term, some issues such as occlusion problem, ordering restriction can not be dealt with very well.

2. GC algorithms obtaining global second optimal solution

To settle the over-smooth problem, [23-25] proposed to adopt unconvex smoothness term to make energy function discontinuity-preserving. So called Potts model $V_{p,q}(f_p, f_q) = \lambda \times T(f_p \neq f_q)$ is a common simple smoothness term, however, even with Potts model, [23,26,28] proved it is NP-hard to optimize such energy function and there is no efficient global optimization algorithm. Therefore, [23,26,27]developed approximating ways to cope this problem by dividing optimization of multivariable energy function into iterative optimization of two-variable energy function, it meanwhile showed that, after certain iteration, the solution we get via this approach is just near the global optimal solution[21]. Because of unconvexness of smoothness term, such algorithm also can deal with occlusion, ordering problems and uniqueness. However, there are still some disadvantages. Approximating approach can only obtain second optimal solution in iterative way, it is hard to measure the computation complexity, and when take occlusion or ordering into consideration, it will bring in more additional computation.

5.3 Graph construction of GC optimization

Graph construction of GC optimization in this section is very similar to the way proposed in [21], as Fig.13 illustrated, where vertexes of graph network are possible matching pixel pairs, and edges of graph network denote neighborhood interaction and restrictions ensuring correspondence between a min cut of graph and a disparity configuration of stereo matching.

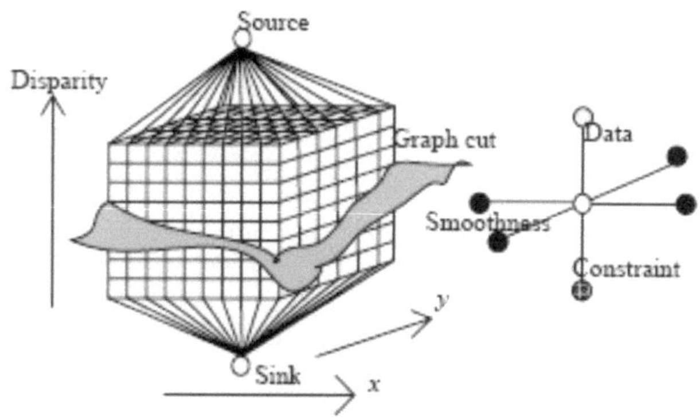

Fig. 13. A graph structure for stereo matching

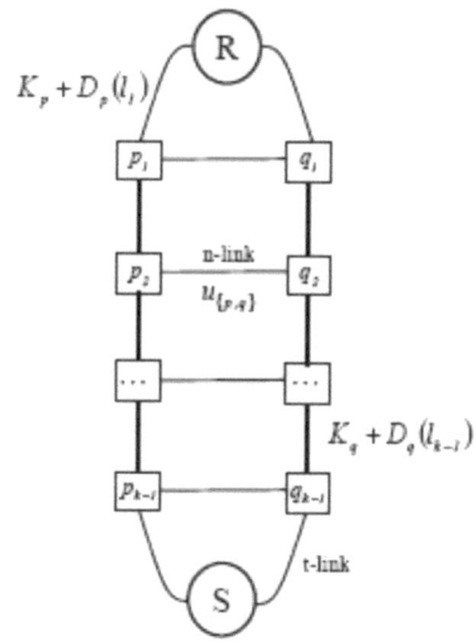

Fig. 14. A subgraph of Fig.13 corresponding to pixels p and q

Fig.14 is a subgraph of Fig.13 corresponding to pixels p and q, and vertexes R and S are terminals *Source* and *Sink* in Fig.13. The detail graph construction process can be defined as follows:

1. For each pixel p, create a set of vertexes $p_1, \ldots\ldots, p_{k-1}$ (k is the number of labels). Connect them by edges which is called *t-links* $\{t_1^p, \ldots, t_k^p\}$ where

   $t_1^p = \{R, p_1\}, t_j^p = \{p_{j-1}, p_j\}, t_k^p = \{p_{k-1}, S\}$;

2. For each pair of neighboring pixels p, q and for each $j \in \{1, \ldots, k-1\}$, create an edge called *n-links* $\{p_j, q_j\}$ with weight $u_{\{p,q\}}$;

3. Each *t-links* t_j^p is assigned a weight $K_p + D_p(l_j)$ where K_p is any constant such that $K_p > (k-1)\sum_{q \in N_p} u_{\{p,q\}}$.

Any cut of graph define in this way corresponds to a disparity configuration of stereo matching, and the cut cost is:

$$|C| = \sum_{p\in I} K_p + \sum_{p\in I} D_p(f_p^C) + \sum_{\{p,q\}\in N} u_{\{p,q\}} \left| f_p^C - f_q^C \right| \tag{13}$$

In Eq.(13), $\sum_{p\in I} K_p$ is a constant, and $\sum_{p\in I} D_p(f_p^C)$ is corresponding data term in Eq.(12). If we define $V_{p,q}(f_p, f_q) = u_{\{p,q\}} \left| f_p^C - f_q^C \right|$, then there is only a constant term dispersion between Eq.(12) and Eq.(13). Therefore, the two equations can get optimal solution simultaneously, i.e. corresponding solution of min cut of constructed graph is also the global optimal solution of energy function. More information can refer to paper [21].

5.4 Stereo matching based on region boundary restriction and GC optimization

For the unconvexness of $u_{\{p,q\}} \left| f_p^C - f_q^C \right|$, energy function with the form of Eq.(13) can obtain global optimal solution via GC, therefore stereo matching algorithm based on region boundary restriction and GC optimization is naturally to represent energy function in the form similar to Eq.(13), but additional, it also need to deal with over-smooth problem meanwhile embody ordering and unique restrictions.

5.4.1 Assumptions

This algorithm assumes that:

1. Most of disparity jump occur at the region of color discontinuity.
2. If the image is over-segmentation based on color information, then it is sensible to consider that pixels in same segment have equal disparity [29,31].
3. Most occlusions in image pair are part-occlusion.

With qualitative analysis, it is clear that the assumptions given above are rational in most of cases.

5.4.2 Algorithm principle

Because pixels in same region have equal disparity after image segmentation, therefore, disparity of whole segment is up to disparity of its boundary pixels, and the key problem of stereo matching can be regarded as find corresponding disparity for every pixel on each segment.

Hence, an approach is region matching, for that if region correspondence between images is known, it is easy to figure out disparities of boundary pixels. [37] proposed a region matching algorithm, which worked as following: (1)segment image based on color information; (2) match regions by region features; (3) compute disparity map of whole image according to region matching result. However, this algorithm is not consistent with the fact. For factors such as imaging process and segmentation algorithm itself, segmentation results of image pairs of same scene may be different in many ways, which will be certainly result in wrong region matching. Fig.15 illustrates the difference in shape and size of segments of image pairs.

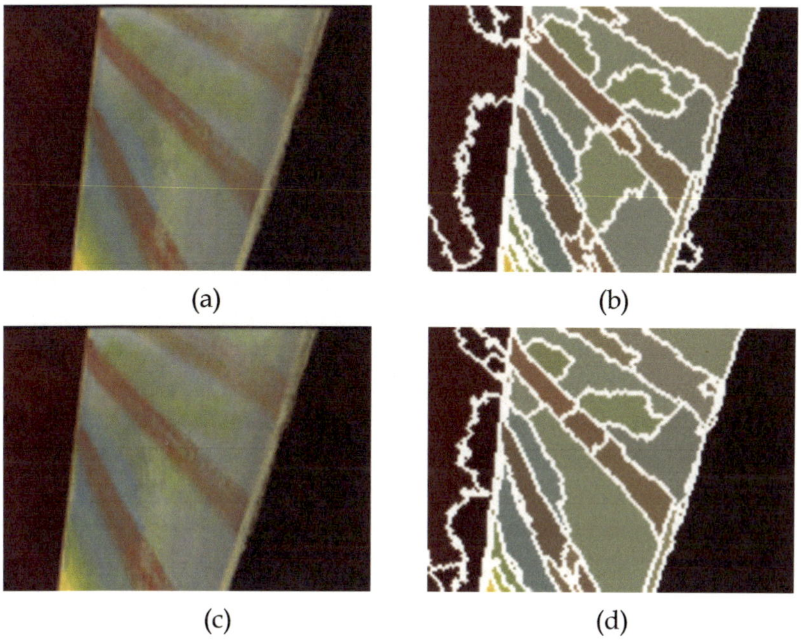

Fig. 15. (a): middle-top part of left view of venus testing image pair; (b): segmentation result of (a) via mean-shift algorithm; (c): middle-top part of right view of venus testing image pair; (d): segmentation result of (c) via mean-shift algorithm

To overcome problem mentioned above, in this section, a new approach for region matching is proposed. It only segments one of reference images (for generality, we can assume it is left image) based on color information, and then constructs energy function according to color-consistency and neighborhood relationship. It will show that, when optimization via graph cuts with this approach, region boundary of left image will close to corresponding region boundary of right image automatically. Constructed energy function is defined as:

$$min\ E(f) = \sum_{p \in BI} D_p(f_p) + \sum_{\{p,q\} \in N_1} V1_{p,q}(f_p, f_q) + \sum_{\{p,q\} \in N_2} V2_{p,q}(f_p, f_q) \qquad (14)$$

Where BI is the image consist of pixels on left and right region boundary (see [37] for definition of left and right region boundary) from one reference image, $D_p(f_p)$ denotes color difference for pixel p with disparity f_p, $V1_{p,q}(f_p, f_q) = u1_{p,q} \times |f_p - f_q|$, $V2_{p,q}(f_p, f_q) = u2_{p,q} \times |f_p - f_q|$ indicate the punish for different disparity of p, q with neighborhood N_1, N_2, where N_1 is neighborhood of pixels along scan line direction on adjacent region(as p, q illustrated in Fig.16(a)), N_2 is neighborhood of pixels on left and right boundary of the same region(as sillustrated in Fig.16(a)), $u1 > u2$. And Fig.16(b) shows how this algorithm works.

(a) (b)

Fig. 16. (a): position relation illustration of pixels on region boundary(part magnified image of Fig.15(b)); (b): principle of region boundary pixels matching illustration(part magnified image of Fig.15(c))

p, q are pixels on boundary of two adjacent region, it is clear that, corresponding points of p, q in Fig.16(a) should lie in the area near central point of the circle in Fig.16(b). If assume correspondence of p, q in optimal configuration f^c is not the case, i.e. corresponding points of p, q in Fig.16(a) are p, q in Fig.16(b) respectively, then according to Eq.(14) , $V1_{p,q}(f_p, f_q) > 0$ and is proportional to distance between p, q, hence it is contradictory to the assumption that f^c is the optimal configuration. Because if choose p, q in Fig.16(b) more close to central point of the circle, $V1_{p,q}(f_p, f_q)$ will certainly reduce and $V2_{p,q}(f_p, f_q)$ and $D_p(f_p)$ should keep the same cost (for pixels in same region are color consistency and $u1 > u2$), therefore, the total cost of energy function $E(f)$ will reduce.

With globally optimizing Eq.(14) via GC, we can get fairly correct result of region matching, but for occlusion between regions, the dense disparity map can not be obtained yet.

5.4.3 Dealing with occlusion

Different depth of scene objects is the essential cause of occlusion, and only pixels in unoccluded part of one image have corresponding point in another image, that is to say, if we can match unoccluded part of reference images correctly, we can get correct disparity map meanwhile. After optimizing Eq.(14) via GC, region matching is fairly accurate, thereby the subsequent key problem is dealing with occlusion. We discuss that in three cases (because there is only horizontal displacement, so we need only analyze occlusion occurring at left and right region boundary):

1. There is no occlusion existing at left or right region boundary, then disparity of pixels on left and right region boundary are equal to each other, and also to disparity of the region.
2. Only left/right region boundary is occluded, in this case, disparity of whole region can be inferred from that of unoccluded region boundary.
3. Both left and right region boundary are occluded. Under this circumstance, we can not certainly get correct region disparity because neither disparity of left or right region boundary is authentic.

Analyze occlusion and disparity estimating in the cases of situation 1 and 2. As Fig.17 illustrated, Fig.17(a) and Fig.17(b) are stereo image pairs. Assume corresponding point pairs after region matching are $\{a1, A1\}$,..., $\{c2, C2\}$, then disparity of pixels on region boundary in Fig.17(a) can be expressed as $(x_{A1} - x_{a1})$,...., $(x_{C1} - x_{c1})$. It is obvious that there is part-occlusion existing in region A, C (labeled with red rectangle), therefore, only disparity of left region boundary of A is authentic, i.e. disparities of pixels between $a1$,$a2$ can be considered to be $(x_{A1} - x_{a1})$. Similarly, disparities of pixels between $c1$, $c2$ can be considered to be $(x_{C2} - x_{c2})$. For $(x_{A2} - x_{a2}) > (x_{A1} - x_{a1}), (x_{C1} - x_{c1}) > (x_{C2} - x_{c2}), (x_{B1} - x_{b1}) = (x_{B2} - x_{b2})$, we can present disparity estimating equation as:

$$D_p = \min((x_{P1} - x_{p1}), (x_{P2} - x_{p2})) \tag{15}$$

where P, p are corresponding pixels on left and right region boundary. As an example ,Fig.17(c) gives the corresponding dense disparity map of Fig.17(a) (disparity of background pixel is set to zero).

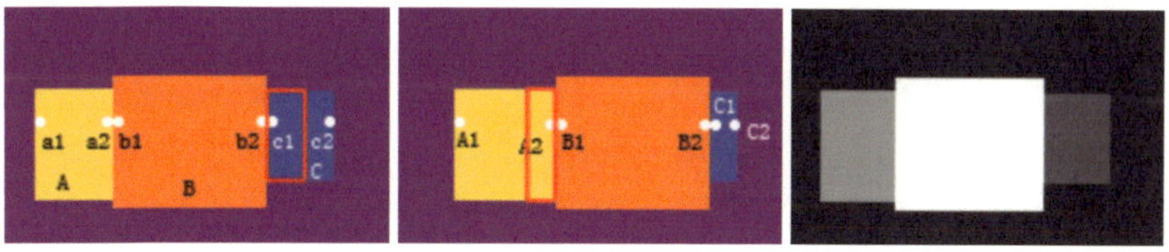

(a) (b) (c)

Fig. 17. Occlusion and disparity calculation. (a): left view of image pair; (b): right view of image pair; (c): corresponding disparity result

As discussed above, with this approach, it can obtain authentic region disparity and meanwhile occlusions occurring within reference image pairs. Additional, although there is punish given for adjacent region boundary, it allows disparity jump between them (as disparity jump existing at the left and right boundary of region B in fiugre17).

5.4.4 Uniqueness

In this algorithm, though it is not defined uniqueness restriction explicitly, uniqueness restriction is still fulfilled in result disparity map for color consistency and neighborhood interactions have been enforced in energy function.

As illustrated in Fig.17, assume boundary pixel $a2$ in Fig.17(a) is (x, y), its corresponding point in Fig.17(b) is $A2 = (x + d, y)$, and $b1 = (x + 1, y)$ is the adjacent boundary pixel of $a2$, hence coordinates of $B1$ as corresponding point to $b1$ should be $(x + d + 1, y)$ (when region B unoccluded) or $(x + d + k, y), k > 1$ (when region B occluded), otherwise, $B1$ will lie in region A and result in more cost of $D_p(f_p)$ for different color within two regions.

To sum up, the process of this algorithm can be described as following:

1. Segment arbitrary one image of stereo image pairs and obtain corresponding region boundaries.
2. Construct graph according to Eq.(14) and segmentation result.
3. Find the min cut of constructed graph and matching regions.
4. Estimate disparity map and analyze occlusion according to Eq.(15).

Among those steps, the second one is the key operation. Although it is similar to approach proposed in [21], it differs from that in graph element and neighborhood system, and the essence of energy function despite of alike equation form.

5.5 Stereo matching experiments

Fig.18 illustrates some examples of stereo matching and disparity estimating with image pairs from Middlebury dataset and real scenes. The results of stereo matching are measured with criteria proposed in [34], i.e. record number of pixel whose disparity discrepancy is beyond one from ground truth(called error). For every pair of reference image, calculate three statistics: (1) error on all pixels in image D_{all} ; (2) error on pixels in undiscontinuity region; (3) error on pixels in untexture region. Experiments result are shown in Fig.18, Fig.19, Fig.20.

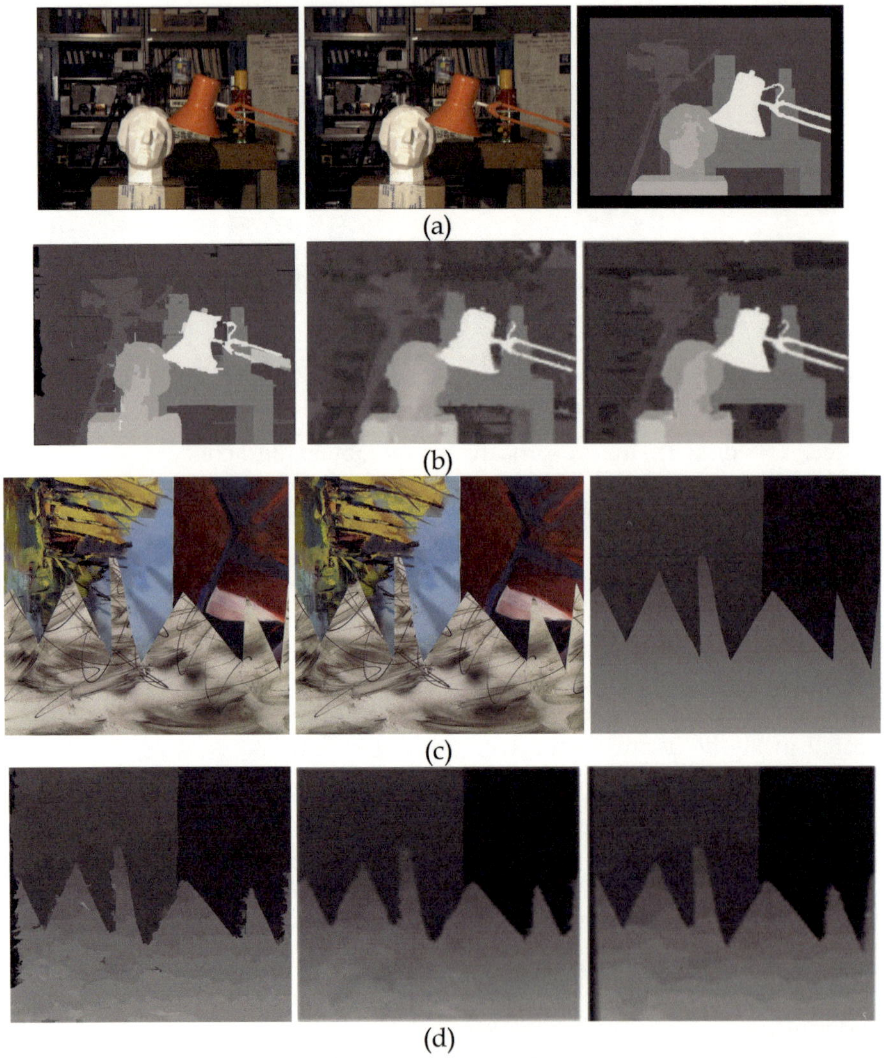

Fig. 18. Result on tsukuba and sawtooth testing image pair. (a): tsukuba testing image pair and corresponding ground truth; (b): corresponding stereo matching results on tsukuba testing image pair via algorithms of proposed, [35-36] from left to right; (c): sawtooth testing image pair and corresponding ground truth; (d): corresponding stereo matching results on sawtooth testing image pair via algorithms of proposed, [35-36] from left to right

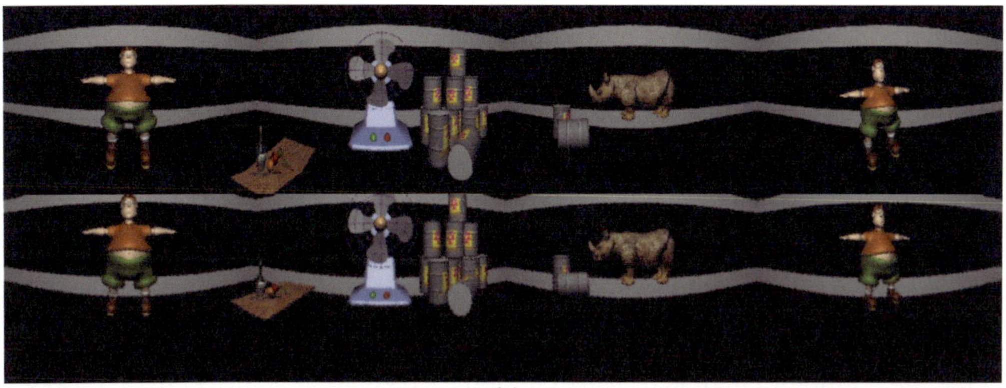

(a)

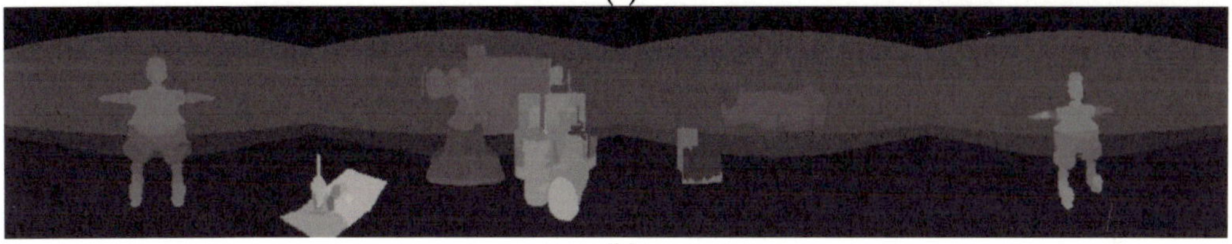

(b)

Fig. 19. Experiment with synthesized scene. (a) synthesized cylindrical panoramic image pair after rectification; (b) disparity map of synthesized cylindrical panoramic image pair.

(a)

(b)

Fig. 20. Experiment with real scene. (a) real cylindrical panoramic image pair after rectification; (b) disparity map of real cylindrical panoramic image pair.

6. Applications on moving object detection and tracking

Moving object detection is a foundation problem in computer vision, and it is also a foundation problem in catadioptric omni-directional stereo vision. So, we will present an application case of moving object detection that is based on the omni-directional stereo vision.

As we know, traditional moving object detection methods that are based on a single camera have some difficulties, including: 1) Need to consider the background change, such as the illumination changes, background disturb (e.g. wind blowing and tree swing), shadow, movement of the cameras, et al. 2) When tracking the moving objects, the object is likely to go beyond the camera resulting in lose of the objects. At this time, we need to rotate the camera and search the object again.

The above problems can be resolved using the omni-directional stereo vision method. In this method, we utilize the depth information from the stereo vision to detect objects, since the depth information calculation is independent from the background image, it is not affected by illumination change and background disturb. Catadioptric omni-directional imaging system captures the 360 degree FOV just in one shot, so it does not need to rotate the camera when tracking moving objects.

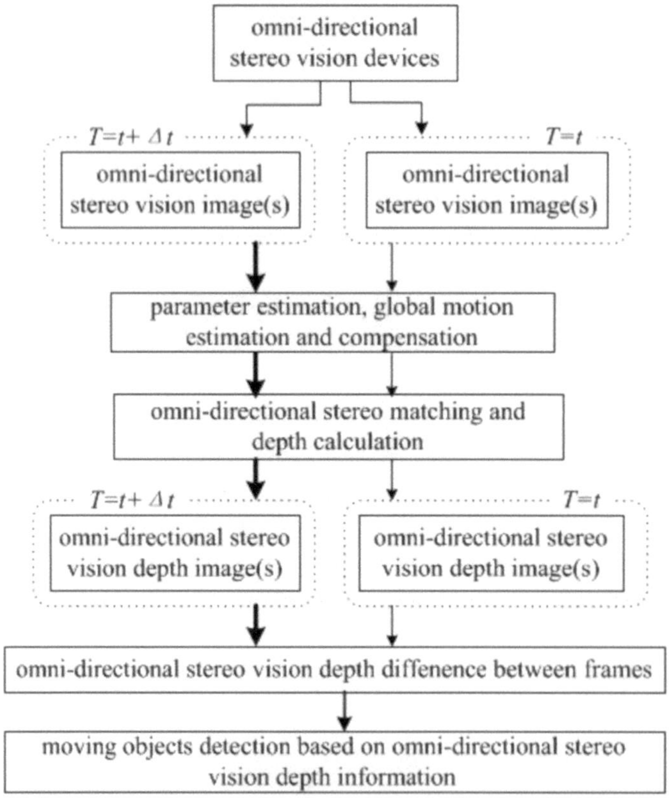

Fig. 21. Overall flow of moving object detection based on omni-directional stereo vision

Fig.21 shows the overall flow of moving object detection based on omni-directional stereo vision. In this figure, the omni-directional stereo vision device takes charge to capture omni-directional stereo vision image (or image pair). After camera parameters estimation, global movement estimation and global movement compensation, we get the omni-directional stereo image (or image pair) that has compensated the global movement of the camera. At this time, there exists no camera movement, and exists only object movement (i.e. local movement). Based on these images, we can perform stereo matching and depth calculation, so as to get the omni-directional stereo depth image at the same time (e.g. $T = t + \Delta t$). Then, we can do differential calculation between frames of the omni-directional stereo depth images at different times, and we can detect and track the moving objects.

7. Acknowledgements

The research is partially supported by National Natural Science Foundation of China (NSFC) project "Moving object detection and tracking based on Stereo omni-directional panorama vision" (Fund. No. 60705013), National Natural Science Foundation of China (NSFC) project "Research on virtual environment construction methods based on stereo parallel mosaicing" (Fund. No. 60773023), Postdoctor Science Foundation of China project "Research on key techniques of stereo omni-directional panorama system" (Fund. No. 20070410977), and Natural Science Foundation of Hunan Province project "Research on Platform-Based SOC Front-End Co-synthesis Techniques" (Fund. No. 08JJ4018).

8. References

A.A. Argyros, C. Bekris, S.C. Orphanoudakis and L.E. Kavraki. Robot homing by exploiting panoramic vision, Journal of Autonomous Robots, 2005, 19(1), 7-25.

H.Y. Shum and L.W. He. Rendering with concentric mosaics, Proceedings of ACM SIGGRAPH, 1999, pp.299-306.

T. Gandhi and M.M. Trivedi. Parametric ego-motion estimation for vehicle surrounds analysis using an omni-directional camera, Machine Vision and Applications, 2005, 16(2), 85-95.

C. Sun and S. Peleg. Fast panoramic stereo matching using cylindrical maximum surfaces, IEEE Transactions on Systems, Man, and Cybernetics, Part B, 2004, 34(2), 760-765.

M.J. Zhang, W. Xu and W. Wang. Real VR space construction and its devices for curve face reflective imaging, P.R. China Patent application No. 200510031552.X, 2005, 5.

R. Benosman, S.B. Kang. Panoramic vision: sensors, theory, and applications. Springer-Verlag New York, Publishing House, 2001.

Zhihui Xiong, Maojun Zhang, Yunli Wang, et al. Fast panorama unrolling of catadioptric omni-directional images for cooperative robot vision systems. Proceedings of IEEE International Conference on Computer Supported Cooperative Work in Design (CSCWD), Melbourne, Australia, Apr. 26-28, 2007(2):1100-1104.

L. Smadja, R. Benosman, J. Devars. Determining epipolar constraint on cylindrical images and using it for 3d reconstruction, Proc. ICAR, Aug 2001.

R. Bunschoten et al.. Range estimation from a pair of omnidirectional images, Proc. IEEE Int. Conf. on Robotics and Automation, Seoul, Korea, 2001:1174~1179.

R. Bunschoten, B. Krose. 3-D scene reconstruction from cylindrical panoramic images, Robotics and Autonomous Systems (special issue), 2002, 41(2/3):111~118.

M. Kimura and H. Saito. 3D reconstruction based on epipolar geometry, IEEE Transactions on Information and Systems, 2001.

L. McMillan and G. Bishop. Plenoptic modeling: An image-based rendering system. ACM SIGGRAPH. 1995: 39~46.

H. Koyasu, J. Miura and Y. Shirai. Real omni-directional stereo for obstacle detection and tracking in dynamic environments. IEEE proceedings, International Conference on Intelligent Robots and System, 2001:31~36.

J. Gluckman, S. K. Nayar and K. Thorek. Real-time omni-directional and panoramic stereo. DARPA Image Understanding Workshop, California, 1998.
A. R. Lawrence and D. C. Nathan. Method and system for panoramic image morphing. United States Patent, 6795090, 2004.
D. Oram. Rectification for any epipolar geometry. 12th British Machine Vision Conference (BMVC), 2001.
S. M. Roy and J. Cox. Cylindrical rectification to minimize epipolar distortion. Computer Vision and Pattern Recognition Proceedings, 1997.
H. H. P. Wu, Y. H. Yu, and W. C. Chen. Projective rectification based on relative modification and size extension for stereo image pairs. IEEE Proceedings, Vision Image and Signal Processing, 2005.
Y. Boykov, O. Veksler and R. Zabih. Markov random fields with efficient approximations. In IEEE Conference on PAMI, 1998, 648-655.
H. Ishikawa and D. Geiger. Segmentation by grouping junctions. In IEEE Conference on PAMI, 1998, 125-131.
O. Veksler. Efficient graph-based energy minimization methods in computer vision. Ph.D. Thesis, Cornell University, 1999
V. Kolmogorov and R. Zabih. What energy functions can be minimized via graph cuts, In IEEE Conference on PAMI 2004, 26(2):147-159
Y. Boykov, O. Veksler and R. Zabih. Fast approximate energy minimization via graph cuts. In IEEE transaction on PAMI, 2001, 23(11):1222-1239.
V. Kolmogorov and R. Zabih. Multi-camera scene reconstruction via graph cuts. In Proc. ECCV, 2002, 82-96.
J. Kim, V. Kolmogorov and R. Zabih. Visual correspondence using energy minimization and mutual information. In Proc. ICCV, 2003.
Y. Boykov, V. Kolmogorov. An experimental comparison of min-cut max-flow algorithms for energy minimization in vision, In IEEE transactions on PAMI, 2004, 26(9):1124-1137.
V. Kolmogorov. Graph based algorithms for scene reconstruction from two or more views. Ph.D. Thesis, Cornell University, 2004.
V. Kolmogorov, R. Zabih. Computing visual correspondence with occlusions using graph cuts. In ICCV, 2001, 2:508-515.
L. Hong, G. Chen. Segment-based stereo matching using graph cuts. In IEEE Computer Society Conference on CVPR, 2004, 74-81.
M. Bleyer, M. Gelauz. A layered stereo matching algorithm using image segmentation and global visibility constraints, ISPRS Journal of Photogrammetry & Remote Sensing, 2005,128-150.
M. Bleyer, M. Gelauz. Graph-cut-based stereo matching using image segmentation with symmetrical treatment of occlusions, Signal Processing: Image Communication, 2007, 127-143.
Y. Deng, Q. Yang, X. Y. Lin and X. O. Tang. Stereo correspondence with occlusion handling in a symmetric patch-based graph-cuts model stereo. In IEEE transaction on PAMI, 2007, 1068-1079.
H. Ishikawa. Exact optimization for Markov random fields with convex priors. In IEEE Transactions on PAMI, 2003, 1333-1336.
D. Scharstein, R. Szeliski. A taxonomy and evaluation of dense two-frame stereo correspondence algorithms, International Journal of Computer Vision, 2002, 47:7-42.
P. Mordohai, G. Medioni. Stereo using monocular cues within the tensor voting framework. In IEEE transaction on PAMI, 2006, 28(6):968-982.
K. J. Yoon, I. S. Kweon. Adaptive support-weight approach for correspondence search. In IEEE transaction on PAMI,2006, 28(4):650-656.
M. Ansari, L. Masmoudi, A. Bensrhair. A new regions matching for color stereo images. Pattern Recognition Letters, 2007, 1679-1687.

27

Person Following Robot with Vision-based and Sensor Fusion Tracking Algorithm

Takafumi Sonoura, Takashi Yoshimi, Manabu Nishiyama,
Hideichi Nakamoto, Seiji Tokura and Nobuto Matsuhira
Corporate R&D Center, Toshiba Corporation
Japan

1. Introduction

Current demographics show that Japan is experiencing a combination of an aging population and a declining birth rate. Therefore, interest is growing in the potential of human symbiotic robots such as daily life support robots that can care for the aged and young children. Human symbiotic robots require sophisticated capabilities to achieve symbiosis and interaction with humans. It is essential for these robots to understand human intentions, and interact with humans and the environment. We call these technologies, which create real value for people and society, "human-centric technologies", and have developed some home robots and human symbiotic robots (Yoshimi et al., 2004; Matsuhira et al., 2005a; Matsuhira et al., 2005b). The development of these robots is a typical target for human-centric technologies, but these technologies are not only applicable for robots but also for all machines that humans use.

In the development of human symbiotic robots, we set one of the target criteria as the ability to recognize individuals using vision, and to understand situations in order to provide various real-life services to humans. To realize this target criterion, we think that the principal capabilities required are accurate vision and recognition of specified individuals who are in the vicinity. Moreover, another important capability common to the human symbiotic robot is that of moving safely near humans.

In light of the above considerations, we have developed ApriAttenda™ shown in Fig.1, a person following robot that finds a specified person using visual tracking functions and follows him/her while avoiding obstacles (Yoshimi et al., 2006). Person following robots developed until now use various types of cameras for detecting a target person, and some of them use other sensors (Schlegl et al., 1998; Sidenbladh et al., 1999; Kwon et al., 2005; Cielniak et al., 2005; Kobilarov et al., 2006). Our newly developed robot adopts a stereo vision system, and additionally a Laser Range Finder (LRF) is mounted on the robot body to enhance the performance of person following motion.

A person following robot has to distinguish the target object from other objects and recognize it by some methods. And the robot has to get the information of the target position, and continue following it quickly so as not to be left behind. At this time, camera information is often used to recognize the target. In addition, in the case of the stereo systems using two or more cameras, the distance information for the person following motion can be obtained.

The stereo vision system generates information on distance to the object being tracked. It is helpful for the person following motion but unsatisfactory, because this information has insufficient accuracy for quick person following motion. Using the image data with a rough pixel limited by the trade-off with the calculation speed, many quantization errors will occur.

So, we designed a tracking system that uses highly accurate measurement information by operating in combination with LRF. Our system has a feature to change the fusion rate of vision and LRF data according to the congestion level of the movement space, and so we achieved quick and stable person following motion.

This article introduces the mobile robot system to which the vision system is applied. And the behaviour of the vision system mounted on the mobile robot is shown. Moreover, the problems of the tracking system applied to the robot system are pointed out, and a new sensor fusion method to overcome the problems is proposed. Additionally, the effect of the proposed method is shown by referring to experiment results.

Fig. 1. Person Following Robot ApriAttenda™ (without LRF)

Size	φ450[mm]×H900[mm]
Weight	approx. 30[kg]
Sensors	CCD Camera×2 with Pan/Tilt Motion Ultrasonic Sensors (8direction) Laser Range Finder×1
Movement	Drive Motors and Wheels×2 (independently driven)
Max Velocity	1.2 [m/s] (4.3[km/h])
Max Acceleration	2.0 [m/s^2]
Interfaces	TFT Liquid Crystal Display, Microphones, Speakers
Power	Lithium-Ion Battery
Operation Time	approx. 1[hour]

Table 1. Specifications of ApriAttenda™

2. Person following robot ~ robotics application of vision systems ~

2.1 Robot specifications

The person following robot, ApriAttenda™, whose shape consists of two spheres, one mounted on top of the other, is shown in Fig.1. It is designed to look friendly and gentle, so many people feel that it is safe and harmonizes with the surrounding environment. The specifications of ApriAttenda™ are shown in Table 1. The robot is approximately 450mm in diameter, 900mm in height, and 30kg in weight, and it moves by two independently driven wheels. The robot gets the image of the target person by means of two CCD cameras on its head with pan/tilt motions. The robot can get higher-resolution images in real time using stereo vision than in the case of using an omnidirectional camera; the accurate recognition of the target person is executed. Furthermore, the robot is equipped with an LRF on its body (Fig.11). It can get high-precision line-scan (direction-distance pare) information.

We have designed the size of this robot to enable it to coexist with people who walk around in the home and public facilities, and to look over the objects on standard height desks or tables. The robot can be commanded through verbal communication, the touch panel display mounted on its back, or wireless LAN from an external PC. The robot is powered by lithium-ion batteries and its operation time is about one hour with full batteries. The robot has an inertia absorbing mechanism to maintain stability in case the robot moves or stops suddenly.

2.2 Functions

ApriAttenda™ finds a specified person and follows him/her. Its basic functions involved in following a person are as follows:

1. Tracking the specified people: A developed proprietary image processing algorithm extracts and recognizes specific individuals, registering the color and texture of their clothing, and distinguishing them from cluttered backgrounds. Additionally, we have strengthened the tracking performance by integration of LRF information. The details are explained below.
2. Following at his/her pace: The robot calculates the distance between the target person and itself using stereo vision and follows him/her with the appropriate speed to keep the distance constant (Fig.2(a)).
3. Avoiding obstacles: The robot uses ultrasonic sensors integrated in the robot's base to detect obstacles and automatically generates a route to avoid them (Fig.2(b)).
4. Resuming contacting when the robot misses him/her: If the robot loses sight of its target, it searches for the person or calls out to re-establish contact.

The person following motion control, including obstacle avoidance and contact resumption, is explained in detail below.

The person following robot equipped with the above mentioned functions is expected to support our daily life from the viewpoints of safety, security and practicality. It will take care of an infant and/or elderly person, and carry baggage as it follows the user in a shopping center as shown in Fig.3.

2.3 System configuration

The system configuration of ApriAttenda™ from the viewpoints of function modules is shown in Fig.4. For the person following function, we have constructed two function modules, the Target Detection Module and the Motion Control Module, in the

ApriAttenda™'s control system. Two camera images of the target person including cluttered backgrounds are captured concurrently by the original versatile multimedia front-end processing board named MFeP (Sato et al., 2005), and sent to the Target Detection Module. At the Target Detection Module, the target person is detected by the newly developed image processing algorithm, and the result (distance and direction data of the target person from the robot) is sent to the Motion Control Module through the network. At the Motion Control Module, the two wheels and the head of the robot are controlled cooperatively to follow the target person smoothly. LRF is mounted and used to track in this module. The Target Detection Module runs on Windows PC and the Motion Control Module runs on Linux PC, because the Windows PC has many image processing applications, and the robot motion control requires real-time processing. The frame rate of the image processing system is about 15 fps, and the control cycle of the motion control system is 1kHz.

a) Moves as the person does (b) Avoid obstacles

Fig. 2. Concept of ApriAttenda™'s Motion

Fig. 3. Assumed Roles of Person Following Robot

Regarding ApriAttenda™'s systemization, the open robot controller architecture (Ozaki, 2003) has been adopted to easily integrate the Target Detection Module and the Motion Control Module, because this distributed object technology based architecture can connect a number of software modules easily even if these modules are located on different CPUs. This architecture has already been successfully applied to ApriAlpha™ (Yoshimi et al., 2004).

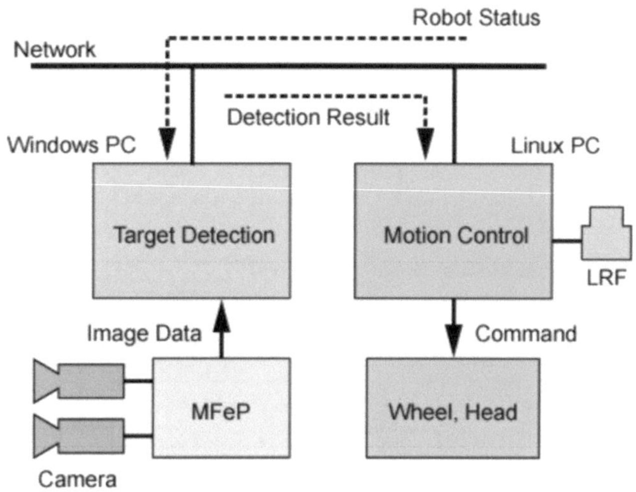

Fig. 4. System Configuration of ApriAttenda™

2.4 Motion controller architecture

A. Person Following Control

The person following robot ApriAttenda™ finds a target person and measures distance and direction to him/her using stereo vision processing and LRF sensing data. The robot controls its speed to keep the distance to the person constant and follows him/her. When the target person moves forward, ApriAttenda™ moves forward, and when the person stops, the robot moves to a point beside the person and also stops. If the person approaches too closely to the robot, ApriAttenda™ backs off. Figure 5 shows the configuration of ApriAttenda™'s motion control system. It consists of two parts, the Body Motion Control Module and the Head Motion Control Module which construct the general position control system. Since the movement of the target person cannot be predicted beforehand, the highest priority of the person following control is to control the camera head module to keep the target person at the center of the visual field, robustly. Next, the robot body is controlled to change its direction to the same direction as the head module, and at the same time, to move its position to keep the distance to the target person constant under the nonholonomic constrained condition of its two independently driven wheels system.

B. Obstacle Avoidance Control

In the person following motion, ApriAttenda™ detects the target person by the image processing and LRF sensing system, and checks for obstacles in its way using ultrasonic sensors in parallel. When an obstacle on the robot's trajectory is found by the ultrasonic sensor, the robot starts to avoid the obstacle, and tries to continue following the person by the vision sensor, so the robot keeps its visual axis to the target person using the degrees of freedom of its head unit and changes the direction of the body and goes around to avoid the obstacle. The avoidance control system is constructed by means of obstacle map written by occupancy grid map and the velocity potential method (Yoshimi et al., 2006). The Avoidance Trajectory Generation Unit in Fig.5 converts the reference information of the robot motion to avoid the obstacle when it exists near the robot.

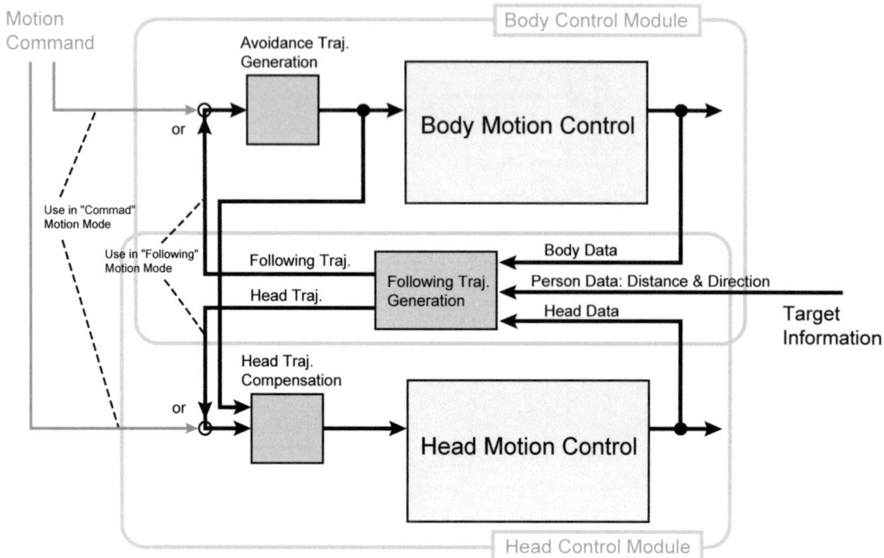

Fig. 5. Motion Control System of ApriAttenda™

3. Vision-based tracking algorithm

A. Feature Parameters for Target Person Detection

The most difficult and important problem for the vision-based target detection of the person following robot is to select the most suitable feature parameter, which expresses the target person in the captured input image (Schlegel et al., 1998). For the detection of the target person's region, we usually check many kinds of features on the specified part of the input image, such as the position (absolute position and distance from the robot), color, and movement speed. If the most suitable feature parameter has been selected, the target detection process is defined to find the part corresponding to the selected parameter from the input image. However, it is difficult to select the most suitable feature parameter to detect the target person's region, because the specified part of the input image moves not only due to the target person's but also the robot's movement; furthermore the detected color of the specified part may change because of shifts in lighting.

Hirai et al. selected a shape of human back and shoulder for visual tracking of the target person (Hirai et al., 2003). We assumed that the target person usually moves and exists before the background, so we defined that the group of feature points on the person's region in the input image moves at a certain speed, and/or exists nearer than the background and its position changes continuously. Once a target person is detected as a region of moving and existing before background, we can follow this region using our definition mentioned above.

B. Dynamic Switching of Feature Parameters for Target Person Detection

To select the most suitable feature parameter for detecting the target person stably while the person following robot is moving, we have introduced a method of dynamically switching the feature parameters. This method selects and switches the most suitable feature parameter for detecting the target person dynamically according to the input image's condition, and achieves robust target person detection.

We have developed a new algorithm to recognize and extract the region of the person from an input image containing a complicated scene for the person following robot ApriAttenda™. We used two kinds of feature parameters, distance from the robot and movement speed, for detecting the person's region, and other feature parameters, color and texture, for specifying the target person. The detection of the target person is executed according to the following sequence (Fig.6):

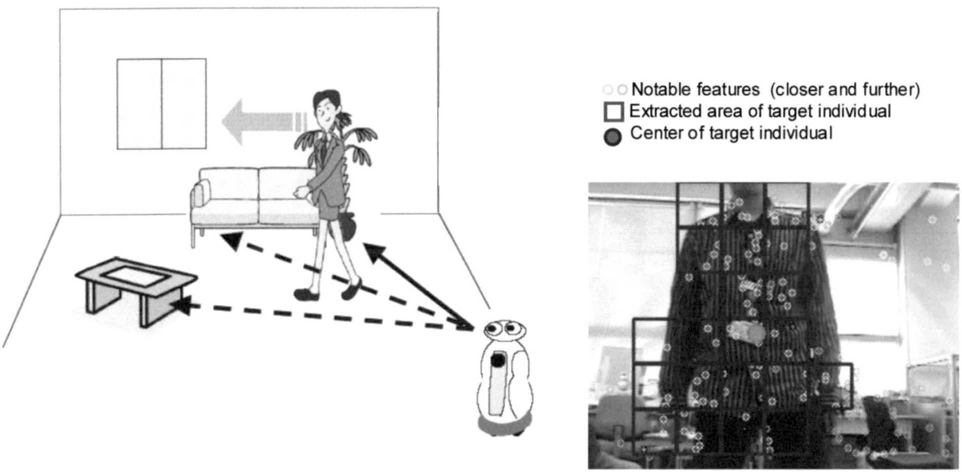

Fig. 6. Image Processing Algorithm of ApriAttenda™

(a)Finding the person , (b) Processing image

1. Feature points extraction: Some feature points are extracted automatically from the input image. The system sets the feature points on the extracted edges or corner points.
2. Velocity calculation of each feature point: The velocity of each feature point is calculated from the history of its motion.
3. Distance measurement to each feature point: The distance from the robot to each feature point is measured by the stereo vision system.
4. Evaluation of the degree of separation for the most suitable feature parameter selection: The most suitable feature parameter for the person region detection is selected by the distribution of the feature points' distance and velocity parameters. The feature parameter that has the largest degree of separation is selected as the most suitable one for the person region detection.
5. Extraction of the region of the person: The person's area is extracted using the most suitable feature parameter selected in the previous step.
6. Recognition of the target person: The area of the target person is identified by combining the information of the pre-registered color and texture of the clothes the target person wears.
7. Data Sending to the Motion Control Module: The distance and direction data to the target person is sent to the Motion Control Module.

A robust method to handle changes in lighting and scene has been achieved by utilizing these variable information data and by importing and updating the feature points of the person's region.

Figure 7 shows examples of the person's area detection, and Fig.8 shows the distribution of the feature points' disparity and velocity parameters. In this case, the feature point's disparity is equivalent to the distance between the robot and the feature point because the distance is a function of the disparity. Figure 7(a) and 8(a) show the case where the distances from the robot to the target person and to the background are almost the same, so the velocity is selected as the feature parameter for the person region detection. Figure 7(b) and 8(b) show the case where the distances from the robot to the target person and to the background are different, so the distance is selected as the feature parameter for the person region detection.

Fig. 7. Results of Target Person Detection

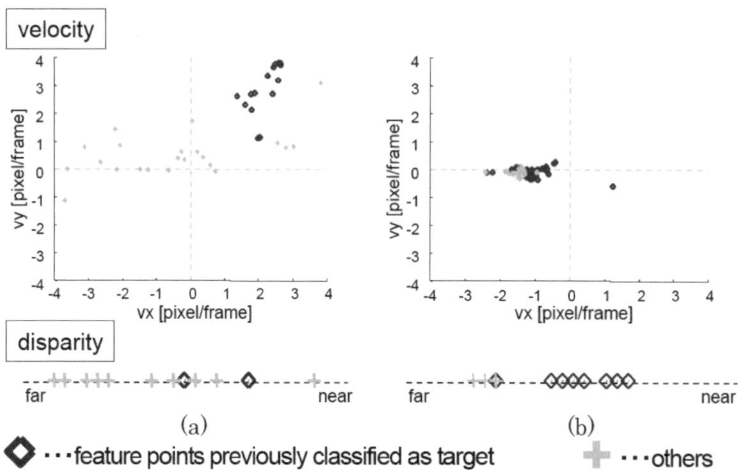

Fig. 8. Distribution of the Feature Points

4. Problems of tracking

4.1 Vision-based tracking problems

When the robot is controlled by feedback using the image processing result, the frame rate and the matching accuracy of the image processing data are big factors to decide the kinematic mobility performance of the robot. The case in which the frame rate is low corresponds to the case in which the sampling rate of the sensor is low. If the response of the feedback operation is worsened by the low rate, it becomes difficult to achieve the person following operation for a quickly moving object. The frame rate of ApriAttenda™ is approx. 15 fps now. This frame rate is fast enough for tracking the movement of a person walking. But the performance is inadequate for a person marching at the double. This frame rate is

decided by the trade-offs of the resolution and CPU performance etc. Moreover, the delay (latency) of the information transmission from the sensor input to the movement output also has a big influence on the kinematic performance. The system design that reduces this delay is needed too, because it is an important factor related to the content of the next frame for the image data processing in the vision-motion cooperative system.
In the visual tracking, the result of the image data processing greatly influences subsequent operation. To begin with, this is one of the most important factors determining whether the tracking object is found accurately. However, even when it keeps detecting the object well, the person following operation might be influenced harmfully by other factors. The aimed direction of the tracking center wobbles when it recognizes only part of the tracking object or included the surroundings of the object, and this wobble becomes a serious problem when real motion is generated. Moreover, when distance information is measured by using the stereo disparity, it is necessary to extract the pair of the same feature point from pictures taken by right and left cameras simultaneously. If another feature point is chosen, a value that is greatly different from an actual distance will be calculated. But even if the process of matching works well, a big error margin will be calculated when the detection accuracy is bad. These wobbles and errors can be reduced by time-average processing such as by low-pass filters. However, the person following response will deteriorate according to the time delay at that time. Because the deterioration of the person following motion performance in the movement system is related to the success or failure of the subsequent image processing, it cannot be disregarded. When tracking is performed only in the stationary camera image, the above-mentioned characteristic is less important. These are new problems in a visual tracking servo motion control system that cooperates with its own movement.
On the other hand, there are some problems concerning the camera sensor. Because the camera sensor captures scenery in angle of view as discrete information in each pixel, the area size in real space that one pixel covers increases as the distance in vision becomes greater, that is, sensor resolution decreases. The above-mentioned characteristic in the stereovision system means that a pixel shift on the image of the far object becomes a big discrete distance jump. This is a problem related to the hardware, so even if the best detection result can be obtained by the image processing, that problem will not be solved. The distance up to about 5m can be resolved in QQVGA (160x120 pixel) image that ApriAttenda™ uses, and the discretization error margin at this time becomes several ten centimeters at the maximum. To decrease the discretization error margin easily, it is only necessary to improve the resolution of the camera, that is, enlarge the size of camera image. However, in this case, a serious trade-off exists. Processing of a large-size image data imposes a huge CPU cost, which causes the frame rate to decrease, and, as a result, the kinematic performance of the robot worsens. From the viewpoint of precise distance measurement, use of another sensor such as an LRF is preferable to using a stereo camera.
The measurement feature of the stereo camera and the laser sensor is shown in the following graphs. The graph shows the distance (Fig.9) and direction (Fig.10) from robot to person with the robot coordinate system when tracking a moving person. The method of tracking with the laser sensor is described below. The person following motion function of the robot is nullified in this experiment. Moreover, note that the true position information is not included in these graphs. However, the calibration has been done respectively beforehand, and the tracking result has been collated with a true value. In Fig.9, in the stereo camera distance data, the influence of the quantization of the image in the circled area "B" is found

besides the error that originates in the failure at the feature point matching in the area "A". For the direction element, almost the same measurement result as LRF is obtained. One reason for this result is thought to be that the resolution that originates in the image size and the angle of view of the camera and the scanning resolution of LRF used in this experiment are almost equal. Additionally, it can be found that the directional element information data of the camera is fluctuating overall more than that of LRF in Fig.10. The reason of this phenomenon is thought to be the above mentioned wobble of the tracking center that is originated from the feature point on the tracking target.

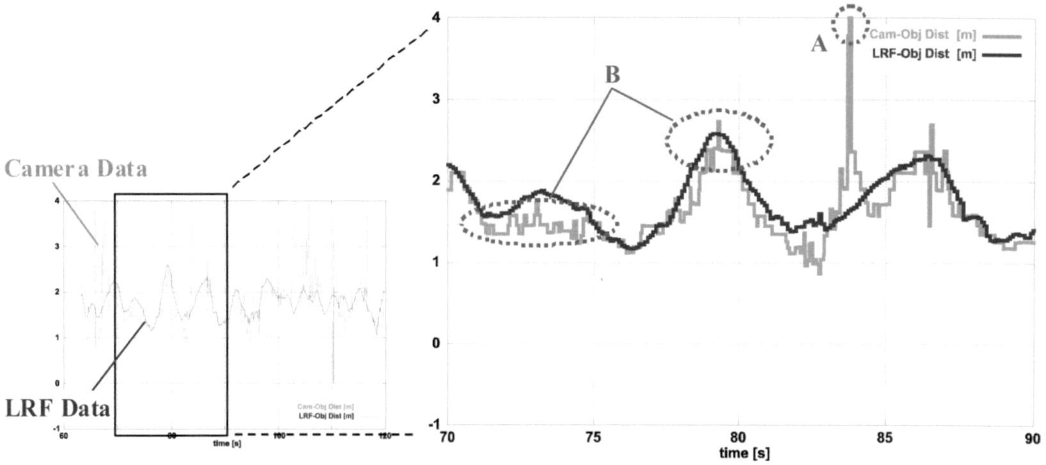

Fig. 9. Person Tracking Result for Robot-Person Distance [m]

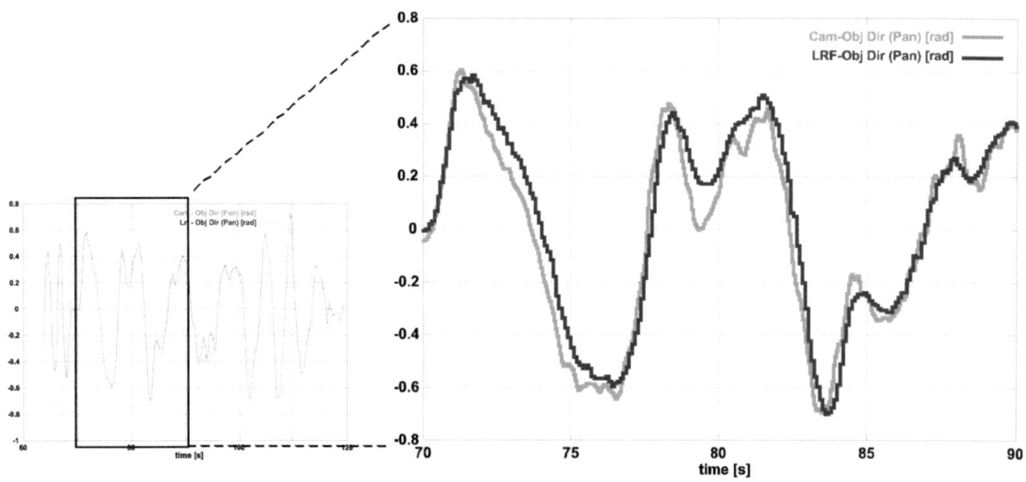

Fig. 10. Person Tracking Result for Robot-Person Horizontal Direction [rad]

4.2 LRF tracking problems

Recently, a Laser Range Finder (LRF) capable of radially measuring straight-line distance in one plane has been miniaturized, and so it can be mounted on a robot easily. The directivity of the LRF is very strong and its accuracy and resolution are also high compared with the ultrasonic sensor, the infrared rays sensor, etc. Good use has been made of these characteristics of the LRF, and many researchers apply LRF to person detection and tracking operations. For instance, there are person detection and a tracking technique that extract the shape of a human's leg and the movement pattern from LRF measurement information and use it. The candidate shape of a human's leg is picked out from LRF data and the truth is judged by searching for the circle pair that has the size of leg section, and using the pattern match with the leg appearance movement model. Lee extracts the set of the LRF detection points based on a dynamic feature from the time series of data, and detects a pair that suits the person's walking step pattern and the leg size from the sets, and finally concludes that the pair is human and continues tracking it (Lee et al., 2006). Okusako detects the person's position by the block match with the template of typical scanning shape of the leg observed during walking (Okusako et al., 2006).

However, many problems remain concerning the person following. Using such techniques, it is difficult to detect the sets of leg shape and decide a pair of legs when two or more people are adjacent. Moreover, the movements of actual people vary. The possibility of confusing various movements such as cut back, side step walking, turning around the place, pivot turning, skip, and movements similar to dance step with the usual movement is incontrovertible. A movement model covering all these possibilities will be complex and huge. It is also a problem that the feature information on which these methods rely is not general. For instance, if the person wears a long skirt or coat, these methods using the leg shape information do not function well. In addition, when the tracking object is a child, there is a possibility that the expected leg shape cannot be detected because the scanning position is different from in the case of an adult. Moreover, the detection of a person carrying luggage might deviate from the model. Moreover it is invalid for a person using assistant apparatus such as a wheelchair. As mentioned above, this technique has many restrictions concerning the state of a tracked target. On the other hand, it is clear that a trade-off exists: the lower the recognition condition set, the higher the rate of misidentification. In the case we envision, namely, that of the service robot acting in an environment in which it coexists with humans, using only LRF to track the person is insufficient.

In a general environment in which the service robot acts, the situation in which the tracking object is completely concealed by another object irrespective of the robot's own behavior must be considered. Using only LRF information, it is almost impossible to re-detect a tracking target once it has been completely lost. For this case, it is effective to employ a method in which another sensor's information, such as camera image, is also used.

5. Vision – LRF sensor fusion tracking

5.1 Consideration of best configuration of sensor fusion system

Generally, when thinking about the sensor fusion of the camera and LRF, the roles of different sensors are clearly distinguished; for instance, to detect the object with the camera, and to measure the distance to the object with LRF. Another method has been devised in which, first, the target is tracked by the image data processing or the LRF leg detection, and next, the normal continuance of the tracking is confirmed by collating the tracking results. However, in the former method the complementation of each defect is insufficient. For instance, LRF may detect the distance on this side wrongly. In the latter method, logical multiplication processing is executed. It will decrease the misidentification rate but not lead to the extension of the continuance time of the tracking.

It is necessary to consider each merit and weak point of the camera and LRF. From the viewpoint of recognition, the image data processing to obtain a lot of feature information such as color, print pattern, texture, and stereo distance is generally dependable and stable. LRF has high possibility of misdetection and misidentification depending on the situation. However, sufficient tracking can be done by LRF alone, using a simple algorithm such as the neighborhood area search based on time continuousness at object position without the high characteristic feature information such as a body shape etc. in an open space where there is no fear of misidentification. Additionally, it is attractive that it is possible to correspond to various movements of people, large range of body height, many kinds of clothes, and assistant apparatus such as wheelchairs for such simple logic. Moreover, in the case of this logic, there is no problem even if the root of the leg or the trunk of the body is scanned. So it is expected that a steadier positional detection result is obtained because the influence of intense movement of the tips of legs is decreased.

On the other hand, from the viewpoint of accuracy of information, LRF detection is overwhelmingly excellent. It becomes an important factor for quick follow motion. This is not limited to the distance element, and also applies to the direction element. Even if the camera resolution is the same level as LRF, the image data processing might hinder the movement compared with the LRF case. Because, generally, the image processing needs to continue tracking, repeatedly detecting and updating the feature points, the wobble and the drift of the tracking center are apt to stand out. The characteristics of the sensors are shown below.

	occlusion	accuracy	human detect and identify	constraint
Camera	good	bad	good	normal
LRF (use leg info.)	bad	good	normal	bad
LRF (no leg info.)	bad	good	bad	good

Table 2. Characteristics of Sensors

We can use the camera system for human detection, whereas tracking using LRF only is problematic. The necessity of the LRF tracking method using leg shape information becomes lower in a system where the camera can be used as in the case of ApriAttenda™. And the general-purpose LRF tracking algorithm is more effective on this system. Thus, according to the situation, the roles of each sensor should be different. So, it is important to develop a strategy based on consideration of the configuration of the entire system.

The rate of misidentification will be decreased by a strategy that takes logical multiplication of each sensor's information. If it is possible, we want to integrate and use the obtained information widely by taking the logical add, for example. However, there is a possibility of adopting the error value through such integration, and fatal misidentification may be generated. If there is an index that judges whether the sensor information can be used for the tracking, we can improve the overall performance by switching sensor information according to the state of the environment.

So, we pay attention to the surrounding congestion situation in the space where the tracking target exists and design a tracking system that adopts the concept of sensor fusion such that the fusion rate changes depending on the congestion degree. When the surrounding space condition is not-congestion, the sensor fusion system gives weight to LRF information. And it shifts to the camera information from LRF when the surroundings are congested.

5.2 Sensor fusion system dependent on congestion degree

A. Entire Structure of Fusion System

We set up LRF on the robot as shown in Fig.11. The view angle of LRF is 240 degrees, and LRF is set such that the measurable area becomes plus or minus 120 degrees horizontally from the robot front direction. The height of the scanning phase is 730mm from the floor surface. Fig.12 shows the control system mounted on ApriAttenda™ that applies the sensor fusion. The direction and the distance between the robot and the tracking object are measured by the stereo camera and LRF. The measured information is passed to the integration processing part and the estimated position of the tracked person to use for the person following motion is calculated in this block. Next, the trajectory for the person following motion is generated in the Following Trajectory Generation Block based on the integration processing result. The trajectories for the wheel base unit and for the head unit are calculated in this block. Additionally, this block includes three block functions, namely, the Trajectory Generation, the Avoidance Trajectory Generation, and the Head Trajectory Compensation, after input of target information in as shown Fig.5. The algorithm introduced in Section 3 is used for the tracking with the stereo camera.

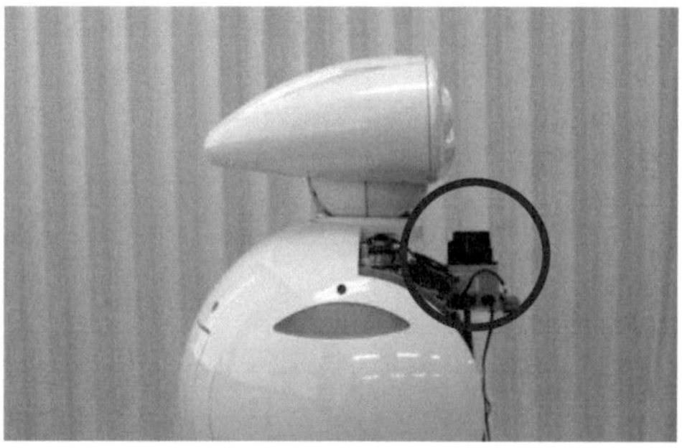

Fig. 11. LRF on ApriAttenda™ (side view)

The tracking by LRF uses the positional estimation method based on time continuousness at the person's global position. Here "Global" means not the movement of parts of the human body such as arms and legs, but the movement of the entire body that approximates the center of gravity position of a human. The model of the tracking is shown in Fig.13 and the flowchart of this algorithm is shown in Fig.14. The following procedures are repeated.

1. Estimate next step position using the movement history until the last step.
2. Set the window that detects the person position information at the estimated next step position.
3. Count the LRF detection points contained in the window.
4. Calculate the distance and direction of the center of gravity of the counted points, and decide the next step reference position of tracking.

It is necessary to set the person position detection window isotropically and widely so that it is possible to adjust to the random and quick person movement. Note that, the larger the size of the window, the higher the rate of the false detection circumstantially. The width of the window area depends on the sampling rate of the sensor. So the faster the sampling rate is, the smaller the window size that can be set. The sampling rate of LRF is 100ms, and we set the size of window as plus and minus 50cm at the center of tracking point. Moreover, in this system the Lost-Counter is prepared against occlusion (covered with another object). If the number of LRF detection point in the window is below the threshold in the step 3), the forecast position calculated in the step 1) is substituted as the next estimated position. And the Lost-Counter counts up. The Lost-Counter is initialized to zero when an effective LRF detection point is detected in the window. As a result, it is possible to endure the momentary occlusion. If the Lost-Counter reached a threshold value, it is judged that the system cannot detect the pursued object again. At this time, the system exits the tracking motion mode, and changes the motion mode to another mode. Various methods are employed in other modes. For instance, the robot wanders in the space and searches for the following target again based on the image template.

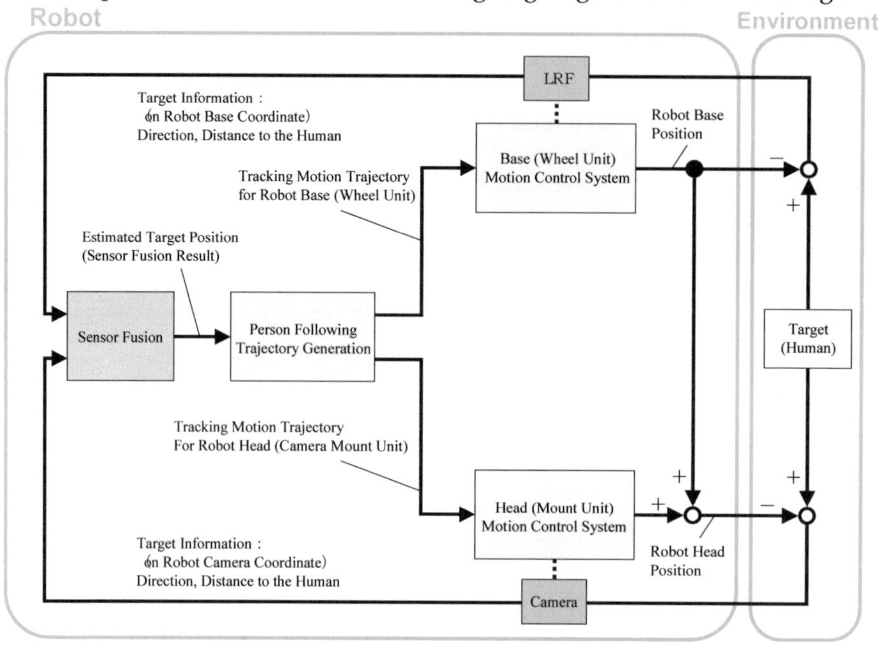

Fig. 12. Motion Control System of ApriAttenda™ Based on Sensor Fusion Data

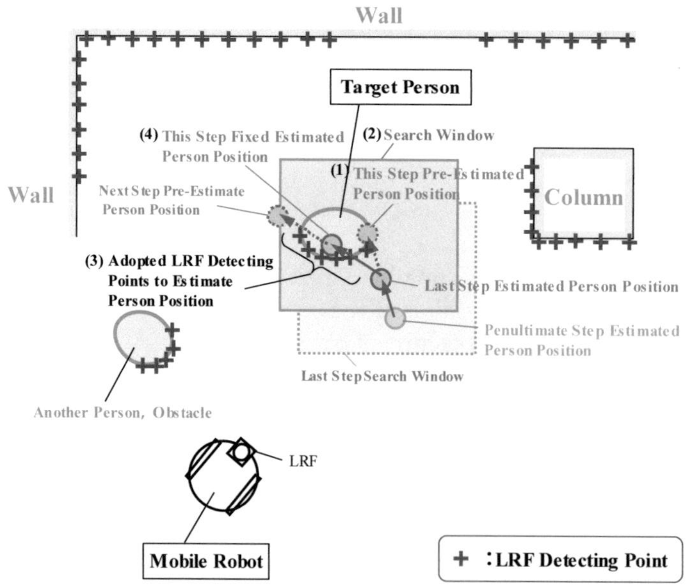

Fig. 13. Model of Person Tracking Algorithm Using LRF Data

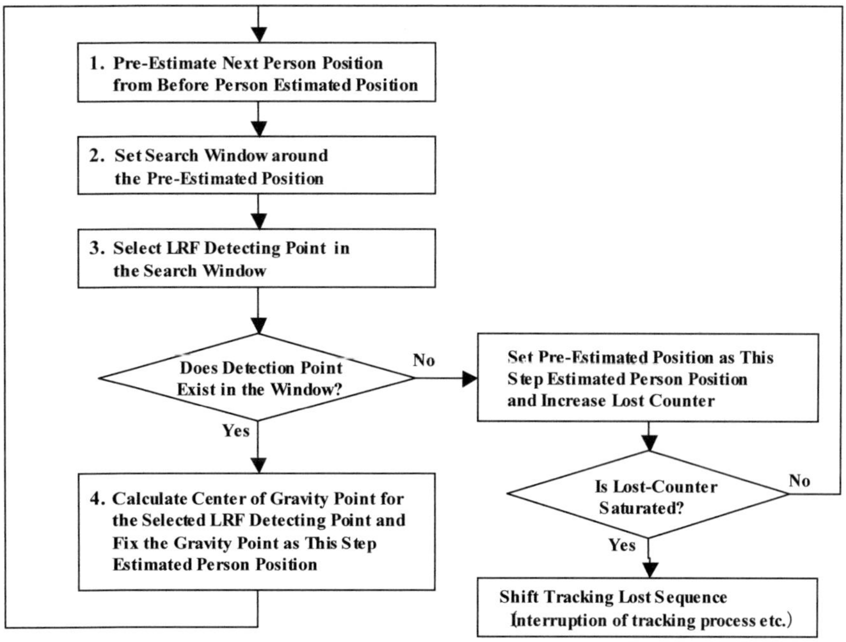

Fig. 14. Flowchart of Person Tracking Algorithm Using LRF Data

B. Sensor Fusion Method

The rate changeable sensor fusion system in which the integrated ratio of vision and LRF information changes depending on the environment state around the tracking target is designed. It is expressed as shown in Fig.15. This processing is executed in the Sensor Fusion block in the system shown in Fig.12. The congestion situation around the tracking target is used as a surrounding environment status that contributes to the fusion ratio "W". And the congestion degree "C" is set as an index that expresses this congestion situation. W and C are the real numbers that take values from 0 to 1. W and C are defined by expression (2). The sensor fusion process shown by expression (1) is executed using these values. Here, "n" in expression (2) is prepared to make the fusion rate nonlinear to the congestion degree. This time the value is set to n=0.4 in the experiment based on experience. "θ_C" and "θ_L" are the direction information that can be obtained from the vision system and the LRF system. "d_C" and "d_L" are the distance information that can also be obtained. "θ" and "d" are the information of the direction and the distance to generate the following motion trajectory.

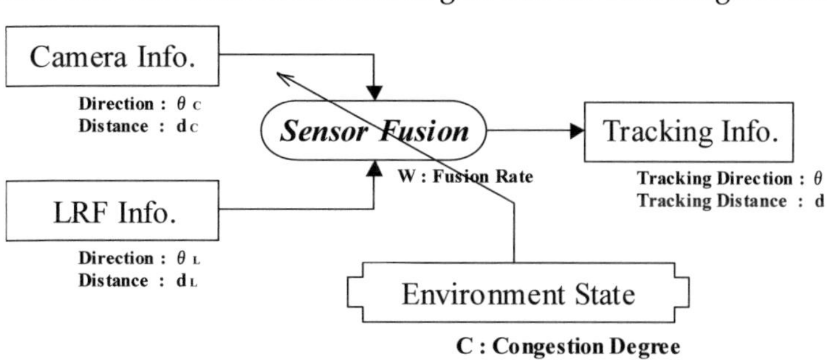

Fig. 15. Rate-Changeable Environmental Adaptive Sensor Fusion Model

$$\theta = \theta_L \cdot W + \theta_C \cdot (1 - W)$$
$$d = d_L \cdot W + d_C \cdot (1 - W) \tag{1}$$

$$W = C^n \tag{2}$$

$$C = \frac{N_{Cong}}{N\max_{Cong}} \tag{3}$$

The congestion degree "C" is defined by the expression (3). This is illustrated in Fig.16. The congestion observation window area is prepared around the person position detection window that used LRF tracking. $N\max_{Cong}$ is the total number of times the scanning laser passes over this area. N_{Cong} is defined as the number of times the scanning laser is able to observe the detection point in the congestion observation window. Here, the congestion observation window is defined such that the area of the window doesn't include the person position detection window area. Therefore, the congestion degree becomes 0 when no other object exists around the tracking target, and it approaches 1 when the number of other objects around the target increases.

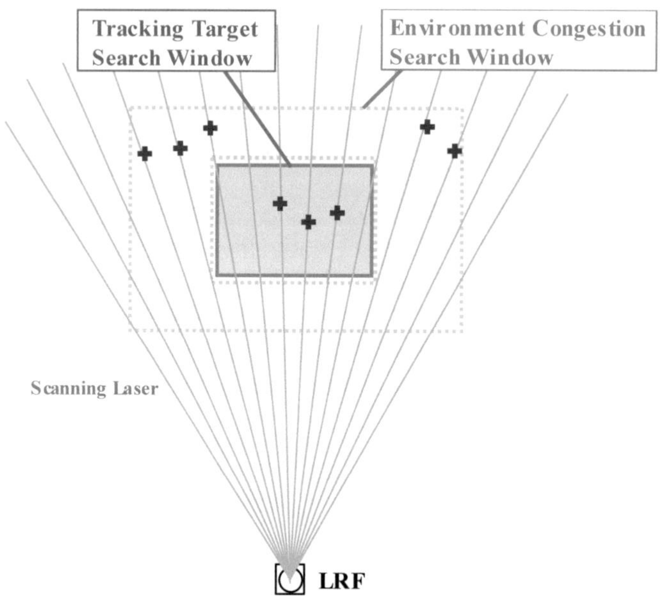

Fig. 16. Definition of Environmental Congestion

C. Person Following Motion

An experiment of person following motion was performed using ApriAttenda™ mounted with this sensor fusion method. From this experiment, in open space, it was confirmed that the robot can follow a person smoothly who moves quickly and randomly. In the experiment, the person moves to the translational direction of the robot at a maximum speed of about 1.2 m/s, and to the rotational direction of the robot at a maximum speed of about 5.0 m/s at a point of 1.5m from the robot.

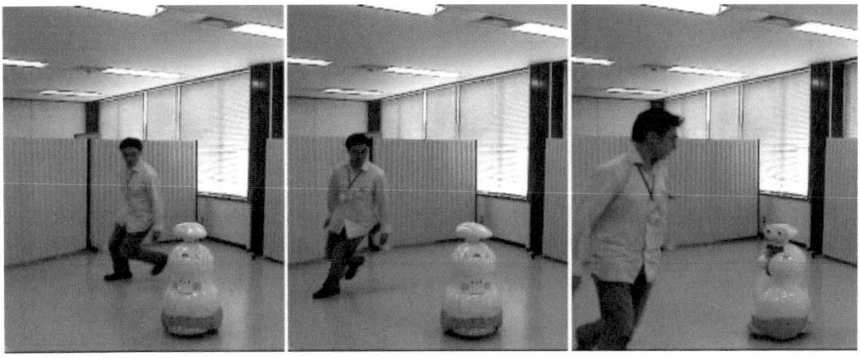

Fig. 17. Fast Person Following Motion

When the person passes over an obstacle in the neighborhood as illustrated in Fig.18, the robot can continue following without losing sight of the person. At this time, the internal state of the robot changes as shown in Fig.19. It is understood that the direction element of the follow reference (heavy-line) smoothly changes from LRF information (deep-color, thin-line) to camera information (light-color, thin-line) according to the congestion degree of the environment (dotted-line) in the figure. We can also understand that the tracking is continued normally from the camera shot shown in Fig.20.

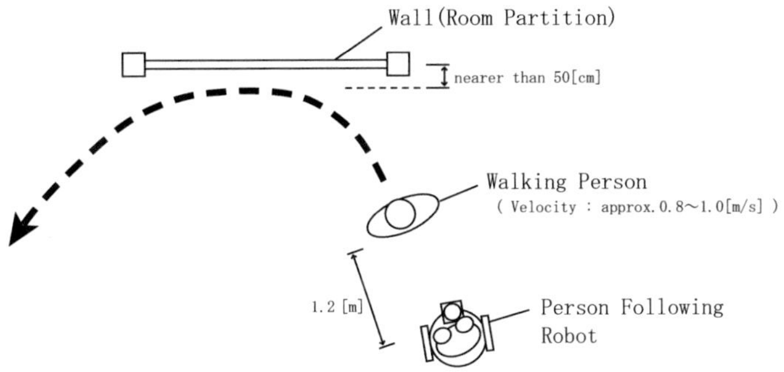

Fig. 18. Experimental Situation: Walking Person Passes near Another Object

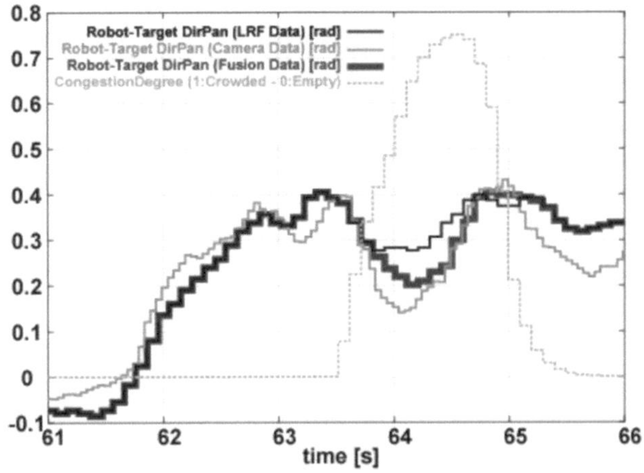

Fig. 19. Person Direction and Congestion Degree in the case of Success Tracking

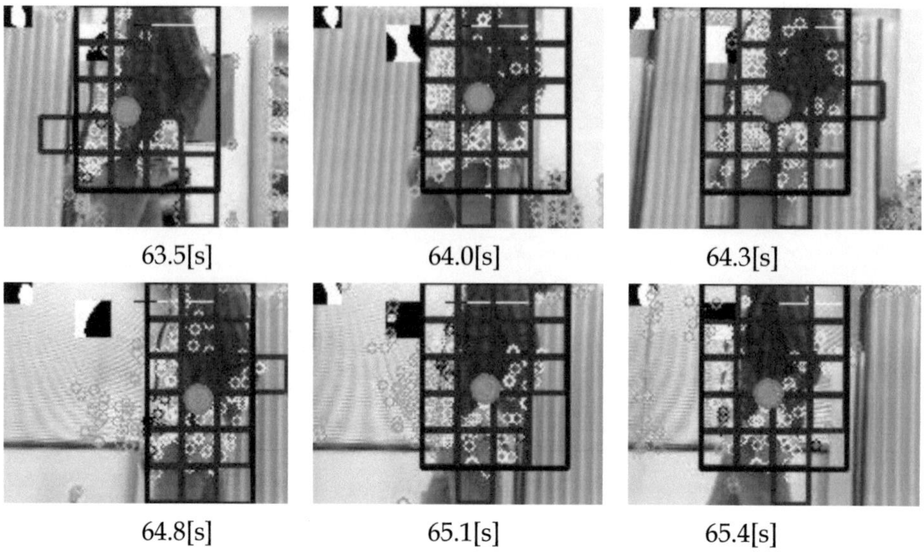

Fig. 20. Robot Camera View during Tracking (Person Passes near Another Object)

In addition, the robot can continue following normally without losing sight of the followed object in the case of the meeting and parting motion (pseudo crossing motion) involving two people as illustrated in Fig.21. And Fig.22 shows the scenery of the experiment of Fig.21. In this experiment, two people who have approached have instantaneously exchanged a rate vector, at the time of the encounter. This motion of the target results in a high probability of misidentification when the robot refers only to the positional history of the target measured by LRF. However, the following motion can be perfectly continued in this system where the designed sensor fusion is mounted. On the other hand, we have confirmed that the robot can follow the target correctly, distinguishing the situation accurately without guessing wrong as to the general cross-motion of the target, too.

Because the above-mentioned movements, such as the nondirectional movement, the fast movement, the crossing and pseudo-crossing motion with other people, and the occlusion are events that occurs naturally in the human coexistence space, it is very important for the service robot to have these person following abilities in these situations.

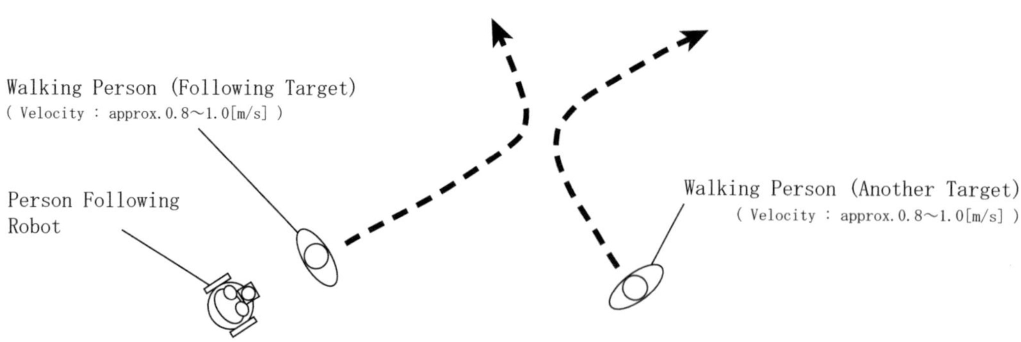

Fig. 21. Experimental Situation: Pseudo Crossing Motion (Two People Walking Meet and Part)

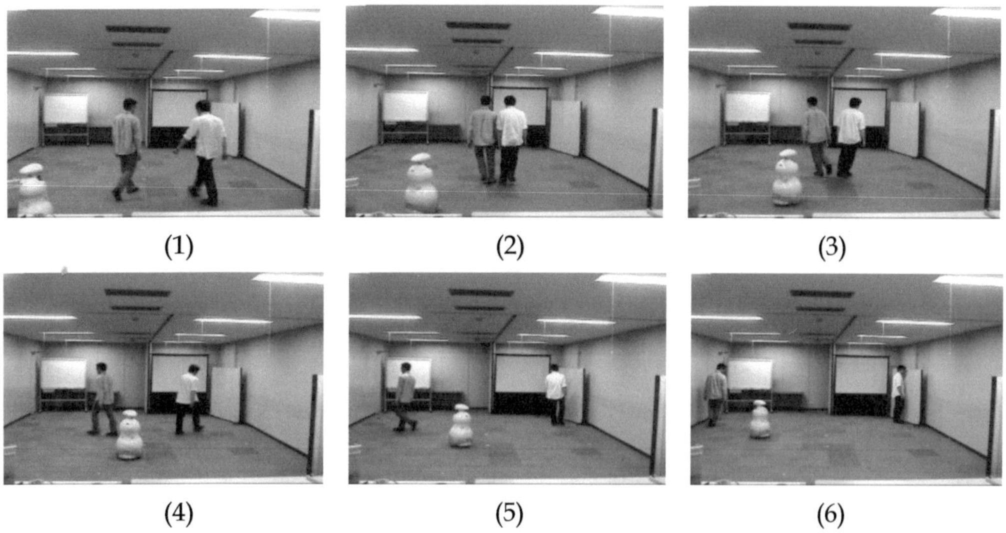

Fig. 22. Experimental Result for Pseudo Crossing Motion

6. Conclusion

The person following robot ApriAttenda™ equipped with a stereo camera and Vision System and LRF is introduced. ApriAttenda™ has the Vision-Based Tracking system and the Vision-Based Motion Control system. ApriAttenda™ can do the person following motion using the tracking information. Moreover, ApriAttenda™ used LRF as another sensor for the tracking performance gain. The respective problems of the vision and LRF tracking systems are pointed out and an improvement method based on the idea of the Vision-LRF Sensor Fusion system is proposed. One feature of this new system is that the fusion rate changes depending on the congestion information of the environment. The experimental movement results of applying these systems to ApriAttenda™ are reported. The efficiency of the proposed method is confirmed by the experiment.

As discussed here, efforts to achieve an advanced application using sensors independently are subject to an unavoidable limit. So, a system design integrating information from two or more types of sensor is required. Because the vision data containing abundant information plays a key role in the complex system, further development of the vision system is desirable.

7. References

Cielniak, G.; Treptow, A. & Duckett T. (2005). Quantitative Performance Evaluation of a People Tracking System on a Mobile Robot, *Proceedings of ECMR05 (2nd European Conference on Mobile Robots)*, Ancona, Italy, September 2005

Hirai, N. & Mizoguchi, H. (2003). Visual Tracking of Human Back and Shoulder for Person Following Robot, *Proceedings of the 2003 IEEE/ASME International Conference on Advanced Intelligent Mechatronics (AIM2003)*, pp. 527-532, Kobe, Japan, July 2003

Kobilarov, M.; Sukhatme, G.; Hyams, J. & Batavia, P. (2006). People tracking and following with mobile robot using an omnidirectional camera and a laser, *Proceedings of the*

2006 IEEE International Conference on Robotics and Automation (ICRA2006), pp. 557-562, Orlando, Florida, May 2006

Kwon, H.; Yoon, Y.; Byung, J.; Park, B. & Kak, C.A. (2005). Person Tracking with a Mobile Robot using Two Uncalibrated Independently Moving Cameras, *Proceedings of the 2005 IEEE International Conference on Robotics and Automation (ICRA2005)*, pp. 2888-2894, Barcelona, Spain, April 2005

Lee, J.; Tsubouchi, T.; Yamamoto, K. & Egawa, S. (2006). People Tracking Using a Robot in Motion with Laser Range Finder, *Proceedings of the 2006 IEEE/RSJ International Conference on Intelligent Robots and Systems (IROS2006)*, pp. 2396-2942, Beijing, China, October 2006

Matsuhira, N.; Ozaki, F.; Ogawa, H.; Yoshimi, T. & Hashimoto, H. (2005a). Expanding Practicability of ApriAlpha in Cooperation with Networked Home Appliances, *Proceedings of IEEE Workshop on Advanced Robotics and its Social Impacts (ARSO '05)*, pp. 254-259, Nagoya, Japan, June 2005

Matsuhira, N.; Ogawa, H.; Yoshimi, T. & Mizoguchi, H. (2005b). Development of Life Support Robots that Coexist in Harmony with People, *Proceedings of the 36th International Symposium on Robotics (ISR2005)*, TU 4H-5, Tokyo, Japan, November 2005

Okusako, S. & Sakane, S. (2006). Human tracking with a mobile robot using a laser range-finder. *Journal of Robotics Society of Japan*, Vol.24, No.5, (July 2006) pp.605-613, (in Japanese)

Ozaki, F. (2003). Open Robot Controller Architecture, *Workshop on Middleware Technology for Open Robot Architecture, 2003 IEEE/ASME International Conference on Advanced Intelligent Mechatronics (AIM2003)*, Kobe, Japan, July 2003

Sato, H; Hashimoto, H; Suzuki, K. & Ozaki, F. (2005). A Versatile Multimedia Front-end Processing Board for Handling Visual and Acoustic Signals Concurrently, *Robotics and Mechatronics Conference 2005 (Robomec2005)*, 2P1-N-053, Kobe, Japan, June 2005 (in Japanese)

Schlegel, C.; Illmann, J.; Jaberg, H.; Schuster, M. & Wörz, R. (1998). Vision Based Person Tracking with a Mobile Robot, *Proceedings of the 9th British Machine Vision Conference*, pp. 418-427, Southampton, UK, 1998

Sidenbladh, H.; Kraqic, D. & Christensen, H.I. (1999). A Person Following Behaviour for a Mobile Robot, *Proceedings of the 1999 IEEE International Conference on Robotics and Automation (ICRA1999)*, pp. 670-675, Detroit, Michigan, May 1999

Yoshimi, T.; Matsuhira, N.; Suzuki, K.; Yamamoto, D.; Ozaki, F.; Hirokawa, J. & Ogawa, H. (2004). Development of a Concept Model of a Robotic Information Home Appliance, ApriAlpha, *Proceedings of the 2004 IEEE/RSJ International Conference on Intelligent Robots and Systems (IROS2004)*, pp.205-211, Sendai, Japan, October 2004

Yoshimi, T.; Nishiyama, M.; Sonoura, T.; Nakamoto, H.; Tokura, S.; Sato, H.; Ozaki, F.; Matsuhira, N. & Mizogushi, H. (2006). Development of a Person Following Robot with Vision Based Target Detection, *Proceedings of the 2006 IEEE/RSJ International Conference on Intelligent Robots and Systems (IROS2006)*, pp. 5286-5291, Beijing, China, October 2006